400k US
300k France ACT ⎤ 1 basket
280k Den Act ⎦
100k FR Div ⎤ another basket
⎦ (passive
_____
$1,080,000 WW income
    X .30%
_____
$324k ⇒ pre credit tax

1 ⇒ foreign taxes

300k x 40% = 120k (F Inc Tax) ⎫ $190
280k x 25% = 70k (") ⎬
                              ⎭
100k x 20% = 20k (")

2 ⇒ foreign tax credit limitation for each basket

324,000 x $\frac{580,000}{1,080,000}$ = $174k
∴ lesser of 174 & 190   excess credit

324 x $\frac{100k}{1,080,000}$ = $30k ∴ lesser of 30 &
                                           20k
                                           excess
                              in in basket   limitation
pre credit tax x $\frac{\text{in in basket}}{WWI}$ = FTC
⇒ then take lesser of foreign tax limit & FTC limitation
total
FTC = $194

UNITED STATES INTERNATIONAL TAXATION

UNITED STATES INTERNATIONAL TAXATION

Third Edition

Philip F. Postlewaite
Professor of Law
Director, Graduate Tax Program
Northwestern University School of Law

Jeffrey T. Sheffield
Senior Lecturer, Graduate Tax Program
Northwestern University School of Law
Partner, Kirkland & Ellis LLP

Julie Green Baumeister
International Tax Services
Ernst & Young LLP

Genevieve A. Tokić
Associate, United States and International Tax
McDermott Will & Emery

CAROLINA ACADEMIC PRESS
Durham, North Carolina

ISBN: 978-1-6328-1542-2
eBook ISBN: 978-1-6328-1543-9

Library of Congress Cataloging-in-Publication Data

Postlewaite, Philip F., 1945- author.
  United States international taxation / Philip F. Postlewaite, Professor of Law Director, Graduate Tax Program, Northwestern University School of Law; Jeffrey T. Sheffield, Senior Lecturer, Graduate Tax Program, Northwestern University School of Law Partner, Kirkland & Ellis LLP; Julie Green Baumeister, International Tax Services, Ernst & Young LLP; Genevieve A. Tokic, Associate, United States and International Tax, McDermott Will & Emery.— Third Edition.
      p. cm.
  Includes index.
  ISBN 978-1-63281-542-2 (hardbound)
  1. Income tax — United States — Foreign income — Cases. 2. Investments, Foreign — Taxation — Law and legislation — United States — Cases. 3. Corporations, Foreign — Taxation — Law and legislation — United States — Cases. 4. Aliens — Taxation — Law and legislation — United States — Cases. 5. Double taxation — United States — Cases. I. Sheffield, Jeffrey T., author. II. Baumeister, Julie Green, author. III. Tokic, Genevieve A., author. IV. Title.
  KF6419.C48 2015
  343.7305'248—dc23

                                                                                              2015015772

Carolina Academic Press, LLC
700 Kent Street
Durham, North Carolina 27701
Telephone (919) 489-7486
Fax (919) 493-5668
www.caplaw.com

Printed in the United States of America
2016 Printing

Dedications

It seems like yesterday
But it was long ago . . .
Wish I didn't know now what I didn't know then
Against the wind
We were running against the wind
We were young and strong, we were running
Against the wind

And the years rolled slowly past . . .
I began to find myself searching
Searching for shelter again and again
Against the wind
A little something against the wind
I found myself seeking shelter against the wind . . .

Well, those drifter's days are past me now
I've got so much more to think about
Deadlines and commitments
What to leave in, what to leave out
Against the wind
I'm still running against the wind
I'm older now but still running
Against the wind

Against the Wind
Bob Seeger

To my Family:
Ruth, Jen, Jess, Eric, Matthew,
Madison, Reid, and Payton

You sometimes created the wind,
but more frequently tried to shelter me from it,
oftentimes without success.
I love you!

PFP

To my wife Hope
With deepest love and affection

JTS

To my Dad, who taught me by example
that hard work will eventually be rewarded,
that it's never too late to chase dreams,
and that nothing is more important than family.

JGB

To S.T., with all my love, and gratitude for your unwavering support.

And to L.E.T., light of my life.

GAT

Preface

This book contains teaching materials for law school courses on the United States federal income taxation of persons engaged in international transactions. It contains 15 separate Units that address fundamental concepts of residency and source, the taxation of United States persons (citizens, residents, and domestic corporations) on their activities abroad, the taxation of foreign persons (non-resident alien individuals and foreign corporations) on their activities within the United States, and the safeguard rules in place to curtail potentially abusive tax deferral in the international context.

The Units in this casebook are arranged so that instructors may assign only those that are consistent with particular course objectives and Units may be presented in an alternative order, as appropriate. Each Unit is organized in four parts:

    A.   Assigned Code and Regulation Provisions

    B.   Problems for Class Discussion

    C.   Overview

    D.   Reference Materials

Students should begin their class preparation by reading the Code and Regulation provisions set forth in Part A of the assigned Unit and working through the Problems in Part B. The overview in Part C and the reference materials in Part D (cases, rulings, and other relevant authorities) provide the context in which the Code and Regulation provisions come into play, how they relate to the assigned Problems, and offers a starting point from which students may conduct further research. Using this added context, students may then review and refine their initial answers to the Problems.

This book is a third successor edition to Philip F. Postlewaite, *International Taxation: Cases, Materials, and Problems* (Anderson Publishing 1999). This edition has been revised to provide a more streamlined approach to the material and to focus on key concepts that can and should reasonably be covered in a one-semester introductory course.

Table of Contents

Table of Contents

Table of Contents

Table of Contents

Table of Contents

Table of Contents

Table of Contents

Table of Contents

Table of Contents

Part I

FOUNDATIONS OF INTERNATIONAL TAXATION

Unit 1

RESIDENCY CLASSIFICATION RULES

A. CODE AND REGULATION PROVISIONS

Code   §§ 2(d); 11(a), (d); 871(a)(1)(A), (a)(1)(D), (a)(2), (b); 877(a), (b); 877A(a)(1), (2); 881(a)(1), (4); 882(a)(1), (2); 7701(a)(4)–(5); 7701(a)(30); 7701(b)(1)–(7).

Reg.   §§ 1.1-1(b), (c); 301.7701-1(a), (b); 301.7701-2(a), (b)(1)–(3), (b)(8)(i), (c)(1)–(2)(i); 301.7701-3(a), (b)(1)–(2), (c)(1)(i); 301.7701-5(a), (b); 301.7701-6(a); 301.7701(b)-1(b)(1)–(2), (c), (e); 301.7701(b)-2(a)–(d)(2); 301.7701(b)-3(a), (b)(1), (3)–(4), (6)–(8); 301.7701(b)-4(a), (c)(3)(i)–(iv).

B. PROBLEMS FOR CLASS DISCUSSION

1-1. Determine the entity classification for United States tax purposes of the following entities:

    (a) A Delaware corporation owned entirely by citizens and residents of Japan.

    (b) A Limited Company formed in Singapore.

    (c) A Gesellschaft mit beschränkter Haftung (GmbH) formed in Germany and owned by two United States persons, with respect to which neither has any personal liability under German law.

    (d) A Limited Company formed in Ghana and owned entirely by two United States persons, one of whom is personally liable for the debts and obligations of the entity under Ghanaian law.

    (e) How would your answer to (d) change if the Ghanaian company was owned by a single United States person who was personally liable for the company's debts?

1-2. Paulina has never been in the United States prior to her move to San Francisco on February 1, Year 1. Paulina moved to San Francisco after having applied for (and received) a green card from United States Citizenship and Immigration Services. She has lived in San Francisco since that time.

    (a) Is Paulina a resident alien for Year 1? Under what test(s) might she be construed to be a resident? What is her residency starting date?

    (b) Would the answer to (a) change if, instead, Paulina moved to San Francisco under a temporary visa on February 1, Year 1, and she lived there until her application for permanent residence was approved on November 15, Year 1?

(c) Would the answer to (a) change if, instead, Paulina moved to San Francisco on October 15, Year 1, and her application for permanent residence in the United States was granted on December 1, Year 1?

1-3. Eduardo, a citizen of Peru, was present in the United States for 90 days during Year 1, 120 days in Year 2, and 125 days in Year 3, with Year 3 being the most recent year. Eduardo was not a lawful permanent resident of the United States during any of those years and was not present in the United States at any time before Year 1.

(a) What is Eduardo's residency status in the United States for each of the three years?

(b) How would the answer to (a) change if Eduardo was present in the United States for 190 days in Year 3?

(c) How would the answer to (a) change if Eduardo was present in the United States for 360 days in Year 1, 300 days in Year 2, and 30 days in Year 3?

(d) How would the answer to (a) change if Eduardo was present in the United States for 90 days in Year 1, 180 days in Year 2, and 150 days in Year 3? Assume Eduardo spent the remainder of each year in Peru where his wife and children live, where he operates a thriving business, and where he is registered to vote and licensed to drive. Eduardo travels to the United States in order to sell the widgets produced by his Peruvian business.

1-4. Geir, a citizen of Ghana, is a student at the University of Arizona and is in the United States on a student visa. He plans to be present in the United States for four years of college, returning home for summers. If he is offered a good job, Geir may stay in Arizona after he graduates.

(a) What is Geir's residency status?

(b) After four years in the United States, Geir's student visa was set to expire upon his graduation on May 1. He did not find a job, so he planned to skip commencement ceremonies and return to Ghana. As Geir was driving to the Tucson airport on April 28 to catch his flight home, he was distracted by the beauty of the Tucson countryside and drove into an embankment. Geir recovered from the accident but only after being immobilized in a body cast until December 28 of the year of his graduation. He flew home on December 31 of that year. What was his residency status for that year?

1-5. Lidia, a citizen and resident of Bolivia, considered moving to the United States even though she had never been to the country. She visited the United States for 15 days in February of Year 1. The trip convinced her to make the move. In May of Year 1, she spent 20 days in Atlanta on a house-hunting trip and on September 3, Year 1, she moved to the United States where she continues to be present and reside domestically.

(a) What is Lidia's residency status for Year 1?

(b) May Lidia elect to be treated as a resident for any portion of Year 1? If so, under what circumstances would she want to make this election?

(c) If Lidia did not arrive permanently in the United States until December 8 of Year 1, what is her residency status? May she elect a different result?

(d) If Lidia arrived permanently on September 3, Year 1, but took a vacation in Bolivia for the entire month of December, Year 1, what is her residency status for Year 1? May she elect a different result?

C. OVERVIEW

A taxpayer's residency classification is a threshold issue for determining the applicability of United States taxation. Broadly speaking, taxpayers are generally considered to be either "domestic" or "foreign," under §§ 7701(a)(4), (5), (14), and (30), and as defined under the Regulations.[1] Depending on the taxpayer's status as domestic or foreign, the tax base varies dramatically, as illustrated in Figure 1-1.

FIGURE 1-1. OVERVIEW OF UNITED STATES TAXING JURISDICTION

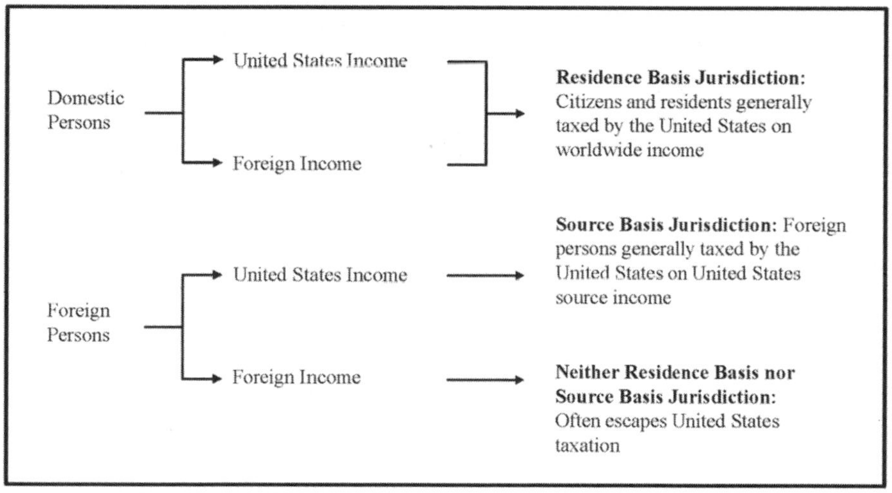

United States citizens, United States residents, and domestic corporations ("domestic persons") are generally subject to tax on their worldwide incomes under § 61, while non-resident alien individuals and foreign corporations ("foreign persons") are typically subject to United States taxation only on specified items or types of income under § 871 (applicable to foreign individuals) and §§ 881 and 882 (applicable to foreign corporations).[2] Thus, if a person is determined to be foreign,

---

[1] Unless otherwise indicated, all section references throughout this text refer to the Internal Revenue Code of 1986, as amended, and all references to Regulation refer to the Treasury Regulations issued thereunder.

[2] The Supreme Court case excerpted in Part D of this Unit, *Cook v. Tait*, discusses Congress's power to tax United States citizens. The discussion herein omits the treatment of trusts and estates, since these entities are beyond the scope of the materials covered in this Casebook. Partnerships are not generally

an integral issue regarding the scope of United States international taxation is the distinction between income that is sourced in the United States and income that is sourced abroad. The source rules are discussed in Unit 2. The United States international tax structure applicable to individuals and corporations is summarized in Figure 1-2.

FIGURE 1-2. UNITED STATES INTERNATIONAL TAX STRUCTURE

Residence	Type of Taxpayer	Tax Base	Tax Rate
United States	Citizen or Resident Alien Individual	Worldwide income	Graduated
	Domestic Corporation		
Non-United States, Non-Treaty Country Resident	Non-Resident Alien Individual	(1) United States source passive income, *and* (2) Income effectively connected with the conduct of a trade or business in the United States	(1) Flat (2) Graduated
	Foreign Corporation	(1) United States source passive income, *and* (2) Income effectively connected with the conduct of a trade or business in the United States, *and* (3) Branch profits tax may apply.	(1) Flat (2) Graduated (3) Flat
Non-United States, Treaty Country Resident	Non-Resident Alien Individual	(1) United States source passive income, *and* (2) Income attributable to a permanent establishment in the United States	(1) Flat (but often lowered by treaty) (2) Graduated
	Foreign Corporation	(1) United States source passive income, *and* (2) Income attributable to a permanent establishment in the United States, *and* (3) Branch profits tax may apply.	(1) Flat (but often lowered by treaty) (2) Graduated (3) Flat (but often lowered by treaty)

One of the most fundamental issues for international taxation has been the potential for double taxation that exists due to persons and transactions crossing borders. United States persons may experience double taxation because the United States imposes tax based on residence while a foreign country may simultaneously impose tax on an item of income derived within its borders. Similarly, a foreign person, subject to income taxation by his home country, may be simultaneously subject to tax on income he derives from activities he pursues in the United States.[3]

---

subject to United States income tax, and their treatment is not specifically discussed. In general, partners of a partnership will be treated as having received their pro rata share of partnership income. *See* Unit 8.

[3] Where one taxpayer is taxed twice on the same item of income, it is referred to as "juridical" double

Double taxation is considered to be so distortive of efficient economic behavior that most countries, including the United States, have addressed it statutorily. Unit 3 of this Casebook introduces one such method, namely, an exclusion from federal income tax for certain foreign-earned income of United States persons. Units 4 through 6 discuss another method, namely, a credit against United States federal income taxes for certain foreign income taxes paid.

The issue of double taxation is also addressed in treaties entered into with other countries, usually on a bilateral basis. Through tax treaties, countries generally agree on a reciprocal basis to reduce their taxation of persons from the other country, thus lowering the foreign tax burdens of their citizens and residents who work or invest abroad. The differential tax treatment of non-residents pursuant to treaties on the one hand versus United States statutory rules on the other is possible because treaties have the same effect as acts of Congress and are equivalent to any other United States law under the Constitution (Art. VI, cl. 2). The interaction between tax treaties and statutory law and the standard terms and provisions of the more than 55 income tax treaties currently in force are the subject of Units 10 through 12.

Because double taxation is addressed both in the Code and in international agreements, the United States taxation of non-residents depends upon whether the person is a resident of a country with which the United States has a tax treaty. If a person is from a country that does *not* have a comprehensive tax treaty with the United States — referred to throughout this Casebook as a "nontreaty country" — the statutory rules of §§ 871 through 885 and related provisions generally impose gross-basis taxes at a rate of 30 percent on passive income items derived from United States sources, while most United States-source business income, including that derived from services, is taxed progressively under §§ 1, 11, and 55.[4]

Because the statutory rules act as a default for those taxpayers and transactions not governed by a tax treaty, the statutory taxation of non-residents and foreign corporations is discussed in Units 7 through 9, before the Units concerning treaties. By learning the default rules first, one can better appreciate the impact of tax treaties.

If a foreign person is from a treaty country (as is frequently the case), United States taxation of that person's income also depends on the terms of the applicable treaty. Typically, both parties to a treaty significantly narrow their taxing jurisdiction through reduced tax rates in the case of passive income and higher thresholds for the imposition of taxation in the case of business income. The United States tax treatment of foreign persons from treaty countries is the subject of Units 10 through 12.

---

taxation. This is in contrast to "economic" double taxation, which refers to the taxation of an item of income in two taxpayers' hands. The classic example of economic double taxation is the distributed corporate profit that is taxed once as income to the corporation and again as dividend income to the shareholder.

[4] As mentioned above and discussed more fully in Unit 9, some entities may also be subject to a 30% branch profits tax.

Because the distinction between foreign and domestic residency is important for the taxation of both individuals and entities, determining residency is a threshold step in virtually every international tax inquiry. This Unit lays out the basic framework for residency classification with respect to individuals and corporations.

1.01 Residency Classification for Individuals

Under § 7701, individuals belong to one of two categories: (1) United States citizens and resident aliens, who are domestic persons; and (2) non-resident aliens, who are foreign persons. According to Regulation § 1.1-1(c), "every person born or naturalized in the United States and subject to its jurisdiction is a citizen."[5] An individual who has filed a declaration of intent to become a citizen, but who has not been admitted to citizenship through naturalization, is deemed an alien and not a citizen. All United States citizens, even if they are also citizens of another jurisdiction, are subject to worldwide income taxation.

While the determination of citizenship has historically proven relatively easy, the determination of residency was for many years much more difficult. Residency was once determined under a facts and circumstances approach. In 1984, Congress formulated an objective determination of whether an alien individual is a non-resident of the United States. There are now two tests by which residency is determined: one based on the individual's legal status, and the other based on his physical presence in the United States.

Under § 7701(b), an alien individual will be considered to be a United States resident with respect to any calendar year if: (1) the individual is a lawful permanent resident of the United States at any time during the calendar year (the "green card test"); or (2) the individual meets a "substantial presence test." In addition, two limited elections are available. The first, found in § 7701(b)(4), provides rules under which an individual may elect to be treated as a resident in the first year of presence even if the substantial presence test is not met. The second, found in § 6013(g), enables non-resident alien spouses of United States citizens or residents to file joint United States tax returns.

In all other cases, an individual is classified as a non-resident alien for tax purposes. If an individual is not described in either of these tests (and does not make a residency election), he will not be considered a United States resident, regardless of the degree or extent of his physical, economic, or commercial contacts with the United States.

1.02 The Green Card Test

The first objective measure of United States residency focuses on the alien's legal status within the jurisdiction. An alien is treated as a United States resident if that individual is a lawful permanent resident of the United States *at any time* during the calendar year at issue. Under this so-called "green card" test, an

---

[5] The definition is consistent with and cross-references Title 8 of the United States Code, "Aliens and Nationality," Chapter 12, "Immigration and Nationality," which defines citizenship by birth and processes for acquiring citizenship by naturalization. *See* 8 U.S.C. §§ 1401–1459.

individual is a lawful permanent resident of the United States if he holds a green card at any time during the year and his status as a green card holder has neither been revoked nor determined administratively or judicially to have been abandoned. A green card is given to an individual who is lawfully granted the privilege of residing in the United States as an immigrant in accordance with the immigration laws. Non-resident aliens in the process of applying for a green card do not meet the green card test.

1.03   The Substantial Presence Test

The substantial presence test focuses on the alien individual's actual physical presence in the United States. The idea is that individuals who spend substantial amounts of time in the United States over a period of years have a sufficiently close relationship with the United States to justify taxing them as residents. Under the substantial presence test, an alien individual is treated as a resident alien in a given year if he is present in the United States on at least 31 days of that year and at least 183 total days during a three-year period, weighted towards the year in question.

Section 7701(b)(3) and the Regulations thereunder determine whether the 183-day test is met using a composite, weighted measure of the days of physical presence in the United States over the three-year period including the year in question and the two preceding years. If an alien individual's presence equals or exceeds 183 days using the multipliers set forth in the statute, and equals or exceeds 31 days during the year in question, the alien individual meets the substantial presence test and is treated as a United States resident, unless an exception applies. In the absence of an exception, actual presence of 183 days or more in any year is incontrovertible evidence of residence. Exceptions are provided for certain exempt individuals and certain individuals whose presence is transitory or temporary.

1.04   The 30-Day De Minimis Rule

Notwithstanding any prior presence by an alien individual, if an alien individual is in the United States for 30 days or less in the current calendar year, a *de minimis* exception to the substantial presence test applies. Under this 30-day exception, if an alien individual is physically present within the United States for such a limited time in the current year, he will be considered a non-resident even if the 183-day formula would otherwise be satisfied.

1.05   The Tax-Home Exception

Section 7701 also negates resident status under the substantial presence test where the facts and circumstances and the individual's physical presence during the current year indicate that the individual has more significant ties to another jurisdiction. Under the "tax-home exception," an alien individual is treated as a non-resident even if he meets the substantial presence test for any current year if the individual (1) is present within the United States on fewer than 183 days during the current year; (2) establishes that, for the current year, his "tax home" is in a foreign country; and (3) has a closer connection to such foreign country than to the United States.

A tax home is defined with reference to the concept employed by § 162(a)(2) (applicable to the deductibility of traveling expenses incurred while away from home). Under these standards, a tax home is located at an individual's regular or principal place of business. If the individual lacks a regular or principal place of business, his tax home is his principal place of abode.

In determining whether an individual has established a "closer connection" to a foreign country than to the United States, the individual must demonstrate a significant lifestyle nexus to that country. Regulation § 301.7701(b)-2(d)(1) lists relevant facts and circumstances to consider in this determination. The tax-home exception is not available for any year in which an individual has applied for a green card, has taken other affirmative steps to become a permanent resident, or has an application for adjustment of status pending.

1.06   Exempt and Other Special Categories of Alien Individuals

Under the objective definition of resident alien contained in § 7701(b), certain alien individuals and their activities are accorded special exemptions from resident status. Certain days of presence of these "exempt" and special aliens are not counted towards the individual's United States residency. Under § 7701(b)(3), special rules apply to four categories of exempt individuals, as well as to individuals unable to leave the United States for medical reasons, and certain individuals commuting to or traveling through the United States. In general, days spent in the United States by such individuals will not be counted for purposes of determining presence under the substantial presence test.

Exempt Individuals. The exempt category of alien individuals includes foreign government-related individuals, teachers or trainees, students, and professional athletes competing in charitable sporting events. Section 7701(b)(5) and Regulation § 301.7701(b)-3 provide detailed definitions of the individuals in these exempt categories. For teachers and students, visa requirements are imposed and substantial compliance with such provisions is mandated. Special timing limitations are imposed on the teacher and student exemptions where such individuals are recurrently present in the United States. Lengthy stays eventually lose the protection of the exemption. These limitations prevent foreign persons from enjoying a timeless pursuit of experience and knowledge in the United States without contributing to national revenues.

Medical Conditions. Presence does not arise for any day on which an individual objectively intended to leave the United States but was unable to leave due to a medical condition or problem arising while the individual was present in the United States. Regulation § 301.7701(b)-3(c) provides that the condition causing the failure to leave must not be a pre-existing problem or condition known at the time the individual entered the United States.

Days in Transit. Pursuant to § 7701(b)(7)(C) and Regulation § 301.7701(b)-3(d), days in transit between foreign points are excluded as days of presence for the substantial presence test, presumably because such a traveler most likely cannot utilize his brief stay in the United States for any purpose sufficiently significant to extend residency nexus. The exemption is designed to protect individuals who must travel between airports to change planes or who experience brief United States layovers. The exemption is conditioned on physical presence of less than 24 hours and the absence of any non-travel activities. Thus, for example, should the individual attend a business meeting while in transit, the exemption will not apply.

Contiguous Country Commuters. Regular commuters residing in Mexico and Canada are also shielded from resident status. Under § 7701(b)(7)(B) and Regulation § 301.7701(b)-3(e), a "regular" commuter is an individual who commutes to his place of employment or self-employment in the United States on more than 75 percent of the workdays during the working period. Commuting is determined on a daily basis, so overnight or extended stays will not qualify as commuting for purposes of this exemption.

1.07 Residency Commencement and Termination

A resident individual's period of residency in the United States depends upon the test under which the individual obtained residency status. If an alien individual satisfies the green card test but does not meet the substantial presence test, the individual's "residency starting date" is the first day of his physical presence during a calendar year as a lawful permanent resident, pursuant to § 7701(b)(2)(A) and Regulation § 301.7701(b)-4. If an alien individual satisfies the green card test for the current year but is not physically present in the United States during the current year, the residency starting date is the first day of the following year.

If the substantial presence test is met, residency generally commences on the first day the individual is present in the United States. However, § 7701(b)(2)(C) provides a *de minimis* rule which disregards nominal presence in some cases for purposes of the substantial presence test. For example, if an individual, during a period of actual presence (for example, a house-hunting trip), can establish that he had a closer connection to a foreign country than to the United States, up to ten days of presence can be disregarded for purposes of determining the residency start date.

Under § 7701(b)(2)(A), if an individual meets both the green card and substantial presence tests, residency commences on the earlier of the residency commencement dates provided under both tests. Similar rules apply for determining the alien individual's residency termination date. Regulation § 301.7701(b)-4(b) provides the general rule that, for an individual who ceases to be a resident during a calendar year and is not a resident at any time during the following calendar year, the residency termination date is the last day of the calendar year.

Section 7701(b)(2)(B) and the Regulations thereunder provide that, notwithstanding the general rule, residency terminates under the green card test on the first day during the calendar year on which the individual is no longer a lawful permanent resident, if the individual establishes that, for the remainder of the calendar year, his tax home was in a foreign country and he maintained a closer connection to that foreign country than to the United States. An alien individual who holds a green card may abandon resident alien status (subject to the substantial presence test) by surrendering the green card to United States Citizenship and Immigration Services (USCIS) or a consular officer. The date of such surrender controls the date of termination of residency, rather than the subsequent date, if any, on which the United States government processes the surrendered green card. According to Regulation § 301.7701(b)-1, abandonment occurs when the individual files an application for abandonment or submits a letter accompanying his green card stating his intent to abandon resident status. If, however, the determination of abandonment is initiated by USCIS or a consular official, the abandonment of lawful permanent residency occurs upon the issuance of a final administrative or judicial order of abandonment (after any appeal has been exhausted).

Under the substantial presence test, § 7701(b)(2) provides that an individual's last day of physical presence will close the period of residency, provided that after such date the individual has a closer connection to a foreign country for the balance of the calendar year and is not a United States resident in the next year. The nominal presence rules may be used to disregard up to ten days of actual presence. Although these days are disregarded for purposes of determining residency commencement and termination dates, they are still considered for determining whether an individual meets the substantial presence test.

Certain United States citizens and residents who give up their status (expatriate) are subject to § 877, which may tax these individuals on certain of their United States-source income under the regular progressive rates applicable to current citizens and residents if this results in a higher total tax than would be achieved if they were taxed as non-residents. Prior rules required the expatriation to be accompanied by a tax-avoidance motive before § 877 would apply, but a 2004 amendment removed that requirement. A 2008 amendment added § 877A, which mandates a one-time mark-to-market tax in certain expatriation cases. Under §§ 7701(n) and 6039G(a), any individual who is subject to § 877 must notify the United States government by giving notice about the termination to the Secretary of State or the Secretary of Homeland Security, and by filing a statement in accordance with § 6039G. Until these requirements are met, residency or citizenship is not terminated even if other termination rules are met.

1.08 First-Year Residency Election

An alien individual can also be treated as a United States resident by making an affirmative election of such treatment under § 7701(b)(1)(A)(iii). The purpose of the election is to assist those in the process of meeting the substantial presence test who, for the year in question, did not accumulate the requisite presence to secure residency status, but nonetheless wish to be considered United States residents for taxation purposes. Section 7701(b)(4) lays out five requirements: (1) the taxpayer must have failed to be a resident under the green card or substantial presence tests; (2) the taxpayer must not have been a resident in the year preceding the election year; (3) the taxpayer must meet the substantial presence test for the year following the election year; (4) the taxpayer must be present for 31 consecutive days in the election year; and (5) the taxpayer must be present for 75 percent of the period beginning with the first day of the 31-day period described in (4) and ending with the last day of the election year. An applicant may claim up to five days of presence for periods in which the applicant was actually absent from the United States.

The residency election is made on the alien individual's tax return for the year for which the election is made. However, since the election depends upon the satisfaction of the substantial presence test in the succeeding taxable year, Regulation § 301.7701(b)-4(c)(3) provides that the election cannot be made before the individual satisfies the substantial presence test for the following year. If the substantial presence test is not satisfied at the original due date for the return to be filed in the year the election is made, the alien individual may request an extension of time to file until the test is satisfied.

Under § 7701(b)(4)(C), the residency start date begins on the first day of the earliest presence period meeting both the 31-day and 75 percent measuring periods. Termination issues are not relevant in the context of the residency election since the election is conditioned upon satisfying the substantial presence test for the following year.

1.09 Spousal Residency Election

As a general rule, favorable tax treatment is accorded to married taxpayers who file a joint tax return. Prior to 1975, citizens or residents who married non-resident aliens were precluded from filing a joint return and thus were not eligible for many important tax benefits. In 1976, Congress enacted §§ 6013(g) and 6013(h) to eliminate the disparate treatment of citizens or residents who marry non-resident aliens. These provisions permit married couples to elect to treat the non-resident alien spouse as a United States resident. An election under § 6013(g) may be made by a spouse who is a non-resident at the close of the taxable year. An election under § 6013(h) may be made by a spouse who is a non-resident at the beginning of the year but becomes a resident by year-end.

If the non-resident alien spouse has little independent income, the § 6013 election may prove beneficial, since it will enable the couple to become eligible for, among other benefits:

1. The usually advantageous rate schedule of § 1(a) for married couples filing jointly;

2. The § 21 household and dependent care credit;

3. The earned income credit of § 32; and

4. With regard to the § 1211(b)(1) limitation upon the deductibility of capital losses, $3,000 of allowable losses rather than $1,500.

The election generally is not beneficial if the non-resident alien spouse has a substantial amount of foreign source income which is lightly taxed by the country of income source. In such a case, the tax benefits to be derived from the election to file jointly are likely outweighed by the detriments of subjecting such foreign source income to United States taxation. Similarly, though subject to some uncertainty, the election is less likely to be beneficial if a non-resident alien spouse's income is subject to more beneficial tax treatment as a foreign person eligible for the benefits of a tax treaty.[6]

1.10 General United States Taxation of Corporations

The distinction between foreign and domestic is as important for corporate entities as it is for individuals. As in the case of United States citizens and residents, a domestic corporation is subject to United States taxation on all of its income from whatever source derived, while § 11(d) limits the application of this provision by interposing taxing thresholds for "foreign" corporations.[7]

A corporate subsidiary is a separate juridical entity from its parent. A domestic corporation's foreign subsidiary is thus subject to limited taxation in the United States, while a foreign corporation's domestic subsidiary is, like any other domestic corporation, subject to tax on its worldwide income. A branch is distinguished: since it is not a separate juridical entity, its income is attributed to the entity that operates the branch. If the entity that operates the branch is classified as a corporation and the corporation is domestic, all of its foreign branch income is subject to tax in the United States. If the corporate entity is foreign, the branch's United States-source income may be subject to various forms of United States taxation, including a branch profits tax (discussed in Unit 9).

The limited jurisdiction of the United States to tax foreign subsidiaries unduly encourages domestic corporations to form foreign subsidiaries instead of foreign branch offices, even though non-tax considerations might weigh in favor of using the latter. In response to this concern, Congress has implemented limited measures to curb this distortive behavior by undercutting the advantages that might arise from the foreign incorporation of investments and activities conducted for the benefit of United States persons. Some examples of these measures include the Controlled Foreign Corporation rules (§§ 951–965 discussed in Units 13 and 14) and the Passive Foreign Investment Companies rules (§§ 1291–1298, discussed in Unit 15), each of which safeguards United States taxation in the case of certain foreign activities of foreign companies that are owned, in whole or in part, by United States persons.

1.11 Classification of Certain Business Entities

It is generally straightforward to determine whether an entity is domestic or foreign, since this inquiry turns exclusively on the jurisdiction of formation under §§ 7701(a)(4) and 7701(a)(5). Section 7701(a)(4) provides that a domestic corporation is one organized or created under the laws of the United States or any of its states. Section 7701(a)(5) provides the (perhaps unnecessary) inverse proposition, that a foreign corporation is one which is not domestic.

---

[6] See Unit 10 for a discussion of how treaties may impact residency rules.

[7] As in the case of individuals, the application of § 11 is further limited if a tax treaty applies. Qualification for tax treaty benefits may significantly reduce a foreign corporation's tax liability to the United States, as discussed in Unit 10.

The main difficulty in this area relates to the threshold determination of whether an entity should be treated for United States tax purposes as a corporation, a partnership, a venture of individuals, or disregarded as separate from its owner or owners, and the effects of any available classification elections on such determination. It is the classification of an entity for United States tax purposes as a corporation or as a non-corporate entity that determines the applicable method of United States taxation.

Generally, business entities are either classified as corporations, or as eligible entities for which the Regulations provide certain default classifications but for which the owners may elect certain alternative classifications, as described in more detail below. Certain domestic entities, such as those organized under a federal or state statute as a corporation, or regulated insurance companies, are treated as corporations and are not eligible entities.

Regulation § 301.7701-2 identifies more than 80 foreign entities that are treated as *"per se"* corporations. If a foreign entity is not automatically classified as a corporation by virtue of its inclusion on the *per se* list, it is an "eligible entity" for which classification may be elected under what are commonly referred to as the "check-the-box" rules, found in Regulation § 301.7701-3. *Per se* corporations are not eligible to elect their classification under the check-the-box rules.

Form 8832, Entity Classification Election, provides the boxes to be checked, by which an eligible entity may elect to be classified as an association taxable as a corporation, as a partnership, or if it has a single owner, as a disregarded entity. Regulation § 301.7701-3(b) explains the classification election rules for eligible entities and provides default rules for classification in the absence of an election. The default rules may be different depending on whether the eligible entity is foreign or domestic.

According to Regulation § 301.7701-3(b)(2), the default classifications and the applicable alternative classifications for foreign eligible entities depend on how many owners the entity has and whether any owner possesses personal liability for the debts of or claims against the entity by reason of ownership.

A foreign eligible entity with a single owner is treated by default as a sole proprietorship, or in other words disregarded as a separate entity, if the owner has personal liability for the debts of or claims against the entity. In such case, the entity may instead elect to be treated as an association taxable as a corporation for United States tax purposes. If the owner has limited liability, the entity will be treated as an association taxable as a corporation by default. In such case, the entity may instead elect to be disregarded as separate from its owner for United States tax purposes.

A foreign entity with more than one owner will be classified as a corporation for United States tax purposes if all the owners have limited liability for the debts and obligations of the entity; but if at least one owner has personal liability, it will be classified as a partnership by default. In either case, the entity can elect the opposite treatment using Form 8832.

Check-the-box elections can be made at formation of the eligible entity or at a later time, as provided under Regulation § 301.7701-3(c). Where an eligible entity already in existence makes an election to change its classification using Form 8832, such election may have United States tax consequences, as provided under Regulation § 301.7701-3(g).

The flexibility accorded to international tax planning created by the check-the-box Regulations has been nothing short of extraordinary. The regime is widely seen as too flexible, giving sophisticated tax planners an open door to exploit inconsistencies in the tax rules between the United States and other countries. The Internal Revenue Service seems to be contending daily with the tax complexities that have arisen since the promulgation of these Regulations. To date, efforts to reign in the excessive latitude of the check-the-box Regulations have been limited.

D. REFERENCE MATERIALS

* *Cook v. Tait*

COOK v. TAIT
Supreme Court of the United States
265 U.S. 47 (1924)

MR. JUSTICE MCKENNA delivered the opinion of the Court. . . .

Plaintiff is a native citizen of the United States, and was such when he took up his residence and became domiciled in . . . Mexico. A demand was made upon him by defendant in error, designated defendant, to make a return of his income for the purpose of taxation under the revenue laws of the United States. Plaintiff complied with the demand, but under protest; the income having been derived from property situated in . . . Mexico. A tax was assessed against him in the sum of $1,193.38, the first installment of which he paid, and for it, as we have said this action was brought.

The question in the case . . . is, as expressed by plaintiff, whether Congress has power to impose a tax upon income received by a native citizen of the United States who, at the time the income was received, was permanently resident and domiciled in . . . Mexico, the income being from real and personal property located in Mexico.

Plaintiff assigns against the power, not only his rights under the Constitution of the United States, but under international law, and in support of the assignments cites many cases. It will be observed that the foundation of the assignments is the fact that the citizen receiving the income and the property of which it is the product are outside of the territorial limits of the United States. These two facts, the contention is, exclude the existence of the power to tax. Or to put the contention another way, to the existence of the power and its exercise, the person receiving the income and the property from which he receives it must both be within the territorial limits of the United States to be within the taxing power of the United States. The contention is not justified, and that it is not justified is the necessary deduction of recent cases. . . .

We may make further exposition of the national power as the case depends upon it. It was illustrated at once in *United States v. Bennett* by a contrast with the power of a state. It was pointed out that there were limitations upon the latter that were not on the national power. The taxing power of a state, it was decided, encountered at its borders the taxing power of other states and was limited by them. There was no such limitation, it was pointed out, upon the national power, and that the limitation upon the states affords, it was said, no ground for constructing a barrier around the United States, "shutting that government off from the exertion of powers which inherently belong to it by virtue of its sovereignty."

The contention was rejected that a citizen's property without the limits of the United States derives no benefit from the United States. The contention, it was said, came from the confusion of thought in "mistaking the scope and extent of the sovereign power of the United States as a nation and its relations to its citizens and their relation to it." And that power in its scope and extent, it was decided, is based on the presumption that government by its very nature benefits the citizen and his property wherever found, and that opposition to it holds on to citizenship while it "belittles and destroys its advantages and blessings by denying the possession by government of an essential power required to make citizenship completely beneficial." In other words, the principle was declared that the government, by its very nature, benefits the citizen and his property wherever found, and therefore has the power to make the benefit complete. Or, to express it another way, the basis of the power to tax was not and cannot be made dependent upon the situs of the property in all cases, it being in or out of the United States, nor was not and cannot be made dependent upon the domicile of the citizen, that being in or out of the United States, but upon his relation as citizen to the United States and the relation of the latter to him as citizen. The consequence of the relations is that the native citizen who is taxed may have domicile, and the property from which his income is derived may have situs, in a foreign country and the tax be legal — the government having power to impose the tax.

Judgment affirmed.

Unit 2

SOURCE RULES

A. CODE AND REGULATION PROVISIONS

Code §§ 861; 862; 863(a), (b); 864(a); 865(a), (b), (c), (d), (g).

Reg. §§ 1.861-2(a); 1.861-3(a)(1); 1.861-7(a), (c), (d); 1.863-1(d)(1)–(3)(iii); 1.863-3(a)–(c).

B. PROBLEMS FOR CLASS DISCUSSION

2-1. Determine the source of each of the following items:

(a) An interest payment of $1,000 made by Ramli, a Malaysian citizen who is present in the United States for the whole year during which the payment was made, and whose only gross income for all years consists of interest and dividend income from investments in Malaysia.

(b) An interest payment of $1,000 made by Texas Co., a corporation organized in Texas, on a general obligation bond.

(c) How would the answer to (b) change if the interest is paid not by Texas Co. but by its Singapore branch on a deposit at that branch? Like Texas Co., the branch is engaged in the commercial banking business.

(d) How would the answer to (b) change if Texas Co.'s interest payment is made in Year 4 and Texas Co. derives both United States source income attributable to the active conduct of its business in the United States and foreign source income attributable to the active conduct of its business outside the United States? Texas Co.'s gross income for Years 1 through 4 is as follows:

Year	United States source gross income	Foreign source gross income
1	$500,000	$3,000,000
2	500,000	3,000,000
3	1,000,000	2,000,000
4	2,000,000	2,000,000
Total	$4,000,000	$10,000,000

2-2. Determine the source of each of the following items:

(a) A cash dividend (out of earnings and profits) paid to shareholders by Wash Co., a corporation organized in Washington.

(b) A cash dividend (out of earnings and profits) of $1,000 paid to shareholders in Year 4 by Foreign Co., a foreign corporation that conducts business in the United States and has the following items of gross income for Years 1 through 4:

Year	Gross income effectively connected with U.S. business	Other gross income
1	$2,000,000	$10,000,000
2	3,000,000	10,000,000
3	5,000,000	10,000,000
4	10,000,000	10,000,000
Total	$20,000,000	$40,000,000

(c) How would the answer to (b) change if the dividend was declared in Year 3 but not paid until Year 4?

2-3. Evita is a citizen and resident of Argentina. Evita came to the United States in Year 1 to sell clothing on behalf of Patagonia, an Argentine corporation. Evita is one of many agents that Patagonia sent to the United States in Year 1. Evita makes $3,000 in commissions on sales to domestic customers during her five-month stay in the United States.

(a) What is the source of Evita's commissions?

(b) How would the answer to (a) change if Evita was in the United States for only 60 days?

2-4. Determine the source of each of the following items:

(a) A fellowship from Duke University awarded to Soledad, a Chilean individual who is not a citizen or resident of the United States. Soledad will use the fellowship to study the economic development of Madagascar.

(b) A $100,000 jackpot from the Oregon State Lottery paid to Soledad.

2-5. Straw Co. is a domestic corporation that sells drinking straws. Determine the source of Straw Co.'s income from the sale of its inventory in each of the following alternative situations:

(a) Straw Co. purchases its inventory from an Ohio manufacturer and sells it to distributors in Nigeria, with title passing in Nigeria.

(b) Straw Co. manufactures its own inventory at a factory plant in Ohio and sells it to distributors in Nigeria, with title passing in Nigeria.

2-6. Determine the source of a $60,000 gain from the sale of an antique automobile located in the United States, with title passing therein, owned by Soledad, a Chilean citizen and resident.

2-7. Tarek, a citizen and resident of Lebanon, composed a symphony while in Turkey for two months. He is now considering various offers from music publishers throughout the world. For each offer described below, determine whether the proposed transaction will produce United States or foreign source income.

(a) A United States publisher offers to pay for the exclusive right to publish and sell the work in the United States. Under the proposed contract, Tarek would receive five percent of the publisher's gross revenues from each sale of Tarek's work.

(b) A Kenyan publisher makes the same offer described in (a).

(c) A United States publisher offers to pay Tarek a fixed sum in exchange for all rights to the composition.

(d) The offers in (a) and (b) were made and accepted before Tarek started composing the symphony.

C. OVERVIEW

As discussed in Unit 1, non-resident aliens and foreign corporations as defined under § 7701 are generally subject to United States taxation only on income that is sourced in the United States or is in some way connected with business conducted in the United States. The rules for sourcing income as either domestic or foreign are thus crucial for foreign taxpayers. The source rules are also important for United States persons due to the pivotal role these rules play in computing the foreign tax credit, as will be seen in Units 4 through 6.

The principal rules for sourcing income are contained in §§ 861, 862, 863, and 865. Underpinning these rules is the general proposition that the source of income is the jurisdiction from which the income is derived. This inquiry poses both factual and jurisdictional issues. The initial issue is whether a sufficient nexus exists between the United States and the income in question to classify the income as United States source.

What factors give rise to income and create such a nexus? Economic analysis might point to the market which creates the demand for services, the capital or other assets which provide the means of paying for services, the social system which fostered the skills and training necessary to perform the services, the financial system which allows for payment to be made, the legal system which protects each party's property rights, and any number of other potential "sources" from which income may be said to derive. Employing a highly analytical tool for determining source thus might produce a rule that separates each payment for services into separate components that must be attributed to one or more jurisdictions. The potential for layers of inquiry and complexity seems infinite.

For example, in the case of income that arises from rendering services, the fact that the recipient of the services (such as an employer) resides in the United States and the fact that this recipient pays for the services with a check drawn on a United States bank provide two significant "jurisdictional contacts" with the United States — namely, the residence of the payor and the place where payment is made. Other significant focal points include where the funds are received and deposited by the service provider, and where the services are rendered.

While each of these contacts provides an economically defensible basis upon which to determine source, it is the last mentioned — the place where services are rendered — that Congress has deemed most relevant for purposes of United States source classification. This rule is probably based as much or more upon ease of administration as it is upon any other framework, but a close study of the source rules reveals the validity and necessity of an inquiry into the theoretical source of income.

The source rules generally classify income as income with a United States source, as income without a United States source (foreign source), or as income partly from within and partly from without the United States (mixed source). The source rules differ based upon type of income, such as interest, dividends, and income from the manufacture and sale of property. Categories of income not expressly addressed by a particular sourcing rule are sourced administratively or judicially, often by reference to the statutory rule which is most congruous with the transaction or income type under consideration.

Sections 861 and 865 describe specific categories of income and determine when such items are United States source income. Section 862 merely confirms the converse. If, after the application of §§ 861 and 865, the item does not have a United States source, then, typically by definition, the income item has a foreign source. These provisions generally adopt a singular focus, categorizing income as either exclusively United States source or exclusively foreign source.

Section 863 addresses income that has significant connections to both the United States and another jurisdiction or jurisdictions. That section provides allocation rules intended to properly reflect the "contributions" of the respective jurisdictions to the derivation of the income. Items of income that are excludable from gross income are not sourced, presumably because the source is irrelevant.

Losses, expenses and other deductions are not separately sourced under § 861 but are allocated and apportioned pursuant to § 861(b). Regulation § 1.861-8 sets forth the general rules for determining proper allocation and apportionment of deductions. Regulation § 1.865-1 imposes separate loss allocation rules for losses recognized on the sale or exchange of personal property. Under that Regulation, any loss recognized with respect to personal property other than stock, inventory, and certain other excluded assets is allocated to the class of gross income to which a gain on the sale of such property would be placed. Losses not subject to this rule include losses from foreign currency transactions and certain financial instruments and losses from inventory. The general allocation rule under Regulation § 1.865-1 is similar for stock losses, which are allocated according to the residence of the seller, as is generally the case with stock gains. The rules for allocating and apportioning deductions are explored further in Units 8 and 12.

Effective tax planning may require scrutiny of the source rules of several countries because not all jurisdictions have the same criteria for source purposes. For instance, while the United States focuses on the jurisdiction where services are rendered, another jurisdiction may employ a different standard, such as the residence of the payor. Thus, in an international setting, it is possible that a single transaction spanning two taxing jurisdictions will possess two countries of source, as each country concludes that the income arises exclusively within its borders. The result is double taxation — a topic addressed most comprehensively by means of a credit for foreign taxes paid, as discussed in Units 4 through 6, and through tax treaties, as discussed in Units 10 through 12.

Before looking into the particular sourcing rules presented in this Unit, it is important to understand that determining the source of an item of income does not necessarily tell us anything about how the item will ultimately be taxed — that is a topic for later Units. The sourcing of income is instead a definitional threshold analysis that, along with residency determinations, will inform subsequent levels of analysis. As you go through the source rules presented in this Unit, it is important to keep in mind this distinction between sourcing something and determining the tax consequences of that source.

2.01   Interest Income

The source of interest income is generally controlled by the residence or the place of incorporation of the obligor (the person paying the interest). Thus, under § 861(a)(1), interest from the United States or the District of Columbia and interest from the obligations of United States residents and domestic corporations possess a United States source. However, Regulation § 1.861-2(a)(2) expands this rule and in so doing complicates the notion of residency introduced in Unit 1.

Under this Regulation, in addition to noncorporate residents and domestic corporations, foreign partnerships and foreign corporations that are engaged in a trade or business in the United States are also considered to be residents of the United States for purposes of the interest sourcing rule. As a result, interest paid by a foreign entity will be considered United States source if the entity is conducting a trade or business in the United States. This potentially surprising result is mitigated by Regulations, as discussed in section 2.02, below.

Special issues may arise if there is more than one obligor in any given debt transaction — a possibility not addressed in § 861. For example, in the context of a joint obligation between a United States resident and a non-resident alien, it is not clear whether the source of the interest should be determined by reference to both obligors regardless of the ultimate payor of the obligation, the ultimate payor of the obligation alone, the ability of each co-obligor to pay the obligation, or some other factor or combination of factors. Neither the statute nor the Regulations pertaining to the source of interest offer guidance in this matter.

For purposes of determining source, the concept of interest is quite broadly defined. Although the statute refers only to "interest on bonds, notes, or other interest-bearing obligations," § 861(a)(1) covers interest imputed under §§ 483 (interest on deferred payments from certain property sales) and 1273 (original issue discount). Other disguised interest payments are also included in the definition pursuant to Regulation § 1.861-2(a)(7).

2.02   Exceptions to the Interest Source Rule

While the residence of the obligor generally dictates the source of interest income, there are a number of exceptions to this general rule. These exceptions are premised on grounds of both policy and practicality.

Active Foreign Business Exception. Until 2010, § 861(a)(1)(A) provided that interest payments would not be deemed to arise from a United States source if they were made by a United States resident or corporation that met the 80-percent foreign business requirements of former § 861(c)(1). Section 861(c) was repealed in 2010 but grandfathered for certain existing companies, an exception which can now be found in §§ 871(i)(2)(B) and 871(l). Further, the repeal did not affect certain payments of interest on obligations issued before August 10, 2010.

Banking Obligors. Pursuant to § 861(a)(1)(A), interest on deposits with certain foreign banking branches of domestic corporations and partnerships will be considered foreign sourced. The effect of this exception is that this interest income will be exempt from United States tax in the hands of foreign investors, even though the amount is paid by a resident obligor.

United States Branches of Foreign Partnerships. Foreign corporations and foreign partnerships are treated as United States residents for purposes of the interest sourcing rules under Regulation § 1.861-2(a)(2) if they are engaged in a trade or business in the United States at any time during the year of payment. Interest paid by these foreign obligors is United States source income to the recipient. As explained more fully in Unit 9, however, § 884(f)(1) treats interest paid by a foreign corporation as having United States source only if it is paid by a United States trade or business of that corporation. Under former law, there was no similar limitation for foreign partnerships, but 2004 legislation amended § 861(a)(1)(B) to extend the same limitation to foreign partnerships.

2.03   Dividends

Dividends are generally sourced according to the situs of incorporation of the payor corporation, under § 861(a)(2). Thus, the dividend source rules make an initial distinction between domestic and foreign corporations. With very minor exceptions, dividends received from domestic corporations are United States source income. However, as discussed below, a more refined attempt is made to track the earnings and profits derived by foreign corporations and to account for the origin of those earnings via the source rules.

As set forth in Regulation § 1.861-3, the term "dividend" for source rule purposes encompasses distributions defined in § 316. Under that section, a dividend is any distribution of property made by a corporation to its shareholders out of current or accumulated earnings and profits. Section 301 provides the tax consequences of corporate distributions. Under that section, dividends are included in gross income under § 301(c)(1) and are thus subject to the dividend sourcing rules. Distributions made in the absence of earnings and profits are applied against and reduce the adjusted basis of the stock under § 301(c)(2), or if the basis is insufficient, they are treated as gain from the sale or exchange of property under § 301(c)(3), implicating the source rules applicable to gains, as discussed in subpart 2.08 below. The source of other kinds of corporate distributions, such as stock redemptions and § 305 stock dividends, should be determined by the dividend source rule to the extent these distributions are treated as dividends for United States tax purposes.

2.04   Exceptions to the Dividend Source Rule

Dividends from foreign corporations with a *de minimis* or no United States business nexus are generally foreign source. However, under § 861(a)(2)(B), dividends paid by a foreign corporation may be United States source if over a three-year period, 25 percent or more of the gross income of the corporation is effectively connected with a United States trade or business (a concept explored in more detail in Unit 9). If this 25 percent threshold is equalled or exceeded, a proportionate share of the dividend received by the shareholder will be United States source, as provided in the statute.

2.05   Personal Services Compensation

As mentioned in the overview, compensation for personal services is generally sourced according to the locale in which the services are performed. Thus, under § 861(a)(3), compensation for labor or personal services performed in the United States has a United States source. Regulation § 1.861-4(a)(1) asserts that this rule holds true irrespective of the residence of the payor, the place in which the contract for services was made, or the place or time of payment. However, § 861(a)(3) provides a *de minimis* exception to the place-of-performance rule. Under this exception, up to $3,000 of certain compensation income earned by foreign persons who are present in the United States for short periods of time is not considered to be sourced in the United States.[1]

This threshold may be intended to foster inbound trade and investment by permitting residents of other countries to make brief visits to the United States for business purposes (such as buying and selling goods) without being subject to tax on the compensation paid them by their home-country employers. The threshold may also ease administrative burdens, both by saving visitors from having to file returns and by saving the Internal Revenue Service from pursuing visitors on small amounts of income.

To the extent it fulfills either of these policy goals, the compensation threshold, though small enough to have little practical effect, raises the question why there are no similar statutory thresholds for other kinds of foreign-owned income. It also raises the question of the appropriate threshold level. The threshold was set at $3,000 in a predecessor statute in the 1939 Code. What was once presumably a rather large exception, never having been indexed for inflation, has gradually eroded in value. Whatever policy this threshold furthered has also surely met with a corresponding erosion.

Special problems may arise in characterizing income as compensation. For example, if an individual performs services that eventually culminate in a patent, trade secret, or other intellectual property right, are subsequent payments more in the nature of a royalty (and therefore subject to a separate source rule discussed in the next subpart) or of compensation (and therefore generally sourced where performed)? *Boulez v. Commissioner*, excerpted in Part D of this Unit, provides

---

[1] See Unit 8 for additional discussion of these rules.

some clues but ultimately may raise more questions than it answers.[2]

2.06   Rents and Royalties

Rents and royalties are generally sourced according to the jurisdiction where the property giving rise to the income is located or used, under §§ 861(a)(4) and 862(a)(4). Regulation § 1.861-5 confirms that rents and royalties derived from the use of or right to use property located in the United States are classified as United States source. This broad source rule ostensibly covers every type of literary and industrial right to use intangible assets. Section 861(a)(4) lists among such intangibles "United States patents, copyrights, secret processes and formulas, good will, trade-marks, trade brands, franchises, and other like property."

The principal classification problem with respect to royalties lies in distinguishing royalties from other kinds of income, as the *Boulez* case illustrates. Differentiating royalty income from sales income poses a challenge particularly when payment is contingent on receipts derived from the use or disposition of the property. Licenses and sales are often distinguished by reference to the bundle of rights relinquished — in the case of complete relinquishment, a sale is deemed to have occurred, while a license may be the proper characterization if some rights are retained.

Significant uncertainty arises in many situations as to what rights comprise a sufficient bundle of rights, the relinquishment of which constitutes a sale. For example, if a foreign author assigns to a domestic corporation in perpetuity the United States and foreign serial rights to a written work but retains movie, stage, and book rights, is the assignment a sale or merely a license of one of the rights stemming from the written work? License characterization appears to be supported by Revenue Ruling 60-226, 1960-1 CB 26, in which the Service stated that "[i]n cases where interests resembling royalties are retained by the copyright proprietor along with other rights in the transferred interest, the transaction may under some conditions fail to have the required characteristics of a sale."

In order to alleviate some of these line-drawing problems, the Code contains a special sourcing rule for most intangible property. Pursuant to the source rules for sales of personal property found in § 865 (discussed in subpart 2.08 below), income arising from a transaction that is in substance a sale of intangible property is nonetheless sourced according to the royalty rule if payment is contingent on the productivity, disposition, or use of the intangible asset. Under this rule, found in § 865(d)(1)(B), income derived from the transfer is therefore generally sourced according to the jurisdiction in which the property is used.

However, the general classification issue remains for all transactions not addressed by the statute, namely those involving dispositions of tangible property, regardless of contingencies, and those involving dispositions of intangible property in which payment is not contingent on use or productivity of the underlying asset.

---

[2] See also *Sergio Garcia v. Commissioner*, 140 T.C. 6 (2013), for a more recent case that further develops the issue and allocates payments between personal services and royalties.

2.07 United States Real Property Interests

Gain from the disposition of real property, or an interest in real property, located in the United States is generally sourced in the United States. If the property is located outside the United States, the gain is foreign source. The critical factor is thus the situs of the real property. As discussed below, different sourcing rules apply to gain on the disposition of personal property. It is therefore necessary to determine whether the property involved is real or personal property. If it is personal property, the situs rule does not apply unless the property is "associated personal property" as defined in § 897. Associated personal property generally includes personal property structurally or operationally associated with the use of real property.

2.08 Sales of Personal Property Generally

Historically, sourcing gain from the sale of personal property — whether inventory or not — depended upon a "title passage rule," under which source was determined according to the location where title to the personal property passed from the seller to the buyer. The title passage rule is still generally relevant with respect to income arising from the sale of certain inventory as provided in § 861(a)(6) and its corollary, § 862(a)(6), but non-inventory property is now generally sourced according to the residence of the seller.

However, § 865(e)(2) adds an additional layer of analysis to the sourcing of income from personal property sales. In essence, § 865(e)(2)(A) may provide an override to the title passage rule (in the case of income from inventory sales) and the residence rule (in the case of income from non-inventory sales) if the income from the sale is primarily attributable to an office or fixed place of business maintained by the seller in the United States. It is important to keep in mind this exception when analyzing the general source rules for inventory and non-inventory property, as discussed below.

2.09 Sales of Inventory Property

Inventory that is purchased and sold to customers is generally sourced, under the long-standing title passage rule, according to the jurisdiction in which legal title passes. The rule itself is contained in Regulation § 1.861-7(c), which provides that a sale takes place "at the time when, and the place where, the rights, title, and interest of the seller in the property are transferred to the buyer." The operation of this title passage rule depends upon its interpretation under local commercial law.

Under § 861(a)(6), income derived from the purchase of inventory property outside the United States and sold within (as determined under the title passage rule) the United States is United States source income, while under § 862(a)(6), inventory property purchased within the United States and sold outside the United States is generally foreign source income.

Regulation § 1.861-7 restates the rule of § 861(a)(6) and provides further that gains derived from the purchase and sale of personal property are treated as derived entirely from the country in which the property is sold. When inventory property is both purchased and sold domestically or both purchased and sold in a foreign country, Revenue Ruling 75-263, 1972-2 CB 287, affirms that the situs of sale controls in those cases as well.

There are two major exceptions to the title passage rule for inventory sales. The first, introduced above, is the statutory override of § 865(e)(2)(A), applicable to all personal property (including inventory) sales by non-residents. This rule provides that if the sales income is attributable to an office or fixed place of business maintained by the seller in the United States, the income is deemed to have United States source. In determining whether an office or fixed place of business exists, § 865(e)(3) refers to § 864(c)(5), which discusses the significance of agents and the need for materiality. In connection with that statute, Regulation § 1.864-7(b) provides that an office or fixed place of business is a "fixed facility" such as a factory, store or site through which a foreign person engages in a trade or business. The Regulation goes on to describe various factors which may enter into the determination of whether a fixed facility, and therefore a United States office or fixed place of business, exists. These rules will be discussed in more detail in Unit 8.

Section 865(e)(2)(B) provides an exception to the § 865(e)(2)(A) override which applies in the case of inventory property: the presence of a domestic office or fixed place of business will not cause the gain to be United States source when such inventory property is destined for export and a foreign office "materially participates" in the sale. There is no guidance in § 865(e) with respect to the level of participation necessary to trigger this exception, but the principles of § 864(c)(4) probably control (as in the case of § 865(c)(5), discussed above and specifically referenced by § 865(e)(3), this provision uses the same phrase and provides a similar function). Under Regulation § 1.864-6(b)(3)(i), participation is material if it involves active participation in solicitation, contract negotiations, or other "significant" services related to the sale, but not if the participation merely involves giving final approval, displaying samples, holding and distributing the sale property, providing a place for title passage, or providing other related clerical functions.

Section 865(e)(2)(A) seems to suggest on its face that, "[n]otwithstanding any other provisions of this part [§§ 861 through 865]," once an office or fixed place of business exists, inventory sales income subject to this provision "shall be sourced in the United States." However, this does not affect the general rule of § 865(b)(1) which provides that in the case of inventory property, § 865 does not apply and instead the income must be sourced according to the rules of §§ 861(a)(6), 862(a)(6), and 863. In other words, if title passes in the United States, the inventory gain will be considered United States source, regardless of the existence of a domestic office; but if title passes outside the United States, the inventory gain may be re-sourced to the United States under § 865(e)(2).

A second limitation on the title passage rule is an anti-abuse provision found in Regulation § 1.861-7. When a sale is arranged primarily to avoid tax, this Regulation provides that "the sale will be treated as having been consummated at the place where the substance of the sale occurred" rather than under the title passage rule. The determination is based on all factors of the transaction, including negotiations, execution of the agreement, location of the property, and place of payment. However, the government has never been successful in these challenges, since risk of loss by definition has substance, albeit minimized through the use of insurance.

Regulation § 1.861-7(a) explains a major distinction that should be noted between purchase-and-sale income and production-and-sale income. When dealing with purchase-and-sale income, as discussed above, only the sale is deemed responsible for generating the income. In production-and-sale situations, some of the income is seen as a result of production activity so that the income is not deemed to derive from the sale alone. As discussed later in this Unit, the source of the income in this latter situation is split between production and sales activities according to specified rules in §§ 863(a) and 863(b)(2).

2.10 Sales of Non-Inventory Property

Income from the sale of personal property other than inventory property (defined in § 865(i)(1) under the principles of § 1221(a)) is generally sourced according to the residence of the seller as defined by § 865, rather than where title passes. Gain derived by a United States resident from the sale of personal property is generally sourced in the United States, and that derived by a non-resident is generally sourced outside the United States. Thus, for dispositions of non-inventory property, a determination of the taxpayer's residence must be made.

As in the case of interest sourcing discussed *supra* in subpart 2.01, § 865(g) contains variations on the rules for determining residence for purposes of applying § 865. For individuals, the standard differs from that described in § 7701(b), discussed in Unit 1. Instead of these bright line rules, the critical factor for § 865 is the location of the taxpayer's "tax home" as that term is defined in § 911 (the subject of Unit 3).

The tax home concept is elusive and often requires a detailed consideration of many relevant facts and circumstances. In addition, application of the tax home concept may give rise to seemingly incongruous results for sourcing purposes. For example, an individual that has a United States tax home will be classified as a resident under § 865(g) even if otherwise classified as a non-resident under § 7701(b). The possibility for confusion is fairly minor because, with a few exceptions, most individuals who are non-residents under § 7701(b) will have a tax home abroad, thus ensuring that the gain from the sale of non-inventory property will be classified as foreign source. Nevertheless, the § 865 residence rule is referred to as a "modified" residence rule because it adds the subjective tax home inquiry to the otherwise objective classification system of § 7701 as outlined in Unit 1.

Finally, § 865(e)(2)(A) once again acts as an override on the use of the residence rule and will treat the gain from the sale of non-inventory property as United States source where a United States office or fixed place of business exists. But unlike the case of inventory property, there is no exception for material participation by a foreign office — if a United States office or fixed place of business exists and the income from the sale of personal property is attributable to that office, the residence rule no longer controls, and the income will be deemed United States source.

2.11 Depreciable Property

Notwithstanding the general rule of § 865(a), which applies to income derived from the sale of personal property, gain from the sale of depreciable personal property is addressed in § 865(c), which bifurcates the gain between (1) gain attributable to adjustments to basis resulting from depreciation deductions and (2) gain in excess of those depreciation adjustments. Gain attributable to depreciation adjustments is generally allocated between sources within the United States and sources outside the United States according to two separate rules: an allocation rule for items used in international commerce and a "predominate use" rule for all other depreciable property. Any gain from the sale of depreciable property in excess of gain attributable to depreciation adjustments is sourced under § 865(c)(2), which applies the title passage rule as if the depreciable property were inventory property.

For certain items used in international commerce and listed in § 168(g)(4), gain attributable to depreciation adjustments is allocated according to a formula set forth in § 865(c)(1), which links the gain to prior depreciation deductions taken by the taxpayer in calculating United States and foreign source taxable income. The taxpayer's residence in such cases is irrelevant.

Table 2-1 provides an example of allocations of gain attributable to depreciation deductions between United States and foreign source according to the formula in § 865(c)(1). The example also demonstrates the bifurcation of gain between gain attributable to depreciation adjustments and gain in excess of depreciation adjustments.

TABLE 2-1. DEPRECIATION RECAPTURE: AN EXAMPLE

A United States resident purchases an aircraft for use in international commerce at a price of $6 million, depreciates $2 million of the cost, and sells it for $7 million (producing gain on the sale in the amount of $3 million):

If depreciation deduction is allocated to . . .	And title passes in . . .	Then the source of the gain is . . .
United States source income	United States	all United States source
United States source income	Foreign jurisdiction	$2 million United States source, $1 million foreign source
Foreign source income	United States	$1 million United States source, $2 million foreign source
Foreign source income	Foreign jurisdiction	all foreign source

If depreciation deduction is allocated to . . .	And title passes in . . .	Then the source of the gain is . . .
60% United States source income and 40% foreign source income	United States	$2.2 million United States source, $0.8 million foreign source
60% United States source income and 40% foreign source income	Foreign jurisdiction	$1.2 million United States source, $1.8 million foreign source

For all other depreciable property, a "predominant use" rule applies, under which all depreciation deductions taken on the property sold are treated as having been allocated to either United States or foreign source income based on the location of the property's use. Thus, under § 865(c)(3)(B), all of the gain attributable to depreciation deductions will be United States source if the property is predominantly used within the United States. Likewise, if the property is predominantly used in another country, all of the gain attributable to depreciation deductions will be foreign source. As a result of this rule, even if depreciation deductions are taken in the United States, none of the gain on the sale of property predominantly used outside the United States is United States source unless title passes in the United States.

2.12 Intangible Property

As in the case of depreciable property, intangible property may also be subject to different treatment than that accorded to other income derived from the sale of personal property. According to § 865(d)(1)(A), gain from the disposition of an intangible asset (other than goodwill) is sourced under the regular § 865(a) rule, but only to the extent the payments in consideration of the sale are not contingent on the productivity, use, or disposition of the intangible. Section 865(d)(1)(B) provides that sales of intangible assets for contingent consideration are sourced under the royalty source rules of § 861(a)(4). However, under § 865(d)(4), gain from the sale of an intangible asset which has been amortized for tax purposes is sourced under the depreciable personal property rule of § 865(c) to the extent of such amortization. This rule applies regardless of whether the sale is contingent upon productivity or use.

Goodwill is classified as an intangible asset under § 865(d)(2), but gain from the sale of goodwill is subject to yet another separate source rule under § 865(d)(3). Under that provision, goodwill is sourced in the country in which it was generated. In cases involving a multi-jurisdictional business, an allocation of the gain among various jurisdictions may be required. However, as goodwill in some cases is amortizable, the depreciable personal property rules of § 865(c) should govern to the extent of any amortization.

2.13   Scholarships and Prizes

Generally, Regulation § 1.863-1(d) sources scholarships, fellowship grants, grants, prizes and awards by reference to the residence of the payor. Thus, a scholarship awarded by a foreign government or an international organization is foreign source income, while similar awards paid by a United States person are sourced in the United States. However, under Regulation § 1.863-1(d)(iii), scholarships, fellowship grants, targeted grants (defined as public interest grants awarded by a domestic nonprofit organization or by the Federal, state, or local government) and achievement awards (defined as targeted grants for past activities) received by a foreign person are foreign source if the scholarship, grant, or award relates to activities conducted outside the United States.

2.14   Mixed-Source Income

Items of income, expenses, losses, and deductions that are not specifically described in §§ 861(a) or 862(a) may still have United States source. Section 863(a) provides that these items must be allocated or apportioned to domestic or foreign sources pursuant to Regulations.

Section 863(b) provides special rules for determining source with respect to three particular types of gains, profits, and income. Under this section, gains, profits, or income may have mixed source when they arise from (1) services rendered partly in and partly outside the United States; (2) production and sale of inventory property involving a foreign jurisdiction; or (3) purchase and sale transactions involving a possession of the United States. In these specific cases, allocable expenses may be deducted from the gross income and the resulting taxable income must be apportioned among foreign and United States sources as described in Regulations §§ 1.863-1 through 1.863-7.

The most significant class of income subject to § 863(b) is that from the sale or exchange of inventory property (1) produced in whole or in part within the United States and sold or exchanged in a foreign jurisdiction or (2) produced outside the United States and sold or exchanged domestically. This income is considered partly from a United States source and partly from a foreign source because it is attributable to both the production activity and the sales activity which occurred in two separate jurisdictions.

Inventory property is defined by reference to § 865(i)(1), which defines it as personal property described in § 1221(a)(1) — in essence, stock in trade and property held for sale to customers. As noted above, § 865(c)(2) may also treat some of the gain from the sale of depreciable property as inventory property. Regulation § 1.863-3(b) specifies three methods for allocating income from § 863(b) inventory sales: the "50/50" method, the independent factory price ("IFP") method, and the taxpayer's own books and records method.

In the absence of an election otherwise, the 50/50 method applies to inventory property sourced under § 863(b). Under Regulation § 1.863-3(b)(1), the 50/50 method divides manufacturing gross income equally between production activity and sales activity. The production half is sourced under Regulation § 1.863-3(c)(1); the sales half under Regulation § 1.863-3(c)(2). Subject to a number of exceptions, paragraph (c)(1) sources production activity income according to where the taxpayer's assets are located, while income from sales activity is sourced according to the title passage rule of Regulation § 1.861-7(c).

In general, the 50/50 method is preferred by taxpayers because it often maximizes foreign source income and therefore foreign tax credits, as discussed in Unit 6. However, a taxpayer may elect out of this method by using either the IFP method or the taxpayer's own books and records method.

Like the 50/50 method, the IFP method apportions gross income between production activity and sales activity. A taxpayer must "fairly establish" an IFP pursuant to Regulation § 1.863-3(b)(2). If the taxpayer elects this method, the IFP is deemed to represent gross income from the production activity, and any proceeds above that price are deemed to represent the sales activity. Under Regulation § 1.863-3(b)(2)(iii), gross income from production activity equals gross receipts from production activity minus the cost of production activity goods sold; gross income from sales activity equals gross receipts from sales activity less the cost of sales activity goods sold. As in the case of the 50/50 method, the source is determined under Regulation § 1.863-3(c)(1) (for production activity income) and Regulation § 1.863-3(c)(2) (for sales activity income).

Finally, upon receiving advance permission from the Service, a taxpayer may instead elect to allocate the income from § 863(b) inventory sales and exchanges based upon its own books and records, according to Regulation § 1.863-3(b)(3). There is a fairly oncrous burden of proof necessary to obtain approval from the Service, so few taxpayers choose this option. If approval is not obtained, the 50/50 or IFP method must be used.

2.15 Transactions Involving Computer Programs

More recently, Treasury has felt pressure to provide more detailed guidance for sourcing income from the license and sale of computer software. Under Regulation § 1.861-18(b)(1), transactions involving computer software are classified within one or more of four possible categories: (1) transfers of copyright rights (including the right to copy the program and sell it to others, the right to prepare derivative programs using the program, and the right to display publicly or make a public performance of the program); (2) transfers of copyrighted articles (meaning a transfer of a copy of the program but not any of the copyright rights described above); (3) the provision of services for the development or modification of the program; or (4) the provision of know-how with respect to programming techniques specifically furnished under conditions preventing unauthorized disclosure because the parties consider such know-how to be a trade secret.

Under Regulation § 1.861-18(f)(1), the first category, transfers of copyright rights, will be sourced as sales of personal property if the seller transfers all substantial rights in the copyright. All other transfers of such rights will be treated as a license producing royalty income. Under Regulation § 1.861-18(f)(2), transfers of copyrighted articles will be sourced as sales of personal property if all the benefits and burdens of ownership are transferred to the buyer. All other transfers of copyrighted articles will be sourced as a lease generating rental income.

Provision of services related to computer programs is sourced as services income; the issue for computer software is the initial characterization of the income as compensation rather than one of the four transactions described in Regulation § 1.861-18(b). This determination must be made based on all relevant facts and circumstances according to Regulation § 1.861-18(d). Finally, the provision of know-how, a concept strictly defined under Regulation § 1.861-18(e), is sourced in the manner applicable to sales of intangible assets under § 865(d) rather than as a provision of a service.

2.16   Other Income

Sections 861, 862, 863, and 865 do not purport to source all types of income. Some payments fall outside the parameters of these statutes, and the practitioner must look to general source principles to determine their source. Historically, it was thought that the controlling factor of source for these payments was the residence of the payor. This view was encouraged by the Service's position in Revenue Ruling 69-108, 1969-1 C.B. 192, in which it was held, apparently to the exclusion of all other factors, that the residence of the obligor decided the source of alimony. While it is clear that this rule still stands for alimony, the Service thereafter abandoned that general position. For example, in Revenue Ruling 73-252, 1973-1 C.B. 337, the Service took the position that the main factor in determining source is the location of the property to which the payment related or the situs of the activities that resulted in the payment being made.

Thus, two source rules exist — one in rem, the other in personam. Difficulty may arise in deciding which source rule applies in a given situation, as illustrated in *Bank of America v. United States*, 680 F.2d 142 (Ct. Cl. 1982). Therein, the court sourced acceptance, confirmation, and negotiation commissions derived by a bank by analogy of each to established source rules. Acceptance and confirmation commissions most resembled interest and were sourced according to those rules. Negotiation commissions mirrored income derived for services and thus were sourced in the United States. In the absence of a specific source rule, one should, where possible, analogize to other source rules for guidance, as illustrated in Revenue Ruling 2004-75, set forth in Part D of this Unit. Only where no other source rule has relevance should resort be made to in rem or in personam jurisdiction principles.

D.   REFERENCE MATERIALS

- *Boulez v. Commissioner*
- Revenue Ruling 2004-75

BOULEZ v. COMMISSIONER

United States Tax Court

83 T.C. 584 (1984)

KORNER, JUDGE:

Respondent determined a deficiency in petitioner's individual income tax for the calendar year 1975 in the amount of $20,685.61. After concessions, the issue which we are called upon to decide is whether certain payments received by petitioner in the year 1975 constitute sale "royalties," . . . and are therefore exempt from tax by the United States, or whether said payments constitute compensation for personal services . . . and are therefore taxable by the United States. . . .

OPINION

Petitioner contends that the payments to him in 1975 by CBS, Inc. were not taxable by the United States, because they were "royalties". . . . Respondent . . . contends that the payments in question were taxable to petitioner by the United States because they represented compensation for personal services performed in the United States by petitioner. . . .

[W]e must decide whether the payments received by petitioner in 1975 from CBS, Inc. constituted royalties or income from personal services. . . . This issue, in turn, involves two facets:

(1) Did petitioner intend and support to license or convey to CBS Records, and did the latter agree to pay for, a property interest in the recordings he was engaged to make, which would give rise to royalties?

(2) If so, did petitioner have a property interest in the recordings which he was capable of licensing or selling?

The first of the above questions is purely factual, depends upon the intention of the parties, and is to be determined by an examination of the record as a whole, including the terms of the contract entered into between petitioner and CBS Records, together with any other relevant and material evidence.

The second question — whether petitioner had a property interest which he could license or sell — is a question of law. . . .

We will examine each of these questions in turn.

1. THE FACTUAL QUESTION

By the contract entered into between petitioner and CBS Records in 1969, as amended, did the parties agree that petitioner was licensing or conveying to CBS Records a property interest in the recordings which he was retained to make, and in return for which he was to receive "royalties?" . . .

The contract between the parties is by no means clear. On the one hand, the contract consistently refers to the compensation which petitioner is to be entitled to receive as "royalties," and such payments are tied directly to the proceeds which CBS Records was to receive from sales of recordings which petitioner was to make. Both these factors suggest that the parties had a royalty arrangement, rather than a compensation arrangement, in mind in entering into the contract. We bear in mind, however, that the labels which the parties affix to a transaction are not necessarily determinative of their true nature, and the fact that a party's remuneration under the contract is based on a percentage of future sales of the product created does not prove that a licensing or sale of property was intended, rather than compensation for services.

On the other hand, the contract between petitioner and CBS Records is replete with language indicating that what was intended here was a contract for personal services. Thus, paragraph 1. . . . clearly states that CBS Records was engaging petitioner "to render your services exclusively for us as a producer and/or performer. . . . It is understood and agreed that such engagement by us shall include your services as a producer and/or performer. . . . " Paragraph 3. of the contract then requires petitioner to "perform" in the making of a certain number of recordings in each year. Most importantly, in the context of the present question, paragraph 4. of the contract . . . makes it clear that CBS considered petitioner's services to be the essence of the contract: petitioner agreed not to perform for others with respect to similar recordings during the term of the contract, and for a period of five years thereafter, and he was required to "acknowledge that your services are unique and extraordinary and that we shall be entitled to equitable relief to enforce the provision of this paragraph 4."

Under paragraph 5. of the contract . . . it was agreed that the recordings, once made, should be entirely the property of CBS Records, "free from any claims whatsoever by you or any person deriving any rights or interests from you." Significantly, nowhere in the contract is there any language of conveyance of any alleged property right in the recordings by petitioner to CBS Records, nor any language indicating a licensing of any such purported right, other than the designation of petitioner's remuneration as being "royalties." The word "copyright" itself is never mentioned. Finally, under paragraph 13. of the contract, CBS Records was entitled to suspend or terminate its payments to petitioner "if, by reason of illness, injury, accident or refusal to work, you fail to perform for us in accordance with the provisions of this agreement. . . . "

Considered as a whole, therefore, and acknowledging that the contract is not perfectly clear on this point, we conclude that the weight of the evidence is that the parties intended a contract for personal services, rather than one involving the sale or licensing of any property rights which petitioner might have in the recordings which were to be made in the future.

2. THE LEGAL QUESTION

Before a person can derive income from royalties, it is fundamental that he must have an ownership interest in the property whose licensing or sale gives rise to the income. . . . [T]his Court held that in order for a payment to constitute a "royalty," the payee must have an ownership interest in the property whose use generates the payment . . .

It is clear, then, that the existence of a property right in the payee is fundamental for the purpose of determining whether royalty income exists. . . .

Did the petitioner have any property rights in the recordings which he made for CBS Records, which he could either license or sell and which would give rise to royalty income here? We think not. . . .

In spite of [a] change in the law in 1971, however, petitioner's contractual relationship with CBS Records went on as before. Neither the amendment to that contract of 1971, nor the further amendment in 1974, made any reference to the change of the copyright laws, nor modified the basic contract in any respect which would be pertinent to the instant question. We conclude, therefore, that the parties saw no need to modify their contract because they understood that even after the Sound Recording Amendment of 1971, petitioner still had no licensable or transferable property rights in the recordings which he made for CBS Records, and we think this was correct.

The Copyright Act of 1909, even after its amendment by the Sound Recording Amendment of 1971, describes the person having a copyrightable interest in property as the "author or proprietor," 17 U.S.C. § 9, and further provides that "the word 'author' shall include an employer in the case of works made for hire." 17 U.S.C. § 26. The above is a statutory enactment of the long recognized rule that where a person is employed for the specific purpose of creating a work, including a copyrightable item, the fruits of his labor, carried out in accordance with the employment, are the property of his employer. The rule creates a rebuttable presumption to this effect, which can be overcome by express contractual provisions between the employee and the employer, reserving to the former the copyrightable interest.

Here, the petitioner, a musical conductor of world wide reputation, was employed to make recordings for CBS Records, and in doing so, was to exercise his peculiar and unique skills in accordance with his experience, talent, and best judgment. In these circumstances, we do not think that petitioner was an "employee" in the common law sense, but rather was an independent contractor, with the same relationship to CBS Records as a lawyer, an engineer, or an architect would have to his client, or a doctor to his patient. This, however, provides no grounds for distinction, since the "works for hire" rule applies to independent contractors just as it does to conventional employees.

In the instant case, the application of the "works for hire" rule means that petitioner had no copyrightable property interest in the recordings which he created for CBS Records, even after 1971. Petitioner was engaged for the specific purpose of making the recordings in question; his contract with CBS Records reserved no property rights in the recordings to him, and indeed made it specific that all such rights, whatever they were, were to reside in CBS Records. Under these circumstances, we do not think that petitioner has overcome the statutory presumption of the "works for hire" rule, nor that he has shown that he had any property interest in the recordings, either before 1971 or thereafter, which he could either license or sell to CBS Records so as to produce royalty income within the meaning of the treaty. This conclusion, in turn, reinforces our belief, which we have found as a fact, that the contract between petitioner and CBS Records was one for the performance of personal services. . . .

REVENUE RULING 2004-75
2004-2 C.B. 109

ISSUES

(1) Whether income received by non-resident alien individuals under life insurance and annuity contracts issued by a foreign branch of a U.S. life insurance company is U.S.-source income. . . .

(2) Whether income received by bona fide residents of Puerto Rico under life insurance and annuity contracts issued by a Puerto Rican branch of a U.S. life insurance company is U.S.-source income. . . .

FACTS

A U.S. life insurance company conducts business in Country A and Puerto Rico through a separate branch in each jurisdiction. The branches sell a wide range of insurance products including, but not limited to, whole life, universal life, and variable life insurance and fixed and variable annuities to individuals living in Country A and Puerto Rico. These products are life insurance and annuity contracts under the Internal Revenue Code. There is no income tax treaty in force between Country A and the United States.

Individuals in Country A and Puerto Rico pay premiums to the U.S. life insurance company in exchange for the benefits set forth in the relevant contracts. For example, under a life insurance contract, the life insurance company generally agrees, in exchange for premiums, to pay a certain amount to a beneficiary upon the death of the insured. Under an annuity contract, the life insurance company typically agrees, in exchange for premiums, to pay a certain amount each year to the owner of the contract beginning upon the owner's retirement and ending upon the owner's death. The life insurance company invests the premiums received with respect to its life insurance and annuity contracts in domestic and foreign income-producing assets, such as stocks and bonds.

The life insurance and annuity contracts issued by the U.S. life insurance company to individuals in Country A and Puerto Rico have cash values. The individuals in Country A and Puerto Rico withdraw amounts from the cash values of their life insurance and annuity contracts, and the amounts withdrawn are gross income under section 61 to the extent provided under section 72. The individuals in Country A and Puerto Rico also receive annuity payments under their annuity contracts that are gross income under section 61 to the extent provided under section 72.

This revenue ruling applies only to annuity payments and withdrawals of cash value that are gross income to the extent provided under section 72, and does not apply to amounts received under life insurance contracts by reason of the death of the insured that are excludible from gross income under section 101.

LAW

Section 861(a) specifies that certain items of income are U.S.-source income. Section 861(a)(1) generally provides that interest is U.S.-source income when paid by a U.S. obligor. Section 861(a)(2) generally provides that dividends are U.S.-source income when paid by a domestic corporation. Section 861(a) does not specify the source of income paid by a U.S. life insurance company under a life insurance or annuity contract.

When the source of an item of income is not specified by statute or by regulation, courts have determined the source of the item by comparison and analogy to classes of income specified within the statute. *Bank of America v. United States*, 680 F.2d 142, 147 (Ct. Cl. 1982); *Howkins v. Commissioner*, 49 T.C. 689 (1968). In *Clayton v. United States*, 33 Fed. Cl. 628 (1995), aff'd, the Court of Federal Claims held that the earnings and accretions component of distributions made by an employee stock ownership plan ("ESOP") to foreign participants was U.S.-source income because the trust underlying the ESOP was a domestic trust.

. . .

ANALYSIS

Because section 861(a) does not include rules specifying the source of income received under a life insurance or annuity contract under section 72, the source of such income is determined by comparison and analogy to classes of income that are specified within the statute. *Bank of America*, 680 F.2d at 147; *Howkins*, 49 T.C. at 689. Income received under a life insurance or annuity contract under section 72 is an investment return on the cash value of the contract and is analogous to (1) interest on a debt obligation, (2) dividends on a stock, and (3) earnings and accretions on pension fund assets. Thus, the source of that income is determined in the same manner as the source of interest, dividends, and earnings and accretions on pension fund assets. Under sections 861(a)(1) and (2), interest or dividends are U.S. source when the obligor or corporation, respectively, is domestic. Earnings and accretions on pension fund assets are also U.S. source when the pension trust is domestic. Accordingly, income received under a life insurance or annuity contract is U.S. source when the issuer of the contract is a domestic corporation.

. . .

Payments made to bona fide residents of Puerto Rico with respect to life insurance and annuity contracts issued by a Puerto Rican branch of a U.S. life insurance company are derived from sources within the United States under the principles described above. . . .

HOLDINGS

(1) Income received by nonresident alien individuals under life insurance or annuity contracts issued by a foreign branch of a U.S. life insurance company is U.S.-source . . . income. . . .

(2) Income received by bona fide residents of Puerto Rico under life insurance or annuity contracts issued by a Puerto Rican branch of a U.S. life insurance company is U.S.-source income. . . .

Part II

INTRODUCTION TO THE TREATMENT OF OUTBOUND ACTIVITIES

Unit 3

FOREIGN EARNED INCOME OF UNITED STATES PERSONS

A. CODE AND REGULATION PROVISIONS

Code   §§ 911(a)–(d)(3), (d)(5)–(7), (e)–(f)(1).
Reg.   §§ 1.871-2(a); 1.911-2(a)–(d); 1.911-3(a)–(d); 1.911-4(a)–(b)(4), (d); 1.911-6(a), (c).

B. PROBLEMS FOR CLASS DISCUSSION

3-1. Casey, an unmarried United States citizen utilizing a calendar year, was transferred to Belgrade, Serbia, to work for her employer's subsidiary for an anticipated four-year period. She arrived on December 31, Year 1 and commenced employment on January 1, Year 2. Her annual salary was $100,000 and her foreign housing expenses, paid by her employer, were $3,000 per month.

(a) To what extent can Casey exclude her salary and housing expenses from her Year 2 United States gross income under § 911?

(b) How would the answer to (a) change if her annual salary was $40,000?

(c) How would the answer to (a) change if Casey arrived in Serbia on January 11, Year 2, and stayed through December 27, Year 3?

(d) How would the answer to (a) change if Casey paid income tax of $12,000 to Serbia on her salary? Is there a difference if, under Serbian law, she was not liable for any tax? If she declared herself to be a non-resident of Serbia and therefore under Serbian law was not liable for tax, should the result be any different?

3-2. On June 30, Year 1, Douglas, a United States citizen employed by an Illinois corporation, transferred to Guyana to work for the corporation's subsidiary. The corporation told Douglas that he should expect to work at the subsidiary in Guyana for approximately 18 months, with a return to the United States scheduled for December 31, Year 2. Douglas's yearly salary is $100,000. He pays foreign housing expenses of $3,000 per month during his stay in Guyana.

(a) To what extent can Douglas exclude some or all of his Year 1 salary and housing expenses from his United States gross income under § 911?

43

(b) How would the answer to (a) change if Douglas invests a portion of his salary in a Guyanese bank, earning interest of $5,000 per year?

(c) How would the answer to (a) change if, at Douglas's request, his employer pays $30,000 of his Year 1 and Year 2 salary in Year 3 and Year 4 respectively?

C. OVERVIEW

As discussed in Unit 1, the United States generally imposes taxation on the worldwide income of its residents, citizens, and domestic corporations, thereby potentially overlapping the tax jurisdiction of other countries. The justification for worldwide taxation is perhaps strongest when applied to a United States citizen and resident who lives and works in the United States but earns foreign income in a passive manner, such as through the ownership of stock in a foreign corporation. From a benefits point of view, these members of society regularly draw on public goods (national defense, physical and financial infrastructure, national parks, etc.) through their mere presence within the country. Similarly, it would violate both equity and efficiency norms if some United States resident taxpayers could avoid United States taxation simply by earning foreign-source rather than domestic-source income.

However, these benefits and equity/efficiency rationales might be less clearly applicable in the case of United States persons who journey abroad to search for employment, to relocate pursuant to their employer's instructions, or even to retire. In these cases, another government might have an equal or stronger claim over the taxpayer's income than the United States. The question thus arises: which country should provide relief from double taxation, and how should such relief be implemented? In the case of United States persons living and working abroad, the United States has determined that it should provide some relief, and, as its mechanism for relief, it has chosen to exempt certain foreign earnings and housing costs pursuant to § 911.

Because § 911 is an exclusion of foreign earned income from the United States tax base, this statute represents the source-based territoriality principle of taxation rather than the residence-based principle of worldwide taxation. The rationale behind providing this form of territorial taxation for United States citizens (and in some cases, resident aliens) working overseas has never been the subject of unanimous agreement. Instead, legislators over the years have been unclear about the basic goal of § 911, and support for the provision has vacillated over the 80-plus years of its existence.

Perhaps the greatest beneficiaries of § 911 are United States employers with employees working abroad. These employers often provide their overseas employees "tax equalization" arrangements under which the employer ensures that the employees will not pay more tax by working abroad than they would pay if they worked exclusively in the United States. To the extent § 911 excludes compensation and housing that would otherwise be taxable, the employer is relieved of the obligation to reimburse the employee for United States tax on those amounts.

Section 911 thus acts in part as a tax subsidy for employers who send employees abroad.

Section 911 has long occupied a precarious position in United States international tax policy. When the concepts of § 911 were first enacted in 1926, the stated intent of Congress was "to take one further step toward increasing our foreign trade." As originally conceived, the foreign earned income exclusion was for "foreign traders," United States citizens employed abroad in selling merchandise produced in the United States. In the years since, there have been frequent ebbs and flows in Congressional support for § 911, with occasional pushes to repeal often followed closely in time by initiatives to broaden the rules. The most frequently cited reasons for granting tax advantages to United States citizens working overseas are that they are required in order to spur United States business overseas and to provide equitable treatment for United States citizens facing higher costs of living abroad. However, one may well question who actually benefits from § 911 and who pays for it. It continues to be difficult to understand what impact § 911 actually has on exports or jobs within or without the United States, and whether the encouragement of exports is a sound tax policy in any event. Additionally, qualification for § 911 is not dependent upon being subject to a foreign tax, and thus it potentially provides a total escape from taxation. Furthermore, double taxation may be relieved without the use of § 911 by a combination of foreign tax credits and, where applicable, treaty benefits. Future Congresses will likely return to § 911 repeatedly in the constant political struggles over revenue needs, equity and efficiency goals, and the ideal base of United States taxation in an increasingly globalized world.

The legislative maneuvering behind § 911 demonstrates the ongoing challenges faced by policymakers to find a balance between a provision's perceived benefits and perceptions of tax equity for United States citizens who work in the United States versus those who work abroad. The history of § 911 illustrates some of the reasons for the length and complexity of the Internal Revenue Code. As a harbinger of additional efforts by some policymakers to move towards a more territorial tax system, § 911 warrants special notice both in terms of substance and process.

The following sections discuss the substantive workings of the foreign earned income exclusion. The policy goals that have influenced legislators should be kept in mind when analyzing the many requirements, definitions, and exceptions of § 911.

3.01 The Elective § 911 Exclusion

As § 911(a) states and Regulation § 1.911-1(a) reiterates, the § 911 exclusion is elective for qualifying taxpayers. Section 911(d)(1) and Regulation § 1.911-2 provide rules for determining eligibility. In general, a United States citizen qualifies for the exclusion by having a foreign tax home as well as either (1) being a bona fide resident of a foreign country (the bona fide residence test) or (2) being present in a foreign country for 330 days in 12 months (the presence test). In addition, resident aliens with a foreign tax home may qualify for the exclusion if they meet the presence test. *See* Figure 3-1.

FIGURE 3-1. THE TWO REQUIREMENTS OF § 911 ELIGIBILITY

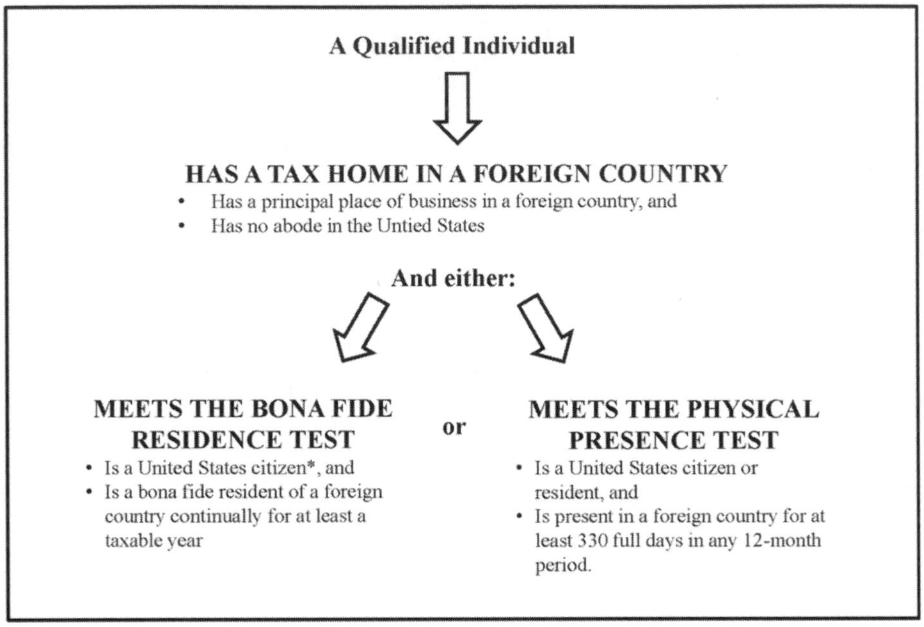

A Qualified Individual

⇩

HAS A TAX HOME IN A FOREIGN COUNTRY
- Has a principal place of business in a foreign country, and
- Has no abode in the Untied States

And either:

⇙   ⇘

MEETS THE BONA FIDE   or   **MEETS THE PHYSICAL**
RESIDENCE TEST   **PRESENCE TEST**
- Is a United States citizen*, and   - Is a United States citizen or
- Is a bona fide resident of a foreign   resident, and
  country continually for at least a   - Is present in a foreign country for at
  taxable year   least 330 full days in any 12-month
                              period.

* Or resident alien that is a citizen or national of an applicable treaty country. *See* subpart 3.04.

A qualifying individual may elect to exclude a maximum of $80,000 per year, as adjusted for inflation, but in no event can one exclude more than his or her foreign earned income for the year. Although these requirements appear fairly straight-forward, not all who are eligible will necessarily claim the benefits of § 911. One reason for this is that a taxpayer claiming the exclusion is not entitled to any attendant exclusions, deductions, or credits against such income. As a result, an individual with a high amount of deductions, credits or other exclusions with respect to his or her foreign earnings might have a lower total tax liability without electing § 911.

3.02   Requirements for Eligibility: Foreign Tax Home

Having a foreign tax home is a prerequisite to § 911 qualification. An individual cannot have a foreign tax home if he or she has an abode in the United States. Section 911(d)(3) states that the tax home concept has the same meaning as the § 162(a)(2) "away from home" requirement applied to business and travel expenses, a requirement that has significant interpretive precedent in the domestic context. Regulation § 1.911-2(b) attempts to flesh out this concept in the international context, but provides limited assistance.

The tax home requirement is probably of minimal significance for meeting the bona fide residence requirement (discussed below), but it may be significant in the context of the physical presence test (also discussed below). At one time, the physical presence test required foreign presence of at least 510 days within 18 months. Congress, in shortening the testing period to the current standard of 330 days in 12 months, may have feared that a person with a minimal foreign presence might qualify for the exclusion. The tax home doctrine acts as an additional safeguard against such an apparently undesirable result.

The Service has successfully invoked the tax home doctrine to support a finding of a United States abode and no foreign tax home in cases of discontinuous living patterns (for example, in the case of employees on an oil rig who spend 28 days abroad followed by a 28-day period in the United States) or attempts to meet the presence test by disguising a vacation abroad as an employment-related matter.[1] *Jones v. Commissioner*, excerpted in Part D of this Unit, provides an example of the tax home doctrine supporting a finding of bona fide residence.

The issue is further complicated by the interaction of § 911 with § 162. In 1992, Congress, in an effort to minimize claims for the deduction of travel expenses, amended § 162(a) to provide that the taxpayer "shall not be treated as being temporarily away from home during any period of employment if such period exceeds one year." The enactment tightened the standards for deductions under § 162: a person who stayed away more than a year would be considered to have established a new tax home. As a result, the person would be denied travel expenses when away from his original home for more than a year.

However, this legislative change may well have broadened the standards for exclusion under § 911, since, as noted above, the term "tax home" for purposes of § 911 has the same meaning as under § 162(a)(2). Thus, a person who stays away from his original home for more than a year will likely be deemed to have established a new tax home for purposes of § 911, regardless of other applicable limitations.

3.03   Bona Fide Residence Test

One means by which a taxpayer evidences his eligibility for the § 911 exclusion is to establish a genuine nexus to or presence in a foreign country. This option is only available to United States citizens and United States resident aliens who are citizens or nationals of a country with which the United States has an applicable income tax treaty in effect. Section 911(d)(1)(A) specifically limits the bona fide residence test to United States citizens. Omitting residents may be understandable since it is unusual — though not impossible — for aliens to maintain simultaneous residency status in the United States and another country. Nevertheless, resident aliens can qualify for § 911 benefits under the bona fide residence test under nondiscrimination clauses (generally prohibiting treaty partners from placing heavier tax burdens on foreign nationals than on their own citizens) in applicable tax treaties. Thus, United States resident aliens from tax treaty partner countries may not be excluded from the bona fide residence test. The non-discrimination clauses of tax treaties are discussed further in Unit 10.

Under Regulation § 1.911-2(c), bona fide residence is determined by applying the principles of § 871 and accompanying Regulations relating to the determination

---

[1] *See, e.g., Lemay v. Commissioner*, 837 F.2d 681 (5th Cir. 1988); *Gelhar v. Commissioner*, T.C. Memo 1992-162.

of the residence of aliens. Section 871, which imposes United States taxation on non-resident alien individuals, is the primary subject of Units 7 through 9. The classification of aliens as resident or non-resident is discussed in Regulations §§ 1.871-2 through -5. These provisions became otherwise obsolete in 1984 due to the enactment of § 7701(b), but, by virtue of their prior incorporation into § 911, they are still controlling for purposes of establishing bona fide residence under this section. These principles provide that the question of bona fide residence is a question of fact that primarily concentrates on the qualitative indicia of having truly established a life in a foreign country.

Claimants have the burden of establishing their foreign residency, and the claimed period must span an entire taxable year. It is possible for a taxpayer to qualify while residing in more than one country during the tax year, so long as foreign residency is not interrupted. Barring death, a taxpayer must possess such residence for the entire taxable year (January 1 through December 31 for persons who file their income tax returns on a calendar year basis, as most individuals do).

Under Regulation § 1.871-2(b), whether an individual is a resident for purposes of § 911 generally depends upon the individual's intentions regarding the purpose of the travel and the nature and length of the stay abroad. The Service determines whether an individual qualifies largely on the basis of relevant facts and circumstances. For example, failure to purchase or rent a house or room abroad will weigh heavily against the establishment of bona fide residence unless the taxpayer can show, considering the demands of employment, that it would be unreasonable to do so. Regulation § 1.871-2(b) seems to suggest that indefinite stays will qualify the taxpayer, but it also allows for an extended stay, if necessary for accomplishing the taxpayer's purpose in going abroad. The purpose need only be of a nature that cannot "be promptly accomplished." Thus if the purpose requires an extended stay, foreign residency may be claimed, regardless of the taxpayer's intent to return and specific return date to the United States.

Under § 911(d)(5), an individual is not a bona fide resident of a foreign country if the person makes a statement to the authorities of that country claiming to be a non-resident, and the tax authority either declines to impose tax by reason of non-residency, or fails to make a final decision on such person's status. Thus, an individual who makes such a statement generally is denied § 911 benefits regardless of any other facts which might support a residency claim.

Physical presence, which is the *sine qua non* of the presence test, is also a factor in determining eligibility under the bona fide residence standard. Excessive absence from the stated jurisdiction of residence undercuts assertions of residency. However, temporary visits to the United States or elsewhere on vacation or business trips should not deprive the citizen of status as a bona fide resident of a foreign country. The crucial question is, of course, when an absence becomes unreasonable, so as to sever foreign residency status. For example, a representative of a domestic employer who is assigned abroad and recalled to the United States for a one-month or shorter consultation with the employer should not forfeit foreign residency status. These rules apply only once bona fide residence has been established.

In the presence of other factors that adequately support a taxpayer's claim of bona fide residence, courts have not accorded great weight to the fact that the taxpayer's stay abroad is limited by visa to a certain time period. In some countries, it may be nearly impossible to obtain a visa enabling an individual to stay for an indefinite period. In such cases, a limited-time visa will be of little significance in determining residency.

Once a person has established bona fide residence in a foreign country for an uninterrupted period that includes an entire tax year, such person will qualify as a bona fide resident for the period starting with the date the residency actually began and ending when the residency actually ended. Such a person could thereby qualify as a bona fide resident for the entire tax year plus portions of the years before and after the tax year that provided the bona fide residence qualification.

3.04   Physical Presence Test

An alternative (and more objective) way to qualify for the § 911 exclusion is via the physical presence test. This test is available to both United States citizens and residents. The physical presence test is not concerned with the taxpayer's intentions or the nature and purpose of the stay abroad. Instead, the test is a mathematical one, focusing only on the length of time a taxpayer stays in a foreign country or countries.

Regulation § 1.911-2(d) provides the rules for determining whether physical presence is met. A citizen or resident meets the physical presence test if, during a period of 12 consecutive months, he or she is physically present in a foreign country (or countries) for 330 "qualifying" days (approximately 11 months). A qualifying day is a period of 24 continuous hours beginning at midnight and ending the following midnight. (A special rule is provided for passing over international waters.) In contrast with the bona fide residence test, which requires residency to be established for a person's full tax year (usually a calendar year), the 12-month period for establishing physical presence may begin with any day and must end on the day before the same calendar day, 12 months later. The 12-month period must be made up of consecutive months but any 12-month period may be used if the 330 days fall into that period. The period may begin before or after the taxpayer's arrival in the foreign jurisdiction and, similarly, may end before or after departure from that jurisdiction. A person's 12-month periods can overlap each other. Finally, the 330-day requirement need not be a consecutive period of presence.

The required presence need not be for business purposes. Thus, for example, vacation time in a foreign country counts towards presence as well as any time spent for any other purpose. The physical presence test is, by virtue of its mechanical nature, undoubtedly more certain than the facts and circumstances approach involved in establishing and determining bona fide residence. Moreover, under the presence test, the whereabouts of the taxpayer at particular times can be easily verified by customs stamps on a passport. Thus, it seems likely that the bona fide residence test is significant only when the taxpayer has spent a substantial amount of time in the United States during the course of a foreign assignment.

3.05   Excludable Income Amounts

Once a foreign tax home and either the bona fide residence test or physical presence test have been satisfied, a taxpayer is eligible to make the election under § 911 to exclude from his gross income (1) the "foreign earned income" and (2) the "housing cost amount." Although listed by the Code in that order, the housing cost amount is determined first because the amount of foreign earned income that can be excluded under § 911 is limited by several factors, one of which is the housing cost amount. More specifically, the amount of foreign earned income excludable is equal to the lesser of (1) the excess of the individual's foreign earned income over the excluded housing cost amount, and (2) the annual exclusion amount prorated to reflect the individual's qualifying days.

3.06   "Housing Cost Amount"

Under § 911(c)(1), an individual's housing cost amount is the amount of the individual's housing expenses that fall between a floor and a cap.[2] Generally, the floor is 16 percent of the exclusion amount, which is $80,000 for 2002 and later, and as adjusted for inflation in years after 2005. The cap is 30 percent of the exclusion amount. Ignoring inflation adjustments, if the exclusion amount is $80,000, the cap is $24,000 (30 percent of $80,000), the floor is $12,800 (16 percent of $80,000), and the maximum allowable housing cost amount is the difference between the cap ($24,000) and the floor ($12,800), or $11,200 on an annual basis.

Housing expenses include all reasonable expenses paid by or on behalf of an individual for housing for the taxpayer, the taxpayer's spouse, and the taxpayer's dependents in a foreign country, including expenses such as rent or fair rental value, utilities, and insurance. Under § 911(c)(3), housing expenses do not include interest, taxes, or co-op expenses which are already deductible under §§ 163, 164, or 216(a). The housing cost amount exclusion applies in addition to the foreign earned income exclusion and is determined prior to the foreign earned income exclusion.

Under Regulation § 1.911-4(b), housing expenses do not include the cost of purchasing a house, capital improvements, and other capital expenditures; the cost of purchased furniture, accessories, or domestic labor; amortized payments of principal with respect to an evidence of indebtedness secured by a mortgage on the taxpayer's housing; and several other items.

The housing cost amount exclusion is also limited to the lesser of the housing cost amount attributable to an individual's employer-provided amounts or his foreign earned income for the taxable year. Employer-provided amounts are defined in the Regulation to include any foreign earned income paid or incurred on behalf of an individual by the employer, including salary, reimbursements for housing expenses, educational expenses, or other specified amounts.

The term "housing cost amount" is sufficiently broad that any employee, even if not compensated specifically for housing purposes, may still qualify to the extent of

---

[2] Adjustments to the floor and cap may be made on the basis of geographic differences in housing costs relative to housing costs in the United States. See Notice 2006-87 excerpted in Part D of this Unit.

his own housing expenditures. The implicit assumption is that like an increase in salary, indirect employer-provided amounts should receive the same treatment as payments to an identically situated taxpayer whose salary does not reflect the amount of the employer-provided housing allowance to the extent the payments are included in the taxpayer's gross income. The only earnings that are not employer-provided are those arising from an individual's self-employment.

3.07 Self-Provided Housing

Housing costs paid by a self-employed qualifying taxpayer are treated as a deduction rather than an exclusion under § 911(c)(4). The deduction is limited to the excess of the foreign earned income of the individual for the year over the amount of income that is excluded under § 911(a). If all of an individual's foreign earned income is excluded under the foreign earned income exclusion, § 911(c)(4)(C) provides a one-year carryover to the succeeding taxable year.

3.08 "Foreign Earned Income"

"Earned income" is generally defined in § 911(d)(2)(A) as cash or property given as compensation for personal services rendered. According to § 911(b)(1)(A), earned income is "foreign" if it is attributable to the individual's services performed in a foreign country or countries during the individual's qualifying period of bona fide residence or presence. Without foreign earned income, no benefits are available under § 911 regardless of the taxpayer's compliance with the foreign tax home and presence or bona fide residence standards.

Income earned for services performed in the United States is not eligible for the exclusion, since such income would generally be United States source, as discussed in Unit 2. In addition, income earned by employees of the United States or an agency of the United States is not included in foreign earned income, even if it is earned abroad and would otherwise be considered foreign-source. Finally, income earned in a "restricted country," which currently includes only Cuba, is also excluded from the definition of foreign earned income.

Traditionally, the Service has interpreted earned income in a manner parallel to that of the concept of compensation under § 861(a)(3) (for example, wages, salaries, and professional fees), as distinguished from passive income (for example, dividends, interest, sales income, royalties, rents, and other particular source rule categories). This approach led to some hair-splitting distinctions in deciding which source rule applied and whether an item of income represented earned income. However, for purposes of the § 911 exclusion, the courts have interpreted earned income more broadly.

3.09 Deferred Payments

Income earned for services performed abroad must be attributed to the taxable year in which the employee performed those services, pursuant to § 911(b)(2)(B). For purposes of computing the foreign earned income limitation, foreign earned income deferred until the taxable year after the year in which the services generating the income were performed is not taken into account in the year of receipt. Instead, the deferred earned income is deemed earned in the year of performance and thus absorbs the limitation for the taxable year of performance. If income is deferred in excess of one taxable year beyond the year in which the services were performed, the income no longer constitutes foreign earned income for purposes of § 911. Individuals engaged in long-term employment contracts involving deferred payments may thus inadvertently forfeit the § 911 exclusion.

3.10   Sole Proprietorship or Partnership

Generally, business income is regarded as a return on capital and thus is not regarded as earned income. However, if a taxpayer performs services for a business, amounts received as compensation may be considered earned income if those amounts reasonably reflect the value of the taxpayer's services, as provided in § 911(d)(2)(A).

In the case of a non-corporate business in which both personal services and capital are material income-producing factors, a reasonable allowance as compensation for the individual's services is treated as earned income, but such allowance is capped at 30 percent of the taxpayer's share of the net profits of the business under § 911(d)(2)(B). However, if capital is not a material income-producing factor and the income of the business was earned in connection with the performance of personal services, all of the income is foreign earned income.

3.11   Computation of Tax Liability Where Exclusion Applies

Where a taxpayer excludes income under § 911(a), the taxpayer's regular tax liability under § 1 and alternative minimum tax liability under § 55 must be computed under § 911(f). The amount computed under § 911(f)(1) will nearly always be higher than the tax computed under §§ 1 and 55 because the excluded foreign earned income pushes the taxable income up into a higher tax bracket. In essence, § 911(f) causes amounts over and above the excluded income amounts to be taxed at the rates that would have applied if the excluded income had been included as the first dollars earned. It may be helpful to think of the foreign earned income as a block of untaxed dollars that consumes the taxpayer's lower tax brackets, leaving the taxable income to be taxed at a higher rate. *See* Figure 3-2.

FIGURE 3-2. EXAMPLE OF TAX LIABILITY UNDER § 911(f)

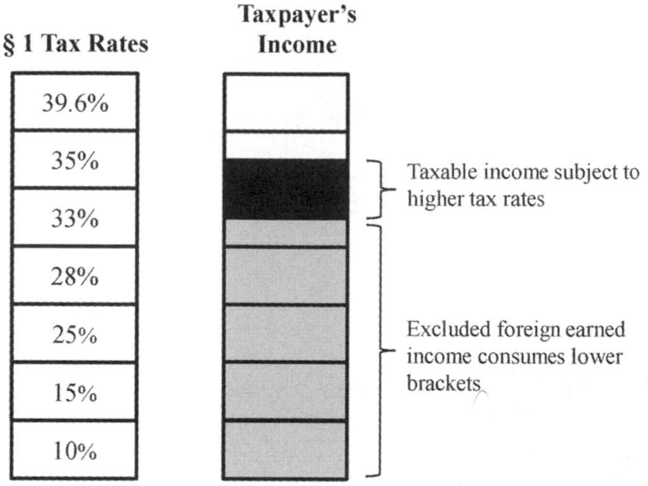

Section 911(f)(2) contains a similar rule for purposes of computing a taxpayer's liability for the alternative minimum tax where the taxpayer excludes income under § 911(a).

D.   REFERENCE MATERIALS

- Notice 2006-87

- *Jones v. Commissioner*

NOTICE 2006-87[3]
2006-2 C.B. 766

DETERMINATION OF HOUSING COST AMOUNT
ELIGIBLE FOR EXCLUSION OR DEDUCTION

This notice provides adjustments to the limitation on housing expenses for purposes of section 911 of the Internal Revenue Code (Code) for specific locations, on the basis of geographic differences in housing costs relative to housing costs in the United States.

[T]he Tax Increase Prevention and Reconciliation Act of 2005 (TIPRA) . . . added a new section 911(c)(2)(A) of the Code, which limits the housing expenses taken into account in section 911(c)(1)(A) to an amount equal to the product of — (i)

---

[3] The Service, under mandate in § 911(c)(2)(B), provides a detailed list of exceptions to the § 911(c)(2)(A) cap. The first such Notice was issued in 2006, and subsequent Notices have been issued each year. *See, e.g.*, Notice 2014-29, 2014-18 I.R.B. 991. We include this heavily excerpted version of the 2006 Notice merely to serve as an alert that the cap may be something other than 30 percent of the § 911(b)(2)(D) amount.

30 percent (adjusted as may be provided under the Secretary's authority under section 911(c)(2)(B)) of the amount in effect under section 911(b)(2)(D) for the calendar year in which the taxable year of the individual begins, multiplied by (ii) the number of days of that taxable year within the applicable period described in section 911(d)(1).

. . .

Section 911(c)(2)(B) of the Code authorizes the Secretary to issue regulations or other guidance to adjust the percentage under section 911(c)(2)(A)(i) based on geographic differences in housing costs relative to housing costs in the United States. . . .

Accordingly, [this Notice] . . . identifies locations within countries with high housing costs relative to housing costs in the United States, and provides an adjusted limitation on housing expenses for a qualified individual incurring housing expenses in one or more of these high cost localities in 2006 to use (in lieu of the otherwise applicable limitation . . .) in determining his or her housing expenses under section 911(c)(2)(A) of the Code. The table will be updated each year by administrative pronouncement (e.g., through issuing a notice, amending Form 2555 or the instructions thereto, or by making a revised table available on the IRS website at http://www.irs.gov), beginning in 2007. . . .

[Table omitted.]

A qualified individual incurring housing expenses in one or more of the high cost localities identified above for the year 2006 may use the adjusted limit provided in the table . . . in determining his or her housing cost amount on Form 2555, Foreign Earned Income.

JONES v. COMMISSIONER
United States Court of Appeals, Fifth Circuit
927 F.2d 849 (1991)

GOLDBERG, CIRCUIT JUDGE:

In a notice dated December 8, 1987, the Commissioner of Internal Revenue (the "Commissioner") determined deficiencies in George H. and Betty A. Jones' (collectively hereinafter referred to as "Taxpayers") income tax for the taxable years ending December 31, 1981, 1982 and 1983, in the amounts of $7,355, $37,513, and $37,031 respectively. The case was subsequently tried before the Tax Court. Finding that Jones failed to prove he was a bona fide resident of Japan during the applicable period, the Tax Court determined deficiencies in Taxpayers' income tax. . . .

I. Facts and Proceedings Below

When George H. Jones ("Jones") retired from the Air Force in 1970, he entered into an employment agreement with International Air Service Company, Ltd. ("IASCO"), a California corporation in the business of furnishing flight crew personnel to aircraft operators. Pursuant to a contract between IASCO and Japanese Air Lines Co., Ltd. ("JAL"), Jones was assigned exclusively to JAL, flying out of Tokyo, Japan. While in Japan on this initial assignment, Taxpayers and their four children resided in a rented house in Japan.

Jones served with JAL, based in Tokyo, from 1971 through March 1972. On March 31, 1972, JAL furloughed Jones. Jones moved his family and belongings back to San Antonio, Texas, so he could attempt to obtain interim employment. On January 1, 1973, JAL recalled Jones to active duty and reassigned him to JAL's Tokyo base. Although he then moved back to Tokyo, his wife remained in San Antonio so that their son could graduate from high school, after which time Mrs. Jones and their youngest daughter anticipated joining Jones in Tokyo. During both his first and second assignment in Tokyo, Jones' flights consisted of routes within Japan and between Japan and Asia.

In March 1974, JAL reassigned Jones to Anchorage, Alaska, its only base located in the United States. Therefore, after Taxpayers' son graduated from high school in San Antonio, Mrs. Jones and Taxpayer's youngest daughter also moved to Anchorage. Taxpayers' youngest daughter only lived in Anchorage until she left for college. After moving to Anchorage, Mrs. Jones began a career for the first time. She eventually went to work for a newly-formed bank and worked directly for the chairman of the bank.

On March 3, 1980, and continuing through the years in issue, JAL transferred Jones back to Tokyo. Although Mrs. Jones had the opportunity to move to Tokyo as well, she decided to remain in Anchorage and pursue her own career until Jones' expected retirement in 1988. She continued to occupy the townhome that Taxpayers jointly owned in Anchorage. Taxpayers filed joint United States income tax returns for the years in question, 1981, 1982, and 1983.

When he moved back to Tokyo, Jones moved into the Hotel Nikko Narita (the "Hotel"), where he stayed until his retirement in 1988. Jones apparently elected to stay at the Hotel instead of renting an apartment or a house for reasons of convenience, economy, and the society of other JAL crewmembers who also lived in the Hotel. He checked into and out of the Hotel in accordance with his schedule, and left his personal belongings in storage at the Hotel when he was away.

Although Taxpayers tried to see each other as frequently as possible, Jones was only able to fly on JAL with discount tickets for approved vacation periods. Unlike many domestic air carriers, JAL did not allow its flight crew members the privilege of flying free anytime a seat was available. This same policy applied to Mrs. Jones.

Although Jones did not own an automobile in Japan during the years in issue, he had renewed his Japanese driver's license so that he could occasionally borrow a car or rent a car when his family came to visit him. Jones also maintained his Alaska driver's license and two cars in the United States were co-titled in his name. Although he did not maintain a bank account in Japan and held no Japanese-based credit cards, he did maintain joint bank accounts with his wife in Alaska and San Antonio, and held U.S.-based credit cards. During the years in question, Jones was registered to vote in Alaska and voted absentee in United States elections.

Jones held a commercial multi-entry visa, renewable every four years, which allowed him to stay in Japan a maximum of three years per entry. The only limitation was a requirement that he leave Japan at least once every three years. Since his profession dictated frequent trips outside Japan, this was not a problem for Jones.

Jones paid both Japanese and United States income taxes for the years at issue. Jones' Japanese income tax returns were prepared at his expense by a Japanese accountant in Japan. After moving to Japan, Jones received a dividend check, representing a 1981 payment under the Alaska Permanent Fund Distribution Program. Because entitlement was based on Alaskan residence, Jones returned the check, explaining that he was no longer an Alaska resident.

During the years in issue, JAL assigned Jones to flights which were either intercontinental between Japan and the United States, or intracontinental segments of such international flights within Japan and the United States. Jones had no control over which flights he was scheduled to fly. During the relevant period, Jones spent less than 165 nights a year in Japan. Since Anchorage was JAL's only U.S. base, and one of the normal stopover cities on Japan/U.S. routes, Jones' job required that he be in Anchorage frequently. When overnight in Anchorage, Jones stayed in the townhouse co-owned by Taxpayers.

During the years in issue, Jones did not have extensive contact with Japanese culture. He did visit a local Japanese doctor for medical attention and he participated in certain recreational activities, including jogging and playing golf. Jones socialized with co-workers also living at the Hotel and occasionally drove into Tokyo for dinner and entertainment. . . . Taxpayers claimed exclusions of $76,050 and $81,272, respectively, under Section 911 of the Code. . . .

II. Discussion

. . . The only issue this court must address is whether Jones was a "qualified individual" within the meaning of section . . . 911 of the Code. To be entitled to . . . the exclusion available under Code Section 911 [for] foreign earned income, a taxpayer had to have a tax home in a foreign country and demonstrate (1) that he had either been a "bona fide resident" of a foreign country for an uninterrupted period including an entire taxable year (the "bona fide residency test"), or (2) that he had been physically present in a foreign country for a certain period of time (the "physical presence test"). Jones concedes that he does not meet the "physical presence test." Therefore, Jones must show that his tax home was in Japan and that he was a bona fide resident of Japan during the applicable period. . . .

This court must determine residence in light of congressional intent, which was to encourage foreign trade by encouraging foreign employment for citizens of the United States, and to place them in an equal position with citizens of other countries going abroad who are not taxed by their own countries.

For purposes of section . . . 911, the test of a taxpayer's bona fide residence in a foreign country is the test of alien residence established in Code Section 871. Treasury Regulation Section 1.871-2(b) provides in pertinent part that:

An alien actually present in the United States who is not a mere transient or sojourner is a resident of the United States for purposes of the income tax. . . . One who comes to the United States for a definite purpose which in its nature may be promptly accomplished is a transient; but, if his purpose is of such a nature that an extended stay may be necessary for its accomplishment, and to that end the alien makes his home temporarily in the United States, he becomes a resident, though it may be his intention at all times to return to his domicile abroad when the purpose for which he came has been consummated or abandoned. Residence is therefore much less than domicile which requires an intent to make a fixed and permanent home.

When determining whether a taxpayer was a bona fide resident of a foreign country, courts consider a number of objective factors, first enunciated in *Sochurek v. Commissioner*, 300 F.2d 34 (7th Cir. 1962). These factors include:

(1)   intention of the taxpayer;

(2)   establishment of his home temporarily in the foreign country for an indefinite period;

(3)   participation in the activities of his chosen community on social and cultural levels, identification with the daily lives of the people and, in general, assimilation into the foreign environment;

(4)   physical presence in the foreign country consistent with his employment;

(5)   nature and duration of his employment . . . ;

(6)   assumption of economic burdens and payment of taxes to the foreign country;

(7)   status of resident contrasted to that of transient or sojourner;

(8)   treatment accorded his income tax status by his employer;

(9)   marital status and residence of his family;

(10)   . . . whether his assignment abroad could be promptly accomplished within a definite or specified time; [and]

(11)   good faith in making his trip abroad; whether for purpose of tax evasion.

While all these factors may not be present in every situation, those appropriate should be properly considered and weighed. A taxpayer must offer "strong proof" of bona fide residence in a foreign country to qualify for the foreign earned income exclusion under section 911.

In upholding the Commissioner's assessment, the Tax Court seemed to place particular emphasis on the fact Jones chose to live in the Hotel, rather than renting an apartment or a home in Japan, and the fact that Jones' wife chose to live in Anchorage, rather than give up her job and move to Japan with her husband. The Tax Court also noted that Jones had a number of ties to the United States, while he remained relatively unassimilated into the Japanese community. The Tax Court's analysis, however, overlooks the other . . . factors.

First, the Tax Court failed to consider Jones' intent. Jones obviously intended to become a resident of Japan and therefore he accordingly returned to the State of

Alaska a dividend check which was based on Alaskan residence. A taxpayer's intent plays perhaps the most important part in determining the establishment and maintenance of a foreign residence.

Jones established his home in Japan, presumably for the remainder of his career. Jones' job as a pilot was ongoing and both JAL and Jones intended Jones to live and work in Japan until his retirement. Therefore, Jones' purpose for being in Japan was of such a nature that an extended stay was necessary. Due to his flight schedule, JAL required his physical presence in Japan and such presence was consistent with his employment.

In addition, Jones argues that he should not be penalized because the economic realities of Japan lead him to choose to live in the Hotel, instead of renting an apartment or buying a home. The Commissioner and the Tax Court seemed bothered by the apparent temporary nature of a hotel, but it is not necessary for a taxpayer to establish a fixed, permanent place of abode in order to be a "resident" of a foreign country.

Furthermore, Jones was apparently only away from his home in Japan when his business required it, or when he was on vacation. The fact that Jones was able to stay at his home in Anchorage during flights was merely fortuitous and should not be held against Jones. If JAL had not previously based Jones in Anchorage, Taxpayers would not have owned property there. In addition, if JAL had scheduled Jones to fly only Asian trips, as he had done when he was previously assigned to Japan, Jones would not have had occasion to layover in Anchorage. Nevertheless, business and vacation trips to the United States should not affect Jones' residency.

Jones paid resident Japanese income taxes. Jones' Japanese income tax returns were prepared at his expense by a Japanese accountant. Both JAL and IASCO viewed Jones as a resident of Japan for Japanese income tax purposes. In fact, JAL required IASCO to withhold Japanese income taxes from Jones' payroll checks. The last . . . factor also arguably supports Jones' claim to bona fide residency because the Commissioner has never suggested that Jones took the job in Japan for the purposes of tax evasion.

Both in his briefs and during oral argument, the Commissioner seemed to rely heavily on the fact that Jones' wife did not move to Japan during his last assignment to Tokyo. The Commissioner seems to argue that Taxpayers should be punished because Mrs. Jones chose to stay in Anchorage and pursue a career, rather than move to Japan with her husband. When JAL reassigned Jones to Japan in 1980, Taxpayers' children were all away at school or married. For the first time in a number of years, Mrs. Jones was free to devote herself to a career. She would most likely not have been able to find comparable employment if she had joined her husband in Japan.

We are besieged with cases and statistics and erudite writing about the necessity for the equalization of rights and opportunities for men and women in our society. It would be strange indeed if the Congress of the United States which has legislated frequently and ardently for the equality of the sexes, should in the field of taxation find that a woman who desires to establish herself in the field of business, and her husband who obviously encouraged her, should be penalized because she is pursuing something which the Congress thinks is in the interest of our nation and its economy. Penalizing Taxpayers for Mrs. Jones' decision in no way furthers the clearly enunciated legislative purpose behind section . . . 911 of encouraging foreign employment of United States citizens.

Although Jones admittedly did not learn to speak Japanese and was relatively unassimilated into the Japanese culture, the majority of . . . factors support Jones' contention that he was a bona fide resident of Japan during the relevant period. Jones was not a mere transient or sojourner in Japan. Even though he intended to eventually return to his domicile in the United States after he retired from JAL, his purpose for being in Japan required him to remain there for at least eight years. Although Jones may have felt a little like a sojourner in a foreign land, as Moses did after he left Egypt and fled to Midian, under the applicable modern day tax statutes we are required to classify him as a bona fide resident of Japan, and not a mere transient or sojourner.

Section 911 . . . speaks to the modern age. . . . Today, husbands and wives, men and women, have the right to separate careers. With respect to Jones' tax residence, he was neither a domiciliary nor a transient. He was a resident of Japan. The Code clearly could have used the word domicile or transient; neither of these are strange to our congressional enactments and legislation. Instead, the Code speaks in terms of residence. Since we find that Jones was a bona fide resident of Japan during the relevant time period, we reverse the Tax Court.

Tax Home

Because the Tax Court determined that Jones was not a bona fide resident of Japan, it did not reach the question of whether Jones' tax home was in Japan. As we stated earlier, however, in order to qualify for the tax benefits available pursuant to section . . . 911, the taxpayer must prove both that he was a bona fide resident of a foreign country and that his tax home was in a foreign country. . . .

Treasury Regulation Section 1.911-2(b) sets forth the general rule that a taxpayer's tax home is at his principal place of business or employment. However, section 911, and the regulations promulgated pursuant to [it], provide the overriding exception that if an individual's abode is in the United States, then he is legally incapable of establishing that his tax home is in a foreign country.

Recently the Tax Court has had an opportunity to discuss the abode limitation, and this court has affirmed at least two of these opinions. In these cases, this court has adopted the following definition of abode:

> "Abode" has been variously defined as one's home, habitation, residence, domicile, or place of dwelling. While an exact definition of "abode" depends upon the context in which the word is used, it clearly does not mean one's principal place of business. Thus, "abode" has a domestic rather than a vocational meaning, and stands in contrast to "tax home." . . .

The facts in this case can easily be distinguished from oil rig and compound worker cases. . . . In those cases, when the taxpayers were on duty on oil rigs or in the oil field compounds, they slept in employer-provided housing, ate employer-provided meals and returned home to the United States after each work period on employer-provided flights. In addition, the taxpayer's family was not allowed to join him abroad. These taxpayers were not incurring any costs associated with living abroad; rather, they were essentially commuting on a regular basis from their homes in the United States.

In contrast, Jones had to pay for his vacation travel to the United States. Jones also paid for his meals and his housing while abroad. Jones also incurred the additional cost of paying Japanese income taxes. In addition, Mrs. Jones had the opportunity to move to Japan if she had so desired, but she elected to keep her job in Anchorage for her own personal reasons. Therefore, Jones' abode was in Japan and not in the United States, and his tax home was also in Japan during the relevant period.

III. Conclusion

We are compelled to conclude that the Tax Court erred as a matter of law. Taxpayers have established that Jones was a bona-fide foreign resident of Japan and had his tax home in Japan during the years in question. Therefore, the Tax Court decision is reversed and remanded with direction to the Tax Court to expunge the deficiency assessed and enter judgment for the Taxpayers.

Unit 4

FOREIGN TAX CREDIT: OVERVIEW

A. CODE AND REGULATION PROVISIONS

Code   §§ 164(a)(3), (b)(3); 275(a)(4); 901(a), (b), (i), (j); 903; 904(a); 909(a), (d).

Reg.   §§ 1.901-1(c); 1.901-2(a), (b), (c)(1), (f); 1.901-3.

B. PROBLEMS FOR CLASS DISCUSSION

4-1. Todd, a United States citizen, opened a coffee shop in Honduras. During the year, Todd incurred the following tax liabilities, which he paid promptly: (i) Honduran real property tax; (ii) Honduran value added tax; (iii) Honduran federal income tax on Todd's business income; (iv) Honduran state income tax; (v) Honduran withholding tax (at a rate of 25 percent) on dividends; and (vi) Honduran "social security" tax imposed on Todd's self-employment from the coffee shop business.

   (a) Which of these taxes are creditable under § 901 or § 903?

   (b) With respect to the creditable taxes, may Todd credit some and deduct others?

4-2. DelCo is a domestic corporation. Its principal business activity consists of the manufacture and sale of industrial machinery, and its main plant and offices are located in Delaware. DelCo also has a branch plant located in France where DelCo manufactures and sells its products in Europe. During the year, DelCo realized $100,000 of taxable income from its United States plant activities, and $75,000 of taxable income from its foreign branch activities. Assume that DelCo's United States tax liability (pre-credit) is $50,000. The foreign branch paid $40,000 in corporate income taxes to France.

   (a) What is DelCo's final United States tax liability for the year?

   (b) What if the taxes paid to France were $20,000?

C. OVERVIEW

Individuals and corporations are commonly subject to double taxation due to the overlap of source and residence: both the jurisdiction in which income is generated (the country of source) and the jurisdiction in which the income earner is resident or organized as a matter of law (the country of residence) claim jurisdiction to tax.

61

The United States international tax system is built upon the principle that the residence country has a primary right to tax its residents on income from whatever source derived. Thus, a United States individual or corporation that earns income in another country might be taxed both by that other country (based on source) and the United States (based on residence). Without relief from one or both of the jurisdictions, the tax bill from this common overlap could destroy any value from engaging in cross-border activity.

Most countries use a number of different methods to prevent, remedy, or reduce this kind of juridical double taxation.[1] First, both in terms of historical use and common practice, countries that impose worldwide taxation on the basis of residence, like the United States, generally provide unilateral statutory relief from double taxation.[2] Second, countries coordinate taxation among themselves by entering into tax treaties, generally on a bilateral (two-country) basis. The bilateral solutions introduced in tax treaties are discussed more fully in Units 10 through 12. Unit 3 focused on unilateral relief through the foreign earned income exclusion. This Unit focuses on the unilateral approach of the foreign tax credit.

If a foreign country (the source country) imposes tax on an item of income earned within its jurisdiction by a resident of another country, that person uses the foreign tax credit in his home country (the residence country) to reduce his home country's tax on that item of income. The basic foreign tax credit approach involves extending a dollar-for-dollar credit for foreign taxes paid against the domestic taxes imposed on foreign-source income. This unilateral solution to double taxation thus represents a voluntary surrender of tax jurisdiction by the country of residence to the country of source — to the extent the source country imposes a tax, the residence country reduces its corresponding tax.

Through the mechanism of the foreign tax credit, the United States declines to collect residence-based tax and allows foreign countries to preserve their source-based tax. If the foreign country does not impose taxation, the United States tax is not reduced, and the residence-based tax is preserved. The residence-based tax thus acts as a default or residual tax — it is only imposed to the extent no corresponding foreign tax is imposed.

The preservation of residence-based taxation as a residual matter distinguishes the United States system from the approach some countries take to double taxation, namely, total exemption from residence-based tax for foreign source income (often referred to as a territorial system). In a pure territorial system, the home country refrains from imposing taxes on income earned abroad, whether or not the foreign country imposes taxation.

---

[1] *See* Unit 1, note 3.

[2] The relief is unilateral in the sense that it is granted independent of the actions of any other country. In the United States, unilateral methods of relief emerged simultaneously with the emergence of the income tax itself. The modern income tax, enacted in 1913, included a deduction for foreign taxes paid, but the law was quickly amended to include additional relief measures such as the foreign tax credit (enacted in 1918) and the exemption for certain foreign earned income (enacted in 1926; see discussion in Unit 3).

Arguments can be made in support of both the credit and the exemption strategies, and there is vigorous debate in the United States about which strategy best enhances this country's position in the global economy. For example, some argue that the imposition of residence-based taxation — especially if combined with a relatively high United States corporate tax rate — puts United States companies at a disadvantage in relation to their foreign counterparts when operating in countries that refrain from imposing taxation as a method of attracting foreign investment. This suggests that the credit system is not sufficient to put United States firms on an equal footing with competitors in foreign markets, and that an exemption system is needed to level this playing field.

Conversely, others argue that a territorial system would unfairly disadvantage purely domestic companies in relation to those that have overseas operations since the former are fully subject to United States taxation, but the latter are not so subject to the extent they earn income abroad. As a result, companies would be encouraged to set up factories and other operations abroad so as to escape United States taxation. This suggests that an exemption system would make domestic firms uncompetitive and drive firms offshore, and that a foreign tax credit system is needed to ensure a (slightly different) level playing field between United States domestic and multinational firms.

As should be clear, no system can satisfy both of these compelling arguments. The tension between the two positions explains much of the international tax system as it exists today. In reality, there are very few purely territorial tax systems — most countries with territorial systems also have special rules that impose residence-based tax on at least some of the income earned by their citizens or residents abroad. On the other hand, there are also very few (if any) purely worldwide tax systems, and the United States is not one, as Unit 3 and later Units make clear. Instead, most countries fall somewhere on a spectrum between the two poles.

In undertaking an analysis of the foreign tax credit rules introduced in this Unit and expanded upon in Units 5 and 6, one should keep in mind the tensions described above. This Unit lays out the basic framework of the foreign tax credit, introduces a number of pressures that arise in the implementation of this theoretically simple yet practically quite complex strategy for relief of double taxation, and identifies the kinds of foreign taxes that may be credited against United States tax obligations.

4.01 Credit versus Deduction

Under § 901(b)(1), a credit against tax may be taken by a United States citizen and a domestic corporation for foreign and possession "income, war profits, and excess profits taxes." Alternatively, a deduction for such taxes is available under § 164(a)(3). A taxpayer must select *either* the credit *or* the deduction. As a rule, § 275(a)(4) prevents their simultaneous use. The election to take either a credit or a deduction is typically made at the time of filing a return but can also be made within certain time frames specified in the Regulations. The election is made on an annual basis. Thus, the taxpayer may alternate annually between the credit and the deduction depending upon which is more favorable. In most cases, the § 901 credit is more advantageous than the deduction because a credit reduces tax on a dollar-for-dollar basis, while a deduction merely reduces the amount of income upon which the tax will be levied. In some cases, however, the deduction may be preferable to the credit. Most notably, the § 901 credit is curtailed by the source rule limitation of § 904, discussed in more detail in Unit 6; however, this limitation does not apply to § 164(a)(3) deductions. Obviously, the deduction is preferable for taxes which are not otherwise creditable.

4.02   Creditable Taxes — General Principles

The Regulations under § 901 construct a two-pronged test to determine whether a foreign levy is a creditable tax. A foreign levy is an "income tax" for which a credit is allowed if (1) it is a tax, and (2) its predominant character is that of an income tax in the United States sense. Paragraphs (a) through (d) of Regulation § 1.901-2 address whether a foreign levy qualifies as an income tax for § 901 purposes. *Wada v. Commissioner*, excerpted in Part D of this Unit, provides some interpretation and analysis of this issue. In addition, paragraphs (e) and (f) of Regulation § 1.901-2 address rules for determining both the amount of tax that is creditable and the identity of the payor of the tax. The definitional issue of which payments constitute an income tax and which do not permeates the discussion of the foreign tax credit.

4.03   Payor of a Tax

Traditionally, a credit has been extended only to the taxpayer incurring a foreign tax liability. A Supreme Court case, *Biddle v. Commissioner*, 302 U.S. 573 (1938), explained that a taxpayer incurs a tax liability if the remedies for non-payment run against him. Regulation § 1.901-2(f) makes clear that legal liability under foreign law is the determinative factor for treatment as payor of a tax, regardless of who actually pays the tax.

The fact that a withholding agent is required under foreign law to remit a tax does not deprive the party actually burdened by the tax from qualifying as the taxpayer for credit purposes. Provided the agent had the right to withhold such funds, the amount of the proceeds withheld constitutes both income to, and a tax payment by, the taxpayer. In essence, the transaction is viewed as though the taxpayer had received the full amount of the proceeds and thereafter personally paid the foreign tax.

For example, assume that a United States citizen invested in the stock of a foreign corporation that declared a $100 dividend. This shareholder would probably not file a return in the foreign country to pay taxes due on any dividends received. Instead, the shareholder might receive only $90 because the corporation was required under foreign law to withhold $10 as potential tax.[3] In that case, he would still be considered to have paid the tax since the legal liability for the tax rests on him. Example (2) in Regulation § 1.901-2(f)(2)(ii) further illustrates that in determining the payor of a tax, beneficial interest is controlling, and nominees and agents are ignored.

---

[3] The United States similarly uses the payor withholding method to collect taxes from passive foreign investors. See Unit 7 for a discussion.

Guardian Industries Corp. v. United States, 477 F.3d 1368 (Fed. Cir. 2007), demonstrates the difficulties that can often arise regarding the identity of the proper taxpayer for tax credit purposes, especially when imposing legal liability is a matter of interpreting foreign law. In that case, the taxpayer, a Delaware corporation, was allowed to claim legal liability, and therefore a foreign tax credit, for foreign taxes that were paid with respect to income earned by several Luxembourg operating subsidiaries. Guardian was entitled to the foreign tax credit because of its sole ownership of GIE, a wholly owned Luxembourg holding company which was treated as a disregarded entity (and hence a branch of Guardian) for United States tax purposes under the check-the-box rules of § 7701. GIE in turn owned the operating subsidiaries, and under Luxembourg law, GIE and the subsidiaries reported their incomes and deductions on a single, consolidated return. This consolidation meant that GIE was liable for the group's taxes under Luxembourg law.

By virtue of its treatment as a disregarded entity for United States tax purposes, GIE's tax liabilities were therefore considered liabilities of its parent company, Guardian. At the same time, the operating subsidiaries were treated as corporations, and their income was not attributed to GIE or Guardian, for United States tax purposes. As a result of this structure, Guardian successfully claimed foreign tax credits in respect of GIE's consolidated tax liability, even though the income that gave rise to the tax was not included in GIE's or Guardian's income for United States tax purposes.

The Treasury viewed Guardian's claim for foreign tax credits based on this structure to be beyond the spirit, if not the letter, of Regulation § 1.901-2(f), which states the rules for determining "the person by whom tax is considered paid." In 2006, the Treasury issued Proposed Regulations, the preamble to which is excerpted in Part D of this Unit, to address concerns about the separation of foreign tax credits from the related income, as illustrated by the result obtained in *Guardian*. The Regulations, finalized in 2012, retain the general principle that tax is considered paid by the person who has legal liability under foreign law for the tax. The Regulations provide further guidance regarding the treatment of foreign taxes paid on the combined income of two or more persons, requiring apportionment of the foreign taxes according to the relative amount of income taken into account by each person.

Congress also responded to structures like that used in *Guardian* with the 2010 enactment of § 909. This provision adopts "matching rules" designed to match foreign tax credits to the income to which they relate. The rule generally prevents taxpayers from taking a foreign tax credit unless and until they also take into account the income that was subject to foreign tax. The dynamic interplay between the foreign tax credit, the deferral regime, and the check-the-box rules continues to be a fascinating and troubling aspect of the United States international tax regime, and one that bears close watching in the years ahead.

4.04 Amount of Tax Paid

Regulation § 1.901-2(e) restricts the types of payments that are creditable, precluding credit for refundable amounts, subsidies, multiple levies, and non-compulsory payments. As this Regulation provides, "an amount is not tax paid to a foreign country to the extent that it is reasonably certain that the amount will be refunded, credited, rebated, abated, or forgiven." Only those taxes that result from a "reasonable approximation" of one's final liability under the foreign tax law are creditable taxes. Anything in excess of that standard constitutes a non-compulsory amount for which the credit is not available. Thus, to maximize the potential for creditability, a taxpayer should apply foreign tax law (including applicable tax treaties) so as to reduce foreign income and taxes. However, a taxpayer is not expected to alter its business form, conduct, or mode of operations in order to demonstrate that an amount is "compulsory."

The examples given in Regulation § 1.901-2 are useful in understanding the parameters of the concept of creditable taxes. For instance, example (1) in Regulation § 1.901-2(e)(5)(ii) describes the need to interpret foreign arm's length pricing rules, and example (2) provides that a taxpayer must seek available refunds of foreign taxes paid. The obvious intent of these rules is to restrict the credit as much as possible and thereby protect the residual residence-based tax imposed in the United States.

4.05 Subsidies

Given the ingenuity of sophisticated tax practitioners advising private industry operating abroad, coupled with the desire of foreign governments to maximize their revenues by facilitating the crediting of payments made to them, the Regulations single out disguised subsidies and render them non-creditable as foreign tax payments. Under Regulation § 1.901-2(e)(3) and § 901(i) (which codified the Regulation), "tax payments" made to a foreign government are not creditable if the government uses the money to provide any direct or indirect benefit to the taxpayer, to a related party, or to any party to the transaction. The Regulation states that a "subsidy" includes benefits in the form of a rebate, refund, credit, deduction, payment, discharge of an obligation, or any other method that is employed to confer a benefit.

4.06 Multiple Levies

A similar focus attends the imposition of multiple charges. Example (5) in Regulation § 1.903-1(b)(3) demonstrates that if a foreign country imposes both an excise and an income tax and the excise tax is creditable against the income tax, the amount of the income tax for purposes of § 901 would not reflect the portion of the income tax sheltered by the excise tax.

Thus, if a United States person incurs foreign income tax liability of $100 and is permitted to credit $30 of an excise tax he paid to the foreign government against that liability, the United States person will be considered to have paid an excise tax of $30 and an income tax of $70. Accordingly, only $70 is a creditable foreign tax. This rule ensures that the amount of taxes eligible for the credit is not inflated. The character of each tax levied is preserved for purposes of assessing its creditability, and the foreign tax credit as adjusted thereby reflects the taxpayer's true income tax burden.

4.07   Refunds and Benefits

If an amount is reasonably certain to be refunded, it does not qualify for the credit. The application of this limitation most frequently arises in the context of taxes withheld at the source. Regulation § 1.901-2(e)(2)(ii) posits as an example the case of $100 of passive income subject to a $25 foreign withholding tax. As the recipient qualifies under a tax treaty for a reduced tax rate of $10, the excess $15, although technically withheld and paid to a foreign government, will not qualify for the credit as it is reasonably certain to be refunded. Other categories which must be taken into account are tax credits authorized by the foreign jurisdiction, such as investment or charitable contribution credits. Additionally, should "other property" be received from the taxing authorities (e.g., anything from televisions to bonds), such rebates also reduce the amount of tax paid.

4.08   Compulsory Payments

To credit a payment to a foreign country, § 901(b) requires a taxpayer to show that the payment is an income tax. As noted below, this determination is made independently for each separate foreign levy. Regulation § 1.901-2(a) provides that in order to constitute a creditable income tax, the levy must be a "tax," the predominant character of which must be "that of an income tax in the U.S. sense." The Regulation further interprets this concept by providing that in order to constitute a tax, the payment must be a compulsory payment to a foreign government which is intended as such. Fines, penalties, interest, royalties, and charges for specific economic benefits do not represent a "tax" for purposes of the credit.

4.09   Economic Benefits

Payments in exchange for specific economic benefits are addressed in Regulation § 1.901-2(a)(2)(ii). The Regulation recognizes that some foreign levies may serve both as a compulsory tax payment and as a payment in exchange for a specific economic benefit. In such a case, the payment is bifurcated into its component parts and a credit is available only if the taxpayer can establish the distinct element of the foreign levy which constitutes a tax. Taxpayers who find themselves in this dilemma are euphemistically referred to as "dual-capacity taxpayers."

A specific economic benefit is one that is not readily available to others subject to the general tax. The Regulation notes that the right to conduct business in the foreign jurisdiction does not represent such a benefit. An economic benefit can take the form of property, services, or other privileges, provided the benefit is distinguishable from that received by others. Indirect benefits garnered through related parties and the like are equally suspect. However, the payment of pension, unemployment, or disability amounts generally is not considered to be paid in return for a specific economic benefit.

4.10   Predominant Character of an Income Tax

A foreign levy qualifies as an income tax for § 901 purposes if its predominant character is that of an income tax in the United States sense. This means that the tax must be designed to reach net gain. Regulation § 1.901-2(b) states that the net gain requirement is determined through compliance with a three-pronged test — a realization test, a gross receipts test, and a net income test. Additionally, Regulation §§ 1.901-2(a)(3)(ii) and (c) prohibit the use of "soak-up" taxes — that is, those for which liability depends upon the availability of the credit against the taxpayer's tax obligation to another country. Regulation § 1.901-2(c)(2) provides four examples to illustrate this concept.

The definitional issue of predominant character has garnered much controversy, and courts have stepped in to offer their views as to what foreign taxes may be credited.[4] In *PPL Corp. v. Commissioner*, excerpted in Part D of this Unit, the Supreme Court relied on the longstanding doctrines that emphasize a tax's predominant character and analyze foreign taxes based on how they would be classified if imposed in the United States finding a certain United Kingdom "windfall" tax creditable in the United States because it would reach net income under its normal or predominant application.

While the overall requirements regarding creditability are generally and technically applicable to all taxes, there are important conceptual distinctions among business, investment, and services income. The following sections discuss creditability issues that arise in each of these three types of income.

4.11   Taxes on Business Income

Generally speaking, the Service has attempted to deny creditability to foreign taxes that are levied on business operations where the taxpayer has suffered a net loss in that country. If, upon review of the language or administration of a foreign tax statute, the Service concludes that the tax might be levied upon a net loss, it may contend that the tax is not a creditable income tax in the United States sense.

To be an income tax within the United States meaning of the term, a foreign tax must meet a "realization test," a "net income test," and a "gross receipts test." These tests are considered below in that order.

The Realization Test. Regulation § 1.901-2(b)(2) provides that the gain on which the foreign tax is levied must be realized in the United States sense. This realization test is met if the event that gives rise to the tax would result in the realization of income under the standards of the Code. A tax that is triggered by a purchase, a tax computed on the basis of rental value, and a tax triggered by the manufacture of a product rather than its sale generally would violate the

---

[4] See *Exxon Corporation v. Commissioner*, 113 T.C. 338 (1999), for an example of the interpretive difficulties involved in this analysis, focused on whether the absence of a deduction for interest under the tax law of a foreign jurisdiction renders a tax uncreditable because the predominant character of the tax failed to meet the net income test.

realization test since none of these events gives rise to realization as expressed by § 1001.

However, Regulation § 1.901-2(b)(2)(i)(C) provides that this standard is relaxed if the tax is levied on a pre-realization event that serves as a substitute for the later triggering event. Thus, for example, if the tax is imposed on a pre-realization event and the tax is based upon a difference in values at the beginning and the end of the period (or the taxing event is the physical transfer or export of readily marketable property), the realization test is waived. Such a tax formulation by a foreign jurisdiction shows an intent to reach some realization event and seems designed simply to relieve the authorities from having to rely upon the taxpayer's honest reporting of the sales price actually obtained outside that jurisdiction. Pre-realization events also include recapture of tax events such as previously permitted deductions, credits, or allowances.

Some additional exceptions to the realization test are afforded under Regulation § 1.901-2(b)(2). First, Regulation § 1.901-2(b)(2)(i) provides that a tax may be credited even if it is sometimes imposed upon the occurrence of events not meeting the United States realization concept as long as the predominant character of the tax is one that is imposed upon an event that would result in the realization of income under United States tax law. Basically, this exception should apply to a tax levied on a wide variety of income types, including both those realized in the United States sense and others not so realized. If the unrealized types (e.g., rental income from a personal residence or receipt of stock dividends) are insignificant in light of the realized items included in the tax base, the tax may be credited. In such a case, the tax is evaluated as a whole because "a tax either is or is not an income tax, in its entirety, for all persons subject to the tax."

A second exception is provided for taxes levied on non-realization events that occur before events which would result in domestic realization. Provided that a second tax is not levied upon the actual realization, the earlier event satisfies the standard. Regulation §§ 1.901-2(b)(2)(ii) and 1.901-2(b)(2)(iv), example (4), illustrate this concept by showing that a tax levied on a deemed distribution by a corporation to its shareholders is creditable, so long as the foreign jurisdiction does not impose a second tax on the later actual distribution of funds. If a tax is later imposed, the second tax, and not the first, would qualify for the credit.

A third exception is provided for taxes levied on the transfer or processing of readily marketable property, even if this occurs prior to the occurrence of a realization event. Readily marketable property is property which (1) is inventory or property primarily held for sale and (2) can be sold on an open market without further processing or is exported from the foreign country.

The Net Income Test. Regulation § 1.901-2(b)(4) provides that the foreign tax must be structured to reach net income. In order to satisfy this test, the tax must permit either recovery of actual significant costs (including capital expenditures) or an allowance that closely approximates these amounts. The critical issues in this area are determining which expenses are significant and when (if ever) the lack of a deduction for significant expenses will be tolerated. Under Regulation § 1.901-2(b)(4), the foreign tax law must permit the recovery of the more significant costs incurred in producing the product. If actual expenses are not permitted, but an alternative procedure that reasonably approximates such costs is employed, the net income test is met. Furthermore, the fact that such costs may be recovered more slowly under foreign law than would be the case under United States law will not prevent the tax from being creditable.

The Gross Receipts Test. Regulation § 1.901-2(b)(3) states that a creditable tax may in some cases be imposed on gross receipts. An alternative calculation of gross receipts is permitted when such receipts may be difficult to determine and the alternative calculation produces a figure not in excess of fair market value.

4.12 Taxes on Dividends, Interest, and Other Passive Income

As noted previously, the creditability of taxes on investment income items in theory is determined by the same requirements discussed above for business taxes (the realization, net income, and gross receipts tests). However, Regulation § 1.901-2(b)(4)(i) makes some distinctions between passive income and business income, providing that a foreign tax will satisfy the net income requirement "where that tax is almost certain to reach some net gain in the normal circumstances in which it applies because costs and expenses will almost never be so high as to offset gross receipts."

Withholding taxes on dividends, interest, royalties, and other types of passive income are thus likely to be creditable taxes, even if taxation of these items is on a gross basis. Examples in the Regulations only use a tax on wages to illustrate the creditability of gross basis taxes, but investment income is probably indistinguishable for these purposes. In addition, gross basis withholding taxes on investment income may also meet the "in lieu of" standard discussed later in this Unit. The Regulations take a comparatively lenient attitude towards gross basis taxes that most likely reflects the desire by the United States to protect the creditability by other countries of tax imposed under the United States' own withholding tax regime, as discussed in Unit 7.

4.13 Taxes on Compensation

Foreign taxes on compensation, like those imposed on passive income, will generally be creditable, even if the tax is imposed on a gross basis. Such taxes are almost certain to reach net income by the very nature of compensation income. As stated by the Court of Claims in *Bank of America v. United States*, 459 F.2d 513 (Ct. Cl. 1972):

> [I]t is almost universally true that a wage or salary employee does not spend more on expenses incident to his job than he earns in pay. A foreign tax upon the gross income of an employee from his work should therefore be creditable by the employee under § 901(b)(1) despite the refusal of the other jurisdiction to permit deduction of job-related expenses. The reason is, of course, that in those circumstances the employee would always (or almost always) have some net gain and, accordingly, the tax, though on gross income, would be designed to pinch net gain in the end — and would in fact have that effect. In those circumstances, a loss (excess of expenses

over profit) is so improbable, and some net gain is so sure, that the tax can be placed on gross income without any real fear or expectation that there will be no net gain or profit to tax.

A similar position, and reasoning, was adopted by the Service in Regulation § 1.901-2(b)(4)(iv). In example (3) of that provision, a gross receipts tax on wages was permitted even though no deductions were allowable.

4.14 Taxes "In Lieu Of" Income Taxes: § 903

Section 903 provides that, for purposes of the foreign tax credit, the term "income, war profits, and excess profits taxes" includes taxes paid in lieu of a foreign income tax. The Senate Finance Committee Report accompanying the adoption of § 903, indicated that the statute was intended to enjoy a broad construction:

> Your committee believes further amendments should be made in [§ 901]. . . . In the interpretation of the term "income tax," the Commissioner, the Board [of Tax Appeals, predecessor to the Tax Court], and the courts have consistently adhered to a concept of income tax rather closely related to our own, and if such foreign tax was not imposed upon a basis corresponding approximately to net income it was not recognized as a basis for such credit. Thus if a foreign country in imposing income taxation authorized, for reasons growing out of the administrative difficulties of determining net income or taxable basis within that country, a United States domestic corporation doing business in such country to pay a tax in lieu of such income tax but measured, for example, by gross income, gross sales or a number of units produced within the country, such tax has not heretofore been recognized as a basis for a credit. Your committee has deemed it desirable to extend the scope of this section. Accordingly [§ 903] provides that the term "income, war profits, and excess profits taxes" shall . . . include a tax paid by a domestic taxpayer in lieu of the tax upon income, war profits, and excess profits taxes which would otherwise be imposed upon such taxpayer.[5]

Under Regulation § 1.903-1, to qualify as a § 903 "in lieu of" tax, the tax must meet the general definition of a "tax" as discussed above. This general definition, it should be recalled, focuses upon compulsory levies not made in exchange for a specific economic benefit. The tax also must be imposed as a substitute for (and not in addition to) an income tax or series of income taxes otherwise imposed. Thus, a tax based on gross income or some unique definition of "income" stands a better chance of being credited under § 903 than under § 901 given that the base of the tax need not bear any relationship to net income.

The foreign jurisdiction's purpose for imposing the tax, whether administrative or otherwise, is irrelevant in assessing creditability. Additionally, the nature of the base upon which the tax is levied — gross income, receipts, units exported, and the like — will not preclude creditability under § 903. Finally, the tax cannot be a

---

[5] S. Rep. No. 1631, 77th Cong., 2d Sess. 130–33 (1942).

"soak-up tax" (i.e., a tax for which liability is dependent upon the availability of the credit). Examples in Regulation § 1.903-1(b)(3) flesh out the boundaries of the concept in this context.

The substitution requirement is the most significant aspect of § 903. However, to date there remains uncertainty as to how strictly it should be applied. In *Compania Embotelladora Coca Cola, SA v. United States*, 139 F. Supp. 953 (Ct. Cl. 1956), for example, the Court of Claims held that a Cuban production tax could be credited under the predecessor of § 903 even though the taxpayer claimed a § 901 credit for not less than two other taxes. Yet, in *Allstate Insurance Co v. United States*, 419 F.2d 409 (Ct. Cl. 1969), the same court denied the creditability of an insurance premiums tax because the taxes "were not 'in lieu' of income taxes otherwise generally imposed, but were an additional levy which the plaintiff was required to pay over and above and apart from its payment of income taxes." The Service appears to stand solidly behind the *Allstate* approach: if a domestic person is subject both to the general tax of a foreign jurisdiction and also a surtax, the surtax should not qualify as a creditable tax under § 903.

4.15   Section 904 Limitation Upon the Amount of Taxes Which May Be Credited

Once the amount of creditable foreign taxes has been ascertained under §§ 901 and 903, the taxpayer must examine the limitations which are imposed upon the credit. The object of the limitation is to protect the United States' ability to tax the domestic source income of its own taxpayers. The provision attempts to accomplish this objective by limiting the foreign tax credit to the United States tax liability that (absent the credit) would be imposed on the taxpayer's foreign source income unreduced by foreign tax credits. Section 904 contains an overall limitation and a series of additional special limitations, discussed in detail in Unit 6. The overall limitation of § 904(a) can be expressed in formula form as follows:

$$\text{Maximum foreign tax credit} = \frac{\text{Foreign source taxable income}}{\text{Worldwide taxable income}} \times \text{United States tax on worldwide income}$$

4.16   Denial of Credit for Taxes Paid to Certain Countries

In order to effectuate various Congressional policies, § 901(j) provides that the foreign tax credit is denied for tax payments to specified countries. The intent of the legislation is to deny the tax benefits for activity in these hostile countries. The denial of the credit makes operations in these disfavored nations more expensive and thus may dampen the enthusiasm of United States enterprises to conduct business operations therein. The section is applicable to countries with which the United States has severed or ceased to conduct diplomatic relations, which are generally not recognized, or which have been designated as engaging in international terrorism.

D.   REFERENCE MATERIALS

- *Wada v. Commissioner*
- *PPL Corporation v. Commissioner*
- Preamble to Proposed Regulation § 1.901-2(f)

WADA v. COMMISSIONER
United States Tax Court
T.C. Memo 1995-241

MEMORANDUM FINDINGS OF FACT AND OPINION

JACOBS, JUDGE:

. . .

After a concession by petitioners, the issues for decision are: . . . (3) whether petitioners are entitled to a foreign tax credit under section 901 for Japanese "social security" payments of $1,047 made during 1988. . . .

FINDINGS OF FACT

. . . Petitioners resided in Honolulu, Hawaii, at the time they filed their petition.

Background

At all relevant times, petitioner Young Sook Wada (Mrs. Wada) was a U.S. citizen; petitioner Takeshi Wada (Mr. Wada) was a Japanese citizen. It is undisputed that Mr. Wada was a resident alien of the United States during the years under consideration.

. . .

Japanese Social Security Payments

During 1988, Mr. Wada received wages from Uokuni Sohonsha totaling 1,380,810 yen ($10,775). Respondent determined such amount to constitute taxable income in the United States. Of this total, Uokuni Sohonsha withheld 40,940 yen ($319) for income tax, 50,000 yen ($390) for insurance, and 134,110 yen ($1,047) for an item that the parties have stipulated to be "social security." On their 1988 Federal income tax return, petitioners neither reported any of Mr. Wada's wage income earned in Japan nor claimed a foreign tax credit.

Petitioners do not dispute the $10,775 addition of foreign earned income to their 1988 gross income. Petitioners' position is that they are entitled to a $1,366 foreign tax credit, which includes $319 of foreign income tax withheld, and $1,047 of foreign "social security." In the notice of deficiency, respondent allowed a $319 credit for foreign income tax paid, but did not allow a foreign tax credit for the $1,047 of foreign "social security."

OPINION

. . .

Issue 3. Foreign Tax Credit

Petitioners acknowledge that Mr. Wada earned $10,775 of wage income during 1988 from his employment with Uokuni Sohonsha in Japan. Petitioners argue, however, that section 901 entitles them to a $1,366 foreign tax credit. Respondent allowed $319 of this amount in the statutory notice of deficiency. The allowability of the remaining $1,047 as a foreign tax credit hinges upon whether "social security" withheld on Mr. Wada's Japanese wage income qualifies for the credit.

Section 901(b)(3) allows an alien resident of the United States to claim as a tax credit against his U.S. Federal income tax the amount of any income, war profits, and excess profits taxes paid or accrued during the taxable year to any foreign country. Accordingly, the foreign tax credit claimed by petitioners under section 901 would have to be based on Mr. Wada's payment of income, war profits, or excess profits taxes to Japan. Therefore, we must determine whether the $1,047 of "social security" paid by Mr. Wada to Japan during 1988 qualifies as income, war profits, or excess profits taxes, such that it is creditable under section 901.

The purpose of the foreign tax credit is the reduction of international double taxation. *See American Chicle Co. v. United States*, 316 U.S. 450, 452 (1942). Nevertheless, permitting a credit for foreign taxes "paid or accrued" is "an act of grace on the part of Congress", and a taxpayer seeking to benefit from such a credit must prove that all the conditions upon which allowance of the credit depends have been fulfilled. *Irving Air Chute Co. v. Commissioner*, 143 F.2d 256, 259 (2d Cir. 1944), affg. 1 T.C. 880 (1943).

For a tax credit to be creditable under section 901, the person claiming the credit must generally establish that the foreign levy with respect to which the credit is claimed is an income tax within the meaning of section 1.901-2(a)(1), Income Tax Regs. Sec. 1.901-2A(b)(1), Income Tax Regs. The payment cannot be a payment for a specific economic benefit. Sec. 1.901-2(a)(2)(i), Income Tax Regs. However, section 1.901-2(a)(2)(ii)(C), Income Tax Regs., states:

> A foreign levy imposed on individuals to finance retirement, old-age, death, survivor, unemployment, illness, or disability benefits, or for some substantially similar purpose, is not a requirement of compulsory payment in exchange for a specific economic benefit, as long as the amounts required to be paid by the individuals subject to the levy are not computed on a basis reflecting the respective ages, life expectancies or similar characteristics of such individuals.

Petitioners have not provided us with any information upon which we could ascertain whether Japanese "social security" meets the requirements of section 1.901-2(a)(2)(ii)(C), Income Tax Regs., or how it is computed. Thus, they have failed to prove that all of the conditions upon which allowance of the foreign tax credit depends have been fulfilled. Accordingly, we are required to sustain respondent's determination that this amount does not qualify for a foreign tax credit under section 901.

PPL CORPORATION v. COMMISSIONER
United States Supreme Court
133 S. Ct. 1897 (2013)

OPINION

JUSTICE THOMAS delivered the opinion of the Court.

In 1997, the United Kingdom (U.K.) imposed a one-time "windfall tax" on 32 U.K. companies privatized between 1984 and 1996. This case addresses whether that tax is creditable for U.S. tax purposes. Internal Revenue Code § 901(b)(1) states that any "income, war profits, and excess profits taxes" paid overseas are creditable against U.S. income taxes. 26 U.S.C. § 901(b)(1). Treasury Regulations interpret this section to mean that a foreign tax is creditable if its "predominant character" "is that of an income tax in the U.S. sense." Treas. Reg. § 1.901-2(a)(1)(ii). Consistent with precedent and the Tax Court's analysis below, we apply the predominant character test using a commonsense approach that considers the substantive effect of the tax. Under this approach, we hold that the U.K. tax is creditable under § 901 and reverse the judgment of the Court of Appeals for the Third Circuit.

I

A

During the 1980's and 1990's, the U.K.'s Conservative Party controlled Parliament and privatized a number of government-owned companies. These companies were sold to private parties through an initial sale of shares, known as a "flotation." As part of privatization, many companies were required to continue providing services at the same rates they had offered under government control for a fixed period, typically their first four years of private operation. As a result, the companies could only increase profits during this period by operating more efficiently. Responding to market incentives, many of the companies became dramatically more efficient and earned substantial profits in the process.

The U.K.'s Labour Party, which had unsuccessfully opposed privatization, used the companies' profitability as a campaign issue against the Conservative Party. In part because of campaign promises to tax what it characterized as undue profits, the Labour Party defeated the Conservative Party at the polls in 1997. Prior to coming to power, Labour Party leaders hired accounting firm Arthur Andersen to structure a tax that would capture excess, or "windfall," profits earned during the initial years in which the companies were prohibited from increasing rates. Parliament eventually adopted the tax, which applied only to the regulated companies that were prohibited from raising their rates. It imposed a 23 percent tax on any "windfall" earned by such companies. . . .

The only variables that changed in the windfall tax formula for all the companies were profits (P) and flotation value (FV); the initial period (D) varied for only a few of the companies subject to the tax. The Labour government . . . claimed (and the Commissioner here reiterates) that the tax was simply a 23 percent tax on the difference between what the companies' flotation values should have been and what they actually were.

B

Petitioner PPL Corporation (PPL) was an owner, through a number of subsidiaries, of 25 percent of South Western Electricity plc, 1 of 12 government-owned electric companies that were privatized in 1990 and that were subject to the tax. . . . In its 1997 federal income-tax return, PPL claimed a credit under § 901 for its share of the bill. The Commissioner of Internal Revenue (Commissioner) rejected the claim, but the Tax Court held that the U.K. windfall tax was creditable for U.S. tax purposes under § 901. See 135 T.C. 304, 342 (2010). The Third Circuit reversed. 665 F.3d 60, 68 (2011). We granted certiorari . . . to resolve a Circuit split concerning the windfall tax's creditability under § 901. Compare *Entergy Corp. & Affiliated Subsidiaries v. Commissioner*, 683 F.3d 233, 239 (CA5 2012).

II

Internal Revenue Code § 901(b)(1) provides that "[i]n the case of . . . a domestic corporation, the amount of any income, war profits, and excess profits taxes paid or accrued during the taxable year to any foreign country or to any possession of the United States" shall be creditable. . . . Under relevant Treasury Regulations, "[a] foreign levy is an income tax if and only if . . . [t]he predominant character of that tax is that of an income tax in the U.S. sense." Treas. Reg. § 1.901-2(a)(1). The parties agree that Treasury Regulation § 1.901-2 applies to this case. That regulation codifies longstanding doctrine dating back to *Biddle v. Commissioner*, 302 U.S. 573 (1938), and provides the relevant legal standard.

The regulation establishes several principles relevant to our inquiry. First, the "predominant character" of a tax, or the normal manner in which a tax applies, is controlling. See *id.*, at 579 ("We are here concerned only with the 'standard' or normal tax"). Under this principle, a foreign tax that operates as an income, war profits, or excess profits tax in most instances is creditable, even if it may affect a handful of taxpayers differently. Creditability is an all or nothing proposition. As the Treasury Regulations confirm, "a tax either is or is not an income tax, in its entirety, for all persons subject to the tax." Treas. Reg. § 1.901-2(a)(1).

Second, the way a foreign government characterizes its tax is not dispositive with respect to the U.S. creditability analysis. See § 1.901-2(a)(1)(ii) (foreign tax creditable if predominantly "an income tax in the U.S. sense"). In *Biddle*, the Court considered the creditability of certain U.K. taxes on stock dividends under the substantively identical predecessor to § 901. The Court recognized that "there is nothing in [the statute's] language to suggest that in allowing the credit for foreign tax payments, a shifting standard was adopted by reference to foreign characterizations and classifications of tax legislation." 302 U.S., at 578–579. See also *United States v. Goodyear Tire & Rubber Co.*, 493 U.S. 132 (1989) (noting in interpreting 26 U.S.C. § 902 that *Biddle* is particularly applicable "where a contrary interpretation would leave" tax interpretation "to the varying tax policies of foreign tax authorities"); *Heiner v. Mellon*, 304 U.S. 271, 279 and n. 7 (1938) (state-law definitions generally not controlling in federal tax context). Instead of the foreign government's characterization of the tax, the crucial inquiry is the tax's economic effect. See *Biddle*, supra, at 579 (inquiry is "whether [a tax] is the substantial equivalent of payment of the tax as those terms are used in our own statute"). In other words, foreign tax creditability depends on whether the tax, if enacted in the U.S., would be an income, war profits, or excess profits tax.

Giving further form to these principles, Treasury Regulation § 1.901-2(a)(3)(i) explains that a foreign tax's predominant character is that of a U.S. income tax "[i]f . . . the foreign tax is likely to reach net gain in the normal circumstances in which it applies." The regulation then sets forth three tests for assessing whether a foreign tax reaches net gain. A tax does so if, "judged on the basis of its predominant character, [it] satisfies each of the realization, gross receipts, and net income requirements set forth in paragraphs (b)(2), (b)(3), and (b)(4), respectively, of this section." Treas. Reg. § 1.901-2(b)(1). . . . The tests indicate that net gain (also referred to as net income) consists of realized gross receipts reduced by significant costs and expenses attributable to such gross receipts. A foreign tax that reaches net income, or profits, is creditable.

III

A

It is undisputed that net income is a component of the U.K.'s "windfall tax" formula. Indeed, annual profit is a variable in the tax formula. . . . It is also undisputed that there is no meaningful difference for our purposes in the accounting principles by which the U.K. and the U.S. calculate profits. The disagreement instead centers on how to characterize the tax formula the Labour Party adopted.

The Third Circuit, following the Commissioner's lead, believed it could look no further than the tax formula that the Parliament enacted and the way in which the Labour government characterized it. Under that view, the windfall tax must be considered a tax on the difference between a company's flotation value (the total amount investors paid for the company when the government sold it) and an imputed "profit-making value," defined as a company's "average annual profit during its 'initial period'. . . times 9, the assumed price-to-earnings ratio." 665 F.3d, at 65. So characterized, the tax captures a portion of the difference between the price at which each company was sold and the price at which the Labour government believed each company should have been sold given the actual profits earned during the initial period. Relying on this characterization, the Third Circuit believed the windfall tax failed at least the Treasury Regulation's realization and gross receipts tests because it reached some artificial form of valuation instead of profits.

In contrast, PPL's position is that the substance of the windfall tax is that of an income tax in the U.S. sense. While recognizing that the tax ostensibly is based on the difference between two values, it argues that every "variable" in the windfall tax formula except for profits and flotation value is fixed. . . . PPL emphasizes that the only way the Labour government was able to calculate the imputed "profit-making value" at which it claimed companies should have been privatized was by looking after the fact at the actual profits earned by each company. In PPL's view, it matters not how the U.K. chose to arrange the formula or what it claimed to be taxing, because a tax based on profits above some threshold is an excess profits tax, regardless of how it is mathematically arranged or what labels foreign law places on it. PPL, thus, contends that the windfall taxes it paid meet the Treasury Regulation's tests and are creditable under § 901.

We agree with PPL and conclude that the predominant character of the windfall tax is that of an excess profits tax, a category of income tax in the U.S. sense. It is important to note that the Labour government's conception of "profit-making value" as a backward-looking analysis of historic profits is not a recognized valuation method; instead, it is a fictitious value calculated using an imputed price-to-earnings ratio. . . . Instead, the windfall tax is a tax on realized net income disguised as a tax on the difference between two values, one of which is completely fictitious. . . .

. . .

The Commissioner argues that any algebraic rearrangement is improper, asserting that U.S. courts must take the foreign tax rate as written and accept whatever tax base the foreign tax purports to adopt. . . . As a result, the Commissioner claims that the analysis begins and ends with the Labour government's choice to characterize its tax base as the difference between "profit-making value" and flotation value. Such a rigid construction is unwarranted. It cannot be squared with the black-letter principle that "tax law deals in economic realities, not legal abstractions." *Commissioner v. Southwest Exploration Co.*, 350 U.S. 308, 315, 76 S. Ct. 395, 100 L. Ed. 347, 134 Ct. Cl. 903, 1956-1 C.B. 614 (1956). Given the artificiality of the U.K.'s method of calculating purported "value," we follow substance over form and recognize that the windfall tax is nothing more than a tax on actual profits above a threshold.

. . .

The economic substance of the U.K. windfall tax is that of a U.S. income tax. The tax is based on net income, and the fact that the Labour government chose to characterize it as a tax on the difference between two values is not dispositive under Treasury Regulation § 1.901-2. Therefore, the tax is creditable under § 901.

The judgment of the Third Circuit is reversed.

It is so ordered.

PREAMBLE TO PROPOSED REGULATION § 1.901-2(f)
2006-2 C.B. 368 (Sept. 5, 2006)

REG-124152-06

AGENCY: Internal Revenue Service (IRS), Treasury.

ACTION: Notice of proposed rulemaking and notice of public hearing.

SUMMARY: These proposed regulations provide guidance relating to the determination of who is considered to pay a foreign tax for purposes of sections 901 and 903. The proposed regulations affect taxpayers that claim direct and indirect foreign tax credits.

. . .

Background

Section 901 of the Internal Revenue Code (Code) permits taxpayers to claim a credit for income, war profits, and excess profits taxes paid or accrued during the taxable year to any foreign country or to any possession of the United States. Section 903 of the Code permits taxpayers to claim a credit for a tax paid in lieu of an income tax.

Section 1.901-2(f)(1) of the current final regulations provides that the person by whom tax is considered paid for purposes of sections 901 and 903 is the person on whom foreign law imposes legal liability for such tax. This legal liability rule applies even if another person, such as a withholding agent, remits the tax. Section 1.901-2(f)(3) provides that if foreign income tax is imposed on the combined income of two or more related persons (for example, a husband and wife or a corporation and one or more of its subsidiaries) and they are jointly and severally liable for the tax under foreign law, foreign law is considered to impose legal liability on each such person for the amount of the foreign income tax that is attributable to its portion of the base of the tax, regardless of which person actually pays the tax.

The existing final regulations were published in 1983. Since that time, numerous questions have arisen regarding the application of the legal liability rule to fact patterns not specifically addressed in the regulations or the case law. These include situations in which the members of a foreign consolidated group may not have in the U.S. sense the full equivalent of joint and several liability for the group's consolidated tax liability, and cases in which the person whose income is included in the foreign tax base is not the person who is obligated to remit the tax. Courts have reached inconsistent conclusions on these matters. Compare *Nissho Iwai American Corp. v. Commissioner*, 89 T.C. 765, 773–74 (1987), *Continental Illinois Corp. v. Commissioner*, 998 F.2d 513 (7th Cir. 1993), *Norwest Corp v. Commissioner*, 69 F.3d 1404 (8th Cir. 1995), *Riggs National Corp. & Subs. v. Commissioner*, 107 T.C. 301 (1996) (all holding that U.S. lenders had legal liability for tax imposed on their interest income from Brazilian borrowers, notwithstanding that under Brazilian law the tax could only be collected from the borrowers) with *Guardian Industries Corp. & Subs. v. United States*, 65 Fed. Cl. 50 (2005), (concluding that the subsidiary corporations in a Luxembourg consolidated group had no legal liability for tax imposed on their income, because under Luxembourg law the parent corporation was solely liable to pay the tax).

. . .

The IRS and the Treasury Department have determined that the regulations should be updated to clarify the application of the legal liability rule in these situations, and request comments on additional matters that should be addressed in published guidance.

Explanation of Provisions

A. Overview

. . .

The proposed regulations would retain the general principle that tax is considered paid by the person who has legal liability under foreign law for the tax. However, the proposed regulations would further clarify application of the legal liability rule in situations where foreign law imposes tax on the income of one person but requires another person to remit the tax. The proposed regulations make clear that foreign law is considered to impose legal liability for income tax on the person who is required to take such income into account for foreign tax purposes even if another person has the sole obligation to remit the tax. . . .

The proposed regulations would provide detailed guidance regarding how to treat taxes paid on the combined income of two or more persons. First, the proposed regulations would clarify the application of § 1.901-2(f) to foreign consolidated-type regimes where the members are not jointly and severally liable in the U.S. sense for the group's tax. The proposed regulations would make clear that the foreign tax must be apportioned among all the members pro rata based on the relative amounts of net income of each member as computed under foreign law. The proposed regulations would provide guidance in determining the relative amounts of net income.

. . .

C. Taxes Imposed on Combined Income

1. Foreign Consolidated Groups

The IRS and Treasury Department believe that § 1.901-2(f)(1) of the current final regulations requires allocation of foreign consolidated tax liability among the members of a foreign consolidated group pro rata based on each member's share of the consolidated taxable income included in the foreign tax base. In addition, the IRS and Treasury Department believe that § 1.901-2(f)(3) confirms this rule in situations in which foreign consolidated regimes impose joint and several liability for the group's tax on each member. With respect to a foreign consolidated-type regime where the members do not have the full equivalent of joint and several liability in the U.S. sense, or where the income of the consolidated group members is attributed to the parent corporation in computing the consolidated taxable income, the current regulations do not include a specific illustration of how the consolidated tax should be allocated among the members of the group for foreign tax credit purposes.

Thus, the IRS and Treasury Department believe that § 1.901-2(f)(1) of the current final regulations requires as a general rule pro rata allocation of foreign tax among the members of a foreign consolidated group, and that § 1.901-2(f)(3) illustrates the application of the general rule in cases where the group members are jointly and severally liable for that consolidated tax. Failure to allocate appropriately the consolidated tax among the members of the group may result in a separation of foreign tax from the income on which the tax is imposed. This type of splitting of foreign tax and income is contrary to the general purpose of the foreign tax credit to relieve double taxation of foreign-source income. Accordingly, § 1.901-2(f)(2) of the proposed regulations would explicitly cover all foreign consolidated-type regimes, including those in which the regime imposes joint and several liability in the U.S. sense, those in which the regime treats subsidiaries as branches of the parent corporation (or otherwise attributes income of subsidiaries to the parent corporation), and those in which some of the group members have limited obligations, or even no obligation, to pay the consolidated tax. Several significant commentators recommended that the regulations be clarified in this manner.

The proposed regulations would define combined income to include cases where the foreign country initially recognizes the subsidiaries as separate taxable entities, but pursuant to the applicable consolidated tax regime treats subsidiaries as branches of the parent, requires or treats all income as distributed to the parent, or otherwise attributes all income to the parent. This approach will minimize the need for extensive analysis of the intricacies of the relevant foreign consolidated tax regime, by treating a foreign subsidiary as legally liable for its share of the consolidated tax without regard to the precise mechanics of the foreign consolidated regime. This approach will not only reduce inappropriate foreign tax credit splitting but will also reduce administrative burdens on taxpayers and the IRS.

Section 1.902-1(f)(2) of the proposed regulations retains the general principle that the foreign tax must be apportioned among the persons whose income is included in the combined base pro rata based on the relative amounts of net income of each person as computed under foreign law. As under current law, this rule would apply regardless of which person is obligated to remit the tax, which person actually remits the tax, and which person the foreign country could proceed against to collect the tax in the event all or a portion of the tax is not paid. Under § 1.902-1(f)(2)(i), person for this purpose includes a disregarded entity.

Ex)   ABC Inc. (US Corp) manu & sells shoes.

(on mid term)

"   "   earns $400k from U.S., many
    - has branch in france, & branch
    has operating income of $300k. and
    passive inc. (dividend) $100k.
    - french tax rate = 20% on div. inc.   [by cat
    & also 40% on operating income.   not country]

ABC Inc has another branch in Denmark.
    - had operating inc. of $280k.
Denmark's tax rate on operating inc = 25%.

U.S. tax rate 30%.

Q: What is the final tax liability of
ABC Inc? Pretax inc, FTC limit

pre credit US tax × $\frac{FSI}{WWI}$

operating inc:
300k (F)
280k (D)

ans first page.

Unit 5

FOREIGN TAX CREDIT: THE "DEEMED PAID" CREDIT

A. CODE AND REGULATION PROVISIONS

Code   §§ 78; 902(a), (b).

Reg.   §§ 1.902-1(a)(1)–(5), (a)(9)(iii), (b)(1).

B. PROBLEMS FOR CLASS DISCUSSION

5-1. Throughout Year 1, USC, a domestic corporation, owned all of the shares of the single class of stock of FC, a Fijian corporation formed on January 1, Year 1. FC engages in the manufacture of machinery in Fiji. The machinery is sold by FC in Fiji and also other countries. FC had gains, profits, and income of $100,000 for Year 1, and paid foreign income taxes imposed on those gains, profits, and income of $40,000. On December 31, Year 1, FC paid a dividend of $30,000 to USC. What is USC's taxable income and net United States tax liability with respect to the dividend, assuming that USC's United States tax rate is 35 percent?

5-2. Assume the same ownership structure and governing tax rates as in Problem 5-1. In addition, assume that throughout Year 1, FC owned all of the shares of the single class of stock of NC, a Nicaraguan corporation. NC had gains, profits, and income of $300,000 in Year 1 and paid foreign income taxes on those gains, profits, and income of $90,000. On December 31, Year 1, NC paid a $100,000 dividend to FC. Assume that FC had $300,000 of gains, profits, and income for Year 1, consisting of $200,000 from its own business operations and the $100,000 dividend received from NC. Assume further that FC paid $50,000 of foreign income tax on those gains, profits, and income. On December 31, Year 1, FC paid a dividend of $125,000 to USC. What is USC's income and net United States tax liability with respect to the dividend?

5-3. Assume the same ownership structure as in Problems 5-1 and 5-2, with the following modifications in ownership: USC owns 25 percent of FC; FC owns 30 percent of NC; and NC owns 40 percent of QC, a corporation organized in Qatar. Assuming dividends are paid by each of FC, NC, and QC to their respective parents, to what extent can USC claim credit for foreign taxes paid by FC, NC, and QC?

C. OVERVIEW

As discussed in Unit 4, the foreign tax credit is generally allowed only to the taxpayer who paid, or on whose behalf were paid, foreign taxes to a foreign government or possession. If United States corporations always operated in foreign countries via a branch, there would be no impediment to the foreign tax credit — since there would be no separate taxpayer, the United States corporation would be the payor of the foreign tax.

In contrast, if a United States corporation establishes a foreign subsidiary and the subsidiary earns foreign-source income and pays the foreign tax, the subsidiary is not entitled to a foreign tax credit in the United States under § 901 since it is not liable for any United States income tax. In addition, in most cases, the United States parent may not take the foreign tax credit with respect to subsidiary earnings, since the United States parent did not pay the tax.[1]

Absent any relief, when the foreign subsidiary distributes its earnings to the parent as a dividend, net of the foreign taxes, United States income tax will apply to the distribution, thereby imposing a second layer of tax on the underlying income.[2] When finally distributed to individual shareholders of the parent corporation as a dividend, yet another layer of tax would apply. The earnings stream would therefore have been subject to at least three layers of tax by the time it reached the hands of the investor.

Section 902 reduces the aggregate amount of United States taxes imposed in this situation by permitting a domestic corporation to claim the credit for foreign taxes paid by certain foreign subsidiaries in respect of earnings distributed to the domestic parent. In essence, the distribution "piggybacks" to the United States distributee corporation the amount of foreign taxes incurred by the foreign subsidiary in earning such amounts. In other words, the dividend carries with it an indirect, or "deemed paid," tax which allows the United States distributee to claim a credit for the taxes actually paid by its subsidiary.

Section 902 also helps equalize the United States tax treatment between foreign branches and foreign subsidiaries of domestic corporations. Where a domestic corporation operating a foreign branch pays foreign taxes, as discussed in Unit 4, the domestic corporation can claim a foreign tax credit under § 901. Where a foreign subsidiary pays the tax, § 902 permits the domestic parent to claim the credit as and to the extent the subsidiary distributes its after-tax earnings to the parent.

The § 902 "deemed paid" provisions have undergone substantial modifications but still bear a resemblance to their original form upon enactment in 1918. Under that 1918 statute, in the precursor to what is now § 902(b), a domestic corporation

---

[1] This was not always the case, however, as the *Guardian Industries* case, discussed in Unit 4, illustrates. The enactment of new § 909 in 2010, discussed briefly in Unit 4, may prevent the use of foreign tax credits in *Guardian*-like structures as well as a broad range of similar structures and transactions.

[2] To the extent a foreign tax is also imposed on the dividend itself, a so-called "direct" foreign tax credit should be available to the United States parent company, as discussed in Unit 4. This Unit, and § 902 generally, is concerned with the crediting by domestic companies of foreign taxes that are imposed on and paid by foreign subsidiaries with respect to earnings that arise in the foreign country.

owning a "majority of the voting stock" of a foreign corporation could claim a foreign credit with respect to dividends received, but only those foreign taxes paid by a first-tier foreign corporation could be deemed paid by the United States parent. The earnings of lower-tier corporations were subject to United States tax when distributed as a dividend through the first-tier corporation to the domestic parent. Congress has revised the statute a number of times since 1918, typically reducing the amount of stock ownership required and adding successively lower tiers to the regime (but imposing additional requirements in the case of subsidiaries below the third tier, as discussed later in this Unit).

5.01   Section 902: Basic Structure

Current law permits a domestic corporation (other than an S corporation) that receives a dividend from a foreign corporation in any taxable year to take a credit for taxes deemed paid if it owns at least 10 percent of the voting stock of the foreign corporation. Within this rule are a number of preliminary considerations: whether the distribution in question is a dividend, whether the distribution is received, and whether the payor corporation is sufficiently connected in the chain of ownership to the distributee corporation.

As was the case in the context of the sourcing rules discussed in Unit 2, dividends are defined for these purposes by reference to domestic, not foreign, law. Thus § 316 controls the determination of whether something is a dividend. Regulation § 1.902-1(a)(12) provides that a dividend is considered received for these purposes when "unqualifiedly made subject to the demands of the distributee."

The deemed paid provisions extend to sixth-tier subsidiaries. For purposes of § 902, the foreign corporation that pays the dividend to its United States parent is designated a "first-tier corporation" under Regulation § 1.902-1(a)(2). A foreign corporation in which a first-tier corporation owns at least 10 percent of the voting stock is a "second-tier" corporation under Regulation § 1.902-1(a)(3). A first-tier corporation to which dividends are paid by a second-tier corporation is deemed to have paid a portion of the taxes actually paid or accrued by the second-tier corporation.

A second-tier corporation to which dividends are paid by a foreign corporation in which the second-tier corporation owns at least 10 percent of the voting stock (a "third-tier" corporation) is deemed to have paid a portion of the third-tier corporation's taxes. The treatment is available similarly through "sixth-tier" corporations.

An additional ownership limitation is imposed for lower-tier subsidiaries. In order to claim the credit for lower-tier corporations, the domestic corporate parent must have at least a five percent indirect ownership interest in those foreign corporations. In a two-tier arrangement, the percentage of stock owned by the domestic corporation in the first-tier corporation multiplied by the percentage of stock held by the first-tier corporation in the second-tier corporation must equal at least five percent. With a three-tier arrangement, the percentage share held by the domestic corporation and each tier corporation when multiplied together must equal at least five percent. Similar requirements apply in determining the indirect ownership standards for lower-tier subsidiaries.

Suppose, for example, that domestic corporation A owns 30 percent of foreign corporation B (the first-tier corporation). Corporation B owns 40 percent of foreign corporation C (the second-tier corporation). Corporation C owns 50 percent of foreign corporation D (the third-tier corporation). In this example, both the 10 percent direct ownership and the five percent indirect ownership requirements are met: the 10 percent direct ownership requirement is met because A owns more than 10 percent of B, B owns more than 10 percent of C, and C owns more than 10 percent of D. The five percent indirect ownership requirement is met because A owns more than five percent of C (the second-tier) through B (the first-tier): A's directly owned 30 percent of B multiplied by B's 40 percent stake in C equals 12 percent. A also owns more than five percent of D (the third-tier) through its stakes in C and B: A's 12 percent indirect ownership of C multiplied by C's 50 percent stake in D equals 6 percent. Thus, A can claim the foreign tax credit for taxes paid and deemed paid by each of B, C, and D, to the extent earnings are distributed up through the chain to A. *See* Figure 5-1.

FIGURE 5-1. THREE-TIERED OWNERSHIP STRUCTURE ALLOWING
PASS-THROUGH OF FOREIGN TAXES PAID

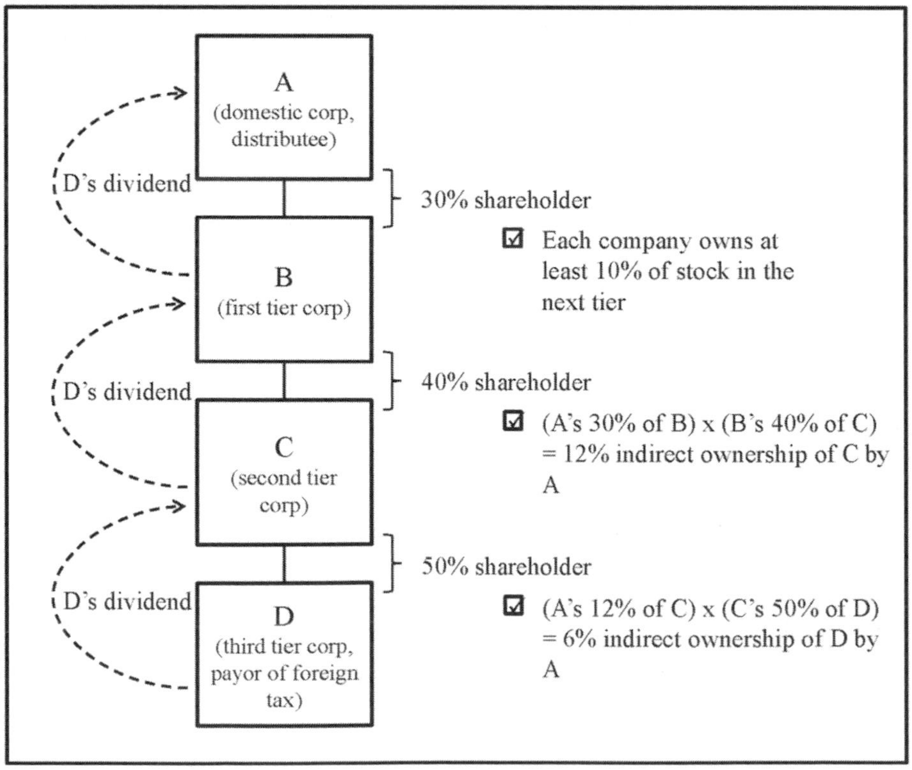

As illustrated above, in cases involving less than 100 percent ownership, the lower the tier, the greater the percentage ownership required for the domestic parent corporation to meet the five percent indirect holding and thus qualify for the deemed paid credit. Using the above example, if C's ownership in D dropped to 40 percent, A's indirect ownership of D would drop to 4.8 percent. A could still claim the foreign tax credit for taxes paid by B and C, but it would no longer be able to claim the credit for taxes paid by D. In addition, as discussed more fully below, A's ability to claim the foreign tax credit depends on the distribution of earnings up through the tiers — i.e., for A to claim a § 902 tax credit with respect to taxes paid by D, D would have to distribute earnings to C, C to B, and B to A.

5.02   Calculating the Taxes Deemed Paid by Domestic Corporations

Section 902(a) provides that a domestic parent corporation generally cannot claim a credit for foreign taxes paid by its foreign subsidiary unless the subsidiary makes a dividend distribution to the parent. Under domestic law, a dividend is viewed as a manifestation of accumulated profits. It is the payment of the dividend that triggers the deemed paid provisions. As a result, determining a corporation's indirect tax credit is a matter of both identifying a dividend that potentially carries a deemed-paid foreign tax with it and calculating the amount of credit that will be allowed with respect to this tax. The amount of the allowable credit is directly proportional to the size of the dividend as a percentage of available undistributed earnings of the foreign subsidiary paying the dividend. Numerically expressed, the computation is:

$$\S\ 902Cr = FTP \quad x \quad \frac{DIV}{UE - FTPA}$$

In this formula, "§ 902Cr" is the § 902 credit, i.e., the amount of tax paid by the first-tier corporation that will be deemed paid by a domestic corporation and therefore eligible for a foreign tax credit. "FTP" refers to the post-1986 foreign taxes paid, accrued, or deemed paid by the first-tier corporation. "DIV" means the dividends paid by the first-tier corporation to the domestic corporation. "UE" refers to the post-1986 undistributed pre-foreign taxes earnings of the first-tier corporation, and "FTPA" means the foreign taxes paid or accrued by such first-tier corporation. Regulation § 1.902-1(a)(9) labels the denominator of the fraction "undistributed earnings," which is defined as the relevant foreign corporation's earnings and profits. These earnings and profits should generally equal pre-tax earnings, less taxes paid or accrued.

Thus, by way of example, assume domestic corporation X owns 100 percent of foreign corporation Y, formed in Year 1. Y distributes its first dividend in Year 8 of $300 at a time in which total undistributed earnings (net of foreign taxes paid) equaled $1,000. If its foreign tax payments during its period of existence had totaled $500, the deemed paid credit for which X is eligible would total $150:

$$\S\ 902Cr = S500 \quad x \quad \frac{\$300}{\$1,500 - \$500} \quad = \quad \$150$$

The reason that the calculation is based on earnings and taxes arising in years after 1986 is that the § 902 computational rules were significantly revised under the Tax Reform Act of 1986. Before the change, foreign taxes were attributed to dividends paid by foreign corporations on an annual basis, so that a dividend was traced to the profits of the particular tax year in which it was made. Under the current rules, earnings, profits, and taxes are combined in perpetual pools, so that dividends carry a deemed paid foreign tax that reflects the average effective foreign tax burden, from 1986 forward, of the dividend-paying corporation.

The same formula is used to calculate the taxes a first-tier corporation is deemed to have paid through a second-tier corporation (as well as a second through a third), as well as the flow-through of taxes paid by lower-tier subsidiaries. Of course, the taxes "deemed" paid by a foreign subsidiary have no direct effect on United States tax liability; however, they may affect the amount of § 902 credit that the domestic parent can claim when the first-tier foreign subsidiary pays a dividend.

A dividend distribution from a foreign subsidiary to its parent corporation may produce *both* direct and indirect credits for the year of distribution. If a foreign jurisdiction taxes shareholders upon the receipt of a dividend from the foreign corporation, a § 901 credit may be available to the distributee corporation in addition to the § 902 determinations discussed above.

The practical significance of the § 902 formula is that a domestic corporation operating through a foreign subsidiary instead of a branch does not entirely forfeit its claim to a foreign tax credit. Furthermore, the formula (when viewed alongside the § 482 allocation provisions, which are beyond the scope of this Casebook) might be seen as an attempt to ensure that the transfer of income from a subsidiary to a parent will occur through the conventional mechanism of the dividend payment, rather than the more circuitous routes of providing loans, goods, or services at a less than arm's-length price.

5.03   Undistributed Earnings and Accumulated Profits

Section 902(c) defines the post-1986 undistributed earnings of a foreign corporation as those accumulated after 1986, computed without reduction for dividends distributed during the year. Undistributed earnings are calculated as of the close of the taxable year in which the dividend is distributed and are determined under United States tax principles and not foreign law. Thus, the regular United States tax rules for calculating earnings and profits generally apply. For example, under the regular rules, accrued taxes reduce earnings and profits in the year of accrual. This rule also applies to undistributed earnings for § 902 purposes: as Regulation § 1.902-1(a)(9)(iii) clarifies, foreign taxes imposed on post-1986 earnings of the corporation in question (but not its lower-tier subsidiaries) reduce its undistributed earnings, regardless of whether the foreign taxes are creditable.[3] In addition, undistributed earnings include earnings only from years

---

[3] As a result, when the term "undistributed earnings" is used in this Casebook and elsewhere, it implies that the stated amount represents accumulated earnings after foreign taxes paid or accrued by the corporation in question.

beginning with the first taxable year in which the § 902 ownership requirements are met.

5.04   The § 78 Gross-Up

When a domestic corporation elects to take the foreign tax credit for taxes paid by a foreign corporation, the amount of taxes deemed paid must be treated and reported as dividend income. That is, the amount of the actual dividends received are "grossed-up" to include an additional amount equal to the tax deemed paid on those dividends. The § 78 gross-up prevents the "overcrediting" of foreign taxes.

This statutory approach is an attempt to insure that the amount of indirect foreign tax credits available through § 902 does not exceed the amount of direct foreign tax credits that would be available if the foreign operations were conducted through a branch. When a foreign branch is used, the foreign tax credit is available, and all income is subject to United States tax. If instead a subsidiary is used, § 902 allows the domestic parent to use the foreign tax credit while domestic taxation applies only to the dividend income. The remainder of the foreign earnings are not subject to domestic taxation. The gross-up concept eliminated this disparity as to distributed earnings of the subsidiary.

For example, assume that D, a domestic corporation, establishes H, a Hong Kong subsidiary. H earns $100 during the taxable year and pays $20 of income tax to Hong Kong. H distributes one-half of its after-tax earnings ($100 - $20 tax = $80 × 50% = $40) to D. By operation of the § 902 deemed paid credit, absent the § 78 gross-up, D would be subject to United States tax on $40 of income, yet receive a § 902 credit of $10, the tax on half of H's undistributed earnings ($20 tax × $40/ $80).

In contrast, if H was merely a branch of D, D would be entitled to credit the $20 tax on H's earnings, but D would also be subject to tax on H's full $100 of earnings. To achieve parity, D is required in the prior example by virtue of the § 78 gross-up to include as additional dividend income the $10 of foreign tax paid by H to Hong Kong. Although the § 78 gross-up eliminates the disparity between branches and subsidiaries with respect to foreign earnings received as dividend distributions, disparity remains in cases of undistributed (retained) foreign earnings.

The grossed-up income is treated as a dividend for all United States tax purposes, except the dividends-received deduction for eligible dividends received from foreign corporations under § 245.

D.   REFERENCE MATERIALS

- *First Chicago Corp. v. Commissioner*
- Revenue Ruling 92-86

FIRST CHICAGO CORP. v. COMMISSIONER
United States Tax Court
96 T.C. 421 (1991)

GERBER, JUDGE:

Respondent . . . determined a. . . . deficiency in petitioner's 1983 corporate income tax. The issue considered in this opinion concerns petitioner's foreign tax credit. . . . The specific foreign tax area under consideration is whether petitioner and/or its affiliated group is entitled to the section 902(a) deemed paid foreign tax credit.

Petitioner, First Chicago Corp. (P), is a bank holding company organized in 1969 with its principal place of business in Chicago, Illinois. P, as the common parent, filed. . . . consolidated returns and the petition in this case on its own behalf and on behalf of the members of its affiliated group. . . . Certain affiliated members of P's consolidated group claimed foreign tax credits under section 902(a) [and] reported equivalent amounts under section 78 as "gross-up" income. Respondent disallowed all of the above-listed credits and correspondingly determined a decrease in the amount of "gross-up" income. . . .

OPINION

The controversy here concerns a question of first impression involving the interpretation of the 10-percent requirement of section 902. . . . We must specifically decide whether [the] provisions would permit petitioner to avail itself of the deemed foreign tax credit.

GENERAL BACKGROUND

Section 901 provides for the allowance to a domestic corporation of a credit on certain foreign taxes paid or accrued during a taxable year to any foreign country or possession of the United States. Section 901 also provides, in the case of a corporate taxpayer, an allowance of a credit for taxes "deemed to have been paid under sections 902 and 960." . . .

Accordingly, section 902, in addition to the foreign tax credit for foreign tax actually paid or accrued by a domestic taxpayer under section 901, imputes a credit, in certain circumstances, to domestic corporations for a proportionate (in relation to the domestic corporation's shareholdings) amount of tax paid by a dividend-paying foreign corporation.

SECTION 902(a): THE STATUTE AND LEGISLATIVE HISTORY

In the face of the statutory language "a domestic corporation which owns at least 10 percent of the voting stock of a foreign corporation," petitioner first argues that "[t]he language . . . and the rationale for section 902(a) together fully support treating the consolidated group as one entity for purposes of determining whether the 10% voting stock requirement of section 902(a) has been met." If we should hold otherwise, petitioner's alternative position is that, factually, [its] affiliates held the shares as agents or nominees on behalf of [it]. Respondent counters that neither the language nor the intent of section 902(a) . . . would permit aggregating the shares of affiliated corporate taxpayers in order to meet the qualifications of section 902(a). Respondent also argues that the facts indicate that . . . subsidiaries and affiliates were not agents or nominees. . . . Respondent also asserts that section 902(a) requires 10-percent voting power rather than 10 percent of the voting stock and that [petitioner] and its affiliates did not have 10 percent of the voting power.

Petitioner argues that the legislative history supports aggregation under section 902(a). First, we consider whether the legislative history regarding section 902(a) should be consulted, and if consulted, whether it supports petitioner's argument that section 902(a) should be read to include an affiliated group.

Normally, there is:

> no more persuasive evidence of the purpose of a statute than the words by which the legislature undertook to give expression to its wishes. Often these words are sufficient in and of themselves to determine the purpose of the legislation. In such cases we have followed their plain meaning. . . .

When, however, the meaning leads to absurd results or the results are "plainly at variance with the policy of the legislation as a whole," courts have followed the purpose, rather than the literal words of the statute.

It is clear that the general congressional intent underlying sections 901 and 902 was to avoid double (foreign and domestic) taxation of foreign income and dividends by allowing a credit for certain taxes paid or deemed paid with respect to dividends received. Moreover, in the legislative history . . . that principle was reaffirmed, but the requirement that a domestic corporation own a majority of the voting stock of the foreign corporation was reduced to the current "ten percent or more" standard.

Petitioner, however, asks us to focus upon what it considers to be part of the legislative history concerning the Revenue Act of 1918. . . . During floor debate of a 1918 Revenue Act predecessor of the current foreign tax credit sections, one senator proposed the aggregation of related domestic taxpayers in order to meet the majority voting requirement (which was required at that time). The proposal did not, however, find its way into enacted legislation, and, to date, has not appeared as part of the statutory language. To the extent one would consider this to be material in the legislative history, it should not be denominated as a reflection of congressional intent because it reflects the view or proposal of only one senator and, more importantly, was not incorporated in the resulting legislation. Accordingly, we find no express or implied congressional intent to include consolidated shareholdings or aggregation of shareholdings in order to meet the 10-percent or more threshold for application of section 902. . . .

PETITIONER'S AGENT OR NOMINEE POSITION

Having decided that petitioner and its affiliated group are not entitled to aggregate, we next consider petitioner's alternative theory that its affiliates held shares . . . as agents and nominees. Petitioner offered this alternative argument, which essentially posits that each subsidiary held the . . . shares as an agent or nominee. . . . Under those circumstances, petitioner contends that it held 10 percent in one shareholder. On this point, the parties' arguments converge upon a recent Supreme Court case which addressed the question of whether the tax attributes of the property held by an agent can be attributed to the principal. . . .

The four indicia of agency status are as follows: (1) Whether the corporation operates in the name and for the account of the principal; (2) whether the corporation binds the principal by its actions; (3) whether the corporation transmits money received to the principal; and (4) whether receipt of income is attributable to the services of employees of the principal and to assets belonging to the principal.

Although a subsidiary corporation satisfying these indicia may be considered a true agent of its parent in a general sense, two other requirements are also imposed. The first requirement mandates that the subsidiary's agency relationship with its parent cannot be derived exclusively from the fact that it is owned by its parent-principal. This factor addresses the separate-entity doctrine. . . . It demands proof positive that the agency relationship exists separate and apart from the subsidiary's ownership by its principal and that it is not in substance a tax-avoiding manipulation of an otherwise independent legal entity. These concerns are satisfied where unequivocal evidence of the genuineness of the agency relationship exists.

Assuming unequivocal evidence of a genuine agency relationship is present, it must lastly be established that the subsidiary's business purpose was the carrying on of the normal duties of an agent. Reference to general agency principles will determine whether this second requirement is satisfied. . . .

To fit within this framework, petitioner first argues that its sole purpose for spreading the ownership of . . . shares amongst several affiliates, rather than having one shareholder, was to obtain a voting benefit under Article 16 of the Articles of Association . . . prohibiting any shareholder, regardless of the number of shares held, more than six votes. Petitioner advances the obvious and convincing business purpose that they wished to protect a sizable investment . . . by exercising their shareholders' rights to cause the election of officers and board members in order to participate in management. Respondent agrees that this was a valid business purpose of petitioner, but points out that certain of the affiliates also obtained business benefits from ownership . . . shares. The "Edge Act subsidiaries," for example, were required to maintain capital of at least $2 million and the . . . shares were counted in the satisfaction of that requirement. Nevertheless, we find that the principal business proposal of placing ownership . . . shares in subsidiaries was to maintain and possibly enhance control over the investment. . . . Having found . . . that the property was held in a manner which reflects that it could have been the subject of an agency (or nominee) relationship, we proceed to see if an agency relationship existed. . . .

The parties' initial controversy over the "six . . . factors" concerns the requirement of whether the corporation's relations with its principal are not dependent upon the fact that it is owned by the principal. Although petitioner acknowledges that the [*Commissioner v.*] *Bollinger*[, 485 U.S. 340 (1988),] court set out the six . . . factors, it argues that the Supreme Court ruled for the taxpayer without deciding whether the fifth one had been met and without holding the taxpayer to a strict or literal compliance with some or all of the remaining "factors." Respondent argues that the Supreme Court did not eliminate or ignore the fifth factor or decide that a wholly owned subsidiary could be an agent for its owner.

After noting that the relationship between a corporation-agent and its owner-principal is always based on ownership and the owner can cause the relationship to be altered or terminated at any time, the Supreme Court stated that this requirement (the fifth factor) was an attempt to protect the separate-entity doctrine. . . . In that connection, the Court expressed the view that it agreed "that it is reasonable for the Commissioner to demand unequivocal evidence of genuineness [of the agency relationship] in the corporation-shareholder context. . . . " The essence of this analysis is that petitioner must show the genuineness of the agency relationship, separate and apart from its general authority to control the corporate subsidiaries.

The facts in our record do contain numerous circumstantial bits of evidence which could be interpreted to imply the existence of an agency relationship [with] and its affiliates. But there is no direct and/or explicit evidence that an agency relationship existed. . . . As pointed out by the Supreme Court, the element of control is always present between a corporation and its owner. That control is similar to the type of control found in an agency relationship. Accordingly, petitioner must decisively show that a "genuine agency" was intended. . . . Petitioner has failed to show such a relationship existed [with] and its affiliates during the years under consideration. . . .

As pointed out above, there are several factors and facts in this record which indicate that the affiliated corporations involved were acting in concert and on behalf of affiliated members. It is most significant that this type of action is usual in consolidated groups with common ownership. . . . [T]he inherent commonality in such relationships requires the showing of a genuine agency relationship. . . . We find in this case that petitioner has not shown an agency relationship (an agency in fact) existed in this case. . . .

To reflect the foregoing,

Decision will be entered under Rule 155.

REVENUE RULING 92-86
1992-2 CB 199

ISSUES:

(1) May a domestic corporation compute foreign taxes deemed paid under section 902 of the Internal Revenue Code of 1986 with respect to a deemed dividend distribution from a foreign corporation in a transaction described in section 304(a)(1) under the facts below?

. . .

FACTS:

P, a domestic corporation, owns all of the outstanding stock of DX, a domestic corporation, and FX, a Country U corporation. DX owns all of the outstanding stock of FY, a Country U corporation. Of the outstanding stock of FX, 90 percent by value is voting stock and 10 percent by value is non-voting stock. FX and FY were incorporated in 1987. P and DX are members of a consolidated group. The functional currency of FX and FY under section 985(b) is the U.S. dollar.

The fair market value of the FY stock owned by DX is $40x, and DX has a basis of $20x in the FY stock. FY has accumulated $30x of post-1986 undistributed earnings, and has paid post-1986 foreign income taxes of $10x. See section 902(c) of the Code. The fair market value of the voting and non-voting stock of FX owned by P is $500x. FX has accumulated post-1986 undistributed earnings of $30x, and has paid post-1986 foreign income taxes of $10x.

DX sells all of its FY stock to FX for $40x.

LAW AND ANALYSIS:

The sale of the FY stock by DX to FX for $40x is a transaction described in section 304(a)(1) of the Code. Under section 304(a)(1), if one or more persons are in control of each of two corporations and, in return for property, one of the corporations acquires stock in the other corporation from the person (or persons) so in control, the receipt of the property is treated for purposes of sections 302 and 303 as a distribution in redemption of the stock of the corporation acquiring such stock. DX directly controls FY through its ownership of FY stock, and indirectly controls FX through the attribution rule of section 318(a)(3)(C). See section 304(c)(1) and (3)(A).

Thus, for purposes of section 302 of the Code, DX's receipt of the $40x is treated as a distribution in redemption of the stock of FX. The determination whether the distribution is treated as in part or full payment in exchange for stock is made by reference to the FY stock. See section 304(b)(1). DX directly owned all of the FY stock before the transaction, and constructively owns all of the FY stock after the transaction under the attribution rules of section 318(a)(2)(C) and (a)(3)(C). Thus, none of the provisions of section 302(b) apply to treat the distribution as in part or full payment in exchange for stock. Accordingly, the redemption is treated as a distribution of property to which section 301 applies.

The distribution received by DX is taxable as a dividend by reference to the earnings and profits of FX and FY. See sections 301(c)(1), 316 and 304(b)(2) of the Code. The amount and source of the portion of the distribution that is treated as a dividend is determined as if the property were distributed by FX to the extent of its earnings and profits, and then by FY to the extent of its earnings and profits. The distribution received by DX is a dividend of $40x. The dividend is deemed to come out of FX's earnings and profits to the extent of $30x, and out of FY's earnings and profits to the extent of $10x. The dividend is considered paid by FX and FY directly to DX, and the earnings and profits of FX and FY are reduced by $30x and $10x, respectively. See H.R. Rep. No. 98-861 (Conf. Rep.), 98th Cong., 2d Sess. 1223 (1984), 1984-3 (Vol. 2) C.B. 477; section 312(a).

A domestic corporation that directly owns 10 percent or more of the voting stock of a foreign corporation from which it receives dividends in any taxable year is deemed to have paid the same proportion of such foreign corporation's post-1986 foreign income taxes as the amount of such dividends (determined without regard to section 78 of the Code) bears to such foreign corporation's post-1986 undistributed earnings. See section 902(a).

Section 902(a) of the Code allows a foreign tax credit for foreign taxes paid by a foreign corporation and deemed paid by a domestic corporate shareholder only where the domestic corporation directly owns at least 10 percent of the voting stock of the distributing foreign corporation. See Rev. Rul. 85-3, 1985-1 C.B. 222. In *First Chicago Corp. v. Commissioner*, 96 T.C. 421 (1991), the Tax Court held that direct ownership is required for purposes of section 902 and thus the ownership of several members of an affiliated group could not be aggregated to reach the 10 percent threshold.

When Congress amended section 304(b)(2) of the Code in 1984 to clarify the characterization and sourcing rules under section 304, it indicated that the foreign tax credit should be allowed to the selling corporation "to the same extent as if the distribution had been made directly by the corporation that is treated as having made the distribution." See H.R. Rep. No. 98-861, supra. . .

Under section 304 of the Code, FX is treated as having made a dividend distribution to DX. Consistent with the legislative history, DX is considered to own, for purposes of section 902 (a), the stock of FX that DX owns actually or constructively under section 304(c) in determining whether DX controls FX. Therefore, DX is considered to own 100 percent of the voting stock of FX. DX may therefore compute foreign taxes deemed paid of $10x with respect to the dividend that is considered received from FX (10x foreign tax x 30x dividend/30x undistributed earnings). If DX computes foreign taxes deemed paid with respect to the dividend from FX, then DX must include the $10x in income as a dividend. See section 78.

Also, for purposes of section 902(a) of the Code, FY is treated as having made a dividend distribution to DX with respect to the FY voting stock actually owned by DX, and DX is entitled to a credit for foreign taxes deemed paid on the dividend that it is considered to receive from FY. See H.R. Rep. No. 98-861, supra. The amount of the credit computed under section 902(a) is $3.33x (10x foreign tax x 10x dividend/30x undistributed earnings). If DX computes foreign taxes deemed paid with respect to the dividend from FY, DX must include the 3.33x in income as a dividend. See section 78.

　. . .

HOLDING:

(1) DX may compute foreign taxes deemed paid under section 902 of the Code on the dividends from FX and FY. See H.R. Rep. No. 98-861. . . .

Unit 6

FOREIGN TAX CREDIT: THE § 904 LIMITATIONS

A. CODE AND REGULATION PROVISIONS

Code   §§ 904(a)–(d)(2), (f)(1)–(3), (5).
Reg.   § 1.904-1(b).

B. PROBLEMS FOR CLASS DISCUSSION

6-1. Jennifer, a United States citizen and resident, operates a pharmacology consulting business as a sole proprietor. In Year 1, Jennifer realized $100,000 of taxable income from Colombia, on which she paid Colombian income taxes of $45,000. Jennifer also realized $150,000 of domestic taxable income.

   (a) Assuming a 35 percent rate of tax is imposed by the United States, compute Jennifer's foreign tax credit for Year 1.[1]

   (b) What result if, in addition to the above transactions, she derived $50,000 of Canadian-source interest income subject to a reduced tax rate of five percent? Assuming she paid $2,500 in Canadian income taxes and a 35 percent rate of tax is imposed by the United States, compute Jennifer's foreign tax credit for Year 1.

6-2. Ewessco Corporation is a domestic corporation engaged in the worldwide manufacture and sale of paper products. In Year 1, Ewessco realized taxable income from its United States plant of $50,000, taxable income from its Brazilian plant of $30,000 (paying $15,000 in Brazilian income taxes), a taxable loss of $20,000 from its Mexican plant (paying no taxes), and $40,000 in gain from the sale of capital assets (that are not real property) held for more than one year and sold in Chile (paying $8,000 in Chilean income taxes). Assume a 35 percent rate of tax by the United States.

   (a) What is Ewessco Corporation's allowable foreign tax credit for Year 1?

   (b) For purposes of (b)–(d), assume that no loss arose in Mexico. How would the answer to (a) change if the Chilean capital gain arose

---

[1] While current income tax rates on capital gain and ordinary income are 20 percent and 39.6 percent, respectively, the problems assume rates of 15 percent and 35 percent, reflecting a 20 percent rate differential.

through the sale of rental real property located in Chile?

(c) How would the answer to (b) change if Ewessco was not a domestic corporation but instead a United States citizen (Emily) operating a sole proprietorship? Assume a 15 percent rate of tax with respect to net capital gain.

(d) How would the answer to (b) change if, in addition to the Chilean capital gain, Ewessco Corporation realized a $40,000 long-term United States capital loss?

6-3. Z Corporation, a domestic corporation, commenced foreign operations in Year 1 by establishing a Brazilian branch, which produced a loss of $40,000, while its domestic operations generated $40,000 of income.

(a) In Year 2, its Brazilian operations resulted in taxable income of $100,000 with an attendant tax payment of $45,000, while its domestic operations generated taxable income of $75,000. What is Z Corporation's tax liability for Year 2 if its pre-credit United States tax liability was $61,250?

(b) Same as (a), except that Z Corporation did not conduct any operations in Brazil in Year 2. Instead, it sold all of the equipment used exclusively in the Brazilian branch to an unrelated purchaser residing in Brazil. Title to the equipment passed in Brazil, and the sale generated a total gain of $50,000 in Year 2. Z Corporation paid $10,000 in federal income taxes to Brazil as a result of the equipment sale. What is its tax liability for Year 2 if its pre-credit United States tax liability was $43,750?

(c) Same as (a), except in Year 1, Z Corporation also realized foreign source rental income of $50,000 from property it owned in Mexico. It does not actively manage the property; it holds the property strictly for the production of rental income with little or no effort. Z Corporation paid a $5,000 (10%) tax liability to Mexico. What is its tax liability for Year 1 if the pre-tax credit United States tax liability was $17,500?

C. OVERVIEW

The United States has a complex system of foreign tax credit limitation rules. Codified in § 904, the object of the foreign tax credit limitation rules is to protect the claim of the United States to tax the domestic source income of its own taxpayers. Thus, § 904(a) basically attempts to limit the allowable foreign tax credit against the United States tax liability to the tax liability imposed on the taxpayer's foreign source taxable income.

The policy reasons for limiting foreign tax credits seem clear, given that the point of having a foreign tax credit is to prevent *double* taxation. If a foreign country imposes a higher tax rate than the United States, only the overlapping tax rate represents double taxation: the excess foreign tax resulting from the foreign country's higher rate of tax is a cost of doing business in that country, but not a double tax. Thus in an ideal world (from the perspective of the revenue raiser, at least), every single item of income would be separately assessed to make sure it was in fact subject to double taxation before applying the credit. This is not practicable, but a number of different strategies could be employed to achieve a similar purpose.

The general, or "overall" limitation of § 904(a) is a typical approach. In addition, some countries (including the United States, at one time) apply a "per country" limitation on foreign tax credits. Under this system, a taxpayer's income is separated according to country of origin and credits are allowed based on comparison to the home country's tax rates. The income may be further separated, and the limitation applied, by type of income. Combinations of these approaches are also possible. The separate application of a limitation on different types of income is referred to as the basket system, the United States version of which is the subject of this Unit.

6.01   Section 904(a): The Overall Limitation

Once the amount of foreign taxes creditable under §§ 901–903 has been ascertained as described in Units 4 and 5, the taxpayer must examine the § 904 limitations that are imposed upon the credit. Section 904 contains an overall limitation and a series of additional special limitations. The overall limitation of § 904(a) can be expressed in formula form as follows:

$$\text{Maximum foreign tax credit} = \frac{\text{Foreign source taxable income}}{\text{Worldwide taxable income}} \times \text{United States tax on worldwide income}$$

Thus, the overall limitation of § 904 limits the amount of the credit taken to an amount of tax that is proportionate to a taxpayer's foreign source taxable income. For example, assume that a domestic corporation subject to an effective United States tax rate of 35 percent derives $30 of domestic source income and $80 of foreign source income subject to an effective tax rate of 50 percent (yielding a foreign tax liability of $40). The taxpayer's worldwide income of $110 would incur a pre-credit United States tax liability of $38.50. In the absence of a limitation, the creditable foreign tax ($40) would eliminate the domestic tax otherwise owing. If this were allowed, the United States would have completely surrendered its claim to tax. Instead, the general § 904 limitation caps the credit at $28 ($80 / $110 x $38.50). The effect of the limitation thus is to prevent the crediting of foreign taxes in excess of United States taxes on foreign source income.

Before proceeding to the mechanics of the basket system, four basic aspects of the overall § 904 limitation deserve comment:

1. *The limitation is based on income subject to tax.* A foreign tax may be considered creditable under § 901 even though it is levied upon income which is exempt from domestic taxation. The general § 904 limitation, however, focuses upon *taxable* income determined under United States tax provisions and thus excludes, from both the numerator and the denominator, income which is exempt from United States tax.

2. *Because the limitation is based upon taxable income, it necessarily involves the allocation of expenses to foreign source income.* The subject of allocating and

apportioning expenses is treated in the very complex rules found in Regulation § 1.861-8, discussed at length in Unit 8. Under that Regulation, expenses are generally allocated to the class of income to which they bear a factual relationship. However, two categories of expenses (research and development and interest) are treated differently. These expenses are deemed to have been incurred for the general financial welfare of the taxpayer and thus are usually allocated among all income. Such is the case even when the expense is actually incurred in making an exclusively foreign investment or in conducting a foreign business operation.

3. *The income sourcing rules control in determining the credit.* As a general rule, the source of income rules discussed in Unit 2 are controlling for purposes of the foreign tax credit. Thus, the taxpayer's transactions are to be tested against the rules of §§ 861–863 and 865. Once sourced, the income is integrated accordingly into the general § 904 limitation as United States or foreign source taxable income.

In some cases, however, Congress for various policy reasons has altered the source of income rules solely for foreign tax credit purposes. Thus, even if a particular transaction otherwise generates foreign source taxable income (generally a preferable result for purposes of the limitation), Congress has selected certain transactions and legislated a different standard to apply for sourcing purposes in determining the allowable foreign tax credit.

One such exception is § 904(h), which is intended to preserve the domestic source character (for § 904 purposes only) of income derived by a United States-owned foreign corporation (defined as a foreign corporation owned 50 percent or more by vote or value by domestic persons). Since dividends and interest from a foreign corporation are typically foreign source, the interposition of a foreign corporation between a domestic taxpayer and its domestic earnings could assist in inflating the numerator of the limitation by a conversion of the character of the income from domestic to foreign.

In general, § 904(h) provides two sourcing rules applicable to United States-owned foreign corporations for § 904 purposes. First, amounts includible in the gross income of United States shareholders under certain "safeguard" Code provisions (*see* Units 13 through 15) are deemed domestic source income to the extent attributable to domestically derived income of the foreign corporation. Second, subject to a *de minimis* exception, dividends and interest paid by such a corporation to a United States shareholder or a related person are viewed as domestic source income to the extent they are properly allocable to the domestically derived income of the foreign corporation.

4. *Some taxpayers are exempted from the general § 904 limitation.* Under § 904(k), individuals whose foreign source income consists entirely of certain types of passive income are not subject to the § 904 limitation if the amount of creditable foreign taxes paid does not exceed $300 ($600 if married filing jointly).

6.02 The Basket System

Various policy considerations have led Congress to specify that the § 904 calculation must be applied separately to special classes of income, often referred to as income "baskets." In effect, the separate application of the § 904 limitation to discrete baskets of income results in several special limitations applicable to United States taxpayers. Broadly speaking, the purpose of the separate basket limitation system is to prevent taxpayers from averaging, or "cross-crediting," low- and high-taxed income.

For example, if a domestic corporation earns foreign source business income which is taxed at a higher rate by the foreign country than by the United States, its allowable United States tax credit will be lower than its actual foreign tax paid, due to the overall limitation of § 904 discussed above. In the absence of other limitations, a simple way to utilize the excess foreign tax credits would be to increase the amount of foreign source income — and therefore the allowable foreign tax credit — without increasing the actual foreign tax paid. How can this be accomplished?

One relatively straightforward method would be to earn some income in a country that will tax it lightly or not at all. For example, the domestic corporation could simply purchase some income-producing securities, such as corporate bonds or government certificates, issued by non-United States obligors. Many countries (including the United States) do not impose taxes on the interest earned by many of these kinds of instruments when earned by non-residents (see discussion in Unit 8). The bonds would produce foreign source interest income to the United States company which would increase the taxpayer's overall percentage of foreign income. The company would thus increase its allowable foreign tax credit even though it paid no additional foreign tax. To be sure, this technique almost invariably increases the amount of tax owing to the United States, because foreign income increases worldwide income. However, the higher amount of United States tax otherwise due is offset by the excess of foreign tax paid which is now creditable. Thus, the technique is helpful to the extent it releases suspended foreign tax credits on other income.

Cross-crediting allows taxpayers to use relatively easily-generated low-or non-taxed income to credit United States taxes beyond the overall limitation ceiling, which is otherwise imposed on higher taxed income. This goes beyond relieving double taxation to the extent that the item of income was virtually certain of receipt yet subject to little or no tax abroad. The example is further illustrated in Figure 6-1, below.

FIGURE 6-1. "CROSS CREDITING" IN THE ABSENCE OF LIMITATIONS

U.S. Corp, a domestic corporation, earns $75,000 in domestic source income. In addition, U.S. Corp earns:		
Scenario 1: $25,000 in foreign source active business income.	*Scenario 2:* $3,500 in foreign source interest income.	*Scenario 3:* both $25,000 in foreign source active business income and $3,500 in foreign source interest income.
U.S. Tax Rate: 35% Foreign Tax Rate: 40% Allowable FTC: $8,750[a] U.S. Tax Due: $0 Foreign Taxes Not Credited: $1,250	U.S. Tax Rate: 35% Foreign Tax Rate: 0% Allowable FTC: $0 U.S. Tax Due: $1,225	U.S. Tax Rate: 35% Foreign Tax Rate: 40%, 0% Allowable FTC: $9,975[b] U.S. Tax Due: $0 Foreign Taxes Not Credited: $25
Total U.S. & Foreign Taxes Paid on Foreign Income: $10,000	Total U.S. & Foreign Taxes Paid on Foreign Income: $1,225	Total U.S. & Foreign Taxes Paid on Foreign Income: $10,000

[a] $35,000 [35% x $100,000] x ($25,000 [foreign source income] / $100,000 [worldwide income])
[b] $36,225 [35% x $103,500] x ($28,500 [foreign source income] / $103,500 [worldwide income])

To preclude this kind of manipulation of the foreign tax credit limitation, Congress has in the past required that separate foreign tax credit calculations be made for as many as nine different kinds of income. Called "baskets," these separate types of income included passive income, high withholding tax interest, financial services income, shipping income, certain dividends received from non-controlled foreign corporations, certain dividends from so-called "domestic international sales corporations" (DISCs) or former DISCs, taxable income attributable to certain foreign trade income, distributions from "foreign sales corporations" attributable to foreign trade income, and, finally, all other income.

Citing the need to simplify reporting and recordkeeping requirements for taxpayers, Congress changed the law in 2004 so that there are only two baskets: the "passive category income" basket and the "general category income" basket. In changing the law and thus allowing greater opportunities for cross-crediting, Congress asserted that requiring taxpayers to separate income and tax credits into nine separate tax baskets created some of the most complex tax reporting and compliance issues in the Code. Simplifying these rules would reduce double taxation, enhance the competitiveness of United States based-businesses, and create jobs in the United States. For details, see the House Report on the 2004 Jobs Act excerpted in Part D of this Unit. However, legislation enacted in 2010 created a separate basket for certain income items that are treated as United States source under the Code but reassigned as foreign source by treaty. Section 904(d)(6) is intended to prevent taxpayers from cross-crediting in situations where foreign source income (and thus the foreign tax credit limitation) is increased by treaty, thus reversing to some extent the generosity created in the 2004 Act.

Cross-crediting would not be needed if every country imposed the same amount of tax on the same base, since the United States foreign tax credit would perfectly match the amount of foreign tax paid — a potential double tax would be encountered and fully eliminated in every situation. But some countries impose higher or lower tax rates than those imposed by the United States on the same base. In scenario 1 of Figure 6-1, the income is subject to double taxation only insofar as it is taxed by both the United States and a foreign jurisdiction. The United States tax rate on that income yielded only an $8,750 tax burden. The income is only subject to a double tax of $8,750 — the other $1,250 represents a single layer of tax imposed, albeit at a higher rate, by the foreign jurisdiction.

The extra tax imposed by the foreign jurisdiction represents an extra cost of doing business in that jurisdiction compared to doing business in the United States. Allowing cross-crediting reduces that extra cost by allowing taxpayers to be indifferent to the high rates imposed by some countries so long as they can earn foreign source income subject to low rates elsewhere. For example, in scenario 3 of Figure 6-1, cross-crediting of active income taxed at high rates in a foreign jurisdiction and passive income taxed at low rates in a foreign jurisdiction reduces the amount of foreign taxes not credited from $1,250 to $25. This goes beyond relieving double taxation and makes investing abroad more attractive from a tax perspective than it otherwise would be, which in some cases could displace investment in the United States.

Under the current rules, cross-crediting of active and passive income is still prohibited, but taxpayers have more flexibility in cross-crediting in general, especially in the case of high- and low-taxed active business income.

6.03 Passive Category Income

When the § 904 limitation was first enacted, one of the most popular ways of cross-crediting was to deposit money and earn interest in a foreign jurisdiction that would impose little or no taxation on the earnings. Doing so would increase the foreign source income numerator of the § 904 limitation ratio without significantly increasing the payment of foreign taxes, as shown in the example above.

To prevent use of this tactic, § 904(d) as originally enacted provided that the limitation must be separately applied against interest income. In 1986, Congress expanded the interest basket to encompass all passive income. Passive category income is currently defined generally as income that is classified as foreign personal holding company income under § 954(c). Therefore, as will become more clear after study of Unit 14, the category includes interest, dividends, royalties, rents, and similar items.

The passive income basket currently also encompasses three specialized types of income that were divided into separate baskets under prior law. These include United States source dividends from a DISC or former DISC, taxable income attributable to certain foreign trade income, and distributions from a foreign sales corporation attributable to foreign trade income. Thus some of the complexity of the old law remains, since taxpayers must still analyze their income items and separate them according to these detailed specifications. The benefit of the change to two baskets is thus not so much in achieving simplicity as in allowing more cross-crediting, which may have the effect of encouraging more United States investment in low tax jurisdictions.

To counter this possible effect, the passive category of income excludes any items that are subject to a higher foreign tax rate than the maximum United States tax rate that would apply on the same income under § 1 or § 11, as applicable. Consistent with the original purpose of § 904 in segregating low tax income from all other income, this "high-taxed income" is appropriately placed in the general income basket.

6.04   General Category Income

Income that is not included in the passive category income under § 904(d) is still subject to the general § 904 calculation. A separate basket is therefore necessary to make sure that the general limitation applies. The general category income basket described in § 904(d)(2) serves this purpose. Generally, to lessen the effect of the § 904 limitation, the tax planning objective is to maximize foreign source income, without running afoul of the special rules just discussed or the ones concerning capital gains and foreign losses described below.

6.05   Special Rules for Capital Gains   *Individuals only*

Foreign source capital gains, like any other type of foreign source income, will increase the numerator and denominator of the overall limitation formula and thereby generally increase the amount of creditable taxes available to offset a United States income tax liability. At the same time, if the recipient of such income is an individual, he may be taxed at a lower rate on capital gains than on ordinary income. Including the full amount of the lower-taxed foreign source capital gain in the numerator of the overall limitation formula would allow the taxpayer to use it to offset domestic income that is subject to a higher rate.

To counter this distortion, § 904(b) includes a special rule, which applies only with respect to persons who are eligible for a reduced rate on certain preferred income items under § 1(h). Corporations, which are not eligible for a reduced rate on capital gains, are not subject to this rule. The effect of this rule, as discussed below, is to reduce the overall foreign limitation by excluding from the calculation a part of the capital gain income. The rule also applies with respect to any § 1231 gain taxed to an individual at long-term capital gains rates.

Under § 904(b)(2)(B), if there is a "capital gain rate differential," the taxpayer's foreign source income only includes the amount of "foreign source net capital gain" in excess of "the rate differential portion" (in other words, a "rate differential portion" must be calculated and is treated as domestic source income). A capital gain rate differential exists if § 1(h) applies.

Foreign source net capital gain is defined in § 904(b)(3)(B) as the lesser of foreign net capital gain or all net capital gain. The rate differential portion is determined by finding the difference between the highest applicable tax rate (defined as the regular § 1 rate) and the alternative tax rate (defined as the § 1(h) rate), dividing that amount by the highest applicable tax rate, and multiplying that amount by the net foreign source capital gain amount.

The rate differential portion is deducted from both foreign source income and overall income. Normally this rule will cause the overall foreign tax credit ceiling to be reduced, but there is no impact unless the foreign country imposes a tax on the capital gains that is higher than the United States preferred rate. That is unlikely to be the case for most types of capital gains. Nevertheless, to the extent foreign tax is imposed on capital gains income, the capital gain differential rule must be applied.

6.06   Special Rule for Capital Losses

Corporations can generally deduct capital losses only to the extent of capital gains. Section 904(b)(2)(A) provides that, in determining the § 904 limitation, foreign source capital gain can be included only to the extent of foreign source capital gain net income, defined as the lesser of capital gain net income from foreign sources or capital gain net income. The purpose of this rule is to prevent domestic capital losses from offsetting foreign capital gain in determining taxable income while the capital gain retains its foreign source character for purposes of the limitation.

6.07   Recapture of Foreign Losses: § 904(f)

Foreign losses reduce a taxpayer's worldwide income and therefore may increase the amount of allowable foreign tax credits in a given year. As such, taxpayers may find it expedient to manipulate the realization of their unrealized losses. For example, to achieve favorable foreign tax credit results, a taxpayer might wish to trigger foreign source taxable losses in a separate limitation category to offset United States source income, trigger a United States source loss to offset foreign source taxable income in a particular category, or trigger a loss in one category to offset income in another. Such flexibility would conflict with the underlying policy of having separate limitation categories as a means of preventing cross-crediting.

To prevent these manipulations, § 904(f) imposes a number of special rules for allocating losses for purposes of the foreign tax credit. Figure 6-2 compares what would happen if a United States source loss were allocated wholly to foreign source active income, wholly to foreign source passive income, or proportionately between them.

FIGURE 6-2. CONSEQUENCES OF VARYING ALLOCATIONS OF LOSSES AMONG BASKETS

U.S. Corp, a domestic corporation, earns $75,000 in foreign source general category income (paying $30,000 in foreign tax) and $80,000 in foreign source passive category income (paying no foreign tax). In addition, U.S. Corp has a $60,000 ordinary loss.		
Scenario 1: Allocate the loss to the general income basket	*Scenario 2:* Allocate the loss to the passive income basket	*Scenario 3:* Allocate the loss proportionately among the baskets according to income ᶜ
U.S. Tax Rate: 35%	U.S. Tax Rate: 35%	U.S. Tax Rate: 35%
Foreign Tax Rate – active / passive: 40% / 0%	Foreign Tax Rate – active / passive: 40% / 0%	Foreign Tax Rate – active / passive: 40% / 0%
Foreign Tax Paid: $30,000	Foreign Tax Paid: $30,000	Foreign Tax Paid: $30,000
Allowable FTC: $5,250 in general basket, $0 in passive basket ᵃ	Allowable FTC: $26,250 in general basket, $0 in passive basket ᵇ	Allowable FTC: $16,170 in general basket, $0 in passive basket ᵈ
U.S. Tax Due: $28,000	U.S. Tax Due: $7,000	U.S. Tax Due: $17,080
Foreign Taxes Not Credited: $24,750	Foreign Taxes Not Credited: $3,750	Foreign Taxes Not Credited: $13,830
Total U.S. & Foreign Taxes Paid on Foreign Income: $58,000 (effective tax rate of 61% on worldwide income)	Total U.S. & Foreign Taxes Paid on Foreign Income: $37,000 (effective tax rate of 39% on worldwide income)	Total U.S. & Foreign Taxes Paid on Foreign Income: $47,080 (effective tax rate of 49.5% on worldwide income)

ᵃ For the general basket, $33,250 [35% x $95,000] x ($15,000 [foreign source income] / $95,000 [worldwide income]); for the passive basket, the maximum allowable credit would be $28,000 ($33,250 [35% x $95,000] x ($80,000 [foreign source income] / $95,000 [worldwide income]), but no foreign taxes were paid in this basket, so none are creditable.
ᵇ For the general basket, $33,250 [35% x $95,000] x ($75,000 [foreign source income] / $95,000 [worldwide income]); for the passive basket, the maximum allowable credit would be $7,000 ($33,250 [35% x $95,000] x ($20,000 [foreign source income] / $95,000 [worldwide income]), but no foreign taxes were paid in this basket, so none are creditable.
ᶜ Total foreign source income equals $155,000, of which foreign source general category income of $75,000 represents 48% and $80,000 of passive income represents 52%. If assigned proportionately on the basis of income, the $60,000 loss would be allocated $28,800 to the general basket and $31, 200 to the passive basket.
ᵈ For the general basket, $33,250 [35% x $95,000] x ($46,200 [$75,000 - $28,800 foreign source income] / $95,000 [worldwide income]); for the passive basket, the maximum allowable credit would be $17,080 ($33,250 [35% x $95,000] x ($48,800 [$80,000 - $31,200 foreign source income] / $95,000 [worldwide income]), but no foreign taxes were paid in this basket, so none are creditable.

This comparison illustrates that allocation of losses can have a significant impact on the worldwide tax burden. Thus the rules of § 904(f) should be carefully analyzed to determine how allocations must be made in a given set of circumstances. Some of the main rules are discussed below.

The Confinement of Losses to Separate Baskets. The foreign tax credit basket limitation is calculated by reference to worldwide income, so the denominator is the same for each basket, but the numerator changes from basket to basket. Without a mechanism to address the use of losses, a loss in one basket would lower the denominator of the limitation fraction in the other basket with no effect on the numerator, creating a greater allowance for the use of any foreign tax credits available in that basket. If, for example, a taxpayer had general income basket loss and passive income basket gain in a given year, the separate basket rule would have the effect of insulating the passive income from the active loss and allowing a full foreign tax credit with respect to the passive income, assuming taxes are paid on that income. Section 904(f) prevents this result by providing a mechanism for allocating foreign losses first to baskets in which the taxpayer has foreign income against which the foreign losses can be offset.

Allocating Foreign Losses. Under § 904(f)(5)(A), losses in one basket can offset domestic source income only to the extent that the aggregate amount of such losses exceeds the aggregate amount of foreign income earned in both baskets. Thus, a mechanism is imposed which keeps losses derived from a foreign source in foreign categories, requiring that they be absorbed by foreign income before they can be utilized in the credit context to reduce only the denominator. By such an ordering approach, the numerator of the credit limitation is reduced first, thereby limiting the amount of the credit.

Recapture Rules. Special recapture rules are provided for allocating income earned in subsequent years to categories that previously absorbed the foreign loss. These rules prevent foreign losses from minimizing the impact of the separate baskets. The allocation rules are applied fairly straightforwardly to losses attributable to either basket. Such "separate limitation losses" are allocated among the foreign source income in the other basket. Thus, foreign source losses offset foreign source income regardless of its basket label and thereby reduce the § 904 numerator and the benefits of the foreign tax credit.

Overall Foreign Loss. If a domestic taxpayer sustains an overall loss from foreign activities during the year, that loss offsets the taxpayer's domestic income in the loss year. If the taxpayer in subsequent years earns an overseas profit, § 904(f)(1) requires that foreign source income in an amount equal to that previously deducted loss be recharacterized as having been derived from a domestic source. The source of the income is thus changed to preclude a double benefit in the foreign tax credit context.

In general, § 904(f) provides that any taxpayer who sustains an overall foreign loss must recapture that loss in later taxable years. Recapture is accomplished by recasting a portion of subsequently derived foreign income as domestic source income. The amount of transformed income is limited to the lesser of the amount of the previously unrecaptured loss or 50 percent of foreign taxable income for that year. A larger percentage may be recaptured if the taxpayer so elects. This election should be advantageous when the taxpayer has a domestic loss which reduces his or her tax liability in a later year. Through acceleration of the recapture, it is possible to exhaust the overall foreign loss account before the arrival of more profitable years.

There are many additional rules for allocating losses for foreign tax credit purposes, and additional complexities in applying the rules discussed in general here. In addition, the foreign tax credit limitation is a dynamic area of law. Much like § 911, which was the subject of Unit 3, the foreign tax credit limitation has been subject to numerous revisions over the years, alternately restricting and loosening the ability to reduce United States tax on the basis of foreign taxes paid. Sometimes, the competitiveness of United States-based businesses is given as a reason for loosening restrictions, while other times the need to protect the United States tax base from erosion is given as a reason to tighten the rules. The current regime, in allowing greater cross-crediting of high- and low-taxed income, is generally more flexible and taxpayer-friendly than it has been in the past.

6.08 Carryback and Carryover of Excess Taxes Paid: § 904(c)

Finally, in most cases, the foreign tax credit does not perfectly offset the foreign taxes actually paid in any given situation. The amount of foreign taxes paid or accrued in a taxable year may exceed the foreign tax credit limitation determined under § 904(a). This scenario results in the taxpayer having excess unused foreign tax credits. On the other hand, the § 904(a) limitation in a given year may exceed the amount of foreign taxes paid, thus resulting in an "excess limitation." Section 904(c) therefore provides rules for carrying excess credits to other taxable years in which the taxpayer has an excess limitation.

D. REFERENCE MATERIALS

- House Rep. No. 108-548, pt. 1 (June 16, 2004)

HOUSE REPORT NO. 108-548
AMERICAN JOBS CREATION ACT OF 2004

. . .

C. REDUCTION TO TWO FOREIGN TAX CREDIT BASKETS

(Sec. 303 of the bill and sec. 904 of the Code.)

E. PRESENT LAW

In general

The United States taxes its citizens and residents on their worldwide income. Because the countries in which income is earned also may assert their jurisdiction to tax the same income on the basis of source, foreign-source income earned by U.S. persons may be subject to double taxation. In order to mitigate this possibility, the United States provides a credit against U.S. tax liability for foreign income taxes paid, subject to a number of limitations. The foreign tax credit generally is limited to the U.S. tax liability on a taxpayer's foreign-source income, in order to ensure that the credit serves its purpose of mitigating double taxation of cross-border income without offsetting the U.S. tax on U.S.-source income.

The foreign tax credit limitation is applied separately to the following categories of income: (1) passive income, (2) high withholding tax interest, (3) financial services income, (4) shipping income, (5) certain dividends received from non-controlled section 902 foreign corporations ('10/50 companies'), (6) certain dividends from a domestic international sales corporation or former domestic international sales corporation, (7) taxable income attributable to certain foreign trade income, (8) certain distributions from a foreign sales corporation or former foreign sales corporation, and (9) any other income not described in items (1) through (8) (so-called 'general basket' income). In addition, a number of other provisions of the Code and U.S. tax treaties effectively create additional separate limitations in certain circumstances.

. . .

F. REASONS FOR CHANGE

The Committee believes that requiring taxpayers to separate income and tax credits into nine separate tax baskets creates some of the most complex tax reporting and compliance issues in the Code. Reducing the number of foreign tax credit baskets to two will greatly simplify the Code and undo much of the complexity created by the Tax Reform Act of 1986. The Committee believes that simplifying these rules will reduce double taxation, make U.S. businesses more competitive, and create jobs in the United States.

G. EXPLANATION OF PROVISION

In general

The provision generally reduces the number of foreign tax credit limitation categories to two: passive category income and general category income. Other income is included in one of the two categories, as appropriate. For example, shipping income generally falls into the general limitation category, whereas high withholding tax interest generally could fall into the passive income or the general limitation category, depending on the circumstances. Dividends from a domestic international sales corporation or former domestic international sales corporation, income attributable to certain foreign trade income, and certain distributions from a foreign sales corporation or former foreign sales corporation all are assigned to the passive income limitation category. The provision does not affect the separate computation of foreign tax credit limitations under special provisions of the Code relating to, for example, treaty-based sourcing rules or specified countries under section 901(j).

Part III

INBOUND TAXATION

Unit 7

TREATMENT OF FOREIGN-OWNED UNITED STATES INVESTMENT INCOME

A. CODE AND REGULATION PROVISIONS

Code   §§ 871(a), (d), (h), (i); 873(a), (b); 881(a), (c), (d).
Reg.   § 1.871-7.

B. PROBLEMS FOR CLASS DISCUSSION

7-1.   Surya, a citizen and bona fide resident of Nepal, has never been present in the United States. During Year 1, he had no United States trade or business, but he owned a number of assets that produced the following items of income:

- $20,000 dividend on the stock of DelCo, a corporation formed in Delaware;

- $5,000 gain on sale of 10 shares of stock in UruCo, a corporation formed in Uruguay;

- $13,000 dividend on the UruCo stock, of which $5,200 is United States source and $7,800 is foreign source;

- $10,000 in rents from rental property located in the United States;

- $1,000 of foreign-source interest on a loan made to Emily, a citizen and resident of Bolivia;

- $2,000 of interest on a deposit at a Chicago, Illinois bank; and

- $8,000 in cash from the sale of the United States rights to a patent Surya created for five percent of the net profits from products produced through its use.

Surya's potential deductions for the year consisted of depreciation and expenses with respect to the rental property of $3,000, a $1,000 loss on the sale of five shares of UruCo stock, and medical expenses incurred abroad of $4,500. Assume that Surya would be subject to a 20 percent effective tax rate on his taxable income if §§ 1 and 55 applied.

(a)   What is Surya's United States taxable income and his tax liability for Year 1?

(b)   What result if Surya elects under § 871(d)?

7-2.   In Year 1, Shaida, a citizen and resident of Guyana, purchased 10 shares of stock in DelCo, a Delaware corporation, for $7,000. In Year 3, Shaida sold the shares for $10,000 in cash to an unrelated individual residing in the United States. To what extent will the United States impose income tax with respect to Shaida's $3,000 gain in Year 3 under each of the following alternative scenarios?

(a)   Shaida was never physically present in the United States at any time in Year 1, Year 2, or Year 3.

(b)   Shaida was not physically present in the United States at any time in Year 1 or Year 2, but she was physically present in the United States for 200 days in Year 3, beginning on January 1 of Year 3.

(c)   Same as (b), except that for 100 of the 200 days of presence in the United States in Year 3, Shaida was a student residing in the United States under a visa issued under the Immigration and Nationality Act.

7-3.   SaudiCo is a corporation organized in Saudi Arabia. Except as otherwise provided, all of SaudiCo's shares are owned by citizens and residents of Saudi Arabia who have no connection to the United States. SaudiCo has a number of investments in the United States, but it does not conduct a trade or business within the United States. For each situation described below, determine whether the interest received by SaudiCo is subject to United States taxation under § 881(a).

(a)   Interest from a certificate of deposit issued by a California bank.

(b)   Interest from a certificate of deposit issued by the Italian branch of a California bank.

(c)   Interest from a loan to an unrelated Delaware corporation.

(d)   Same as (c), except that the amount of interest payable to SaudiCo is dependent upon the domestic corporation's net profits each year.

(e)   Same as (c), except that the amount of interest payable to SaudiCo is determined with reference to changes in the Dow Jones Industrial Average index.

(f)   Interest from a loan to its wholly-owned United States subsidiary corporation.

C. OVERVIEW

As discussed in Units 1 and 2, in contrast to the worldwide taxation the United States imposes on its citizens and residents, its taxation of foreign persons is considerably more restricted, and generally limited to items of income generated in the United States, namely, income derived from certain domestic investment-related sources and income derived from domestic trade or business activities. These items may be taxed on either a gross or net basis, depending on the nature of the income derived.[1]

---

[1] This Unit explores the common themes underpinning the taxation of investment income earned by

A non-resident alien individual is subject to United States tax only on specifically defined categories of income under § 871. The major category is found in § 871(a)(1), which includes items generally associated with passive investment assets, including interest, dividends, and rents, but also other forms of income such as wages, premiums, annuities, and "other fixed or determinable annual or periodic gains, profits and income," commonly collectively referred to as FDAP. A second category, found in § 871(a)(2), consists of domestic source income from the sale or exchange of capital assets, but only if the non-resident individual is present in the United States for at least 183 days during the taxable year. Section 871(a)(3) constitutes a third category — social security benefits received — which may be subject to tax depending on the level of benefits, tax filing status, and other income received.

Unless otherwise exempt, FDAP, capital gains, and social security benefits are taxed under § 871(a) on a gross basis at a flat 30 percent tax rate, without setoff for deductions or credits.[2] This tax is sometimes referred to as a "withholding tax" because in most cases it is enforced via §§ 1441 and 1442 by imposing an obligation to withhold on the payor of the income item rather than by collecting the tax directly from the recipient.

Foreign corporations, like non-resident individuals and unlike domestic corporations, incur United States tax only on specific categories of income derived from United States sources or activities. Foreign corporations are subject to tax on specified domestic source investment income items described in § 881, which generally parallel the investment-related items listed in § 871(a)(1) for individuals. As in the case of individuals, domestic source investment income items are taxed on a gross basis at a 30 percent rate without setoff for deductions or credits, and the tax is enforced by withholding at the source.

Non-resident alien individuals and foreign corporations are also subject to United States tax on a net basis and at the graduated tax rates of §§ 1, 11, and 55, as applicable, on income that is effectively connected with a United States trade or business. The taxation of effectively connected business income is the subject of Unit 8. In some cases, foreign corporations may also face a branch profits tax with respect to earnings and profits effectively connected to a United States trade or business, as discussed in Unit 9. This Unit 7 focuses on the various types of income that are subject to a source-based, gross basis tax (enforced generally through withholding by the payor). Subparts 7.01 through 7.06 examine the major categories of income subject to gross basis tax and the major exceptions within these categories. Subpart 7.07 discusses the enforcement mechanism of withholding.

---

foreign persons who are not eligible for tax benefits under a tax treaty. If a treaty applies, the United States taxation of investment income may be significantly reduced. The impact of treaties on investment income is the subject of Unit 11.

[2] In the case of Social Security benefits, the 30 percent tax applies to a maximum of 85 percent of the gross benefit amount, for an effective rate of 25.5 percent.

7.01   Income Items Included in §§ 871(a) and 881(a)

To be subject to the gross basis tax imposed under § 871(a) or § 881(a), income must be derived from United States sources and *not* effectively connected to a United States trade or business. The items described in these sections encompass primarily income from passive, non-business activities.

7.02   Income from Intangible Property

United States source royalties (as distinct from rents) are not listed in the statute as FDAP income, but Regulation § 1.871-7(b) makes clear that these royalties are so included. Section 871(a)(1)(D) also includes gains from the sale or exchange of intangible assets or of any interest therein, to the extent such gains are contingent on the productivity, use, or disposition of the property, but gains from the sale or exchange of all other property are excluded from the scope of § 871(a)(1)(D).

Section 1235 contains a special rule that impacts the taxation of gains derived from the sale or exchange of patents and patent rights. Under § 1235, any transfer of a patent or patent right is considered to be the sale or exchange of a capital asset even if the payments in consideration for the transfer are contingent on the productivity, use, or disposition of the transferred property. Regulation § 1.1235-1(d) confirms this rule, stating that payments made pursuant to a § 1235 transfer are "payments of the purchase price and are not the payment of royalties." As a result, gain derived from transfers of patents and patent rights governed by § 1235 would generally be addressed not under § 871(a)(1), which addresses income other than capital gain, but under § 871(a)(2), which addresses capital gain. However, as discussed in Unit 2, § 865(d)(1)(B) overrides this rule in the case of contingent gains, stating that such gains are treated as royalty payments for sourcing purposes. This treatment is repeated and clarified in Regulation § 1.871-11(c) and (e). As a result, in the case of patents, § 865(d)(1)(A) causes non-contingent gain to be sourced as a sale of personal property under § 865 and potentially subject to tax under § 871(a)(2). In contrast, contingent sale gain is sourced under §§ 865(d)(1)(B) and 861(a)(4) and potentially subject to tax under § 871(a)(1)(D).

Although § 871(a)(1)(A) purports to reach all forms of FDAP income, special exceptions have been overlaid by legislation and judicial decisions, most notably in the context of interest, as discussed below, and insurance premiums, as demonstrated in Revenue Ruling 89-91, set forth in Part D of this Unit. On the other hand, the Service and the courts have also expanded the list of FDAP income items on a case by case basis. For example, alimony is FDAP income, as are lottery winnings.

7.03   Exception for Most Interest Payments

Although it is the first item listed in both §§ 871(a) and 881(a), most United States source interest is not in fact taxable to foreign persons due to the portfolio interest exceptions. These exceptions, found in §§ 871(h) and (i) (for individuals) and 881 (c) and (d) (for corporations), serve as an example of tax legislation responding to global competition in international commerce, as opposed to other policy questions such as neutrality, efficiency, or equity.

Prior to the mid-1980s, many countries, including the United States, imposed taxes on interest and dividends earned by foreign persons on their United States investment portfolios. Even so, investors could use financial intermediaries in certain countries with favorable United States tax treaty relationships to obtain tax-free access to the United States bond market. In 1984, the United States terminated these treaties and adopted a tax exemption for United States-sourced portfolio interest, making United States debt more attractive in the global market. The international reaction to the repeal was swift and remarkable. For example, before the repeal, foreign persons held about $25.8 billion in treasury securities, while two years after the repeal, foreign persons held $96.1 billion. In the process, the United States set in motion a global "race to the bottom," since any country competing for capital against the United States would be disadvantaged to the extent their interest rates were still eroded by taxation. As a result, most countries now do not impose tax on interest earned on debt instruments held by foreign persons.

The portfolio interest exception repealed the tax on most types of interest, provided such interest is not effectively connected with the payee's United States trade or business and provided it is not received by a person who owns 10 percent or more of the stock of the payor, measured by voting power. Additional rules apply for United States source interest received by foreign corporations under § 881(c)(3). The exception only applies if the payor or other withholding agent receives a statement that the beneficial owner of the obligation is not a United States person. The withholding obligation and the effect of payee statements are discussed in subpart 7.07 below.

The preferences provided by statute may also prove beneficial to residents of a treaty country. While treaty provisions impose a tax rate on investment income typically lower than the statutory rate of 30 percent, certain income such as portfolio interest income may qualify for a United States statutory rate lower than the treaty rate. As discussed more fully in Unit 10, under most income tax treaties, nothing in the treaty will preclude or preempt an exemption, income, or credit otherwise available. If the statute exempts interest income entirely, such income will remain exempt even though the terms of an applicable income tax treaty might, for example, subject such income to a flat tax rate of five or 10 percent.

7.04   Exception for Certain Dividends

Dividends from United States sources are typically subject to taxation as FDAP under § 871(a), with exceptions provided in §§ 871(i) and 881(d). First, a transition rule exists for dividends paid by certain domestic corporations that meet the active foreign business income test of former § 861(c)(1). As former § 861(c)(1) was repealed in 2010, this transition rule applies to tax years beginning after December 31, 2010. Second, dividends paid by a foreign corporation that are treated as United States source under § 861(a)(2)(B) are also exempt from withholding tax under §§ 871 and 881.

Thus, even though the source rules require an assessment of the extent to which foreign corporations earn income that is effectively connected with a United States trade or business, the designation may have no gross basis tax implications for foreign recipients, due to the operation of §§ 871(i) and 881(d). As discussed in Units 4 through 6, creditability for foreign taxes on dividends will be determined by the source designation. As a result, the designation as United States source is not without consequence for United States recipients of these dividends. But for purposes of foreign investors in the United States, the special sourcing rules of §§ 871(i) and 881(d) are generally inconsequential.

7.05   Capital Gains

The taxation of capital gains earned by non-resident alien individuals is addressed in § 871(a)(2). The general rule is that non-resident alien individuals are subject to tax of 30 percent on net capital gains derived from domestic sources if such individuals are present in the United States for 183 days or more during the taxable year. In practice, however, the 183-day presence requirement will generally result in a determination that the taxpayer is a United States resident under § 7701(b). Accordingly, such individuals will generally be taxed under § 1, including the preferential capital gains rates provided in § 1(h)(1), and not under § 871. Section 871(a)(2) is typically imposed only on non-resident alien individuals whose presence is excluded for purposes of determining residency under § 7701(b)(5), but whose presence is counted for purposes of § 871(a)(2), such as foreign government officials, teachers, students, and certain professional athletes.

However, even for non-resident aliens whose presence exceeds 183 days, presence alone will not lead to taxation under § 871(a)(2). This is because of the rather complex source rules that apply for gains from the sale of non-inventory property. As discussed in Unit 2, income from the sale of personal property other than inventory property is generally sourced according to the residence of the seller as defined by § 865, and § 865(g) determines residence for these purposes not on the basis of presence and other tests of § 7701 but on the location of the taxpayer's "tax home." As more fully discussed in Unit 3, this term generally refers to the taxpayer's principal place of business. As a result, the 183 day standard of § 871(a)(2) only applies to non-resident alien individuals after it has been determined that the individual has a United States tax home, such that the sale of the property would give rise to United States source gain in the first place. In other words, if the taxpayer has no United States tax home, the gain will not be United States source under § 865, and therefore § 871(a)(2) would not apply.

7.06   Income from Real Property

While real property might typically be considered a passive investment, two special statutes permit or require certain income derived from real property by foreign persons to be treated as effectively connected income rather than investment income. First, §§ 871(d) (for individuals) and 881(d) (for corporations) permit foreign persons to elect to treat income derived from United States real property as effectively connected income. This may be desirable because, for example, it permits the foreign person to compute taxable income on the basis of net income rather than gross income.

Second, § 897(a) treats gains and losses derived from sales and other dispositions of United States real property interests as effectively connected income. The treatment of real property income is quite complex, and therefore addressed separately in Unit 9.

7.07 Withholding of 30 Percent Tax at Source

The 30 percent tax imposed under §§ 871(a) and 881(a) is generally enforced by means of withholding at the source of the payment. This tax collection mechanism is generally considered the best approach since the tax is imposed on foreign persons outside of United States jurisdiction. Without a withholding mechanism, it might be difficult to enforce the tax imposed by §§ 871 and 881, since the purported taxpayer is not generally within the practical administrative reach of the Service.

Under §§ 1441 and 1442, any foreign or domestic person having "control, receipt, custody, disposal, or payment" of any item of United States source income described in § 871 or § 881 is responsible for withholding the 30 percent tax from such payment and for remitting that tax to the Service. To encourage compliance, persons required to withhold such tax are themselves liable for the tax.

Regulations under §§ 1441 and 1442 offer comprehensive guidance on the information reporting and withholding rules applicable to payments of FDAP income and taxable capital gains to foreign persons. Very generally, the Regulations require the person who last touches the United States source FDAP income item before it is paid to a foreign person (or to such foreign person's foreign agent) to withhold the applicable amount of tax from the payment and to pay such tax to the United States. The person required to withhold tax is referred to as the "withholding agent."

As a result of the withholding requirements, United States payors of income must determine the residency status of persons to whom they will make payments. Since, as discussed in Unit 1, residency determinations can sometimes involve complications, payors typically determine a payee's status on the basis of a withholding certificate filed with the payor by the payee. A foreign person provides this certificate on Form 8233 (for compensation income) or Form W-8BEN (for all other FDAP income). Payees are not required to certify or file Form W-8BEN with the Service, and, unless they know that the certificate contains false statements, withholding agents may rely on the statements made by payees in determining whether to withhold United States tax. If the payee does not furnish a certificate, payments may be subject to the withholding tax if payable to a foreign address.

Where the recipient of United States source FDAP income is a domestic partnership with one or more foreign partners, the partnership itself becomes the withholding agent. Withholding must occur when the partnership furnishes Forms K-1 reporting the distributive shares of the partners or, if earlier, upon a distribution of the FDAP income to a foreign partner. If the recipient of United States source FDAP income is a foreign partnership, of course, the payor generally must serve as the withholding agent. But where the foreign partnership has made a "withholding agreement" with the Service, the foreign partnership itself will become the withholding agent and the payor is relieved of the obligation to withhold United States tax.

Under § 1461, a withholding agent is personally liable for any amount required to be withheld under § 1441 or § 1442. If the recipient pays the tax on behalf of the withholding agent, the agent is relieved from liability for payment of the tax but remains liable for any applicable penalties and assessed interest. A withholding agent must provide a Form 1042-S to each recipient reporting the amount of tax withheld, and all of the Forms 1042-S must be attached to a separate information return (Form 1042) filed by the withholding agent.

D. REFERENCE MATERIALS

- Revenue Ruling 89–91

REVENUE RULING 89-91
1989-2 C.B. 129

ISSUE

Are the insurance premiums that are received by a foreign corporation in the circumstances described below subject to the income tax imposed on premiums by section 881(a) of the Internal Revenue Code of 1986?

FACTS

X is a foreign casualty insurance company organized under the laws of foreign country FC. In 1987, X insured United States risks as defined in section 861(a)(7) of the Code, and the income derived from this activity was therefore from sources within the United States.

The insurance policies issued by X were not signed or countersigned in the United States by any officer or agent of X. During 1987, X was not engaged in a trade or business in the United States within the meaning of section 864(b) of the Code. Premiums on the policies were subject to the excise tax of section 4371.

LAW AND ANALYSIS

Section 881(a)(1) of the Code imposes an income tax of 30 percent on certain kinds of gross income, including premiums, that foreign corporations receive from sources within the United States, to the extent not effectively connected with the corporation's United States trade or business. Section 1442 requires the payor of the income to withhold this tax.

Chapter 34 of the Code (sections 4371–4374), as in effect in 1987, imposed an excise tax on certain premiums paid to foreign insurers and reinsurers of United States risks. Policies that were signed or countersigned in the United States by an officer or agent of the insurer were generally exempt from the tax. (Section

1012(q)(13) of the Technical and Miscellaneous Revenue Act of 1988, Pub. L. No. 100-647, 102 Stat. 3342, 3525, prospectively amended section chapter 34 to exempt from the excise tax any amount effectively connected with the conduct of a trade or business within the United States, subject to exceptions.)

Rev. Rul. 80-222, 1980-2 C.B. 211, holds that premiums for the insurance of United States risks by foreign insurers not engaged in a United States trade or business are subject to excise tax under section 4371 of the Code, but not to income tax and withholding under sections 881 and 1442 Rev. Rul. 80-222 restates the conclusions and reasoning of I.T. 1359, I-1 C.B. 292 (1922). The two reasons given for the holding are: (1) Congress intended to impose income tax and withholding on items of gross income only if the items have a high content of net income, and insurance premiums do not; and (2) the premiums are subject to a stamp or excise tax that Congress intended as a substitute for an income tax.

Only the second of these reasons finds explicit support in the legislative history of the excise tax (and the stamp tax that preceded it) on premiums paid to foreign insurers having no United States trade or business. Congress believed that such premiums were not subject to an income tax, and the excise and stamp taxes were intended to reduce the competitive advantage of a foreign insurer's otherwise tax-free operation. See H.R. Rep. No. 2333, 77th Cong., 2d Sess., at 61 (1942); 61 Cong. Rec. 7180–81 (1921).

The Service has re-examined the legislative history described above and concluded that the "high content of net income" theory is unnecessary to the holding of Rev. Rul. 80-222. Rev. Rul. 80-222 is therefore modified to eliminate reliance on this theory.

HOLDING

The insurance premiums received by a foreign corporation in the circumstances described above are not subject to the income tax imposed on premiums by section 881(a) of the Code.

. . .

Unit 8

TREATMENT OF FOREIGN-OWNED UNITED STATES BUSINESS INCOME

A. CODE AND REGULATION PROVISIONS

Code §§ 864(b)(1), (c)(1)–(5); 865(e)(2)(B); 871(b); 873(a), (b); 875; 882(a), (c).

Reg. §§ 1.861-4(b)(1), (2); 1.861-8(a)(1)–(4), (b), (c); 1.861-9T(a); 1.864-2(a), (b); 1.864-4(a), (c).

B. PROBLEMS FOR CLASS DISCUSSION

8-1. Reconsider the facts from Problem 7-1 regarding Surya, a citizen and bona fide resident of Nepal, who has never been present in the United States. During Year 1, he owned a number of assets that produced the following items of income:

- $20,000 dividend on the stock of DelCo, a corporation formed in Delaware;

- $5,000 gain on sale of 10 shares of stock in UruCo, a corporation formed in Uruguay;

- $13,000 dividend on the UruCo stock, of which $5,200 is United States source and $7,800 is foreign source;

- $10,000 in rents from rental property located in the United States;

- $1,000 of foreign-source interest on a loan made to Emily, a citizen and resident of Bolivia;

- $2,000 of interest on a deposit at a Chicago, Illinois bank; and

- $8,000 in cash from the sale of the United States rights to a patent Surya created for five percent of the net profits from products produced through its use.

Surya's potential deductions for the year consisted of depreciation and expenses with respect to the rental property of $3,000, a $1,000 loss on the sale of five shares of UruCo stock, and medical expenses incurred abroad of $4,500.

(a) The facts of Problem 7-1 assumed that Surya did not have a trade or business in the United States. Without that assumption, would Surya be engaged in a domestic trade or business with respect to any of his activities in Year 1?

(b) Would Surya be engaged in a domestic trade or business if either DelCo or UruCo conducted a trade or business in the United States? Does the result depend upon whether Surya is a minority shareholder? A significant shareholder? A majority shareholder? The sole shareholder?

(c) Would Surya be engaged in a domestic trade or business if DelCo and UruCo are general partnerships or limited liability companies (rather than corporations) that conducted a trade or business in the United States? Does the result depend upon whether Surya had a minority interest in the entities? A majority interest? What if both entities are limited partnerships and Surya is the general partner?

(d) Assume that Surya is engaged in a trade or business in the United States with respect to the rental property. What is Surya's federal income tax liability to the United States, if he is subject to a 20 percent effective tax rate on his taxable income under §§ 1 and 55?

8-2. To what extent is each taxpayer described below engaged in a trade or business within the United States?

(a) X Corp is organized in Ecuador. X Corp entered into a contract with DomCo, a domestic corporation, under which DomCo serves as X Corp's exclusive agent in selling its products in the United States. DomCo receives a commission for each sale to a United States customer. The contract prohibits DomCo from selling any competing products in the United States and from acting as the agent for another in selling any competing products in the United States.

(b) Y Corp is organized in Panama, but has a branch office in the United States. Y Corp's products are sold in the United States by domestic employees working out of a rented office building in Tulsa, Oklahoma. All orders from United States customers must be approved by Y Corp's home office in Panama, and no domestic employee has the power to bind Y Corp in any way.

(c) Z Corp is organized in Belize. Z Corp purchases goods in the United States for sale to customers in foreign countries. Z Corp maintains an office in San Diego, California, that is staffed by domestic employees who facilitate purchases and arrange for shipping.

8-3. Fabio, a citizen and resident of Paraguay, is a professional model. Last summer, Fabio posed in front of the Washington Monument for the cover of a forthcoming romance novel to be published exclusively in Paraguay by a Paraguayan publisher that is not engaged in a trade or business within the United States. To what extent is Fabio liable for United States income tax in each of the following alternative scenarios?

(a) The photo shoot took only a single day and Fabio received total compensation of $2,000 from the publisher.

(b) The photo shoot took three days and Fabio received total compensation of $6,000 from the publisher.

(c) How would the answers to (a) and (b) change if Fabio received his compensation under a contract with a United States modeling company which performed the photo shoot on behalf of the Paraguayan publisher?

8-4. ForCo is a Bolivian corporation that purchases zippers for sale. It has facilities in the United States, Argentina, and Bolivia. The zippers bought in the United States are sold exclusively in the United States. Likewise, the zippers from Argentina are sold exclusively there, and the zippers from Bolivia are sold exclusively within Bolivian borders. ForCo generates all of its income from these three countries. ForCo does not have a separate division that oversees operations in the United States. In addition, ForCo purchases wine from a distributor in Argentina and sells it exclusively therein. For Year 1, ForCo incurred $50,000 in general administrative expenses related to both United States and non-United States operations. ForCo incurred $80,000 in deductible interest expense in Year 1 from its borrowings used to improve the Bolivian facility. It has $150,000 expense for labor/wages regarding the zippers: $90,000 in the United States, $40,000 in Argentina, and $20,000 in Bolivia, and $70,000 expense for labor/wages regarding the wine. ForCo 's sales and gross income from each country in Year 1 were as follows:

Country	Asset Bases	Zippers Sales	Zippers Gross Income	Wine Gross Income
United States	$50,000	$250,000	$100,000	$0
Argentina	$100,000	$1,500,000	$200,000	$600,000
Bolivia	$200,000	$800,000	$300,000	$0

Assuming the income from the sale of zippers in Argentina and Bolivia is not effectively connected with ForCo's United States operations, what is ForCo's taxable income in Year 1 for United States income tax purposes?

C. OVERVIEW

As discussed in Unit 7, United States-source investment income that is not effectively connected to a United States trade or business may be subject to a flat 30 percent tax. In contrast, income that is effectively connected with the conduct of a trade or business in the United States is potentially taxed on a net income basis at the regular graduated rates. This Unit is concerned with the determination of whether a foreign person is engaged in trade or business within the United States and, if so, the rules for identifying whether and to what extent the person has effectively connected income (ECI).

8.01   Engaged in a Trade or Business in the United States

Whether a foreign person is engaged in trade or business within the United States is generally a question of fact for which there are no hard and fast rules. In fact, the Code avoids an affirmative definition of the concept, opting instead to present several discrete situations that do, or do not, give rise to a trade or business. By necessity the Service and courts have been left to establish the parameters for this determination. A few of the key cases and rulings are excerpted in Part D of this Unit. The first, Revenue Ruling 88-3, makes it clear that the facts and circumstances are determinative — a thorough analysis must be made in every case.

The analysis of whether conduct constitutes a United States trade or business may draw, in some circumstances, upon the distinction between activities giving rise to § 162 business expenses and those giving rise to deductions under § 212 related to the production of income. In appropriate cases, analogous authorities construing the distinction between business versus investment expenses under §§ 162 or 212, respectively, may prove to be valuable interpretive tools for counsel representing foreign taxpayers with United States activities.

Some general guidance can also be gleaned from the body of cases construing the trade or business standard for general income tax purposes. First, a United States trade or business is generally characterized by progression, continuity, or sustained activity that occurs during some substantial portion of the taxable year. Courts have broadly focused primarily upon the degree and significance of the activity undertaken by the person under scrutiny in assessing whether that person is engaged in a trade or business. Yet Revenue Ruling 58-63 (excerpted in Part D) illustrates that in some cases, just one instance of activity — such as the entry of a horse in a race in the United States — can constitute a domestic trade or business.

If a foreign person's presence in the United States is limited to maintaining an office for merely ministerial or collection functions, it is probably not a United States trade or business. For example, many foreign companies maintain a domestic representative office, which typically does not solicit business or participate meaningfully in any specific profit-motivated transaction, but simply reports on market conditions or performs bookkeeping and other ministerial functions in the United States. A representative office thus should not amount to the conduct of a trade or business. *Scottish American Investment Co., Ltd. v. Commissioner* (excerpted in Part D) lays out a number of factors relevant to this analysis.

If a foreign person's domestic activities are directly related or pivotal to the active pursuit of profit, however, a trade or business probably exists. In order for a domestic trade or business to exist, its "core activities" (those activities that are essential to deriving profit) must be conducted in the United States. For example, a foreign person rendering material services or soliciting sales domestically is probably engaged in a trade or business.

8.02   Attribution through Agents

Activities of agents and employees add a layer of complexity to the trade or business analysis. For example, no trade or business should typically arise from isolated sales by employees or minimal operational or export activity in the United States. On the other hand, extensive sales activity or domestic marketing conducted through dependent agents (such as employees) has been found to constitute a trade or business for the principal or employer. To be considered a dependent agent, it is not necessary for the United States person or entity to be related or affiliated with the foreign person. Instead, it is sufficient that the United States-based person or entity acts exclusively (or nearly exclusively) for such foreign person in order to be considered such foreign person's dependent agent.

It is less clear whether the activities of an *independent* agent should be imputed to a foreign person for purposes of determining whether the principal is engaged in a domestic trade or business. The activities of licensees and lessees are not typically imputed to the foreign licensor or lessor (licensees and lessees are not agents of the foreign person), but the treatment of other independent relationships is not clear-cut. The case of *United States v. Balanovski* (excerpted in Part D) illustrates some of the various relationships and activities that might give rise to a trade or business through the actions of agents.

Finally, the trade or business activity of a pass-through entity is generally imputed to its foreign owners under § 875(1), in the case of both general and limited partners. Thus in the trade or business analysis, a partnership is akin to an agent, with the partners as principals. However, the corporate form is typically respected, so the Code offers no similar look-through rule for corporations and their shareholders. Thus, a foreign person, whether corporate or individual, and regardless of the level of ownership interest, will not typically be considered to be engaged in a trade or business by virtue of its ownership of shares in a domestic corporation that is so engaged.

8.03   Performance of Services as a Trade or Business

Under the criteria discussed above for determining whether activity constitutes a trade or business, it might seem that not all services would necessarily constitute a trade or business — continuity, regularity, and significance of the services performed would all come into play. But aside from a special *de minimis* rule discussed below, § 864(b) provides that a foreign person who provides services in the United States at any time within a taxable year is automatically deemed to be engaged in a domestic trade or business, regardless of duration, frequency, or other factors. This is the case whether the person performs services as an employee or as an independent contractor.

While the basic rule that performing services means being engaged in trade or business is simply stated, numerous issues arise in identifying the nature of income from services, the location where the services were performed, and whether an amount is really attributable to services or more properly represents some other form of income, such as license fees. For example, if a foreign company makes available some of its workers to provide know-how and training to the workers of a domestic company, it might be difficult to determine the extent to which inter-company payments constitute compensation income versus license fees. In Revenue Ruling 55-17, 1955-1 C.B. 388, the Service found that license treatment should prevail if the personal services are only nominally valuable apart from the license of the know-how itself.

The *de minimis* rule mentioned above is found in § 864(b)(1), which provides a special exception from trade or business status for nominal or incidental services performed by a non-resident alien individual. This is a threshold rule that echoes the one for source that was discussed in Unit 2: presence and employer status limitations must be met and the compensation must not exceed $3,000. If an individual satisfies the criteria, he will not be deemed to be engaged in a domestic trade or business (and he will not be taxed in the United States on the compensation, since it is also foreign source under the rules discussed in Unit 2).

However, if a non-resident alien's domestic source services income exceeds $3,000, a trade or business exists. Compensation for services is normally deemed ECI and thus is generally subject to tax at the regular graduated tax rates of §§ 1 and 55, as applicable. Thus, once the *de minimis* threshold is exceeded, the full amount of compensation is ECI, not just the excess over $3,000.

Recalling the discussion regarding the policy behind the similar *de minimis* source rule of § 861(a)(3) discussed in Unit 2, it seems clear that these thresholds, if they were ever significant, have been eroded to the point of near irrelevance today, as they have never been adjusted to account for inflation. But they do raise the question of whether thresholds are appropriate and if so, why this ever-increasingly obsolete rule persists on the books.

8.04   Real Property Activity as a Trade or Business

Unlike performing services, merely owning United States real property does not automatically mean that a person is engaged in a domestic trade or business. As discussed in Units 7 and 9, however, two rules permit or require certain income derived from real property by foreign persons to be treated as ECI even if no trade or business exists. First, under §§ 871(d) (for individuals) and 881(d) (for corporations), foreign persons may make a "net income election" to treat income derived from United States real property as ECI. Second, § 897(a) treats gains and losses derived from sales and other dispositions of United States real property interests as if that gain or loss were ECI.

In Unit 7, Problem 7-1 illustrated why a foreign person might prefer to make a net income election under §§ 871(d) or 881(d) (as applicable). The reason is that as ECI, deductions are allowed for related expenses and the graduated rates apply; otherwise, no deductions are allowed and the flat rate of 30 percent applies.

However, § 897(a) is not a pro-taxpayer rule. In the absence of § 897(a), foreign persons might avoid United States tax on their gains from the sale of United States real property altogether, since these gains (if sourced on the basis of the seller's residency) would likely be foreign-source or might avoid the tax under § 871(a)(2). Instead of reducing a potentially higher gross basis tax to a lower net basis graduated one as the §§ 871 and 881 net income election does, § 897 serves to allow

United States taxation where none would otherwise be imposed.

The net income election treats certain income as ECI, but it does not cause a person to be otherwise engaged in a trade or business. A foreign person's real property activity will be considered to be engaged in a trade or business only if it meets the criteria discussed above. Additional rules that apply to foreign holders of interests in United States real property are discussed in Unit 9.

8.05   Sales Activity as a Trade or Business

Limited authority exists regarding when activity involving the sale of inventory within the United States constitutes a domestic trade or business. It is generally assumed that a domestic trade or business probably exists if a foreign person maintains a stock of inventory in the United States and has a dependent agent pursuing sales efforts (such as an employee or an unrelated person acting on an exclusive or near exclusive basis for the person).

Although less clear-cut, a foreign person will also probably have a domestic trade or business if it or its dependent agents conduct significant marketing activity and maintain a stock of inventory in the United States from which it fills orders. If a foreign person ships inventory to a United States-based dependent or independent agent on a consignment basis, such shipments, coupled with the sales efforts of the agent, will probably constitute a domestic trade or business. In a consignment arrangement, the foreign seller ships its products to a United States sales agent who has possession of the products and markets them to customers, but title remains with the foreign seller. Using agency theory, the foreign seller will be viewed as maintaining a stock of inventory in the United States.

8.06   Purchasing Activity as a Trade or Business

A foreign person should not be viewed as being engaged in a United States trade or business simply because it purchases products in the United States for sale outside the United States. However, a high volume of purchases and a highly sophisticated service component together with certain sales activity (even if such sales are not to United States persons) may lead to a finding of a trade or business, as occurred in the *Balanovski* case (excerpted in Part D of this Unit).

8.07   The Force of Attraction Doctrine

At one time, if a foreign person was engaged in a domestic trade or business, all of his United States source income, business-related or not, was attributed to his business under a concept called the "force of attraction" rule. When this was the rule, all domestic source income was subject to United States tax under the regular graduated rates, regardless of its connection to the trade or business. For foreign persons doing business in the United States, it was thought that the force of attraction rule would tend to stifle unrelated passive investment activity. As a result, the rule has long since changed so that income must bear an "effective connection" to the taxpayer's business before being subject to tax in the United States. However, some remnants of the force of attraction doctrine remain in the rules relating to ECI, discussed below.

8.08   Effectively Connected Income

Without a trade or business, a foreign person cannot generally have ECI. This simple rule is confirmed in Regulation § 1.864-3(a). However, if a domestic trade or business exists, it is treated in much the same manner as a United States person conducting a domestic trade or business. Under §§ 871(b) and 882, all of the income effectively connected with a domestic trade or business is taxed on a net basis at graduated rates. This ensures that a foreign person bears a tax burden on domestic business income roughly equivalent to that borne by domestic persons.

Nevertheless, a number of variations apply in computing a foreign person's effectively connected net income ultimately subject to tax. Generally, a foreign person determines its ECI following a sequence of three or four steps, depending on the circumstances.

First, the gross ECI derived in the foreign person's domestic trade or business is segregated from other foreign and domestic source income which is not effectively connected with the business. Second, expenses related to the domestic trade or business are segregated. Third, these expenses are allocated among categories of gross income. Fourth, if necessary, the expenses may be further apportioned among foreign and domestic source income within a class of income. The net ECI thereby determined is taxed under the graduated tax rates applicable to domestic corporations or citizens and residents, as the case may be. The following sections address each of the four steps to determining net ECI.

8.09   Step One: Identification of Gross Effectively Connected Income

The first step in taxing a foreign person engaged in a United States trade or business involves separating the ECI from other income. Under § 864(c), ECI encompasses three principal categories of income: capital gain or loss from United States sources and fixed or determinable income (FDAP income); all other United States source income; and certain foreign source income. Some income items relating to real property also constitute ECI; these more complex rules are discussed in Unit 9.

8.10   FDAP Income as ECI

In general, under § 864(c)(2), a foreign person who conducts a domestic trade or business and receives domestic source FDAP income items described in §§ 871 or 881 may be required to treat these items as ECI. In some cases, § 864(c)(2) is advantageous to foreign taxpayers since it causes their FDAP income items to be taxed on a net basis at graduated rates rather than subject to a gross basis tax.

Regulation § 1.864-4 provides rules for segregating domestic source passive income from other domestic source income and establishes two tests for assessing whether FDAP income items will be treated as ECI. The "asset use" test, described in part (c)(2) of the Regulation, applies mainly to determinations involving investment income that does not directly derive from the business activity. This test seeks to distinguish income derived from holding investment assets from that generated by using assets in the day-to-day operation of the business. It is primarily relevant to foreign persons engaged in manufacturing or selling tangible goods in the United States.

The "business activities" test, described in part (c)(3) of the Regulation, applies mainly to passive income that arises directly from the active conduct of the trade or business. This test is primarily relevant to foreign persons conducting service-intensive businesses or dealing with the licensing of intangible assets. For example, dividends, interest, and gains derived from buying and selling stock and securities by an investment company is ECI as described in example 1 of Regulation § 1.864-4(c)(3). The business activities test looks to whether the activities of the domestic trade or business are a material factor in realizing the investment income. If so, the income is ECI. Unlike the asset use test, which focuses narrowly on the role of particular income-generating assets in business operations, the business activities test focuses on broader measures of the degree of correlation between the business activities and the investment income.

8.11   All Other United States Source Income as ECI

The two tests of § 864(c)(2) omit perhaps the most significant class of business profits: that derived from sales of inventory. Gain realized from manufacturing or buying and selling inventory goods is not considered FDAP income. Inventory gain is therefore the main subject of § 864(c)(3), which introduces what is sometimes referred to as the residual force of attraction rule. In essence, if a foreign person has a United States trade or business, § 864(c)(3) treats all of the person's United States source income, gain, or loss which is not described in §§ 871 and 881 (other than the items already included under § 864(c)(2)), as ECI. However, § 865(e)(2) provides a major exception to this rule if the inventory sale originates from a foreign office or other fixed place of business which materially participates in the sale. In that case, if the sale is by a non-resident, the property is sold for use, disposition, or consumption outside the United States, and title passes outside of the United States, the inventory may be deemed foreign source.

8.12   Effectively Connected Foreign Source Income

Section 864(c)(4) sets out the final significant category of ECI. Normally, income, gain, or loss from foreign sources is not considered ECI, but § 864(c)(4) provides a list of types of foreign source income that may be treated as such.

The main types of foreign source income that will be treated as ECI are listed in § 864(c)(4)(B): certain rents or royalties from intangibles, certain dividends or interest derived in banking, financing, or trading activities, and gains from foreign inventory sales. These kinds of income are treated as ECI only if the foreign person maintains a United States office or other fixed place of business (OFPB) and the income is attributable to that OFPB.

The rule of § 864(c)(4) was introduced as a means of preventing foreign persons from using the United States as a tax haven. Without § 864(c)(4) in place, a foreign company from a country that did not tax foreign income could set up a sales office in the United States through which it sold inventory to customers in other countries, with title passing outside the United States. Under the old title passage rules, the sales income was foreign source from a United States perspective and presumably foreign source from the home country's perspective as well. As a result, neither the home country nor the United States imposed tax. The rule of § 865(e)(2) has reduced the impact of § 864(c)(4) because § 865(e)(2) will usually cause such transactions to result in domestic source income.

Section 864(c)(4) was designed to prevent this conduit structure and is intended to capture only income that has its economic genesis in the United States. Thus, under § 864(c)(5)(B), income will not be attributable to a United States OFPB unless that establishment was a material factor in the realization of that income. A United States office will not satisfy this standard unless it provides a significant contribution to the production of the income and its activities are an essential economic element in the production of the income in question.

Regulation § 1.864-7(a)(2) provides that whether an OFPB exists depends on the facts and circumstances of each case, with particular regard to "the nature of the taxpayer's trade or business and the physical facilities actually required by the taxpayer in the ordinary course of the conduct of his trade or business." In general, a fixed facility is needed, but where management functions occur is not necessarily determinative. Special rules are provided in § 864(c)(5)(A) with regard to the offices in the United States of various agents employed by foreign persons.

8.13 Step Two: Segregating Expenses

Once the taxpayer ascertains the amount of gross ECI, the next step is to determine the extent to which deductions against that income are permitted. As a general rule, foreign persons may only deduct expenses to the extent they are related to the ECI. Thus, if a foreign person is engaged in a domestic trade or business and is also engaged in some other activity (such as investment activity or foreign activity), the person must allocate expenses between income derived from its United States trade or business and income earned from the other activities. *Stemkowski v. Commissioner*, excerpted in Part D of this Unit, explores some of the difficulties in identifying deductible expenses.

The allocation of deductions is often a matter of vital importance for foreign persons. The procedures for the allocation of deductions are set forth in Regulation § 1.861-8. These Regulations apply to both inbound and outbound transactions, but the discussion below is confined to the treatment of inbound transactions. In general, with respect to inbound transactions, the Regulation creates a two-tiered method for dealing with deductions: first, *allocation* and then, if necessary, *apportionment*.

The allocation process is a threshold determination that focuses on whether an expense is directly related to a particular class of gross income. In effect, the task of allocating deductions involves matching deductions with the gross income to which they most directly relate. Once deductions are matched with a particular class, the composition of that class must be analyzed to determine whether it is comprised solely of United States source income (a "residual grouping"), solely foreign source income (a "statutory grouping"), or some combination thereof.

Apportionment of allocated deductions within a class of gross income is required only in the last scenario, when a class of income is determined to include both United States and foreign source income. When apportionment is required, the deduction already allocated to that mixed-source class of gross income under the first-tier allocation procedure is, in effect, "sub-allocated" between the foreign and United States source income in the class.

Expenses directly related to the rendition of services (such as salaries and rents) are allocable to the class of gross income derived from services. Some expenses, such as supervisory or general and administrative expense, are not definitely related to any class of income and are thus most likely allocable to *all* classes of gross income. As various classes of gross income (e.g., income from services and interest income) may include both foreign and United States source gross income, allocated expenses must further be apportioned between those two types of income. The mechanics of these processes are discussed in the following sections.

8.14   Step Three: Allocation

The allocation process essentially entails matching deductions to the category of gross income to which those deductions most factually relate. As a general rule, a deduction is allocated to the gross income category to which that deduction is "definitely related." A deduction is definitely related to a class of gross income if it is incurred as a result of, or incident to, an activity or in connection with property from which such class of gross income is derived.

Classes of gross income to which deductions are allocated are not predetermined. The Regulations provide that the gross income to which a specific deduction is definitely related is referred to as a "class of gross income." Instead of first delineating certain classes of gross income and allocating deductions amongst these classes, the classes of gross income to which deductions are allocated is driven and defined by the nature of the deduction being allocated. A class of gross income may consist of one or more items (or subdivisions thereof) of the gross income categories enumerated in § 61. For instance, deductions for real estate taxes on a rental property would directly relate to the rental class of gross income.

To compound the ambiguity permeating this Regulation and, in particular, the definitely related standard, it is entirely possible under the Regulations that a deduction may not bear a definite relationship to *any* particular class of gross income. In such a case, the deduction is treated as definitely related and allocable to *all* of the taxpayer's gross income. For example, such an expense could include certain general and administrative salaries for top level management of a foreign corporation that cannot be traced to a given class of income.

Such unmatched expenses, by definition, bypass the allocation process, but are ratably apportioned between the statutory groupings (i.e., foreign and United States source gross income) comprising the taxpayer's gross income. Allocations must be made even if no gross income has been received or accrued within the relevant class of gross income. Moreover, allocation is appropriate even though the deduction to be allocated exceeds the amount of income in the gross income class.

8.15 Step Four: Apportionment

The process of apportioning deductions occurs within a class of gross income and matches deductions with the foreign or United States source income to which they are related. The apportionment of deductions is crucial in many settings. For foreign taxpayers, the apportionment process bears on distinguishing effectively connected gross income from other gross income.

For these purposes, once a deduction has been allocated to a class of gross income, the source of the gross income item(s) comprising that class must be determined. If the class consists exclusively of foreign source (or effectively connected) income (the "statutory grouping") or exclusively of United States source (or non-effectively connected) income (the "residual grouping"), the taxpayer fortunately may end its analysis after the allocation process is completed. The deduction is allocated in its entirety to the income in the statutory or residual grouping, whichever is appropriate.

Taxpayers analyzing deductions which bear no direct relationship to *any* gross income are also fortunate from a computational vantage point. These expenses bypass the initial allocation process and are merely apportioned on a ratable basis between groupings.

If the class of gross income to which a deduction has been allocated is comprised of both United States and foreign source income (or effectively connected and non-effectively connected income), the deduction must be apportioned between those two groupings of income. The apportionment process must be accomplished in a fact-based manner which "reflects to a reasonably close extent the factual relationship" between the deduction and the gross income grouping. Examples of bases and factors which may be considered in making this factual determination include comparisons of sales, gross receipts, cost of goods sold, profit contributions, expenses and intangible costs incurred in generating the activity, and gross income.

These possible apportionment bases are by no means exclusive. This open-ended list of bases, coupled with the malleable factual relationship standard, renders the apportionment process ripe for tax planning. Of course, fields ripe for planning are fallow for certainty. The tax adviser should explore and analyze all possible apportionment bases which suggest a relationship between the grouping and the deduction to ascertain the most advantageous apportionment method.

Finally, additional rules apply for allocating and apportioning certain specific types of expenses, the principal one being interest expense. The allocation of interest expense is generally described in Regulation § 1.861-8(e)(2) and the rules are laid out in Regulations §§ 1.861-9T through 1.861-13T. As a general rule, Regulation § 1.861-9T(a) adopts the view that interest expense is fungible, reasoning that borrowing money for one activity allows more money to be devoted to other activities. This means that borrowing for one activity really serves to facilitate multiple activities. Accordingly, deductible interest expense is usually allocated among all activities.

There are a number of rules and exceptions to the interest expensing rules, including separate rules for foreign corporations and a number of anti-abuse provisions designed to protect the United States tax base from overly creative tax planning. As always, the particular facts and circumstances of a given transaction will require a thorough analysis of the Code and Regulations, as well as all available guidance.[1] Some key cases and rulings regarding the issues that arise in determining net ECI are included in Part D below, but these provide merely an overview of the breadth and depth of issues involved in the treatment of foreign-owned United States business income.

D. REFERENCE MATERIALS

- Revenue Ruling 88-3
- Revenue Ruling 58-63
- *Stemkowski v. Commissioner*
- *United States v. Balanovski*
- *Scottish American Investment Company, Ltd. v. Commissioner*

REVENUE RULING 88-3
1988-1 C.B. 268

Rev. Rul. 73-227, 1973-1 C.B. 338, examines the activities of X, the foreign financing subsidiary of a United States parent, and holds that the United States source interest income that X earns is effectively connected with a United States trade or business under section 864(c) of the Internal Revenue Code of 1954.

Section 864(b) of the Code and the regulations promulgated thereunder provide rules for determining whether a foreign taxpayer is engaged in a trade or business within the United States. (These rules may differ in some respects from those used in determining whether a taxpayer is engaged in a trade or business under other sections of the Code.) The determination whether X is engaged in a trade or business within the United States must therefore be made by applying these rules to the facts described in the ruling. Rev. Rul. 73-227, however, does not do so. The ruling simply concludes without discussion of the applicable statute and regulations that X is engaged in a trade or business within the United States. Because the ruling does not discuss and apply the proper legal standard, its conclusion may be unsound.

In addition, the determination whether a taxpayer is engaged in a trade or business within the United States is highly factual. Such a determination is not ordinarily made in an advance ruling. See sections 2.01 and 4.01(2) of Rev. Proc. 87-6, 1987-1 I.R.B. 45.

Accordingly, Rev. Rul. 73-227 is revoked. Determinations under section 864 of the

---

[1] This complex and often changing area of the law is beyond the scope of this casebook, but for further guidance, see PHILIP F. POSTLEWAITE, INTERNATIONAL TAXATION, CORPORATE AND INDIVIDUAL (Carolina Academic Press, 9th ed. 2014).

Code must be made by applying the regulations promulgated thereunder to the facts and circumstances of each case.

REVENUE RULING 58-63
1958-1 C.B. 624

Advice has been requested whether a nonresident alien individual, owning a racing stable in France and engaged in the operation of same for profit, who enters a horse in a race in the United States, is exempt from United States income tax on the winnings therefrom.

A citizen and resident of France owned and operated a horse racing stable, located in France, for profit. He was invited to enter an outstanding horse in a race to be held in the United States. He and the racing association agreed that the horse would not compete in any other races while in the United States. The racing association invited him to view the race and participate in the social events connected therewith. The invitation was accepted. The horse won the race and the owner was paid the winner's purse.

The operation of a racing stable for profit is a business enterprise. The entry of a horse in a race in this country constitutes being "engaged in trade or business within the United States," within the meaning of section 871(c) of the Internal Revenue Code of 1954. Accordingly, income derived therefore is subject to United States income tax unless exempted by some other provision of law.

STEMKOWSKI v. COMMISSIONER
United States Court of Appeals, Second Circuit
690 F.2d 40 (1982)

OAKES, CIRCUIT JUDGE:

This supposed test case involves the taxability of a Canadian citizen who formerly played professional hockey for the New York Rangers of the National Hockey League (NHL). As a nonresident alien, Stemkowski was subject to United States tax on that portion of his income connected with his performance of services in this country, and entitled to deduct expenditures relating to such United States income. . . . We affirm in part, and reverse and remand in part.

The . . . major issues on appeal are:

. . .

2. Whether the Tax Court correctly held that taxpayer was not entitled to deduct certain off season physical conditioning expenses claimed as ordinary and necessary business expenses.

3. Whether the Tax Court correctly held that taxpayer was not entitled to various other deductions for what he claimed were ordinary and necessary business expenses, including those for newspapers, magazines, telephone, television, "promotional" activities, and gifts to trainers.

4. Whether the Tax Court correctly held that taxpayer was not entitled to deduct

sales taxes because they were not connected with the conduct of his trade or business within the United States, or to deduct amounts withheld from his salary to pay premiums on disability insurance. . . .

DISCUSSION

. . .

2. Off Season Physical Conditioning Expenses

Stemkowski claims deductions for his off season expenses on golf, bowling, tennis, running, swimming, and using a YMCA and a health club, as business expenses under I.R.C. § 162, on the theory that they were necessary to meet an obligation in the NHL contract to keep in good physical condition throughout the year. The Tax Court reasoned, however, that off season conditioning was related only to arriving fit at training camp and therefore held that Stemkowski's conditioning expenses were nondeductible because [they were] allocable to income earned in Canada. This holding is clearly erroneous. Off season conditioning contributes not only to the fitness required of players on the first day of training camp under Paragraph 2(a) of the contract but also to the fitness required throughout the regular season under Paragraph 2(b) of the contract. Thus, Stemkowski's off season conditioning expenses were at least in part connected to United States income.

Because of its erroneous reasoning the Tax Court did not reach the question, on which both sides presented evidence, whether Stemkowski's off season conditioning expenses were deductible under § 162 as ordinary and necessary for business, or were nondeductible under § 262 as for personal fun and relaxation. Not everything that is done to develop one's body, even if one is a professional athlete, is necessarily for business. For a hockey player, weight lifting, jogging, bicycling, and other exercises to strengthen and coordinate the body may well be at the business end of the spectrum, because these activities may contribute directly to professional hockey playing ability. Golf, tennis, squash, or bowling, however, at least for a hockey player, may well be at the fun and relaxation end of the spectrum, especially in light of Stemkowski's testimony that he played golf to relax, played tennis and squash for fun, and bowled with a girlfriend.

There is no general rule that can be laid down in connection with such expenses, and we remand to the Tax Court to make a factual determination, on the basis of its familiarity with the record and the demeanor of the witnesses, as to which of these expenses were deductible. We remand also for allocation of the off season conditioning expenses between Canadian and United States source income. With respect to some of the claimed conditioning expenses, e.g., club membership, the Tax Court will also need to determine whether the taxpayer has satisfied the substantiation requirements of § 274.

3. Miscellaneous Business Expenses

Stemkowski also sought to deduct as business expenses the costs of magazines and newspapers in which he read hockey news; the costs of "promotional" activities such as entertaining fans, team members, and media people, purchasing hockey tickets for friends, having his hair styled, and answering fan mail; the tips he paid his trainers; and some of the costs of maintaining a telephone and television. The Tax Court disallowed these deductions on the erroneous ground that they were not required by the employer. While a requirement by an employer that an employee make an expenditure may be one factor weighing in favor of the employee's right to a deduction, it is not a prerequisite for the deduction. Section 162(a) requires only that the expense be a necessary and ordinary expense paid or incurred during the taxable year in carrying on a trade or business. For all expenses except those for hockey publications and for fan mail, Stemkowski either failed to establish deductibility, or failed to meet the substantiation requirements of § 274(d), which applies to travel expenses, expenditures on activities or facilities generally considered for entertainment, amusement, or recreation, or gift expenses.

The purchase of general newspapers is personal and cannot be deducted. Because Stemkowski's claimed purchase of hockey journals might be deductible as relating to his work, however, and because no substantiation under § 274(d) is required for such expenses, we remand for a determination whether Stemkowski's "hockey news" deduction meets the "ordinary and necessary" business expense standard of § 162. . . .

4. Sales Tax and Disability Insurance Deductions

Only three types of expenses not related to income from a trade or business in the United States are allowed as deductions to nonresident aliens under § 873(b): casualty or theft losses; charitable contributions; and personal exemption(s). A nonresident alien's United States sales taxes are not deductible unless shown to be business related. Stemkowski failed to make this showing; for example, taxpayer's sales taxes were not shown to be business related, he specifically deducted the sales tax on wedding ring purchases, and these expenses are not otherwise deductible under § 873(b). Disability insurance premiums, even for hockey players, are personal and not business expenses. Thus, the Tax Court properly disallowed Stemkowski's sales tax and disability insurance deductions. . . .

UNITED STATES v. BALANOVSKI
United States Court of Appeals, Second Circuit
236 F.2d 298 (1956)

. . .

Defendants Balanovski and Horenstein were copartners in the Argentine partnership, Compania Argentina de Intercambio Comercial (CADIC), Balanovski having an 80 per cent interest and Horenstein, a 20 per cent interest. Balanovski, an Argentine citizen, came to the United States on or about December 20, 1946, and remained in this country for approximately ten months, except for an absence of a few weeks in the spring of 1947 when he returned to Argentina. His purpose in coming here was the transaction of partnership business; and while here, he made extensive purchases and sales of trucks and other equipment resulting in a profit to the partnership of some $7,763,702.20.

His usual mode of operation in the United States was to contact American suppliers and obtain offers for the sale of equipment. He then communicated the offers to his father-in-law, Horenstein, in Argentina. Horenstein, in turn, submitted them at a markup to an agency of the Argentine Government, Instituto Argentino de Promocion del Intercambio (IAPI), which was interested in purchasing such equipment. If IAPI accepted an offer, Horenstein would notify Balanovski and the latter would accept the corresponding original offer of the American supplier. In the meantime IAPI would cause a letter of credit in favor of Balanovski to be opened with a New York bank. Acting under the terms of the letter of credit Balanovski would assign a portion of it, equal to CADIC's purchase price, to the United States supplier. The supplier could then draw on the New York bank against the letter of credit by sight draft for 100 per cent invoice value accompanied by (1) a commercial invoice billing Balanovski, (2) an inspection certificate, (3) a nonnegotiable ware-house or dock receipt issued in the name of the New York bank for the account of IAPI's Argentine agent, and (4) an insurance policy covering all risks to the merchandise up to delivery F.O.B. New York City. Then, if the purchase was one on which CADIC was to receive a so-called quantity discount or commission, the supplier would pay Balanovski the amount of the discount. These discounts, paid after delivery of the goods and full payment to the suppliers, amounted to $858,595.90, constituting funds which were delivered in the United States.

After the supplier had received payment, Balanovski would draw on the New York bank for the unassigned portion of the letter of credit, less 1 per cent of the face amount, by submitting a sight draft accompanied by (1) a commercial invoice billing IAPI, (2) an undertaking to ship before a certain date, and (3) an insurance policy covering all risks to the merchandise up to delivery F.A.S. United States Sea Port. The bank would then deliver the nonnegotiable warehouse receipt that it had received from the supplier to Balanovski on trust receipt and his undertaking to deliver a full set of shipping documents, including a clean on board bill of lading issued to the order of IAPI's Argentine agent, with instructions to notify IAPI. It would also notify the warehouse that Balanovski was authorized to withdraw the merchandise. Upon delivery of these shipping documents to the New York bank Balanovski would receive the remaining 1 per cent due under the terms of the letter of credit. Although Balanovski arranged for shipping the goods to Argentina, IAPI paid shipping expenses and made its own arrangement there for marine insurance. The New York bank would forward the bill of lading, Balanovski's invoice billing IAPI, and the other documents required by the letter of credit (not including the supplier's invoice billing Balanovski) to IAPI's agent in Argentina.

Twenty-four transactions following substantially this pattern took place during 1947. Other transactions were also effected which conformed to a substantially similar pattern, except that CADIC engaged the services of others to facilitate the acquisition of goods and their shipment to Argentina. And other offers were sent to Argentina, for which no letters of credit were opened. Several letters of credit were opened which remained either in whole or in part unused. In every instance of a completed transaction Balanovski was paid American money in New York, and in every instance he deposited it in his own name with New York banks. Balanovski never ordered material from a supplier for which he did not have an order and letter of credit from IAPI.

Balanovski's activities on behalf of CADIC in the United States were numerous and varied and required the exercise of initiative, judgment, and executive responsibility. They far transcended the routine or merely clerical. Thus he conferred and bargained with American bankers. He inspected goods and made trips out of New York State in order to buy and inspect the equipment in which he was trading. He made sure the goods were placed in warehouses and aboard ship. He tried to insure that CADIC would not repeat the errors in supplying inferior equipment that had been made by some of its competitors. And while here he attempted "to develop" "other business" for CADIC.

Throughout his stay in the United States Balanovski employed a Miss Alice Devine as a secretary. She used, and he used, the Hotel New Weston in New York City as an office. His address on the documents involved in the transactions was given as the Hotel New Weston. His supplier contacted him there, and that was the place where his letters were typed and his business appointments arranged and kept. Later Miss Devine opened an office on Rector Street in New York City, which he also used. When he returned to Argentina for a brief time in 1947 he left a power of attorney with Miss Devine. This gave her wide latitude in arranging for shipment of goods and in signing his name to all sorts of documents, including checks. When he left for Argentina again at the end of his 10-month stay, he left with Miss Devine the same power of attorney, which she used throughout the balance of 1947 to arrange for and complete the shipment of goods and bank the profits.

When Balanovski left the United States in October 1947 he filed a departing alien income tax return, on which he reported no income. In March 1948 the Commissioner of Internal Revenue assessed $2,122,393.91 as taxes due on income for the period during which Balanovski was in the United States. In May 1953 the Commissioner made a jeopardy assessment against Balanovski in the amount of $3,954,422.41 and gave him notice of it. At the same time a similar jeopardy assessment, followed by a timely notice of deficiency, was made against Horenstein in the amount of $1,672,209.90, representing his alleged share of CADIC's profits on the above described sales of United States goods.

The government brought the present action to foreclose a federal tax lien on $511,655.58 and $42,529.49 — amounts of partnership funds held in two United States banks — and to obtain personal judgments against Balanovski and Horenstein in the sums of $6,722,625.54 (of which $5,050,415.64 is now sought on appeal) and $1,672,209.90 respectively. Balanovski and Horenstein were served with process by mail in Argentina . . . ; and Miss Devine, the purported agent of Balanovski, was personally served in New York. Defendants then appeared by their attorneys and proceeded to defend the action.

. . .

The district court held that CADIC was not engaged in a trade or business within the United States . . . but that each of the partners was liable for certain taxes because Balanovski as an individual was so engaged in business and therefore taxable . . . , while Horenstein received "fixed or determinable annual or periodical gains, profits, and income" . . . . We, on the contrary, hold that the partnership CADIC was engaged in business in the United States and that hence the two copartners were taxable for their share of its profits from sources within the United States.

. . .

CADIC was actively and extensively engaged in business in the United States in 1947. Its 80 per cent partner, Balanovski, under whose hat 80 per cent of the business may be thought to reside, was in this country soliciting orders, inspecting merchandise, making purchases, and (as will later appear) completing sales. While maintaining regular contact with his home office, he was obviously making important business decisions. He maintained a bank account here for partnership funds. He operated from a New York office through which a major portion of CADIC's business was transacted.

We cannot accept the view of the trial judge that, since Balanovski was a mere purchasing agent, his presence in this country was insufficient to justify a finding that CADIC was doing business in the United States. We need not consider the question whether, if Balanovski (an 80 per cent partner) were merely engaged in purchasing goods here, the partnership could be deemed to be engaged in business, since he was doing more than purchasing. Acting for CADIC he engaged in numerous transactions wherein he both purchased and sold goods in this country, earned his profits here, and participated in other activities, pertaining to the transaction of business.

. . .

As copartners of CADIC, Balanovski and Horenstein are taxable for the amount of partnership profits from sources within the United States under the statutory provisions cited above. The district court held them taxable only upon the "discounts" or "commissions" paid CADIC by the suppliers after completion of the sales transactions, not upon the total profits of the sales. This solution of the problem is in seeming conflict with the usual rule that discounts received as inducements for quality purchasing are considered as reducing the purchasers' cost for tax purposes. Further, isolation of the discount from the sales transaction is not in accord with preferred accounting technique. Isolation of the discount for tax purposes would be more appropriate if the court considered the partnership as a broker receiving commissions, rather than as a vendor. But we need not consider whether the circumstances here justified the segregation for tax purposes of the discounts from the remainder of the sales profits . . . for we hold the total profits on these transactions, including the discounts, to be taxable in full.

. . .

On the appeal of the defendant taxpayers the decision below is affirmed. On the appeal of the United States of America the judgment of the district court is reversed and the action is remanded for the entry of a judgment of recovery based upon a computation of taxes due in accordance with this opinion.

SCOTTISH AMERICAN INVESTMENT CO., LTD.
v. COMMISSIONER
United States Tax Court
12 T.C. 49 (1949)

FINDINGS OF FACT

. . .

Petitioners are investment trusts, organized under the laws of Great Britain, with principal offices in Edinburgh, Scotland. . . .

Each has been engaged in the business of investing the funds of its security holders for the primary purpose of deriving income from investments.

During the years before us each had a board of directors, which met at the home offices. All decisions as to the purchase and sale of securities and as to investment policies were made by the home offices. All purchases and sales were handled directly by petitioners through resident brokers, with confirmatory advices usually being sent to petitioners' United States office, located in Jersey City, New Jersey.

. . .

Late in 1936 petitioners arranged for the establishment of an office in the United States, which, during the years involved, was located at 26 Journal Square in Jersey City. The purpose for the establishment of the office was "to enable petitioners to keep in closer touch with their large United States investments, to do themselves what had formerly been done for them by others, and to gain certain tax advantages."

. . .

From the inception, the American office was managed by a member of an accounting firm, who was appointed assistant secretary of each of the petitioners.

In 1942 and 1943 J. Wallace Gentles, C. P. A., a partner in the accounting firm of Barrow, Wade, Guthrie & Co., was the active assistant secretary. He succeeded Walter A. Cooper, who resigned from the position in 1941. The duties remained the same. In order to facilitate his work, there was a trunk telephone line between petitioners' office and the office of the accounting firm of which Gentles was a partner.

As assistant secretary, he received remuneration from petitioners, which, pursuant to his agreement with his accounting firm, was paid over to it, and was used in part by it to pay the salaries of the staff working in the Jersey City office, all of whom were on the accounting firm's pay roll.

Each petitioner conferred upon the assistant secretary general authority to attend to its United States affairs and represent its interests in this country, and specific authority with respect to the following matters: [t]he collection of interest and dividends, and the deposit of such income in each petitioner's bank account; the maintenance of complete records in respect of all the security holdings and all the transactions of each petitioner in the United States; the execution and filing of proxies in connection with each petitioner's securities; the making of periodical reports by cable and letter to the home office of each petitioner on economic, political, or other developments in the United States; the payment of all local expenses of petitioners, such as office expenses, salaries, telephone and telegraph bills, and the general miscellaneous expenses of running an office in the United States; the completion and filing of tax returns for each petitioner; and the withdrawal of funds from each petitioner's bank account in the United States in amounts up to $5,000 in any calendar month on the assistant secretary's signature and up to any amount with the countersignature of a director.

Petitioners' American securities were not in the custody of their assistant secretary, but were in the custody of J. P. Morgan & Co. and the National City Bank of New York, which reported periodically to the Jersey City office on the securities in their possession. The list of these securities was checked and confirmed by the Jersey City office.

The registered securities of each petitioner held in the United States were, with minor exceptions, registered in the names of nominees designated by J. P. Morgan & Co. and the bank. With minor exceptions in the case of British and Second British, the only securities registered in the names of the nominees so designated were petitioners' securities.

The income from the securities registered in the names of nominees which was paid to, and collected by, each petitioner was paid to each petitioner pursuant to standing directions given by the nominees to the respective paying corporations.

Prior to the opening of petitioners' American office in 1936, the functions undertaken by that office were performed by the banks.

The activities regularly carried on by petitioners in their American office after its establishment were primarily of a clerical nature and consisted of the following:

1. Dividends on each petitioner's securities held in the United States as received at the Jersey City office were deposited by that office in the petitioners' bank accounts. Interest received on coupon bonds was usually collected by the bank having custody of such securities, while interest on registered bonds was collected by the Jersey City office. All amounts of income, whether dividends or interest, were entered in petitioners' books of account and in each case it was ascertained by reference to financial publications and dividend services that the income collected by each petitioner was correct and the exact amount to which it was entitled.

2. Original books and records were maintained in the United States, in which were recorded all of petitioners' transactions in this country. The books of each petitioner consisted of a security ledger, a general ledger, and a cash book, which were looseleaf, and a general journal, which was a bound volume. In addition, each petitioner maintained in its United States office debit and credit vouchers in which all sales and purchases of securities and disbursements of every character were entered.

3. Requests for proxies were studied to determine whether or not it was in the best interests of petitioners to grant the proxy, and generally the assistant secretary in this country exercised his own judgment as to the granting of proxies.

In doubtful cases, the home offices were consulted, but in most of these cases the home offices instructed the assistant secretary to act according to his individual judgment.

4. From published material received from corporations, the stock of which was held by petitioners, the Jersey City office obtained information as to stock dividends and stock rights. Such of this information as seemed important was sent on to the home offices. Annual reports of these corporations were also sent to the home offices; and also occasional reports on conditions in the United States, including statistical data published by the Federal Reserve Bank and the New York Times. Reports and recommendations were made in connection with corporate reorganizations in which petitioners were interested.

5. All United States tax returns were prepared, executed, filed, and the tax liability paid, by or under the supervision of the assistant secretary in this country. These included income taxes, withholding taxes, social security taxes, property taxes, and franchise taxes.

6. On or about the 15th of December of each year, information was sent to the home offices for inclusion in the annual reports of petitioners. This information contained advice as to transactions which had taken place up to the date it was sent and an estimate of income and expenses anticipated between that date and the end of December. On the last day of the year, to avoid delay, the information previously submitted was brought up to date by cablegram.

. . .

During 1942 and 1943 each petitioner used the American office as in previous years for the regular performance in this country of routine and clerical functions incident and helpful to the business which it carried on in Scotland.

In 1942 and 1943 petitioners were not engaged in trade or business in the United States. . . .

OPINION

. . . We must decide whether, during 1942 and 1943, petitioners were "engaged in trade or business within the United States" and, therefore, are resident foreign corporations and entitled to the tax treatment accorded such corporations. The question before us is not whether any foreign investment trust can, under any circumstances, be considered as being engaged in business within the United States under the applicable code sections. It is, rather, whether these particular foreign investment trusts, petitioners herein, can be said, on the record before us, to be engaged in business within the United States, notwithstanding the following facts: All judgments as to investments, the purchase and sale of securities, and substantially all other major policy decisions were made by officers in the home office of the trusts situated outside of the United States; orders for purchase and sale of securities were executed by petitioners directly through resident banks in the United States; one of the principal purposes for the establishment of the American office was "to gain certain tax advantages;" and the American office's activities were, according to a realistic appraisal of the evidentiary facts, confined to routine and clerical functions performed by the banks prior to 1936.

Since our factual conclusions that all of the major decisions as to petitioners' businesses were made in Scotland and that the activities of the American office were confined to routine and clerical functions are crucial to our decision herein, some discussion in connection therewith is pertinent.

Petitioners, on brief, ascribe the following activities to the business of an investment trust: (1) The investment of funds, (2) the collection of income, (3) the exercise of voting rights, (4) the maintenance of records, (5) the obtaining of information, and (6) miscellaneous activities such as the preparation of tax returns. Petitioners concede that the determination of investment policies was made in Scotland. The record is clear that all decisions as to purchases and sales of securities were made by petitioners' directors or managing secretaries at their home offices, and orders in connection therewith were sent directly from Scotland to resident brokers in the United States. The Jersey City office was advised of these transactions so that it would make the proper entries on its books.

Before the establishment of the Jersey City office, the income of petitioners was collected by the banks. Afterwards, the dividends and interest on petitioners' investments (other than the interest on coupon bonds) were collected by that office, checked as to accuracy of amount, deposited in the bank accounts which it maintained, and remitted to petitioners in Scotland. Nothing in the record indicates that this was other than a routine operation.

With regard to the exercise of voting rights, the certified public accountant who acted as assistant secretary of petitioners in charge of the Jersey City office testified as follows:

Q: Who had authority to deal with proxies received from corporations in whose shares the company had invested?

A: Oh, as Assistant Secretary for each of those companies, the proxies came to my desk and I had to determine whether or not it was the best interests of the company to exercise or grant the proxy. In some cases, where the thing was involved, I would give Edinburg an opportunity to express itself, but on quite a number of occasions they said "we merely leave it to your judgment," or rather in a few cases, because I didn't ask in too many cases. In a few cases in which I asked, they left it to my individual judgment.

Q: Is it fair to state that you acted on proxies without, in the majority of cases, without consulting the head office?

A: Oh, yes.

This quotation constitutes the entire record as to this activity incident to petitioners' business. We draw from it the conclusion that, with regard to the usual case in which no question appeared, proxies were acted upon by the assistant secretary, but with regard to cases in which a question appeared calling for the exercise of judgment as to policy, the matter was referred to the home offices; and in the latter case the home offices usually deferred to the recommendation of the assistant secretary.

The maintenance of records was obviously a routine and clerical activity. The same would be true concerning the information given to petitioners in Edinburgh "in order that they could make out their annual balance sheets and reports . . . to their security holders."

With regard to the obtaining of information, the record shows the testimony of the same witness to be as follows:

Q: Did you send any other information, or make any other reports to the home office periodically?

A: Oh, yes, we keep them fully informed as to the published material received in the Jersey City office from the companies whose stocks we own, whose bonds we own, and kept them informed as to stock dividends and stock rights, and information that appeared to us to be sufficient import to send along to Edinburg.

Bearing in mind that neither this witness (who was a certified public accountant), nor any other employee of petitioners' Jersey City office, was a business analyst or an investment counselor, it would seem that information was forwarded to petitioners in the same routine way as that in which income was remitted.

The only "miscellaneous activities" specified were the preparation of tax returns, the leasing of the Jersey City office, and the payment of expenses, which are routine and, so far as the record shows, incidental activities.

. . .

It seems quite clear . . . that, but for the operation of the Jersey City office, petitioners could not [be deemed to be engaged in a trade or business within the United States]. Whether the establishment of such office and the activities there carried on are sufficient to change this result is a question not free from all doubt. But we believe, under the facts of these proceedings, that those activities are of themselves inadequate, and hence petitioners cannot be considered as resident foreign corporations. It is true that language was used in prior opinions by way of dicta to the effect that the United States office "was used for the regular transaction of business" and "performed vital functions in the taxpayers' investment trust business." But these functions, although of such character and consequence as to permit the conclusion that the office was used for the regular and not casual transaction of business, do not require and do not warrant the conclusion that the business of petitioners was carried on in the United States. . . . In our opinion, the real business of petitioners, the doing of what they were principally organized to do in order to realize profit, was the cooperative management in Scotland of British capital, a large part of which was invested by them in American securities through transactions effected through resident brokers. To this business of petitioners, the business activities of the American office were merely helpfully adjunct. No consequential transactions were effected through or by the direction of the Jersey City office. It functioned primarily as a clerical department performing a number of useful routine and incidental services for petitioners. But it cannot be said here that the local office, even though we look at its activities as a whole, was doing what was principally required to be done by petitioners in order to realize profit, or that its activities constituted a business which petitioners carried on within the United States.

In cases such as these, it is a matter of degree, based upon both a quantitative and a qualitative analysis of the services performed, as to where the line of demarcation should be drawn. It is not so much the volume of the activities of the Jersey City office, although volume of activities may, in some cases, be a factor, but rather their character and the purpose for which the office is established that we believe are determinative. We are not convinced that the services of this local office, quantitatively extensive and useful as they may have been, approached that quality which is necessary in order that petitioners can be characterized as having engaged in business in the United States during the years involved. . . .

. . .

Our conclusion . . . is consistent with the cases and other authorities construing the phrases "doing business" or "engaged in business" in the field of corporation law. We recognize that these cannot be controlling of our question, although their helpfulness need not be entirely disregarded. There, the problem frequently arises under various state constitutional and statutory provisions regulating out-of-state corporations. Such activities as the establishment of an office, performance of incidental transactions, the doing of acts relating solely to internal management, the appointment of an agent, and the acquiring or holding of stock in domestic corporations, have generally been held not to be sufficient to hold that the corporation is doing or engaging in business in the state. Petitioners have done little, if anything, more.

Respondent's determination must be sustained.

Decisions will be entered for respondent.

Unit 9

TAXATION OF BRANCH PROFITS AND INVESTMENT IN UNITED STATES REAL PROPERTY

A. CODE AND REGULATION PROVISIONS

Code   §§ 884(a)–(d), (f)(1)–(2); 897(a)–(c)(4)(A), (e), (g); 1031(h).
Reg.   §§ 1.884-1; 1.897-1(b)(1)–(4)(ii)(A); 1.897-1(d)(1)–(2); 1.897-2(a)–(c)(1); 1.897-6T(a)(1)–(3).

B. PROBLEMS FOR CLASS DISCUSSION

9-1. Vietindo Corporation is a privately-held corporation organized in Vietnam that sells luxury automobiles in its showroom in New York City to United States customers. In all cases, title passes to the customers in the United States. Vietindo rented a showroom and funded its branch operation with a $200,000 contribution. For Year 1, it earned $100,000 of United States net income, paid tax of $35,000, and invested the rest of its earnings in its United States showroom. In Year 2, it earned $200,000 of such net income, paid tax of $70,000, placed the excess earnings in a bank account, and repatriated $50,000 to Vietnam. In Year 3, Vietindo earned $300,000 of net income, paid tax of $105,000, and repatriated $250,000. What is the amount of the branch profits tax, if any, for Years 1–3?

9-2. FC, a foreign corporation, has $100,000 of interest expense allocated to effectively connected income from a United States trade or business for Year 1. Its interest expense payments consist of $55,000 of interest to N, a non-resident individual not engaged in a United States trade or business; $25,000 interest to C Corporation, a foreign corporation owning 15 percent of FC's voting stock; and $20,000 to D Corporation, a Delaware corporation. To what extent is the branch interest tax applicable?

9-3. FC Corporation, a foreign corporation, has $120,000 of interest expense allocable to effectively connected income from a United States trade or business. It pays branch interest in the same amounts as specified in problem 9-2. To what extent is the branch excess interest tax applicable?

9-4. Teo, an individual, is a citizen and resident of Argentina who has never been present in the United States. Teo owned the following assets: (i) 100 shares of the common stock of Y Corporation, a foreign corporation; and (ii) vacant land located in Oregon held as investment property.

149

(a) Assume that Teo realized a $13,000 gain on the sale of the vacant land in Oregon. What are the United States income tax consequences, if any, to Teo?

(b) How would the answer to (a) change if Teo exchanged the vacant land in Oregon for vacant land in Ireland?

(c) How would the answer to (a) change if Teo contributed the vacant land in Oregon to Z Corporation, a domestic corporation, in return for all of its stock?

(d) Assume the facts in (c) occurred in Year 1. In Year 2, Teo sold the Z stock for a gain of $20,000. What are the United States income tax consequences to Teo in Year 2?

(e) How would the answer to (a) change if Teo contributed the vacant land in Oregon to Q Corporation, a foreign corporation, in return for all of its stock?

(f) Assume that Y Corporation, a foreign corporation, owned exclusively real property located in the United States. If Y Corporation sells a parcel of real property to an unrelated purchaser, what United States income tax consequences, if any, arise?

(g) How would the answer to (f) change if Y Corporation did not sell any of its holdings but Teo sold all or a portion of his shares in Y Corporation?

(h) Assume that Teo buys 30 percent of the stock in W Corporation, a domestic corporation, the exclusive holdings of which are United States real property. If Teo sells the stock four years later for a gain of $5,000, what are the United States income tax consequences, if any?

(i) How would the answer to (h) change if Teo purchased and sold a 10-year debenture rather than stock?

(j) How would the result in (h) change if W Corporation was publicly traded?

(k) How would the result in (h) change if W Corporation's real estate holdings comprised only 30 percent of its asset base on the date of sale?

(l) How would the result in (k) change if Teo sold his stock 10 years after its purchase?

C. OVERVIEW

This Unit discusses two important topics that add some complexity to the fundamental rules developed in Units 7 and 8: (1) the "branch profits taxes," and (2) the taxation of United States real property interests. A few items of interest in each of these specialized areas are highlighted but an exhaustive analysis is not provided — many special rules are omitted, and others are dealt with in a simplifying manner. This Unit thus serves as a mere introduction to some of the topics that exist beyond the general principles of the United States inbound taxation of business income covered in this text. As is probably plain to readers by now, it is with good reason that the United States international tax regime is widely considered one of the most complex in the world, and this Unit is but one window on that complexity.

9.01   Branch Profits Taxes — In General

Foreign corporations engaged in a United States trade or business are generally subject to the branch profits tax rules contained in § 884. These rules are designed to impose United States tax treatment on foreign corporations doing business through a United States branch that is similar to the tax treatment of foreign corporations operating in the United States through a United States subsidiary. In the latter case, the subsidiary is subject to corporate-level tax on worldwide income plus a tax on dividends repatriated to its foreign owners. In the former case, absent some mechanism like the branch profits tax, the foreign corporation may only be subject to United States taxation on effectively connected income. The branch profits taxes impose on foreign corporations doing business in the United States in an unincorporated form an additional tax of 30 percent that simulates the additional tax that would be imposed on earnings repatriated by a United States subsidiary via dividends or interest payments to a foreign corporation. The branch profits taxes are imposed in addition to the regular corporate income tax on income effectively connected with a domestic trade or business.

The branch profits taxes involve a tripartite regime. The first branch profits tax equals 30 percent (or a lower treaty rate, if applicable — see discussion in Unit 11) of a foreign corporation's "dividend equivalent amount." The dividend equivalent amount generally represents the foreign corporation's current earnings and profits from a domestic trade or business, as adjusted for net increases and decreases in United States net equity and as adjusted in certain other ways. The dividend equivalent amount is essentially the amount available for repatriation (i.e., the amount that would be treated as a dividend if distributed to the foreign parent if the branch were a subsidiary corporation).

The second branch profits tax, the branch interest tax, is a 30 percent tax (or a lower tax treaty rate if applicable) on interest paid by a foreign corporation's domestic trade or business. The branch interest tax applies if the recipient of the interest payment is a foreign person not engaged in a domestic trade or business. This tax similarly closes the subsidiary/branch gap by converting repatriated interest into interest paid by a United States subsidiary.[1] As such, that interest would be subject to tax and parity is achieved.

The third branch profits tax is imposed at the corporate level on "branch excess interest." A foreign corporation is liable for a 30 percent tax (or a lower tax treaty rate if applicable) if the amount of the interest deduction allowed to the foreign corporation against effectively connected income under § 882 exceeds the amount of interest paid by that corporation's domestic trade or business. Such excess is treated as interest paid to that foreign corporation by a wholly-owned United

---

[1] Interest payments from a domestic subsidiary to a foreign parent would not be eligible for the portfolio interest exception. *See* § 881(c)(3).

States subsidiary.[2] This tax treats the foreign branch as having paid the amount of interest deducted from effectively connected income under § 882 as United States source income. Any excess deduction is, in essence, treated as if a foreign parent were financing a United States subsidiary.

9.02   Branch Profits Tax on the Dividend Equivalent Amount

Under § 884(a), a foreign corporation that operates a United States trade or business is generally subject to a 30 percent tax on its annual "dividend equivalent amount." Its basic purpose is to impose a 30 percent tax on the annual effectively connected earnings of a foreign corporation which are not reinvested in the assets of a domestic trade or business and which are thus considered repatriated to shareholders in some fashion. Under § 884(b), the dividend equivalent amount, the measurement base for the tax, is equal to the foreign corporation's current effectively connected earnings and profits adjusted for increases or decreases in its "U.S. net equity" as defined in § 884(c). A foreign corporation's U.S. net equity is determined by reducing, but not below zero, the amount of money and the adjusted basis of its effectively connected assets ("U.S. assets") by its effectively connected liabilities ("U.S. liabilities").

The computation of the dividend equivalent amount and the concept of U.S. net equity are best illustrated by an example. As the starting point for computing the dividend equivalent amount, the normal annual determination of earnings and profits is made pursuant to § 312 (discussed more fully below). The reliance on earnings and profits as a computational base seems quite logical as it measures the base of earnings available for distribution as a dividend for United States tax purposes, which is what § 884 is designed to reach. For example, if a newly-formed foreign corporation has $500 of effectively connected earnings and profits from the conduct of its domestic trade or business in Year 1, its Year 1 dividend equivalent amount begins at $500.

The branch profits tax is avoided if these earnings remain in the United States (i.e., U.S. net equity increases) since the parity-breaking removal of earnings without tax has not occurred. Thus, if the foreign corporation's U.S. net equity increases during its taxable year, the corporation's effectively connected earnings and profits and thus its taxable base is reduced (but not below zero) by the amount of this reinvestment in the United States. In the above example, if $500 is invested in United States property, the dividend equivalent amount would be zero in Year 1, properly reflecting the fact that the branch profits tax should not apply when United States earnings have merely been reinvested in a domestic trade or business rather than repatriated.

Conversely, if the foreign corporation's U.S. net equity decreases during the taxable year (thereby signaling the withdrawal of the corporation's investment of earnings in the United States targeted by § 884), its effectively connected earnings and profits are *increased* by the amount of the reduction. This repatriation represents the appropriate juncture at which to impose tax. Thus, in the preceding

---

[2] Thus, again, the portfolio interest exception would not apply, and the full 30 percent tax would be imposed.

example, if in Year 2 the corporation withdrew $150 from its domestic branch and had no effectively connected earnings for the year, the $150 decrease in U.S. net equity appropriately increases the dividend equivalent amount and the branch profits tax base. Thus, a 30 percent tax would be imposed on the $150 withdrawal.

Any such increase in the dividend equivalent amount, however, cannot exceed the foreign corporation's accumulated effectively connected earnings and profits (the excess of the corporation's post-1986 aggregate earnings and profits derived from its domestic trade or business over its aggregate dividend equivalent amounts as determined for prior years). In the above example, if the corporation withdrew $700, it should not give rise to a dividend equivalent amount of $700 since this would exceed the corporation's domestic earnings component (to date, $500).

9.03   Effectively Connected Earnings and Profits

Pursuant to § 884(d)(1), effectively connected earnings and profits represents the foreign corporation's earnings and profits attributable to its effectively connected income. Section 884(d)(2) and Regulation § 1.884-1(f)(1) provide that, subject to several modifications, the general rules for computing earnings and profits under § 312 apply for this purpose. As is the case in many other important definitional areas, earnings and profits is not affirmatively defined in the Code but guidance is available in Regulations and under case law.

In general, all corporate expenditures are allowable as deductions from earnings and profits, no matter whether they are deductible for income tax purposes, while items of income that would otherwise be exempt from tax (such as tax-exempt interest income) are included. The regular corporate income tax is deducted in computing effectively connected earnings and profits, but the branch taxes are not, per Regulation § 1.884-1(f)(1). In addition, § 884(d)(1) makes clear that effectively connected earnings and profits are not reduced by distributions made by the foreign corporation during the year. If this were permitted, the offending act, repatriation, would serve to reduce the taxable base.

9.04   The Branch Interest Tax

Continuing its theme of placing domestic and foreign corporations on equal tax footing, § 884(f) imposes two branch profits taxes on the interest expense of foreign corporations engaged in a domestic trade or business (or treated as having income effectively connected therewith). The first such tax, commonly called the "branch interest tax," is generally a 30 percent withholding tax on interest paid by a foreign corporation's United States trade or business.

The branch interest tax applies to foreign corporations engaged in a United States trade or business or treated as having effectively connected income. This tax effectively treats any interest paid by a foreign corporation engaged in a United States trade or business (i.e., branch interest) as if it were paid by a United States corporation. Thus, the interest will generally be subject to a 30 percent tax. This tax again serves to create parity between the treatment of interest paid by a United States corporation and a foreign branch by simulating the withholding tax generally applicable to United States corporations.

The amount of branch interest subject to tax under § 884(f)(1)(A) is generally capped at the amount of interest apportioned to effectively connected income under the provisions of Regulation § 1.882-5. As with the other branch profits taxes, the branch interest tax rate is subject to modification by tax treaty.

Several practical exceptions apply to exclude interest derived from ordinary course foreign business dealings from the branch interest tax regime. For instance, no branch interest arises from liabilities incurred in the ordinary course of the foreign corporation's foreign business operations (e.g., accounts payable incurred for inventory). Similarly, no branch interest generally arises from liabilities secured by non-United States assets or from inter-branch liabilities.

9.05   The Branch Excess Interest Tax

The second branch profits tax on interest is the "branch excess interest tax." It generally imposes on a foreign corporation a 30 percent tax on the amount by which the interest deduction allowed to a foreign corporation under § 882 exceeds the amount of interest paid by that foreign corporation's United States trade or business (as determined for purposes of the branch interest tax). Such excess is treated as if it were interest paid to that foreign corporation by a wholly-owned United States subsidiary. This tax ensures that branch operations are not used as vehicles by which to funnel interest tax-free into foreign hands. As with the other branch profits taxes, the tax is subject to modification by tax treaty. Unlike the branch interest tax, the excess interest tax does not operate by recharacterizing interest as domestic source income subject to potential tax to the recipient under §§ 871 and 881. Rather, the foreign corporation accounts for and itself pays the tax along with its United States tax return.

9.06   Background on the Taxation of United States Real Property Interests

The remainder of this Unit discusses a second topic: the taxation of United States real property interests. Prior to 1980, it was often possible for foreign corporations to invest in United States real property free of United States tax so long as they avoided gains that were effectively connected to the conduct of a domestic trade or business. Similarly, foreign individuals could sell domestic real property without consequence because they were generally immune from tax on capital gains unless the gain was effectively connected to a domestic trade or business or unless the individual had been present in the United States for 183 days or more.

Thus, because the mere ownership and sale (without development efforts or active management) of unimproved real property generally would not rise to the level of the conduct of a United States trade or business, it was possible for a foreign investor to sell United States real property without paying United States tax. In the same vein, a foreign investor who "triple net leased" a building to a lessee (i.e., by requiring that the lessee pay all expenses) was not deemed to be engaged in a United States trade or business by virtue of that net lease, apparently on the theory that the activities of the lessee should not be imputed to the foreign lessor.[3] Thus, a triple net leased building could similarly be sold by a foreign investor without being subject to United States tax.

In order to prevent such tax-free dispositions of United States real property by foreign investors and to put domestic and foreign investors on equal tax footing with respect to such property, Congress enacted the Foreign Investment in Real Property Tax Act of 1980 (FIRPTA). Under FIRPTA (codified in § 897), gain or loss from the disposition of a "United States real property interest" by a foreign investor is treated as if the gain or loss were effectively connected with a United States trade or business. The amount of gain or loss realized on such a disposition is determined under § 1001 and is recognized for tax purposes unless one of the § 897 non-recognition exceptions applies to shield it from taxation. The practical effect of this rule is to expose such gain to United States tax.

This characterization of the gain controls even if the foreign person's domestic activities do not otherwise constitute an actual trade or business and even if the gain is not otherwise deemed to be effectively connected to a domestic trade or business under the principles of § 864(c). Moreover, a non-resident need not satisfy a physical presence test or have a United States tax home to be subject to the tax.

FIRPTA, then, prevents tax-favored disposal of interests in United States real property by foreign investors. While the statutory reach of § 897 is broad and all-encompassing with regard to *direct* investment in United States real property, significant distinctions exist with respect to *indirect* investment (i.e., the formation by foreign persons of a foreign or domestic corporation through which to invest in United States real property). Depending upon whether a United States or a foreign holding company is employed, certain transfers are exempt from the coverage of § 897.

While FIRPTA as originally drafted blocked numerous tax-avoidance techniques, some of its provisions became redundant with the passage of more general corporate tax reform in 1986, which curtailed some of the circumvention techniques previously available to foreign investors (without reference to FIRPTA). Since the FIRPTA provisions were not revised or repealed simultaneously or thereafter, it is not unusual to encounter redundancies among the § 897 provisions and overlapping corporate tax provisions. Some of these redundancies are highlighted in the discussion that follows.

9.07 Section 897: The Big Picture

The gain or loss of a foreign taxpayer from the disposition of a United States real property interest, as defined in § 897, is considered effectively connected to a domestic trade or business under § 871(b)(1) (for individuals) or § 882(a)(1) (for corporations). As such, absent a special non-recognition exception, the gain will be taxed at the graduated rates normally applicable to individuals and corporations. As is otherwise true for effectively connected income, deductions are allowed under § 873 (for individuals) or § 882(c) (for corporations).

---

[3] *See, e.g.*, Rev. Rul. 73-522, 1973-2 C.B. 226; *Neill v. Commissioner*, 46 B.T.A. 197 (1942).

9.08   Direct Investment in United States Real Property

Various modes of investment are available through which foreign taxpayers may acquire United States real property interests — direct investment by the taxpayer or indirect investment through the property holdings of a foreign or domestic corporation or partnership. The simplest case, a disposition of a direct investment in property actually and directly owned by the taxpayer, is clearly subject to tax under § 897(a). In the direct investment setting, two critical definitional issues for the application of § 897 arise — (1) the determination of whether a "United States real property interest" is involved, and (2) whether a "disposition" of that interest has occurred.

9.09   United States Real Property Interests

The statutory prerequisite for the application of § 897 is a disposition of a United States real property interest. Under § 897(c)(1), this term generally is defined as any interest in real property (including an interest in a mine, well, or other natural deposit) located in the United States or the Virgin Islands and any interest (other than an interest solely as a creditor) in any *domestic* corporation that is (or was, during certain specified time periods) a United States real property holding corporation. Thus, the term includes both direct and indirect investment via outright ownership, co-ownership, options, and leaseholds.

9.10   Tangible Property

The term "United States real property interest" includes not only land, but also any un-severed natural products, improvements, and any personal property associated with the use of land. It also includes leaseholds of land and improvements and options to acquire such land or leaseholds. In keeping with the legislative purpose, the term is particularly broad and far reaching. Local law definitions are not controlling. Furthermore, the term "improvements" is liberally construed so that buildings, permanent structures, and the structural components thereof are subject to § 897.

"Associated personal property" encompassed by the definition of "United States real property interest" results in a significant expansion of the statute's reach to include personal property. Under the Regulations, such property is limited to four basic categories of tangible property. The first category relates to property predominantly used in mining, farming, and forestry. These properties are generally of the type used to extract minerals and to farm and harvest crops. This category does not, however, include property used to transport severed natural resources.

Property used predominantly in the improvement of real property is also subject to § 897. Such property includes, for example, razing equipment used to improve or construct real property. Property used predominantly in the operation of a lodging facility is also governed by § 897. It encompasses furniture, appliances, and personal property used in common areas of apartments, hotels, motels, dorms, residences, or other permanent structures offering lodging for consideration.

Finally, property used predominantly in the rental of a furnished office and other work space is subject to § 897. Such property includes office equipment and furniture used by the lessor to provide rental space. However, property described in any of these four categories does not constitute a United States real property interest if it is disposed of more than one year before or more than one year after the disposition of the realty with which it is associated or, if within those time periods, separate dispositions of the personalty and realty are made to unrelated taxpayers.

9.11   Intangible Property

As previously discussed, the definition of a real property interest is broadly focused and easily determined as regards tangible property. However, if intangible interests were not included in the term as well, circumvention techniques could easily be employed. For example, instead of an outright sale of domestic real property, a foreign investor might employ an installment sale and shortly thereafter liquidate its investment by disposing of the installment obligation to a third party. Section 897 would have little impact but to foster tax planning if such a simple structuring technique could prevent its application. The Regulations therefore extend the statute's coverage to include various intangible ownership interests.

In general, interests held solely as a creditor are immune from the reach of FIRPTA, on the theory that a creditor's investment return is in the nature of interest rather than capital appreciation and should be regulated as such. Again, such a bright line rule creates opportunity for avoidance. For example, Regulations to § 897 provide in general terms that a mortgage may run afoul of § 897 to the extent it has an equity feature (e.g., participation in appreciation). Additional rules deal with situations where an interest that appears in form to represent a creditor relationship might otherwise escape FIRPTA, even if in substance the return was tied to the profitability of the company, which in turn relied on the performance of the real property held by the company.

Installment sales may also be subject to § 897. If the taxpayer elects out of § 453, the installment notes are not real property interests since the sale is fully subject to § 897 at the time it occurs. However, if gain is reported under the installment method, the notes are classified as a United States real property interest in order to ensure both that subsequent collections on the notes fall subject to § 897 and that any disposition of the installment notes which cashes out the investment is also subject to § 897.

Finally, as indirect investments under § 897 focus generally on stock ownership in United States corporations, a definitional issue arises as to the classification of investment through the ownership of conduit entities — partnerships, trusts, and estates. In contrast to stock ownership, the ownership *per se* of an interest in a conduit entity is not a United States real property interest. This potential gap in the legislation is closed by § 897(g), which uses a look-through rule under which the disposition of an interest in a pass-through entity, to the extent that the consideration received by the taxpayer is attributable to United States real property interests held by the entity, is considered to be received directly by the taxpayer and thus is subject to the rules applicable to direct investment.

Regulation § 1.897-1(e)(2)–(3), although not issued specifically pursuant to § 897(g), provides detailed guidance on similar issues and may be used to determine the taxpayer's proportionate share of the assets held by the entity. The imputation is required regardless of whether the partnership, trust, or estate is foreign or domestic. Thus, from a planning standpoint, a foreign corporation may prove to be a superior investment vehicle than a foreign partnership or trust, because the imputation rules do not apply to foreign corporations.

9.12 Dispositions

Regulation § 1.897-1(g) provides that a disposition of a United States real property interest is "any transfer that would constitute a disposition by the transferor for any purpose of the Internal Revenue Code and regulations thereunder." This broad definition forecloses a number of means by which taxpayers might arrange their affairs so as to sever ownership and prevent the application of § 897. Thus, an outright sale of property, its transfer in satisfaction of a claim, or any other taxable transfer will constitute a disposition. Similarly, non-recognition transfers which produce as a corollary taxable gain such as the receipt of boot in a like-kind exchange or, with regard to a gift, the relief of a liability in excess of the taxpayer's basis in the property should constitute a disposition. Moreover, certain transactions which would normally be afforded non-recognition treatment under the Code may trigger § 897 re-characterization into taxable events.

More difficult questions arise with respect to less traditional types of transfers — gifts, bequests, non-taxable transfers to trusts, partnerships, corporations, and other entities, and like-kind exchanges without boot. As a general rule, non-recognition transactions are respected so long as the United States real property interest is exchanged for an interest which similarly carries the § 897 taint upon its disposition. However, in those cases not specifically addressed by FIRPTA, the resolution of the issue of whether such a transfer constitutes a disposition should turn on an analysis of the policy behind the enactment of § 897.

As long as the transfer does not remove the transferor's (or transferee's) subsequent gain from the taxing jurisdiction of the United States or generate an increased basis which would shield a portion of the gain from domestic taxation upon a subsequent disposition, it generally should not constitute a disposition for purposes of § 897. Consequently, a gift of a United States real property interest should be exempt from § 897 as the property's basis will transfer to the donee. The donee, even if a non-resident with no United States activity, will itself be subject to tax under § 897 upon any subsequent disposition of the property. Such an interpretive approach is consistent with § 897(e) which conditions any otherwise available non-recognition treatment upon the continued application of § 897 to the property received in the non-recognition event.

9.13   Indirect Investment — Interests Held Through Domestic Corporations

Indirect investment through domestic corporations is also targeted by FIRPTA. In keeping with the statutory purpose, the interposition of a United States corporation between the foreign taxpayer and a United States real property interest will not insulate the foreign investor from the application of § 897. In fact, in such settings, taxation may result both at the corporate level upon the domestic corporation's sale of the property, and at the shareholder level upon the shareholder's sale of the shares in the corporation if the sale of the corporate stock precedes the corporation's sale of the property.

Gain from the sale by a foreign person of shares in a United States corporation will be taxed under § 897 if that corporation has at any time within the past five years (or, if shorter, the taxpayer's holding period) been a "United States real property holding corporation." This determination is predicated upon the extent of the corporation's investment in United States real property interests. This treatment generally applies regardless of the foreign shareholder's percentage ownership in the corporation and regardless of whether he disposes of all or only a portion of his holdings. Even a one percent foreign shareholder in a domestic United States real property holding corporation is subject to § 897.

9.14   United States Real Property Holding Corporations

A United States real property holding corporation is any corporation, if the fair market value of its United States real property interests equals or exceeds 50 percent of the value of all of its combined foreign and domestic real property interests and business assets.[4] However, if the holding corporation is publicly traded, its shares will not constitute an interest in a real property holding corporation unless the shareholder owns more than five percent of the stock. One reason for this rule is that small shareholders probably lack information about and control over the investment decisions of publicly traded corporations. Such shareholders are probably not using their stock ownership as a means to circumvent the FIRPTA rules, and an onerous application of FIRPTA to them might unduly discourage foreign persons from buying stock in United States public companies.

In determining whether a domestic corporation is a United States real property holding corporation, holdings by that domestic corporation in other business entities are taken into account. For example, if the United States corporation owns an interest in a partnership, trust, or estate, whether foreign or domestic, it is treated as holding directly its proportionate share of that entity's assets.

---

[4] Importantly, both foreign and domestic corporations can be United States real property holding corporations, but, as noted in subpart 9.13, only the disposition of an interest in a *domestic* United States real property holding corporation will be subject to tax under § 897. The determination of whether a foreign corporation constitutes a United States real property holding corporation is only relevant for purposes of determining whether a domestic corporation, whose assets include the stock of such foreign corporation, is itself a United States real property holding corporation, as discussed below. *See* § 897(c)(4).

If the United States corporation owns an interest in another corporation, whether domestic or foreign, different imputation rules apply depending upon the degree of ownership. If the corporation owns a controlling interest of 50 percent or more of the value of the stock of another corporation, an imputation rule similar to that applicable to other entities applies to attribute a proportionate share of the subsidiary's assets to the parent corporation. If the United States corporation owns less than a controlling interest, the attribution of assets becomes an all-or-nothing proposition. In such a case, the sole issue is whether the shares in the domestic or foreign subsidiary constitute a United States real property interest. If so, the value of the entire interest is considered a real property interest; if not, none of the interest is so considered.

In examining whether a corporation has been a United States real property holding corporation during the statutory testing period, the Service looks to the shorter of the period during which the foreign investor held the shares or the five-year period ending on the date of disposition of the shares. Thus, a corporation will be classified as a United States real property holding corporation if it had the requisite level of United States real property interests on any of the applicable determination dates during the shorter of those periods.

9.15   Indirect Investment — Interests Held Through Foreign Corporations

In contrast to the gain recognition imposed by § 897 on foreign shareholders upon the sale of their stock in a domestic corporation having significant holdings of United States real property interests, no gain or loss is recognized under § 897 when a foreign taxpayer disposes of shares in a foreign corporation. Foreign shareholders in a foreign corporation holding a United States real property interest thus enjoy greater latitude in the disposition of their ownership interests (which are not subject to § 897) than do similarly situated foreign taxpayers whose investment vehicle is a domestic corporation (which are subject to § 897). The distinction in tax treatment between these two vehicles most likely stems from enforcement and detection difficulties particular to foreign corporations. However, the foreign corporation remains subject to tax under § 897 even if its shares have been sold. Thus, a potential buyer of the shares should discount the price paid to reflect this inherited potential tax burden.

9.16   Distributions by Foreign Corporations

Under §§ 311(b) and 336(a), a foreign corporation that distributes a United States real property interest will recognize gain equal to the full unrealized appreciation in the distributed property at distribution. However, such gain would not ordinarily be subject to tax absent FIRPTA, except in those cases where the gain was otherwise effectively connected with a United States trade or business, since under § 882 the capital gains of a foreign corporation not effectively connected with the conduct of a domestic trade or business are not subject to tax. Section 897(d) therefore provides an important safeguard, by imputing the requisite trade or business and effective connection status to encompass any such gain.

Examples in which a foreign corporate transferor must recognize income under § 897(d) include distributions "with respect to" a shareholder's stock (§ 301); distributions in redemption of a shareholder's interest § 302); and distributions in liquidation where the transferee receives a stepped-up basis (e.g., under §§ 331 and 334). The crux of § 897(d), then, is to prevent a distributee from obtaining a stepped-up basis in domestic realty while the foreign corporate distributor escapes United States tax on the appreciation attributable to that property. If the recipient obtains a stepped-up basis, the foreign transferor is taxed via § 897 even if the transfer would not otherwise be taxable.

D. REFERENCE MATERIALS

- Revenue Ruling 2008-31
- Revenue Ruling 84-160

REVENUE RULING 2008–31
2008-1 C.B. 1180

ISSUE

Is an interest in a notional principal contract, the return on which is calculated by reference to an index described below referencing data from a geographically and numerically broad range of United States real estate a United States real property interest ("USRPI") under section 897(c)(1) of the Code?

FACTS

X maintains and widely publishes an index (the "Index") that seeks to measure the appreciation and depreciation of residential or commercial real estate values within [a specified large] geographic area within the United States. The . . . large geographic area has a population exceeding one million people. The Index is calculated by reference to (1) sales prices (obtained from various public records), (2) appraisals and reported income, or (3) similar objective financial information, each with respect to a broad range of real property holdings of unrelated owners within the relevant geographic area during a relevant testing period. Using proprietary methods, this information is weighted, aggregated, and mathematically translated into the Index.

Because of the broad-based nature of the Index, an investor cannot, as a practical matter, directly or indirectly, own or lease a material percentage of the real estate, the values of which are reflected by the Index.

On January 1, Year 1, FC, a foreign corporation, enters into a notional principal contract ("NPC"), within the meaning of sections 1.446-3(c)(1) and 1.863-7(a)(1) of the Income Tax regulations, with unrelated counterparty DC, a domestic corporation. Neither FC nor DC is related to X. Pursuant to the NPC, FC profits if the Index appreciates (that is, to the extent the underlying United States real property in the particular geographic region appreciates in value) over certain levels. Conversely, FC suffers a loss if the Index depreciates (or fails to appreciate more than at a specified rate). During the term of the NPC, DC does not, directly or indirectly, own or lease a material percentage of the real property, the values of which are reflected by the Index.

LAW AND ANALYSIS

Section 897(a) provides that gain or loss from the disposition of a USRPI of a nonresident alien individual or a foreign corporation shall be taken into account as effectively connected income under section 871(b)(1) or section 882(a)(1), respectively, as if the taxpayer were engaged in a trade or business within the United States during the taxable year and as if such gain or loss were effectively connected with such trade or business.

A USRPI is generally defined under section 897(c)(1)(A) as either an interest in real property located in the United States or the Virgin Islands, or any interest (other than an interest solely as a creditor) in any domestic corporation unless the taxpayer establishes that such corporation was at no time a USRPHC during certain periods.

The term "interest in real property" under section 897(c)(6)(A) includes fee ownership and co-ownership of land or improvements thereon, leaseholds of land or improvements thereon, options to acquire land or improvements thereon, and options to acquire leaseholds of land or improvements thereon.

Section 1.897-1(c)(1) of the regulations generally defines USRPIs to include any interest, other than an interest solely as a creditor, in real property located in the United States or the Virgin Islands. Section 1.897-1(d)(2)(i) provides that an interest in real property other than solely as a creditor includes a fee ownership, co-ownership, or leasehold interest in real property, a time sharing interest in real property, and a life estate, remainder, or reversionary interest in such real property. The term also includes any direct or indirect right to share in the appreciation in the value, or in the gross or net proceeds or profits generated by, the real property.

HOLDING

Because of the broad-based nature of the Index, the NPC does not represent a "direct or indirect right to share in the appreciation in the value . . . [of] the real property" within the meaning of Treas. Reg. § 1.897-1(d)(2). Accordingly, FC's interest in the NPC calculated by reference to the Index is not a USRPI under section 897(c)(1).

REVENUE RULING 84-160
1984-2 C.B. 125

ISSUE

Whether section 897(e) of the Internal Revenue Code permits nonrecognition of tax in the fact situation set forth below.

FACTS

FX is a corporation organized under the laws of a foreign country (FC), which does not have an income tax treaty with the United States. *FX* holds 100 percent of the stock of corporation *S*, a domestic corporation. *S* is engaged in real estate development and has determined that it constitutes a U.S. real property holding corporation as defined in section 897(c)(2) of the Code. Therefore, the stock of *S* constitutes a U.S. real property interest pursuant to section 897(c)(1). For business purposes *FX* wishes to interpose a holding company between itself and *S*. Therefore, on December 1, 1984, in a transaction qualifying for nonrecognition under section 351, *FX* transfers all of the shares of *S* to *H*, a corporation newly organized in the United States, solely in exchange for the stock of *H*. Because the shares of *S* are the only assets of *H*, *H* constitutes a U.S. real property holding corporation as defined in section 897(c)(2).

LAW and ANALYSIS

Under section 897(a) of the Code, a foreign corporation's gain or loss from the disposition of a U.S. real property interest is treated as if the foreign corporation were engaged in a trade or business within the United States and as if the gain or loss were effectively connected with the trade or business. . . .

Section 897(e) of the Code provides that except to the extent otherwise provided in section 897(d) and section 897(e)(2), any nonrecognition provision shall apply for purposes of section 897 to a transaction only in the case of an exchange of a United States real property interest for an interest the sale of which would be subject to taxation under this chapter, i.e., chapter 1 of the Code. Section 897(e)(2) provides that the Secretary shall prescribe regulations (which are necessary or appropriate to prevent the avoidance of Federal income taxes) providing the extent to which nonrecognition provisions shall, and shall not, apply for purposes of section 897, and the extent to which the transfers of property in reorganization and changes in interest in, or distributions from, a partnership, trust, or estate, shall be treated as sales of property at fair market value. Section 897(e)(3) defines the term "nonrecognition provision" as meaning any provision of this title, i.e., the Internal Revenue Code, for not recognizing gain or loss.

Section 897(e) of the Code provides that any nonrecognition provision shall apply for purposes of this section to a transaction only in the case of an exchange of a United States real property interest for an interest the sale of which would be subject to taxation under chapter 1 of the Code. This provision is intended to preserve otherwise available nonrecognition in cases where it is clear that gain inherent in a U.S. real property interest will remain subject to U.S. taxation. In the present case, *FX* has exchanged, in a transaction qualifying for nonrecognition under section 351, one U.S. real property interest for another U.S. real property interest, the sale of which will be clearly subject to U.S. taxation. Therefore, *FX* is entitled to receive nonrecognition treatment pursuant to section 897(e) of the Code.

HOLDING

In accordance with section 897(e) of the Code, in the above fact situation, the nonrecognition provision will apply for purposes of section 897. . . .

Unit 10

OVERVIEW OF TAX TREATIES

A. CODE AND REGULATION PROVISIONS

Code   §§ 871(a)(1), (2); 871(b); 894(a); 7852(d).
Relevant portions of the United States-Canada Tax Treaty.

B. PROBLEMS FOR CLASS DISCUSSION

10-1. In what ways do income tax treaties fulfill their articulated objective of "eliminating double taxation?" What other avenues (besides treaties) are available for eliminating double taxation? If unilateral measures are available, what role does the treaty serve? Do treaties defer to the country of residence or the country of source?

10-2. Melinda, a United States citizen, retired to Canada on January 1, Year 1. If Melinda derives $30,000 of dividend income from a United States corporation in Year 3, what country or countries might tax that income and at what rate(s)?

10-3. Hans, a citizen and resident of Canada, works in the United States each year from January 1 to July 31. During his stay in the United States, Hans rents an apartment in New York City. He owns a home in Canada, where his spouse and children live year round. Hans is a registered voter in Canada, and Canada is the location of his bank accounts, stocks, and automobiles. Is Hans subject to United States taxation on the dividends he receives from his Canadian stock?

10-4. Eduardo, a citizen and resident of Argentina, forms Eduardo Inc., a wholly-owned Canadian corporation, which invests in a United States corporation and receives dividends annually. Are benefits under the Canada Treaty available? Explain the policy implicated by this situation.

10-5. Review the titles of the 31 articles in the Canada-United States tax treaty. What are the similarities and differences between the United States statutory treatment of foreign persons and the treaty treatment of Canadian residents? What is the impact of the treaty on United States citizens and residents?

C. OVERVIEW

The United States has entered into more than 55 income tax treaties with other countries.[1] The purpose of these agreements is to mitigate the potential for double taxation that arises in conjunction with international activities. They do so by providing consistent rules specifically governing which treaty country has the primary right to tax income items (such as business profits, income from real property, dividends, interest, royalties, and other items) or certain classes of persons (such as students, teachers, athletes, artists, and apprentices).

Double taxation arises most often when one country asserts taxing authority on the basis of the residence of the person receiving the income (the home country) and another on the basis of source of the income (the host country). *See* Figure 10-1. It also arises when, in a certain set of circumstances, each country asserts residence jurisdiction, or each views the income as sourced in their own jurisdiction.

FIGURE 10-1. EXAMPLE OF TYPICAL "DOUBLE TAXATION"

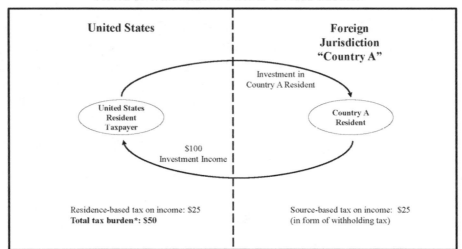

*Total tax burden on United States resident taxpayer, absent foreign tax credit or other relief from double taxation

By alleviating double taxation, tax treaties are intended to stimulate trade and investment between the two signatory countries and add a degree of certainty to cross border transactions. For example, the United States treaty with Egypt (effective 1982) was entered into for the purposes of "the avoidance of double taxation of income . . . and the elimination of obstacles to international trade and investment." The United States treaties with the Czech Republic (effective 1993), Hungary (effective 1979), Poland (effective 1976), and the Slovak Republic (effective 1993) claim an intention to "further expand and facilitate mutual economic relations" between the partner countries. Similarly, in 2004 testimony before the Senate Committee on Foreign Relations on pending income tax agreements with

---

[1] These can generally be found on the IRS website; however, the website is not always up to date. For instance, the treaties with Bangladesh and Sri Lanka were not listed for over a year after their entry into force.

Japan (an update to an old treaty) and Sri Lanka (a treaty that had been variously in negotiation or tabled since 1985), the United States negotiator suggested that the goal of these treaties is to increase the amount and efficiency of activity between treaty partner countries so that each country's situation is improved.

At the same time, tax treaties introduce complexities in international taxation because they provide a second source of authority that can be equal in weight to that of other laws. Treaties have the same effect as acts of Congress and possess authority that overrides the tax treatment otherwise provided by the Internal Revenue Code. Moreover, as is the case with statutory law, the treaty language is often only the starting point for analysis — interpretation will pose many challenges to the application of international tax rules.

In the United States, tax treaties are generally drawn from model income tax treaties formulated by the Treasury, the most current version of which was released in 2006 (referred to in this Casebook as the 2006 Model Tax Treaty). However, most of the world's tax treaties, including the 2006 Model Tax Treaty and all of the United States tax treaties currently in effect, are also based on model income tax conventions promulgated by the Organization for Economic Cooperation and Development (OECD), an international organization of which the United States is a member.

An additional model tax convention, designed for use between developed and developing countries, is published by the United Nations (referred to herein as the UN Model Tax Convention). This model is similar in most respects to the United States and OECD models but contains provisions that may be more favorable to developing country treaty partners. The Treasury Department, in its official explanation of United States tax treaties, often refers to the UN Model Tax Convention when explaining deviations from the model, which it refers to as "concessions," such as greater allocation of taxing jurisdiction to the source country.[2]

The OECD and UN model conventions are fairly frequently updated as international tax law develops in response to trends in business activity and diplomatic efforts between countries. The United States Model Income Tax Convention is also updated but on a less frequent basis: the current model was published in 2006 and previous models were published in 1996, 1981, and 1977.

Both the 2006 Model Tax Treaty and the actual tax treaty in force between the United States and Canada are included in the Appendix to this book, together with the Technical Explanations to both treaties. It is worthwhile to scan the provisions of these treaties to get a sense of their structures, functions, and scope.

---

[2] In general, the UN Model Tax Convention tends to favor greater allocation of taxing jurisdiction to source countries, reflecting that the typical flow of capital is from developed to developing countries. For example, see the United States tax treaties with India, Sri Lanka, and the Philippines.

10.01   The Treaty Process

United States income tax treaties are the culmination of extensive, complex, and often protracted negotiations between representatives of the United States and other countries. Primary responsibility for the negotiation of tax treaties and their related protocols rests with the staffs of the Treasury Department's Office of International Tax Counsel and the Office of Tax Analysis (International). Personnel of the Internal Revenue Service and the State Department also play pivotal advisory roles in the negotiation process.

As treaty provisions emerge from negotiations, the agreed upon text is initialed, signifying the signatories' acquiescence to certain provisions. Once the State Department translates and approves the treaty text, the treaty is signed by the appropriate officials of the United States (i.e., the Secretary of State or the United States Ambassador) and the foreign country. The signed treaty is then forwarded to the President. Signed treaties are submitted by the President to the Senate for advice and consent to ratification. Once the treaty is submitted to the Senate, it is referred to the Senate Foreign Relations Committee. The Committee reviews the explanations of the treaty prepared by the Treasury Department and the Joint Committee on Taxation, as well as the comments and statements of interested parties. The Committee may hold hearings on the proposed treaty.

After its review, the Committee submits the treaty to the Senate floor for consent to ratification, either on its negotiated terms or as amended by the Committee. The full Senate then deliberates on the proposed treaty and ultimately must consent by a vote of two thirds of the members present. The Senate may adopt a tax treaty in whole or may enter a reservation on specific provisions of the treaty, which then may be further negotiated between the treaty partners.

After Senate ratification, the President confirms the treaty by signing a ratification instrument. The treaty only comes into force after both treaty countries ratify the treaty (according to their respective internal legal procedures) and exchange ratification instruments. The date that ratification instruments are exchanged generally marks the date upon which the treaty is considered to be "in force." A treaty which is in force is not, however, always "in effect." Treaties may contain prospective or retroactive effective dates.

10.02   Interpretative Resources

The principal interpretive and supplemental sources arising in conjunction with tax treaties are Protocols, which may amend existing and proposed tax treaties and must be duly enacted via proper ratification procedures, and Treasury Department Technical Explanations, which serve as official guides to the tax treaties. In the past, Treasury has also issued Regulations interpreting some tax treaties.

Similar to legislative history behind a statute, Technical Explanations discuss, interpret, and give examples regarding the particular provisions of the treaty. They also highlight the policy, compromises, and understandings driving particular treaty provisions. Additional legislative history includes reports from the Senate Foreign Relations Committee and the Joint Committee on Taxation, as well as transcripts of debate held in the Senate on pending treaties. Case law interpreting existing treaties is a less prevalent but important additional resource for understanding and applying tax treaties.

In addition to United States legislative and judicial materials, the OECD publishes a commentary to its model convention. This commentary provides interpretive resources for all of the model tax conventions and it is frequently updated to reflect developments in international tax law. Although the OECD commentary is not legally binding on the United States, the interpretations it contains reflect international consensus on many of the nuances found in tax treaties. As such, it is an important tool in tax treaty interpretation.

Like any other type of treaty, a tax treaty is to be interpreted according to the provisions of international law relating to treaties. That law has been codified in the Vienna Convention on the Law of Treaties (1986). The United States signed but did not ratify the Vienna Convention. Nevertheless, the United States has acknowledged that it is bound by this agreement to the extent that it embodies or reflects customary international law.

10.03 Relationship of Tax Treaties to United States Federal Law

According to the Supreme Court, "a treaty is primarily a compact between independent nations [that] depends for the enforcement of its provisions on the interest and the honor of the governments which are parties of it."[3] Thus a tax treaty is an international agreement between the United States and another sovereign nation or nations. Globally, most tax treaties are bilateral rather than multilateral, although exceptions exist.

The countries that enter into a tax treaty are generally referred to in the treaty and elsewhere as the Contracting States. This can lead to confusion, as the respective governments are referred to as "the first Contracting State" and "the other Contracting State." In its Technical Explanation to the 2006 Model Tax Treaty, Treasury suggests that "the actual name of the other Contracting State should be used throughout the text of the Technical Explanation to an actual treaty." This seemingly simple idea is sometimes difficult to achieve in practice, as most provisions are reciprocal, so that which Contracting State is which will depend on the direction of the particular income item. Establishing the directional flow of the income item is therefore an imperative first step in analyzing how the treaty will apply.

Article VI, paragraph 2 of the United States Constitution states that treaties, along with the Constitution itself and all laws in pursuance thereof, "shall be the supreme law of the land." Thus, treaties and the Internal Revenue Code are generally accorded equal weight, as §§ 894(a)(1) and 7852(d) of the Code acknowledge. To deal with potential inconsistencies and conflicts between the two authorities, courts have adopted a "last in time" rule of construction which provides that the later enacted provision controls. Since virtually all of the current income tax treaties of the United States were entered or renegotiated after the adoption of

---

[3] *See Edye v. Robertson*, 112 U.S. 580, 598 (1884).

the Internal Revenue Code of 1954 (the Code referenced in § 7852(d)), generally treaty provisions will control.[4] However, under the last in time approach, if a treaty and a later enacted Code provision conflict, the Code provision will prevail unless the subsequent enactment does not plainly indicate an intent to supersede the treaty.

As a result, international taxation issues must be studied in light of any controlling income tax treaty. Answers derived from interpretation of the treaty must be double checked against the statutory regime to ensure that an overriding provision has not been subsequently enacted by Congress.

10.04   Double Taxation

Tax treaties attempt to ameliorate double taxation in two ways. First, these agreements delineate specific types of income (i.e., business profits, dividends, interest, etc.) and provide precise rules for the taxation of these items. Regarding passive income, the country where the income is derived (the source country) generally gives way under the treaty regime to the recipient's country of domicile (the residence country). Treaties generally provide that under certain conditions the recipient of a particular item of income will be taxed at a lesser tax rate or will be exempt from taxation in the source country. Regarding active income, generally the source country refrains from such concessions.

Second, treaties establish "competent authority" procedures that afford taxpayers the opportunity to present disputes regarding treaty provisions to the officials of either country for resolution. In most United States tax treaties, disputes are to be resolved by diplomatic means. Under Article 25 of the 2006 Model Tax Treaty, upon petition from the taxpayer, the competent authorities are to "endeavor . . . to resolve the case by mutual agreement." Other procedural remedies, such as international arbitration, are rarely invoked.

10.05   Saving Clause

The basic premise of tax treaties is that the United States extends tax benefits to foreign residents of a tax treaty country in exchange for that country's reciprocal grant of benefits to United States persons. However, the United States reserves its right to subject its own citizens, including those permanently living abroad, to domestic tax on their worldwide income as if the treaty were not in effect, as provided in Article 1, paragraph 4 of the 2006 Model Tax Treaty. This clause is called a saving clause, presumably because it saves United States taxing jurisdiction over its citizens. United States citizens are thus generally not permitted to avoid taxation by establishing foreign residency and claiming United States treaty benefits extended to foreign residents.

---

[4] The one exception is the treaty with Greece, which entered into force in 1953 and, other than a technical correction made in 1961, has remained unchanged since then.

10.06   Treaty Benefit Eligibility

Signatory countries expressly limit the categories of persons eligible for the benefits of tax treaties in a number of ways. In most cases, only a corporation or other person that is a "resident" of one of the foreign signatory countries may claim the benefits of an income tax treaty. Treaties generally define those individuals and entities that qualify as residents: in the 2006 Model Tax Treaty, the definition appears in Article 4. An individual is typically considered a resident of a treaty country if the individual is within the taxing jurisdiction of that country as a resident. Because a person may be a resident of both signatory countries, most treaties contain a "tiebreaker rule" to place a dual resident in only one country for purposes of applying the treaty. In addition, Article 22 of the 2006 Model Tax Treaty limits benefits eligibility, as discussed below.

10.07   Anti-Treaty Shopping Measures

The "anti-treaty shopping" provisions of most tax treaties present another hurdle to be cleared by a claimant of the treaty benefit. Such provisions, often found in "limitation of benefits" clauses, operate to restrict treaty benefits to those individuals and entities legitimately connected to the treaty countries. Treaty shopping limitations prevent citizens of other countries that do not have United States tax treaties from exploiting treaty benefits by selectively conducting their affairs in favorable treaty countries.

The treaty shopping targeted by such provisions typically involves the establishment of a corporation or other entity entitled to tax treaty benefits by "third country investors" not directly entitled to the tax treaty benefits being claimed by the corporation or entity. For example, as discussed in Unit 8, under the Code, dividends paid by a United States corporation to a foreign corporation which is not a resident of a treaty signatory are subject to a 30 percent tax. Under Article 10(3) of the United States-Netherlands tax treaty, however, dividends paid by a wholly-owned United States subsidiary to its Dutch parent are generally eligible for elimination of this tax. To avoid United States tax on the dividend, a resident of a third country that does not have a tax treaty with the United States could merely interpose a Dutch corporation between himself and the dividend-paying United States corporation. Absent an anti-treaty shopping clause to prevent this, the third country investor could thereby successfully obtain advantageous treaty benefits.

Treaty shopping is discouraged by the United States for both policy and pragmatic reasons. As a matter of broad tax treaty policy, the United States intends that particular treaty benefits be available only to individual residents and entities established within the signatory country. Moreover, on a strategic level, tax treaty negotiators contend that, if treaty shopping continues unabated, the incentive for countries to step forward and meaningfully negotiate a treaty with the United States is eroded. In the prior example, for instance, if third country residents could merely avail themselves of United States-Netherlands tax treaty benefits by using Dutch intermediary corporations, the United States and its citizens would be effectively deprived of any reciprocally favorable tax treatment in that third country.

Given the unintended benefits accruing to third country beneficiaries via treaty shopping, it is now established United States treaty policy to include anti-treaty shopping clauses in new or revised tax treaties. For example, under a typical limitation of benefits clause, an entity which is a resident of a treaty jurisdiction is not entitled to relief from taxation in the other jurisdiction unless more than 50 percent of the beneficial interest in such entity is owned, directly or indirectly, by one or more individual residents of that jurisdiction and the entity's income is not used in substantial part, directly or indirectly, to meet liabilities to persons who are residents of a third jurisdiction. These restrictions prevent the use of entities as mere conduits or leveraged shells through which income is funneled to third country investors after enjoying a brief tax holiday in a treaty country.

10.08   Non-Discrimination

Aside from reducing international double taxation, tax treaties also attempt to ensure that the residents of each signatory country are not discriminated against in a tax sense by the tax authorities of the other country. This protection is afforded in most tax treaties by operation of a "non-discrimination clause." In a typical clause, the United States promises on a reciprocal basis not to tax a foreign person residing in a treaty country at a higher rate than a United States person in the same circumstances, nor to deprive that person of any deduction or credit available to United States citizens in the same circumstances.

The relatively imprecise language contained in typical non-discrimination clauses raises the question of when a foreign person is "in the same circumstances" as a United States person and thus is entitled to parallel tax treatment. The Service has shed some light on the proper construction of this phrase, albeit negatively, by defining what circumstances are not "the same circumstances." For instance, it appears that a non-resident person seldom can rely on a non-discrimination clause, because that non-resident, subject to limited taxation by the United States, seldom is in the same circumstances as a United States citizen or resident who is subject to worldwide taxation.

10.09   Competent Authority Procedures

Double taxation can arise in several ways which may not be specifically addressed in the articles of a treaty. To safeguard against the effects of such omissions as well as to ensure the intended application of the treaty, most tax treaties contain a "mutual agreement procedure" provision which designates consultation between competent authorities to resolve treaty disputes. In the 2006 Model Tax Treaty, this procedure is contained in Article 25.

Mutual agreement provisions set forth procedures by which a taxpayer that is subject to double taxation or other inconsistent treatment by a signatory country and who lacks specific relief via the treaty can petition for relief. To invoke these procedures, the taxpayer presents his or her case to the designated competent authority. If the taxpayer's prayer for relief is meritorious, the authority may present the matter to its foreign counterpart with a view toward finding an equitable solution.

Resolving differences through competent authority diplomacy may be time-consuming and costly to the taxpayer. As a result, there is some international interest in adopting mandatory arbitration as an alternative procedure to be invoked when competent authorities fail to obtain a resolution within two years. A few United States tax treaties, including those with France, Germany, Ireland, Kazakhstan, Mexico, the Netherlands, and Switzerland, provide simply that if "any difficulty or doubt arising as to the interpretation or application of [the treaty] cannot be resolved by the competent authorities in a mutual agreement procedure . . . , the case may, if both competent authorities and all affected taxpayers agree, be submitted for arbitration." Arbitration procedures are not spelled out in these treaties, but are to be established by diplomatic means. The taxpayer must agree to be bound by the decision of the arbitration board, and the decision is binding on both Contracting States. Mandatory arbitration clauses were added by protocols to amend the United States tax treaties with Germany, Belgium, Canada, and France. As a practical matter, the United States has had relative success with the competent authority process, and the inclusion of mandatory arbitration clauses has the effect of encouraging the competent authorities to negotiate with greater intent to reach principled and timely resolution of treaty disputes.

D.   REFERENCE MATERIALS

- Revenue Ruling 91-58

REVENUE RULING 91-58
1991-2 C.B. 340

ISSUE

May nationals of the United Kingdom who are residents of the United States within the meaning of section 7701(b) of the Code qualify for the exclusions and deduction provided by section 911 by establishing that they have been bona fide residents of a foreign country or countries for an uninterrupted period that includes an entire taxable year?

FACTS

X is a domestic corporation that provides specialized services in the United States and foreign countries. X employs nationals (citizens) of the United Kingdom whose tax homes are in the United Kingdom or other foreign countries. Although these nationals are employed by X in the United Kingdom and other foreign countries, they are residents of the United States, within the meaning of section 7701(b).

LAW AND ANALYSIS

Section 911 of the Code provides that a "qualified individual" may elect to exclude or deduct certain amounts from gross income. A citizen of the United States is a qualified individual if either of the following tests is met: (1) the individual's tax home is in a foreign country and the individual establishes to the satisfaction of the Secretary that he or she has been a bona fide resident of a foreign country or countries for an uninterrupted period which includes an entire taxable year (the "bona fide residence test"); or (2) the individual's tax home is in a foreign country and, during any period of 12 consecutive months, he or she is present in a foreign country or countries during at least 330 full days in such period (the "physical presence test"). The determination of whether a United States citizen is a bona fide resident of a foreign country is made by applying the principles of section 871 and the regulations thereunder. By its terms, section 911(d)(1)(B) provides that an alien resident of the United States is a qualified individual only if he or she satisfies the requirements of the physical presence test. . . .

The principles set forth in Rev. Rul. 72-330 are applicable to the instant situation. Therefore, absent a specific treaty provision or a provision of the regulations under the treaty to the contrary, the non-discrimination article in a United States income tax treaty will be applied without regard to the saving clause in the treaty..

Paragraph (1) of Article 24 (Non-discrimination) of the United States United Kingdom Income Tax Convention (the Treaty) provides that individuals who are nationals of a Contracting State and who are residents of the other Contracting State shall not be subjected in that other State to any taxation or any requirement connected therewith which is other or more burdensome than the taxation and connected requirements to which nationals of that other State in the same circumstances are or may be subjected. Paragraph (3) (Personal Scope) of the Treaty contains the saving clause and provides that a Contracting State may tax its residents and its nationals as if the Treaty had not come into effect. However, paragraph (4) of Article I of the Treaty provides, in part, that the saving clause shall not affect the application of Article 24 (Non-discrimination).

Because citizens of the United States may be treated as qualified individuals for purposes of section 911(d) of the Code under either the bona fide residence test or the physical presence test, requiring nationals of the United Kingdom to satisfy the physical presence test subjects them to a requirement connected with section 911 which is more burdensome than the taxation and connected requirements to which citizens of the United States in the same circumstances are subjected. Accordingly, nationals of the United Kingdom must be treated as qualified individuals for purposes of section 911 if they satisfy the requirements of the bona fide residence test.

HOLDING

Nationals of the United Kingdom who are residents of the United States within the meaning of section 7701(b) of the Code may qualify for the exclusion and deduction provided by section 911 by establishing to the satisfaction of the Secretary that they have been bona fide residents of a foreign country or countries under the residency rules of section 1.871-2(b) of the regulations for a period that includes an entire taxable year. . . .

Unit 11

TAX TREATIES AND INVESTMENT INCOME

A. CODE AND REGULATION PROVISIONS

Relevant portions of the United States-Canada Tax Treaty.

B. PROBLEMS FOR CLASS DISCUSSION

11-1. Tom, a Canadian citizen and bona fide resident, has never been present in the United States. During Year 1, he had no United States trade or business, but owned a number of assets that produced the following items of income:

- $20,000 dividend on the stock of DelCo, a corporation formed in Delaware;

- $5,000 gain on sale of ten shares of stock in UruCo, a corporation formed in Uruguay;

- $13,000 dividend on the UruCo stock, of which $5,200 is United States source and $7,800 is foreign source;

- $10,000 in rents from rental property located in the United States;

- $1,000 of foreign-source interest on a loan made to Emily, a citizen and resident of Bolivia;

- $2,000 of interest on a deposit at a Chicago, Illinois bank; and

- $8,000 in cash from the sale of the United States rights to a patent Tom created for five percent of the net profits from products produced through its use.

Tom's potential deductions for the year consisted of depreciation and expenses with respect to the rental property of $3,000, a $1,000 loss on the sale of five shares of UruCo stock, and medical expenses incurred in Canada of $4,500. Assume that under §§ 1 and 55, Tom would be subject to a 20 percent effective rate on his taxable income.

(a) What is Tom's United States taxable income and his tax liability for Year 1, assuming none of his holdings constitutes a permanent establishment under the United States-Canada treaty?

(b) Can he elect to treat his real property activity as business income/ profits?

11-2.   Shaida is a citizen and resident of Canada. In Year 1, Shaida purchased 10 shares of stock in DelCo, a Delaware Corporation, for $7,000. In Year 3, Shaida sold the shares for $10,000 cash to an unrelated individual residing in the United States. To what extent will the United States impose income tax with respect to Shaida's $3,000 gain in Year 3 under each of the following scenarios?

(a)   Shaida was never physically present in the United States at any time in Year 1, Year 2, or Year 3.

(b)   Shaida was not physically present in the United States at any time in Year 1 or Year 2, but she was physically present in the United States for 200 days in Year 3.

(c)   Same as (b), except that for 100 of the 200 days of presence in the United States in Year 3, Shaida was a student residing in the United States with a visa issued under the Immigration and Nationality Act.

11-3.   ForCo is a corporation organized in Canada. All of ForCo's shares are owned by citizens and residents of Canada who have no connections to the United States. ForCo has a number of investments in the United States, but it does not have a permanent establishment therein. For each situation described below, determine whether the interest received by ForCo is subject to United States taxation.

(a)   Interest from a certificate of deposit issued by a California bank.

(b)   Interest from a certificate of deposit issued by the Italian branch of a California bank.

(c)   Interest from a loan to an unrelated United States corporation.

(d)   Same as (c), except that the amount of interest payable to ForCo is dependent upon the domestic corporation's net profits each year.

(e)   Same as (c), except that the amount of interest payable to ForCo is determined with reference to changes in the Dow Jones Industrial Average index.

(f)   Interest from a loan to its wholly-owned United States subsidiary corporation.

C.   OVERVIEW

In contrast to United States citizens and residents who are taxed on worldwide income, foreign persons are generally taxable only on items of income generated in the United States: passive income derived from United States sources and income derived from domestic trade or business activities. Taxation may be reduced or eliminated altogether pursuant to tax treaties between the United States and other countries.

As discussed in Unit 10, tax treaties generally classify a taxpayer as a resident of one of the signatory countries, thus characterizing the taxpayer's country as the country of residence and the other country as the country of source. Tax treaties also characterize income items either as passive (investment-type) or active (business-type), and generally assign the right to tax investment income to the residence country and active income to the source country. Because they are essentially contracts between two parties, treaties address the taxation of persons in both countries. Thus from each country's perspective, treaties address both outbound (domestic residents deriving income from a foreign jurisdiction) and inbound (foreign residents deriving income from domestic sources) transactions.

The reduction of rates and other provisions found in tax treaties are generally reciprocal (for exceptions, see the treaty with Egypt, which provides non-reciprocal rates for dividends, or the treaty with the Philippines, which provides non-reciprocal rates for royalties). As a result, the foreign taxation of a United States investor can generally be ascertained from the provisions discussed herein in the context of foreign persons investing in the United States. However, the complexities of international taxation are such that in determining the foreign taxation of a United States person, care should be taken regarding the interpretation of the treaty in the absence of knowledge of the foreign country's laws. In most cases, a foreign lawyer should be consulted when advising United States persons about the tax results of their cross-border activities, even if a tax treaty is available.

This Unit addresses transactions involving passive investment income from the perspective of the United States. Since, as discussed in Unit 10, the saving clause in United States tax treaties prevents these agreements from applying to reduce the taxation of United States citizens or residents, or both (and sometimes including former citizens or residents), the transactions discussed in this Unit generally focus on inbound transactions, that is, the United States taxation of United States-source investment income earned by foreign persons.

As discussed in Unit 7, the Code generally taxes passive income of foreign persons at a flat 30 percent rate of tax (for individuals, the rate is imposed by § 871; for corporations, it is imposed by § 881). However, foreign persons of countries with whom the United States has a tax treaty may be entitled to a reduced rate of tax under the treaty, since these agreements impose a rate that is far lower than the statutory 30 percent rate for most types of passive income, subject (of course) to various exceptions and limitations.

The 2006 Model Tax Treaty (reproduced in the Appendix), promulgated and periodically updated by the Treasury Department, serves as the template for new treaties. However, guidance from other model treaties may be relied upon, as discussed in Unit 10. As a result, treaties currently in force reflect the official policies as of the time they were entered into and may not reflect current policy. In this Unit, references to Articles refer to those found in the 2006 Model Tax Treaty, which itself does not always incorporate all of the policy choices evidenced in current treaties.[1]

---

[1] For instance, the 2006 Model Tax Treaty does not exempt source country taxation of controlled corporation dividends, even though a number of existing tax treaties do. In addition, the Model does not incorporate an arbitration provision, even though several current United States tax treaties have such provisions.

11.01   A Note on Interpretation

As discussed in Unit 10, the countries that enter into a tax treaty are generally referred to in the treaty and elsewhere as the Contracting States. This can lead to confusion, as the respective governments are referred to as "the first Contracting State" and "the other Contracting State." In its Technical Explanation to the 2006 Model Tax Treaty (also excerpted in the Appendix), Treasury suggests that "the actual name of the other Contracting State should be used throughout the text of the Technical Explanation to an actual treaty." While this advice seems simple, it is in practice difficult to do, since most provisions are reciprocal — which Contracting State is which will depend on the direction of the particular income item. Establishing the directional flow of the income item is therefore an imperative first step in analyzing how the treaty will apply.

11.02   Dividends — Treaty Article 10

Absent a tax treaty, United States source dividends (other than those sourced under § 861(a)(2)(B); *see* § 871(i)(2)(D)) that are not effectively connected to the conduct of a domestic trade or business are generally subject to a 30 percent tax, pursuant to § 871(a)(1)(A) for individuals and § 881(a)(1) for corporations. United States tax treaties generally reduce the statutory tax rate significantly. The recent trend has been towards complete exemption of dividends with respect to certain inter-company dividends paid between companies resident in contracting states, as evidenced in the treaties with countries such as Australia, Mexico, the Netherlands, and the United Kingdom.

Most treaties, pursuant to the 2006 Model Tax Treaty and its predecessors, do not provide complete exemption but do reduce the 30 percent rate to a 15 percent "general rate" for individual shareholders and for corporate shareholders holding less than 10 percent of the company's shares (there is a five percent "direct dividend rate" for dividends paid to corporate recipients that own at least 10 percent of the stock of the paying corporation, so long as the dividend is not attributable to a permanent establishment, as discussed below).

For exceptions to this rule, see the United States treaties with Greece (both general and direct dividends are taxed at 30 percent), the U.S.S.R. (still in force with respect to Armenia, Azerbaijan, Belarus, Georgia, Kyrgyzstan, Moldova, Tajikistan, Turkmenistan and Uzbekistan, and providing for 30 percent on dividends of both kinds), Pakistan (general dividends are taxed at 30 percent, direct at 15 percent), the Philippines (general at 25 percent, direct at 20 percent), India (general at 25 percent, direct at 15 percent), and Israel (general at 25 percent, direct at 12.5 percent).

It is the United States' position that higher tax rates on dividends under treaty may be granted as a concession to developing countries. This is because developing countries are generally importers of capital and the reduced rates under treaties tend to allocate tax revenues to capital exporting countries, like the United States. However, many of the above-mentioned treaties that provide for higher dividend tax rates are not with countries considered to be developing by the United States.

The determination of whether a payee corporation is or should be entitled to a lower tax rate on dividends under a particular treaty, especially where a corporate structure is used in order to achieve treaty benefits, has been the subject of several Revenue Rulings. One example is Revenue Ruling 75-118, which is reproduced in Part D of this unit. In that Ruling, the Service ruled that a foreign corporation was entitled to the direct dividend rate under the treaty even though the company had restructured its subsidiary from Canada to the United States solely to take advantage of the treaty with the United States. However, qualifying for a lower tax rate based solely on the formal structure of corporate ownership creates an opportunity for abuse. The Service is generally reluctant to apply the lower treaty rate in the case of a parent-subsidiary relationship that has been established primarily (or solely) for the purpose of securing the favorable tax rate.

Finally, the reduced rate for dividends applies only if the dividends are not attributable to the operation of a permanent establishment. If the dividends are attributable to a permanent establishment, the provisions of Article 7 (Business Profits) apply. The tax treatment of this kind of income is the subject of Unit 12.

11.03   Interest — Treaty Article 11

Even though it is the first item listed in the definition of passive income items subject to the flat 30 percent statutory tax, most United States source interest is not in fact taxable to foreign persons due to the bank deposit and portfolio interest exceptions, discussed in Unit 7. In the unusual event that a foreign person's United States source interest income is subject to tax, treaty relief may be available.

The 2006 Model Tax Treaty generally provides that interest received from a United States payor and beneficially owned and derived by a treaty country resident may be subject to tax of up to 15 percent, so long as the interest is not attributable to a permanent establishment. As in the case of dividends, if the interest is attributable to a permanent establishment, the provisions of Article 7 (Business Profits) apply.

For treaty purposes, "interest" is generally construed quite broadly. It includes not only traditional interest payments for the use or forbearance of money but may also include unstated interest, such as original issue discount and imputed interest. Absent language to the contrary, interest does not, however, include call premiums, swap payments, or guarantee fees, since these items do not represent compensation for the use of money.

The majority of tax treaties currently in force do not completely exempt domestic source interest income from taxation, but provide a reduced tax rate, typically between 10 and 15 percent.

A number of treaties include one or more "anti-abuse" exceptions to the source-country reduction or exemption for tax on interest. The first exception is for so-called contingent interest, defined in the 2006 Model Tax Treaty as interest calculated on the basis of profits, cash flow, property appreciation, and similar items. Source country taxation of this kind of interest is typically preserved at the same rate as that for regular dividends. United States tax would only be imposed on contingent interest that is not portfolio interest under statutory law. The second exception is for certain interest payments connected to a real estate mortgage investment conduit (REMIC), which are typically subject to full source country taxation both because these investment vehicles create many opportunities for tax avoidance and because a reduced rate of source country tax would disadvantage domestic purchasers in relation to foreign investors in real property.

11.04   Royalties — Treaty Article 12

As discussed in Unit 7, royalties are typically subject to the 30 percent tax under domestic law. However, royalties derived from the United States are generally exempt from tax or subject to a reduced rate of tax under most tax treaties. The 2006 Model Tax Treaty, like its 1996 predecessor, provides for complete source country exemption of royalties derived and beneficially owned by a resident of the other contracting state. Under the treaties that follow this model, royalties derived by a foreign licensor from United States sources are exempt from United States taxation. Accordingly, so long as the royalties are not attributable to a permanent establishment, they are also exempt from the flat 30 percent tax. However, a number of treaties (including, for example, those with Australia, India, and Mexico) only reduce source country withholding, typically to between 5 and 20 percent. As in the case of interest and dividends, royalties that are attributable to a permanent establishment are not dealt with in Article 12 but are business profits, addressed in Article 7 (*see* Unit 12).

Under domestic law, the term "royalties" generally encompasses payments received for the use of (or the right to use): (1) any copyright of literary, artistic, or scientific work (often excluding cinematographic, radio, or television films); (2) any patent, trademark, secret formula, process, or other like right or property; or (3) information concerning industrial, commercial, or scientific experience. Treaties provide a separate definition that is generally independent of domestic law, but that typically cover the same range of items. Many treaties also treat as royalties any gains derived from the alienation of any right or property that are contingent on the productivity, use, or disposition thereof.

11.05   Gains from the Disposition of Property — Treaty Article 13

The flat 30 percent tax of §§ 871 and 881 applies to gain from the sale or exchange of intangible assets (but only to a limited extent) and to gain from the sale or exchange of capital assets (but only if held by foreign individuals meeting certain tax home requirements). Under most treaties, gains derived from the transfer of property are generally taxable only in the country of the transferor's residence. However, in many treaties, the United States retains jurisdiction to tax those gains derived from the transfer of intangible assets where the amount of gain is contingent on the productivity, use, or disposition of the intangible asset, on the theory that this kind of property interest possess a sufficient nexus to the United States to warrant the reservation of a right to tax the gain received upon their disposition.

11.06   Income from Real Property — Treaty Articles 6 and 13

Most treaties do not provide for a reduction of the statutory rate for income derived from real property. The income is typically subject to tax in the situs jurisdiction regardless of whether the income is derived annually (e.g., rental income) or whether the income is derived from a disposition of the property (e.g., gain from the sale of the property).

11.07   Residual Income — Treaty Article 21

To the extent that miscellaneous types of income might be classified as passive income (such as prizes and awards), the "Other Income" article of a treaty will typically eliminate the United States tax on such income, generally granting taxing authority to the recipient's home country only. As in the case of dividends, royalties, and interest, however, this rule only applies so long as the income is not attributable to a permanent establishment in the United States. Where a permanent establishment exists, Article 7 will apply to the income attributable to it.

It should be fairly clear that, when dealing with treaties, it is imperative to ascertain whether a permanent establishment exists and, if so, whether income items are attributable to it. If so, these income items will be characterized as business profits and may be subject to taxation under regular statutory rules. Permanent establishments and attributable business profits are therefore the subject of the next Unit.

D.   REFERENCE MATERIALS

- Revenue Ruling 75-118

REVENUE RULING 75-118
1975-1 CB 390

Advice has been requested whether, under the circumstances described below, a dividend paid by a United States subsidiary corporation to its Netherlands parent corporation is subject to the reduced rate of tax of 5 percent provided by Article VII(1)(b) of the Income Tax Convention between the United States and the Netherlands (the "Convention"), T.D. 5778, 1950-1 C.B. 92, and United States-Netherlands Supplementary Income Tax Convention, 1967-2 C.B. 472.

S2 is a domestic corporation all of whose stock is owned by S1, a corporation organized under the laws of the Netherlands. P, a Netherlands corporation, owns all of the stock of S1.

S1 was organized in 1947 and is a holding company holding the stock of three United States corporations including S2 and numerous foreign corporations. S1 does not have a permanent establishment in the United States. S1 acquired the stock of S2 in 1965 as a partial liquidation distribution from a Canadian subsidiary of P. This liquidation was effected upon a belief that Canada might amend its income tax law in a way that the Canadian corporation would be taxed on dividends received from *S2* and taxed on capital gain arising from a later disposition of the *S2* stock.

S1 has complete dominion and control over dividends which it receives from *S2* and is under no obligation to transfer such dividends to *P.*

S2 had gross income from manufacturing in 1973 and in each year since its incorporation. However, such gross income has included neither interest nor dividend income. *S2* paid a dividend to *S1* on December 1, 1973.

Article VII of the Convention provides, in part, that dividends paid by a United States corporation to a Netherlands corporation shall be subject to tax by the United States at a rate not exceeding 5 percent if (1) during the part of the taxable year preceding payment of the dividend and during the whole of the prior taxable year the Netherlands corporation owned at least 25 percent of the voting stock of the United States corporation; (2) not more than 25 percent of the gross income of the United States corporation for such year consisted of interest and dividends; and (3) the shares of stock with respect to which the dividends are paid are not effectively connected with any permanent establishment that the Netherlands corporation has in the United States.

Accordingly, the dividend paid in 1973 by *S2* to *S1* falls within the scope of Article VII(1)(b) of the Convention and is subject to the reduced rate of tax of 5 percent.

Unit 12

TAX TREATIES AND BUSINESS INCOME

A. CODE AND REGULATION PROVISIONS

Relevant portions of the United States-Canada Tax Treaty.

B. PROBLEMS FOR CLASS DISCUSSION

12-1. CanCo was organized under the laws of Canada and is owned entirely by Canadian citizens and residents. Its principal business activity consists of the worldwide sale of goods purchased in Canada. All of CanCo's office facilities are located in Canada.

(a) If CanCo receives unsolicited orders from United States residents, is its income subject to taxation in the United States?

(b) How does the answer to (a) change if CanCo sends catalogues to various individuals in the United States and advertises on United States television, all of which leads to the placement of orders by United States residents?

(c) How does the answer to (a) change if, regarding its sales made in the United States, orders for CanCo's goods are solicited by its traveling salespersons operating out of the home office in Canada on a commission basis? Assume that purchase orders are sent to the Canadian office where they are accepted by CanCo and filled from inventory warehoused in Canada. Also assume that CanCo maintains no inventory, plant, office, or other facilities in the United States.

(d) How does the answer to (c) change if CanCo maintains a branch office located in leased office space in Chicago, the branch maintains a leased warehouse for storage of purchased inventory, and United States sales staff operates out of the Chicago office, but all orders must be accepted in Canada?

(e) Would CanCo have a permanent establishment in the United States if it were a shareholder in a corporation conducting a trade or business through a permanent establishment in the United States?

(f) Would the answer to (e) change if CanCo was a significant shareholder? A majority shareholder? The sole shareholder?

(g) Would the answer to (e) change if CanCo instead invested in a general partnership or limited liability company rather than a corporation?

(h) X Corporation is organized in Canada. It entered into a contract with DomCo, an unrelated domestic corporation, under which DomCo serves as X's exclusive agent in selling X's products in the United States. DomCo receives a commission for each sale to a United States customer. The contract prohibits DomCo from selling any competing products in the United States and from acting as the agent for another in selling any competing products in the United States. Is its income subject to tax in the United States?

(i) Z Corporation is organized in Canada. It purchases goods in the United States for sale to customers in foreign countries. Z Corporation maintains an office in San Diego, California, that is staffed by domestic employees who facilitate purchases and arrange for shipping. Is its income subject to tax in the United States?

12-2. George is a Canadian architect representing a client that is constructing a building in San Francisco. As part of his services, George was on site on six different days during the year.

(a) Is George subject to taxation by the United States?

(b) Would the answer to (a) change if George was on site for nine consecutive months during the year?

(c) Suppose instead that George is a commissioned salesperson who works for a Canadian corporation that sells products in the United States. George spends 130 days in the United States during the year in pursuit of his employment. Is George subject to taxation in the United States?

12-3. ForCo is a Canadian corporation that purchases zippers for sale. It has facilities in the United States, Argentina, and Bolivia. The zippers bought in the United States are sold exclusively in the United States. Likewise, the zippers bought in Argentina are sold exclusively there, and the zippers bought in Bolivia are sold exclusively within Bolivian borders. ForCo generates all of its income from these three countries. ForCo does not have a United States branch or separate division that oversees operations in the United States. In addition, ForCo purchases wine from a distributor in Argentina and sells it exclusively therein. For Year 1, ForCo incurred $50,000 in general administrative expenses related to both United States and non-United States operations. In addition, ForCo incurred $80,000 in deductible interest expense in Year 1 from its borrowings used to improve the Bolivian facility. Additionally, it has a $150,000 expense for labor/wages regarding the zippers, $90,000 in the United States, $40,000 in Argentina, and $20,000 in Bolivia, and $70,000 expense for labor and wages regarding the wine. ForCo's sales and gross income from each country in Year 1 are as follows:

| Country | Zippers | | | Wine |
	Asset Bases	Sales	Gross Income	Gross Income
United States	$50,000	$250,000	$100,000	$0
Argentina	$100,000	$1,500,000	$200,000	$600,000
Bolivia	$200,000	$800,000	$300,000	$0

Assuming the income from the purchase and sale of zippers in Argentina and Bolivia is not attributable to ForCo's United States operations, what is ForCo's taxable income in Year 1 for United States income tax purposes?

C. OVERVIEW

As discussed in previous Units, in contrast to the worldwide taxation the United States imposes on its citizens and residents, foreign persons are generally taxable only on items of income derived from United States sources or from the conduct of domestic trade or business activities. Units 7 through 9 explained that United States trade or business income may be "effectively connected" with the conduct of such trade or business, and thus potentially taxed at the regular United States rates, or it may not be effectively connected, but still potentially subject to a flat 30 percent tax. Unit 10 introduced treaties as a second source of international tax law, and Unit 11 showed how a treaty might change the tax consequences for foreign persons investing in the United States. Of course treaties not only cover passive-type investments; they also address cross-border business activities.

This Unit is concerned with the general tax treaty principles governing the receipt of business income (which includes income from the performance of dependent and independent services). As mentioned in previous Units, while tax treaties address both outbound transactions (United States residents deriving income from a foreign jurisdiction) and inbound transactions (foreign residents deriving income from within the United States), the discussion in this Unit focuses primarily on the latter: how will the United States tax business income earned in the United States by foreign persons who are eligible for the benefits of a tax treaty with the United States?

Usually, having a treaty in place means having a higher threshold to United States taxation: the treaty tends to tighten the scope of source based (or host country) jurisdiction in favor of residence based (or home country) jurisdiction. In other words, when the United States signs a treaty, it usually foregoes some of its taxing rights with the idea that reciprocal concessions by the other contracting state will reduce tax burdens on United States persons doing business in the other country. Accordingly, under statutory law, foreign persons are subject to United States taxation on all income derived from the conduct of trade or business in the United States, while under most treaties, income derived from the conduct of a trade or business is taxable by the United States only if it constitutes "business profits" that are "attributable to" a "permanent establishment" maintained in the United States.

While the concepts of "trade or business" and "effectively connected" discussed more fully in Unit 8 are similar to the concepts of "permanent establishment" and "attributable to" discussed in this Unit, the treaty concepts generally require a greater nexus or immersion in the host country than do the statutory standards. Figure 12-1 compare the relevant treaty and statutory language.

FIGURE 12-1. UNITED STATES TAXATION OF UNITED STATES BUSINESS INCOME

	Residents of Treaty Countries	Residents of Non-Treaty Countries
Required presence in the United States	Must have a PERMANENT ESTABLISHMENT in the United States to be subject to taxation	Need only be ENGAGED IN TRADE OR BUSINESS within the United States to be subject to taxation
What is taxed?	BUSINESS PROFITS that are ATTRIBUTABLE TO the permanent establishment	Income EFFECTIVELY CONNECTED with the conduct of a trade or business in the United States
Rate of tax	Graduated rates (§ 1 or § 11)	Graduated rates (§ 1 or § 11)
Deductions allowed?	Yes	Yes

Determining how a treaty impacts the United States taxation of business income thus involves a number of interpretive steps before the ultimate tax consequences can be determined. First, it must be determined whether a person is carrying on a business in the United States for treaty purposes. If so, it must be determined whether that business is conducted through a "permanent establishment." If it is not, the income will not be taxed as business profits (but might be taxed under another treaty provision). If, however, the business is carried on through a permanent establishment, profits must be appropriately attributed to the permanent establishment. Finally, deductions must also be appropriately allocated to the permanent establishment. Only after each of these steps has been determined can the tax consequences of a treaty-resident person operating a business in the United States be assessed.

It is important to remember that a corporation is typically respected as a separate taxpayer for United States tax purposes, so a foreign person — whether individual or corporate — investing in a domestic corporation that carries on a trade or business will not need to invoke a treaty with respect to the business profits of the domestic corporation. Generally speaking, it is only when a foreign person is itself involved in carrying on a domestic business that a treaty would be invoked to limit the taxing jurisdiction of the United States.

12.01 United States Trade or Business

The standard for determining whether a foreign person is carrying on a business in the United States for tax treaty purposes is likely the same standard employed in determining if a person is engaged in a domestic trade or business under § 864, discussed in Unit 8. As a generalization, the standard is similar to that required for deductibility of expenses under § 162 (i.e., regularity and continuity). If a foreign person does not conduct a trade or business under § 864, it will be exempt from domestic tax on its active business profits without the need for a treaty exemption.

12.02   Permanent Establishment — Treaty Article 5

Generally, income tax treaties provide that business income is taxable in a country only if an enterprise possesses a "permanent establishment" in such country. Revenue Ruling 58-63, excerpted in Part D of this Unit, illustrates that there is a qualitative difference between a trade or business and a permanent establishment. The Ruling might seem familiar — it was also excerpted, albeit more heavily — in Unit 8. There, the excerpt demonstrated that a United States trade or business could be found even in the context of a single instance of activity (entering a horse in a race). In this Unit, more of the Ruling is included — the same activity that constituted a trade or business did not constitute a permanent establishment under the United States-France tax treaty, so none of the income was subject to United States tax. The Ruling demonstrates that the permanent establishment provision serves as a higher threshold to the taxation of business profits. Instead of triggering United States tax upon meeting the more easily satisfied trade or business standard, a foreign person will be able to avoid triggering United States tax if the activities do not constitute a permanent establishment.

United States treaties generally equate a permanent establishment with a fixed place of business through which the business of an enterprise is wholly or partly carried on.[1] An enterprise will possess a permanent establishment in the United States if it either maintains such a fixed place of business in the United States itself, or if the activities of another person who maintains such a fixed place of business are imputed to the enterprise. The permanent establishment concept has thus been summarily described as a "physical presence test supplemented by an agency rule and restricted by an activity rule."[2]

A permanent establishment may include a place of management, a branch, an office, a factory, a workshop, a warehouse, or a place of extraction of natural resources. A historical view of the concept suggests that some sort of physical presence is required, but currently under debate is whether human presence is likewise essential. For example, the Organization for Economic Cooperation and Development (OECD) has taken the position that in certain cases computer servers may create a permanent establishment if the business of an enterprise is wholly or partly carried on through such servers.

The OECD adopted changes to its model tax convention in 2001 to reflect this position. The OECD's theory is that a server is a piece of equipment that has a physical location, which may constitute a "fixed place of business" for the enterprise that operates it. However, the United States Treasury Department has not similarly revised its model treaty, having taken the position that the use of a

---

[1] *See, e.g.*, Art. 5(1) of the 2006 Model Tax Treaty.

[2] Remarks of Jacques Sasseville, head of tax treaty matters at the OECD, at the Conference Board of Canada's 1999 Conference on Advanced E-Commerce Tax Policy in New York, New York. *See* "OECD Working Group Proposes Web Site Not Be Treated as 'Permanent Establishment,'" Bloomberg BNA Tax Management Weekly Report (Nov. 22, 1999).

computer server is a passive activity, analogous to the use of a warehouse. The United States and other OECD and non-OECD countries continue to consider whether servers should be, by themselves, capable of giving rise to a permanent establishment.

Treaties also provide some guidance as to what activities will not constitute a permanent establishment. Many common arrangements with respect to merchandise or goods do not constitute a permanent establishment. For instance, the use of facilities or the maintenance of a stock of goods solely for the purpose of storage, display, or delivery is not a permanent establishment. Neither does the use of a facility for ancillary business purposes generally give rise to a permanent establishment.

Likewise, no permanent establishment arises from the maintenance of a fixed place of business solely for the purpose of purchasing goods or merchandise, collecting information, or carrying on any other activity of a preparatory or auxiliary character. Finally, in the context of electronic commerce, unlike a computer server, a website is not a physical location and therefore is generally thought not to create a permanent establishment.

Some treaties permit inventory to be stored by a foreign person in a United States warehouse for quick delivery to domestic customers without that inventory stock (or the warehouse in which it is stored) constituting a permanent establishment. Similarly, the use by a foreign person of a United States showroom or a demonstration room to display or demonstrate the use of its products to domestic customers will not constitute a United States permanent establishment. Perhaps for pragmatic reasons, the Service has broadly construed the scope of the "preparatory or auxiliary activities" that do not give rise to a permanent establishment (compare Revenue Ruling 72-418 and Revenue Ruling 77-45, each of which are excerpted in Part D of this Unit).

A permanent establishment may indirectly arise by virtue of a foreign person's ownership interest in a pass-through entity. For instance, a permanent establishment may be imputed to a foreign partner in a limited or general partnership if the partnership itself has a United States permanent establishment. See, for example, *Unger v. Commissioner*, excerpted in Part D of this Unit. If the partnership earns business profits, the foreign partner's distributive share of such profits retains its partnership-level character upon pass-through. As that partner is deemed to have a United States permanent establishment, the partner's share of partnership business profits will not be insulated from taxation under a treaty in the hands of the distributee partner.

In contrast, stock ownership of, or affiliation with, entities or persons with a United States permanent establishment does not in and of itself appear to be sufficient grounds to impute a permanent establishment to the owner or affiliate, as suggested by Revenue Rulings 76-322 and 86-156, also excerpted in Part D.

12.03   Duration

Even if a foreign person uses a United States office or other fixed place of business, a permanent establishment should not arise if the use of that office or fixed place of business is brief or transitory rather than permanent. What represents brief (as opposed to permanent) use will vary based on the facts and circumstances of each particular case. Conducting significant business operations at a site for abbreviated time periods has been found to give rise to a permanent establishment.[3]

12.04   Use of Another's Fixed Place of Business

Business exigencies, particularly for multinational entities, often necessitate the use by foreign employees of the domestic offices or establishments of a United States affiliate or other United States person. At issue in such cases is the permitted extent of such use before the foreign entity is found to have a permanent establishment. The use of United States hotel rooms by the employees of a foreign person on a temporary and transient basis should not give rise to a domestic permanent establishment. Recall that this scenario likewise would probably not constitute a trade or business according to *The Scottish American Investment Co., Ltd. v. Commissioner*, excerpted and discussed in Unit 8.

By analogy, the temporary and transient use of a domestic subsidiary's office by employees of a foreign parent corporation should not constitute a permanent establishment. However, a permanent establishment may arise if the employees of a foreign corporation make frequent and continuous use of another's domestic office or fixed place of business for substantial periods of time. In that case, the fact that the office is not owned by the foreign corporation is not likely to be sufficient detachment to negate the existence of a permanent establishment.

12.05   Use of Agents

A permanent establishment may arise if the employees of a foreign person use a United States office or other fixed place of business. Likewise, a permanent establishment will exist when a foreign person conducts business through an agent who effectively serves as its United States alter-ego. Most treaties generally provide that the office of a person (an "agent") who acts on behalf of a foreign taxpayer (the "principal") may be imputed to that taxpayer under certain circumstances, with two pertinent and typical limitations.

First, consistent with Article 5(6) of the 2006 Model Tax Treaty, a foreign person does not have a permanent establishment solely because it conducts business in the United States through a broker, general commission agent, or any other independent agent, so long as that agent acts in the ordinary course of its business.[4]

---

[3] *See, e.g.*, Rev. Rul. 67-322, 1967-2 C.B. 469 (Danish corporation that operated a restaurant in the United States for a period of six months in each of two consecutive years was considered to carry on a trade or business in the United States through a permanent establishment).

[4] *See also* Article 5(7) of the United States-Canada Tax Treaty.

Second, consistent with Article 5(5) of the 2006 Model Tax Treaty (and Article 5(5) of the United States-Canada Tax Treaty),[5] a dependent agent's activities are imputed to a foreign principal only if the agent has and habitually exercises in the United States the authority to conclude contracts in the name of the principal and the agent's activities themselves constitute a permanent establishment. For an example, see Revenue Ruling 90-80, excerpted in Part D of this Unit.

An independent agent is one who is paid, in pursuance of his or her usual trade or business, to sell goods or merchandise consigned or entrusted to the agent for that purpose by or for the owner of such goods or merchandise.

A dependent agent is one that truly stands in the stead of the principal, conducting business in its place. A dependent agent may have the authority to negotiate and conclude contracts in the name of the principal or hold stock or merchandise of the principal and regularly fill orders from that stock on behalf of the principal. Incidental or occasional contractual or merchandising activity is insufficient to render an agent a dependent agent. The dependent agent's power to conclude contracts on behalf of the principal or its power to fill orders must be exercised with "some frequency over a continuous period of time." Occasional or incidental activity does not evidence regularity.

12.06 Dependent Agents

United States tax treaties often provide for a fairly generous cushion of dependent agent activity that may take place before a principal is deemed to have a permanent establishment. The mere fact that an agent concludes certain contracts in the United States is not *per se* evidence of a permanent establishment. Rather, a permanent establishment arises only if the agent regularly executes contracts setting forth the name of its foreign principal as the contracting party. An internet services provider therefore is probably not a dependent agent because its activities do not generally include such contractual authority.

Agents Versus Purchasers. Agents are clearly distinguished from purchasers for purposes of imputing a permanent establishment to a principal. A bona fide purchaser of goods is not an agent of the seller. If a domestic entity purchases goods from a foreign manufacturer and resells the goods on terms and conditions established by the domestic purchaser, the domestic activities of that purchaser are not imputed to the foreign manufacturer for treaty purposes and do not translate to a permanent establishment for the foreign manufacturer.

Agents Versus Lessees. For tax treaty purposes, lessees are also distinguished from agents. A bona fide lessee of property or equipment is not an agent of the lessor. Thus, if a domestic entity leases personal property from a foreign lessor eligible for treaty benefits, neither the existence of the lease nor the presence of leased personal property within the United States should give rise to a United States permanent establishment for the lessor. In contrast, the lease of domestic real property by a foreign person may give rise to a permanent establishment

---

[5] Where appropriate, this text may specifically refer to the Canada treaty, as that treaty is used in the problems for class discussion.

merely by virtue of the United States nexus of that property.

12.07   Income from Employment — Treaty Article 14[6]

Tax treaties typically contain special threshold rules governing the taxation of income derived by an individual from performing personal services. These rules distinguish between dependent and independent personal services. "Dependent personal services" generally includes those performed by employees. Under Article 14(2) of the 2006 Model Tax Treaty, compensation derived by a foreign individual eligible for treaty benefits is not subject to United States income taxation if the recipient is present in the United States for 183 days or less in the taxable year, the compensation is paid by or on behalf of a foreign employer, and it is not borne by a United States permanent establishment or fixed base. Some treaties also contain dollar thresholds, in some cases limited to wages earned by students or entertainers.

Some treaties exempt dependent services from taxation if the employee is present in the United States for a limited time period. Durational thresholds were considered by the Service in Revenue Ruling 86-145, reproduced in Part D of this Unit. Treaties may also differentiate between employees based on the status of their employers. For instance, an individual who performs services on behalf of a foreign employer may be eligible for treaty benefits only if the employee provides services for a treaty country employer that is resident in that country. In contrast, exemption may not apply to an individual who comes to the United States and works for a domestic employer.

A bona fide employer-employee relationship must exist in order to ensure treaty exemptions. For example, if a foreign individual establishes a foreign corporation to "employ" him or her shortly before a United States tour, the Service will likely assert that no true employer-employee relationship exists. If the corporate employer lacks substance (i.e., it merely serves as a shell for the efforts of the individual), the Service will likely treat the foreign corporate employer as an agent of the "employee" when the employer receives United States source payments. This recharacterization serves to deny the application of the dependent services exemption to the foreign individual. However, under some treaties, the foreign individual's United States source compensation may still be exempt under an independent services article, as discussed below.

In some situations, treaty benefits cannot be extended if the compensation sought to be excluded is deducted on a United States tax return filed by the foreign employer or by another person. Such a limitation prevents double dipping into tax benefits both by exempting the recipient's income from taxation and claiming a corresponding deduction from the payor's United States taxable income.

---

[6] Article 14 of the United States-Canada Tax Treaty, addressing independent personal services, was deleted by the Fifth Protocol to the treaty, which entered into force in 2008. Such independent personal services are dealt with under Articles 5 and 7 relating to permanent establishments and business profits. Subsequent treaty articles were not re-numbered, so dependent personal services (i.e., income from employment) are addressed in Article 15 of the United States-Canada Tax Treaty, the analogue to Article 14 of 2006 Model Tax Treaty.

Some tax treaties limit the amount of income that may be received by a claimant for dependent services. For example, a treaty may impose a $10,000 limit on domestic services. If the limit is exceeded, all United States source compensation is taxable; the first $10,000 may not be excluded. Certain exclusions may also apply in computing the income limitation.

12.08   Independent Personal Services (Independent Contractors)

In accordance with prior United States and OECD model tax treaties, some of the United States tax treaties currently in force address income from independent personal services in a separate article, typically subjecting this kind of income to tax only if the services are performed in the United States and the income is attributable to a domestic fixed base that is regularly available to the individual for the purpose of performing the services.

Under these treaties, independent services are analyzed by reference to whether a "fixed base" existed, while other business profits are analyzed by reference to whether a permanent establishment existed. In most cases, the two concepts are thought to be analogous if not identical. Because of this overlap, treaty formulators at the OECD decided to collapse the independent services article of that model treaty (Article 14) into its business profits article (Article 7), beginning with the 2001 OECD model. The United States 2006 Model Tax Treaty (as well as subsequent new or recently amended United States treaties) follows suit.

The OECD Commentary explains that the integration of the two concepts was adopted because it was not always clear which activities should fall into which provision, and it was decided that in any case there were no intended differences between the concepts of fixed base and permanent establishment, nor in how profits and taxation were to be computed under the two articles. The Treasury Technical Explanation notes that the language in the 2006 Model Tax Treaty is now identical to that in the OECD model tax convention, and that the change similarly "is intended to clarify that income from the performance of professional services or other activities of an independent character is dealt with under Article 7 (Business Profits). . . ."

Thus, although the term "business" is not comprehensively defined anywhere in the 2006 Model Tax Treaty, Article 3(1)(e) provides that it includes the performance of professional and other independent services. As a result, the taxation of income from such services is addressed in Article 7 of the 2006 Model Tax Treaty (and of subsequent new or amended United States treaties), discussed below.

Some United States tax treaties contain specific rules in Article 5 that address when a permanent establishment will arise from the provision of services. For example, the United States-Canada Tax Treaty, as amended by the Fifth Protocol, contains two separate tests for when services will be considered provided through a permanent establishment. Under the first test, services provided in one contracting state by an individual on behalf of an enterprise for 183 days or more during any 12-month period will be deemed conducted through a permanent establishment, if, during that period, more than 50 percent of the gross business revenue of the enterprise is derived from such services. The second test will deem services to be conducted through a permanent establishment where the services are provided in the other contracting state for 183 days or more in any 12-month period for the same or a connected project, for customers resident in that other contracting state, or who maintain a permanent establishment therein, if the services are provided in respect of that permanent establishment. If either of these tests is met, income from the services is taxed under Article 7 (Business Profits).

12.09   Consequences of Having a Permanent Establishment

After having determined that a foreign taxpayer has a "permanent establishment" in the United States, the next step is to ascertain the "business profits" of the taxpayer that are "attributable to" the permanent establishment. Under most treaties, only these business profits may be taxed by the United States (*see* Article 7 of the 2006 Model Tax Treaty; most treaties currently in force use identical language). Some treaties also include a permanent establishment force of attraction rule as an anti-avoidance measure (for example, the treaties with India, Indonesia, Kazakhstan, Latvia, Mexico, and Thailand contain such a provision). Under these treaties, in addition to business profits attributable to a permanent establishment, the United States may treat income as business profits attributable to that permanent establishment if it arises from sales of goods or merchandise that are similar to those sold through the permanent establishment or from business activities that are similar to those conducted through the permanent establishment.

In the absence of a force of attraction provision, however, only those business profits that are attributable to the permanent establishment will generally be taxed by the United States. Treaties are fairly ambiguous regarding how the United States will tax these business profits. Article 7(2) of the 2006 Model Tax Treaty provides that profits should be attributed to the permanent establishment as if the permanent establishment were a "distinct and independent enterprise" in the United States, and Article 7(3) provides that expenses "incurred for the purposes of the permanent establishment," regardless of where they are incurred, should be allowed as deductions against the business profits so attributed.

The treaty offers no further guidance regarding the ultimate taxation of these profits, but according to the principles of anti-discrimination (*see* Article 24), the United States must generally tax these profits in the same manner as business profits earned by domestic enterprises, namely, on a net basis using the graduated tax rates available to residents and domestic corporations.

Although the fundamental taxing framework applicable to a foreign person's business income parallels that applicable to domestic persons, the method of computing a foreign person's net income from a permanent establishment is distinct and complex. Generally, the determination of such income follows a three step sequence. First, and as described in greater detail in Subpart 12.12, below, the gross income derived by the foreign person attributable to a permanent establishment must be segregated from any other foreign or domestic source income which is not attributable to that permanent establishment. Second, the foreign person's expenses related to the permanent establishment must be segregated. Finally, these expenses must be allocated between income attributable to the permanent establishment and other income.

12.10   Business Profits — Treaty Article 7

The term "business profits" generally includes income derived from any trade or business, including the rental of tangible personal property and the performance of personal services. Therefore, any income derived from the conduct of an active business is characterized as business profits. As discussed briefly in Unit 11, the business profits article generally overrides other treaty articles dealing with specific types of income. Under the 2006 Model Tax Treaty and most United States treaties currently in force, if a foreign person maintains and derives income through a permanent establishment in the United States, the income typically will be subject to tax on a net basis under the business profits article even if it is exempt under a separate treaty article. For instance, royalties might be exempt from United States tax under Article 12 of the 2006 Model Tax Treaty, but if characterized as business profits attributable to a permanent establishment, this income would be taxable under Article 7.

Conversely, if a foreign person does not maintain a United States permanent establishment (or derives United States source income unrelated to a permanent establishment), the treaty article dealing with that specific type of income (if any) generally controls. For example, if a foreign corporation maintains a permanent establishment and receives a dividend from a United States portfolio investment that is unrelated to that permanent establishment, the dividend income will be subject to a flat withholding tax under the dividends article (Article 10 in the 2006 Model Tax Treaty) rather than the business profits article (Article 7).

12.11   The "Attributable to" Concept

Business profits are "attributable to" a permanent establishment if the assets or activities of the permanent establishment play a meaningful role in generating those profits. For example, if a foreign taxpayer is engaged in a domestic trade or business through a permanent establishment and that taxpayer makes an isolated sale of inventory in the United States from an unrelated business wholly independent of the assets or activities of the permanent establishment, the domestic source profit realized is not attributable to the foreign person's permanent establishment.

In the tax treaty context, income must be attributable to the taxpayer's permanent establishment before subjecting that income to the graduated rates. This treatment ensures that passive income retains its status as such and bears a treaty rate of (generally) zero to 15 percent, while "true" business income is computed on a net basis and subjected to the graduated rates of §§ 1, 11, and 55, as the case may be. This distinction also ensures that a foreign person conducting a domestic trade or business does not confront the disincentive of high tax rates with respect to the person's non-business investment in the United States.

12.12   Gross Income Attributable to a Permanent Establishment

The first step in taxing a foreign person deriving business profits from a permanent establishment involves separating the income attributable to that business from other income. "Attributable to" income encompasses two principal categories of income: (1) fixed or determinable income and capital gain or loss from sources within the United States; and (2) some foreign source income.

The determination of whether income is attributable to a permanent establishment is discussed in the Technical Explanations of many treaties. Generally, only income from assets used, risks assumed, and activities performed by, the permanent establishment will be attributable to the permanent establishment.[7]

Many treaties provide that the determination of whether income is attributable to a permanent establishment incorporates the domestic rules that attribute income to the taxing jurisdiction. As a result, Unit 8, which outlines the framework for attributing income to a United States trade or business, should be revisited when analyzing whether business profits will be attributed to a permanent establishment.

As discussed in Unit 8, domestic rules provide mechanisms for segregating passive income from business income. They generally employ two tests: one to be applied to taxpayers such as foreign sellers or manufacturers dealing with tangible goods in the United States (the "asset-use" test) and the other to be applied to taxpayers such as those conducting service-intensive businesses or those dealing with the licensing of intangible assets (the "material-factor" test).

Foreign persons engaged in the manufacture or sale of tangible goods in the United States who concomitantly derive passive income items in the course of that business generally face the asset-use test. This test seeks to distinguish income derived from holding investment assets from income generated from assets used in the day-to-day operation of the permanent establishment. The asset-use test focuses on whether the income is derived from assets used, or held for use, in the conduct of a United States trade or business through a permanent establishment.

Three factors are considered in deciding whether an asset is used, or held for use, in a United States business: (1) whether the asset is held for the principal purpose of promoting the *present* conduct of a United States trade or business; (2) whether the asset is acquired and held in the ordinary course of the trade or business; and (3) whether the asset is otherwise held in some direct relationship to the trade or business. If the asset is deemed to be a business asset under one of these standards, all income flowing from its use is attributable to the permanent establishment.

A rebuttable presumption generally exists that the requisite relationship is present for purposes of the asset-use test if the asset is acquired with funds generated by the trade or business, the income generated from the asset is

---

[7] *See, e.g.*, Technical Explanation to the 2006 Model Tax Treaty, Art. 7(2).

reinvested in that trade or business, and United States personnel actively involved in that business exercise significant management and control over the investment of the asset. This presumption can be rebutted if the foreign person demonstrates that an asset is held to carry out some future business purpose and not to meet present business needs.

Unlike the asset-use test, which focuses narrowly on the role of particular income-generating assets in business operations, the material-factor test focuses on the more overarching measure of the degree of correlation with the business activities of the foreign person's United States permanent establishment. Such income is considered "attributable to" if the United States activities of that business are a material factor in the realization of such items of income, gain, or loss.

Generally, a United States permanent establishment will not be a material factor in generating income if the core activities incident to the transaction are conducted abroad. Such would be the case in a patent licensing context where the license negotiation and consummation occurs abroad by foreign employees and the United States branch plays no role in otherwise arranging for the licenses.

12.13   Waiver of Business Profits Article Protection

A foreign person not maintaining a United States permanent establishment may decline to use an otherwise available tax treaty exemption for business profits. This approach may prove beneficial, for example, in creating a United States net operating loss carryforward. A waiver may also dislodge income attributable to a permanent establishment to absorb losses not so attributable.

D.   REFERENCE MATERIALS

- Revenue Ruling 58-63
- Revenue Ruling 72-418
- Revenue Ruling 77-45
- *Unger v. Commissioner*
- Revenue Ruling 90-80
- Revenue Ruling 76-322
- Revenue Ruling 86-156
- Revenue Ruling 86-145

REVENUE RULING 58-63
1958-1 C.B. 624

. . .

Advice has been requested whether a nonresident alien individual, owning a racing stable in France and engaged in the operation of same for profit, who enters a horse in a race in the United States, is exempt from United States income tax on the winnings therefrom.

A citizen and resident of France owned and operated a horse racing stable, located in France, for profit. He was invited to enter an outstanding horse in a race to be held in the United States. He and the racing association agreed that the horse would not compete in any other races while in the United States. The racing association invited him to view the race and participate in the social events connected therewith. The invitation was accepted. The horse won the race and the owner was paid the winner's purse.

The operation of a racing stable for profit is a business enterprise. The entry of a horse in a race in this country constitutes being "engaged in trade or business within the United Sates," within the meaning of section 871(c) of the Internal Revenue Code of 1954. Accordingly, income derived therefore is subject to United States income tax unless exempted by some other provision of law.

Article 3 of the income tax convention between the United States and France provides, in part, that an enterprise of one of the contracting states is not subject to taxation by the other contracting state in respect of its industrial and commercial profits except in respect of such profits allocable to its permanent establishment in the latter state. A "French enterprise" includes every form of undertaking carried on by an individual resident of France in France. "Industrial and commercial profits" include profits derived from the industrial activity of a French enterprise. The term "permanent establishment" includes branches, mines and oil wells, plantations, factories, workshops, stories, purchasing and selling and other offices, agencies, warehouses, and other fixed places of business.

Accordingly, it is held that a nonresident alien individual does not have a permanent establishment in the United States merely by entering a race horse in a single race in the United States and coming to the United States to view the race and to participate in the social events connected therewith. While the winner's purse received by the owner of a racing stable operated for profit constitutes industrial or commercial profits, this income is exempt from United States income tax under Article 3 of the income tax convention between the United States and France.

REVENUE RULING 72-418
1972-2 C.B. 661

. . .

Advice has been requested whether, for purposes of United States income taxation, the activities of an office maintained in the United States by a German bank under the circumstances described below cause that office to be a "permanent establishment" of the bank in the United States within the meaning of Article II(1)(c) of the [United States-Germany income tax treaty].

A German bank, a foreign corporation which has its business management or seat in the Federal Republic of Germany, maintains a representative's office in the United States. The lease of the office space is in the name of an individual who is acting as the bank's representative. The German bank maintains an account with a bank incorporated in the United States out of which the expenses of the representative's office are paid by checks drawn on such United States bank.

The bank's office in the United States performs the following activities, all without fees:

1. Investigates and obtains information regarding various commercial and financial matters in the United States of interest to the bank, and submits reports thereon to its head office in Germany. The nature of these reports covers a large field varying from specific credit reports on American banks to reports on general financial conditions in the United States.

2. Assists the bank's United States and German customers with information, and furnishes German customers with letters of introduction to American banks or manufacturing corporations. On occasions, it authenticates signatures on letters or cables to the home office in Germany.

3. Establishes and maintains contracts with banks, financial institutions, business corporations and government agencies in the United States, and furnishes them with information regarding German banking, financial, and business matters, and current interest and discount rates generally prevailing in Germany.

4. On rare occasions, communicates with the bank's debtors in the United States and obtains information regarding the possibility of repayment of past due obligations.

5. Advertises for the bank throughout the United States in newspapers, periodicals and by personal contacts.

The bank's office in the United States does not engage in buying, selling, paying, or collecting bills of exchange; issuing letters of credit or receiving money for transmission or transmitting money by draft, check, cable, or otherwise, making loans; receiving deposits or exercising fiduciary powers; keeping or maintaining any books of account for the bank except a record of its own expenses; concluding any contracts on behalf of the bank; or soliciting business on behalf of the bank.

Article II(1)(c) of the [United States-Germany income tax treaty] provides that the term "permanent establishment" means a fixed place of business in which the business of an enterprise of one of the contracting States is wholly or partly carried on, and includes an "office." However, such article further provides that a permanent establishment shall be deemed not to include the maintenance of a fixed place of business for the collection of information for the enterprise, or for the purpose of advertising, for the supply of information, for scientific research or for similar activities, if they have a preparatory or auxiliary character, for the enterprise.

Article II(1)(d) of the [treaty] defines an "enterprise of one of the contracting States" to mean, as the case may be, a "United States enterprise" or a "German enterprise."

Article II(1)(f) of the [treaty] defines a "German enterprise" to mean an industrial or commercial enterprise or undertaking carried on in the Federal Republic by a natural person resident in the Federal Republic or by a German company. A "German company" is defined as a juridical person or an entity treated as a juridical person for tax purposes under the laws of the Federal Republic if the company has its business management or seat in the Federal Republic.

It is held in the instant case that the above-mentioned business activities of the representative's office maintained by the German bank in the United States do not cause that office to be a "permanent establishment" of the bank in the United States within the meaning of Article II(1)(c) of the [treaty].

REVENUE RULING 77-45
1977-1 C.B. 413

. . .

Advice has been requested whether a Canadian corporation that performs engineering services in the United States is subject to Federal income tax with respect to such activities in accordance with the provisions of the United States-Canada Income Tax Convention and Protocol . . . under the circumstances described below.

M, a corporation organized under the laws of Canada, is a consulting engineering firm engaged in the planning and design of manufacturing plants. *M* contracted to plan and design a plant located in the United States. The preponderance of *M*'s services on the plant is accomplished in Canada, including significant modifications of design resulting from re-evaluation of on-site conditions. Although the plant is constructed by a general contractor under contract with *M*'s United States client, *M* has employees at the United States construction site who inspect contractor work performance and the quality of materials, make minor changes in plans and specifications, check contractor billings, keep account of job progress, and prepare reports for the home office.

The on-site employees of *M* are not authorized to make major decisions that would affect basic plan design or result in significant departures from the construction contract. These employees are under the supervision of and in continual contact with higher level project managers in Canada.

The on-site employees work in a construction shed or an area inside a warehouse or workshop provided by the client who also provides office furniture and equipment. Neither the work space nor furniture and equipment is the subject of separately bargained for consideration by *M*.

M has only one project in progress in the United States during the taxable year, and the duration of the project will not exceed 1 year.

Article I of the Convention provides that industrial and commercial profits of enterprises of the contracting States are mutually exempted from taxation, except in respect of such profits allocable to a permanent establishment.

Section 3(f) of the Protocol of the Convention states, that:

> The term "permanent establishment" includes branches, mines, and oil wells, farms, timber lands, plantations, factories, workshops, warehouses, offices, agencies, and other fixed places of business of an enterprise but does not include a subsidiary corporation. * * *

When an enterprise of one of the contracting States carries on business in the other contracting State through an employee or agent established there, who has general authority to contract for his employer or principal or has a stock of merchandise from which he regularly fills orders which he receives, such enterprise shall be deemed to have a permanent establishment in the latter State.

The fact that an enterprise of one of the contracting States has business dealings in the other contracting State through a commission agent, broker, or other independent agent or maintains therein an office used solely for the purchase of merchandise shall not be held to mean that such enterprise has a permanent establishment in the latter State.

The specific question is whether *M* has a permanent establishment in the United States within the meaning of section 3(f) of the Protocol to the Convention.

The definition of "permanent establishment" in section 3(f) of the Protocol does not specifically include a construction site. It is the view of the Internal Revenue Service that, in the absence of specific treaty language to the contrary, a construction site of any significant duration is generally considered to constitute a permanent establishment even if a treaty's permanent establishment article is silent as to such site. It is also the view of the Service that planning and supervision carried on by a building contractor are part of the activity allocable to its construction site permanent establishment. Planning and supervision of construction work do not of themselves, however, make a construction site a construction site of the enterprise that plans and supervises construction. Thus, since *M*'s activities are restricted to supervision and planning, whether they constitute a permanent establishment must be considered without regard to determinations applicable to construction sites.

In the instant case, the activities of *M* and its employees consist primarily of planning and supervision of the construction activities. *M*'s employees in the United States are not authorized to make major decisions concerning basic plan design. In addition, *M*'s employees use a building and furniture provided by *M*'s client without separately bargained for consideration; and the duration of the project will not exceed 1 year. Thus, the presence and activities of *M*'s employees do not constitute the maintenance of a permanent establishment by *M* in the United States within the meaning of section 3(f) of the Protocol to the Convention.

Accordingly, *M* is not subject to Federal income tax with respect to income attributable to engineering services performed by its employees at the construction site in the United States pursuant to Article I of the Convention.

. . .

UNGER v. COMMISSIONER
United States Court of Appeals, District of Columbia Circuit
936 F.2d 1316 (1991)

BUCKLEY, CIRCUIT JUDGE:

We are asked to determine whether the United States-Canada Income Tax Convention of 1942 permits the United States to tax a Canadian resident's distributable share of capital gain realized by a Massachusetts partnership in which he is a limited partner. On the settled authority of *Donroy, Ltd. v. United States*, 301 F.2d 200 (9th Cir.1962), we hold that it does.

I. Background

In 1984, the Charles River Park "C" Company ("Company"), a Massachusetts limited partnership, sold real estate in Boston, Massachusetts. The sale produced a long-term capital gain that was distributed among the Company's seven general and twenty-two limited partners. Among those limited partners was Robert Unger, a resident of British Columbia, Canada. His share of the gain totaled $289,260.

Mr. Unger did not include this sum as taxable income on his 1984 United States Nonresident Alien Income Tax Return. Instead, he indicated that as he had no "permanent establishment" in the United States, this income was exempt from taxation by the United States under the Tax Convention. The Internal Revenue Service disagreed. . . .

II. Discussion

Article I of the Tax Convention provides in relevant part:

> An enterprise of one of the contracting States is not subject to taxation by the other contracting State in respect of its industrial and commercial profits except in respect of such profits allocable in accordance with the Articles of this Convention to its permanent establishment in the latter State.

As defined in the Convention's first Protocol, "the term 'enterprise' includes every form of undertaking, whether carried on by an individual, partnership, corporation or any other entity," Protocol Section 3(b); "the term 'permanent establishment' includes branches, . . . offices, agencies and other fixed places of business of an enterprise," id. Section 3(f).

The question, then, turns on the nature of a limited partnership. If Mr. Unger's interest as a limited partner in the Company gives him an interest in its offices, he has a permanent establishment in Boston that makes his share of the Company's profits taxable by the United States. If he has no permanent establishment here, this income is exempt.

Two views have long competed regarding the basic nature of a partnership. The "aggregate theory" considers a partnership to be no more than an aggregation of individual partners. Under this theory, each partner has an interest in the property of the partnership; thus, Mr. Unger would be deemed to have a permanent establishment in the United States. The "entity theory" characterizes a partnership as a separate entity; under this view, the offices would be attributable to the partnership but not the partners, and Mr. Unger would not be deemed to have a permanent establishment in this country. Courts remain ambivalent in their treatment of partnerships, dealing with them as aggregates for certain purposes and as entities for others. . . .

The Internal Revenue Code . . . treats partnerships as aggregates for some purposes and as separate entities for others. A partnership must calculate income as a discrete entity. The obligation to pay taxes, however, passes through the partnership to the individual partners. The conflict between the aggregate and the entity views, then, carries over to the realm of federal taxation.

Mr. Unger argues that whatever the merits of the aggregate theory where ordinary partnerships are concerned, it should not be applied to limited partnerships. He maintains that a limited partner should be likened to (and taxed the same way as) a corporate shareholder, as both risk only the capital they have chosen to put at stake. In contrast, a general partner has full personal liability for partnership debts. Moreover, like a shareholder, a limited partner may not participate in the active management of the enterprise; indeed, if he should, he will lose his protected status and become fully liable as a general partner. Mr. Unger also points out that the distinctions between general and limited partnerships can be dispositive. Courts have chosen, for example, to protect partnership assets from execution by judgment creditors of a limited partner, and to ignore the citizenship of limited partners, but not that of general partners, in determining diversity jurisdiction.

Mr. Unger makes a number of valid observations about the intricacies and inconsistencies that exist in the law of partnership as it has evolved in various jurisdictions, but he fails to provide any persuasive reason, based on either Massachusetts partnership law or the facts of this case, for us to disregard what has come to be viewed as settled law under the Tax Convention.

In 1962, in *Donroy*, the Ninth Circuit was called upon to deal with an almost identical case. It involved Canadian corporations that were limited partners of two California partnerships whose principal offices were located in San Francisco. The court examined the relevant California partnership law and concluded that the aggregate theory was to be applied in determining whether the Canadian partners had a permanent establishment in the United States. It concluded that "the office or permanent establishment of the partnership is, in law, the office of each of the partners — whether general or limited." The court also noted that "the United States and Canada look, not to the partnership as such, but to the distributive income of the individual partners for income tax purposes." Thus the application of the aggregate theory in *Donroy* was consistent with the manner in which partnership income was actually taxed by both parties to the Convention. . . .

Although Mr. Unger attempts to draw factual distinctions between the two cases, we find no material differences between them. Mr. Unger chose limited partnership interest as a form of passive investment, and asserts that the Canadian corporations in *Donroy* became limited partners in California limited partnerships in order to expand their business. This assertion apparently rests on statements the district court mentioned as issues for future litigation, and on the Canadian partners' compliance with California's rule that a limited partnership will not be licensed as a liquor wholesaler unless each of the limited partners is qualified to transact business in California. The requirement applied regardless of whether the limited partners actually engaged in the conduct of business. These slim reeds cannot support a conclusion that these limited partners were so actively involved in the conduct of business as to make *Donroy* inapplicable here.

As the Tax Court noted, the factual distinctions between these cases are inconsequential. Whatever their reasons, both Mr. Unger and the Canadian limited partners in *Donroy* participated in the same form of business organization; and *Donroy* held that, as a matter of law, it was the ownership of a limited partnership interest that resulted in a permanent establishment in the United States. As Mr. Unger has failed to cite any legal authority or factual differences that would require a contrary conclusion, we find that *Donroy* is dispositive of this case; and we do so for reasons that go beyond the respect that one circuit will normally accord the decisions of another. . . .

III. Conclusion

We hold that as a result of his limited partnership interest in the Company, Mr. Unger had a permanent establishment in the United States within the meaning of the United States-Canada Income Tax Convention. As a consequence, his share of the partnership gains is taxable by the United States. The Tax Court's decision is therefore affirmed.

. . .

REVENUE RULING 90-80
1990-2 C.B. 170

ISSUE

Are the foreign persons in the two situations described below subject to United States tax on gain from barter transactions in the United States? . . .

FACTS

. . .

Situation 2

D, a citizen and resident of FC [a treaty country], wished to invest $20,000 in the United States. On January 1, 1989, D entered into a written agreement (the Agreement) with C, a citizen and resident of the United States. The Agreement gives C the authority to negotiate and conclude barter transactions in D's name. C will act only on behalf of D in these transactions, will be under D's management and control, and will have no other employment during 1989.

Acting under the Agreement, C maintained an office and performed bartering activities. After paying C for his services, D made a profit of $70,000 on the 1989 barter transactions.

LAW AND ANALYSIS

Under section 1001 of the Code, gain or loss will be recognized on each separate barter exchange. The amount of gain or loss will be the difference between the adjusted basis of the property exchanged and the fair market value of the property received. . . .

Situation 2

C has and habitually exercises in the United States the authority to conclude barter contracts and transactions in D's name. C is not an independent agent because C has no other employment during 1989 and is under D's management and control. Therefore, under Article 5 of the Convention, D has a permanent establishment in the United States in 1989 by virtue of the activities C undertakes for D and the office maintained by C for the purpose of conducting D's barter transactions.

Since D is treated as having a permanent establishment in the United States, under Article 7(1) of the Convention, the 1989 business profits of D that are attributable to its United States permanent establishment are taxable in the United States. The $70,000 profit that D derived from the barter transactions is attributable to D's United States permanent establishment, and thus, those profits are subject to tax . . . D must file a 1989 United States tax return.

HOLDING

. . .

Situation 2

For 1989, D is subject to tax . . . on its $70,000 profit from the barter transactions.

REVENUE RULING 76-322
1976-2 C.B. 487

Advice has been requested whether an Australian corporation that ships goods to the United States on a consignment basis for sale therein is subject to the Federal income tax with respect to such activity under the provisions of the Income Tax Convention between the United States and Australia (the Convention).

P, a foreign corporation organized under the laws of Australia, manufactures products distributed in various countries. *S*, a domestic corporation whose principal place of business is in the United States, is a wholly owned subsidiary of *P*. *P* sells its products at arm's-length prices to *S*, a United States distributor for the products. *S*, on its own behalf, then sells such products (at prices it determines) to independent retailers and wholesalers throughout the United States. In addition, *P* sells its products at arm's-length prices to other unrelated and independent distributors in the United States. These distributors do not constitute permanent establishments of *P* under the Convention.

The agreement between *P* and *S* provides, among other things, that products will be delivered to a carrier at *P*'s plant in Australia, to be forwarded by such carrier for and on behalf of, and at the expense and risk of, *S* to such point or points in the

United States as S may designate. All responsibility for such products is assumed by S which may from time to time and without notice to or consent of P move such products to such locations as it desires.

The products are held by S on consignment. The title to and ownership of such products is in P until purchased by S in accordance with the provisions of the agreement. The purchase by S from P takes place immediately prior to the sale of such products by S.

The agreement further provides that S is responsible to P for damage, destruction, theft, or loss of goods prior to purchase by S. S bears the cost of insurance of the consigned goods with the loss payable to P. Upon request, S furnishes P with an inventory of all products held on consignment, but it is not liable to account to P for the proceeds of sales made by S. Also, S is under no obligation to purchase the consigned products. P has the right to recall any consigned products prior to the time of their purchase by S.

P has no employees in the United States and conducts no other business in the United States. S sells in its own name to its own customers.

Article III(1) of the Convention provides, in part, that an Australian enterprise shall not be subject to United States tax in respect of its industrial or commercial profits unless it is engaged in trade or business in the United States through a permanent establishment therein.

Article II(1)(o) of the Convention defines the term "permanent establishment," in part, as meaning a branch, agency, management or fixed place of business. Where an enterprise of one of the Contracting States has a subsidiary corporation that is engaged in trade or business in the other State, whether through a permanent establishment or otherwise, or has an agent in that other State (other than an agent who has and habitually exercises, a general authority to negotiate and conclude contracts on behalf of that enterprise, or regularly fills orders on its behalf from a stock of goods located in that other State), that enterprise shall not, merely by reason thereof, be deemed to have a permanent establishment in that other State.

Under the concepts of the Convention, the absence of a permanent establishment, on the part of an enterprise having business dealings in the country concerned, is based in part upon the premise that such business dealings are handled through a commission agent, broker or other independent agent. A subsidiary corporation will be treated as an independent agent, as distinguished from an agent of the parent, under similar circumstances. The subsidiary corporation's presence in the country concerned, where it is engaged in trade or business, is by itself no basis to hold that the parent corporation has a permanent establishment in such country, unless the subsidiary has and habitually exercises a general authority to contract for its parent, or as an agent of the parent regularly fills orders of goods on behalf of the parent from a stock of the parent's goods located in such country.

Under the agreement in the instant case, neither a limited agency nor a general agency is established. The relationship between P and S is that of seller and purchaser, since the power that S has in determining when title to the consigned goods passes from P is exercisable only as a purchaser. Further, since S is not considered *P*'s agent, although *P* has a 'stock of goods" in the United States, *P* has no employee or agent in the United States that could fill orders from such stock of goods.

Accordingly, *P* does not have a permanent establishment in the United States within the meaning of the Convention. Therefore, the income derived by *P* from transactions with *S*, its subsidiary, in accordance with the terms of the agreement discussed herein, is not subject to Federal income tax.

REVENUE RULING 86-156
1986-2 C.B. 297

ISSUE

Whether photocopy machines are "other like property" within the meaning of Article IX of the United States-Netherlands Income Tax Convention (the Treaty) and, if not, whether payments for the lease thereof constitute industrial or commercial profits within the meaning of Article III of the Treaty.

FACTS

P, a corporation organized under the laws of the Netherlands, owns 100 percent of the stock of *S*, a corporation organized under the laws of the United States. *P* manufactures photocopy machines and leases them to *S*, and *S* makes periodic rental payments to *P*. *P* carries on a portion of its manufacturing operations in the Netherlands. *P* is not engaged in a trade or business within the United States through a permanent establishment. *S* subleases the photocopy machines to its United States customers.

LAW AND ANALYSIS

Article IX of the Treaty . . . specifically exempted United States source royalties paid to a Netherlands corporation for the use of industrial, commercial, or scientific equipment, provided that the Netherlands corporation was not engaged in a trade or business within the United States through a permanent establishment.

Article IX(2) . . . exempts United States source royalties, rentals, or amounts paid as consideration for the use of, or right to use, copyrights, artistic or scientific works, patents, designs, plans, secret processes or formulae, trademarks, motion picture films, films or tapes for radio or television broadcasting, or other like property or rights, or information concerning industrial, commercial or scientific knowledge, experience or skill, provided that the Netherlands corporation does not have a permanent establishment within the United States to which such amounts are attributable.

Article III(1) of the Treaty . . . exempts industrial or commercial profits derived by a Netherlands enterprise to the extent not attributable to a permanent establishment in the United States. Article II(1)(g) defines a Netherlands enterprise as an industrial or commercial enterprise or undertaking carried on in the

Netherlands by the taxpayer. Article III(5) of the Treaty . . . provides that industrial or commercial profits means income derived from the active conduct of a trade or business, but does not include income described in Article IX(2). . . .

Where payments for the use of industrial, commercial or scientific equipment are to be exempted by the royalties article in a treaty, that article specifically states that such property is included within its scope. Therefore, the phrase "other like property or rights" contained in Article IX(2) of the Treaty . . . modifies only the items specifically enumerated in Article IX(2). The items of tangible property included in Article IX(2) are tapes, films, and artistic or scientific works. None of the items enumerated could possibly incorporate equipment. Consequently, the phrase "other like property or rights" cannot be interpreted to refer to industrial, commercial, or scientific equipment. Payments for the use of industrial, commercial or scientific equipment, therefore, are not covered by Article IX(2) and are exempt, if at all, under the business profits article (Article III) of the Treaty.

Article III(5) of the Treaty defines "industrial or commercial profits" as "income derived from the active conduct of a trade or business." Article III(1) provides that the exemption for industrial or commercial profits derived by a Netherlands enterprise is applicable only to income that is not attributable to a permanent establishment in the United States.

The phrases "industrial or commercial profits" and "income derived from the active conduct of a trade or business" do not require such profits or income of the Netherlands enterprise be derived by an active trade or business within the United States, but merely require that the income be derived from the active conduct of a trade or business conducted in whole or in part in the Netherlands by the Netherlands enterprise.

Article III of the Treaty, therefore, exempts United States source rentals or other payments for the use of industrial, commercial, or scientific equipment, provided that such amounts are attributable to a trade or business actively conducted in whole or in part in the Netherlands by the Netherlands enterprise and are not attributable to a permanent establishment in the United States.

HOLDING

Under the facts of this case, the rentals for photocopy machines derived by P from S constitute industrial or commercial profits derived by a Netherlands enterprise. Furthermore, the rentals are not attributable to a permanent establishment of P in the United States. Therefore, the rentals are exempt from United States tax under Article III of the Treaty.

REVENUE RULING 86-145
1986-2 C.B. 297

ISSUE

Whether the term "tax year concerned" as used in Article 15(2)(a) of the United States-United Kingdom Income Tax Convention ("Convention") . . . refers to the tax year in which personal services are performed or to the tax year in which compensation for those services is received.

FACTS

A, a United Kingdom resident, was present in the United States for more than 183 days in 1985. *A* performed personal services during that period for an employer who was not a resident of the United States and who had no permanent establishment or fixed base in the United States. With respect to 1985, *A* was a resident of the United Kingdom and was not deemed a resident of the United States under Article 4 of the Convention. *A* was present in the United States for 30 days in 1986 and during that period was paid for the services performed when present in the United States in 1985. In each of those years, *A*'s United States tax year was the calendar year.

LAW AND ANALYSIS

Article 15(1) of the Convention provides the general rule that remuneration in respect of employment is taxable in the Contracting State where the employment is performed.

Article 15(2) of the Convention provides that, notwithstanding Article 15(1), remuneration derived by a resident of a Contracting State in respect of an employment exercised in the other Contracting State shall be taxable only in the first-mentioned State if:

(a) the recipient is present in that other State for a period not exceeding in the aggregate 183 days *in the tax year concerned*; and

(b) the remuneration is paid by, or on behalf of, an employer who is not a resident of that other State; and

(c) the remuneration is not borne as such by a permanent establishment or a fixed base which the employer has in that other State. [Emphasis added.]

The Treasury Department Technical Explanation of the Convention states that Article 15 of the Convention is based on Article 15 (Dependent Persons Services) of the 1977 OECD Model Convention (Model Convention). Article 15(1) of the Model Convention has a rule and exception similar to Article 15(2)(a) of the Convention. The focus of this exception is "employment of short duration abroad. . . . The exemption is limited to the 183-day period." Thus, the use of the term "in the tax year concerned" as part of the limitation on that exemption refers to the tax year in which the employment services being compensated are performed, and not to the tax year in which the compensation for the services is received.

Since *A* was present in the United States for more than 183 days in 1985, the exemption from United States taxation under Article 15(2) of the Convention is unavailable to *A* with respect to the services *A* rendered during that year. The exemption is unavailable with respect to those services notwithstanding that *A* was paid for them in 1986 when *A* was present in the United States for less than 183 days.

HOLDING

For purposes of the 183-day limitation to the exemption under Article 15(2)(a) of the Convention, the term "tax year concerned" refers to the tax year in which the services being compensated are performed in a Contracting State by a resident of the other Contracting State and not to the tax year in which compensation for services is received.

Part IV

SAFEGUARDS

Unit 13

INTRODUCTION TO CONTROLLED FOREIGN CORPORATIONS

A. CODE AND REGULATION PROVISIONS

Code   §§ 951(a)(1), (b); 957(a), (c); 958(a), (b).
Reg.   § 1.957-1.

B. PROBLEMS FOR CLASS DISCUSSION

13-1.   X Corporation is a foreign corporation with three classes of capital stock outstanding, consisting of 60 shares of Class A stock, 40 shares of Class B stock, and 150 shares of Class C stock. The owners of a majority of Class A stock are entitled to elect three of the five corporate directors, and the owners of a majority of the Class B stock are entitled to elect the other two. The Class C stock has no voting rights. Dividends are paid on a per share basis and there are no liquidation preferences.

       Y Corporation is a foreign corporation with one class of stock outstanding, consisting of 90 shares. Danielle, a United States citizen, owns 25 shares of X Corporation Class A stock and 45 shares of Y Corporation stock for the year. Y Corporation owns 15 shares of X Corporation Class A stock for the year. The remaining shares of stock are owned by unrelated foreign persons.

       Determine the status of Danielle, X Corporation, and Y Corporation in Year 1 for purposes of § 951.

13-2.   At all times in Year 1, three individuals owned all of the outstanding shares of FC Corporation, a French corporation. As of January 1, Year 1, Jacques, a citizen and resident of France, owned 50 shares of the stock, while Ken and Lisa, both United States citizens and residents, each owned 25 shares. On July 1, Year 1, FC Corporation redeemed 10 shares held by Jacques. On July 2, Year 1, American counsel warned of potential United States income tax problems associated with the redemption. Accordingly, on July 4, Year 1, FC Corporation redeemed five shares from each of Ken and Lisa. The holdings of the shareholders remained unchanged for the balance of the Year 1. Were there tax problems and, if so, do the July 4, Year 1, redemption transactions avert the United States income tax problems?

C. OVERVIEW

As discussed in Unit 1, a taxpayer's residency classification is a threshold issue for determining the applicability of United States taxation. Domestic persons (United States citizens, residents, and domestic corporations) are generally subject to tax on worldwide income, while foreign persons (non-resident alien individuals and foreign corporations) are often only subject to United States taxation on specified items or types of income. Since corporate entities can generally choose their classification as foreign or domestic according to the formal jurisdiction of their incorporation, United States residents can fairly easily avoid United States taxation on foreign earnings simply by creating foreign corporations to engage in foreign income-producing activities.

Because the corporation is generally respected as a separate taxpayer, the foreign income produced would be income of the foreign corporation, but would not be part of the United States taxpayer's worldwide income. Only when the United States taxpayer "repatriates" the income, either by causing the corporation to pay a dividend or by the taxpayer selling the stock, would the taxpayer realize income for United States income tax purposes. Thus, the United States tax system inherently provides opportunities for "deferral" of taxation on foreign income to the extent the separate existence of the corporation and its residence according to situs of incorporation are respected.

Deferral is not the same as a complete exemption of foreign income (as would be allowed under a pure territorial system where only United States source income is taxed) because tax may apply upon repatriation. However, repatriation is often within the control of the shareholder, so that the ability to permanently avoid United States taxation is correspondingly within his control. For instance, a shareholder can often determine whether and when to sell stock in a corporation and may even (depending upon the shareholder's level of control over the corporation) compel or prevent the payment of a dividend.

This Unit and the next discuss subpart F, one of the main measures the United States employs to prevent deferral of taxation on foreign-source income. Subpart F and its regime for controlled foreign corporations (CFCs) were introduced to the Code in 1962. The term "subpart F" refers simply to the placement of the rules governing the taxation of United States shareholders that own controlling interests in foreign corporations: subpart F of Part III of Subchapter N of Chapter 1 of Title 26. As in this Casebook, it is usually referred to by the shorter name of subpart F.

The purpose of subpart F is to accelerate United States taxation of certain earnings of foreign corporations that are controlled by United States shareholders. Thus, subpart F is an exception to the general rule that the United States does not impose tax on foreign-source income earned by foreign persons (see discussion in Unit 1).

Under § 951(a)(1), subpart F subjects certain United States shareholders of CFCs to current taxation on certain of the CFC's earnings and investments, regardless of whether they are distributed to the shareholder. Because subpart F only encompasses certain shareholders and certain types of income, the definitional aspects of this regime are central to the ultimate imposition of tax. The threshold issue for the application of subpart F, and the topic of this Unit, is therefore whether a CFC exists.

If no CFC exists, there is no need to examine subpart F further, since no United States tax consequences thereunder will arise absent this definitional threshold. But if a CFC does exist, further issues arise in determining whether and to what extent its shareholders will face tax consequences as a result of their ownership interests. Thus, this Unit is focused solely on identifying CFCs and their United States shareholders, while the consequences of these determinations are addressed in Unit 14. Subpart F is arguably one of the most commonly encountered and complex provisions of United States international tax law, and great care must be taken to observe the detailed structure of this regime.

13.01   CFC Defined

Section 957(a) defines a CFC as any foreign corporation of which more than 50 percent of the stock, as measured by either vote or value, is owned or considered to be owned by "United States shareholders" on any day during the corporation's taxable year. Therefore, in order to determine whether a foreign corporation is a CFC, it is necessary to identify whether it has United States shareholders, and, if so, to determine whether they collectively are considered to own the requisite amount of stock during the relevant period. The steps for determining whether a foreign corporation is a CFC are summarized in flow-chart form in Figure 13-1 at the end of this Part C.

13.02   United States Shareholder Defined

Pursuant to § 951(b), a United States shareholder is a United States person who owns, or is considered to own due to attribution rules (discussed at Subpart 13.04 below), 10 percent or more of the foreign corporation's total combined voting power of all classes of stock entitled to vote. Section 957(c) further provides that, for these purposes, a United States person is generally defined as provided in § 7701(a)(30), with some exceptions. As discussed in Unit 1, § 7701(a)(30) defines a United States person as a resident, a domestic partnership or corporation, or a domestic estate or trust. Ownership of the CFC is determined under § 958(a) and (b), which includes in its scope shares held directly, indirectly through other entities, and constructively by attribution from other shareholders.

13.03   Direct Ownership

Although § 951(b) provides bright-line percentage ownership rules for determining the status of foreign entities and their owners, taxpayers could employ a broad range of formal and informal control arrangements to circumvent these rules. As a result, determining what constitutes "ownership" for purposes of determining CFC status requires a substance-over-form approach. Regulations under § 957 provide a set of standards for determining whether the greater-than-50-percent United States ownership test is met.

For example, Regulation § 1.957-1(b) mandates a facts-and-circumstances analysis of the voting structure. This Regulation addresses arrangements taxpayers might use in order to nominally shift formal voting power away from United States shareholders even though actual control is retained. Conversely, the Regulation provides that a shareholder could own stock entitled to vote yet not have the voting power of such stock for purposes of § 957. The standards provided under this Regulation are designed to prevent taxpayers from avoiding CFC status by manipulating ownership interests through techniques such as weighted voting, cumulative voting, irrevocable proxies, or special issue veto power.

Pursuant to Regulation § 1.957-1, the requisite level of voting power is found in all cases in which United States shareholders have the power to elect, appoint, or replace a majority of the board of directors (or comparable governing body). Even if the shareholders nominally lack authority to appoint a majority of the foreign corporation's board, the corporation will nonetheless be a CFC if its United States shareholders actually possess the power through contractual or other arrangements.

Finally, a foreign corporation will be a CFC if the United States ownership threshold is met on any day during the corporation's taxable year. Thus, even a one-day shift of ownership pursuant to a sale or redemption of a foreign shareholder's stock could result in the requisite ownership by United States shareholders and cause a corporation to be a CFC.

13.04   Indirect and Constructive Ownership

In addition to manipulating ownership interests through various allocations of voting power, taxpayers may also attempt to avoid CFC status by shifting their shares to other taxpayers, especially entities which they control. Attribution rules provide the safeguard against these manipulations. First, § 958(a) provides that stock owned by or for foreign corporations, partnerships, trusts, or estates is considered proportionately owned by its shareholders, partners, or beneficiaries. Second, § 958(b) incorporates the constructive ownership rules of § 318, with some modifications, for purposes of determining whether a person holds a 10 percent ownership interest.

13.05   Limitations of the Subpart F Regime

The subpart F regime is a very incomplete mechanism, allowing numerous foreign corporations owned by United States shareholders to fall outside of its technical reach despite the broad nature of the provisions defining control and ownership. In practice, the rules can be readily circumvented in many circumstances. For example, a foreign corporation is not a CFC so long as no single United States shareholder owns 10 percent or more of its stock, even if more than 50 percent of its total voting power or value is owned by United States persons (for example, if all of a foreign corporation's stock is held equally by 11 unrelated United States persons). Similarly, a foreign corporation is not a CFC even if a United States person owns exactly 50 percent of its stock, so long as all other United States persons each own less than 10 percent of the stock in the corporation and are unrelated to all the other shareholders.

Nevertheless, many foreign corporations are classified as CFCs for United States tax purposes. In such cases, it is not a foregone conclusion that the shareholders will face United States tax consequences as a result of their ownership. Instead, the company's income items will be scrutinized to determine whether United States taxation will ultimately apply under § 951. The focus of this scrutiny and the general taxing provisions applicable to the United States shareholders of CFCs are discussed in the next Unit.

Finally, given the complex rules of subpart F and its common moniker as an "anti" statute (i.e., anti-deferral), which indicates that it exists to prevent taxpayers from doing something they would otherwise prefer to do, it is easy to assume that obtaining CFC status is universally considered a situation to be avoided at all costs in tax planning. The *Framatome Connectors* case, excerpted in Part D of this Unit, illustrates not only that this is not always the case (although the tax benefit sought by the taxpayer in that case is no longer available under current law), but also that taxpayers might even encounter some difficulty in obtaining CFC status in the (typically unlikely) event that such status is desirable.[1]

FIGURE 13-1. SUMMARY FLOWCHART FOR DETERMINING CFC STATUS

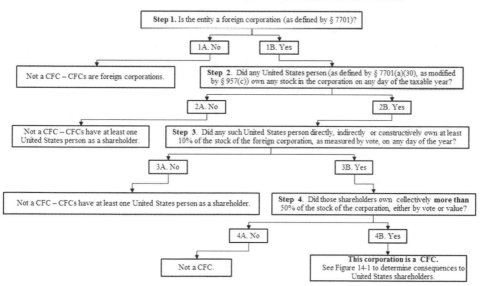

D. REFERENCE MATERIALS

- *Framatome Connectors USA, Inc. v. Commissioner*

---

[1] However, Example 3 of Treasury Regulation § 1.701-2(f) provides an example of a situation where affirmative use of a domestic partnership to subject oneself to the CFC regime, and the attendant foreign tax credit look-through rules of sections 904(d)(2)(E) and 904(d)(3), is still expressly permitted under both Subchapter K and Subchapter N.

FRAMATOME CONNECTORS USA, INC. v. COMMISSIONER
United States Tax Court
118 TC. 32 (2002)

COLVIN, JUDGE:

Respondent determined deficiencies in petitioners' income and withholding taxes and a penalty . . . .

. . .

After concessions, we must decide:

1. Whether Burndy-Japan Ltd. (Burndy-Japan) was a controlled foreign corporation (CFC) of Burndy Corp. (Burndy-US) in 1992. We hold that it was not because Burndy-US did not own more than 50 percent of the voting power of Burndy-Japan stock or more than 50 percent of the value of Burndy-Japan stock in 1992.

. . .

Petitioner Framatome US is a New York corporation, the principal place of business of which was in Connecticut when the petitions were filed. Framatome S.A., a French company, owned 100 percent of FCI, another French company, which owned 100 percent of Framatome US during the years in issue. . . . Burndy-US was a predecessor corporation of Framatome US and Framatome Connectors USA Holding, Inc. . . .

Burndy-US wanted to enter the Japanese market in the early 1960s. To do so, Burndy-US believed that it needed a distribution system in Japan that was owned and operated by a Japanese company. [Sumitomo Electric Industries, Ltd. (Sumitomo), and Furukawa Electric Co., Ltd. (Furukawa)] had sales organizations and distribution systems for their products throughout Japan. On September 28, 1961, Burndy-US, Furukawa, and Sumitomo agreed to form Burndy-Japan to manufacture and sell Burndy-US products in Japan. Burndy-US, Furukawa, and Sumitomo each became the owner of 100,000 shares of common stock (i.e., a one-third interest) in Burndy-Japan. [In 1973, Burndy-US purchased additional shares and increased its ownership in Burndy-Japan to 50 percent.]

The Burndy-Japan articles of incorporation (as amended) provide: (a) Burndy-Japan shall have not more than 15 directors and not more than 3 auditors; (b) the board of directors shall elect one president and may elect one chairman and some (i.e., an unspecified number of) executive directors; (c) the chairman shall preside over meetings of the board of directors; (d) the president shall act for the chairman if there is no chairman or the chairman is unable to act; (e) the president shall preside over general meetings of shareholders; and (f) each shareholder shall have one vote per share.

The articles of incorporation also provide that a majority of the votes of the shareholders is required to adopt resolutions, except for the following, which require approval by shareholders who have shares representing more than 80 percent of the issued shares: (a) Amendment of the articles of incorporation; (b) election of directors and auditors; (c) change in capital; (d) assignment of the entire or essential part of the business of the company; (e) entrusting a third party with management; (f) disposition of profits; (g) acquisition or disposition of shares of other companies; and (h) conclusion or alteration of license agreements. The articles of incorporation authorized one class of stock consisting of 1,500,000 shares of common stock with a par value of [Yen] 500 per share.

. . .

For the taxable year 1992, respondent reclassified foreign tax credits related to Burndy-Japan from the general limitation foreign tax credit basket under section 904(d)(1)(I) to a separate non-controlled corporation foreign tax credit basket under section 904(d)(1)(E). Respondent reclassified the Burndy-Japan foreign tax credits solely on the ground that Burndy-Japan was not a CFC within the meaning of section 957(a). The effect of this reclassification was to reduce petitioners' allowable foreign tax credit from Burndy-Japan for 1992 (including carryovers from 1988 and 1989) from $1,802,524 to $381,790.

1. *Voting Power Test and Stock Value Test*

Petitioners contend Burndy-Japan was a CFC in 1992. A foreign corporation is a CFC if U.S. shareholders own more than 50 percent of the voting power of all classes of its stock (the voting power test), § 957(a)(1), or if U.S. shareholders own more than 50 percent of the total value of its stock (the stock value test), § 957(a)(2).

Burndy-US owned 50 percent of the stock of Burndy-Japan in 1992. For petitioners to prevail, they must show that, in 1992, either the voting power of Burndy-Japan stock held by Burndy-US exceeded 50 percent of the total combined voting power of Burndy-Japan stock, or the value of Burndy-Japan stock held by Burndy-US exceeded 50 percent of the total value of Burndy-Japan stock. Petitioners contend that Burndy-US met both tests. We disagree for the following reasons.

2. *Whether Burndy-US Owned More Than 50 Percent of the Total Combined Voting Power of the Stock of Burndy-Japan*

Petitioners contend that Burndy-US owned more than 50 percent of the total combined voting power of Burndy-Japan because Burndy-US owned 50 percent of the stock of Burndy-Japan and, according to petitioners, had the following powers: (a) Burndy-US could select Burndy-Japan's board of directors and president and control the board's tie-breaking vote; (b) Burndy-US could dissolve Burndy-Japan; and (c) Burndy-US had management control of Burndy-Japan. Petitioners point out that neither Furukawa nor Sumitomo exercised the veto powers created by the 1973 agreement and contend that Burndy-US paid Furukawa and Sumitomo a control premium in 1973 when Burndy-US obtained 50 percent of the stock of Burndy-Japan.

a. *Petitioners May Not Rely on the Doctrine of Substance Over Form*

In 1973, Burndy-US, Sumitomo and Furukawa changed the structure of their ownership of Burndy-Japan so that Burndy-US would own 50 percent of the stock of Burndy-Japan and the two other Japanese companies would each own 25 percent. It is clear that this change did not give Burndy-US more than 50 percent of the voting power of Burndy-Japan if "voting power" refers to the shareholders' percentage of stock ownership. Nonetheless, petitioners now contend that Burndy-US owned more than 50 percent of the voting power of Burndy-Japan.

Petitioners rely on several cases in which the government successfully invoked the substance over form doctrine. In those cases, the issue was whether a U.S. shareholder or shareholders owning 50 percent or less of the stock of a foreign corporation had more than 50 percent of the voting power of the corporation for purposes of section 957(a)(1). The theme running through these cases was the arrangement by the U.S. shareholders to have the foreign corporation issue a new class of voting preferred stock to foreign persons so as to avoid or terminate CFC status of the foreign corporation. The Commissioner contended, and the courts in those cases held, that the foreign corporation remained a CFC because in substance the U.S. shareholders retained control of the corporation, notwithstanding the reduction of their nominal percentage ownership of stock having 50 percent or less of the voting power.

Petitioners contend that those cases support their position that Burndy had more than 50 percent of the voting power and value of stock of Burndy-Japan. We disagree. The Government prevailed in those cases by relying on section 1.957-1(b)(2), Income Tax Regs., and by invoking the doctrine of substance over form. That doctrine generally allows the Commissioner to recharacterize a transaction according to its substance but does not allow a taxpayer to disavow a transactional form of the taxpayer's own choosing. Generally, the Commissioner, not the taxpayer, can assert the doctrine of substance over form. As the U.S. Court of Appeals for the Second Circuit (the court to which these cases are appealable) stated:

> It would be quite intolerable to pyramid the existing complexities of tax law by a rule that the tax shall be that resulting from the form of transaction taxpayers have chosen or from any other form they might have chosen, whichever is less. [*Television Indus., Inc. v. Commissioner*, 284 F.2d 322, 325 (2d Cir. 1960).]

Petitioners made inconsistent claims concerning Burndy-Japan's CFC status. Before 1987, Burndy-US owned 50 percent of the stock of Burndy-Japan but it did not treat Burndy-Japan as a CFC. Burndy-US first claimed Burndy-Japan as a CFC on its 1987 return. Petitioners changed their position even though Burndy-US continued to own 50 percent of the stock of Burndy-Japan from 1987 to 1992, and the operational relationship between Burndy-US and Burndy-Japan did not change during those years; the only change was the tax law.

Petitioners contend that they derived no U.S. tax benefit by not treating Burndy-Japan as a CFC before 1987. However, their representations regarding the pre-1987 years are incomplete and unconvincing. They deny having Subpart F income for the years 1987 through 1992, and they ask us to infer that they had little or no Subpart F income from 1983 to 1986. They cite nothing in the record relating to 1983 through 1986 to support their contention, and they made no reference to the years before 1983. . . . We are not persuaded that petitioners derived no U.S. tax benefit from not treating Burndy-Japan as a CFC before 1987.

A taxpayer may be permitted to invoke the doctrine of substance over form if the motive of the taxpayer is not primarily tax avoidance. Petitioners' reversal of position regarding whether Burndy-Japan was a CFC was tax motivated. Petitioners may not invoke the doctrine of substance over form here, and we need not consider petitioners' contention that Burndy-US, in substance, controlled Burndy-Japan in deciding whether Burndy-US owned more than 50 percent of the voting power of Burndy-Japan.

. . .

We conclude that Burndy-US did not own more than 50 percent of the voting power of Burndy-Japan in 1992.

3. *Whether Burndy-US Owned More Than 50 Percent of the Value of Burndy-Japan Stock*

A foreign corporation is a CFC if U.S. shareholders own more than 50 percent of the total value of its stock. Sec. 957(a)(2). Petitioners contend that Burndy-US owned more than 50 percent of the value of Burndy-Japan stock in 1992. We disagree.

. . .

Petitioners contend that the value of Burndy-Japan stock owned by Burndy-US was more than 50 percent of the value of the three blocks of stock owned by its three shareholders. Petitioners contend that a control premium applies in valuing the Burndy-Japan stock owned by Burndy-US because Burndy-US owned 50 percent of the stock and controlled Burndy-Japan during the years in issue. Similarly, petitioners contend that a minority discount or discount for lack of marketability applies to Furukawa's and Sumitomo's holdings.

We find the testimony of respondent's experts, Bajaj and Alan C. Shapiro (Shapiro), about the rationale for applying control premiums and minority discounts to be useful in analyzing this issue. They testified that a premium applies in valuing a large block of stock if the holder of that block has the power to extract private benefits that are disproportionate to benefits available to minority shareholders (private benefits analysis). Petitioners did not offer any expert testimony relating to the merits of the private benefits analysis and did not cross-examine respondent's experts on this point.

Burndy-US could not extract private benefits from Burndy-Japan because Furukawa and Sumitomo could veto several important types of corporate actions. These veto powers gave Furukawa and Sumitomo leverage over actions not subject to veto through the indirect or "log-rolling" effect; i.e., the ability of Furukawa or Sumitomo to pressure Burndy-US to act as requested on a matter not subject to veto to keep Furukawa or Sumitomo from vetoing an action subject to their veto powers.

Petitioners contend we should disregard Bajaj's testimony because he was biased. We disagree and find Bajaj's analysis to be helpful in deciding this issue.

. . .

c. Conclusion Relating to the Stock Value Test

We conclude that Burndy-US did not own more than 50 percent of the value of Burndy-Japan stock in 1992.

. . .

4. Conclusion

We conclude that petitioners are liable for withholding tax on $20,881,431 of constructive dividends that Burndy-US paid to FCI in 1993.

Unit 14

CONTROLLED FOREIGN CORPORATIONS — SUBPART F INCOME

A. CODE PROVISIONS

Code   §§ 951; 952(a); 954(a), (b)(3)–(4), (c)(1)(a), (d)(1), (3), (e); 957(a), (c); 958; 959(a); 960(a); 961; 1248(a), (c), (d).

B. PROBLEMS FOR CLASS DISCUSSION

14-1. A, B, and C, each United States citizens and residents, own one-third of the stock of Z Corporation, a Bolivian corporation formed as a Sociedad Anonima.

(a) In Year 1, Z Corporation earns $100,000 in interest income and $200,000 in dividend income. What United States income result?

(b) In Year 2, Z Corporation again earns $100,000 in interest and $200,000 in dividend income. It also opens a travel business in Bolivia, which generates $7,000,000 in gross income. What United States income result? What if it generates $90,000 of such gross income?

14-2. Abe, a United States citizen, and DomCo, a domestic corporation wholly-owned by Abe, form Chala Co., a corporation under Peruvian law, on January 1, Year 1, with a contribution of $5,000 each in return for 50 shares of common stock. Chala Co. purchases equipment in the United States from DomCo and sells the equipment to independent parties in Peru and other South American countries. In Year 1, Chala Co. made $50,000 of net income from sales in other South American countries and $100,000 of net income from sales in Peru. Chala Co. is classified as a corporation for United States tax purposes. No foreign income taxes are paid by Chala Co. on its income.

(a) What are the United States income tax consequences for Abe, DomCo, and Chala Co. in Year 1?

(b) What result in (a) if Chala Co. paid income tax to the other South American countries of $20,000 on its income from sales in those countries?

(c) What result in (a) if Chala Co. in Year 2 derives no income for the year but distributes to Abe and DomCo $25,000 each?

    (d)   How would the answer to (a) change if Damien, an unrelated share-holder, owned eight percent of the stock of Chala Co., and Abe and DomCo owned 46 percent each?

    (e)   Suppose Chala Co., owned solely by Abe and DomCo, makes the same $150,000 of income for each of Years 1 through 5. On January 1, Year 6, Abe sells his 50 shares to Martin, an unrelated Peruvian citizen, for $400,000.

        (1)   What are the United States income tax consequences of the sale to Abe?

        (2)   What result if DomCo (instead of Abe) sold its shares?

    (f)   How would the answer to (e) change if Damien owned eight percent of the stock of Chala Co., Abe and DomCo owned 46 percent each, and Damien sells his shares?

C. OVERVIEW

Subpart F accelerates United States taxation of certain undistributed earnings of certain foreign corporations as a way to reduce any tax incentives to invest capital overseas rather than in the United States. As discussed in Unit 13, subpart F is an anti-deferral regime designed to protect the tax base against erosion that can occur when United States persons, instead of holding foreign assets directly, place them in foreign corporations to avoid current United States taxation on associated income. Unit 13 focused on identifying the United States persons who are subject to subpart F due to being defined as "United States shareholders" of "controlled foreign corporations" (CFCs). These designations are requisite thresholds to United States taxation under subpart F: if they are not met, no tax consequences arise under these provisions. But if they are met, the inquiry has only begun: the tax consequences must still be determined. The general structure for determining these consequences is the focus of this Unit.

The general rule of subpart F is that, if a corporation is a CFC for 30 consecutive days or more during any taxable year, its United States shareholders that hold stock on the last day in the year on which the corporation is a CFC must include in gross income a "pro rata share" of its "subpart F income" under § 951. (United States shareholders must also include certain other items of income, including their share of earnings from investments in United States property, but subpart F income is the most expansive category.) In other words, whether or not the CFC actually distributes any money to these United States shareholders, they will be deemed to have received an amount of income from the CFC, and will be taxed under the regular income tax rules as if they received that income. This rule has several collateral effects, impacting, for example, related foreign tax credits. A more detailed discussion of all such effects is beyond the scope of this Unit.

As indicated by the terms used in § 951, determining the tax consequences of being a United States shareholder of a CFC requires a two-step analysis. First, the CFC's subpart F income must be identified. Second, any United States sharehold-er's pro rata share of such income must be determined. This Unit explores these concepts as well as one additional consideration for determining the United States tax consequences of being a United States shareholder in a CFC, namely, the treatment of sale proceeds on disposition of CFC stock. A summary flowchart of the two-step analysis and tax consequences to shareholders of a CFC is provided in Figure 14-1.

FIGURE 14-1. SUMMARY FLOWCHART OF TAX CONSEQUENCES TO SHAREHOLDERS OF CFCS

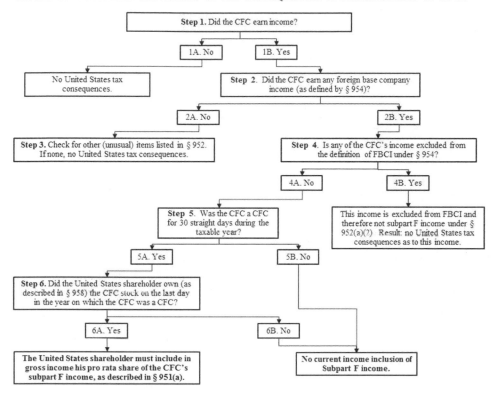

14.01   Subpart F Income

Subpart F income is defined in § 952 as the sum of "insurance income" as defined under § 953, "foreign base company income" as determined under § 954, bribes, kickbacks and the like, income earned by CFCs organized in countries that the United States does not recognize or which are otherwise subject to the provisions of § 901(j), and certain income of CFCs earned in countries that participate in international boycotts as described in § 999. Foreign base company income, the main category of subpart F income, generally targets situations in which a domestic owner, instead of operating directly (through a branch operation), establishes a foreign "base company" subsidiary in a low-tax jurisdiction in order to avoid United States and foreign taxation on certain types of income. Figure 14-2 presents a basic comparison, where the owner is a United States corporation, in the absence of subpart F.

FIGURE 14-2. UNITED STATES TAXATION OF BRANCH VERSUS BASE COMPANY PROFITS,
IN THE ABSENCE OF SUBPART F

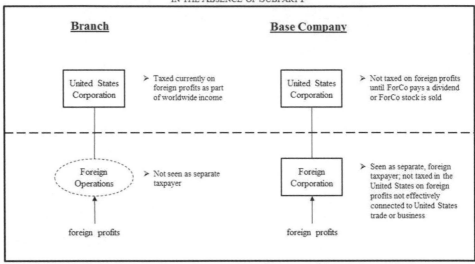

Foreign base company income is defined in § 954 as the sum of the company's (1) foreign personal holding company income, (2) foreign base company sales income, (3) foreign base company services income, and (4) foreign base company oil related income. Some of these categories are further defined in § 954. Income in each category may be reduced by allocable expenses under § 954(b)(5).

14.02   Foreign Personal Holding Company Income

Foreign personal holding company income ("FPHCI") is defined in § 954(c) and includes several categories of items, most of which are passive or otherwise easily moveable to another jurisdiction for source purposes. The main categories are dividends, interest, royalties, rents and annuities, and net gains from certain dispositions of property.

Section 954(c) provides several exclusions from foreign personal holding company income, such as rents and royalties derived in the active conduct of a CFC's trade or business from unrelated parties. Perhaps the broadest exclusion is that for certain passive income derived from related corporations, provided in § 954(c)(3)(A). Section 954(d)(3) defines a related corporation for these purposes as one that is a corporation controlling, or controlled by, the CFC, or controlled by the same persons who control the CFC. Dividends and interest from a related corporation are generally excluded from the definition of foreign personal holding company income if the related corporation is incorporated in the same country as the CFC and a substantial part of that corporation's trade or business assets are located in that jurisdiction.[1] Similarly, rents and royalties received from a related

---

[1] Section 954(c)(6) contains an additional, more expansive exception for FPHCI received from related parties, but this provision expired at the end of 2014, and to date efforts to extend the provision have been unsuccessful.

corporation are excluded if such amounts relate to the use of property within the CFC's country of incorporation. Some restrictions apply to these exclusions.

At one time, disposition gains included net gains from the disposition of interests in most flow-through entities, while net gains from the disposition of property held in the ordinary course of business were not considered FPHCI. Under these rules, for example, if a CFC sold a partnership interest at a gain, the entire gain would be FPHCI regardless of the categories of assets held by the partnership. In contrast, if the partnership sold its underlying assets, or if the CFC sold its interest in a disregarded entity, at a gain, the CFC's entire gain would not be FPHCI. Instead, the partnership assets sold (or deemed sold) would be separately assessed, and only the gains from the sale of partnership assets that either gave rise to passive income or did not give rise to any income would be FPHCI. This inconsistency was resolved in favor of like treatment with the enactment of § 954(c)(4), which treats the sale of a partnership interest by a CFC as a sale of the proportionate share of partnership assets attributable to that interest if the CFC owns, directly, indirectly, or by attribution, at least 25 percent of a capital or profits interest in the partnership. This situation is illustrated in Figure 14-3.

FIGURE 14-3. SALE OF PARTNERSHIP INTEREST BY A CFC

United States
Shareholders

CFC

Unrelated
Partner

At least
25%

Partnership

x% of income

y% of
income

FPHCI-generating
assets (such as
stocks and bonds)

Active-income-
generating assets
(such as a factory)

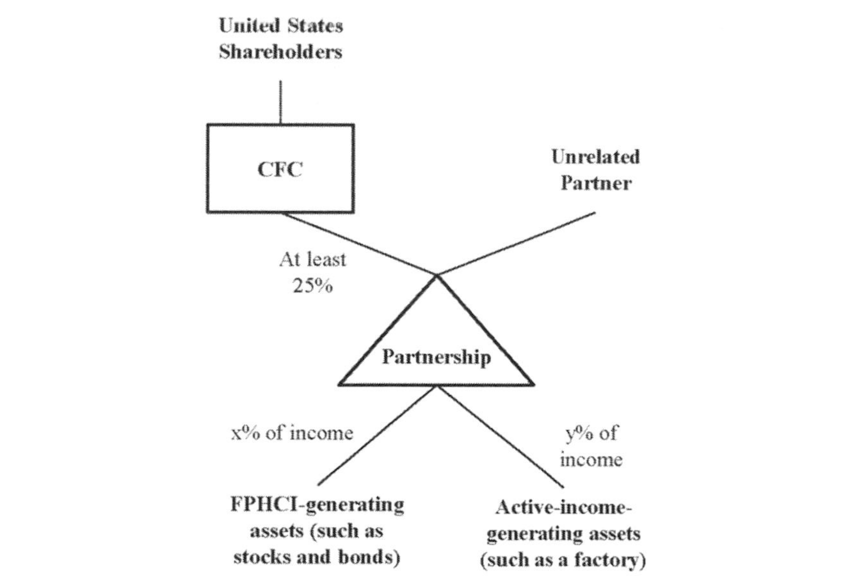

If the CFC sells its partnership interest, the gain will be FPHCI to the extent of x% of the gain attributable to the CFC's proportionate interest; the remaining y% gain will not constitute FPHCI.

The definition of FPHCI excludes several items, most of which are not considered to be easily movable. For instance, rents and royalties received from unrelated third parties and derived in the active conduct of a trade or business are excluded under § 954(c)(2)(A), under the general theory that an actively-conducted trade or business is relatively captive to a jurisdiction that supports a market for the goods or services provided by that trade or business. Therefore, that trade or business is not easily moved offshore. The determination of whether rents or royalties are actively derived is generally made on a facts-and-circumstances basis.

14.03 Foreign Base Company Sales Income

The second main category of foreign base company income is income attributable to sales of personal property, as defined in § 954(a)(2) and (d). This category was designed to prevent United States corporations from avoiding United States taxation by setting up foreign subsidiaries as distribution centers, through which goods would be distributed to other countries and ultimately to consumers. Figure 14-4 presents a basic comparison between direct sales and sales through a foreign base company, in the absence of subpart F.

FIGURE 14-4. DIRECT SALES VERSUS FOREIGN BASE COMPANY SALES
IN THE ABSENCE OF SUBPART F

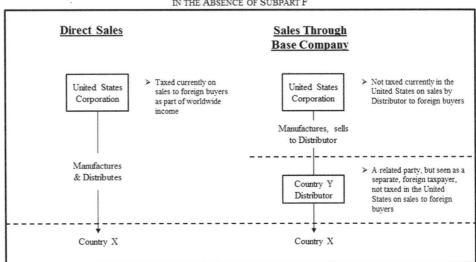

In the absence of subpart F, the use of foreign base companies as conduits for the sale of the parent company's goods to consumers outside of the base country permitted business profits to be indefinitely lodged in the foreign sales entity, thereby deferring United States taxation on profits until they were repatriated to the domestic owner. By including certain sales activity as foreign base company income, and therefore subpart F income, subpart F prevents this easy avoidance of current United States taxation.

For income to constitute foreign base company sales income, four requirements must be met. First, under § 954(d)(1), purchases or sales must be made to, from, or on behalf of, a person related to the CFC (any entity or individual owning, directly or indirectly, more than 50 percent of the CFC's stock, and any entity controlled by the CFC or controlled by the same persons as the CFC). Second, the transaction must involve personal property. Third, the personal property must be manufactured or produced outside of the CFC's country of incorporation. Finally, the purchase or sale must be for use or destination outside the base company's jurisdiction.

Thus, to avoid having foreign base company sales income, a company should avoid setting up a distributing company in one country to sell products manufactured by a related person in another country, to customers located in a third country (as illustrated in Figure 14-3). Income derived from the sale of goods by the CFC inside the country of its incorporation is not foreign base company sales income. The theoretical rationale for this rule is that multinationals should locate manufacturing and sales activities in countries that afford them the greatest market opportunities — that is, they should choose the locations of their business activities based on economic, not tax, factors.

For example, a company may be able to expand its sales if it manufactures its product in close physical proximity to its customers. In such case, it makes sense for a company to have multiple factories in multiple countries to serve multiple markets. Subpart F supports this kind of firm expansion by allowing deferral of United States taxation on the sales income earned by subsidiaries organized in the same country as the manufacturing or production facilities, or the same country as its customers, or both. Similarly, it may make economic sense to locate a sales or distribution subsidiary close to the source of supply for the goods it sells (for example, in the same country where the coffee beans it purchases and sells to customers are grown, in which case sales from those beans, even if to related persons in another country, will not be subpart F income). However, subpart F prevents firms from avoiding current United States taxation when there is thought to be no economic reason to locate a distributing corporation in a country, for instance, because there is neither production capacity nor a customer base in that country.

In addition to the definitional exception to subpart F for sales income earned by a CFC organized in the same country where the products it sells are produced or manufactured, there is an exception under the Regulations for any sales income earned by a CFC that itself performs manufacturing or production functions with respect to the products sold, regardless of where those functions are carried out, and even where the raw materials are purchased from a related person. There are obvious difficulties in determining the amount of manufacturing efforts required by the base company to remove the transaction from the statute's reach. Regulation § 1.954-3(a)(4) requires either complete manufacture or production by the CFC or a "substantial transformation of the property." Substantial transformation occurs most clearly when the resulting product sold is not the product purchased. The Regulation cites as examples such processes as the conversion of wood pulp into paper, steel into bolts and screws, and raw fish into canned fish. This analysis is undoubtedly more qualitative than quantitative, and thus may suffer from lack of predictability.

Additional uncertainty arises regarding the necessary degree of manufacturing when the property sold is comprised of purchased component parts. Regulation § 1.954-3(a)(4) provides two basic tests in such situations: first, a general test of facts and circumstances, and second, an overriding 20 percent cost of goods sold test.

Under the first test, if purchased property is used as a component part in the personal property that is ultimately sold, the integration activity is deemed to constitute manufacturing if it is substantial in degree. Incidental manufacturing activities such as packaging, repackaging, labeling, or minor assembly are insufficient to claim the exclusion. For an example of operations that will not constitute manufacturing, production, or construction, see Regulation § 1.954-3(a)(4)(iii) Example 3. This facts and circumstances test seems to be generously applied by the courts.

The second test represents a significant safe harbor rule for manufacturing that involves component parts. Under the general rule, no foreign base company sales income arises if 20 percent or more of the total costs of goods sold is comprised of direct labor and overhead incurred by the CFC in converting the purchased item into the finished product. Regulation § 1.954-3(a)(4)(iii) Example 1 cites as an example the manufacturing of industrial engines using purchased engine components. The Regulation states that although the finished product is not sufficiently distinguishable from the components to constitute a substantial transformation, if the labor and overhead costs to convert the components to the finished product account for 20 percent or more of the total cost of goods sold, they will nevertheless be considered to have been manufactured by the CFC doing the converting.

14.04 Foreign Base Company Services Income

Foreign base company income also includes "foreign base company services income" under § 954(a)(3). Foreign base company services income is defined in § 954(e) as that derived in connection with the performance of services which are performed for, or on behalf of, any related person and performed outside the country under the laws of which the CFC is created or organized.

This category of income was originally included to prevent manufacturers from improperly shifting offshore the income they derive from certain services performed on their behalf. The primary concern was that United States persons could shift profits out of the United States tax base by arranging transactions so that a foreign CFC was the nominal service provider (for example, it might be listed as the provider on a contract) while its United States parent company provided most of the services (for example, by using its employees to provide services described as "supervisory" in nature but which actually constituted the bulk of the services to be provided under the contract). With the shift to an increasingly service-based economy since the original enactment of the subpart F provisions, the foreign base company services income rules have become more and more relevant.

Foreign base company services income includes (but is not limited to) income from services performed by the CFC in four specific cases listed under Regulation § 1.954-4(b): (1) services paid for or reimbursed by a person related to the CFC; (2) services which a related person is obligated to perform; (3) services which were a condition of a related-party sale of property; and (4) services to which a related person gave "substantial assistance." Under these rules, assistance is deemed substantial if it is either a principal element in producing the services income or exceeds 50 percent of the cost of the performed services.

Regulation § 1.954-4(b)(2)(ii) currently identifies eight kinds of assistance that might be considered substantial including the provision of intangible benefits such as supervision and know how, and tangible assets such as supplies and equipment. The Regulation also provides a number of objective and subjective tests and examples for determining whether assistance to the CFC will be deemed substantial. However, under Notice 2007-13 (excerpted in Part D of this Unit), Treasury has indicated that it is significantly rewriting the substantial assistance rules to eliminate their subjective components and focus instead on an objective, bright line, cost-based rule for multinational service arrangements.

According to Notice 2007-13, change is appropriate because the current rules are overly broad in the context of the increasingly integrated nature of multinational business in today's global economy, and because these rules apparently do little more than force United States-based multinational companies to structure their transactions in artificial ways to avoid the Regulation's reach — i.e., the rules do not ultimately prevent the behavior they target, but merely impose an additional regulatory hurdle to be navigated by tax experts. A major concern with the current rules is that since income from services performed in the country in which the CFC is organized is not foreign base company services income, current law may force United States-based multinationals to set up full-service firms in every country in which they want to provide services, even if such firms are duplicative or superfluous to the global operations of the firm, or tend to favor foreign employment over domestic jobs. Query whether such an outcome is consistent with the rationale described above with respect to foreign base company sales income, namely, that multinational planning should be based on economic reasons rather than tax reasons.

Thus, for example, under the current rules, if a United States company enters into a contractual obligation to build a highway in a foreign country and assigns this contract to a subsidiary located in a country other than the one in which the highway is to be built, the CFC's services might be deemed to have been performed on behalf of the domestic parent and give rise to foreign base company services income. The determination would depend on a facts-and-circumstances-based inquiry that would include deciding whether the services provided by the parent company were a principal element in producing the income from the construction contract.

Under the standard laid out in Notice 2007-13, however, the income would only constitute foreign base company services income if the cost to the CFC of the assistance furnished by the related United States person equals or exceeds 80 percent of the total cost to the CFC of performing the services. To state the inverse proposition, no foreign base company services income will result so long as more than 20 percent of the costs incurred by the CFC in performing the services are attributable to services it performs directly or through a related CFC. This minimal standard both simplifies and significantly reduces the reach of the current rules, so that most service fees earned by CFCs can likely escape current taxation under subpart F with a minimum of planning.

14.05 Allocation of Deductions to Base Company Income: Rules and Limitations

Foreign base company income is reduced by "properly allocable" deductions pursuant to § 954(b)(5). Deductions are allocated according to Regulations §§ 1.861-8 and 1.904-5, in a fashion that parallels the allocation and apportionment scheme applicable for purposes of computing the foreign tax credit limitation. Deductions are logically allocated to the gross base company income category to which they directly relate. If no such relationship exists, a next-best rule is triggered (i.e., ratably apportioning deductions among all gross income categories). The allocation process is limited in that it cannot create a "loss" with respect to a given category of base company income.

A special rule applies, however, if the CFC's foreign base company income exceeds 70 percent of its gross income. In such a case, under § 954(b)(3)(B) all of the CFC's gross income is treated as foreign base company income. It thus follows that all of the CFC's deductions may be offset against gross foreign base company income.

Under § 954(b)(5), interest paid to United States shareholders is allocated first to foreign personal holding company income that is passive income within the meaning of § 904(d)(2). Any remainder is allocated to other subpart F or non-subpart F income.

14.06 Special Rules Applicable to Foreign Base Company Income

Foreign base company income is not automatically included in subpart F income, but, as noted above, an excessive amount of foreign base company income can cause all of the CFC's gross income to be cast as subpart F income. Section 954(b) provides three special provisions that determine the extent to which foreign base company income will be included in subpart F income.

The first of these is the *de minimis* rule of § 954(b)(3)(A), as interpreted under Regulation § 1.954-1(b)(1)(i). Under this rule, if gross foreign base company income is less than the lesser of five percent of the CFC's gross income or $1,000,000, the CFC's foreign base company (or insurance) income will be deemed to be zero. Under this test, for example, if a CFC has gross income of $4,000,000 and gross foreign base company income of $100,000, its adjusted foreign base company income is deemed to equal zero.

The second provision is the full inclusion test of § 954(b)(3)(B), as interpreted under Regulation § 1.954-1(b)(1)(ii). This test offers a sharp contrast to the *de minimis* test. In general, the full inclusion test provides that if the CFC's gross foreign base company income exceeds 70 percent of its total gross income, all of its gross income will be considered gross foreign base company income. Under this test, if a CFC had gross income of $4,000,000 of which $3,000,000 was gross foreign base company income, it would be deemed to have realized $4,000,000 in foreign base company income.

The third provision is the high-taxed income exception of § 954(b)(4), as interpreted under Regulation § 1.954-1(d). As the foreign base company provisions are geared toward discouraging the use of tax havens to locate base companies and avoid domestic taxation, Congress crafted an elective exception to exclude from subpart F any foreign base company income that is not taxed at a significantly lower rate than would be imposed domestically. Under this exception, a taxpayer may elect to exclude from the subpart F income computation any item of income subject to an effective tax rate that exceeds 90 percent of the maximum domestic corporate tax rate. Under Regulation § 1.954-1(d)(5), the election, which must be made by controlling United States shareholders, is binding on all the United States shareholders of the CFC.

There are, of course, many other exceptions and limitations applicable to the computation of foreign base company income and subpart F income, which are beyond the scope of this Unit.

14.07 Pro Rata Share

If a CFC has earned subpart F income for the year, the next step is to determine the portion of that income that must be included as gross income by the United States shareholders under § 951. Only United States shareholders who own (directly or indirectly) CFC stock on the last day in a tax year, on which the foreign corporation was a CFC must include this pro rata share of subpart F income. *See* Section 951(a)(1). A United States shareholder's pro rata share is calculated on the basis of both direct and indirect ownership, but not on the basis of constructive ownership, under § 951(a)(2). The regulations address how to compute pro rata shares in cases where the CFC has more than one class of stock outstanding. *See* Regulation § 1.951-1(e)(3).

14.08 Basis Adjustments

The CFC rules cause United States shareholders to be taxed on a hypothetical, rather than an actual, distribution. As a result, these shareholders could be subject to double tax on the amount deemed distributed, either when earnings are subsequently distributed or, if not subsequently distributed, when the shareholders sell their stock, the value of which should include the undistributed earnings. Section 961 provides for basis adjustments to prevent such double taxation.

First, under § 961(a), a shareholder's basis for each share of CFC stock or other property is increased by the amount of income imputed to the shareholder under § 951. The basis adjustment applies to "other property" when the United States shareholder is only deemed to own stock of the CFC under the indirect ownership rules of § 958. Such property includes stock in a foreign corporation and any interest in a foreign partnership, trust, or estate, as provided in Regulations §§ 1.961-1(b)(1) and 1.961-2. Since this upward basis adjustment reduces the gain recognized on an ultimate sale of the stock, such a sale prior to receipt of actual distributions will prevent double taxation.

Second, under § 961(b), a shareholder's basis in each share of CFC stock or other property is reduced when subsequent dividend distributions comprised of previously taxed earnings are actually made. As the following section describes, distributions of previously taxed income are excluded from gross income, so when the distribution is made, a corresponding basis reduction must ensue to reverse the earlier effect of § 961(a). In effect, this restores the taxpayer's basis in his CFC stock to the same amount it would have been, had he avoided having currently-includible distributions from the corporation under subpart F.

14.09 Exclusions from Gross Income — Previously Taxed Earnings and Profits

The CFC provisions impute income to United States shareholders even if the corporation does not actually distribute any income to these owners. When no actual distribution occurs, § 961 treats the shareholder as if he contributed the deemed dividend back to the corporation, in turn increasing his basis in the stock. If, after the imputation of income, a distribution of dividends from the CFC actually occurs, a mechanism is necessary to ensure that distributions representing earnings which have previously been imputed to the CFC shareholder are not again taxed, and that the corresponding basis increase mandated by § 961 is reversed.

Section 959 supplies this mechanism. In situations where particular earnings and profits have been subjected to imputation, it provides that such earnings and profits (and the distributions from them) are thereafter insulated from taxation (i.e., the dividend distribution represented by these earnings and profits will not be taxed). The exclusion shields those earnings from a second layer of taxation upon actual distribution. Another exclusion applies to those earnings and profits attributable to imputed amounts which have been reinvested by the CFC in United States property. Amounts imputed from investment in United States property are excludable to the extent such earnings are attributable to income derived from the other categories of imputed income.

As it is possible for actual and constructive distributions to occur during the same year, priority rules respecting such distributions have been enacted. Section 959 invokes the normal ordering rules of § 316: distributions are deemed to come first from current earnings and profits to the extent thereof and thereafter from accumulated earnings and profits. Through this priority scheme, previously taxed earnings are deemed distributed to shareholders first. Until distributions exceed the amount of previously taxed income, actual distributions will not be taxable as dividends to the shareholder.

14.10 Sale of CFC Stock

A final issue for consideration is the tax treatment of a sale or disposition of CFC stock by a United States shareholder. As should be apparent at this point, subpart F is not a comprehensive anti-deferral statute. In many cases, CFCs earn income which is not subject to current United States taxation under this regime, and which may benefit from deferral so long as the earnings are retained offshore and not distributed to the United States shareholders. These untaxed retained earnings could then be converted into capital gain upon the sale of the stock.

While this result is fairly common in the case of domestic stock ownership, the advantage of retaining earnings in the corporation to avoid current shareholder taxation in the domestic context is tempered to the extent the corporation itself is taxed on its worldwide income as it is earned. Since the basic premise of the CFC is to earn and retain income offshore where it will be subject neither to United States taxation nor, potentially, foreign taxation, the ability to convert deferred retained earnings into capital gain may create an additional distortion that renders holding stock in foreign corporations more tax-advantaged than holding stock in domestic corporations.

The statutory response to this potential distortion is found in § 1248. Upon certain dispositions of CFC stock, this provision recharacterizes a portion of gain, representing the previously deferred earnings, as a dividend. To the extent that the dividend is not eligible for the reduced rate currently available to individual taxpayers under § 1(h)(11), this could result in ordinary treatment for this portion of the stock gain, thus potentially eroding (but probably not erasing) much of the benefit of deferral.

In general, § 1248 provides that if the sale of stock or the liquidation of a CFC occurs and if the taxpayer owned 10 percent or more of the stock, whether directly, indirectly, or constructively, at any time during the five-year period preceding the sale, the portion of the taxpayer's gain equal to the earnings and profits attributable to that ownership period will be treated as a dividend. The foreign corporation must have been a CFC for some portion of that 10 percent ownership period, but not necessarily on the date of the disposition or exchange. Section 1248 includes a number of rules to prevent evasion through creative tax planning, but the most straightforward means to avoid § 1248 (though not necessarily the most easily attainable means) is to sell stock after the CFC has ceased to be a CFC for the requisite five-year period.

Section 1248(a) provides detailed rules for determining the amount of gain that will be recharacterized as dividend income. In general, the statute may recharacterize earnings and profits accumulated by a CFC after 1962 while the United States shareholder held the stock. Gain realized in excess of this amount would retain its character (generally, capital gain). Section 1248 only applies to gain, so any loss recognized on a transaction involving CFC stock will be characterized under other provisions (typically as capital loss). Section 1248 presents a number of additional rules and exceptions for the treatment of gains realized from the sale of CFC stock, so one is well advised to examine the statute and regulatory guidance carefully in light of the particular factual context.

D.   REFERENCE MATERIALS

- Notice 2007-13

NOTICE 2007-13
2007-5 I.R.B. 410 (Jan. 29, 2007)

Modification of the Substantial Assistance Rules

SECTION 1. OVERVIEW

This notice announces that the Treasury Department and the Internal Revenue Service (the IRS) will amend Treas. Reg. § 1.954-4(b)(1)(iv) and (b)(2)(ii) and the examples thereunder, which provide that substantial assistance rendered by a related person or persons to a controlled foreign corporation ("CFC") is included within the definition of foreign base company services income under section 954(e) of the Internal Revenue Code (Code). These amended regulations will limit the types of activities that constitute substantial assistance to certain assistance rendered, directly or indirectly, by a United States person or persons (as the term is defined in section 957(c) of the Code) to a related CFC. Until regulations reflecting these changes are issued, taxpayers may rely on this notice.

. . .

SECTION 2. SUBSTANTIAL ASSISTANCE RULES

A. BACKGROUND

Under section 951(a)(1)(A)(i) of the Code, a United States shareholder of a CFC includes in gross income each year its *pro rata* share of the CFC's subpart F income for the taxable year of the CFC which ends with or within such taxable year of the shareholder. Section 952(a)(2) defines the term "subpart F income" to mean, in part, foreign base company income (as defined under section 954).

Section 954(a)(3) of the Code defines "foreign base company income" to include "foreign base company services income" for the taxable year. Section 954(e)(1) defines "foreign base company services income" for purposes of section 954(a)(3) to mean income derived in connection with the performance of services which are performed (1) for, or on behalf of, any related person and (2) outside the country under the laws of which the CFC is created or organized. The statute does not explicitly provide for substantial assistance rules under section 954(e). Those rules are promulgated under the Secretary's authority under section 7805(a) to issue regulations interpreting the term "for, or on behalf of, any related person" under section 954(a)(3).

Treas. Reg. § 1.954-4(b)(1)(iv) defines "services which are performed for, or on behalf of, a related person" to include substantial assistance contributing to the performance of services by a CFC that has been furnished by a related person or persons. Treas. Reg. § 1.954-4(b)(2)(ii) sets forth the rules for the application of the substantial assistance test. Treas. Reg. § 1.954-4(b)(2)(ii)(*a*) states, in general, that assistance "shall include, but shall not be limited to, direction, supervision, services, know-how, financial assistance (other than contributions to capital), and equipment, material, or supplies." Treas. Reg. § 1.954-4(b)(2)(ii)(*b*) and (*c*) then provide separate tests depending on whether the assistance provided by the related person or persons is in the form of (1) direction, supervision, services or know-how, or (2) financial assistance, equipment, material or supplies.

Treas. Reg. § 1.954-4(b)(2)(ii)(*b*) provides that assistance in the form of direction, supervision, services or know-how may be substantial under either a subjective or an objective test. Under the subjective test, assistance in the form of direction, supervision, services or know-how will be considered substantial if the assistance provides the CFC with skills which are a principal element in producing the income from the performance of such services by such CFC (the principal element test). For example, a CFC enters into a contract with an unrelated person to drill an oil well. The technical and supervisory personnel who oversee the drilling of the well are employees of M, a person related to CFC. In such an instance, the services performed by CFC for the unrelated party are considered foreign base company services because the services performed by M substantially assist CFC in the performance of the contract and the services performed by M are a principal element in producing the income from the performance of the drilling contract. *Cf.* Treas. Reg. § 1.954-4(b)(3), Ex. 2.

Alternatively, under the objective test, assistance in the form of direction, supervision, services or know-how may be substantial if the cost to the CFC of the assistance furnished by persons related to the CFC equals 50 percent or more of the total cost to the CFC of performing the services performed by such CFC (the cost test). For these purposes, costs are determined after taking into account adjustments (if any) made under section 482. *See* Treas. Reg. § 1.954-4(b)(2)(ii)(*b*).

Treas. Reg. § 1.954-4(b)(2)(ii)(*c*) states, in general, that financial assistance, equipment, material, or supplies furnished by a person related to the CFC shall be considered assistance only in the amount, after taking into account adjustments (if any) made under section 482, by which the consideration actually paid by the CFC to the related person for the purchase or use of such item is less than the arm's length charge for such purchase or use. The total of all such amounts from all related persons is compared with the profits derived by the CFC from the performance of the services to determine whether the related party's contributions qualify as substantial assistance.

Treas. Reg. § 1.954-4(b)(2)(ii)(*d*) expands on the tests in Treas. Reg. § 1.954-4(b)(2)(ii)(*b*) and (*c*) by providing that, even if assistance furnished by a related person or persons to a CFC is not considered substantial under paragraphs (*b*) or (*c*) in isolation, it may nevertheless constitute substantial assistance when taken together or in combination with other assistance furnished by a related person or persons to the CFC. Treas. Reg. § 1.954-4(b)(2)(ii)(*e*) provides that, in applying Treas. Reg. § 1.954-4(b)(2)(ii)(*b*) and (*d*), assistance in the form of direction, supervision, services, or know-how shall not be taken into account, unless the assistance so furnished assists the CFC directly in the performance of the services performed. Treas. Reg. § 1.954-4(b)(3) sets forth examples, including examples addressing the application of the substantial assistance test.

B. DISCUSSION

The substantial assistance rules were published as final regulations in 1968 (T.D. 6981, 1968-2 C.B. 314). The purpose of the substantial assistance rules is to treat as foreign base company services income, income received by a CFC from rendering services to an unrelated person where in rendering those services a related person substantially contributes to the CFC's performance of such services in a manner that suggests that the CFC, rather than the related party, entered into the contract to obtain a lower rate of tax on the service income. Since the regulations were published in 1968, there has been a substantial expansion in the reach of the global economy, particularly in the provision of global services. As a result, many of the U.S. multinationals that provide services outside of the United States currently have globally integrated businesses with support capabilities for unrelated customer projects in different geographic locations, largely based on factors such as expertise and cost efficiencies.

For example, a CFC may contract with an unrelated person to provide installation and subsequent repair services. A related CFC, however, is the foreign corporation that provides the repair services. Although the foreign related CFC that is providing the support services will continue to have foreign base company services income to the extent that it performs those services outside of its country of incorporation, it does not seem appropriate in the current global economy to continue to treat the profits of the CFC contracting to furnish services to the unrelated person as foreign base company services income because of the support services provided by a related foreign person. If the substantial assistance regulations are not amended to deal with these types of businesses structures, the regulations may cause taxpayers to change the way they do business or structure their operations in light of the substantial assistance rules, even if such a structure would be less efficient from a business perspective by, for example, requiring a taxpayer to duplicate a full service infrastructure in each country.

The Treasury Department and the IRS, however, remain concerned about the ability of related United States persons to shift profits offshore to CFCs organized in low tax jurisdictions in cases where the related United States person or persons provides so much assistance to the CFC that the CFC cannot be said to be providing services on its own account and thus acting as an independent entity. Accordingly, the Treasury Department and the IRS will revise the regulations to eliminate the substantial assistance rules, except in certain limited instances in which a United States person or persons provide sufficient assistance directly or indirectly to a related CFC.

C. PROPOSED GUIDANCE

The Treasury Department and the IRS will amend Treas. Reg. § 1.954-4(b)(1)(iv) and (b)(2)(ii) and the examples thereunder. Treas. Reg. § 1.954-4(b)(1)(iv) as amended will provide that services performed by a CFC in a case where substantial assistance by a related United States person or persons (as the term is defined in section 957(c) of the Code) contributes to the performance of such service will constitute "services which are performed for, or on behalf of, a related person." Treas. Reg. § 1.954-4(b)(2)(ii) as amended will provide that "substantial assistance" consists of assistance furnished (directly or indirectly) by a related United States person or persons to the CFC if the assistance satisfies an objective cost test. The subjective "principal element" test will no longer apply to determine substantial assistance. For purposes of the objective cost test, the definition of the term "assistance" will include, but will not be limited to, direction, supervision, services, know-how, financial assistance (other than contributions to capital), and equipment, material, or supplies provided directly or indirectly by a related United States person to a CFC.

The cost test will be satisfied if the cost to the CFC of the assistance furnished by the related United States person or persons equals or exceeds 80 percent of the total cost to the CFC of performing the services. The term "cost" will be determined after taking into account adjustments, if any, made under section 482 of the Code. Taxpayers may apply the cost test either by demonstrating that the assistance provided, directly or indirectly, by related United States persons is below the 80 percent cost threshold, or, alternatively, by demonstrating that the cost of the services provided by the CFC itself, and/or by a related CFC, is more than 20 percent of the total cost to the CFC of performing the services. For this purpose, services provided by a CFC itself are not assistance provided "indirectly" by a related United States person (or persons). However, employees, officers, or directors of the CFC who are concurrently employees, officers, or directors of a related United States person during a taxable year of the CFC will be considered employees, officers or directors solely of the related United States person for such taxable year for purposes of this notice.

The examples under Treas. Reg. § 1.954-4(b)(2)(ii) will be amended to reflect the amendments to the regulations. The application of the proposed cost test is illustrated by the following examples.

Example 1: USP, a U.S. corporation, wholly owns CFC1 and CFC2, each a foreign corporation. CFC1 enters into a contract with FP, an unrelated foreign person, to design a bridge for FP in Country Y, a foreign country that is not CFC1's country of organization. CFC1 incurs a total of $100x of costs to design the bridge for FP. USP performs supervisory services in Country Y for CFC1 with respect to the contract for which CFC1 pays USP a fee. CFC1 directly performs services related to the performance of that contract that cost CFC1 $15x. CFC2 performs centralized support services related to the performance of that contract in Country X, its country of organization, for which CFC1 pays CFC2 $10x. CFC1 is not treated as receiving substantial assistance in the performance of that contract because more than 20% of the cost of that contract is attributable to services furnished directly by CFC1 or a related CFC (CFC2).

Example 2: USP, a U.S. corporation, wholly owns CFC1 and CFC2, each a foreign corporation. CFC2 enters into a contract with FP, an unrelated person, to design a bridge in Country Y, a foreign country that is not CFC2's country of organization. With respect to the contract with FP, USP performs services in Country Y for CFC1 in the form of design and technical services for which CFC1 pays USP $85x. CFC1 contracts with CFC2 to provide those services and others to CFC2 for $90x. CFC2 uses those services together with services it performs itself that cost CFC2 $10x to design the bridge for FP. Pursuant to the cost test, USP provides substantial assistance to CFC2 in the performance of its contract for FP because USP indirectly furnishes assistance to CFC2 (through CFC1) that exceeds 80 percent of the total cost to CFC2 for performing the contract.

Example 3: USP, a U.S. corporation, wholly owns CFC1 and CFC2, each a foreign corporation. CFC2 enters into a contract with FP, an unrelated person, to design a bridge in Country Y, a foreign country that is not CFC2's country of organization. With respect to the contract with FP, USP performs services in Country Y for CFC1 in the form of design and technical services for which CFC1 pays USP $60x. CFC1 contracts with CFC2 to provide those services and others to CFC2 for $70x. CFC2 uses those services together with services it performs itself that cost CFC2 $30x to design the bridge for FP. CFC2 is not treated as receiving substantial assistance in the performance of that contract because more than 20% of the cost of that contract is attributable to services furnished directly by CFC2.

Unit 15

PASSIVE FOREIGN INVESTMENT COMPANIES

A. CODE AND REGULATION PROVISIONS

Code   §§ 954(c); 1291(a)–(d); 1293(a)–(e); 1295; 1296(a)–(e), (k); 1297.
Reg.   § 1.1296-1(c)–(d).
Prop. Reg.   §§ 1.1291-1(a)–(c); 1.1291-2(e); 1.1291-4(a), (c)–(e).

B. PROBLEMS FOR CLASS DISCUSSION

15-1. All of the single class of stock in Venn Corporation, a Venezuelan corporation, is owned by Theo (6 percent), Remi (47 percent), and Paloma (47 percent) (all unrelated United States citizens and residents). Venn's only asset is an office building in Brazil that is currently leased to an unrelated Brazilian operating company under a 50-year lease. Venn derives substantial rental income from the property but does not make distributions to its shareholders.

  (a) Are the shareholders subject to the CFC rules and/or the PFIC rules?

  (b) How would the answer to (a) change if Remi was a citizen and resident of Brazil?

15-2. Assume the same general facts from Problem 15-1(b). In addition, assume the following:

  • Theo purchased his Venn stock on January 1, Year 1, from an unrelated seller for $5,000 and sold all of his stock on December 31, Year 10, to an unrelated purchaser for $15,000.

  • No election was made under § 1295 or § 1296.

  • The United States tax rate on long-term capital gain at all relevant times was 15 percent.

  • The highest marginal tax rate under § 1 in each of Years 1–10 was 35 percent, and Theo's taxable income placed him in the 28 percent bracket each year.

  • The interest rate under § 6621 for underpayments of tax was seven percent. Ignore the compounding aspect of the determination, and round up to the nearest dollar.

  (a) What are the United States income tax consequences of Theo's ownership of the Venn stock in Years 1–10 and the gain from his stock sale in Year 10?

(b)   How would the answer to (a) change if Theo made a § 1295 election with respect to the Venn stock in Year 1? Assume that the earnings attributable to Theo's stock are as follows:

Year	Ordinary Income	Long Term Capital Gain
1	$100	$900
2	200	800
3	300	700
4	400	600
5	500	500
6	600	400
7	700	300
8	800	200
9	900	100
10	1000	0
TOTAL	$5,500	$4,500

(c)   How would the answer to (a) change if Theo made a § 1295 election at the beginning of Year 6? Assume that Theo's Venn stock was worth $10,000 on that day.

(d)   How would the answer to (a) change if in Year 1 Theo made a § 1296 election with respect to the Venn stock, which was publicly traded, and the stock appreciated $1,000 annually and has the earnings pattern similar to that described in (b)?

C.   OVERVIEW

As discussed in prior Units, the basic United States tax regime applicable to foreign corporations has a relatively narrow focus, generally reaching only certain domestic source income and income effectively connected with a United States trade or business. As such, domestic investors have found foreign corporations to be an attractive vehicle for deferring or even completely avoiding United States taxation on foreign earnings. Congress has enacted a litany of statutory mechanisms to prevent what may be considered an excessive amount of tax-motivated offshore investment, but, as we have seen, these regimes may often be avoided with attentive tax planning. For instance, as discussed in Unit 13, because the controlled foreign corporation (CFC) regime applies only to United States persons owning at least 10 percent of the voting power of the foreign corporation, these rules can be avoided by structuring the ownership of the foreign corporation so that no United States person holds the requisite amount. Likewise, as discussed in Unit 14, the ordinary income conversion rules of § 1248 applicable to the disposition of CFC stock can be circumvented by limiting United States ownership.

One way to limit ownership is simply to expand the pool of investors — i.e., use a mutual fund model to bring investors together and dilute any one person's share of the whole. In the 1980s, many United States investors began doing just that. Foreign investment companies were established in favorable tax jurisdictions (those imposing little or no taxation on investment earnings), where shareholders could both accumulate untaxed earnings and convert ordinary income items, such as interest and dividends, to capital gain on the sale of the investment company shares.

In response, Congress enacted the passive foreign investment company (PFIC) provisions in 1986. These provisions are targeted at the deferral benefits accruing to United States shareholders who (by design or coincidence) escape the CFC regime by holding less than a 10 percent stake in a foreign corporation that invests in passive assets. The PFIC rules are secondary to the CFC rules — if a person is subject to income inclusion under the CFC rules as a United States shareholder in a CFC, the PFIC rules will not apply.

The PFIC regime thus serves essentially as a backstop to the objective ownership-based tests of the CFC regime. The PFIC provisions parallel the classic anti-deferral regimes by recapturing deferral benefits enjoyed by domestic shareholders and preventing the conversion of PFIC ordinary income to capital gain upon the shareholder's disposition of its PFIC investment.

The classification of a foreign corporation as a PFIC derives from the predominantly passive nature of the investments and resulting income of the entity. In contrast to the CFC regime that it is intended to supplement, application of the PFIC rules does not depend on particular levels of United States ownership, but hinges instead on income and assets held by domestic shareholders through foreign corporations. The PFIC regime focuses on the character of the entity and its capacity for providing opportunities for deferral and favorable income characterization.

If a foreign corporation constitutes a PFIC for a given taxable year, certain tax consequences may apply as described below. However, the PFIC regime also provides two elections that result in current taxing schemes for United States shareholders. In each case, annual United States tax consequences are imposed upon the shareholder, designed to roughly approximate how the PFIC's earnings would have been taxed had the assets been held directly by the shareholders. As a result, before delving into what constitutes a PFIC, it may be helpful to understand how the tax consequences differ among these various possibilities. This Unit briefly introduces the alternative taxing schemes available under the PFIC regime, and then provides an overview of the major definitional and analytical aspects of the relevant statutes.

15.01   The § 1291 Tax and Interest Regime   — *Default*

Section 1291 provides the default tax regime for PFICs, which applies unless a shareholder makes an election to prevent its application. In general, § 1291 imposes a special shareholder tax and interest charge on deferred income, essentially reversing the deferral benefits achieved by United States persons by virtue of their PFIC investment. The § 1291 tax and interest regime is triggered upon the realization of gain from the disposition of PFIC stock and upon the shareholder's receipt of certain PFIC distributions attributable to earnings in post-1986 years on which the shareholder enjoyed tax deferral (so-called "excess distributions"). Thus, under this statutory default regime, shareholders may invest through PFICs and take advantage of deferral, but they will pay a cost upon exit in the form of back taxes and interest payments.

15.02   The § 1295 QEF Election

To avoid these default rules, § 1295 allows domestic shareholders to elect to have their share of PFIC earnings taxed currently if certain requirements are met. Under this provision, shareholders must elect to treat the PFIC as a "qualifying electing fund" (QEF). In general, the result of QEF status is to create a current year ordinary income and net capital gain inclusion for United States shareholders.

Pros

Overall, the QEF election presents a number of tradeoffs for taxpayers. For example, a lower rate of tax may be imposed on the earnings, both as a result of the segregation of ordinary income and net capital gain and because the default regime applies the highest taxable rate in effect. However, while ordinary income taxed under the QEF election may be subject to a lower tax rate than under § 1291, the taxpayer might be able to earn more interest on the deferred tax amount than the amount of the underpayment interest that will be ultimately assessed.   *But*

15.03   The § 1296 Mark-to-Market Regime

FMV − basis = inc/ded.

A domestic shareholder of PFIC stock may also avoid the default regime of § 1291 if the stock is marketable on a public exchange and the shareholder makes an election under § 1296(k) to recognize income or loss on the PFIC stock on an annual basis. Under § 1296(a), the difference at year-end between the basis of the stock and its fair market value constitutes either income or a deduction. Deductions, however, are limited to the extent of prior income inclusions ("unreversed inclusions"). The income or loss under the election is characterized as ordinary income or ordinary loss, and the source of the gain or loss is determined as if derived from the sale of the PFIC stock. Basis adjustments to the PFIC stock are provided under § 1296(b) for any income or loss taken into account.

Pro

Cons

The § 1296 mark-to-market election also presents a number of tradeoffs for taxpayers. For example, under the election, income is recognized as the stock actually appreciates, so the timing of the gain is not controlled by any artificial pro-rata allocation of such gain as occurs under § 1291. On the other hand, the electing shareholder may be subject to taxation even when no distributions are made and no stock is sold, and the shareholder is taxed at ordinary income rates on all appreciation.

Thus, when considering the implications of PFIC status, it bears keeping in mind that tax consequences may vary, depending on what elections may be available and which taxation regime may provide the most favorable result for the taxpayer. The next sections turn to the definitional questions regarding PFIC status.

15.04   Classification of a PFIC: The Passive Income and Passive Assets Tests

The classification of a foreign corporation as a PFIC derives from the passive nature of the investments and the resulting income generated from those investments. PFIC status is imposed on any foreign corporation that meets either a passive income test or a passive assets test, regardless of its domestic ownership or lack thereof. As a result, it is often significantly more difficult for a foreign corporation to escape PFIC status than it would to escape status as a CFC.

15.05   Passive Income Test

Under § 1297(a)(1), a foreign corporation constitutes a PFIC if 75 percent or more of its gross income for the taxable year consists of passive income. In general, passive income is any income comprising foreign personal holding company income as defined by § 954(c). This so-called "tainted" income includes dividends, interest and interest equivalents, rents, royalties, annuities, and net gains from certain property, commodities, and foreign currency transactions.

[margin note: Test]

Passive income does not, however, include any income derived from the active conduct of certain businesses which by their nature generate income items normally considered passive. For instance, § 1297(b) provides that income (e.g., interest income) derived in the active conduct of a banking business does not generally constitute passive income. Similarly, income derived by a corporation predominantly engaged in the insurance business from the active conduct of that business is not passive income if that business would be subject to domestic taxation if conducted by a domestic corporation.

[margin note: exception – active banking biz.]

Section 1297(b) also provides an important exemption for certain passive income derived by foreign corporations from related parties. Under this provision, passive income generally does not include income derived by a foreign corporation from a related party if the related party generated the income in the active conduct of a business. Interest, dividend, rental, or royalty income received or accrued from a related person is not passive income in the hands of the recipient to the extent that the income is allocable to non-passive income of that related person. Because the PFIC regime is mainly designed to prevent deferral on easily mobile capital rather than active business income, this look-through rule is meant to insulate income received by a foreign corporation holding stock in an active operating subsidiary, to the extent the income does not constitute passive income in the hands of the subsidiary. Thus, stock ownership in tiered-entity structures is not unduly penalized.

[margin note: related parties]

15.06   Passive Assets Test

A foreign corporation constitutes a PFIC if the average annual percentage of the fair market value or adjusted basis of its passive income-producing assets represents at least 50 percent of the value or adjusted basis, as applicable, of all of the entity's assets. *See* §§ 1297(a)(2) and 1297(e). To prevent year-end manipulation of assets, the percentage of passive assets is determined quarterly on a gross basis.

[margin note: Test]

See Notice 88-22 (excerpted in Part D).[1] If assets are dual-natured, the proportionate amount of passive income generated dictates the includable portion of the value of such assets as passive assets.

The passive assets test is generally applied on a fair market value basis. However, if an eligible foreign corporation so elects, the passive assets test may be applied with reference to the adjusted basis of its assets under § 1297(e). This election allows taxpayers to avoid complicated and uncertain valuation issues. Though no Regulations have been issued to date to guide taxpayers in applying the passive assets test, the Service has provided some guidance by notice.

15.07   Special Look-Through Rule

The PFIC provisions contain a special look-through rule for applying the passive income and passive assets tests. This rule, found in § 1297(c), is intended to prevent the sheltering of passive-income generating assets in a subsidiary. It provides that for purposes of determining whether a foreign corporation is a PFIC, a foreign corporation is deemed to own its proportionate share of the assets of a subsidiary of which it owns directly or indirectly, by value, 25 percent or more of the subsidiary's stock. It is also deemed to receive its proportionate share of the subsidiary's income. The look-through rule applies regardless of whether the subsidiary is a domestic or foreign corporation. If the rule applies, the subsidiary's underlying assets and income factor into the foreign parent's passive asset and income calculations for testing purposes. However, because the look-through rule is not meant to penalize PFICs that own stock in, or receive dividends from, an active subsidiary (again, the main focus is easily mobile capital), stock ownership and dividends are not factored in to the parent's assets and income for PFIC determination purposes.

Depending on the investments and activities of a foreign corporation's subsidiary, the look-through rule may benefit or burden the taxpayer. If the subsidiary has a minimal amount of passive assets and generates little or no passive income, attributing its assets and income to the foreign parent may favorably dilute the parent's overall passive income and investment structure. However, tiered structures in which a subsidiary has a significant amount of investment in passive assets should be avoided, since that subsidiary, viewed separately or combined with that subsidiary's subsidiaries, might be classified as a PFIC.

15.08   Exceptions to Passive Foreign Investment Company Status

Owing to the broad PFIC definition, § 1298 contains two important relief provisions for newly-formed corporations and those corporations undergoing a change in the nature of their business operations. These exceptions are critical for investors in new business ventures which during their initial start-up period may

---

[1] Despite its age, this Notice continues to be relied upon by the Service as the principal source of guidance in determining the assets that produce passive income for PFIC purposes. For an example, see PLR 200813036 (December 19, 2007) (excerpted in Part D of this Unit).

generate only passive income and thereby expose their investors to the risk of being deemed to hold a PFIC investment.

The first relief provision, found in § 1298(b)(2), shields a start-up foreign corporation from PFIC status for the first taxable year in which it derives gross income (i.e., its "start-up year"). The exemption is extended only to those start-up corporations with no past or future ties to PFIC status. A qualifying foreign corporation cannot have had a PFIC predecessor, and it must also establish that it will not be, and is in fact not, a PFIC for either of its two taxable years following the year in which the corporation first earns gross income.

The start-up corporation exception thus spares investments in newly formed corporations that are generating cash from stock subscriptions and loan proceeds and garnering interest and other passive income from temporary investment of that cash pending full-scale active business operations. However, the exception is difficult to apply given its forward looking requirements and its potential retroactive application if taxpayers miss the mark in predicting the results of the two-year operating window.

For comparable policy reasons, the PFIC provisions are similarly relaxed for certain foreign corporations that are embarking upon a new business course. Under § 1298(b)(3), a foreign corporation in the process of changing businesses will not constitute a PFIC for any taxable year if all ties to PFIC status are severed. A qualifying corporation cannot itself (nor can its predecessors) have been a PFIC for any prior taxable year. Moreover, the corporation must establish that substantially all of its passive income for the taxable year is attributable to proceeds from the disposition of one or more active trades or businesses. It must also assure the Service that it will not be a PFIC for either of the two subsequent taxable years and must, in fact, not be so classified.

15.09   The § 1291 Tax and Interest Regime — Excess Distributions and Dispositions

The goal of the PFIC provisions is to eliminate the deferral benefits obtained by United States investors through the use of foreign investment companies as vehicles for passive investment. Accordingly, § 1291 recoups the tax on income previously subject to deferral and tacks on a penalizing interest charge when that income is repatriated from the PFIC. These results ensue either when income is realized by United States shareholders through certain "excess distributions" of PFIC income, or upon a shareholder's actual or deemed disposition of PFIC stock.

15.10   Mechanics of § 1291

The § 1291 deferral tax and interest regime are triggered by an "excess distribution" to a United States person. An excess distribution captures for tax purposes PFIC income which has effectively been lodged in the PFIC during the shareholder's holding period of the stock, and thus has been subject to tax deferral with respect to that shareholder. A direct or indirect disposition of PFIC stock likewise triggers § 1291. The gain recognized by the shareholder on such a disposition is deemed to be an excess distribution.

In numerical terms, the excess distribution subject to the special tax and interest provisions is generally the shareholder's ratable portion of the excess, if any, of the amount of PFIC distributions received during the taxable year over 125 percent of the average amount of PFIC distributions received by the taxpayer during the three preceding taxable years (or the shareholder's holding period, if shorter). The excess distribution on a disposition is the amount of gain, if any, realized on the transaction. This determination is made on a share-by-share basis, and the total excess distribution with respect to any stock is zero for the taxable year in which the taxpayer's holding period for the PFIC stock begins.

15.11   The Deferred Tax Amount

If either a distribution from a PFIC or the gain from a disposition of PFIC stock is included in the shareholder's gross income under § 1291(a), the shareholder will be taxable in the current year on this amount at ordinary income rates. However, the amount of the tax owed by the PFIC shareholder is further increased by a specially computed tax on the excess distribution allocated to PFIC taxable years within the shareholder's holding period (i.e., the "deferred tax amount"). This tax recaptures the deferral benefits enjoyed by the shareholder in prior tax years. The deferred tax amount is computed at the highest tax rates that would have applied had the PFIC income actually been received in those years. It also reflects an appropriate interest charge.

The deferred tax amount is the sum of the tax on the excess distribution allocated to each relevant prior PFIC taxable year computed at the highest applicable tax rate in effect for that year plus interest on the tax so computed. The interest is computed using the § 6621 rates and methods for the computation of underpayments of tax.

The § 1291 deferred tax and interest regime gives rise to an interesting anomaly. Excess distributions are computed simply based upon the absolute amount of the distribution, rather than its composition. Accordingly, even if a distribution represents a tax-free return of capital under normal taxing rules, it may still give rise to a tax and interest liability. Such a result is counterintuitive to general taxing principles, yet there is no corrective mechanism to remedy this aberration.

The default PFIC regime presented in § 1291 is thus distinguished from the alternative income imputation mechanism employed in the CFC rules. Instead of taxing shareholders currently on most undistributed earnings and thus permitting only limited deferral as occurs under subpart F (subject to the later application of § 1248 upon a sale of the CFC stock, as explained in Unit 14), the PFIC rules allow the deferral to continue, making up the difference by both imposing the foregone tax and taking into account the time value of the deferral via an interest charge.

Congress was concerned that imposing current taxation on domestic investors may not be appropriate to the extent these may be small shareholders who lack access to the foreign corporation's earnings and profits records, who lack authority to compel dividend distributions, or who lack liquidity (i.e., proceeds from which to pay tax currently) with respect to an imputed dividend. Thus, § 1291 recaptures deferral benefits only upon the receipt of income from gain on the disposition of PFIC stock or from actual distributions on PFIC stock at a time when the taxpayer theoretically has the means to pay the tax.

15.12   QEF Election

Section 1291 generally steers taxpayers to the QEF current taxation regime by imposing relatively punitive tax consequences, which can be avoided by making a QEF election. For instance, if a United States shareholder makes a QEF election with respect to a PFIC in the first year in which the shareholder holds such stock, the shareholder is exclusively governed by the current imputation and taxing regime of § 1293 (discussed in the following section), so direct or indirect distributions from the PFIC and gain on the disposition of its stock are expressly immune from § 1291. This result makes sense, since PFIC shareholders will not have deferred taxation of PFIC earnings if a QEF election is in place.

In contrast, if the shareholder does not elect to treat a PFIC as a qualified electing fund until some later taxable year, the potential for deferral of taxation arises with regard to PFIC earnings accumulated during the corporation's non-QEF period. The shareholder in such a fund is essentially subject to hybrid tax treatment to account for the deferral opportunity enjoyed in non-QEF years: the shareholder is taxed currently on his or her imputed PFIC earnings under § 1293, but is also subject to § 1291 with respect to PFIC distributions and dispositions of such stock attributable to the non-QEF period. The potential for current taxation coupled with a special add-on tax and interest charge thus encourages the taxpayer to make the QEF election if possible.

15.13   Removing the § 1291 Taint

If a PFIC shareholder owns shares at some point during his or her holding period during which a QEF election was not in effect, the shareholder remains subject to the § 1291 regime for that ownership period even if he or she makes a valid QEF election for later taxable years. Two elective statutory devices are available to enable shareholders to cleanse PFIC shares of their § 1291 fund taint. These devices are the so-called "deemed sale" and the "deemed dividend" elections. Upon making one of these QEF elections, the shareholder will be treated prospectively as a shareholder subject solely to the § 1293 current taxation regime.

15.14   The Deemed Sale Election

The first remedial election available to PFIC shareholders is the deemed sale election, which is described in Regulation § 1.1291-10. This election enables United States shareholders to elect to recognize gain with respect to stock in a QEF held on the first day of the QEF's first taxable year as such. Upon filing an election, a shareholder who held stock in the PFIC on the first day of the election year is deemed to have sold its stock on a specified qualification date. To eradicate any accrued deferral benefits, the hypothetical gain is included in the shareholder's gross income as ordinary income. The gain is treated as a disposition, thus forcing the shareholder to also pay the appropriate § 1291 deferred taxes and interest on any gain allocated to the shareholder's post-1986 tax years in which the corporation was a PFIC. In determining this allocation, the gain is deemed to be earned in a pro rata fashion over the shareholder's holding period. If the stock has experienced minimal appreciation, the deemed sale election is a cost-efficient means of avoiding the continued application of the § 1291 deferral tax and interest regime.

15.15   The Deemed Dividend Election

A similar cleansing election is available to shareholders in a PFIC that is also a CFC. Under § 1291(d)(2)(B), if the shareholder holds the stock on the first day of a given year, the shareholder may elect to include in gross income for that year a deemed dividend equal to the post-1986 earnings and profits attributable to that stock. The shareholder's pro rata share of post-1986 earnings and profits need not be positive in order to make the election.

The § 1291 taint is stripped from the PFIC stock as the deemed dividend is treated as an excess distribution to be allocated to the days in the holding period underlying the post-1986 earnings and profits. For these purposes, post-1986 earnings and profits include not only undistributed earnings and profits accumulated in such years but also those accumulated during the holding period of the shareholder in which the corporation was a PFIC. As in the deemed sale context, the excess distribution is subject to tax and to the special deferral tax and interest provisions of § 1291.

15.16   Requirements for Making the QEF Election

A PFIC is treated as a qualified electing fund (and thus its income will be subject to current taxation under § 1293 with respect to an electing United States shareholder) if two general requirements are satisfied. First, the shareholder must make an election on a timely filed tax return for the election year. Second, the PFIC must comply with all reporting and other requirements for both determining its ordinary earnings and net capital gain and for otherwise carrying out the purposes of the PFIC rules. Once made with respect to a particular PFIC, the QEF election is irrevocable without the consent of the Service. It applies to all subsequent taxable years of the electing shareholder. The election is shareholder-specific, and applies only to the particular shareholder making the election and not to subsequent transferees. Furthermore, it generally applies only with respect to current and subsequent shareholdings in the PFIC specified in the election.

15.17   Current § 1293 Taxation of United States Shareholders Electing QEF Status

Section 1293 essentially requires an electing shareholder to include in gross income (and thereby subjects currently to taxation) its imputed pro rata share of the PFIC's current earnings and profits regardless of whether the PFIC actually distributes any earnings to the shareholder. To approximate the tax treatment of a domestic mutual fund, the PFIC's earnings are not treated in their entirety as a dividend or ordinary income. Rather, the shareholder includes in gross income his or her pro rata share of the PFIC's ordinary earnings and net capital gain to be taxed to the shareholder, respectively, as ordinary income and long-term capital gain.

These amounts are included in income in the taxable year of the shareholder which ends with or within the PFIC's taxable year. The taxpayer's pro rata share of ordinary earnings and net capital gain is the amount of such items that would have been distributed with respect to the shareholder's stock if on each day of the PFIC's taxable year it had distributed that shareholder's share of daily PFIC income and gain. Any gain realized on the disposition of stock in a QEF will be treated as a capital gain.

15.18   Safeguards Against Double Taxation of PFIC Earnings

Section 1293 contains two specific safeguards to prevent double taxation of PFIC earnings and profits when those earnings are actually distributed. Any amount distributed by a PFIC is treated as a non-dividend distribution to the extent the taxpayer establishes that the actual distribution is paid out of earnings and profits previously taxed under the QEF regime.

For example, assume that D, a domestic corporation, purchased stock in P, a PFIC, in Year 1. D immediately elected QEF status with respect to its investment in P. D, by operation of § 1293, included $100 in income in Year 1, but no actual distribution was made to D by P. However, in Year 2, P distributed $50 to D. The $50 is treated as previously taxed to D and is not treated as a dividend under § 1293(c). As such, the distribution escapes taxation under § 1293(a)(1)(A) in Year 2.

Non-dividend characterization is available to a shareholder if such earnings were previously taxed to *any* United States person. It is not limited solely to those earnings taxed to the electing shareholder receiving the distribution. Moreover, concomitant basis adjustments to the shareholder's PFIC stock investment follow the § 1293 inclusions. The basis in the PFIC stock is increased by the amount of any § 1293(a) inclusion and decreased by any tax-free non-dividend distribution under § 1293(c). These adjustments insulate against subsequent double taxation upon the shareholder's disposition of its PFIC shares.

D.   REFERENCE MATERIALS

- Notice 88-22
- Private Letter Ruling 200813036

NOTICE 88-22
1988-1 C.B. 489

. . .

The Internal Revenue Service recognizes the need for taxpayer guidance under the passive foreign investment company provisions, effective for taxable years beginning after 1986, in advance of the publication of the regulations. In particular, taxpayers require guidance concerning the operation of the definitional tests in section 129[7](a) of the Code in order to determine whether the foreign corporations in which they hold stock are passive foreign investment companies. A foreign corporation determined to be a passive foreign investment company under section 129[7](a) may elect under section 1295 to be a qualified electing fund for its taxable year beginning in 1987. . . .

. . .

The absence of guidance in this document on particular aspects of the definitional tests in section 1296 should not be construed as implying that the regulation will not contain guidance on such matters.

Asset Test

Section 129[7](a)(2) of the Internal Revenue Code provides that a foreign corporation is a passive foreign investment company if the average percentage of the assets (by value) held by the corporation during the taxable year which produce passive income or are held for the production of passive income ("passive assets") is at least 50 percent of all assets (by value) held by the corporation during the taxable year.

Basis for Asset Test

The regulations will provide that the asset test will be applied on a gross basis. No liabilities, whether secured by particular assets or otherwise traceable to particular assets, will be taken into account.

Average Value of Assets

The average value of assets for the taxable year of the foreign corporation will be the average of the fair market values of the assets determined as of the end of each quarterly period during the taxable year of the corporation. The regulations, in general, will not require that the fair market value of the assets be determined by independent appraisal.

Characterization of Assets

The regulations will establish rules for the characterization of assets as either passive or nonpassive assets. In general, an asset will be characterized as passive if it has generated (or is reasonably expected to generate in the reasonably foreseeable future) passive income as defined in section 129[7](b) in the hands of the foreign corporation. Assets held by foreign corporations described in section 129[7](b)(2)(A) and (B) that are utilized to produce income in the active conduct of a banking or insurance business will be treated as nonpassive assets. Assets which generate both passive and nonpassive income in a taxable year shall be treated as partly passive and partly nonpassive assets in proportion to the relative amounts of income generated by those assets in that year. The regulations will give specific guidance with respect to certain kinds of assets, including those described below.

Depreciable property used in a trade or business

Any asset that constitutes "property used in the trade or business" within the meaning of section 1231(b) will be considered a nonpassive asset, provided that the trade or business in question is one that does not produce passive income as defined in section 129[7](b).

Trade or service receivable

A trade or service receivable will be characterized as a passive or nonpassive asset based on the character of the income derived by the corporation from the transaction that generated the receivable. Accordingly, a trade or service receivable derived from sales or services provided by the corporation in the ordinary course of its trade or business which produce nonpassive income will be treated as a nonpassive asset for purposes of the asset test. The regulations will provide that interest incidentally received on a trade or service receivable that is otherwise treated as a nonpassive asset will not affect the characterization of the receivable.

Intangible assets

Subject to further consideration in prospectively applied regulations, the regulations will provide for the inclusion of intangible assets in testing for passive foreign investment company status. Generally, intangible assets that produce identifiable amounts of income, such as patents and licenses, will be characterized on the basis of the income derived from the intangible assets. Goodwill or going concern value must be identified with a specific income-producing activity of the corporation and characterized as a passive or nonpassive asset based on the income derived from the activity. For purposes of applying the asset test under section 129[7](a)(2), intangible assets must be valued according to the guidelines provided in Rev. Rul. 59-60, 1959-1 C.B. 237, as amplified by subsequent revenue rulings published by the Internal Revenue Service.

Working capital

Cash and other current assets readily convertible into cash, including assets which may be characterized as the working capital of an active business, produce passive income, as defined in section 904(d)(2)(A). These assets are, therefore, passive assets for purposes of the section 129[7](a)(2) asset test.

Dealer inventory and investment assets

Trading in stock or securities by a foreign corporation for its own account produces passive income. Therefore, under the regulations, stock, securities and other assets related to trading and similar investment activities of a foreign corporation conducted for its own account will be considered passive assets for purposes of the asset test.

The regulations will distinguish the assets of regular dealers in stock and securities held for sale to customers in the ordinary course of their business from the assets held for investment purposes. Any dividend or interest income earned on stock and securities designated as inventory will not affect the characterization of such assets as nonpassive assets.

A foreign corporate dealer's inventory of stock and securities held for sale to customers will be treated as nonpassive assets provided the dealer specifically identifies in its books and records the stock and securities that it holds for sale to customers in the ordinary course of its trade or business and the stock and securities that it holds for investment on its own account. The dealer may not change the initial designation of any share of stock or security as an inventory or an investment asset. Starting 90 days after the publication of this notice, the dealer must specifically identify the inventory and investment assets on the date of acquisition of such assets. If the inventory assets and investment assets are not properly identified or the corporation changes the characterization of a share of stock or a security, all stock and securities will be treated as passive assets. The quantity of stock and securities identified by the dealer as inventory will be treated as inventory only to the extent it does not exceed the reasonable needs of the dealer's trade or business.

Tax-exempt assets

Securities which produce tax-exempt income, such as municipal bonds, will be characterized as passive assets unless: (1) they represent an appropriately identified inventory asset in the hands of a regular dealer in such securities, or (2) the active banking and insurance exception of section 129[7](b)(2) applies.

PRIVATE LETTER RULING 200813036
(Dec. 19, 2007)

This is in response to a letter dated October 10, 2007, submitted on behalf of Corporation A by its authorized representative, requesting rulings as to the federal income tax consequences of a disposition of stock.

. . .

FACTS

Through a series of wholly and non-wholly owned subsidiaries, Corporation A, a foreign corporation, held a greater than 25 percent interest in the value of Corporation B, a foreign corporation engaged in Business X. On Date 1, the stock of a wholly owned indirect subsidiary of Corporation A, which held the majority of Corporation A's indirectly held shares of Corporation B, was sold (the Sale) to Buyer, along with certain loan amounts due, for an amount equaling the Sales Proceeds. Corporation A intends to invest a portion of the Sales Proceeds in assets that can be used in Business X.

Corporation A has a substantial U.S. shareholder base. Applying the look-through rule of section 1297(c) of the Internal Revenue Code (Code), Corporation A is treated as if it received directly the income from the Sale and is treated as if it holds the Sales Proceeds. Due to the Sales Proceeds, if tested quarterly pursuant to the provisions of 1988-1 C.B. 489, Notice 88-22, Corporation A may hold 50 percent or more passive assets in either Year 1 or Year 2, but is unlikely to hold 50 percent or more passive assets in both years. In the absence of an exception, Corporation A may therefore qualify as a passive foreign investment company (PFIC) in Year 1 or Year 2 with respect to its U.S. shareholders under the asset test provided in Code section 1297(a)(2). Corporation A wants to provide guidance to its U.S. shareholders regarding the anticipated U.S. federal income tax consequences of the Sale, its ownership of the Sales Proceeds, and a dividend paid out of the Sales Proceeds.

Corporation A makes the following representations:

1. Corporation A was not a PFIC in any prior taxable year.

2. During the period of Corporation A's ownership of Corporation B, Corporation B was engaged in an active trade or business.

3. Based on current projections, substantially all of Corporation A's passive income for Year 1 and for Year 2 will be attributable to proceeds from the disposition of the Corporation B stock.

4. If Corporation A would qualify as a PFIC under Code section 1297(a)(2) in either Year 1 or Year 2, Corporation A does not expect to be a PFIC in either of the first two taxable years following that year.

. . .

RULINGS REQUESTED

1. Under Code section 1297(c), the disposition of Corporation B stock will be treated, for purposes of Code section 1297(a), as a disposition of Corporation's A's proportionate share of the assets of Corporation B attributable to that stock.

2. For purposes of Code section 1298(b)(3), the disposition of Corporation B stock will be treated as a disposition of an active trade or business by Corporation A.

3. Code section 1298(b)(3) may be applied to except Corporation A from PFIC status in either Year 1 or Year 2, but not both years.

LAW

Code section 1297(a) defines a PFIC as any foreign corporation if either (1) 75 percent or more of the gross income of such corporation for the taxable year is passive income (income test), or (2) the average percentage of assets held by such corporation during the taxable year which produce passive income or which are held for the production of passive income is at least 50 percent (asset test).

Code section 1297(b)(1) defines passive income as any income which is of a kind which would be foreign personal holding company income as defined in Code section 954(c). Code section 954(c)(1)(B)(i) and Treas. Reg. § 1.954-2(e)(1)(i)(A) provide that gain from the sale of stock is foreign personal holding company income.

Code section 1297(c) provides that if a foreign corporation owns at least 25 percent of the value of the stock of another corporation, for purposes of Code section 1297(a), the foreign corporation will be treated as holding its proportionate share of the assets and receiving directly its proportionate share of the income of the 25-percent owned subsidiary (the look-through subsidiary).

Code section 1298(b)(3) provides that a corporation will not be treated as a PFIC for any taxable year if (A) neither such corporation (nor any predecessor) was a PFIC for any prior taxable year, (B) it is established to the satisfaction of the Secretary that substantially all of the passive income of the corporation for the taxable year is attributable to the proceeds from the disposition of one or more active businesses, and that such corporation will not be a PFIC for either of the first 2 taxable years following such taxable year, and (C) such corporation is not a PFIC for either of such 2 taxable years.

ANALYSIS

The PFIC provisions were enacted as part of the Tax Reform Act of 1986 (The Act), P.L. 99514, to eliminate the deferral advantage achieved by U.S. investors making passive investments through foreign corporations. In enacting the PFIC provisions, Congress did not intend to affect foreign corporations operating active businesses. To achieve these goals, Congress enacted Code section 1297(a) which defines a PFIC as any foreign corporation with 75 percent or more passive income or 50 percent or more passive assets. To further distinguish active from passive foreign corporations, Code sections 1297(c) and 1298(b)(3) were enacted to address holding company structures and change of business years.

Code section 1297(c) addresses holding company structures, providing that for purposes of determining PFIC status, instead of being treated as owning stock (a passive asset), a foreign corporation is instead treated as owning its proportionate share of the assets, and receiving directly its proportionate share of the income, of any subsidiary in which it owns at least 25 percent (by value).

The policy intent behind Code section 1297(c) is stated in the Conference Report to the Act:

> The conferees do not intend that foreign corporations owning the stock of subsidiaries engaged in active businesses be classified as PFICs. To this end, the agreement attributes a proportionate part of assets and income of a 25-percent owned corporation to the corporate shareholder in determining whether the corporate shareholder is a PFIC under either the asset test or income test.

H.R. Conf. Rep. No. 99-841, Vol. II, at 644 (1986).

Although Code section 1297(c) treats a foreign corporation as holding the assets of a look-through subsidiary instead of the stock of the look-through subsidiary, it is silent on whether a foreign corporation is considered to dispose of the stock or assets of a look-through subsidiary. In PLR 200604020 (January 27, 2006) the Service addressed the application of the income and asset tests of Code section 1297(a) to the disposition of look-through stock, ruling that it is considered a disposition of the foreign corporation's proportionate share of the assets of the look-through subsidiary and of those subsidiaries with respect to which the foreign corporation owns (by value) at least 25 percent. Based on the intent of Congress in crafting the special rule applicable to look-through subsidiaries, the Service continues to believe that this is the correct approach. Thus, in applying Code section 1297(a) to Corporation A, the character (active vs. passive) of the gain attributable to the disposition of the Corporation B stock should be determined by reference to the percentage of active and passive assets in Corporation B at the time of the Sale.

Code section 1298(b)(3) addresses change of business years by providing a special rule for foreign corporations in transition from one active business to another active business. Code section 1298(b)(3) provides that such a transitioning corporation will not be treated as a PFIC if (1) the corporation (or a predecessor) was not a PFIC in any prior taxable year; (2) it is established to the satisfaction of the Secretary that (a) substantially all of the passive income of the corporation in the taxable year is attributable to the disposition of an active business and (b) the corporation will not be a PFIC in either of the first two taxable years following the taxable year; and (3) the corporation is not a PFIC for either of the two taxable years following the taxable year. The policy intent behind Code section 1298(b)(3) is also stated in the Conference Report to the Act:

> The conference agreement follows the Senate amendment by excluding . . . corporations in a start-up phase of an active business. The agreement expands this . . . exception by excluding from PFIC classification corporations in transition from one active business to another active business.

Id. at 644 (1986).

Code section 1298(b)(3) does not specify the manner in which an active trade or business is to be disposed of in order to qualify for the change of business exception. Specifically, Code section 1298(b)(3) does not address whether a foreign corporation's disposition of stock of a look-through subsidiary that is engaged in an active trade or business should be considered to be a disposition of an active trade or business by the foreign corporation. The Service, however, has addressed this question, ruling in PLR 200015028 (April 14, 2000) that Code section 1298(b)(3) was applicable to a disposition of stock of a wholly-owned subsidiary that was conducting an active trade or business. The Service believes the ruling in PLR 200015028 is consistent with Congressional intent that corporations engaged in active business, either directly or through a subsidiary, be eligible to avoid PFIC classification. Thus, it is appropriate that the disposition of stock of Corporation B, a look-through subsidiary engaged in an active trade or business, constitute the disposition of an active trade or business by Corporation A for purposes of applying the change of business exception provided by Code section 1298(b)(3).

In addition to its silence with respect to the manner of disposition, Code section 1298(b)(3) is also ambiguous as to the taxable year to which the exception can be applied. One reading would limit the exception's applicability to the taxable year in which the disposition occurs. However, such a reading favors early year dispositions over late year ones. For example, a calendar year corporation that made a disposition on January 1 would have more time to reinvest and take advantage of the exception than a corporation that made a disposition on November 1. There is no indication in the legislative history that Congress intended preferential treatment towards early year dispositions. Accordingly, it is the Service's position that, while Code section 1298(b)(3) can only exclude a single year from PFIC status, that year may be the year of disposition or alternatively, the year subsequent to disposition.

Therefore, if Corporation A would be treated as a PFIC in Year 1, under either the income or asset test of Code section 1297(a), the exception to PFIC status provided in Code section 1298(b)(3) will apply (subject to Corporation A meeting all the conditions set forth in that section). Alternatively, if due to the date of the disposition of the Corporation B stock, Corporation A would not be treated as a PFIC in Year 1 under either the income or asset test of Code section 1297(a), but due to a failure to timely re-invest the Sales Proceeds in Year 2, would be treated as a PFIC in Year 2, the exception to PFIC status provided by Code section 1298(b)(3) will apply in that year (again, subject to Corporation A meeting all the conditions set forth in that section).

RULINGS

Based on the information submitted and the representations made, we rule as follows:

1. Under Code section 1297(c), the disposition of Corporation B stock will be treated, for purposes of Code section 1297(a), as a disposition of Corporation's A's proportionate share of the assets of Corporation B attributable to that stock.

2. For purposes of Code section 1298(b)(3), the disposition of Corporation B stock will be treated as a disposition of an active trade or business by Corporation A.

3. Code section 1298(b)(3) may be applied to except Corporation A from PFIC status in either Year 1 or Year 2, but not both years.

Appendix

UNITED STATES MODEL INCOME TAX CONVENTION
(November 15, 2006)

The Government of the United States of America and the Government of _____, desiring to conclude a Convention for the avoidance of double taxation and the prevention of fiscal evasion with respect to taxes on income, have agreed as follows:

Article 1   GENERAL SCOPE

1. This Convention shall apply only to persons who are residents of one or both of the Contracting States, except as otherwise provided in the Convention.

2. This Convention shall not restrict in any manner any benefit now or hereafter accorded:

    a) by the laws of either Contracting State; or

    b) by any other agreement to which the Contracting States are parties.

3.   a) Notwithstanding the provisions of subparagraph b) of paragraph 2 of this Article:

      i) for purposes of paragraph 3 of Article XXII (Consultation) of the General Agreement on Trade in Services, the Contracting States agree that any question arising as to the interpretation or application of this Convention and, in particular, whether a taxation measure is within the scope of this Convention, shall be determined exclusively in accordance with the provisions of Article 25 (Mutual Agreement Procedure) of this Convention; and

      ii) the provisions of Article XVII of the General Agreement on Trade in Services shall not apply to a taxation measure unless the competent authorities agree that the measure is not within the scope of Article 24 (Non-Discrimination) of this Convention.

    b) For the purposes of this paragraph, a "measure" is a law, regulation, rule, procedure, decision, administrative action, or any similar provision or action.

4. Except to the extent provided in paragraph 5, this Convention shall not affect the taxation by a Contracting State of its residents (as determined under Article 4 (Resident)) and its citizens. Notwithstanding the other provisions of this Convention, a former citizen or former long-term resident of a Contracting State may, for the period of ten years following the loss of such status, be taxed in accordance with the laws of that Contracting State.

5. The provisions of paragraph 4 shall not affect:

    a) the benefits conferred by a Contracting State under paragraph 2 of Article 9 (Associated Enterprises), paragraphs 1 b), 2, and 5 of Article 17

(Pensions, Social Security, Annuities, Alimony, and Child Support), paragraphs 1 and 4 of Article 18 (Pension Funds), and Articles 23 (Relief From Double Taxation), 24 (Non-Discrimination), and 25 (Mutual Agreement Procedure); and

b)   the benefits conferred by a Contracting State under paragraph 2 of Article 18 (Pension Funds), Articles 19 (Government Service), 20 (Students and Trainees), and 27 (Members of Diplomatic Missions and Consular Posts), upon individuals who are neither citizens of, nor have been admitted for permanent residence in, that State.

6. An item of income, profit or gain derived through an entity that is fiscally transparent under the laws of either Contracting State shall be considered to be derived by a resident of a State to the extent that the item is treated for purposes of the taxation law of such Contracting State as the income, profit or gain of a resident.

Article 2   TAXES COVERED

1. This Convention shall apply to taxes on income imposed on behalf of a Contracting State irrespective of the manner in which they are levied.

2. There shall be regarded as taxes on income all taxes imposed on total income, or on elements of income, including taxes on gains from the alienation of property.

3. The existing taxes to which this Convention shall apply are:

a)   in the case of _____:

b)   in the case of the United States: the Federal income taxes imposed by the Internal Revenue Code (but excluding social security and unemployment taxes), and the Federal excise taxes imposed with respect to private foundations.

4. This Convention shall apply also to any identical or substantially similar taxes that are imposed after the date of signature of the Convention in addition to, or in place of, the existing taxes. The competent authorities of the Contracting States shall notify each other of any changes that have been made in their respective taxation or other laws that significantly affect their obligations under this Convention.

Article 3   GENERAL DEFINITIONS

1. For the purposes of this Convention, unless the context otherwise requires:

a)   the term "person" includes an individual, an estate, a trust, a partnership, a company, and any other body of persons;

b)   the term "company" means any body corporate or any entity that is treated as a body corporate for tax purposes according to the laws of the state in which it is organized;

c)   the terms "enterprise of a Contracting State" and "enterprise of the other Contracting State" mean respectively an enterprise carried on by a resident of a Contracting State, and an enterprise carried on by a resident of the other Contracting State; the terms also include an enterprise carried on by a resident of a Contracting State through an entity that is treated as fiscally transparent in that Contracting State;

d) the term "enterprise" applies to the carrying on of any business;

e) the term "business" includes the performance of professional services and of other activities of an independent character;

f) the term "international traffic" means any transport by a ship or aircraft, except when such transport is solely between places in a Contracting State;

g) the term "competent authority" means:

   i) in _____, _____; and

   ii) in the United States: the Secretary of the Treasury or his delegate;

h) the term "_____" means;

i) the term "United States" means the United States of America, and includes the states thereof and the District of Columbia; such term also includes the territorial sea thereof and the sea bed and subsoil of the submarine areas adjacent to that territorial sea, over which the United States exercises sovereign rights in accordance with international law; the term, however, does not include Puerto Rico, the Virgin Islands, Guam or any other United States possession or territory;

j) the term "national" of a Contracting State means: i) any individual possessing the nationality or citizenship of that State; and ii) any legal person, partnership or association deriving its status as such from the laws in force in that State;

k) the term "pension fund" means any person established in a Contracting State that is:

   i) generally exempt from income taxation in that State; and

   ii) operated principally either:

      A) to administer or provide pension or retirement benefits; or

      B) to earn income for the benefit of one or more persons described in clause A).

2. As regards the application of the Convention at any time by a Contracting State any term not defined therein shall, unless the context otherwise requires, or the competent authorities agree to a common meaning pursuant to the provisions of Article 25 (Mutual Agreement Procedure), have the meaning which it has at that time under the law of that State for the purposes of the taxes to which the Convention applies, any meaning under the applicable tax laws of that State prevailing over a meaning given to the term under other laws of that State.

Article 4   RESIDENT

1. For the purposes of this Convention, the term "resident of a Contracting State" means any person who, under the laws of that State, is liable to tax therein by reason of his domicile, residence, citizenship, place of management, place of incorporation, or any other criterion of a similar nature, and also includes that State

and any political subdivision or local authority thereof. This term, however, does not include any person who is liable to tax in that State in respect only of income from sources in that State or of profits attributable to a permanent establishment in that State.

2. The term "resident of a Contracting State" includes:

a) a pension fund established in that State; and

b) an organization that is established and maintained in that State exclusively for religious, charitable, scientific, artistic, cultural, or educational purposes, notwithstanding that all or part of its income or gains may be exempt from tax under the domestic law of that State.

3. Where, by reason of the provisions of paragraph 1, an individual is a resident of both Contracting States, then his status shall be determined as follows:

a) he shall be deemed to be a resident only of the State in which he has a permanent home available to him; if he has a permanent home available to him in both States, he shall be deemed to be a resident only of the State with which his personal and economic relations are closer (center of vital interests);

b) if the State in which he has his center of vital interests cannot be determined, or if he does not have a permanent home available to him in either State, he shall be deemed to be a resident only of the State in which he has an habitual abode;

c) if he has an habitual abode in both States or in neither of them, he shall be deemed to be a resident only of the State of which he is a national;

d) if he is a national of both States or of neither of them, the competent authorities of the Contracting States shall endeavor to settle the question by mutual agreement.

4. Where by reason of the provisions of paragraph 1 a company is a resident of both Contracting States, then if it is created or organized under the laws of one of the Contracting States or a political subdivision thereof, but not under the laws of the other Contracting State or a political subdivision thereof, such company shall be deemed to be a resident of the first-mentioned Contracting State. In all other cases involving dual resident companies, the competent authorities of the Contracting States shall endeavor to determine the mode of application of the Convention to such company. If the competent authorities do not reach such an agreement, that company will not be treated as a resident of either Contracting State for purposes of its claiming any benefits provided by the Convention.

5. Where by reason of the provisions of paragraphs 1 and 2 of this Article a person other than an individual or a company is a resident of both Contracting States, the competent authorities of the Contracting States shall by mutual agreement endeavor to determine the mode of application of this Convention to that person.

Article 5   PERMANENT ESTABLISHMENT

1. For the purposes of this Convention, the term "permanent establishment" means a fixed place of business through which the business of an enterprise is wholly or partly carried on.

2. The term "permanent establishment" includes especially:

a) a place of management;

b) a branch;

c) an office;

d) a factory;

e) a workshop; and

f) a mine, an oil or gas well, a quarry, or any other place of extraction of natural resources.

3. A building site or construction or installation project, or an installation or drilling rig or ship used for the exploration of natural resources, constitutes a permanent establishment only if it lasts, or the exploration activity continues for more than twelve months.

4. Notwithstanding the preceding provisions of this Article, the term "permanent establishment" shall be deemed not to include:

a) the use of facilities solely for the purpose of storage, display or delivery of goods or merchandise belonging to the enterprise;

b) the maintenance of a stock of goods or merchandise belonging to the enterprise solely for the purpose of storage, display or delivery;

c) the maintenance of a stock of goods or merchandise belonging to the enterprise solely for the purpose of processing by another enterprise;

d) the maintenance of a fixed place of business solely for the purpose of purchasing goods or merchandise, or of collecting information, for the enterprise;

e) the maintenance of a fixed place of business solely for the purpose of carrying on, for the enterprise, any other activity of a preparatory or auxiliary character;

f) the maintenance of a fixed place of business solely for any combination of the activities mentioned in subparagraphs a) through e), provided that the overall activity of the fixed place of business resulting from this combination is of a preparatory or auxiliary character.

5. Notwithstanding the provisions of paragraphs 1 and 2, where a person — other than an agent of an independent status to whom paragraph 6 applies — is acting on behalf of an enterprise and has and habitually exercises in a Contracting State an authority to conclude contracts that are binding on the enterprise, that enterprise shall be deemed to have a permanent establishment in that State in respect of any activities that the person undertakes for the enterprise, unless the activities of such person are limited to those mentioned in paragraph 4 that, if exercised through a fixed place of business, would not make this fixed place of business a permanent

establishment under the provisions of that paragraph.

6. An enterprise shall not be deemed to have a permanent establishment in a Contracting State merely because it carries on business in that State through a broker, general commission agent, or any other agent of an independent status, provided that such persons are acting in the ordinary course of their business as independent agents.

7. The fact that a company that is a resident of a Contracting State controls or is controlled by a company that is a resident of the other Contracting State, or that carries on business in that other State (whether through a permanent establishment or otherwise), shall not be taken into account in determining whether either company has a permanent establishment in that other State.

Article 6   INCOME FROM REAL PROPERTY

1. Income derived by a resident of a Contracting State from real property, including income from agriculture or forestry, situated in the other Contracting State may be taxed in that other State.

2. The term "real property" shall have the meaning which it has under the law of the Contracting State in which the property in question is situated. The term shall in any case include property accessory to real property (including livestock and equipment used in agriculture and forestry), rights to which the provisions of general law respecting landed property apply, usufruct of real property and rights to variable or fixed payments as consideration for the working of, or the right to work, mineral deposits, sources and other natural resources. Ships and aircraft shall not be regarded as real property.

3. The provisions of paragraph 1 shall apply to income derived from the direct use, letting, or use in any other form of real property.

4. The provisions of paragraphs 1 and 3 shall also apply to the income from real property of an enterprise.

5. A resident of a Contracting State who is liable to tax in the other Contracting State on income from real property situated in the other Contracting State may elect for any taxable year to compute the tax on such income on a net basis as if such income were business profits attributable to a permanent establishment in such other State. Any such election shall be binding for the taxable year of the election and all subsequent taxable years unless the competent authority of the Contracting State in which the property is situated agrees to terminate the election.

Article 7   BUSINESS PROFITS

1. The profits of an enterprise of a Contracting State shall be taxable only in that State unless the enterprise carries on business in the other Contracting State through a permanent establishment situated therein. If the enterprise carries on business as aforesaid, the profits of the enterprise may be taxed in the other State but only so much of them as are attributable to that permanent establishment.

2. Subject to the provisions of paragraph 3, where an enterprise of a Contracting State carries on business in the other Contracting State through a permanent

establishment situated therein, there shall in each Contracting State be attributed to that permanent establishment the profits that it might be expected to make if it were a distinct and independent enterprise engaged in the same or similar activities under the same or similar conditions. For this purpose, the profits to be attributed to the permanent establishment shall include only the profits derived from the assets used, risks assumed and activities performed by the permanent establishment.

3. In determining the profits of a permanent establishment, there shall be allowed as deductions expenses that are incurred for the purposes of the permanent establishment, including executive and general administrative expenses so incurred, whether in the State in which the permanent establishment is situated or elsewhere.*

4. No profits shall be attributed to a permanent establishment by reason of the mere purchase by that permanent establishment of goods or merchandise for the enterprise.

5. For the purposes of the preceding paragraphs, the profits to be attributed to the permanent establishment shall be determined by the same method year by year unless there is good and sufficient reason to the contrary.

6. Where profits include items of income that are dealt with separately in other Articles of the Convention, then the provisions of those Articles shall not be affected by the provisions of this Article.

7. In applying this Article, paragraph 6 of Article 10 (Dividends), paragraph 4 of Article 11 (Interest), paragraph 3 of Article 12 (Royalties), paragraph 3 of Article 13 (Gains) and paragraph 2 of Article 21 (Other Income), any income or gain attributable to a permanent establishment during its existence is taxable in the Contracting State where such permanent establishment is situated even if the payments are deferred until such permanent establishment has ceased to exist.

---

* Protocol or Notes should include the following language:

It is understood that the business profits to be attributed to a permanent establishment shall include only the profits derived from the assets used, risks assumed and activities performed by the permanent establishment. The principles of the OECD Transfer Pricing Guidelines will apply for purposes of determining the profits attributable to a permanent establishment, taking into account the different economic and legal circumstances of a single entity. Accordingly, any of the methods described therein as acceptable methods for determining an arm's length result may be used to determine the income of a permanent establishment so long as those methods are applied in accordance with the Guidelines. In particular, in determining the amount of attributable profits, the permanent establishment shall be treated as having the same amount of capital that it would need to support its activities if it were a distinct and separate enterprise engaged in the same or similar activities. With respect to financial institutions other than insurance companies, a Contracting State may determine the amount of capital to be attributed to a permanent establishment by allocating the institution's total equity between its various offices on the basis of the proportion of the financial institution's risk-weighted assets attributable to each of them. In the case of an insurance company, there shall be attributed to a permanent establishment not only premiums earned through the permanent establishment, but that portion of the insurance company's overall investment income from reserves and surplus that supports the risks assumed by the permanent establishment.

Article 8   SHIPPING AND AIR TRANSPORT

1. Profits of an enterprise of a Contracting State from the operation of ships or aircraft in international traffic shall be taxable only in that State.

2. For purposes of this Article, profits from the operation of ships or aircraft include, but are not limited to:

   a) profits from the rental of ships or aircraft on a full (time or voyage) basis;

   b) profits from the rental on a bareboat basis of ships or aircraft if the rental income is incidental to profits from the operation of ships or aircraft in international traffic; and

   c) profits from the rental on a bareboat basis of ships or aircraft if such ships or aircraft are operated in international traffic by the lessee.

Profits derived by an enterprise from the inland transport of property or passengers within either Contracting State shall be treated as profits from the operation of ships or aircraft in international traffic if such transport is undertaken as part of international traffic.

3. Profits of an enterprise of a Contracting State from the use, maintenance, or rental of containers (including trailers, barges, and related equipment for the transport of containers) shall be taxable only in that Contracting State, except to the extent that those containers are used for transport solely between places within the other Contracting State.

4. The provisions of paragraphs 1 and 3 shall also apply to profits from participation in a pool, a joint business, or an international operating agency.

Article 9   ASSOCIATED ENTERPRISES

1. Where:

   a) an enterprise of a Contracting State participates directly or indirectly in the management, control or capital of an enterprise of the other Contracting State; or

   b) the same persons participate directly or indirectly in the management, control, or capital of an enterprise of a Contracting State and an enterprise of the other Contracting State,

and in either case conditions are made or imposed between the two enterprises in their commercial or financial relations that differ from those that would be made between independent enterprises, then any profits that, but for those conditions, would have accrued to one of the enterprises, but by reason of those conditions have not so accrued, may be included in the profits of that enterprise and taxed accordingly.

2. Where a Contracting State includes in the profits of an enterprise of that State, and taxes accordingly, profits on which an enterprise of the other Contracting State has been charged to tax in that other State, and the other Contracting State agrees that the profits so included are profits that would have accrued to the enterprise of the first-mentioned State if the conditions made between the two enterprises had been those that would have been made between independent enterprises, then that

other State shall make an appropriate adjustment to the amount of the tax charged therein on those profits. In determining such adjustment, due regard shall be had to the other provisions of this Convention and the competent authorities of the Contracting States shall if necessary consult each other.

Article 10　DIVIDENDS

1. Dividends paid by a company that is a resident of a Contracting State to a resident of the other Contracting State may be taxed in that other State.

2. However, such dividends may also be taxed in the Contracting State of which the company paying the dividends is a resident and according to the laws of that State, but if the dividends are beneficially owned by a resident of the other Contracting State, except as otherwise provided, the tax so charged shall not exceed:

   a)　5 percent of the gross amount of the dividends if the beneficial owner is a company that owns directly at least 10 percent of the voting stock of the company paying the dividends;

   b)　15 percent of the gross amount of the dividends in all other cases.

This paragraph shall not affect the taxation of the company in respect of the profits out of which the dividends are paid.

3. Notwithstanding paragraph 2, dividends shall not be taxed in the Contracting State of which the company paying the dividends is a resident if:

   a)　the beneficial owner of the dividends is a pension fund that is a resident of the other Contracting State; and

   b)　such dividends are not derived from the carrying on of a trade or business by the pension fund or through an associated enterprise.

4.　a) Subparagraph a) of paragraph 2 shall not apply in the case of dividends paid by a U.S. Regulated Investment Company (RIC) or a U.S. Real Estate Investment Trust (REIT). In the case of dividends paid by a RIC, subparagraph b) of paragraph 2 and paragraph 3 shall apply. In the case of dividends paid by a REIT, subparagraph b) of paragraph 2 and paragraph 3 shall apply only if:

   i)　the beneficial owner of the dividends is an individual or pension fund, in either case holding an interest of not more than 10 percent in the REIT;

   ii)　the dividends are paid with respect to a class of stock that is publicly traded and the beneficial owner of the dividends is a person holding an interest of not more than 5 percent of any class of the REIT's stock; or

   iii)　the beneficial owner of the dividends is a person holding an interest of not more than 10 percent in the REIT and the REIT is diversified.

   b)　For purposes of this paragraph, a REIT shall be "diversified" if the value of no single interest in real property exceeds 10 percent of its total interests in real property. For the purposes of this rule, foreclosure property shall not be considered an interest in real property. Where a

REIT holds an interest in a partnership, it shall be treated as owning directly a proportion of the partnership's interests in real property corresponding to its interest in the partnership.

5. For purposes of this Article, the term "dividends" means income from shares or other rights, not being debt-claims, participating in profits, as well as income that is subjected to the same taxation treatment as income from shares under the laws of the State of which the payer is a resident.

6. The provisions of paragraphs 2 through 4 shall not apply if the beneficial owner of the dividends, being a resident of a Contracting State, carries on business in the other Contracting State, of which the payer is a resident, through a permanent establishment situated therein, and the holding in respect of which the dividends are paid is effectively connected with such permanent establishment. In such case the provisions of Article 7 (Business Profits) shall apply.

7. A Contracting State may not impose any tax on dividends paid by a resident of the other State, except insofar as the dividends are paid to a resident of the first-mentioned State or the dividends are attributable to a permanent establishment, nor may it impose tax on a corporation's undistributed profits, except as provided in paragraph 8, even if the dividends paid or the undistributed profits consist wholly or partly of profits or income arising in that State.

8.   a) A company that is a resident of one of the States and that has a permanent establishment in the other State or that is subject to tax in the other State on a net basis on its income that may be taxed in the other State under Article 6 (Income from Real Property) or under paragraph 1 of Article 13 (Gains) may be subject in that other State to a tax in addition to the tax allowable under the other provisions of this Convention.

   b)   Such tax, however, may be imposed:

   i)   on only the portion of the business profits of the company attributable to the permanent establishment and the portion of the income referred to in subparagraph a) that is subject to tax under Article 6 or under paragraph 1 of Article 13 that, in the case of the United States, represents the dividend equivalent amount of such profits or income and, in the case of _____, is an amount that is analogous to the dividend equivalent amount; and

   ii)   at a rate not in excess of the rate specified in paragraph 2 a).

Article 11   INTEREST

1. Interest arising in a Contracting State and beneficially owned by a resident of the other Contracting State may be taxed only in that other State.

2. Notwithstanding the provisions of paragraph 1:

   a)   interest arising in _____ may be taxed in the Contracting State in which it arises, and according to the laws of that State, but if the beneficial owner is a resident of the other Contracting State, the interest may be taxed at a rate not exceeding 15 percent of the gross amount of the interest;

b) interest arising in the United States that is contingent interest of a type that does not qualify as portfolio interest under United States law may be taxed by the United States but, if the beneficial owner of the interest is a resident of _____, the interest may be taxed at a rate not exceeding 15 percent of the gross amount of the interest; and

c) interest that is an excess inclusion with respect to a residual interest in a real estate mortgage investment conduit may be taxed by each State in accordance with its domestic law.

3. The term "interest" as used in this Article means income from debt-claims of every kind, whether or not secured by mortgage, and whether or not carrying a right to participate in the debtor's profits, and in particular, income from government securities and income from bonds or debentures, including premiums or prizes attaching to such securities, bonds or debentures, and all other income that is subjected to the same taxation treatment as income from money lent by the taxation law of the Contracting State in which the income arises. Income dealt with in Article 10 (Dividends) and penalty charges for late payment shall not be regarded as interest for the purposes of this Convention.

4. The provisions of paragraphs 1 and 2 shall not apply if the beneficial owner of the interest, being a resident of a Contracting State, carries on business in the other Contracting State, in which the interest arises, through a permanent establishment situated therein, and the debt-claim in respect of which the interest is paid is effectively connected with such permanent establishment. In such case the provisions of Article 7 (Business Profits) shall apply.

5. Where, by reason of a special relationship between the payer and the beneficial owner or between both of them and some other person, the amount of the interest, having regard to the debt-claim for which it is paid, exceeds the amount which would have been agreed upon by the payer and the beneficial owner in the absence of such relationship, the provisions of this Article shall apply only to the last-mentioned amount. In such case the excess part of the payments shall remain taxable according to the laws of each State, due regard being had to the other provisions of this Convention.

Article 12   ROYALTIES

1. Royalties arising in a Contracting State and beneficially owned by a resident of the other Contracting State may be taxed only in that other State.

2. The term "royalties" as used in this Article means:

a) payments of any kind received as a consideration for the use of, or the right to use, any copyright of literary, artistic, scientific or other work (including cinematographic films), any patent, trademark, design or model, plan, secret formula or process, or for information concerning industrial, commercial or scientific experience; and

b) gain derived from the alienation of any property described in subparagraph a), to the extent that such gain is contingent on the productivity, use, or disposition of the property.

3. The provisions of paragraph 1 shall not apply if the beneficial owner of the royalties, being a resident of a Contracting State, carries on business in the other Contracting State through a permanent establishment situated therein and the right or property in respect of which the royalties are paid is effectively connected with such permanent establishment. In such case the provisions of Article 7 (Business Profits) shall apply.

4. Where, by reason of a special relationship between the payer and the beneficial owner or between both of them and some other person, the amount of the royalties, having regard to the use, right, or information for which they are paid, exceeds the amount which would have been agreed upon by the payer and the beneficial owner in the absence of such relationship, the provisions of this Article shall apply only to the last-mentioned amount. In such case the excess part of the payments shall remain taxable according to the laws of each Contracting State, due regard being had to the other provisions of the Convention.

Article 13   GAINS

1. Gains derived by a resident of a Contracting State that are attributable to the alienation of real property situated in the other Contracting State may be taxed in that other State.

2. For the purposes of this Article the term "real property situated in the other Contracting State" shall include:

a)   real property referred to in Article 6 (Income from Real Property);

b)   where that other State is the United States, a United States real property interest; and

c)   where that other State is _____,

    i)   shares, including rights to acquire shares, other than shares in which there is regular trading on a stock exchange, deriving their value or the greater part of their value directly or indirectly from real property referred to in subparagraph a) of this paragraph situated in _____; and

    ii)   an interest in a partnership or trust to the extent that the assets of the partnership or trust consist of real property situated in _____, or of shares referred to in clause i) of this subparagraph.

3. Gains from the alienation of movable property forming part of the business property of a permanent establishment that an enterprise of a Contracting State has in the other Contracting State, including such gains from the alienation of such a permanent establishment (alone or with the whole enterprise), may be taxed in that other State.

4. Gains derived by an enterprise of a Contracting State from the alienation of ships or aircraft operated or used in international traffic or personal property pertaining to the operation or use of such ships or aircraft shall be taxable only in that State.

5. Gains derived by an enterprise of a Contracting State from the alienation of containers (including trailers, barges and related equipment for the transport of containers) used for the transport of goods or merchandise shall be taxable only in that State, unless those containers are used for transport solely between places within the other Contracting State.

6. Gains from the alienation of any property other than property referred to in paragraphs 1 through 5 shall be taxable only in the Contracting State of which the alienator is a resident.

Article 14   INCOME FROM EMPLOYMENT

1. Subject to the provisions of Articles 15 (Directors' Fees), 17 (Pensions, Social Security, Annuities, Alimony, and Child Support) and 19 (Government Service), salaries, wages, and other similar remuneration derived by a resident of a Contracting State in respect of an employment shall be taxable only in that State unless the employment is exercised in the other Contracting State. If the employment is so exercised, such remuneration as is derived therefrom may be taxed in that other State.

2. Notwithstanding the provisions of paragraph 1, remuneration derived by a resident of a Contracting State in respect of an employment exercised in the other Contracting State shall be taxable only in the first-mentioned State if:

   a) the recipient is present in the other State for a period or periods not exceeding in the aggregate 183 days in any twelve month period commencing or ending in the taxable year concerned;

   b) the remuneration is paid by, or on behalf of, an employer who is not a resident of the other State; and

   c) the remuneration is not borne by a permanent establishment which the employer has in the other State.

3. Notwithstanding the preceding provisions of this Article, remuneration described in paragraph 1 that is derived by a resident of a Contracting State in respect of an employment as a member of the regular complement of a ship or aircraft operated in international traffic shall be taxable only in that State.

Article 15   DIRECTORS' FEES

Directors' fees and other compensation derived by a resident of a Contracting State for services rendered in the other Contracting State in his capacity as a member of the board of directors of a company that is a resident of the other Contracting State may be taxed in that other Contracting State.

Article 16   ENTERTAINERS AND SPORTSMEN

1. Income derived by a resident of a Contracting State as an entertainer, such as a theater, motion picture, radio, or television artiste, or a musician, or as a sportsman, from his personal activities as such exercised in the other Contracting State, which income would be exempt from tax in that other Contracting State under the provisions of Articles 7 (Business Profits) and 14 (Income from Employment) may be taxed in that other State, except where the amount of the

gross receipts derived by such entertainer or sportsman, including expenses reimbursed to him or borne on his behalf, from such activities does not exceed twenty thousand United States dollars ($20,000) or its equivalent in _____ for the taxable year of the payment.

2. Where income in respect of activities exercised by an entertainer or a sportsman in his capacity as such accrues not to the entertainer or sportsman himself but to another person, that income, notwithstanding the provisions of Article 7 (Business Profits) or 14 (Income from Employment), may be taxed in the Contracting State in which the activities of the entertainer or sportsman are exercised unless the contract pursuant to which the personal activities are performed allows that other person to designate the individual who is to perform the personal activities.

Article 17   PENSIONS, SOCIAL SECURITY, ANNUITIES, ALIMONY, AND CHILD SUPPORT

1. a) Pensions and other similar remuneration beneficially owned by a resident of a Contracting State shall be taxable only in that State.

   b)   Notwithstanding subparagraph a), the amount of any such pension or remuneration arising in a Contracting State that, when received, would be exempt from taxation in that State if the beneficial owner were a resident thereof shall be exempt from taxation in the Contracting State of which the beneficial owner is a resident.

2. Notwithstanding the provisions of paragraph 1, payments made by a Contracting State under provisions of the social security or similar legislation of that State to a resident of the other Contracting State or to a citizen of the United States shall be taxable only in the first-mentioned State.

3. Annuities derived and beneficially owned by an individual resident of a Contracting State shall be taxable only in that State. The term "annuities" as used in this paragraph means a stated sum paid periodically at stated times during a specified number of years, or for life, under an obligation to make the payments in return for adequate and full consideration (other than services rendered).

4. Alimony paid by a resident of a Contracting State to a resident of the other Contracting State shall be taxable only in that other State. The term "alimony" as used in this paragraph means periodic payments made pursuant to a written separation agreement or a decree of divorce, separate maintenance, or compulsory support, which payments are taxable to the recipient under the laws of the State of which he is a resident.

5. Periodic payments, not dealt with in paragraph 4, for the support of a child made pursuant to a written separation agreement or a decree of divorce, separate maintenance, or compulsory support, paid by a resident of a Contracting State to a resident of the other Contracting State, shall be exempt from tax in both Contracting States.

Article 18   PENSION FUNDS

1. Where an individual who is a resident of one of the States is a member or beneficiary of, or participant in, a pension fund that is a resident of the other State, income earned by the pension fund may be taxed as income of that individual only when, and, subject to the provisions of paragraph 1 of Article 17 (Pensions, Social Security, Annuities, Alimony and Child Support), to the extent that, it is paid to, or for the benefit of, that individual from the pension fund (and not transferred to another pension fund in that other State).

2. Where an individual who is a member or beneficiary of, or participant in, a pension fund that is a resident of one of the States exercises an employment or self-employment in the other State:

   a) contributions paid by or on behalf of that individual to the pension fund during the period that he exercises an employment or self-employment in the other State shall be deductible (or excludible) in computing his taxable income in that other State; and

   b) any benefits accrued under the pension fund, or contributions made to the pension fund by or on behalf of the individual's employer, during that period shall not be treated as part of the employee's taxable income and any such contributions shall be allowed as a deduction in computing the taxable income of his employer in that other State.

The relief available under this paragraph shall not exceed the relief that would be allowed by the other State to residents of that State for contributions to, or benefits accrued under, a pension plan established in that State.

3. The provisions of paragraph 2 of this Article shall not apply unless:

   a) contributions by or on behalf of the individual, or by or on behalf of the individual's employer, to the pension fund (or to another similar pension fund for which the first-mentioned pension fund was substituted) were made before the individual began to exercise an employment or self-employment in the other State; and

   b) the competent authority of the other State has agreed that the pension fund generally corresponds to a pension fund established in that other State.

4.

   a) Where a citizen of the United States who is a resident of _____ exercises an employment in _____ the income from which is taxable in _____, the contribution is borne by an employer who is a resident of _____ or by a permanent establishment situated in _____, and the individual is a member or beneficiary of, or participant in, a pension plan established in _____,

      i) contributions paid by or on behalf of that individual to the pension fund during the period that he exercises the employment in _____, and that are attributable to the employment, shall be deductible (or excludible) in computing his taxable income in the United States; and

ii) any benefits accrued under the pension fund, or contributions made to the pension fund by or on behalf of the individual's employer, during that period, and that are attributable to the employment, shall not be treated as part of the employee's taxable income in computing his taxable income in the United States.

b) The relief available under this paragraph shall not exceed the lesser of:

    i) the relief that would be allowed by the United States to its residents for contributions to, or benefits accrued under, a generally corresponding pension plan established in the United States; and

    ii) the amount of contributions or benefits that qualify for tax relief in _____.

c) For purposes of determining an individual's eligibility to participate in and receive tax benefits with respect to a pension plan established in the United States, contributions made to, or benefits accrued under, a pension plan established in _____ shall be treated as contributions or benefits under a generally corresponding pension plan established in the United States to the extent relief is available to the individual under this paragraph.

d) This paragraph shall not apply unless the competent authority of the United States has agreed that the pension plan generally corresponds to a pension plan established in the United States.

Article 19 GOVERNMENT SERVICE

1. Notwithstanding the provisions of Articles 14 (Income from Employment), 15 (Directors' Fees), 16 (Entertainers and Sportsmen) and 20 (Students and Trainees):

a) Salaries, wages and other remuneration, other than a pension, paid to an individual in respect of services rendered to a Contracting State or a political subdivision or local authority thereof shall, subject to the provisions of subparagraph b), be taxable only in that State;

b) such remuneration, however, shall be taxable only in the other Contracting State if the services are rendered in that State and the individual is a resident of that State who:

    i) is a national of that State; or

    ii) did not become a resident of that State solely for the purpose of rendering the services.

2. Notwithstanding the provisions of paragraph 1 of Article 17 (Pensions, Social Security, Annuities, Alimony, and Child Support):

a) any pension and other similar remuneration paid by, or out of funds created by, a Contracting State or a political subdivision or a local authority thereof to an individual in respect of services rendered to that State or subdivision or authority (other than a payment to which paragraph 2 of Article 17 applies) shall, subject to the provisions of subparagraph b), be taxable only in that State;

b) such pension, however, shall be taxable only in the other Contracting State if the individual is a resident of, and a national of, that State.

3. The provisions of Articles 14 (Income from Employment), 15 (Directors' Fees), 16 (Entertainers and Sportsmen) and 17 (Pensions, Social Security, Annuities, Alimony, and Child Support) shall apply to salaries, wages and other remuneration, and to pensions, in respect of services rendered in connection with a business carried on by a Contracting State or a political subdivision or a local authority thereof.

Article 20   STUDENTS AND TRAINEES

1. Payments, other than compensation for personal services, received by a student or business trainee who is, or was immediately before visiting a Contracting State, a resident of the other Contracting State, and who is present in the first-mentioned State for the purpose of his full-time education or for his full-time training, shall not be taxed in that State, provided that such payments arise outside that State, and are for the purpose of his maintenance, education or training. The exemption from tax provided by this paragraph shall apply to a business trainee only for a period of time not exceeding one year from the date the business trainee first arrives in the first-mentioned Contracting State for the purpose of training.

2. A student or business trainee within the meaning of paragraph 1 shall be exempt from tax by the Contracting State in which the individual is temporarily present with respect to income from personal services in an aggregate amount equal to $9,000 annually. The competent authorities shall, every five years, adjust the amount provided in this subparagraph to the extent necessary to take into account changes in the U.S. personal exemption and the standard deduction.

3. For purposes of this Article, a business trainee is an individual:

a) who is temporarily in a Contracting State for the purpose of securing training required to qualify the individual to practice a profession or professional specialty; or

b) who is temporarily in a Contracting State as an employee of, or under contract with, a resident of the other Contracting State, for the primary purpose of acquiring technical, professional, or business experience from a person other than that resident of the other Contracting State (or a person related to such resident of the other Contracting State).

Article 21   OTHER INCOME

1. Items of income beneficially owned by a resident of a Contracting State, wherever arising, not dealt with in the foregoing Articles of this Convention shall be taxable only in that State.

2. The provisions of paragraph 1 shall not apply to income, other than income from real property as defined in paragraph 2 of Article 6 (Income from Real Property), if the beneficial owner of the income, being a resident of a Contracting State, carries on business in the other Contracting State through a permanent establishment situated therein and the income is attributable to such permanent establishment. In such case the provisions of Article 7 (Business Profits) shall apply.

Article 22 LIMITATION ON BENEFITS

1. Except as otherwise provided in this Article, a resident of a Contracting State shall not be entitled to the benefits of this Convention otherwise accorded to residents of a Contracting State unless such resident is a "qualified person" as defined in paragraph 2.

2. A resident of a Contracting State shall be a qualified person for a taxable year if the resident is:

a) an individual;

b) a Contracting State, or a political subdivision or local authority thereof;

c) a company, if:

    i) the principal class of its shares (and any disproportionate class of shares) is regularly traded on one or more recognized stock exchanges, and either: A) its principal class of shares is primarily traded on one or more recognized stock exchanges located in the Contracting State of which the company is a resident; or B) the company's primary place of management and control is in the Contracting State of which it is a resident; or

    ii) at least 50 percent of the aggregate vote and value of the shares (and at least 50 percent of any disproportionate class of shares) in the company is owned directly or indirectly by five or fewer companies entitled to benefits under clause i) of this subparagraph, provided that, in the case of indirect ownership, each intermediate owner is a resident of either Contracting State;

d) a person described in paragraph 2 of Article 4 of this Convention, provided that, in the case of a person described in subparagraph a) of that paragraph, more than 50 percent of the person's beneficiaries, members or participants are individuals resident in either Contracting State; or

e) a person other than an individual, if: i) on at least half the days of the taxable year, persons who are residents of that Contracting State and that are entitled to the benefits of this Convention under subparagraph a), subparagraph b), clause i) of subparagraph c), or subparagraph d) of this paragraph own, directly or indirectly, shares or other beneficial interests representing at least 50 percent of the aggregate voting power and value (and at least 50 percent of any disproportionate class of shares) of the person, provided that, in the case of indirect ownership, each intermediate owner is a resident of that Contracting State, and ii) less than 50 percent of the person's gross income for the taxable year, as determined in the person's State of residence, is paid or accrued, directly or indirectly, to persons who are not residents of either Contracting State entitled to the benefits of this Convention under subparagraph a), subparagraph b), clause i) of subparagraph c), or subparagraph d) of this paragraph in the form of payments that are deductible for purposes of the taxes covered by this Convention in the person's State of residence (but not including arm's length payments in the ordinary course of business for services or tangible property).

3.

    a) A resident of a Contracting State will be entitled to benefits of the Convention with respect to an item of income derived from the other State, regardless of whether the resident is a qualified person, if the resident is engaged in the active conduct of a trade or business in the first-mentioned State (other than the business of making or managing investments for the resident's own account, unless these activities are banking, insurance or securities activities carried on by a bank, insurance company or registered securities dealer), and the income derived from the other Contracting State is derived in connection with, or is incidental to, that trade or business.

    b) If a resident of a Contracting State derives an item of income from a trade or business activity conducted by that resident in the other Contracting State, or derives an item of income arising in the other Contracting State from a related person, the conditions described in subparagraph a) shall be considered to be satisfied with respect to such item only if the trade or business activity carried on by the resident in the first-mentioned Contracting State is substantial in relation to the trade or business activity carried on by the resident or such person in the other Contracting State. Whether a trade or business activity is substantial for the purposes of this paragraph will be determined based on all the facts and circumstances.

    c) For purposes of applying this paragraph, activities conducted by persons connected to a person shall be deemed to be conducted by such person. A person shall be connected to another if one possesses at least 50 percent of the beneficial interest in the other (or, in the case of a company, at least 50 percent of the aggregate vote and value of the company's shares or of the beneficial equity interest in the company) or another person possesses at least 50 percent of the beneficial interest (or, in the case of a company, at least 50 percent of the aggregate vote and value of the company's shares or of the beneficial equity interest in the company) in each person. In any case, a person shall be considered to be connected to another if, based on all the relevant facts and circumstances, one has control of the other or both are under the control of the same person or persons.

4. If a resident of a Contracting State is neither a qualified person pursuant to the provisions of paragraph 2 nor entitled to benefits with respect to an item of income under paragraph 3 of this Article the competent authority of the other Contracting State may, nevertheless, grant the benefits of this Convention, or benefits with respect to a specific item of income, if it determines that the establishment, acquisition or maintenance of such person and the conduct of its operations did not have as one of its principal purposes the obtaining of benefits under this Convention.

5. For purposes of this Article:

    a) the term "recognized stock exchange" means:

        i) the NASDAQ System owned by the National Association of Securities Dealers, Inc. and any stock exchange registered with the U.S. Securities and Exchange Commission as a national securities exchange under the U.S. Securities Exchange Act of 1934;

ii)   stock exchanges of _____; and

iii)   any other stock exchange agreed upon by the competent authorities;

b)   the term "principal class of shares" means the ordinary or common shares of the company, provided that such class of shares represents the majority of the voting power and value of the company. If no single class of ordinary or common shares represents the majority of the aggregate voting power and value of the company, the "principal class of shares" are those classes that in the aggregate represent a majority of the aggregate voting power and value of the company

c)   the term "disproportionate class of shares" means any class of shares of a company resident in one of the Contracting States that entitles the shareholder to disproportionately higher participation, through dividends, redemption payments or otherwise, in the earnings generated in the other State by particular assets or activities of the company; and

d)   a company's "primary place of management and control" will be in the Contracting State of which it is a resident only if executive officers and senior management employees exercise day-to-day responsibility for more of the strategic, financial and operational policy decision making for the company (including its direct and indirect subsidiaries) in that State than in any other state and the staff of such persons conduct more of the day-to-day activities necessary for preparing and making those decisions in that State than in any other state.

Article 23   RELIEF FROM DOUBLE TAXATION

1. In the case of _____, double taxation will be relieved as follows:

2. In accordance with the provisions and subject to the limitations of the law of the United States (as it may be amended from time to time without changing the general principle hereof), the United States shall allow to a resident or citizen of the United States as a credit against the United States tax on income applicable to residents and citizens:

a)   the income tax paid or accrued to _____ by or on behalf of such resident or citizen; and

b)   in the case of a United States company owning at least 10 percent of the voting stock of a company that is a resident of _____ and from which the United States company receives dividends, the income tax paid or accrued to _____ by or on behalf of the payer with respect to the profits out of which the dividends are paid.

For the purposes of this paragraph, the taxes referred to in paragraphs 3 a) and 4 of Article 2 (Taxes Covered) shall be considered income taxes.

3. For the purposes of applying paragraph 2 of this Article, an item of gross income, as determined under the laws of the United States, derived by a resident of the United States that, under this Convention, may be taxed in _____ shall be deemed to be income from sources in _____.

4. Where a United States citizen is a resident of _____:

a)   with respect to items of income that under the provisions of this Convention are exempt from United States tax or that are subject to a reduced rate of United States tax when derived by a resident of _____ who is not a United States citizen, _____ shall allow as a credit against _____ tax, only the tax paid, if any, that the United States may impose under the provisions of this Convention, other than taxes that may be imposed solely by reason of citizenship under the saving clause of paragraph 4 of Article 1 (General Scope);

b)   for purposes of applying paragraph 2 to compute United States tax on those items of income referred to in subparagraph a), the United States shall allow as a credit against United States tax the income tax paid to _____ after the credit referred to in subparagraph a); the credit so allowed shall not reduce the portion of the United States tax that is creditable against the _____ tax in accordance with subparagraph a); and

c)   for the exclusive purpose of relieving double taxation in the United States under subparagraph b), items of income referred to in subparagraph a) shall be deemed to arise in _____ to the extent necessary to avoid double taxation of such income under subparagraph b).

Article 24   NON-DISCRIMINATION

1. Nationals of a Contracting State shall not be subjected in the other Contracting State to any taxation or any requirement connected therewith that is more burdensome than the taxation and connected requirements to which nationals of that other State in the same circumstances, in particular with respect to residence, are or may be subjected. This provision shall also apply to persons who are not residents of one or both of the Contracting States. However, for the purposes of United States taxation, United States nationals who are subject to tax on a worldwide basis are not in the same circumstances as nationals of _____ who are not residents of the United States.

2. The taxation on a permanent establishment that an enterprise of a Contracting State has in the other Contracting State shall not be less favorably levied in that other State than the taxation levied on enterprises of that other State carrying on the same activities.

3. The provisions of paragraphs 1 and 2 shall not be construed as obliging a Contracting State to grant to residents of the other Contracting State any personal allowances, reliefs, and reductions for taxation purposes on account of civil status or family responsibilities that it grants to its own residents.

4. Except where the provisions of paragraph 1 of Article 9 (Associated Enterprises), paragraph 5 of Article 11 (Interest), or paragraph 4 of Article 12 (Royalties) apply, interest, royalties, and other disbursements paid by a resident of a Contracting State to a resident of the other Contracting State shall, for the purpose of determining the taxable profits of the first-mentioned resident, be deductible under the same conditions as if they had been paid to a resident of the first-mentioned State. Similarly, any debts of a resident of a Contracting State to a resident of the other Contracting State shall, for the purpose of determining the

taxable capital of the first-mentioned resident, be deductible under the same conditions as if they had been contracted to a resident of the first-mentioned State.

5. Enterprises of a Contracting State, the capital of which is wholly or partly owned or controlled, directly or indirectly, by one or more residents of the other Contracting State, shall not be subjected in the first-mentioned State to any taxation or any requirement connected therewith that is more burdensome than the taxation and connected requirements to which other similar enterprises of the first-mentioned State are or may be subjected.

6. Nothing in this Article shall be construed as preventing either Contracting State from imposing a tax as described in paragraph 8 of Article 10 (Dividends).

7. The provisions of this Article shall, notwithstanding the provisions of Article 2 (Taxes Covered), apply to taxes of every kind and description imposed by a Contracting State or a political subdivision or local authority thereof.

Article 25 MUTUAL AGREEMENT PROCEDURE

1. Where a person considers that the actions of one or both of the Contracting States result or will result for such person in taxation not in accordance with the provisions of this Convention, it may, irrespective of the remedies provided by the domestic law of those States, and the time limits prescribed in such laws for presenting claims for refund, present its case to the competent authority of either Contracting State.

2. The competent authority shall endeavor, if the objection appears to it to be justified and if it is not itself able to arrive at a satisfactory solution, to resolve the case by mutual agreement with the competent authority of the other Contracting State, with a view to the avoidance of taxation which is not in accordance with the Convention. Any agreement reached shall be implemented notwithstanding any time limits or other procedural limitations in the domestic law of the Contracting States. Assessment and collection procedures shall be suspended during the period that any mutual agreement proceeding is pending.

3. The competent authorities of the Contracting States shall endeavor to resolve by mutual agreement any difficulties or doubts arising as to the interpretation or application of the Convention. They also may consult together for the elimination of double taxation in cases not provided for in the Convention. In particular the competent authorities of the Contracting States may agree:

    a)   to the same attribution of income, deductions, credits, or allowances of an enterprise of a Contracting State to its permanent establishment situated in the other Contracting State;

    b)   to the same allocation of income, deductions, credits, or allowances between persons;

    c)   to the settlement of conflicting application of the Convention, including conflicts regarding:

        i)   the characterization of particular items of income;

        ii) the characterization of persons;

    iii) the application of source rules with respect to particular items of income;

    iv) the meaning of any term used in the Convention;

    v) the timing of particular items of income; d) to advance pricing arrangements; and

  e) to the application of the provisions of domestic law regarding penalties, fines, and interest in a manner consistent with the purposes of the Convention.

4. The competent authorities also may agree to increases in any specific dollar amounts referred to in the Convention to reflect economic or monetary developments.

5. The competent authorities of the Contracting States may communicate with each other directly, including through a joint commission, for the purpose of reaching an agreement in the sense of the preceding paragraphs.

Article 26   EXCHANGE OF INFORMATION AND ADMINISTRATIVE ASSISTANCE

1. The competent authorities of the Contracting States shall exchange such information as may be relevant for carrying out the provisions of this Convention or of the domestic laws of the Contracting States concerning taxes of every kind imposed by a Contracting State to the extent that the taxation thereunder is not contrary to the Convention, including information relating to the assessment or collection of, the enforcement or prosecution in respect of, or the determination of appeals in relation to, such taxes. The exchange of information is not restricted by paragraph 1 of Article 1 (General Scope) or Article 2 (Taxes Covered).

2. Any information received under this Article by a Contracting State shall be treated as secret in the same manner as information obtained under the domestic laws of that State and shall be disclosed only to persons or authorities (including courts and administrative bodies) involved in the assessment, collection, or administration of, the enforcement or prosecution in respect of, or the determination of appeals in relation to, the taxes referred to above, or the oversight of such functions. Such persons or authorities shall use the information only for such purposes. They may disclose the information in public court proceedings or in judicial decisions.

3. In no case shall the provisions of the preceding paragraphs be construed so as to impose on a Contracting State the obligation:

  a) to carry out administrative measures at variance with the laws and administrative practice of that or of the other Contracting State;

  b) to supply information that is not obtainable under the laws or in the normal course of the administration of that or of the other Contracting State;

  c) to supply information that would disclose any trade, business, industrial, commercial, or professional secret or trade process, or information the disclosure of which would be contrary to public policy (ordre public).

4. If information is requested by a Contracting State in accordance with this Article, the other Contracting State shall use its information gathering measures to obtain the requested information, even though that other State may not need such information for its own purposes. The obligation contained in the preceding sentence is subject to the limitations of paragraph 3 but in no case shall such limitation be construed to permit a Contracting State to decline to supply information because it has no domestic interest in such information.

5. In no case shall the provisions of paragraph 3 be construed to permit a Contracting State to decline to supply information requested by the other Contracting State because the information is held by a bank, other financial institution, nominee or person acting in an agency or a fiduciary capacity or because it relates to ownership interests in a person.

6. If specifically requested by the competent authority of a Contracting State, the competent authority of the other Contracting State shall provide information under this Article in the form of depositions of witnesses and authenticated copies of unedited original documents (including books, papers, statements, records, accounts, and writings).

7. Each of the Contracting States shall endeavor to collect on behalf of the other Contracting State such amounts as may be necessary to ensure that relief granted by the Convention from taxation imposed by that other State does not inure to the benefit of persons not entitled thereto. This paragraph shall not impose upon either of the Contracting States the obligation to carry out administrative measures that would be contrary to its sovereignty, security, or public policy.

8. The requested State shall allow representatives of the requesting State to enter the requested State to interview individuals and examine books and records with the consent of the persons subject to examination.

9. The competent authorities of the Contracting States may develop an agreement upon the mode of application of this Article, including agreement to ensure comparable levels of assistance to each of the Contracting States, but in no case will the lack of such agreement relieve a Contracting State of its obligations under this Article.

Article 27   MEMBERS OF DIPLOMATIC MISSIONS AND CONSULAR POSTS

Nothing in this Convention shall affect the fiscal privileges of members of diplomatic missions or consular posts under the general rules of international law or under the provisions of special agreements.

Article 28   ENTRY INTO FORCE

1. This Convention shall be subject to ratification in accordance with the applicable procedures of each Contracting State, and instruments of ratification will be exchanged as soon thereafter as possible.

2. This Convention shall enter into force on the date of the exchange of instruments of ratification, and its provisions shall have effect:

a) in respect of taxes withheld at source, for amounts paid or credited on or after the first day of the second month next following the date on which the Convention enters into force;

b) in respect of other taxes, for taxable periods beginning on or after the first day of January next following the date on which the Convention enters into force.

3. Notwithstanding paragraph 2, the provisions of Article 26 (Exchange of Information and Administrative Assistance) shall have effect from the date of entry into force of this Convention, without regard to the taxable period to which the matter relates.

Article 29   TERMINATION

This Convention shall remain in force until terminated by a Contracting State. Either Contracting State may terminate the Convention by giving notice of termination to the other Contracting State through diplomatic channels. In such event, the Convention shall cease to have effect:

a) in respect of taxes withheld at source, for amounts paid or credited after the expiration of the 6 month period beginning on the date on which notice of termination was given; and

b) in respect of other taxes, for taxable periods beginning on or after the expiration of the 6 month period beginning on the date on which notice of termination was given.

IN WITNESS WHEREOF, the undersigned, being duly authorized thereto by their respective Governments, have signed this Convention.

DONE at in duplicate, in the English and _____ languages, both texts being equally authentic, this _____ day of _____, 20_____

FOR THE GOVERNMENT OF   FOR THE GOVERNMENT OF
THE UNITED STATES OF AMERICA: _____:

UNITED STATES MODEL TECHNICAL EXPLANATION ACCOMPANYING THE UNITED STATES MODEL INCOME TAX CONVENTION OF NOVEMBER 15, 2006

This is a technical explanation of the Convention between the United States and [the other Contracting State][1] for the avoidance of double taxation and the prevention of fiscal evasion with respect to taxes on income, signed on [date] (the "Convention").

Negotiations took into account the U.S. Department of the Treasury's current tax treaty policy, and the United States Model Income Tax Convention of November 15, 2006. Negotiations also took into account the Model Tax Convention on Income and on Capital, published by the Organisation for Economic Cooperation and Development (the "OECD Model"), and recent tax treaties concluded by both countries.

The Technical Explanation is an official guide to the Convention. It reflects the policies behind particular Convention provisions, as well as understandings reached with respect to the application and interpretation of the Convention. References in the Technical Explanation to "he" or "his" should be read to mean "he or she" or "his and her."

ARTICLE 1   (GENERAL SCOPE)

Paragraph 1

Paragraph 1 of Article 1 provides that the Convention applies only to residents of the United States or the other Contracting State except where the terms of the Convention provide otherwise. Under Article 4 (Resident) a person is generally treated as a resident of a Contracting State if that person is, under the laws of that State, liable to tax therein by reason of his domicile, citizenship, residence, or other similar criteria. However, if a person is considered a resident of both Contracting States, Article 4 provides rules for determining a State of residence (or no State of residence). This determination governs for all purposes of the Convention.

Certain provisions are applicable to persons who may not be residents of either Contracting State. For example, paragraph 1 of Article 24 (Non-Discrimination) applies to nationals of the Contracting States. Under Article 26 (Exchange of Information and Administrative Assistance), information may be exchanged with respect to residents of third states.

Paragraph 2

Paragraph 2 states the generally accepted relationship both between the Convention and domestic law and between the Convention and other agreements

---

[1] To enhance readability, this Model Technical Explanation uses the term "the other Contracting State"; the actual name of the other Contracting State should be used throughout the text of the Technical Explanation to an actual treaty.

between the Contracting States. That is, no provision in the Convention may restrict any exclusion, exemption, deduction, credit or other benefit accorded by the tax laws of the Contracting States, or by any other agreement between the Contracting States. The relationship between the non-discrimination provisions of the Convention and other agreements is addressed not in paragraph 2 but in paragraph 3.

Under paragraph 2, for example, if a deduction would be allowed under the U.S. Internal Revenue Code (the "Code") in computing the U.S. taxable income of a resident of the other Contracting State, the deduction also is allowed to that person in computing taxable income under the Convention. Paragraph 2 also means that the Convention may not increase the tax burden on a resident of a Contracting States beyond the burden determined under domestic law. Thus, a right to tax given by the Convention cannot be exercised unless that right also exists under internal law.

It follows that, under the principle of paragraph 2, a taxpayer's U.S. tax liability need not be determined under the Convention if the Code would produce a more favorable result. A taxpayer may not, however, choose among the provisions of the Code and the Convention in an inconsistent manner in order to minimize tax. For example, assume that a resident of the other Contracting State has three separate businesses in the United States. One is a profitable permanent establishment and the other two are trades or businesses that would earn taxable income under the Code but that do not meet the permanent establishment threshold tests of the Convention. One is profitable and the other incurs a loss. Under the Convention, the income of the permanent establishment is taxable in the United States, and both the profit and loss of the other two businesses are ignored. Under the Code, all three would be subject to tax, but the loss would offset the profits of the two profitable ventures. The taxpayer may not invoke the Convention to exclude the profits of the profitable trade or business and invoke the Code to claim the loss of the loss trade or business against the profit of the permanent establishment. (See Rev. Rul. 84-17, 1984-1 C.B. 308.) If, however, the taxpayer invokes the Code for the taxation of all three ventures, he would not be precluded from invoking the Convention with respect, for example, to any dividend income he may receive from the United States that is not effectively connected with any of his business activities in the United States.

Similarly, nothing in the Convention can be used to deny any benefit granted by any other agreement between the United States and the other Contracting State. For example, if certain benefits are provided for military personnel or military contractors under a Status of Forces Agreement between the United States and the other Contracting State, those benefits or protections will be available to residents of the Contracting States regardless of any provisions to the contrary (or silence) in the Convention.

Paragraph 3

Paragraph 3 specifically relates to non-discrimination obligations of the Contracting States under the General Agreement on Trade in Services (the "GATS"). The provisions of paragraph 3 are an exception to the rule provided in paragraph

2 of this Article under which the Convention shall not restrict in any manner any benefit now or hereafter accorded by any other agreement between the Contracting States.

Subparagraph (a) of paragraph 3 provides that, unless the competent authorities determine that a taxation measure is not within the scope of the Convention, the national treatment obligations of the GATS shall not apply with respect to that measure. Further, any question arising as to the interpretation of the Convention, including in particular whether a measure is within the scope of the Convention shall be considered only by the competent authorities of the Contracting States, and the procedures under the Convention exclusively shall apply to the dispute. Thus, paragraph 3 of Article XXII (Consultation) of the GATS may not be used to bring a dispute before the World Trade Organization unless the competent authorities of both Contracting States have determined that the relevant taxation measure is not within the scope of Article 24 (Non-Discrimination) of the Convention.

The term "measure" for these purposes is defined broadly in subparagraph (b) of paragraph 3. It would include, for example, a law, regulation, rule, procedure, decision, administrative action or guidance, or any other form of measure.

Paragraph 4

Paragraph 4 contains the traditional saving clause found in all U.S. treaties. The Contracting States reserve their rights, except as provided in paragraph 5, to tax their residents and citizens as provided in their internal laws, notwithstanding any provisions of the Convention to the contrary. For example, if a resident of the other Contracting State performs professional services in the United States and the income from the services is not attributable to a permanent establishment in the United States, Article 7 (Business Profits) would by its terms prevent the United States from taxing the income. If, however, the resident of the other Contracting State is also a citizen of the United States, the saving clause permits the United States to include the remuneration in the worldwide income of the citizen and subject it to tax under the normal Code rules (*i.e.*, without regard to Code section 894(a)). However, subparagraph 5(a) of Article 1 preserves the benefits of special foreign tax credit rules applicable to the U.S. taxation of certain U.S. income of its citizens resident in the other Contracting State. See paragraph 4 of Article 23 (Relief from Double Taxation).

For purposes of the saving clause, "residence" is determined under Article 4 (Resident). Thus, an individual who is a resident of the United States under the Code (but not a U.S. citizen) but who is determined to be a resident of the other Contracting State under the tie-breaker rules of Article 4 would be subject to U.S. tax only to the extent permitted by the Convention. The United States would not be permitted to apply its statutory rules to that person to the extent the rules are inconsistent with the treaty.

However, the person would be treated as a U.S. resident for U.S. tax purposes other than determining the individual's U.S. tax liability. For example, in determining under Code section 957 whether a foreign corporation is a controlled foreign corporation, shares in that corporation held by the individual would be considered to be held by a U.S. resident. As a result, other U.S. citizens or residents might be deemed to be United States shareholders of a controlled foreign corporation subject to current inclusion of Subpart F income recognized by the corporation. See, Treas. Reg. section 301.7701(b)-7(a)(3).

Under paragraph 4, each Contracting State also reserves its right to tax former citizens and former long-term residents for a period of ten years following the loss of such status. Thus, paragraph 4 allows the United States to tax former U.S. citizens and former U.S. long-term residents in accordance with Section 877 of the Code. Section 877 generally applies to a former citizen or long-term resident of the United States who relinquishes citizenship or terminates long-term residency if either of the following criteria exceed established thresholds: (a) the average annual net income tax of such individual for the period of 5 taxable years ending before the date of the loss of status, or (b) the net worth of such individual as of the date of the loss of status. The thresholds are adjusted annually for inflation. The United States defines "long-term resident" as an individual (other than a U.S. citizen) who is a lawful permanent resident of the United States in at least 8 of the prior 15 taxable years. An individual is not treated as a lawful permanent resident for any taxable year if such individual is treated as a resident of a foreign country under the provisions of a tax treaty between the United States and the foreign country and the individual does not waive the benefits of such treaty applicable to residents of the foreign country.

Paragraph 5

Paragraph 5 sets forth certain exceptions to the saving clause. The referenced provisions are intended to provide benefits to citizens and residents even if such benefits do not exist under internal law. Paragraph 5 thus preserves these benefits for citizens and residents of the Contracting States.

Subparagraph (a) lists certain provisions of the Convention that are applicable to all citizens and residents of a Contracting State, despite the general saving clause rule of paragraph 4:

(1) Paragraph 2 of Article 9 (Associated Enterprises) grants the right to a correlative adjustment with respect to income tax due on profits reallocated under Article 9.

(2) Paragraphs 1 b), 2, and 5 of Article 17 (Pensions, Social Security, Annuities, Alimony and Child Support) provide exemptions from source or residence State taxation for certain pension distributions, social security payments and child support.

(3) Paragraph 1 of Article 18 (Pensions Funds) provides an exemption for certain investment income of pension funds located in the other Contracting State, while paragraph 4 provides benefits for certain contributions by or on behalf of a U.S. citizen to certain pension funds established in the other Contracting State.

(4) Article 23 (Relief from Double Taxation) confirms to citizens and residents of one Contracting State the benefit of a credit for income taxes paid to the other or an exemption for income earned in the other State.

(5) Article 24 (Non-Discrimination) protects residents and nationals of one Contracting State against the adoption of certain discriminatory practices in the other Contracting State.

(6) Article 25 (Mutual Agreement Procedure) confers certain benefits on citizens and residents of the Contracting States in order to reach and implement solutions to disputes between the two Contracting States. For example, the competent authorities are permitted to use a definition of a term that differs from an internal law definition. The statute of limitations may be waived for refunds, so that the benefits of an agreement may be implemented.

Subparagraph (b) of paragraph 5 provides a different set of exceptions to the saving clause. The benefits referred to are all intended to be granted to temporary residents of a Contracting State (for example, in the case of the United States, holders of non-immigrant visas), but not to citizens or to persons who have acquired permanent residence in that State. If beneficiaries of these provisions travel from one of the Contracting States to the other, and remain in the other long enough to become residents under its internal law, but do not acquire permanent residence status (i.e., in the U.S. context, they do not become "green card" holders) and are not citizens of that State, the host State will continue to grant these benefits even if they conflict with the statutory rules. The benefits preserved by this paragraph are: (1) the host country exemptions for government service salaries and pensions under Article 19 (Government Service), certain income of visiting students and trainees under Article 20 (Students and Trainees), and the income of diplomatic agents and consular officers under Article 27 (Members of Diplomatic Missions and Consular Posts); and (2) the beneficial tax treatment of pension fund contributions under paragraph 2 of Article 18 (Pension Funds).

Paragraph 6

Paragraph 6 addresses special issues presented by fiscally transparent entities such as partnerships and certain estates and trusts. Because different countries frequently take different views as to when an entity is fiscally transparent, the risk of both double taxation and double non-taxation are relatively high. The intention of paragraph 6 is to eliminate a number of technical problems that arguably would have prevented investors using such entities from claiming treaty benefits, even though such investors would be subject to tax on the income derived through such entities. The provision also prevents the use of such entities to claim treaty benefits in circumstances where the person investing through such an entity is not subject to tax on the income in its State of residence. The provision, and the corresponding requirements of the substantive rules of Articles 6 through 21, should be read with those two goals in mind.

In general, paragraph 6 relates to entities that are not subject to tax at the entity level, as distinct from entities that are subject to tax, but with respect to which tax may be relieved under an integrated system. This paragraph applies to any resident of a Contracting State who is entitled to income derived through an entity that is treated as fiscally transparent under the laws of either Contracting State. Entities falling under this description in the United States include partnerships, common investment trusts under section 584 and grantor trusts. This paragraph also applies to U.S. limited liability companies ("LLCs") that are treated as partnerships or as disregarded entities for U.S. tax purposes.

Under paragraph 6, an item of income, profit or gain derived by such a fiscally transparent entity will be considered to be derived by a resident of a Contracting State if a resident is treated under the taxation laws of that State as deriving the item of income. For example, if a company that is a resident of the other Contracting State pays interest to an entity that is treated as fiscally transparent for U.S. tax purposes, the interest will be considered derived by a resident of the U.S. only to the extent that the taxation laws of the United States treats one or more U.S. residents (whose status as U.S. residents is determined, for this purpose, under U.S. tax law) as deriving the interest for U.S. tax purposes. In the case of a partnership, the persons who are, under U.S. tax laws, treated as partners of the entity would normally be the persons whom the U.S. tax laws would treat as deriving the interest income through the partnership. Also, it follows that persons whom the United States treats as partners but who are not U.S. residents for U.S. tax purposes may not claim a benefit for the interest paid to the entity under the Convention, because they are not residents of the United States for purposes of claiming this treaty benefit. (If, however, the country in which they are treated as resident for tax purposes, as determined under the laws of that country, has an income tax convention with the other Contracting State, they may be entitled to claim a benefit under that convention.) In contrast, if, for example, an entity is organized under U.S. laws and is classified as a corporation for U.S. tax purposes, interest paid by a company that is a resident of the other Contracting State to the U.S. entity will be considered derived by a resident of the United States since the U.S. corporation is treated under U.S. taxation laws as a resident of the United States and as deriving the income.

The same result obtains even if the entity were viewed differently under the tax laws of the other Contracting State (*e.g.*, as not fiscally transparent in the first example above where the entity is treated as a partnership for U.S. tax purposes). Similarly, the characterization of the entity in a third country is also irrelevant, even if the entity is organized in that third country. The results follow regardless of whether the entity is disregarded as a separate entity under the laws of one jurisdiction but not the other, such as a single owner entity that is viewed as a branch for U.S. tax purposes and as a corporation for tax purposes under the laws of the other Contracting State. These results also obtain regardless of where the entity is organized (*i.e.*, in the United States, in the other Contracting State or, as noted above, in a third country).

For example, income from U.S. sources received by an entity organized under the laws of the United States, which is treated for tax purposes under the laws of the other Contracting State as a corporation and is owned by a shareholder who is a resident of the other Contracting State for its tax purposes, is not considered derived by the shareholder of that corporation even if, under the tax laws of the United States, the entity is treated as fiscally transparent. Rather, for purposes of the treaty, the income is treated as derived by the U.S. entity.

These principles also apply to trusts to the extent that they are fiscally transparent in either Contracting State. For example, if X, a resident of the other Contracting State, creates a revocable trust in the United States and names persons resident in a third country as the beneficiaries of the trust, the trust's income would be regarded as being derived by a resident of the other Contracting State only to the extent that the laws of the other Contracting State treat X as deriving the income for its tax purposes, perhaps through application of rules similar to the U.S. "grantor trust" rules.

Paragraph 6 is not an exception to the saving clause of paragraph 4. Accordingly, paragraph 6 does not prevent a Contracting State from taxing an entity that is treated as a resident of that State under its tax law. For example, if a U.S. LLC with members who are residents of the other Contracting State elects to be taxed as a corporation for U.S. tax purposes, the United States will tax that LLC on its worldwide income on a net basis, without regard to whether the other Contracting State views the LLC as fiscally transparent.

ARTICLE 2   (TAXES COVERED)

This Article specifies the U.S. taxes and the taxes of the other Contracting State to which the Convention applies. With two exceptions, the taxes specified in Article 2 are the covered taxes for all purposes of the Convention. A broader coverage applies, however, for purposes of Articles 24 (Non-Discrimination) and 26 (Exchange of Information and Administrative Assistance). Article 24 (Non-Discrimination) applies with respect to all taxes, including those imposed by state and local governments. Article 26 (Exchange of Information and Administrative Assistance) applies with respect to all taxes imposed at the national level.

Paragraph 1

Paragraph 1 identifies the category of taxes to which the Convention applies. Paragraph 1 is based on the OECD Model and defines the scope of application of the Convention. The convention applies to taxes on income, including gains, imposed on behalf of a Contracting State, irrespective of the manner in which they are levied. Except with respect to Article 24 (Non-Discrimination), state and local taxes are not covered by the Convention.

Paragraph 2

Paragraph 2 also is based on the OECD Model and provides a definition of taxes on income and on capital gains. The Convention covers taxes on total income or any part of income and includes tax on gains derived from the alienation of property. The Convention does not apply, however, to social security charges, or any other charges where there is a direct connection between the levy and individual benefits. Nor does it apply to property taxes, except with respect to Article 24 (Non-Discrimination).

Paragraph 3

Paragraph 3 lists the taxes in force at the time of signature of the Convention to which the Convention applies.

The existing covered taxes of the other Contracting State are identified in subparagraph (a) of paragraph 3.

Subparagraph 3(b) provides that the existing U.S. taxes subject to the rules of the Convention are the Federal income taxes imposed by the Code, together with the excise taxes imposed with respect to private foundations (Code sections 4940 through 4948). Social security and unemployment taxes (Code sections 1401, 3101, 3111 and 3301) are specifically excluded from coverage.

Paragraph 4

Under paragraph 4, the Convention will apply to any taxes that are identical, or substantially similar, to those enumerated in paragraph 3, and which are imposed in addition to, or in place of, the existing taxes after [_____], the date of signature of the Convention. The paragraph also provides that the competent authorities of the Contracting States will notify each other of any changes that have been made in their laws, whether tax laws or non-tax laws, that affect significantly their obligations under the Convention. Non-tax laws that may affect a Contracting State's obligations under the Convention may include, for example, laws affecting bank secrecy.

ARTICLE 3   (GENERAL DEFINITIONS)

Article 3 provides general definitions and rules of interpretation applicable throughout the Convention. Certain other terms are defined in other articles of the Convention. For example, the term "resident of a Contracting State" is defined in Article 4 (Resident). The term "permanent establishment" is defined in Article 5 (Permanent Establishment). These definitions are used consistently throughout the Convention. Other terms, such as "dividends," "interest" and "royalties" are defined in specific articles for purposes only of those articles.

Paragraph 1

Paragraph 1 defines a number of basic terms used in the Convention. The introduction to paragraph 1 makes clear that these definitions apply for all purposes of the Convention, unless the context requires otherwise. This latter condition allows flexibility in the interpretation of the treaty in order to avoid results not intended by the treaty's negotiators.

Subparagraph 1(a) defines the term "person" to include an individual, a trust, a partnership, a company and any other body of persons. The definition is significant for a variety of reasons. For example, under Article 4, only a "person" can be a "resident" and therefore eligible for most benefits under the treaty. Also, all "persons" are eligible to claim relief under Article 25 (Mutual Agreement Procedure).

The term "company" is defined in subparagraph 1(b) as a body corporate or an entity treated as a body corporate for tax purposes in the state where it is organized. The definition refers to the law of the state in which an entity is organized in order to ensure that an entity that is treated as fiscally transparent in its country of residence will not get inappropriate benefits, such as the reduced withholding rate provided by subparagraph 2(b) of Article 10 (Dividends). It also ensures that the Limitation on Benefits provisions of Article 22 will be applied at the appropriate level.

The terms "enterprise of a Contracting State" and "enterprise of the other Contracting State" are defined in subparagraph 1(c) as an enterprise carried on by a resident of a Contracting State and an enterprise carried on by a resident of the other Contracting State. An enterprise of a Contracting State need not be carried on in that State. It may be carried on in the other Contracting State or a third state (e.g., a U.S. corporation doing all of its business in the other Contracting State would still be a U.S. enterprise).

Subparagraph 1(c) further provides that these terms also encompass an enterprise conducted through an entity (such as a partnership) that is treated as fiscally transparent in the Contracting State where the entity's owner is resident. The definition makes this point explicitly to ensure that the purpose of the Convention is not thwarted by an overly technical application of the term "enterprise of a Contracting State" to activities carried on through partnerships and similar entities. In accordance with Article 4 (Resident), entities that are fiscally transparent in the country in which their owners are resident are not considered to be residents of a Contracting State (although income derived by such entities may be taxed as the income of a resident, if taxed in the hands of resident partners or other owners). It could be argued that an enterprise conducted by such an entity is not conducted by a resident of a Contracting State, and therefore would not benefit from provisions applicable to enterprises of a Contracting State. The definition is intended to make clear that an enterprise conducted by such an entity will be treated as carried on by a resident of a Contracting State to the extent its partners or other owners are residents. This approach is consistent with the Code, which under section 875 attributes a trade or business conducted by a partnership to its partners and a trade or business conducted by an estate or trust to its beneficiaries.

Subparagraph (d) defines the term "enterprise" as any activity or set of activities that constitutes the carrying on of a business. The term "business" is not defined, but subparagraph (e) provides that it includes the performance of professional services and other activities of an independent character. Both subparagraphs are identical to definitions recently added to the OECD Model in connection with the deletion of Article 14 (Independent Personal Services) from the OECD Model. The inclusion of the two definitions is intended to clarify that income from the performance of professional services or other activities of an independent character is dealt with under Article 7 (Business Profits) and not Article 21 (Other Income).

Subparagraph 1(f) defines the term "international traffic." The term means any transport by a ship or aircraft except when such transport is solely between places within a Contracting State. This definition is applicable principally in the context of Article 8 (Shipping and Air Transport). The definition combines with paragraphs 2 and 3 of Article 8 to exempt from tax by the source State income from the rental of ships or aircraft that is earned both by lessors that are operators of ships and aircraft and by those lessors that are not (e.g., a bank or a container leasing company).

The exclusion from international traffic of transport solely between places within a Contracting State means, for example, that carriage of goods or passengers solely between New York and Chicago would not be treated as international traffic, whether carried by a U.S. or a foreign carrier. The substantive taxing rules of the Convention relating to the taxation of income from transport, principally Article 8 (Shipping and Air Transport), therefore, would not apply to income from such carriage. Thus, if the carrier engaged in internal U.S. traffic were a resident of the other Contracting State (assuming that were possible under U.S. law), the United States would not be required to exempt the income from that transport under Article 8. The income would, however, be treated as business profits under Article 7 (Business Profits), and therefore would be taxable in the United States only if attributable to a U.S. permanent establishment of the foreign carrier, and then only on a net basis. The gross basis U.S. tax imposed by section 887 would never apply under the circumstances described. If, however, goods or passengers are carried by a carrier resident in the other Contracting State from a non-U.S. port to, for example, New York, and some of the goods or passengers continue on to Chicago, the entire transport would be international traffic. This would be true if the international carrier transferred the goods at the U.S. port of entry from a ship to a land vehicle, from a ship to a lighter, or even if the overland portion of the trip in the United States was handled by an independent carrier under contract with the original international carrier, so long as both parts of the trip were reflected in original bills of lading. For this reason, the U.S. Model refers, in the definition of "international traffic," to "such transport" being solely between places in the other Contracting State, while the OECD Model refers to the ship or aircraft being operated solely between such places. The U.S. Model language is intended to make clear that, as in the above example, even if the goods are carried on a different aircraft for the internal portion of the international voyage than is used for the overseas portion of the trip, the definition applies to that internal portion as well as the external portion.

Finally, a "cruise to nowhere," i.e., a cruise beginning and ending in a port in the same Contracting State with no stops in a foreign port, would not constitute international traffic.

Subparagraph 1(g) designates the "competent authorities" for the other Contracting State and the United States. The U.S. competent authority is the Secretary of the Treasury or his delegate. The Secretary of the Treasury has delegated the competent authority function to the Commissioner of Internal Revenue, who in turn has delegated the authority to the Deputy Commissioner (International) LMSB. With respect to interpretative issues, the Deputy Commissioner (International) LMSB acts with the concurrence of the Associate Chief Counsel (International) of the Internal Revenue Service.

The geographical scope of the Convention with respect to the United States is set out in subparagraph 1(i). It encompasses the United States of America, including the states, the District of Columbia and the territorial sea of the United States. The term does not include Puerto Rico, the Virgin Islands, Guam or any other U.S. possession or territory. For certain purposes, the term "United States" includes the sea bed and subsoil of undersea areas adjacent to the territorial sea of the United States. This extension applies to the extent that the United States exercises sovereignty in accordance with international law for the purpose of natural resource exploration and exploitation of such areas. This extension of the definition applies, however, only if the person, property or activity to which the Convention is being applied is connected with such natural resource exploration or exploitation. Thus, it would not include any activity involving the sea floor of an area over which the United States exercised sovereignty for natural resource purposes if that activity was unrelated to the exploration and exploitation of natural resources. This result is consistent with the result that would be obtained under Section 638, which treats the continental shelf as part of the United States for purposes of natural resource exploration and exploitation.

The term "national," as it relates to the United States and to the other Contracting State, is defined in subparagraphs 1(j). This term is relevant for purposes of Articles 19 (Government Service) and 24 (Non-Discrimination). A national of one of the Contracting States is (1) an individual who is a citizen or national of that State, and (2) any legal person, partnership or association deriving its status, as such, from the law in force in the State where it is established.

Subparagraph (k) defines the term "pension fund" to include any person established in a Contracting State that is generally exempt from income taxation in that State and that is operated principally to provide pension or retirement benefits or to earn income for the benefit of one or more such arrangements. In the case of the United States, the term "pension fund" includes the following: a trust providing pension or retirement benefits under a Code section 401(a) qualified pension plan, profit sharing or stock bonus plan, a trust providing pension or retirement benefits under a Code section 403(b) plan, a trust that is an individual retirement account under Code section 408, a Roth individual retirement account under Code section 408A, or a simple retirement account under Code section 408(p), a trust providing pension or retirement benefits under a simplified employee pension plan under Code section 408(k), a trust described in section 457(g) providing pension or retirement benefits under a Code section 457(b) plan, and the Thrift Savings Fund (section 7701(j)). Section 401(k) plans and group trusts described in Revenue Ruling 81-100 and meeting the conditions of Revenue Ruling 2004-67 qualify as pension funds because they are covered by Code section 401(a).

Paragraph 2

Terms that are not defined in the Convention are dealt with in paragraph 2.

Paragraph 2 provides that in the application of the Convention, any term used but not defined in the Convention will have the meaning that it has under the law of the Contracting State whose tax is being applied, unless the context requires otherwise, or the competent authorities have agreed on a different meaning pursuant to Article 25 (Mutual Agreement Procedure). If the term is defined under both the tax and non-tax laws of a Contracting State, the definition in the tax law will take precedence over the definition in the non-tax laws. Finally, there also may be cases where the tax laws of a State contain multiple definitions of the same term. In such a case, the definition used for purposes of the particular provision at issue, if any, should be used.

If the meaning of a term cannot be readily determined under the law of a Contracting State, or if there is a conflict in meaning under the laws of the two States that creates difficulties in the application of the Convention, the competent authorities, as indicated in paragraph 3(c)(iv) of Article 25 (Mutual Agreement Procedure), may establish a common meaning in order to prevent double taxation or to further any other purpose of the Convention. This common meaning need not conform to the meaning of the term under the laws of either Contracting State.

The reference in paragraph 2 to the internal law of a Contracting State means the law in effect at the time the treaty is being applied, not the law as in effect at the time the treaty was signed. The use of "ambulatory" definitions, however, may lead to results that are at variance with the intentions of the negotiators and of the Contracting States when the treaty was negotiated and ratified. The reference in both paragraphs 1 and 2 to the "context otherwise requir[ing]" a definition different from the treaty definition, in paragraph 1, or from the internal law definition of the Contracting State whose tax is being imposed, under paragraph 2, refers to a circumstance where the result intended by the Contracting States is different from the result that would obtain under either the paragraph 1 definition or the statutory definition. Thus, flexibility in defining terms is necessary and permitted.

ARTICLE 4   (RESIDENT)

This Article sets forth rules for determining whether a person is a resident of a Contracting State for purposes of the Convention. As a general matter only residents of the Contracting States may claim the benefits of the Convention. The treaty definition of residence is to be used only for purposes of the Convention. The fact that a person is determined to be a resident of a Contracting State under Article 4 does not necessarily entitle that person to the benefits of the Convention. In addition to being a resident, a person also must qualify for benefits under Article 22 (Limitation on Benefits) in order to receive benefits conferred on residents of a Contracting State.

The determination of residence for treaty purposes looks first to a person's liability to tax as a resident under the respective taxation laws of the Contracting States. As a general matter, a person who, under those laws, is a resident of one Contracting State and not of the other need look no further. For purposes of the Convention, that person is a resident of the State in which he is resident under internal law. If, however, a person is resident in both Contracting States under their respective taxation laws, the Article proceeds, where possible, to use tie-breaker rules to assign a single State of residence to such a person for purposes of the Convention.

Paragraph 1

The term "resident of a Contracting State" is defined in paragraph 1. In general, this definition incorporates the definitions of residence in U.S. law and that of the other Contracting State by referring to a resident as a person who, under the laws of a Contracting State, is subject to tax there by reason of his domicile, residence, citizenship, place of management, place of incorporation or any other similar criterion. Thus, residents of the United States include aliens who are considered U.S. residents under Code section 7701(b). Paragraph 1 also specifically includes the two Contracting States, and political subdivisions and local authorities of the two States, as residents for purposes of the Convention.

Certain entities that are nominally subject to tax but that in practice are rarely required to pay tax also would generally be treated as residents and therefore accorded treaty benefits. For example, a U.S. Regulated Investment Company (RIC) and a U.S. Real Estate Investment Trust (REIT) are residents of the United States for purposes of the treaty. Although the income earned by these entities normally is not subject to U.S. tax in the hands of the entity, they are taxable to the extent that they do not currently distribute their profits, and therefore may be regarded as "liable to tax." They also must satisfy a number of requirements under the Code in order to be entitled to special tax treatment.

A person who is liable to tax in a Contracting State only in respect of income from sources within that State or capital situated therein or of profits attributable to a permanent establishment in that State will not be treated as a resident of that Contracting State for purposes of the Convention. Thus, a consular official of the other Contracting State who is posted in the United States, who may be subject to U.S. tax on U.S. source investment income, but is not taxable in the United States on non-U.S. source income (see Code section 7701(b)(5)(B)), would not be considered a resident of the United States for purposes of the Convention. Similarly, an enterprise of the other Contracting State with a permanent establishment in the United States is not, by virtue of that permanent establishment, a resident of the United States. The enterprise generally is subject to U.S. tax only with respect to its income that is attributable to the U.S. permanent establishment, not with respect to its worldwide income, as it would be if it were a U.S. resident.

Paragraph 2

Paragraph 2 provides that certain tax-exempt entities such as pension funds and charitable organizations will be regarded as residents of a Contracting State regardless of whether they are generally liable to income tax in the State where they are established. The paragraph applies to legal persons organized under the laws of a Contracting State and established and maintained in that State to provide pensions or other similar benefits pursuant to a plan, or exclusively for religious, charitable, scientific, artistic, cultural, or educational purposes. Thus, a section 501(c) organization organized in the United States (such as a U.S. charity) that is generally exempt from tax under U.S. law is a resident of the United States for all purposes of the Convention.

Paragraph 3

If, under the laws of the two Contracting States, and, thus, under paragraph 1, an individual is deemed to be a resident of both Contracting States, a series of tie-breaker rules are provided in paragraph 3 to determine a single State of residence for that individual. These tests are to be applied in the order in which they are stated. The first test is based on where the individual has a permanent home. If that test is inconclusive because the individual has a permanent home available to him in both States, he will be considered to be a resident of the Contracting State where his personal and economic relations are closest (i.e., the location of his "centre of vital interests"). If that test is also inconclusive, or if he does not have a permanent home available to him in either State, he will be treated as a resident of the Contracting State where he maintains an habitual abode. If he has an habitual abode in both States or in neither of them, he will be treated as a resident of the Contracting State of which he is a national. If he is a national of both States or of neither, the matter will be considered by the competent authorities, who will assign a single State of residence.

Paragraph 4

Paragraph 4 seeks to settle dual-residence issues for companies. A company is treated as resident in the United States if it is created or organized under the laws of the United States or a political subdivision. If, as is frequently the case, a company is treated as a resident of the other Contracting State if it is either incorporated or managed and controlled there, dual residence can arise in the case of a U.S. company that is managed and controlled in the other Contracting State. In other cases, a company may be a dual resident because it was originally incorporated in one Contracting State but has "continued" into the other Contracting State. Paragraph 4 thus attempts to deal with each of these situations.

Under paragraph 4, the residence of a dual resident company will be in the Contracting State under the laws of which it is created or organized if it is created or organized under the laws of only one of the other Contracting States. Thus, if a company is a resident of the United States because it is incorporated under the laws of one of the states and is a resident of the other Contracting State because its place of effective management is in that State, then it will be a resident only of the United States. However, if the incorporation test does not resolve the question because, for example, the company was incorporated in one Contracting State and continued into the other Contracting State, but the first-mentioned Contracting State does not recognize the migration and continues to treat the company as a resident, then the competent authorities will try to determine a single State of residence for the company.

If the competent authorities do not reach an agreement on a single State of residence, that company may not claim any benefit accorded to residents of a Contracting State by the Convention. The company may, however, claim any benefits that are not limited to residents, such as those provided by paragraph 1 of Article 24 (Non-Discrimination). Thus, for example, a State cannot discriminate against a dual resident company.

Dual resident companies also may be treated as a resident of a Contracting State for purposes other than that of obtaining benefits under the Convention. For example, if a dual resident company pays a dividend to a resident of the other Contracting State, the U.S. paying agent would withhold on that dividend at the appropriate treaty rate because reduced withholding is a benefit enjoyed by the resident of the other Contracting State, not by the dual resident company. The dual resident company that paid the dividend would, for this purpose, be treated as a resident of the United States under the Convention. In addition, information relating to dual resident companies can be exchanged under the Convention because, by its terms, Article 26 (Exchange of Information and Administrative Assistance) is not limited to residents of the Contracting States.

Paragraph 5

Dual residents other than individuals or companies (such as trusts or estates) are addressed by paragraph 5. If such a person is, under the rules of paragraph 1, resident in both Contracting States, the competent authorities shall seek to determine a single State of residence for that person for purposes of the Convention.

ARTICLE 5   (PERMANENT ESTABLISHMENT)

This Article defines the term "permanent establishment," a term that is significant for several articles of the Convention. The existence of a permanent establishment in a Contracting State is necessary under Article 7 (Business Profits) for the taxation by that State of the business profits of a resident of the other Contracting State. Articles 10, 11 and 12 (dealing with dividends, interest, and royalties, respectively) provide for reduced rates of tax at source on payments of these items of income to a resident of the other State only when the income is not attributable to a permanent establishment that the recipient has in the source State. The concept is also relevant in determining which Contracting State may tax certain gains under Article 13 (Gains) and certain "other income" under Article 21 (Other Income).

Paragraph 1

The basic definition of the term "permanent establishment" is contained in paragraph 1. As used in the Convention, the term means a fixed place of business through which the business of an enterprise is wholly or partly carried on. As indicated in the OECD Commentary to Article 5 (see paragraphs 4 through 8), a general principle to be observed in determining whether a permanent establishment exists is that the place of business must be "fixed" in the sense that a particular building or physical location is used by the enterprise for the conduct of its business, and that it must be foreseeable that the enterprise's use of this building or other physical location will be more than temporary.

Paragraph 2

Paragraph 2 lists a number of types of fixed places of business that constitute a permanent establishment. This list is illustrative and non-exclusive. According to paragraph 2, the term permanent establishment includes a place of management, a branch, an office, a factory, a workshop, and a mine, oil or gas well, quarry or other place of extraction of natural resources.

Paragraph 3

This paragraph provides rules to determine whether a building site or a construction, assembly or installation project, or an installation or drilling rig or ship used for the exploration of natural resources constitutes a permanent establishment for the contractor, driller, etc. Such a site or activity does not create a permanent establishment unless the site, project, etc. lasts, or the exploration activity continues, for more than twelve months. It is only necessary to refer to "exploration" and not "exploitation" in this context because exploitation activities are defined to constitute a permanent establishment under subparagraph (f) of paragraph 2. Thus, a drilling rig does not constitute a permanent establishment if a well is drilled in only six months, but if production begins in the following month the well becomes a permanent establishment as of that date.

The twelve-month test applies separately to each site or project. The twelve-month period begins when work (including preparatory work carried on by the enterprise) physically begins in a Contracting State. A series of contracts or projects by a contractor that are interdependent both commercially and geographically are to be treated as a single project for purposes of applying the twelve-month threshold test. For example, the construction of a housing development would be considered as a single project even if each house were constructed for a different purchaser.

In applying this paragraph, time spent by a sub-contractor on a building site is counted as time spent by the general contractor at the site for purposes of determining whether the general contractor has a permanent establishment. However, for the sub-contractor itself to be treated as having a permanent establishment, the sub-contractor's activities at the site must last for more than 12 months. If a sub-contractor is on a site intermittently, then, for purposes of applying the 12-month rule, time is measured from the first day the sub-contractor is on the site until the last day (*i.e.*, intervening days that the sub-contractor is not on the site are counted).

These interpretations of the Article are based on the Commentary to paragraph 3 of Article 5 of the OECD Model, which contains language that is substantially the same as that in the Convention. These interpretations are consistent with the generally accepted international interpretation of the relevant language in paragraph 3 of Article 5 of the Convention.

If the twelve-month threshold is exceeded, the site or project constitutes a permanent establishment from the first day of activity.

Paragraph 4

This paragraph contains exceptions to the general rule of paragraph 1, listing a number of activities that may be carried on through a fixed place of business but which nevertheless do not create a permanent establishment. The use of facilities solely to store, display or deliver merchandise belonging to an enterprise does not constitute a permanent establishment of that enterprise. The maintenance of a stock of goods belonging to an enterprise solely for the purpose of storage, display or delivery, or solely for the purpose of processing by another enterprise does not give rise to a permanent establishment of the first-mentioned enterprise. The maintenance of a fixed place of business solely for the purpose of purchasing goods or merchandise, or for collecting information, for the enterprise, or for other activities that have a preparatory or auxiliary character for the enterprise, such as advertising, or the supply of information, do not constitute a permanent establishment of the enterprise. Moreover, subparagraph 4(f) provides that a combination of the activities described in the other subparagraphs of paragraph 4 will not give rise to a permanent establishment if the combination results in an overall activity that is of a preparatory or auxiliary character.

Paragraph 5

Paragraphs 5 and 6 specify when activities carried on by an agent or other person acting on behalf of an enterprise create a permanent establishment of that enterprise. Under paragraph 5, a person is deemed to create a permanent establishment of the enterprise if that person has and habitually exercises an authority to conclude contracts that are binding on the enterprise. If, however, for example, his activities are limited to those activities specified in paragraph 4 which would not constitute a permanent establishment if carried on by the enterprise through a fixed place of business, the person does not create a permanent establishment of the enterprise.

The OECD Model uses the term "in the name of that enterprise" rather than "binding on the enterprise." This difference is intended to be a clarification rather than a substantive difference. As indicated in paragraph 32 to the OECD Commentaries on Article 5, paragraph 5 of the Article is intended to encompass persons who have "sufficient authority to bind the enterprise's participation in the business activity in the State concerned."

The contracts referred to in paragraph 5 are those relating to the essential business operations of the enterprise, rather than ancillary activities. For example, if the person has no authority to conclude contracts in the name of the enterprise with its customers for, say, the sale of the goods produced by the enterprise, but it can enter into service contracts in the name of the enterprise for the enterprise's business equipment, this contracting authority would not fall within the scope of the paragraph, even if exercised regularly.

Paragraph 6

Under paragraph 6, an enterprise is not deemed to have a permanent establishment in a Contracting State merely because it carries on business in that State through an independent agent, including a broker or general commission agent, if the agent is acting in the ordinary course of his business as an independent agent. Thus, there are two conditions that must be satisfied: the agent must be both legally and economically independent of the enterprise, and the agent must be acting in the ordinary course of its business in carrying out activities on behalf of the enterprise.

Whether the agent and the enterprise are independent is a factual determination. Among the questions to be considered are the extent to which the agent operates on the basis of instructions from the enterprise. An agent that is subject to detailed instructions regarding the conduct of its operations or comprehensive control by the enterprise is not legally independent.

In determining whether the agent is economically independent, a relevant factor is the extent to which the agent bears business risk. Business risk refers primarily to risk of loss. An independent agent typically bears risk of loss from its own activities. In the absence of other factors that would establish dependence, an agent that shares business risk with the enterprise, or has its own business risk, is economically independent because its business activities are not integrated with those of the principal. Conversely, an agent that bears little or no risk from the activities it performs is not economically independent and therefore is not described in paragraph 6.

Another relevant factor in determining whether an agent is economically independent is whether the agent acts exclusively or nearly exclusively for the principal. Such a relationship may indicate that the principal has economic control over the agent. A number of principals acting in concert also may have economic control over an agent. The limited scope of the agent's activities and the agent's dependence on a single source of income may indicate that the agent lacks economic independence. It should be borne in mind, however, that exclusivity is not in itself a conclusive test; an agent may be economically independent notwithstanding an exclusive relationship with the principal if it has the capacity to diversify and acquire other clients without substantial modifications to its current business and without substantial harm to its business profits. Thus, exclusivity should be viewed merely as a pointer to further investigation of the relationship between the principal and the agent. Each case must be addressed on the basis of its own facts and circumstances.

Paragraph 7

This paragraph clarifies that a company that is a resident of a Contracting State is not deemed to have a permanent establishment in the other Contracting State merely because it controls, or is controlled by, a company that is a resident of that other Contracting State, or that carries on business in that other Contracting State. The determination whether a permanent establishment exists is made solely on the basis of the factors described in paragraphs 1 through 6 of the Article. Whether a company is a permanent establishment of a related company, therefore, is based solely on those factors and not on the ownership or control relationship between the companies.

ARTICLE 6   (INCOME FROM REAL PROPERTY)

Paragraph 1

The first paragraph of Article 6 states the general rule that income of a resident of a Contracting State derived from real property situated in the other Contracting State may be taxed in the Contracting State in which the property is situated. The paragraph specifies that income from real property includes income from agriculture and forestry. Given the availability of the net election in paragraph 5, taxpayers generally should be able to obtain the same tax treatment in the situs country regardless of whether the income is treated as business profits or real property income.

This Article does not grant an exclusive taxing right to the situs State; the situs State is merely given the primary right to tax. The Article does not impose any limitation in terms of rate or form of tax on the situs State, except that, as provided in paragraph 5, the situs State must allow the taxpayer an election to be taxed on a net basis.

Paragraph 2

The term "real property" is defined in paragraph 2 by reference to the internal law definition in the situs State. In the case of the United States, the term has the meaning given to it by Reg. § 1.897-1(b). In addition to the statutory definitions in the two Contracting States, the paragraph specifies certain additional classes of property that, regardless of internal law definitions, are within the scope of the term for purposes of the Convention. This expanded definition conforms to that in the OECD Model. The definition of "real property" for purposes of Article 6 is more limited than the expansive definition of "real property" in paragraph 1 of Article 13 (Capital Gains). The Article 13 term includes not only real property as defined in Article 6 but certain other interests in real property.

Paragraph 3

Paragraph 3 makes clear that all forms of income derived from the exploitation of real property are taxable in the Contracting State in which the property is situated. This includes income from any use of real property, including, but not limited to, income from direct use by the owner (in which case income may be imputed to the owner for tax purposes) and rental income from the letting of real property. In the case of a net lease of real property, if a net election has not been made, the gross rental payment (before deductible expenses incurred by the lessee) is treated as income from the property.

Other income closely associated with real property is covered by other Articles of the Convention, however, and not Article 6. For example, income from the disposition of an interest in real property is not considered "derived" from real property; taxation of that income is addressed in Article 13 (Gains). Interest paid on a mortgage on real property would be covered by Article 11 (Interest). Distributions by a U.S. Real Estate Investment Trust or certain regulated investment companies would fall under Article 13 (Gains) in the case of distributions of U.S. real property gain or Article 10 (Dividends) in the case of distributions treated as dividends. Finally, distributions from a United States Real Property Holding Corporation are not considered to be income from the exploitation of real property; such payments would fall under Article 10 or 13.

Paragraph 4

This paragraph specifies that the basic rule of paragraph 1 (as elaborated in paragraph 3) applies to income from real property of an enterprise. This clarifies that the situs country may tax the real property income (including rental income) of a resident of the other Contracting State in the absence of attribution to a permanent establishment in the situs State. This provision represents an exception to the general rule under Articles 7 (Business Profits) that income must be attributable to a permanent establishment in order to be taxable in the situs state.

Paragraph 5

The paragraph provides that a resident of one Contracting State that derives real property income from the other may elect, for any taxable year, to be subject to tax in that other State on a net basis, as though the income were attributable to a permanent establishment in that other State. The election may be terminated with the consent of the competent authority of the situs State. In the United States, revocation will be granted in accordance with the provisions of Treas. Reg. section 1.871-10(d)(2).

ARTICLE 7   (BUSINESS PROFITS)

This Article provides rules for the taxation by a Contracting State of the business profits of an enterprise of the other Contracting State.

Paragraph 1

Paragraph 1 states the general rule that business profits of an enterprise of one Contracting State may not be taxed by the other Contracting State unless the enterprise carries on business in that other Contracting State through a permanent establishment (as defined in Article 5 (Permanent Establishment)) situated there. When that condition is met, the State in which the permanent establishment is situated may tax the enterprise on the income that is attributable to the permanent establishment.

Although the Convention does not include a definition of "business profits," the term is intended to cover income derived from any trade or business. In accordance with this broad definition, the term "business profits" includes income attributable to notional principal contracts and other financial instruments to the extent that the income is attributable to a trade or business of dealing in such instruments or is otherwise related to a trade or business (as in the case of a notional principal contract entered into for the purpose of hedging currency risk arising from an active trade or business). Any other income derived from such instruments is, unless specifically covered in another article, dealt with under Article 21 (Other Income).

The term "business profits" also includes income derived by an enterprise from the rental of tangible personal property (unless such tangible personal property consists of aircraft, ships or containers, income from which is addressed by Article 8 (Shipping and Air Transport)). The inclusion of income derived by an enterprise from the rental of tangible personal property in business profits means that such income earned by a resident of a Contracting State can be taxed by the other Contracting State only if the income is attributable to a permanent establishment maintained by the resident in that other State, and, if the income is taxable, it can be taxed only on a net basis. Income from the rental of tangible personal property that is not derived in connection with a trade or business is dealt with in Article 21 (Other Income).

In addition, as a result of the definitions of "enterprise" and "business" in Article 3 (General Definitions), the term includes income derived from the furnishing of personal services. Thus, a consulting firm resident in one State whose employees or partners perform services in the other State through a permanent establishment may be taxed in that other State on a net basis under Article 7, and not under Article 14 (Income from Employment), which applies only to income of employees. With respect to the enterprise's employees themselves, however, their salary remains subject to Article 14.

Because this article applies to income earned by an enterprise from the furnishing of personal services, the article also applies to income derived by a partner resident in a Contracting State that is attributable to personal services performed in the other Contracting State through a partnership with a permanent establishment in that other State. Income which may be taxed under this article includes all income attributable to the permanent establishment in respect of the performance of the personal services carried on by the partnership (whether by the partner himself, other partners in the partnership, or by employees assisting the partners) and any income from activities ancillary to the performance of those services (*e.g.*, charges for facsimile services).

The application of Article 7 to a service partnership may be illustrated by the following example: a partnership formed in the other Contracting State has five partners (who agree to split profits equally), four of whom are resident and perform personal services only in the other Contracting State at Office A, and one of whom performs personal services at Office B, a permanent establishment in the United States. In this case, the four partners of the partnership resident in the other Contracting State may be taxed in the United States in respect of their share of the income attributable to the permanent establishment, Office B. The services giving rise to income which may be attributed to the permanent establishment would include not only the services performed by the one resident partner, but also, for example, if one of the four other partners came to the United States and worked on an Office B matter there, the income in respect of those services. Income from the services performed by the visiting partner would be subject to tax in the United States regardless of whether the visiting partner actually visited or used Office B while performing services in the United States.

Paragraph 2

Paragraph 2 provides rules for the attribution of business profits to a permanent establishment. The Contracting States will attribute to a permanent establishment the profits that it would have earned had it been a distinct and separate enterprise engaged in the same or similar activities under the same or similar conditions and dealing wholly independently with the enterprise of which it is a permanent establishment.

The "attributable to" concept of paragraph 2 provides an alternative to the analogous but somewhat different "effectively connected" concept in Code section 864(c). In effect, paragraph 2 allows the United States to tax the lesser of two amounts of income: the amount determined by applying U.S. rules regarding the calculation of effectively connected income and the amount determined under Article 7 of the Convention. That is, a taxpayer may choose the set of rules that results in the lowest amount of taxable income, but may not mix and match.

In some cases, the amount of income "attributable to" a permanent establishment under Article 7 may be greater than the amount of income that would be treated as "effectively connected" to a U.S. trade or business under section 864. For example, a taxpayer that has a significant amount of foreign source royalty income attributable to a U.S. branch may find that it will pay less tax in the United States by applying section 864(c) of the Code, rather than the rules of Article 7, if the foreign source royalties are not derived in the active conduct of a trade or business and thus would not be effectively connected income. But, as described in the Technical Explanation to Article 1(2), if it does so, it may not then use Article 7 principles to exempt other income that would be effectively connected to the U.S. trade or business. Conversely, if it uses Article 7 principles to exempt other effectively connected income that is not attributable to its U.S. permanent establishment, then it must include the foreign source royalties in its net taxable income even though such royalties would not constitute effectively connected income.

In the case of financial institutions, the use of internal dealings to allocate income within an enterprise may produce results under Article 7 that are significantly different than the results under the effectively connected income rules. For example, income from interbranch notional principal contracts may be taken into account under Article 7, notwithstanding that such transactions may be ignored for purposes of U.S. domestic law. Under the consistency rule described above, a financial institution that conducts different lines of business through its U.S. permanent establishment may not choose to apply the rules of the Code with respect to some lines of business and Article 7 of the Convention with respect to others. If it chooses to use the rules of Article 7 to allocate its income from its trading book, it may not then use U.S. domestic rules to allocate income from its loan portfolio.

The profits attributable to a permanent establishment may be from sources within or without a Contracting State. However, as stated in paragraph 2, the business profits attributable to a permanent establishment include only those profits derived from the assets used, risks assumed, and activities performed by, the permanent establishment.

The language of paragraph 2, when combined with paragraph 3 dealing with the allowance of deductions for expenses incurred for the purposes of earning the profits, incorporates the arm's-length standard for purposes of determining the profits attributable to a permanent establishment. As noted below with respect to Article 9, the United States generally interprets the arm's length standard in a manner consistent with the OECD Transfer Pricing Guidelines.

The notes confirm that the arm's length method of paragraphs 2 and 3 consists of applying the OECD Transfer Pricing Guidelines, but taking into account the different economic and legal circumstances of a single legal entity (as opposed to separate but associated enterprises). Thus, any of the methods used in the Transfer

Pricing Guidelines, including profits methods, may be used as appropriate and in accordance with the Transfer Pricing Guidelines. However, the use of the Transfer Pricing Guidelines applies only for purposes of attributing profits within the legal entity. It does not create legal obligations or other tax consequences that would result from transactions having independent legal significance.

For example, an entity that operates through branches rather than separate subsidiaries will have lower capital requirements because all of the assets of the entity are available to support all of the entity's liabilities (with some exceptions attributable to local regulatory restrictions). This is the reason that most commercial banks and some insurance companies operate through branches rather than subsidiaries. The benefit that comes from such lower capital costs must be allocated among the branches in an appropriate manner. This issue does not arise in the case of an enterprise that operates through separate entities, since each entity will have to be separately capitalized or will have to compensate another entity for providing capital (usually through a guarantee).

Under U.S. domestic regulations, internal "transactions" generally are not recognized because they do not have legal significance. In contrast, the rule provided by the notes is that such internal dealings may be used to allocate income in cases where the dealings accurately reflect the allocation of risk within the enterprise. One example is that of global trading in securities. In many cases, banks use internal swap transactions to transfer risk from one branch to a central location where traders have the expertise to manage that particular type of risk. Under the Convention, such a bank may also use such swap transactions as a means of allocating income between the branches, if use of that method is the "best method" within the meaning of regulation section 1.482-1(c). The books of a branch will not be respected, however, when the results are inconsistent with a functional analysis. So, for example, income from a transaction that is booked in a particular branch (or home office) will not be treated as attributable to that location if the sales and risk management functions that generate the income are performed in another location.

Because the use of profits methods is permissible under paragraph 2, it is not necessary for the Convention to include a provision corresponding to paragraph 4 of Article 7 of the OECD Model.

Paragraph 3

This paragraph is the same as paragraph 3 of Article 7 of the OECD Model. Paragraph 3 provides that in determining the business profits of a permanent establishment, deductions shall be allowed for the expenses incurred for the purposes of the permanent establishment, ensuring that business profits will be taxed on a net basis. This rule is not limited to expenses incurred exclusively for the purposes of the permanent establishment, but includes expenses incurred for the purposes of the enterprise as a whole, or that part of the enterprise that includes the permanent establishment. Deductions are to be allowed regardless of which accounting unit of the enterprise books the expenses, so long as they are incurred for the purposes of the permanent establishment. For example, a portion of the interest expense recorded on the books of the home office in one State may be deducted by a permanent establishment in the other if properly allocable thereto.

The amount of expense that must be allowed as a deduction is determined by applying the arm's length principle.

As noted above, the notes provide that the OECD Transfer Pricing Guidelines apply, by analogy, in determining the profits attributable to a permanent establishment. Accordingly, a permanent establishment may deduct payments made to its head office or another branch in compensation for services performed for the benefit of the branch. The method to be used in calculating that amount will depend on the terms of the arrangements between the branches and head office. For example, the enterprise could have a policy, expressed in writing, under which each business unit could use the services of lawyers employed by the head office. At the end of each year, the costs of employing the lawyers would be allocated to each business unit according to the amount of services used by that business unit during the year. Since this appears to be a kind of cost-sharing arrangement and the allocation of costs is based on the benefits received by each business unit, it would be an acceptable means of determining a permanent establishment's deduction for legal expenses. Alternatively, the head office could agree to employ lawyers at its own risk, and to charge an arm's length price for legal services performed for a particular business unit. If the lawyers were under-utilized, and the "fees" received from the business units were less than the cost of employing the lawyers, then the head office would bear the excess cost. If the "fees" exceeded the cost of employing the lawyers, then the head office would keep the excess to compensate it for assuming the risk of employing the lawyers. If the enterprise acted in accordance with this agreement, this method would be an acceptable alternative method for calculating a permanent establishment's deduction for legal expenses.

The notes also specify that a permanent establishment cannot be funded entirely with debt, but must have sufficient capital to carry on its activities as if it were a distinct and separate enterprise. To the extent that the permanent establishment does not have such capital, a Contracting State may attribute such capital to the permanent establishment and deny an interest deduction to the extent necessary to reflect that capital attribution. The method prescribed by U.S. domestic law for making this attribution is found in Treas. Reg. Section 1.882-5. Both Section 1.882-5 and the method prescribed in the notes start from the premise that all of the capital of the enterprise supports all of the assets and risks of the enterprise, and therefore the entire capital of the enterprise must be allocated to its various businesses and offices.

However, section 1.882-5 does not take into account the fact that some assets create more risk for the enterprise than do other assets. An independent enterprise would need less capital to support a perfectly-hedged U.S. Treasury security than it would need to support an equity security or other asset with significant market and/or credit risk. Accordingly, in some cases section 1.882-5 would require a taxpayer to allocate more capital to the United States, and therefore would reduce the taxpayer's interest deduction more, than is appropriate. To address these cases, the notes allow a taxpayer to apply a more flexible approach that takes into account the relative risk of its assets in the various jurisdictions in which it does business. In particular, in the case of financial institutions other than insurance companies, the amount of capital attributable to a permanent establishment is determined by allocating the institution's total equity between its various offices on the basis of the proportion of the financial institution's risk-weighted assets attributable to each of them. This recognizes the fact that financial institutions are in many cases required to risk-weight their assets for regulatory purposes and, in other cases, will do so for business reasons even if not required to do so by regulators. However, risk-weighting is more complicated than the method prescribed by Section 1.882-5. Accordingly, to ease this administrative burden, taxpayers may choose to apply the principles of Treas. Reg. Section 1.882-5(c) to determine the amount of capital allocable to its U.S. permanent establishment, in lieu of determining its allocable capital under the risk-weighed capital allocation method provided by the notes, even if it has otherwise chosen to apply the principles of Article 7 rather than the effectively connected income rules of U.S. domestic law.

Paragraph 4

Paragraph 4 provides that no business profits can be attributed to a permanent establishment merely because it purchases goods or merchandise for the enterprise of which it is a part. This paragraph is essentially identical to paragraph 5 of Article 7 of the OECD Model. This rule applies only to an office that performs functions for the enterprise in addition to purchasing. The income attribution issue does not arise if the sole activity of the office is the purchase of goods or merchandise because such activity does not give rise to a permanent establishment under Article 5 (Permanent Establishment). A common situation in which paragraph 4 is relevant is one in which a permanent establishment purchases raw materials for the enterprise's manufacturing operation conducted outside the United States and sells the manufactured product. While business profits may be attributable to the permanent establishment with respect to its sales activities, no profits are attributable to it with respect to its purchasing activities.

Paragraph 5

Paragraph 5 provides that profits shall be determined by the same method each year, unless there is good reason to change the method used. This rule assures consistent tax treatment over time for permanent establishments. It limits the ability of both the Contracting State and the enterprise to change accounting methods to be applied to the permanent establishment. It does not, however, restrict a Contracting State from imposing additional requirements, such as the rules under Code section 481, to prevent amounts from being duplicated or omitted following a change in accounting method. Such adjustments may be necessary, for example, if the taxpayer switches from using the domestic rules under section 864 in one year to using the rules of Article 7 in the next. Also, if the taxpayer switches from Convention-based rules to U.S. domestic rules, it may need to meet certain deadlines for making elections that are not necessary when applying the rules of the Convention.

Paragraph 6

Paragraph 6 coordinates the provisions of Article 7 and other provisions of the Convention. Under this paragraph, when business profits include items of income that are dealt with separately under other articles of the Convention, the provisions of those articles will, except when they specifically provide to the contrary, take precedence over the provisions of Article 7. For example, the taxation of dividends will be determined by the rules of Article 10 (Dividends), and not by Article 7, except where, as provided in paragraph 6 of Article 10, the dividend is attributable to a permanent establishment. In the latter case the provisions of Article 7 apply. Thus, an enterprise of one State deriving dividends from the other State may not rely on Article 7 to exempt those dividends from tax at source if they are not attributable to a permanent establishment of the enterprise in the other State. By the same token, if the dividends are attributable to a permanent establishment in the other State, the dividends may be taxed on a net income basis at the source State full corporate tax rate, rather than on a gross basis under Article 10 (Dividends).

As provided in Article 8 (Shipping and Air Transport), income derived from shipping and air transport activities in international traffic described in that Article is taxable only in the country of residence of the enterprise regardless of whether it is attributable to a permanent establishment situated in the source State.

Paragraph 7

Paragraph 7 incorporates into the Convention the rule of Code section 864(c)(6). Like the Code section on which it is based, paragraph 7 provides that any income or gain attributable to a permanent establishment during its existence is taxable in the Contracting State where the permanent establishment is situated, even if the payment of that income or gain is deferred until after the permanent establishment ceases to exist. This rule applies with respect to paragraphs 1 and 2 of Article 7 (Business Profits), paragraph 6 of Article 10 (Dividends), paragraph 4 of Article 11 (Interest), paragraph 3 of Articles 12 (Royalties) and 13 (Gains) and paragraph 2 of Article 21 (Other Income).

The effect of this rule can be illustrated by the following example. Assume a company that is a resident of the other Contracting State and that maintains a permanent establishment in the United States winds up the permanent establishment's business and sells the permanent establishment's inventory and assets to a U.S. buyer at the end of year 1 in exchange for an interest-bearing installment obligation payable in full at the end of year 3. Despite the fact that Article 13's threshold requirement for U.S. taxation is not met in year 3 because the company has no permanent establishment in the United States, the United States may tax the deferred income payment recognized by the company in year 3.

Relationship to Other Articles

This Article is subject to the saving clause of paragraph 4 of Article 1 (General Scope) of the Model. Thus, if a citizen of the United States who is a resident of the other Contracting State under the treaty derives business profits from the United States that are not attributable to a permanent establishment in the United States, the United States may, subject to the special foreign tax credit rules of paragraph 4 of Article 23 (Relief from Double Taxation), tax those profits, notwithstanding the provision of paragraph 1 of this Article which would exempt the income from U.S. tax.

The benefits of this Article are also subject to Article 22 (Limitation on Benefits). Thus, an enterprise of the other Contracting State and that derives income effectively connected with a U.S. trade or business may not claim the benefits of Article 7 unless the resident carrying on the enterprise qualifies for such benefits under Article 22.

ARTICLE 8   (SHIPPING AND AIR TRANSPORT)

This Article governs the taxation of profits from the operation of ships and aircraft in international traffic. The term "international traffic" is defined in subparagraph 1(f) of Article 3 (General Definitions).

Paragraph 1

Paragraph 1 provides that profits derived by an enterprise of a Contracting State from the operation in international traffic of ships or aircraft are taxable only in that Contracting State. Because paragraph 6 of Article 7 (Business Profits) defers to Article 8 with respect to shipping income, such income derived by a resident of one of the Contracting States may not be taxed in the other State even if the enterprise has a permanent establishment in that other State. Thus, if a U.S. airline has a ticket office in the other State, that State may not tax the airline's profits attributable to that office under Article 7. Since entities engaged in international transportation activities normally will have many permanent establishments in a number of countries, the rule avoids difficulties that would be encountered in attributing income to multiple permanent establishments if the income were covered by Article 7 (Business Profits).

Paragraph 2

The income from the operation of ships or aircraft in international traffic that is exempt from tax under paragraph 1 is defined in paragraph 2.

In addition to income derived directly from the operation of ships and aircraft in international traffic, this definition also includes certain items of rental income. First, income of an enterprise of a Contracting State from the rental of ships or aircraft on a full basis (i.e., with crew) is income of the lessor from the operation of ships and aircraft in international traffic and, therefore, is exempt from tax in the other Contracting State under paragraph 1. Also, paragraph 2 encompasses income from the lease of ships or aircraft on a bareboat basis (i.e., without crew), either when the income is incidental to other income of the lessor from the operation of ships or aircraft in international traffic, or when the ships or aircraft are operated in international traffic by the lessee. If neither of those two conditions apply, income from the bareboat rentals would constitute business profits. The coverage of Article 8 is therefore broader than that of Article 8 of the OECD Model, which covers bareboat leasing only when it is incidental to other income of the lessor from the operation of ships of aircraft in international traffic.

Paragraph 2 also clarifies, consistent with the Commentary to Article 8 of the OECD Model, that income earned by an enterprise from the inland transport of property or passengers within either Contracting State falls within Article 8 if the transport is undertaken as part of the international transport of property or passengers by the enterprise. Thus, if a U.S. shipping company contracts to carry property from the other Contracting State to a U.S. city and, as part of that contract, it transports the property by truck from its point of origin to an airport in the other Contracting State (or it contracts with a trucking company to carry the property to the airport) the income earned by the U.S. shipping company from the overland leg of the journey would be taxable only in the United States. Similarly, Article 8 also would apply to all of the income derived from a contract for the international transport of goods, even if the goods were transported to the port by a lighter, not by the vessel that carried the goods in international waters.

Finally, certain non-transport activities that are an integral part of the services performed by a transport company, or are ancillary to the enterprise's operation of ships or aircraft in international traffic, are understood to be covered in paragraph 1, though they are not specified in paragraph 2. These include, for example, the provision of goods and services by engineers, ground and equipment maintenance and staff, cargo handlers, catering staff and customer services personnel. Where the enterprise provides such goods to, or performs services for, other enterprises and such activities are directly connected with or ancillary to the enterprise's operation of ships or aircraft in international traffic, the profits from the provision of such goods and services to other enterprises will fall under this paragraph.

For example, enterprises engaged in the operation of ships or aircraft in international traffic may enter into pooling arrangements for the purposes of reducing the costs of maintaining facilities needed for the operation of their ships or aircraft in other countries. For instance, where an airline enterprise agrees (for example, under an International Airlines Technical Pool agreement) to provide spare parts or maintenance services to other airlines landing at a particular location (which allows it to benefit from these services at other locations), activities carried on pursuant to that agreement will be ancillary to the operation of aircraft in international traffic by the enterprise.

Also, advertising that the enterprise may do for other enterprises in magazines offered aboard ships or aircraft that it operates in international traffic or at its business locations, such as ticket offices, is ancillary to its operation of these ships or aircraft. Profits generated by such advertising fall within this paragraph. Income earned by concessionaires, however, is not covered by Article 8. These interpretations of paragraph 1 also are consistent with the Commentary to Article 8 of the OECD Model.

Paragraph 3

Under this paragraph, profits of an enterprise of a Contracting State from the use, maintenance or rental of containers (including equipment for their transport) are exempt from tax in the other Contracting State, unless those containers are used for transport solely in the other Contracting State. This result obtains under paragraph 3 regardless of whether the recipient of the income is engaged in the operation of ships or aircraft in international traffic, and regardless of whether the enterprise has a permanent establishment in the other Contracting State. Only income from the use, maintenance or rental of containers that is incidental to other income from international traffic is covered by Article 8 of the OECD Model.

Paragraph 4

This paragraph clarifies that the provisions of paragraphs 1 and 3 also apply to profits derived by an enterprise of a Contracting State from participation in a pool, joint business or international operating agency. This refers to various arrangements for international cooperation by carriers in shipping and air transport. For example, airlines from two countries may agree to share the transport of passengers between the two countries. They each will fly the same number of flights per week and share the revenues from that route equally, regardless of the number of passengers that each airline actually transports. Paragraph 4 makes clear that with respect to each carrier the income dealt with in the Article is that carrier's share of the total transport, not the income derived from the passengers actually carried by the airline. This paragraph corresponds to paragraph 4 of Article 8 of the OECD Model.

Relationship to Other Articles

The taxation of gains from the alienation of ships, aircraft or containers is not dealt with in this Article but in paragraph 4 of Article 13 (Gains).

As with other benefits of the Convention, the benefit of exclusive residence country taxation under Article 8 is available to an enterprise only if it is entitled to benefits under Article 22 (Limitation on Benefits).

This Article also is subject to the saving clause of paragraph 4 of Article 1 (General Scope) of the Model. Thus, if a citizen of the United States who is a resident of the other Contracting State derives profits from the operation of ships or aircraft in international traffic, notwithstanding the exclusive residence country taxation in paragraph 1 of Article 8, the United States may, subject to the special foreign tax credit rules of paragraph 4 of Article 23 (Relief from Double Taxation), tax those profits as part of the worldwide income of the citizen. (This is an unlikely situation, however, because non-tax considerations (e.g., insurance) generally result in shipping activities being carried on in corporate form.)

ARTICLE 9   (ASSOCIATED ENTERPRISES)

This Article incorporates in the Convention the arm's-length principle reflected in the U.S. domestic transfer pricing provisions, particularly Code section 482. It provides that when related enterprises engage in a transaction on terms that are not arm's-length, the Contracting States may make appropriate adjustments to the taxable income and tax liability of such related enterprises to reflect what the income and tax of these enterprises with respect to the transaction would have been had there been an arm's-length relationship between them.

Paragraph 1

This paragraph is essentially the same as its counterpart in the OECD Model. It addresses the situation where an enterprise of a Contracting State is related to an enterprise of the other Contracting State, and there are arrangements or conditions imposed between the enterprises in their commercial or financial relations that are different from those that would have existed in the absence of the relationship. Under these circumstances, the Contracting States may adjust the income (or loss) of the enterprise to reflect what it would have been in the absence of such a relationship.

The paragraph identifies the relationships between enterprises that serve as a prerequisite to application of the Article. As the Commentary to the OECD Model makes clear, the necessary element in these relationships is effective control, which is also the standard for purposes of section 482. Thus, the Article applies if an enterprise of one State participates directly or indirectly in the management, control, or capital of the enterprise of the other State. Also, the Article applies if any third person or persons participate directly or indirectly in the management, control, or capital of enterprises of different States. For this purpose, all types of control are included, i.e., whether or not legally enforceable and however exercised or exercisable.

The fact that a transaction is entered into between such related enterprises does not, in and of itself, mean that a Contracting State may adjust the income (or loss) of one or both of the enterprises under the provisions of this Article. If the conditions of the transaction are consistent with those that would be made between independent persons, the income arising from that transaction should not be subject to adjustment under this Article.

Similarly, the fact that associated enterprises may have concluded arrangements, such as cost sharing arrangements or general services agreements, is not in itself an indication that the two enterprises have entered into a non-arm's-length transaction that should give rise to an adjustment under paragraph 1. Both related and unrelated parties enter into such arrangements (e.g., joint venturers may share some development costs). As with any other kind of transaction, when related parties enter into an arrangement, the specific arrangement must be examined to see whether or not it meets the arm's-length standard. In the event that it does not, an appropriate adjustment may be made, which may include modifying the terms of the agreement or re-characterizing the transaction to reflect its substance.

It is understood that the "commensurate with income" standard for determining appropriate transfer prices for intangibles, added to Code section 482 by the Tax Reform Act of 1986, was designed to operate consistently with the arm's-length standard. The implementation of this standard in the section 482 regulations is in accordance with the general principles of paragraph 1 of Article 9 of the Convention, as interpreted by the OECD Transfer Pricing Guidelines.

This Article also permits tax authorities to deal with thin capitalization issues. They may, in the context of Article 9, scrutinize more than the rate of interest charged on a loan between related persons. They also may examine the capital structure of an enterprise, whether a payment in respect of that loan should be treated as interest, and, if it is treated as interest, under what circumstances interest deductions should be allowed to the payor. Paragraph 2 of the Commentary to Article 9 of the OECD Model, together with the U.S. observation set forth in paragraph 15, sets forth a similar understanding of the scope of Article 9 in the context of thin capitalization.

Paragraph 2

When a Contracting State has made an adjustment that is consistent with the provisions of paragraph 1, and the other Contracting State agrees that the adjustment was appropriate to reflect arm's-length conditions, that other Contracting State is obligated to make a correlative adjustment (sometimes referred to as a "corresponding adjustment") to the tax liability of the related person in that other Contracting State. Although the OECD Model does not specify that the other Contracting State must agree with the initial adjustment before it is obligated to make the correlative adjustment, the Commentary makes clear that the paragraph is to be read that way.

As explained in the Commentary to Article 9 of the OECD Model, Article 9 leaves the treatment of "secondary adjustments" to the laws of the Contracting States. When an adjustment under Article 9 has been made, one of the parties will have in its possession funds that it would not have had at arm's length. The question arises as to how to treat these funds. In the United States the general practice is to treat such funds as a dividend or contribution to capital, depending on the relationship between the parties. Under certain circumstances, the parties may be permitted to restore the funds to the party that would have the funds had the transactions been entered into on arm's length terms, and to establish an account payable pending restoration of the funds. See Rev. Proc. 99-32, 1999-2 C.B. 296.

The Contracting State making a secondary adjustment will take the other provisions of the Convention, where relevant, into account. For example, if the effect of a secondary adjustment is to treat a U.S. corporation as having made a distribution of profits to its parent corporation in the other Contracting State, the provisions of Article 10 (Dividends) will apply, and the United States may impose a 5 percent withholding tax on the dividend. Also, if under Article 23 the other State generally gives a credit for taxes paid with respect to such dividends, it would also be required to do so in this case.

The competent authorities are authorized by paragraph 3 of Article 25 (Mutual Agreement Procedure) to consult, if necessary, to resolve any differences in the application of these provisions. For example, there may be a disagreement over whether an adjustment made by a Contracting State under paragraph 1 was appropriate.

If a correlative adjustment is made under paragraph 2, it is to be implemented, pursuant to paragraph 2 of Article 25 (Mutual Agreement Procedure), notwithstanding any time limits or other procedural limitations in the law of the Contracting State making the adjustment. If a taxpayer has entered a closing agreement (or other written settlement) with the United States prior to bringing a case to the competent authorities, the U.S. competent authority will endeavor only to obtain a correlative adjustment from the other Contracting State. See, Rev. Proc. 200252, 2002-31 I.R.B. 242, Section 7.04.

Relationship to Other Articles

The saving clause of paragraph 4 of Article 1 (General Scope) does not apply to paragraph 2 of Article 9 by virtue of an exception to the saving clause in paragraph 5(a) of Article 1. Thus, even if the statute of limitations has run, a refund of tax can be made in order to implement a correlative adjustment. Statutory or procedural limitations, however, cannot be overridden to impose additional tax, because paragraph 2 of Article 1 provides that the Convention cannot restrict any statutory benefit.

ARTICLE 10   (DIVIDENDS)

Article 10 provides rules for the taxation of dividends paid by a company that is a resident of one Contracting State to a beneficial owner that is a resident of the other Contracting State. The article provides for full residence country taxation of such dividends and a limited source-State right to tax. Article 10 also provides rules for the imposition of a tax on branch profits by the State of source. Finally, the article prohibits a State from imposing taxes on a company resident in the other Contracting State, other than a branch profits tax, on undistributed earnings.

Paragraph 1

The right of a shareholder's country of residence to tax dividends arising in the source country is preserved by paragraph 1, which permits a Contracting State to tax its residents on dividends paid to them by a company that is a resident of the other Contracting State. For dividends from any other source paid to a resident, Article 21 (Other Income) grants the residence country exclusive taxing jurisdiction (other than for dividends attributable to a permanent establishment in the other State).

Paragraph 2

The State of source also may tax dividends beneficially owned by a resident of the other State, subject to the limitations of paragraphs 2 and 3. Paragraph 2 generally limits the rate of withholding tax in the State of source on dividends paid by a company resident in that State to 15 percent of the gross amount of the dividend. If, however, the beneficial owner of the dividend is a company resident in the other State and owns directly shares representing at least 10 percent of the voting power of the company paying the dividend, then the rate of withholding tax in the State of source is limited to 5 percent of the gross amount of the dividend. Shares are considered voting shares if they provide the power to elect, appoint or replace any person vested with the powers ordinarily exercised by the board of directors of a U.S. corporation.

The benefits of paragraph 2 may be granted at the time of payment by means of reduced rate of withholding tax at source. It also is consistent with the paragraph for tax to be withheld at the time of payment at full statutory rates, and the treaty benefit to be granted by means of a subsequent refund so long as such procedures are applied in a reasonable manner.

The determination of whether the ownership threshold for subparagraph (a) of paragraph 2 is met for purposes of the 5 percent maximum rate of withholding tax is made on the date on which entitlement to the dividend is determined. Thus, in the case of a dividend from a U.S. company, the determination of whether the ownership threshold is met generally would be made on the dividend record date.

Paragraph 2 does not affect the taxation of the profits out of which the dividends are paid. The taxation by a Contracting State of the income of its resident companies is governed by the internal law of the Contracting State, subject to the provisions of paragraph 4 of Article 24 (Non- Discrimination).

The term "beneficial owner" is not defined in the Convention, and is, therefore, defined as under the internal law of the country imposing tax (*i.e.*, the source country). The beneficial owner of the dividend for purposes of Article 10 is the person to which the income is attributable under the laws of the source State. Thus, if a dividend paid by a corporation that is a resident of one of the States (as determined under Article 4 (Residence)) is received by a nominee or agent that is a resident of the other State on behalf of a person that is not a resident of that other State, the dividend is not entitled to the benefits of this Article. However, a dividend received by a nominee on behalf of a resident of that other State would be entitled to benefits. These limitations are confirmed by paragraph 12 of the Commentary to Article 10 of the OECD Model. See also paragraph 24 of the Commentary to Article 1 of the OECD Model.

Special rules, however, apply to shares that are held through fiscally transparent entities. In that case, the rules of Article 1(6) will apply to determine whether the dividends should be treated as having been derived by a resident of a Contracting State. If so, then the source country rules will apply to determine whether that person, or another resident of the other Contracting State, is the beneficial owner of the income, as required by paragraph 2, and satisfies any other requirements for the specified benefits, such as the ownership threshold of subparagraph 2(a).

For example, assume that PCo, a company that is a resident of the other Contracting State, owns all of the outstanding shares in ThirdDE, an entity that is disregarded for U.S. tax purposes that is resident in a third country. ThirdDE owns 100% of the stock of USCo. The other Contracting State views ThirdDE as fiscally transparent under its domestic law, and taxes PCo currently on the income derived by ThirdDE. In this case, PCo is treated as deriving the dividends paid by USCo under Article 1(6). PCo is also the beneficial owner of the dividends under U.S. law, because an entity with a single owner that has made an election under Treas. Reg. Section 301.7701-3(a) is disregarded as an entity separate from its owner.[2] Moreover, PCo is treated as owning the shares of USCo directly. The Convention does not address what constitutes direct ownership for purposes of Article 10. As a result, whether ownership is direct is determined under the internal law of the country imposing tax (i.e., the source country) unless the context otherwise requires. Accordingly, a company that holds stock through such an entity will generally be considered to directly own such stock for purposes of Article 10.

---

[2] It is assumed in each of these examples that none of the parties has entered into an arrangement that would shift the benefits and burdens of ownership to a third party.

This result may change, however, if ThirdDE is regarded as non-fiscally transparent under the laws of the other Contracting State. Assuming that ThirdDE is treated as non-fiscally transparent by the other Contracting State, the income will not be treated as derived by a resident of the other Contracting State for purposes of the Convention. However, ThirdDE may still be entitled to the benefits of the U.S. tax treaty, if any, with its country of residence.

In the case of hybrid entities (that is, an entity that is treated as fiscally transparent under the laws of one State and non-fiscally transparent under the laws of the other, or of a third State), it may be that the person who "derives" the income under Article 1(6) is not the same person as the "beneficial owner" under Article 10. This will not prevent a claim for treaty benefits, so long as each of the requirements is met by one or more residents of the other Contracting State. For example, assume the same facts, except that the intermediate entity is SubDE, an entity organized in the other Contracting State, but treated as a disregarded entity for U.S. tax purposes. Paragraph 2(a) provides that the reduced withholding rate is available to a company that is the beneficial owner of the dividend and, which owns, directly, at least 10 percent of the shares of USCo. Under the laws of the other Contracting State, SubDE is taxable as a corporation. Accordingly, the dividend is treated as derived by a resident of the other Contracting State, SubDE, under the rules of Article 1(6). From the U.S. perspective, SubDE does not exist as a separate entity. Accordingly, the combined entity that is SubDE and PCo satisfy the requirements that the beneficial owner be a resident of the other Contracting State and that the shares of USCo be held directly. In addition, the analysis and result are unchanged if all of the outstanding shares in SubDE are owned by an individual who is a resident of the other Contracting State.

If PCo were not a resident of the other Contracting State, the analysis would be slightly different. From the U.S. perspective, the combined entity that is PCo and SubDE meets the 10 percent ownership requirement, and it owns the shares directly. From the perspective of the other Contracting State, SubDE is a resident of the other Contracting State. Accordingly, all of the requirements of Articles 1(6) and 10(2)(a) are met, and the 5% withholding rate applies to the dividends paid by USCo. Alternatively, PCo might be able to claim an exemption from the withholding tax altogether under another tax treaty to which the United States is a party. That would be the case if PCo were established in, and a resident of, a country with which the United States has entered into a tax treaty eliminating the withholding tax on dividends, and that other country viewed SubDE as fiscally transparent.

The same principles would apply in determining whether companies holding shares through fiscally transparent entities such as partnerships, trusts, and estates would qualify for benefits. As a result, companies holding shares through such entities may be able to claim the benefits of subparagraph (a) under certain circumstances. The lower rate applies when the company's proportionate share of the shares held by the intermediate entity meets the 10 percent threshold, and the company meets the requirements of Article 1(6) (i.e., the company's country of residence treats the intermediate entity as fiscally transparent) with respect to the dividend. Whether this ownership threshold is satisfied may be difficult to determine and often will require an analysis of the partnership or trust agreement.

Paragraph 3

Paragraph 3 provides that dividends received by a pension fund may not be taxed in the Contracting State of which the company paying the tax is a resident, unless such dividends are derived from the carrying on of a business, directly or indirectly, by the pension fund or through an associated enterprise. For these purposes, the term "pension fund" is defined in subparagraph 1(k) of Article 3 (General Definitions).

The rule is necessary because pension funds normally do not pay tax (either through a general exemption or because reserves for future pension liabilities effectively offset all of the fund's income), and therefore cannot benefit from a foreign tax credit. Moreover, distributions from a pension fund generally do not maintain the character of the underlying income, so the beneficiaries of the pension are not in a position to claim a foreign tax credit when they finally receive the pension, in many cases years after the withholding tax has been paid. Accordingly, in the absence of this rule, the dividends would almost certainly be subject to unrelieved double taxation.

Paragraph 4

Paragraph 4 imposes limitations on the rate reductions provided by paragraphs 2 and 3 in the case of dividends paid by RIC or a REIT.

The first sentence of subparagraph 4(a) provides that dividends paid by a RIC or REIT are not eligible for the 5 percent rate of withholding tax of subparagraph 2(a).

The second sentence of subparagraph 4(a) provides that the 15 percent maximum rate of withholding tax of subparagraph 2(b) applies to dividends paid by RICs and that the elimination of source-country withholding tax of paragraph 3 applies to dividends paid by RICs and beneficially owned by a pension fund.

The third sentence of subparagraph 4(a) provides that the 15 percent rate of withholding tax also applies to dividends paid by a REIT and that the elimination of source-country withholding tax of paragraph 3 applies to dividends paid by REITs and beneficially owned by a pension fund, provided that one of the three following conditions is met. First, the beneficial owner of the dividend is an individual or a pension fund, in either case holding an interest of not more than 10 percent in the REIT. Second, the dividend is paid with respect to a class of stock that is publicly traded and the beneficial owner of the dividend is a person holding an interest of not more than 5 percent of any class of the REIT's shares. Third, the beneficial owner of the dividend holds an interest in the REIT of not more than 10 percent and the REIT is "diversified."

Subparagraph (b) provides a definition of the term "diversified", which is necessary because the term is not defined in the Code. A REIT is diversified if the gross value of no single interest in real property held by the REIT exceeds 10 percent of the gross value of the REIT's total interest in real property. Foreclosure property is not considered an interest in real property, and a REIT holding a partnership interest is treated as owning its proportionate share of any interest in real property held by the partnership.

The restrictions set out above are intended to prevent the use of these entities to gain inappropriate U.S. tax benefits. For example, a company resident in the other Contracting State that wishes to hold a diversified portfolio of U.S. corporate shares could hold the portfolio directly and would bear a U.S. withholding tax of 15 percent on all of the dividends that it receives. Alternatively, it could hold the same diversified portfolio by purchasing 10 percent or more of the interests in a RIC. If the RIC is a pure conduit, there may be no U.S. tax cost to interposing the RIC in the chain of ownership. Absent the special rule in paragraph 4, such use of the RIC could transform portfolio dividends, taxable in the United States under the Convention at a 15 percent maximum rate of withholding tax, into direct investment dividends taxable at a 5 percent maximum rate of withholding tax or eligible for the elimination of source-country withholding tax on dividends paid to pension funds.

Similarly, a resident of the other Contracting State directly holding U.S. real property would pay U.S. tax upon the sale of the property either at a 30 percent rate of withholding tax on the gross income or at graduated rates on the net income. As in the preceding example, by placing the real property in a REIT, the investor could, absent a special rule, transform income from the sale of real estate into dividend income from the REIT, taxable at the rates provided in Article 10, significantly reducing the U.S. tax that otherwise would be imposed. Paragraph 4 prevents this result and thereby avoids a disparity between the taxation of direct real estate investments and real estate investments made through REIT conduits. In the cases in which paragraph 4 allows a dividend from a REIT to be eligible for the 15 percent rate of withholding tax, the holding in the REIT is not considered the equivalent of a direct holding in the underlying real property.

Paragraph 5

Paragraph 5 defines the term dividends broadly and flexibly. The definition is intended to cover all arrangements that yield a return on an equity investment in a corporation as determined under the tax law of the state of source, as well as arrangements that might be developed in the future.

The term includes income from shares, or other corporate rights that are not treated as debt under the law of the source State, that participate in the profits of the company. The term also includes income that is subjected to the same tax treatment as income from shares by the law of the State of source. Thus, a constructive dividend that results from a non-arm's length transaction between a corporation and a related party is a dividend. In the case of the United States the term dividend includes amounts treated as a dividend under U.S. law upon the sale or redemption of shares or upon a transfer of shares in a reorganization. See, e.g., Rev. Rul. 92-85, 1992-2 C.B. 69 (sale of foreign subsidiary;s stock to U.S. sister company is a deemed dividend to extent of the subsidiary's and sister company's earnings and profits). Further, a distribution from a U.S. publicly traded limited partnership, which is taxed as a corporation under U.S. law, is a dividend for purposes of Article 10. However, a distribution by a limited liability company is not taxable by the United States under Article 10, provided the limited liability company is not characterized as an association taxable as a corporation under U.S. law.

Finally, a payment denominated as interest that is made by a thinly capitalized corporation may be treated as a dividend to the extent that the debt is recharacterized as equity under the laws of the source State.

Paragraph 6

Paragraph 6 excludes from the general source country limitations under paragraphs 2 through 4 dividends paid with respect to holdings that form part of the business property of a permanent establishment. In such case, the rules of Article 7 (Business Profits) shall apply. Accordingly, the dividends will be taxed on a net basis using the rates and rules of taxation generally applicable to residents of the State in which the permanent establishment is located, as such rules may be modified by the Convention. An example of dividends paid with respect to the business property of a permanent establishment would be dividends derived by a dealer in stock or securities from stock or securities that the dealer held for sale to customers.

Paragraph 7

The right of a Contracting State to tax dividends paid by a company that is a resident of the other Contracting State is restricted by paragraph 7 to cases in which the dividends are paid to a resident of that Contracting State or are attributable to a permanent establishment or fixed base in that Contracting State. Thus, a Contracting State may not impose a "secondary" withholding tax on dividends paid by a nonresident company out of earnings and profits from that Contracting State. In the case of the United States, the secondary withholding tax was eliminated for payments made after December 31, 2004 in the American Jobs Creation Act of 2004.

The paragraph also restricts the right of a Contracting State to impose corporate level taxes on undistributed profits, other than a branch profits tax. The paragraph does not restrict a State's right to tax its resident shareholders on undistributed earnings of a corporation resident in the other State. Thus, the authority of the United States to impose taxes on subpart F income and on earnings deemed invested in U.S. property, and its tax on income of a passive foreign investment company that is a qualified electing fund is in no way restricted by this provision.

Paragraph 8

Paragraph 8 permits a Contracting State to impose a branch profits tax on a company resident in the other Contracting State. The tax is in addition to other taxes permitted by the Convention. The term "company" is defined in subparagraph 1(b) of Article 3 (General Definitions).

A Contracting State may impose a branch profits tax on a company if the company has income attributable to a permanent establishment in that Contracting State, derives income from real property in that Contracting State that is taxed on a net basis under Article 6 (Income from Real Property), or realizes gains taxable in that State under paragraph 1 of Article 13 (Gains). In the case of the United States, the imposition of such tax is limited, however, to the portion of the aforementioned items of income that represents the amount of such income that is the "dividend equivalent amount." This is consistent with the relevant rules under the U.S. branch profits tax, and the term dividend equivalent amount is defined under U.S. law. Section 884 defines the dividend equivalent amount as an amount for a particular year that is equivalent to the income described above that is included in the corporation's effectively connected earnings and profits for that year, after payment of the corporate tax under Articles 6 (Income from Real Property), 7 (Business Profits) or 13 (Gains), reduced for any increase in the branch's U.S. net equity during the year or increased for any reduction in its U.S. net equity during the year. U.S. net equity is U.S. assets less U.S. liabilities. See Treas. Reg. section 1.884-1.

The dividend equivalent amount for any year approximates the dividend that a U.S. branch office would have paid during the year if the branch had been operated as a separate U.S. subsidiary company. In the case that the other Contracting State also imposes a branch profits tax, the base of its tax must be limited to an amount that is analogous to the dividend equivalent amount.

As discussed in the Technical Explanations to Articles 1(2) and 7(2), consistency principles require that a taxpayer may not mix and match the rules of the Code and the Convention in an inconsistent manner. In the context of the branch profits tax, the consistency requirement means that an enterprise that uses the principles of Article 7 to determine its net taxable income also must use the principles in determining the dividend equivalent amount. Similarly, an enterprise that uses U.S. domestic law to determine its net taxable income must also use U.S. domestic law in complying with the branch profits tax. As in the case of Article 7, if an enterprise switches between domestic law and treaty principles from year to year, it will need to make appropriate adjustments or recapture amounts that otherwise might go untaxed.

Subparagraph b) provides that the branch profits tax shall not be imposed at a rate exceeding the direct investment dividend withholding rate of five percent.

Relationship to Other Articles

Notwithstanding the foregoing limitations on source country taxation of dividends, the saving clause of paragraph 4 of Article 1 permits the United States to tax dividends received by its residents and citizens, subject to the special foreign tax credit rules of paragraph 4 of Article 23 (Relief from Double Taxation), as if the Convention had not come into effect.

The benefits of this Article are also subject to the provisions of Article 22 (Limitation on Benefits). Thus, if a resident of the other Contracting State is the beneficial owner of dividends paid by a U.S. corporation, the shareholder must qualify for treaty benefits under at least one of the tests of Article 22 in order to receive the benefits of this Article.

ARTICLE 11   (INTEREST)

Article 11 specifies the taxing jurisdictions over interest income of the States of source and residence and defines the terms necessary to apply the article.

Paragraph 1

Paragraph 1 generally grants to the State of residence the exclusive right to tax interest beneficially owned by its residents and arising in the other Contracting State.

The term "beneficial owner" is not defined in the Convention, and is, therefore, defined under the internal law of the State of source. The beneficial owner of the interest for purposes of Article 11 is the person to which the income is attributable under the laws of the source State. Thus, if interest arising in a Contracting State is received by a nominee or agent that is a resident of the other State on behalf of a person that is not a resident of that other State, the interest is not entitled to the benefits of Article 11. However, interest received by a nominee on behalf of a resident of that other State would be entitled to benefits. These limitations are confirmed by paragraph 8 of the OECD Commentary to Article 11. See also paragraph 24 of the OECD Commentary to Article 1.

Paragraph 2

Paragraph 2 provides anti-abuse exceptions to the source-country exemption in paragraph 1 for two classes of interest payments.

The first class of interest, dealt with in subparagraphs (a) and (b) is so-called "contingent interest." With respect to the other Contracting State, such interest is defined in subparagraph (a) as any interest arising in that State that is determined by reference to the receipts, sales, income, profits or other cash flow of the debtor or a related person, to any change in the value of any property of the debtor or a related person or to any dividend, partnership distribution or similar payment made by the debtor or a related person. Any such interest may be taxed in that Contracting State according to the laws of that State. If the beneficial owner is a resident of the other Contracting State, however, the gross amount of the interest may be taxed at a rate not exceeding 15 percent. With respect to interest arising in the United States, subparagraph (b) refers to contingent interest of a type that does not qualify as portfolio interest under U.S. domestic law. The cross-reference to the U.S. definition of contingent interest, which is found in section 871(h)(4) of the Code, is intended to ensure that the exceptions of section 871(h)(4)(c) will be applicable.

The second class of interest is dealt with in subparagraph c) of paragraph 2. This exception is consistent with the policy of Code sections 860E(e) and 860G(b) that excess inclusions with respect to a real estate mortgage investment conduit (REMIC) should bear full U.S. tax in all cases. Without a full tax at source foreign purchasers of residual interests would have a competitive advantage over U.S. purchasers at the time these interests are initially offered. Also, absent this rule, the U.S. fisc would suffer a revenue loss with respect to mortgages held in a REMIC because of opportunities for tax avoidance created by differences in the timing of taxable and economic income produced by these interests.

Paragraph 3

The term "interest" as used in Article 11 is defined in paragraph 2 to include, *inter alia*, income from debt claims of every kind, whether or not secured by a mortgage. Penalty charges for late payment are excluded from the definition of interest. Interest that is paid or accrued subject to a contingency is within the ambit of Article 11. This includes income from a debt obligation carrying the right to participate in profits. The term does not, however, include amounts that are treated as dividends under Article 10 (Dividends).

The term interest also includes amounts subject to the same tax treatment as income from money lent under the law of the State in which the income arises. Thus, for purposes of the Convention, amounts that the United States will treat as interest include (i) the difference between the issue price and the stated redemption price at maturity of a debt instrument (*i.e.*, original issue discount ("OID")), which may be wholly or partially realized on the disposition of a debt instrument (section 1273), (ii) amounts that are imputed interest on a deferred sales contract (section 483), (iii) amounts treated as interest or OID under the stripped bond rules (section 1286), (iv) amounts treated as original issue discount under the below-market interest rate rules (section 7872), (v) a partner's distributive share of a partnership's interest income (section 702), (vi) the interest portion of periodic payments made under a "finance lease" or similar contractual arrangement that in substance is a borrowing by the nominal lessee to finance the acquisition of property, (vii) amounts included in the income of a holder of a residual interest in a REMIC (section 860E), because these amounts generally are subject to the same taxation treatment as interest under U.S. tax law, and (viii) interest with respect to notional principal contracts that are re-characterized as loans because of a "substantial non-periodic payment."

Paragraph 4

Paragraph 4 provides an exception to the exclusive residence taxation rule of paragraph 1 and the source-country gross taxation rule of paragraph 2 in cases where the beneficial owner of the interest carries on business through a permanent establishment in the State of source situated in that State and the interest is attributable to that permanent establishment. In such cases the provisions of Article 7 (Business Profits) will apply and the State of source will retain the right to impose tax on such interest income.

In the case of a permanent establishment that once existed in the State but that no longer exists, the provisions of paragraph 4 also apply, by virtue of paragraph 7 of Article 7 (Business Profits), to interest that would be attributable to such a permanent establishment or fixed base if it did exist in the year of payment or accrual. See the Technical Explanation of paragraph 7 of Article 7.

Paragraph 5

Paragraph 5 provides that in cases involving special relationships between the payor and the beneficial owner of interest income, Article 11 applies only to that portion of the total interest payments that would have been made absent such special relationships (i.e., an arm's-length interest payment). Any excess amount of interest paid remains taxable according to the laws of the United States and the other Contracting State, respectively, with due regard to the other provisions of the Convention. Thus, if the excess amount would be treated under the source country's law as a distribution of profits by a corporation, such amount could be taxed as a dividend rather than as interest, but the tax would be subject, if appropriate, to the rate limitations of paragraph 2 of Article 10 (Dividends).

The term "special relationship" is not defined in the Convention. In applying this paragraph the United States considers the term to include the relationships described in Article 9, which in turn corresponds to the definition of "control" for purposes of section 482 of the Code.

This paragraph does not address cases where, owing to a special relationship between the payer and the beneficial owner or between both of them and some other person, the amount of the interest is less than an arm's-length amount. In those cases a transaction may be characterized to reflect its substance and interest may be imputed consistent with the definition of interest in paragraph 3. The United States would apply section 482 or 7872 of the Code to determine the amount of imputed interest in those cases.

Relationship to Other Articles

Notwithstanding the foregoing limitations on source country taxation of interest, the saving clause of paragraph 4 of Article 1 permits the United States to tax its residents and citizens, subject to the special foreign tax credit rules of paragraph 4 of Article 23 (Relief from Double Taxation), as if the Convention had not come into force.

As with other benefits of the Convention, the benefits of exclusive residence State taxation of interest under paragraph 1 of Article 11, or limited source taxation under subparagraphs 2(a) and (b), are available to a resident of the other State only if that resident is entitled to those benefits under the provisions of Article 22 (Limitation on Benefits).

ARTICLE 12   (ROYALTIES)

Article 12 provides rules for the taxation of royalties arising in one Contracting State and paid to a beneficial owner that is a resident of the other Contracting State.

Paragraph 1

Paragraph 1 generally grants to the State of residence the exclusive right to tax royalties beneficially owned by its residents and arising in the other Contracting State.

The term "beneficial owner" is not defined in the Convention, and is, therefore, defined under the internal law of the State of source. The beneficial owner of the royalty for purposes of Article 12 is the person to which the income is attributable under the laws of the source State. Thus, if a royalty arising in a Contracting State is received by a nominee or agent that is a resident of the other State on behalf of a person that is not a resident of that other State, the royalty is not entitled to the benefits of Article 12. However, a royalty received by a nominee on behalf of a resident of that other State would be entitled to benefits. These limitations are confirmed by paragraph 4 of the OECD Commentary to Article 12. See also paragraph 24 of the OECD Commentary to Article 1.

Paragraph 2

Paragraph 2 defines the term "royalties," as used in Article 12, to include any consideration for the use of, or the right to use, any copyright of literary, artistic, scientific or other work (such as cinematographic films), any patent, trademark, design or model, plan, secret formula or process, or for information concerning industrial, commercial, or scientific experience. The term "royalties" also includes gain derived from the alienation of any right or property that would give rise to royalties, to the extent the gain is contingent on the productivity, use, or further alienation thereof. Gains that are not so contingent are dealt with under Article 13 (Gains). The term "royalties," however, does not include income from leasing personal property.

The term royalties is defined in the Convention and therefore is generally independent of domestic law. Certain terms used in the definition are not defined in the Convention, but these may be defined under domestic tax law. For example, the term "secret process or formulas" is found in the Code, and its meaning has been elaborated in the context of sections 351 and 367. See Rev. Rul. 55- 17, 1955-1 C.B. 388; Rev. Rul. 64-56, 1964-1 C.B. 133; Rev. Proc. 69- 19, 1969-2 C.B. 301.

Consideration for the use or right to use cinematographic films, or works on film, tape, or other means of reproduction in radio or television broadcasting is specifically included in the definition of royalties. It is intended that, with respect to any subsequent technological advances in the field of radio or television broadcasting, consideration received for the use of such technology will also be included in the definition of royalties.

If an artist who is resident in one Contracting State records a performance in the other Contracting State, retains a copyrighted interest in a recording, and receives payments for the right to use the recording based on the sale or public playing of the recording, then the right of such other Contracting State to tax those payments is governed by Article 12. See Boulez v. Commissioner, 83 T.C. 584 (1984), aff'd, 810 F.2d 209 (D.C. Cir. 1986). By contrast, if the artist earns in the other Contracting State income covered by Article 16 (Entertainers and Sportsmen), for example, endorsement income from the artist's attendance at a film screening, and if such income also is attributable to one of the rights described in Article 12 (*e.g.*, the use of the artist's photograph in promoting the screening), Article 16 and not Article 12 is applicable to such income.

Computer software generally is protected by copyright laws around the world. Under the Convention, consideration received for the use, or the right to use, computer software is treated either as royalties or as business profits, depending on the facts and circumstances of the transaction giving rise to the payment.

The primary factor in determining whether consideration received for the use, or the right to use, computer software is treated as royalties or as business profits is the nature of the rights transferred. See Treas. Reg. section 1.861-18. The fact that the transaction is characterized as a license for copyright law purposes is not dispositive. For example, a typical retail sale of "shrink wrap" software generally will not be considered to give rise to royalty income, even though for copyright law purposes it may be characterized as a license.

The means by which the computer software is transferred are not relevant for purposes of the analysis. Consequently, if software is electronically transferred but the rights obtained by the transferee are substantially equivalent to rights in a program copy, the payment will be considered business profits.

The term "industrial, commercial, or scientific experience" (sometimes referred to as "know-how") has the meaning ascribed to it in paragraph 11 *et seq.* of the Commentary to Article 12 of the OECD Model. Consistent with that meaning, the term may include information that is ancillary to a right otherwise giving rise to royalties, such as a patent or secret process.

Know-how also may include, in limited cases, technical information that is conveyed through technical or consultancy services. It does not include general educational training of the user's employees, nor does it include information developed especially for the user, such as a technical plan or design developed according to the user's specifications. Thus, as provided in paragraph 11.3 of the Commentary to Article 12 of the OECD Model, the term "royalties" does not include payments received as consideration for after-sales service, for services rendered by a seller to a purchaser under a warranty, or for pure technical assistance.

The term "royalties" also does not include payments for professional services (such as architectural, engineering, legal, managerial, medical, software development services). For example, income from the design of a refinery by an engineer (even if the engineer employed know-how in the process of rendering the design) or the production of a legal brief by a lawyer is not income from the transfer of know-how taxable under Article 12, but is income from services taxable under either Article 7 (Business Profits) or Article 14 (Income from Employment). Professional services may be embodied in property that gives rise to royalties, however. Thus, if a professional contracts to develop patentable property and retains rights in the resulting property under the development contract, subsequent license payments made for those rights would be royalties.

Paragraph 3

This paragraph provides an exception to the rule of paragraph 1 that gives the state of residence exclusive taxing jurisdiction in cases where the beneficial owner of the royalties carries on business through a permanent establishment in the state of source and the royalties are attributable to that permanent establishment. In such cases the provisions of Article 7 (Business Profits) will apply.

The provisions of paragraph 7 of Article 7 (Business Profits) apply to this paragraph. For example, royalty income that is attributable to a permanent establishment and that accrues during the existence of the permanent establishment, but is received after the permanent establishment no longer exists, remains taxable under the provisions of Article 7 (Business Profits), and not under this Article.

Paragraph 4

Paragraph 4 provides that in cases involving special relationships between the payor and beneficial owner of royalties, Article 12 applies only to the extent the royalties would have been paid absent such special relationships (i.e., an arm's-length royalty). Any excess amount of royalties paid remains taxable according to the laws of the two Contracting States, with due regard to the other provisions of the Convention. If, for example, the excess amount is treated as a distribution of corporate profits under domestic law, such excess amount will be taxed as a dividend rather than as royalties, but the tax imposed on the dividend payment will be subject to the rate limitations of paragraph 2 of Article 10 (Dividends).

Relationship to Other Articles

Notwithstanding the foregoing limitations on source country taxation of royalties, the saving clause of paragraph 4 of Article 1 (General Scope) permits the United States to tax its residents and citizens, subject to the special foreign tax credit rules of paragraph 4 of Article 23 (Relief from Double Taxation), as if the Convention had not come into force.

As with other benefits of the Convention, the benefits of exclusive residence State taxation of royalties under paragraph 1 of Article 12 are available to a resident of the other State only if that resident is entitled to those benefits under Article 22 (Limitation on Benefits).

ARTICLE 13   (GAINS)

Article 13 assigns either primary or exclusive taxing jurisdiction over gains from the alienation of property to the State of residence or the State of source.

Paragraph 1

Paragraph 1 of Article 13 preserves the non-exclusive right of the State of source to tax gains attributable to the alienation of real property situated in that State. The paragraph therefore permits the United States to apply section 897 of the Code to tax gains derived by a resident of the other Contracting State that are attributable to the alienation of real property situated in the United States (as defined in paragraph 2). Gains attributable to the alienation of real property include gains from any other property that is treated as a real property interest within the meaning of paragraph 2.

Paragraph 1 refers to gains "attributable to the alienation of real property" rather than the OECD Model phrase "gains from the alienation" to clarify that the United States will look through distributions made by a REIT and certain RICs. Accordingly, distributions made by a REIT or certain RICs are taxable under paragraph 1 of Article 13 (not under Article 10 (Dividends)) when they are attributable to gains derived from the alienation of real property.

Paragraph 2

This paragraph defines the term "real property situated in the other Contracting State." The term includes real property referred to in Article 6 (i.e., an interest in the real property itself), a "United States real property interest" (when the United States is the other Contracting State under paragraph 1), and an equivalent interest in real property situated in the other Contracting State.

Under section 897(c) of the Code the term "United States real property interest" includes shares in a U.S. corporation that owns sufficient U.S. real property interests to satisfy an asset-ratio test on certain testing dates. The term also includes certain foreign corporations that have elected to be treated as U.S. corporations for this purpose. Section 897(i).

Paragraph 3

Paragraph 3 of Article 13 deals with the taxation of certain gains from the alienation of movable property forming part of the business property of a permanent establishment that an enterprise of a Contracting State has in the other Contracting State. This also includes gains from the alienation of such a permanent establishment (alone or with the whole enterprise). Such gains may be taxed in the State in which the permanent establishment is located.

A resident of the other Contracting State that is a partner in a partnership doing business in the United States generally will have a permanent establishment in the United States as a result of the activities of the partnership, assuming that the activities of the partnership rise to the level of a permanent establishment. Rev. Rul. 91-32, 1991-1 C.B. 107. Further, under paragraph 3, the United States generally may tax a partner's distributive share of income realized by a partnership on the disposition of movable property forming part of the business property of the partnership in the United States.

The gains subject to paragraph 3 may be taxed in the State in which the permanent establishment is located, regardless of whether the permanent establishment exists at the time of the alienation. This rule incorporates the rule of section 864(c)(6) of the Code. Accordingly, income that is attributable to a permanent establishment, but that is deferred and received after the permanent establishment no longer exists, may nevertheless be taxed by the State in which the permanent establishment was located.

Paragraph 4

This paragraph limits the taxing jurisdiction of the State of source with respect to gains from the alienation of ships or aircraft operated in international traffic by the enterprise alienating the ship or aircraft and from property (other than real property) pertaining to the operation or use of such ships, aircraft, or containers.

Under paragraph 4, such income is taxable only in the Contracting State in which the alienator is resident. Notwithstanding paragraph 3, the rules of this paragraph apply even if the income is attributable to a permanent establishment maintained by the enterprise in the other Contracting State. This result is consistent with the allocation of taxing rights under Article 8 (Shipping and Air Transport).

Paragraph 5

Paragraph 5 provides a rule similar to paragraph 4 with respect to gains from the alienation of containers and related personal property. Such gains derived by a enterprise of a Contracting State shall be taxable only in that Contracting State unless the containers were used for the transport of goods or merchandise solely within the other Contracting State. The other Contracting State may not tax even if the gain is attributable to a permanent establishment maintained by the enterprise in that other Contracting State.

Paragraph 6

Paragraph 6 grants to the State of residence of the alienator the exclusive right to tax gains from the alienation of property other than property referred to in paragraphs 1 through 5. For example, gain derived from shares, other than shares described in paragraphs 2 or 3, debt instruments and various financial instruments, may be taxed only in the State of residence, to the extent such income is not otherwise characterized as income taxable under another article (e.g., Article 10 (Dividends) or Article 11 (Interest)). Similarly gain derived from the alienation of tangible personal property, other than tangible personal property described in paragraph 3, may be taxed only in the State of residence of the alienator.

Gain derived from the alienation of any property, such as a patent or copyright, that produces income covered by Article 12 (Royalties) is governed by the rules of Article 12 and not by this article, provided that such gain is of the type described in paragraph 2(b) of Article 12 (i.e., it is contingent on the productivity, use, or disposition of the property). Thus, under either article, such gain is taxable only in the State of residence of the alienator.

Gains derived by a resident of a Contracting State from real property located in a third state are not taxable in the other Contracting State, even if the sale is attributable to a permanent establishment located in the other Contracting State.

Relationship to Other Articles

Notwithstanding the foregoing limitations on taxation of certain gains by the State of source, the saving clause of paragraph 4 of Article 1 (General Scope) permits the United States to tax its citizens and residents as if the Convention had not come into effect. Thus, any limitation in this Article on the right of the United States to tax gains does not apply to gains of a U.S. citizen or resident.

The benefits of this Article are also subject to the provisions of Article 22 (Limitation on Benefits). Thus, only a resident of a Contracting State that satisfies one of the conditions in Article 22 is entitled to the benefits of this Article.

ARTICLE 14   (INCOME FROM EMPLOYMENT)

Article 14 apportions taxing jurisdiction over remuneration derived by a resident of a Contracting State as an employee between the States of source and residence.

Paragraph 1

The general rule of Article 14 is contained in paragraph 1. Remuneration derived by a resident of a Contracting State as an employee may be taxed by the State of residence, and the remuneration also may be taxed by the other Contracting State to the extent derived from employment exercised (*i.e.*, services performed) in that other Contracting State. Paragraph 1 also provides that the more specific rules of Articles 15 (Directors' Fees), 17 (Pensions, Social Security, Annuities, Alimony and Child Support), and 19 (Government Service) apply in the case of employment income described in one of those articles. Thus, even though the State of source has a right to tax employment income under Article 14, it may not have the right to tax that income under the Convention if the income is described, for example, in Article 17 (Pensions, Social Security, Annuities, Alimony and Child Support) and is not taxable in the State of source under the provisions of that article.

Article 14 applies to any form of compensation for employment, including payments in kind. Paragraph 1.1 of the Commentary to Article 16 of the OECD Model now confirms that interpretation.

Consistent with section 864(c)(6) of the Code, Article 14 also applies regardless of the timing of actual payment for services. Consequently, a person who receives the right to a future payment in consideration for services rendered in a Contracting State would be taxable in that State even if the payment is received at a time when the recipient is a resident of the other Contracting State. Thus, a bonus paid to a resident of a Contracting State with respect to services performed in the other Contracting State with respect to a particular taxable year would be subject to Article 14 for that year even if it was paid after the close of the year. An annuity received for services performed in a taxable year could be subject to Article 14 despite the fact that it was paid in subsequent years. In that case, it would be necessary to determine whether the payment constitutes deferred compensation, taxable under Article 14, or a qualified pension subject to the rules of Article 17 (Pensions, Social Security, Annuities, Alimony, and Child Support). Article 14 also applies to income derived from the exercise of stock options granted with respect to services performed in the host State, even if those stock options are exercised after the employee has left the source country. If Article 14 is found to apply, whether such payments were taxable in the State where the employment was exercised would depend on whether the tests of paragraph 2 were satisfied in the year in which the services to which the payment relates were performed.

Paragraph 2

Paragraph 2 sets forth an exception to the general rule that employment income may be taxed in the State where it is exercised. Under paragraph 2, the State where the employment is exercised may not tax the income from the employment if three conditions are satisfied: (a) the individual is present in the other Contracting State for a period or periods not exceeding 183 days in any 12-month period that begins or ends during the relevant taxable year (i.e., in the United States, the calendar year in which the services are performed); (b) the remuneration is paid by, or on behalf of, an employer who is not a resident of that other Contracting State; and (c) the remuneration is not borne as a deductible expense by a permanent establishment that the employer has in that other State. In order for the remuneration to be exempt from tax in the source State, all three conditions must be satisfied. This exception is identical to that set forth in the OECD Model.

The 183-day period in condition (a) is to be measured using the "days of physical presence" method. Under this method, the days that are counted include any day in which a part of the day is spent in the host country. (Rev. Rul. 56-24, 1956-1 C.B. 851.) Thus, days that are counted include the days of arrival and departure; weekends and holidays on which the employee does not work but is present within the country; vacation days spent in the country before, during or after the employment period, unless the individual's presence before or after the employment can be shown to be independent of his presence there for employment purposes; and time during periods of sickness, training periods, strikes, etc., when the individual is present but not working. If illness prevented the individual from leaving the country in sufficient time to qualify for the benefit, those days will not count. Also, any part of a day spent in the host country while in transit between two points outside the host country is not counted. If the individual is a resident of the host country for part of the taxable year concerned and a non-resident for the remainder of the year, the individual's days of presence as a resident do not count for purposes of determining whether the 183-day period is exceeded.

Conditions (b) and (c) are intended to ensure that a Contracting State will not be required to allow a deduction to the payor for compensation paid and at the same time to exempt the employee on the amount received. Accordingly, if a foreign person pays the salary of an employee who is employed in the host State, but a host State corporation or permanent establishment reimburses the payor with a payment that can be identified as a reimbursement, neither condition (b) nor (c), as the case may be, will be considered to have been fulfilled.

The reference to remuneration "borne by" a permanent establishment is understood to encompass all expenses that economically are incurred and not merely expenses that are currently deductible for tax purposes. Accordingly, the expenses referred to include expenses that are capitalizable as well as those that are currently deductible. Further, salaries paid by residents that are exempt from income taxation may be considered to be borne by a permanent establishment notwithstanding the fact that the expenses will be neither deductible nor capitalizable since the payor is exempt from tax.

Paragraph 3

Paragraph 3 contains a special rule applicable to remuneration for services performed by a resident of a Contracting State as an employee aboard a ship or aircraft operated in international traffic. Such remuneration may be taxed only in the State of residence of the employee if the services are performed as a member of the regular complement of the ship or aircraft. The "regular complement" includes the crew. In the case of a cruise ship, for example, it may also include others, such as entertainers, lecturers, etc., employed by the shipping company to serve on the ship throughout its voyage. The use of the term "regular complement" is intended to clarify that a person who exercises his employment as, for example, an insurance salesman while aboard a ship or aircraft is not covered by this paragraph.

If a U.S. citizen who is resident in the other Contracting State performs services as an employee in the United States and meets the conditions of paragraph 2 for source country exemption, he nevertheless is taxable in the United States by virtue of the saving clause of paragraph 4 of Article 1 (General Scope), subject to the special foreign tax credit rule of paragraph 4 of Article 23 (Relief from Double Taxation).

ARTICLE 15   (DIRECTORS' FEES)

This Article provides that a Contracting State may tax the fees and other compensation paid by a company that is a resident of that State for services performed in that State by a resident of the other Contracting State in his capacity as a director of the company. This rule is an exception to the more general rules of Articles 7 (Business Profits) and 14 (Income from Employment). Thus, for example, in determining whether a director's fee paid to a non-employee director is subject to tax in the country of residence of the corporation, it is not relevant to establish whether the fee is attributable to a permanent establishment in that State.

The analogous OECD provision reaches different results in certain cases. Under the OECD Model provision, a resident of one Contracting State who is a director of a corporation that is resident in the other Contracting State is subject to tax in that other State in respect of his directors' fees regardless of where the services are performed. Under the provision in the Convention, the State of residence of the corporation may tax nonresident directors with no time or dollar threshold, but only with respect to remuneration for services performed in that State. The United States has entered a reservation with respect to the OECD provision.

This Article is subject to the saving clause of paragraph 4 of Article 1 (General Scope). Thus, if a U.S. citizen who is a resident of the other Contracting State is a director of a U.S. corporation, the United States may tax his full remuneration regardless of where he performs his services.

ARTICLE 16   (ENTERTAINERS AND SPORTSMEN)

This Article deals with the taxation in a Contracting State of entertainers and sportsmen resident in the other Contracting State from the performance of their services as such. The Article applies both to the income of an entertainer or sportsman who performs services on his own behalf and one who performs services on behalf of another person, either as an employee of that person, or pursuant to any other arrangement. The rules of this Article take precedence, in some circumstances, over those of Articles 7 (Business Profits) and 14 (Income from Employment).

This Article applies only with respect to the income of entertainers and sportsmen. Others involved in a performance or athletic event, such as producers, directors, technicians, managers, coaches, etc., remain subject to the provisions of Articles 7 and 14. In addition, except as provided in paragraph 2, income earned by juridical persons is not covered by Article 16.

Paragraph 1

Paragraph 1 describes the circumstances in which a Contracting State may tax the performance income of an entertainer or sportsman who is a resident of the other Contracting State. Under the paragraph, income derived by an individual resident of a Contracting State from activities as an entertainer or sportsman exercised in the other Contracting State may be taxed in that other State if the amount of the gross receipts derived by the performer exceeds $20,000 (or its equivalent in [the currency of the other Contracting State]) for the taxable year. The $20,000 includes expenses reimbursed to the individual or borne on his behalf. If the gross receipts exceed $20,000, the full amount, not just the excess, may be taxed in the State of performance.

The OECD Model provides for taxation by the country of performance of the remuneration of entertainers or sportsmen with no dollar or time threshold. This Convention introduces the monetary threshold to distinguish between two groups of entertainers and athletes — those who are paid relatively large sums of money for very short periods of service, and who would, therefore, normally be exempt from host country tax under the standard personal services income rules, and those who earn relatively modest amounts and are, therefore, not easily distinguishable from those who earn other types of personal service income. The United States has entered a reservation to the OECD Model on this point.

Tax may be imposed under paragraph 1 even if the performer would have been exempt from tax under Article 7 (Business Profits) or 14 (Income from Employment). On the other hand. if the performer would be exempt from host-country tax under Article 16, but would be taxable under either Article 7 or 14, tax may be imposed under either of those Articles. Thus, for example, if a performer derives remuneration from his activities in an independent capacity, and the performer does not have a permanent establishment in the host State, he may be taxed by the host State in accordance with Article 16 if his remuneration exceeds $20,000 annually, despite the fact that he generally would be exempt from host State taxation under Article 7. However, a performer who receives less than the $20,000 threshold amount and therefore is not taxable under Article 16 nevertheless may be subject to tax in the host country under Article 7 or 14 if the tests for host-country taxability under the relevant Article are met. For example, if an entertainer who is an independent contractor earns $14,000 of income in a State for the calendar year, but the income is attributable to his permanent establishment in the State of performance, that State may tax his income under Article 7.

Since it frequently is not possible to know until year-end whether the income an entertainer or sportsman derived from performances in a Contracting State will exceed $20,000, nothing in the Convention precludes that Contracting State from withholding tax during the year and refunding it after the close of the year if the taxability threshold has not been met.

As explained in paragraph 9 of the Commentary to Article 17 of the OECD Model, Article 16 of the Convention applies to all income connected with a performance by the entertainer, such as appearance fees, award or prize money, and a share of the gate receipts. Income derived from a Contracting State by a performer who is a resident of the other Contracting State from other than actual performance, such as royalties from record sales and payments for product endorsements, is not covered by this Article, but by other articles of the Convention, such as Article 12 (Royalties) or Article 7 (Business Profits). For example, if an entertainer receives royalty income from the sale of live recordings, the royalty income would be exempt from source state tax under Article 12, even if the performance was conducted in the source country, although the entertainer could be taxed in the source country with respect to income from the performance itself under Article 16 if the dollar threshold is exceeded.

In determining whether income falls under Article 16 or another article, the controlling factor will be whether the income in question is predominantly attributable to the performance itself or to other activities or property rights. For instance, a fee paid to a performer for endorsement of a performance in which the performer will participate would be considered to be so closely associated with the performance itself that it normally would fall within Article 16. Similarly, a sponsorship fee paid by a business in return for the right to attach its name to the performance would be so closely associated with the performance that it would fall under Article 16 as well. As indicated in paragraph 9 of the Commentary to Article 17 of the OECD Model, however, a cancellation fee would not be considered to fall within Article 16 but would be dealt with under Article 7 (Business Profits) or 14 (Income from Employment).

As indicated in paragraph 4 of the Commentary to Article 17 of the OECD Model, where an individual fulfills a dual role as performer and non-performer (such as a player-coach or an actor-director), but his role in one of the two capacities is negligible, the predominant character of the individual's activities should control the characterization of those activities. In other cases there should be an apportionment between the performance-related compensation and other compensation.

Consistent with Article 14 (Income from Employment), Article 16 also applies regardless of the timing of actual payment for services. Thus, a bonus paid to a resident of a Contracting State with respect to a performance in the other Contracting State during a particular taxable year would be subject to Article 16 for that year even if it was paid after the close of the year. The determination as to whether the $20,000 threshold has been exceeded is determined separately with respect to each year of payment. Accordingly, if an actor who is a resident of one Contracting State receives residual payments over time with respect to a movie that was filmed in the other Contracting State, the payments do not have to be aggregated from one year to another to determine whether the total payments have finally exceeded $20,000. Otherwise, residual payments received many years later could retroactively subject all earlier payments to tax by the other Contracting State.

Paragraph 2

Paragraph 2 is intended to address the potential for circumvention of the rule in paragraph 1 when a performer's income does not accrue directly to the performer himself, but to another person. Foreign performers frequently perform in the United States as employees of, or under contract with, a company or other person.

The relationship may truly be one of employee and employer, with no circumvention of paragraph 1 either intended or realized. On the other hand, the "employer" may, for example, be a company established and owned by the performer, which is merely acting as the nominal income recipient in respect of the remuneration for the performance (a "star company"). The performer may act as an "employee," receive a modest salary, and arrange to receive the remainder of the income from his performance from the company in another form or at a later time. In such case, absent the provisions of paragraph 2, the income arguably could escape host-country tax because the company earns business profits but has no permanent establishment in that country. The performer may largely or entirely escape host-country tax by receiving only a small salary, perhaps small enough to place him below the dollar threshold in paragraph 1. The performer might arrange to receive further payments in a later year, when he is not subject to host-country tax, perhaps as dividends or liquidating distributions.

Paragraph 2 seeks to prevent this type of abuse while at the same time protecting the taxpayers' rights to the benefits of the Convention when there is a legitimate employee-employer relationship between the performer and the person providing his services. Under paragraph 2, when the income accrues to a person other than the performer, the income may be taxed in the Contracting State where the performer's services are exercised, without regard to the provisions of the Convention concerning business profits (Article 7) or income from employment (Article 14), unless the contract pursuant to which the personal activities are performed allows the person other than the performer to designate the individual who is to perform the personal activities. This rule is based on the U.S. domestic law provision characterizing income from certain personal service contracts as foreign personal holding company income in the context of the foreign personal holding company provisions. See Code section 954(c)(1)(I). The premise of this rule is that, in a case where a performer is using another person in an attempt to circumvent the provisions of paragraph 1, the recipient of the services of the performer would contract with a person other than that performer (*i.e.*, a company employing the performer) only if the recipient of the services were certain that the performer himself would perform the services. If instead the person is allowed to designate the individual who is to perform the services, then likely the person is a service company not formed to circumvent the provisions of paragraph 1. The following example illustrates the operation of this rule.

Example. Company O, a resident of the other Contracting State, is engaged in the business of operating an orchestra. Company O enters into a contract with Company A pursuant to which Company O agrees to carry out two performances in the United States in consideration of which Company A will pay Company O $200,000. The contract designates two individuals, a conductor and a flutist, that must perform as part of the orchestra, and allows Company O to designate the other members of the orchestra. Because the contract does not give Company O any discretion to determine whether the conductor or the flutist perform personal services under the contract, the portion of the $200,000 which is attributable to the personal services of the conductor and the flutist may be taxed by the United States pursuant to paragraph 2. The remaining portion of the $200,000, which is attributable to the personal services of performers that Company O may designate, is not subject to tax by the United States pursuant to paragraph 2.

In cases where paragraph 2 is applicable, the income of the "employer" may be subject to tax in the host Contracting State even if it has no permanent establishment in the host country. Taxation under paragraph 2 is on the person providing the services of the performer. This paragraph does not affect the rules of paragraph 1, which apply to the performer himself. The income taxable by virtue of paragraph 2 is reduced to the extent of salary payments to the performer, which fall under paragraph 1.

For purposes of paragraph 2, income is deemed to accrue to another person (*i.e.*, the person providing the services of the performer) if that other person has control over, or the right to receive, gross income in respect of the services of the performer.

Since pursuant to Article 1 (General Scope) the Convention only applies to persons who are residents of one of the Contracting States, income of the star company would not be eligible for benefits of the Convention if the company is not a resident of one of the Contracting States.

Relationship to Other Articles

This Article is subject to the provisions of the saving clause of paragraph 4 of Article 1 (General Scope). Thus, if an entertainer or a sportsman who is resident in the other Contracting State is a citizen of the United States, the United States may tax all of his income from performances in the United States without regard to the provisions of this Article, subject, however, to the special foreign tax credit provisions of paragraph 4 of Article 23 (Relief from Double Taxation). In addition, benefits of this Article are subject to the provisions of Article 22 (Limitation on Benefits).

ARTICLE 17   (PENSIONS, SOCIAL SECURITY, ANNUITIES, ALIMONY, AND CHILD SUPPORT)

This Article deals with the taxation of private (i.e., non-government service) pensions and annuities, social security benefits, alimony and child support payments.

Paragraph 1

Paragraph 1 provides that distributions from pensions and other similar remuneration beneficially owned by a resident of a Contracting State in consideration of past employment are taxable only in the State of residence of the beneficiary. The term "pensions and other similar remuneration" includes both periodic and single sum payments.

The phrase "pensions and other similar remuneration" is intended to encompass payments made by qualified private retirement plans. In the United States, the plans encompassed by Paragraph 1 include: qualified plans under section 401(a), individual retirement plans (including individual retirement plans that are part of a simplified employee pension plan that satisfies section 408(k), individual retirement accounts and section 408(p) accounts), section 403(a) qualified annuity plans, and section 403(b) plans. Distributions from section 457 plans may also fall under Paragraph 1 if they are not paid with respect to government services covered by Article 19.

In the other Contracting State, the term pension applies to: [_____]. The competent authorities may agree that distributions from other plans that generally meet similar criteria to those applicable to the listed plans also qualify for the benefits of Paragraph 1.

Pensions in respect of government services covered by Article 19 are not covered by this paragraph. They are covered either by paragraph 2 of this Article, if they are in the form of social security benefits, or by paragraph 2 of Article 19 (Government Service). Thus, Article 19 generally covers section 457, 401(a), 403(b) plans established for government employees, and the Thrift Savings Plan (section 7701(j)).

However, the State of residence, under subparagraph (b), must exempt from tax any amount of such pensions or other similar remuneration that would be exempt from tax in the Contracting State in which the pension fund is established if the recipient were a resident of that State. Thus, for example, a distribution from a U.S. "Roth IRA" to a resident of the other Contracting State would be exempt from tax in the other Contracting State to the same extent the distribution would be exempt from tax in the United States if it were distributed to a U.S. resident. The same is true with respect to distributions from a traditional IRA to the extent that the distribution represents a return of non-deductible contributions. Similarly, if the distribution were not subject to tax when it was "rolled over" into another U.S. IRA (but not, for example, to a pension fund in the other Contracting State), then the distribution would be exempt from tax in the other Contracting State.

Paragraph 2

The treatment of social security benefits is dealt with in paragraph 2. This paragraph provides that, notwithstanding the provision of paragraph 1 under which private pensions are taxable exclusively in the State of residence of the beneficial owner, payments made by one of the Contracting States under the provisions of its social security or similar legislation to a resident of the other Contracting State or to a citizen of the United States will be taxable only in the Contracting State making the payment. The reference to U.S. citizens is necessary to ensure that a social security payment by the other Contracting State to a U.S. citizen who is not resident in the United States will not be taxable by the United States.

This paragraph applies to social security beneficiaries whether they have contributed to the system as private sector or Government employees. The phrase "similar legislation" is intended to refer to United States tier 1 Railroad Retirement benefits.

Paragraph 3

Under paragraph 3, annuities that are derived and beneficially owned by a resident of a Contracting State are taxable only in that State. An annuity, as the term is used in this paragraph, means a stated sum paid periodically at stated times during a specified number of years, under an obligation to make the payment in return for adequate and full consideration (other than for services rendered). An annuity received in consideration for services rendered would be treated as either deferred compensation that is taxable in accordance with Article 14 (Income from Employment) or a pension that is subject to the rules of Article 17 (Pensions, Social Security, Annuities, Alimony, and Child Support).

Paragraphs 4 and 5

Paragraphs 4 and 5 deal with alimony and child support payments. Both alimony, under paragraph 4, and child support payments, under paragraph 5, are defined as periodic payments made pursuant to a written separation agreement or a decree of divorce, separate maintenance, or compulsory support. Paragraph 4, however, deals only with payments of that type that are taxable to the payee. Under that paragraph, alimony paid by a resident of a Contracting State to a resident of the other Contracting State is taxable under the Convention only in the State of residence of the recipient. Paragraph 5 deals with those periodic payments that are for the support of a child and that are not covered by paragraph 4. These types of payments by a resident of a Contracting State to a resident of the other Contracting State are taxable in neither Contracting State.

Relationship to Other Articles

Paragraphs 1(a), 3 and 4 of Article 17 are subject to the saving clause of paragraph 4 of Article 1 (General Scope). Thus, a U.S. citizen who is resident in the other Contracting State, and receives either a pension, annuity or alimony payment from the United States, may be subject to U.S. tax on the payment, notwithstanding the rules in those three paragraphs that give the State of residence of the recipient the exclusive taxing right. Paragraphs 1(b), 2 and 5 are excepted from the saving clause by virtue of subparagraph 5(a) of Article 1. Thus, the United States will not tax U.S. citizens and residents on the income described in those paragraphs even if such amounts otherwise would be subject to tax under U.S. law.

ARTICLE 18   (PENSION FUNDS)

Article 18 deals with cross-border pension contributions. It is intended to remove barriers to the flow of personal services between the Contracting States that could otherwise result from discontinuities in the laws of the Contracting States regarding the deductibility of pension contributions. Such discontinuities may arise where countries allow deductions or exclusions to their residents for contributions, made by them or on their behalf, to resident pension plans, but do not allow deductions or exclusions for payments made to plans resident in another country, even if the structure and legal requirements of such plans in the two countries are similar.

Paragraph 1

Paragraph 1 provides that, if a resident of a Contracting State participates in a pension fund established in the other Contracting State, the State of residence will not tax the income of the pension fund with respect to that resident until a distribution is made from the pension fund. Thus, for example, if a U.S. citizen contributes to a U.S. qualified plan while working in the United States and then establishes residence in the other Contracting State, paragraph 1 prevents the other Contracting State from taxing currently the plan's earnings and accretions with respect to that individual. When the resident receives a distribution from the pension fund, that distribution may be subject to tax in the State of residence, subject to paragraph 1 of Article 17 (Pensions, Social Security, Annuities, Alimony, and Child Support).

Paragraph 2

Paragraph 2 provides certain benefits with respect to cross-border contributions to a pension fund, subject to the limitations of paragraphs 3 and 4 of the Article. It is irrelevant for purposes of paragraph 2 whether the participant establishes residence in the State where the individual renders services (the "host State").

Subparagraph (a) of paragraph 2 allows an individual who exercises employment or self-employment in a Contracting State to deduct or exclude from income in that Contracting State contributions made by or on behalf of the individual during the period of employment or self-employment to a pension fund established in the other Contracting State. Thus, for example, if a participant in a U.S. qualified plan goes to work in the other Contracting State, the participant may deduct or exclude from income in the other Contracting State contributions to the U.S. qualified plan made while the participant works in the other Contracting State. Subparagraph (a), however, applies only to the extent of the relief allowed by the host State (*e.g.*, the other Contracting State in the example) for contributions to a pension fund established in that State.

Subparagraph (b) of paragraph 2 provides that, in the case of employment, accrued benefits and contributions by or on behalf of the individual's employer, during the period of employment in the host State, will not be treated as taxable income to the employee in that State. Subparagraph (b) also allows the employer a deduction in computing its taxable income in the host State for contributions to the plan. For example, if a participant in a U.S. qualified plan goes to work in the other Contracting State, the participant's employer may deduct from its taxable income in the other Contracting State contributions to the U.S. qualified plan for the benefit of the employee while the employee renders services in the other Contracting State.

As in the case of subparagraph (a), subparagraph (b) applies only to the extent of the relief allowed by the host State for contributions to pension funds established in that State. Therefore, where the United States is the host State, the exclusion of employee contributions from the employee's income under this paragraph is limited to contributions not in excess of the amount specified in section 402(g) for elective contributions. Deduction of employer contributions is subject to the limitations of sections 415 and 404. The section 404 limitation on deductions is calculated as if the individual were the only employee covered by the plan.

Paragraph 3

Paragraph 3 limits the availability of benefits under paragraph 2. Under subparagraph (a) of paragraph 3, paragraph 2 does not apply to contributions to a pension fund unless the participant already was contributing to the fund, or his employer already was contributing to the fund with respect to that individual, before the individual began exercising employment in the host State. This condition would be met if either the employee or the employer was contributing to a fund that was replaced by the fund to which he is contributing. The rule regarding successor funds would apply if, for example, the employer has been taken over by a company that replaces the existing fund with its own fund, rolling membership in the old fund over into the new fund.

In addition, under subparagraph (b) of paragraph 3, the competent authority of the host State must determine that the recognized plan to which a contribution is made in the other Contracting State generally corresponds to the plan in the host State. For this purpose the U.S. pension funds eligible for the benefits of paragraph 2 include qualified plans under section 401(a), individual retirement plans (including individual retirement plans that are part of a simplified employee pension plan that satisfies section 408(k)), individual retirement accounts, individual retirement annuities, section 408(p) accounts and Roth IRAs under section 408A), section 403(a) qualified annuity plans, section 403(b) plans, section 457(b) plans and the Thrift Savings Plan (section 7701(j)).

Paragraph 4

Paragraph 4 generally provides U.S. tax treatment for certain contributions by or on behalf of U.S. citizens resident in the other Contracting State to pension funds established in the other Contracting State that is comparable to the treatment that would be provided for contributions to U.S. funds. Under subparagraph (a), a U.S. citizen resident in the other Contracting State may exclude or deduct for U.S. tax purposes certain contributions to a pension fund established in the other Contracting State. Qualifying contributions generally include contributions made during the period the U.S. citizen exercises an employment in the other Contracting State if expenses of the employment are borne by an employer or permanent establishment in that other Contracting State. Similarly, with respect to the U.S. citizen's participation in the pension fund in the other Contracting State, accrued benefits and contributions during that period generally are not treated as taxable income in the United States.

The U.S. tax benefit allowed by paragraph 4, however, is limited under subparagraph (b) to the lesser of the amount of relief allowed for contributions and benefits under a pension fund established in the other Contracting State and the amount of relief that would be allowed for contributions and benefits under a generally corresponding pension fund established in the United States.

Subparagraph (c) provides that the benefits an individual obtains under paragraph 4 are counted when determining that individual's eligibility for benefits under a pension fund established in the United States. Thus, for example, contributions to a pension fund in the other Contracting State may be counted in determining whether the individual has exceeded the annual limitation on contributions to an individual retirement account.

Under subparagraph (d), paragraph 4 does not apply to pension contributions and benefits unless the competent authority of the United States has agreed that the pension fund established in the other Contracting State generally corresponds to a pension fund established in the United States. The notes provide that certain pension funds have been determined to "generally correspond" to funds in the other country. Since paragraph 4 applies only with respect to employees, however, the relevant plans are those that correspond to employer plans in the United States.

Relationship to Other Articles

Paragraphs 1 and 4 of Article 18 are excepted from the saving clause of paragraph 4 of Article 1 by virtue of paragraph 5(a) of Article 1. Thus, the United States will allow U.S. citizens and residents the benefits of paragraphs 1 and 4. Paragraph 2 is excepted from the saving clause by subparagraph 5(b) of Article 1 with respect only to persons who are not admitted for permanent residence or citizens. Accordingly, a person who becomes a U.S. permanent resident or citizen will no longer receive a deduction for contributions to a pension fund established in the other Contracting State.

ARTICLE 19   (GOVERNMENT SERVICE)

Paragraph 1

Subparagraphs (a) and (b) of paragraph 1 deal with the taxation of government compensation (other than a pension addressed in paragraph 2). Subparagraph (a) provides that remuneration paid to any individual who is rendering services to that State, political subdivision or local authority is exempt from tax by the other State. Under subparagraph (b), such payments are, however, taxable exclusively in the other State (i.e., the host State) if the services are rendered in that other State and the individual is a resident of that State who is either a national of that State or a person who did not become resident of that State solely for purposes of rendering the services. The paragraph applies to anyone performing services for a government, whether as a government employee, an independent contractor, or an employee of an independent contractor.

Paragraph 2

Paragraph 2 deals with the taxation of pensions paid by, or out of funds created by, one of the States, or a political subdivision or a local authority thereof, to an individual in respect of services rendered to that State or subdivision or authority.

Subparagraph (a) provides that such pensions are taxable only in that State. Subparagraph (b) provides an exception under which such pensions are taxable only in the other State if the individual is a resident of, and a national of, that other State.

Pensions paid to retired civilian and military employees of a Government of either State are intended to be covered under paragraph 2. When benefits paid by a State in respect of services rendered to that State or a subdivision or authority are in the form of social security benefits, however, those payments are covered by paragraph 2 of Article 17 (Pensions, Social Security, Annuities, Alimony, and Child Support). As a general matter, the result will be the same whether Article 17 or 19 applies, since social security benefits are taxable exclusively by the source country and so are government pensions. The result will differ only when the payment is made to a citizen and resident of the other Contracting State, who is not also a citizen of the paying State. In such a case, social security benefits continue to be taxable at source while government pensions become taxable only in the residence country.

Paragraph 3

Paragraph 3 provides that the remuneration described in paragraph 1 will be subject to the rules of Articles 14 (Income from Employment), 15 (Directors' Fees), 16 (Entertainers and Sportsmen) or 17 (Pensions, Social Security, Annuities, Alimony, and Child Support) if the recipient of the income is employed by a business conducted by a government.

Relationship to Other Articles

Under paragraph 5(b) of Article 1 (General Scope), the saving clause (paragraph 4 of Article 1) does not apply to the benefits conferred by one of the States under Article 19 if the recipient of the benefits is neither a citizen of that State, nor a person who has been admitted for permanent residence there (i.e., in the United States, a "green card" holder). Thus, a resident of a Contracting State who in the course of performing functions of a governmental nature becomes a resident of the other State (but not a permanent resident), would be entitled to the benefits of this Article. However, an individual who receives a pension paid by the Government of the other Contracting State in respect of services rendered to that Government shall be taxable on this pension only in the other Contracting State unless the individual is a U.S. citizen or acquires a U.S. green card.

ARTICLE 20   (STUDENTS AND TRAINEES)

This Article provides rules for host-country taxation of visiting students and business trainees. Persons who meet the tests of the Article will be exempt from tax in the State that they are visiting with respect to designated classes of income. Several conditions must be satisfied in order for an individual to be entitled to the benefits of this Article.

First, the visitor must have been, either at the time of his arrival in the host State or immediately before, a resident of the other Contracting State.

Second, the purpose of the visit must be the full-time education or training of the visitor. Thus, if the visitor comes principally to work in the host State but also is a part-time student, he would not be entitled to the benefits of this Article, even with respect to any payments he may receive from abroad for his maintenance or education, and regardless of whether or not he is in a degree program. Whether a student is to be considered full-time will be determined by the rules of the educational institution at which he is studying.

The host-country exemption in the Article applies to payments received by the student or business trainee for the purpose of his maintenance, education or training that arise outside the host State. A payment will be considered to arise outside the host State if the payer is located outside the host State. Thus, if an employer from one of the Contracting States sends an employee to the other Contracting State for training, the payments the trainee receives from abroad from his employer for his maintenance or training while he is present in the host State will be exempt from tax in the host State. Where appropriate, substance prevails over form in determining the identity of the payer. Thus, for example, payments made directly or indirectly by a U.S. person with whom the visitor is training, but which have been routed through a source outside the United States (*e.g.*, a foreign subsidiary), are not treated as arising outside the United States for this purpose.

The Article also provides a limited exemption for remuneration from personal services rendered in the host State with a view to supplementing the resources available to him for such purposes to the extent of $9,000 United States dollars (or its equivalent in the currency of the other Contracting State) per taxable year. The specified amount is intended to equalize the position of a U.S. resident who is entitled to the standard deduction and the personal exemption with that of a student who files as a non-resident alien and therefore does not. Accordingly, the competent authorities are instructed to adjust this amount every five years, if necessary, to take into account changes in the amount of the U.S. standard deduction and personal exemption.

In the case of a business trainee, the benefits of the Article will extend only for a period of one year from the time that the visitor first arrives in the host country. If, however, a trainee remains in the host country for a second year, thus losing the benefits of the Article, he would not retroactively lose the benefits of the Article for the first year. The term "business trainee" is defined as a person who is in the country temporarily for the purpose of securing training that is necessary to qualify to pursue a profession or professional specialty. Moreover, the person must be employed or under contract with a resident of the other Contracting State and must be receiving the training from someone who is not related to its employer. Thus, a business trainee might include a lawyer employed by a law firm in one Contracting State who works for one year as a *stagiare* in an unrelated law firm in the other Contracting State. However, the term would not include a manager who normally is employed by a parent company in one Contracting State who is sent to the other Contracting State to run a factory owned by a subsidiary of the parent company.

Relationship to Other Articles

The saving clause of paragraph 4 of Article 1 (General Scope) does not apply to this Article with respect to an individual who is neither a citizen of the host State nor has been admitted for permanent residence there. The saving clause, however, does apply with respect to citizens and permanent residents of the host State. Thus, a U.S. citizen who is a resident of the other Contracting State and who visits the United States as a full-time student at an accredited university will not be exempt from U.S. tax on remittances from abroad that otherwise constitute U.S. taxable income. A person, however, who is not a U.S. citizen, and who visits the United States as a student and remains long enough to become a resident under U.S. law, but does not become a permanent resident (i.e., does not acquire a green card), will be entitled to the full benefits of the Article.

ARTICLE 21   (OTHER INCOME)

Article 21 generally assigns taxing jurisdiction over income not dealt with in the other articles (Articles 6 through 20) of the Convention to the State of residence of the beneficial owner of the income. In order for an item of income to be "dealt with" in another article it must be the type of income described in the article and, in most cases, it must have its source in a Contracting State. For example, all royalty income that arises in a Contracting State and that is beneficially owned by a resident of the other Contracting State is "dealt with" in Article 12 (Royalties). However, profits derived in the conduct of a business are "dealt with" in Article 7 (Business Profits) whether or not they have their source in one of the Contracting States.

Examples of items of income covered by Article 21 include income from gambling, punitive (but not compensatory) damages and covenants not to compete. The article would also apply to income from a variety of financial transactions, where such income does not arise in the course of the conduct of a trade or business. For example, income from notional principal contracts and other derivatives would fall within Article 21 if derived by persons not engaged in the trade or business of dealing in such instruments, unless such instruments were being used to hedge risks arising in a trade or business. It would also apply to securities lending fees derived by an institutional investor. Further, in most cases guarantee fees paid within an intercompany group would be covered by Article 21, unless the guarantor were engaged in the business of providing such guarantees to unrelated parties.

Article 21 also applies to items of income that are not dealt with in the other articles because of their source or some other characteristic. For example, Article 11 (Interest) addresses only the taxation of interest arising in a Contracting State. Interest arising in a third State that is not attributable to a permanent establishment, therefore, is subject to Article 21.

Distributions from partnerships are not generally dealt with under Article 21 because partnership distributions generally do not constitute income. Under the Code, partners include in income their distributive share of partnership income annually, and partnership distributions themselves generally do not give rise to income. This would also be the case under U.S. law with respect to distributions from trusts. Trust income and distributions that, under the Code, have the character of the associated distributable net income would generally be covered by another article of the Convention. See Code section 641 et seq.

Paragraph 1

The general rule of Article 21 is contained in paragraph 1. Items of income not dealt with in other articles and beneficially owned by a resident of a Contracting State will be taxable only in the State of residence. This exclusive right of taxation applies whether or not the residence State exercises its right to tax the income covered by the Article.

The reference in this paragraph to "items of income beneficially owned by a resident of a Contracting State" rather than simply "items of income of a resident of a Contracting State," as in the OECD Model, is intended merely to make explicit the implicit understanding in other treaties that the exclusive residence taxation provided by paragraph 1 applies only when a resident of a Contracting State is the beneficial owner of the income. Thus, source taxation of income not dealt with in other articles of the Convention is not limited by paragraph 1 if it is nominally paid to a resident of the other Contracting State, but is beneficially owned by a resident of a third State. However, income received by a nominee on behalf of a resident of that other State would be entitled to benefits.

The term "beneficially owned" is not defined in the Convention, and is, therefore, defined as under the internal law of the country imposing tax (*i.e.*, the source country). The person who beneficially owns the income for purposes of Article 21 is the person to which the income is attributable for tax purposes under the laws of the source State.

Paragraph 2

This paragraph provides an exception to the general rule of paragraph 1 for income that is attributable to a permanent establishment maintained in a Contracting State by a resident of the other Contracting State. The taxation of such income is governed by the provisions of Article 7 (Business Profits). Therefore, income arising outside the United States that is attributable to a permanent establishment maintained in the United States by a resident of the other Contracting State generally would be taxable by the United States under the provisions of Article 7. This would be true even if the income is sourced in a third State.

Relationship to Other Articles

This Article is subject to the saving clause of paragraph 4 of Article 1 (General Scope). Thus, the United States may tax the income of a resident of the other Contracting State that is not dealt with elsewhere in the Convention, if that resident is a citizen of the United States. The Article is also subject to the provisions of Article 22 (Limitation on Benefits). Thus, if a resident of the other Contracting State earns income that falls within the scope of paragraph 1 of Article 21, but that is taxable by the United States under U.S. law, the income would be exempt from U.S. tax under the provisions of Article 21 only if the resident satisfies one of the tests of Article 22 for entitlement to benefits.

ARTICLE 22   (LIMITATION ON BENEFITS)

Article 22 contains anti-treaty-shopping provisions that are intended to prevent residents of third countries from benefiting from what is intended to be a reciprocal agreement between two countries. In general, the provision does not rely on a determination of purpose or intention but instead sets forth a series of objective tests. A resident of a Contracting State that satisfies one of the tests will receive benefits regardless of its motivations in choosing its particular business structure.

The structure of the Article is as follows: Paragraph 1 states the general rule that residents are entitled to benefits otherwise accorded to residents only to the extent provided in the Article. Paragraph 2 lists a series of attributes of a resident of a Contracting State, the presence of any one of which will entitle that person to all the benefits of the Convention. Paragraph 3 provides that, regardless of whether a person qualifies for benefits under paragraph 2, benefits may be granted to that person with regard to certain income earned in the conduct of an active trade or business. Paragraph 4 provides that benefits also may be granted if the competent authority of the State from which benefits are claimed determines that it is appropriate to provide benefits in that case. Paragraph 5 defines certain terms used in the Article.

Paragraph 1

Paragraph 1 provides that a resident of a Contracting State will be entitled to the benefits otherwise accorded to residents of a Contracting State under the Convention only to the extent provided in the Article. The benefits otherwise accorded to residents under the Convention include all limitations on source-based taxation under Articles 6 through 21, the treaty-based relief from double taxation provided by Article 23, and the protection afforded to residents of a Contracting State under Article 24. Some provisions do not require that a person be a resident in order to enjoy the benefits of those provisions. Article 25 is not limited to residents of the Contracting States, and Article 27 applies to diplomatic agents or consular officials regardless of residence. Article 22 accordingly does not limit the availability of treaty benefits under these provisions.

Article 22 and the anti-abuse provisions of domestic law complement each other, as Article 22 effectively determines whether an entity has a sufficient nexus to the Contracting State to be treated as a resident for treaty purposes, while domestic anti-abuse provisions (*e.g.*, business purpose, substance-over-form, step transaction or conduit principles) determine whether a particular transaction should be recast in accordance with its substance. Thus, internal law principles of the source Contracting State may be applied to identify the beneficial owner of an item of income, and Article 22 then will be applied to the beneficial owner to determine if that person is entitled to the benefits of the Convention with respect to such income.

Paragraph 2

Paragraph 2 has six subparagraphs, each of which describes a category of residents that are entitled to all benefits of the Convention.

It is intended that the provisions of paragraph 2 will be self executing. Unlike the provisions of paragraph 4, discussed below, claiming benefits under paragraph 2 does not require advance competent authority ruling or approval. The tax authorities may, of course, on review, determine that the taxpayer has improperly interpreted the paragraph and is not entitled to the benefits claimed.

Individuals — Subparagraph 2(a)

Subparagraph (a) provides that individual residents of a Contracting State will be entitled to all treaty benefits. If such an individual receives income as a nominee on behalf of a third country resident, benefits may be denied under the respective articles of the Convention by the requirement that the beneficial owner of the income be a resident of a Contracting State.

Governments — Subparagraph 2(b)

Subparagraph (b) provides that the Contracting States and any political subdivision or local authority thereof will be entitled to all benefits of the Convention.

Publicly-Traded Corporations — Subparagraph 2(c)(i)

Subparagraph (c) applies to two categories of companies: publicly traded companies and subsidiaries of publicly traded companies. A company resident in a Contracting State is entitled to all the benefits of the Convention under clause (i) of subparagraph (c) if the principal class of its shares, and any disproportionate class of shares, is regularly traded on one or more recognized stock exchanges and the company satisfies at least one of the following additional requirements: first, the company's principal class of shares is primarily traded on one or more recognized stock exchanges located in the Contracting State of which the company is a resident; or, second, the company's primary place of management and control is in its State of residence.

The term "recognized stock exchange" is defined in subparagraph (a) of paragraph 5. It includes (i) the NASDAQ System and any stock exchange registered with the Securities and Exchange Commission as a national securities exchange for purposes of the Securities Exchange Act of 1934; (ii) [certain exchanges located in the other Contracting State]; and (iii) any other stock exchange agreed upon by the competent authorities of the Contracting States.

If a company has only one class of shares, it is only necessary to consider whether the shares of that class meet the relevant trading requirements. If the company has more than one class of shares, it is necessary as an initial matter to determine which class or classes constitute the "principal class of shares". The term "principal class of shares" is defined in subparagraph (b) of paragraph 5 to mean the ordinary or common shares of the company representing the majority of the aggregate voting power and value of the company. If the company does not have a class of ordinary or common shares representing the majority of the aggregate voting power and value of the company, then the "principal class of shares" is that class or any combination of classes of shares that represents, in the aggregate, a majority of the voting power and value of the company. Although in a particular case involving a company with several classes of shares it is conceivable that more than one group of classes could be identified that account for more than 50% of the shares, it is only necessary for one such group to satisfy the requirements of this subparagraph in order for the company to be entitled to benefits. Benefits would not be denied to the company even if a second, non-qualifying, group of shares with more than half of the company's voting power and value could be identified.

A company whose principal class of shares is regularly traded on a recognized stock exchange will nevertheless not qualify for benefits under subparagraph (c) of paragraph 2 if it has a disproportionate class of shares that is not regularly traded on a recognized stock exchange.

The term "disproportionate class of shares" is defined in subparagraph (c) of paragraph 5. A company has a disproportionate class of shares if it has outstanding a class of shares which is subject to terms or other arrangements that entitle the holder to a larger portion of the company's income, profit, or gain in the other Contracting State than that to which the holder would be entitled in the absence of such terms or arrangements. Thus, for example, a company resident in the other Contracting State meets the test of subparagraph (c) of paragraph 5 if it has outstanding a class of "tracking stock" that pays dividends based upon a formula that approximates the company's return on its assets employed in the United States.

The following example illustrates this result.

Example. OCo is a corporation resident in the other Contracting State. OCo has two classes of shares: Common and Preferred. The Common shares are listed and regularly traded on the principal stock exchange of the other Contracting State. The Preferred shares have no voting rights and are entitled to receive dividends equal in amount to interest payments that OCo receives from unrelated borrowers in the United States. The Preferred shares are owned entirely by a single investor that is a resident of a country with which the United States does not have a tax treaty. The Common shares account for more than 50 percent of the value of OCo and for 100 percent of the voting power. Because the owner of the Preferred shares is entitled to receive payments corresponding to the U.S. source interest income earned by OCo, the Preferred shares are a disproportionate class of shares. Because the Preferred shares are not regularly traded on a recognized stock exchange, OCo will not qualify for benefits under subparagraph (c) of paragraph 2.

The term "regularly traded" is not defined in the Convention. In accordance with paragraph 2 of Article 3 (General Definitions), this term will be defined by reference to the domestic tax laws of the State from which treaty benefits are sought, generally the source State. In the case of the United States, this term is understood to have the meaning it has under Treas. Reg. section 1.884-5(d)(4)(i)(B), relating to the branch tax provisions of the Code. Under these regulations, a class of shares is considered to be "regularly traded" if two requirements are met: trades in the class of shares are made in more than de minimis quantities on at least 60 days during the taxable year, and the aggregate number of shares in the class traded during the year is at least 10 percent of the average number of shares outstanding during the year. Sections 1.884-5(d)(4)(i)(A), (ii) and (iii) will not be taken into account for purposes of defining the term "regularly traded" under the Convention.

The regular trading requirement can be met by trading on any recognized exchange or exchanges located in either State. Trading on one or more recognized stock exchanges may be aggregated for purposes of this requirement. Thus, a U.S. company could satisfy the regularly traded requirement through trading, in whole or in part, on a recognized stock exchange located in the other Contracting State. Authorized but unissued shares are not considered for purposes of this test.

The term "primarily traded" is not defined in the Convention. In accordance with paragraph 2 of Article 3 (General Definitions), this term will have the meaning it has under the laws of the State concerning the taxes to which the Convention applies, generally the source State. In the case of the United States, this term is understood to have the meaning it has under Treas. Reg. section 1.884-5(d)(3), relating to the branch tax provisions of the Code. Accordingly, stock of a corporation is "primarily traded" if the number of shares in the company's principal class of shares that are traded during the taxable year on all recognized stock exchanges in the Contracting State of which the company is a resident exceeds the number of shares in the company's principal class of shares that are traded during that year on established securities markets in any other single foreign country.

A company whose principal class of shares is regularly traded on a recognized exchange but cannot meet the primarily traded test may claim treaty benefits if its primary place of management and control is in its country of residence. This test should be distinguished from the "place of effective management" test which is used in the OECD Model and by many other countries to establish residence. In some cases, the place of effective management test has been interpreted to mean the place where the board of directors meets. By contrast, the primary place of management and control test looks to where day-to-day responsibility for the management of the company (and its subsidiaries) is exercised. The company's primary place of management and control will be located in the State in which the company is a resident only if the executive officers and senior management employees exercise day-to-day responsibility for more of the strategic, financial and operational policy decision making for the company (including direct and indirect subsidiaries) in that State than in the other State or any third state, and the staff that support the management in making those decisions are also based in that State. Thus, the test looks to the overall activities of the relevant persons to see where those activities are conducted. In most cases, it will be a necessary, but not a sufficient, condition that the headquarters of the company (that is, the place at which the CEO and other top executives normally are based) be located in the Contracting State of which the company is a resident.

To apply the test, it will be necessary to determine which persons are to be considered "executive officers and senior management employees". In most cases, it will not be necessary to look beyond the executives who are members of the Board of Directors (the "inside directors") in the case of a U.S. company or the members of the [_____] in the case of the other Contracting State. That will not always be the case, however; in fact, the relevant persons may be employees of subsidiaries if those persons make the strategic, financial and operational policy decisions. Moreover, it would be necessary to take into account any special voting arrangements that result in certain board members making certain decisions without the participation of other board members.

Subsidiaries of Publicly-Traded Corporations — Subparagraph 2(c)(ii)

A company resident in a Contracting State is entitled to all the benefits of the Convention under clause (ii) of subparagraph (c) of paragraph 2 if five or fewer publicly traded companies described in clause (i) are the direct or indirect owners of at least 50 percent of the aggregate vote and value of the company's shares (and at least 50 percent of any disproportionate class of shares). If the publicly-traded companies are indirect owners, however, each of the intermediate companies must be a resident of one of the Contracting States.

Thus, for example, a company that is a resident of the other Contracting State, all the shares of which are owned by another company that is a resident of that State, would qualify for benefits under the Convention if the principal class of shares (and any disproportionate classes of shares) of the parent company are regularly and primarily traded on a recognized stock exchange in that Contracting State. However, such a subsidiary would not qualify for benefits under clause (ii) if the publicly traded parent company were a resident of a third state, for example, and not a resident of the United States or the other Contracting State. Furthermore, if a parent company in the other Contracting State indirectly owned the bottom-tier company through a chain of subsidiaries, each such subsidiary in the chain, as an intermediate owner, must be a resident of the United States or the other Contracting State in order for the subsidiary to meet the test in clause (ii).

Tax Exempt Organizations — Subparagraph 2(d)

Subparagraph 2(d) provides rules by which the tax exempt organizations described in paragraph 2 of Article 4 (Resident) will be entitled to all the benefits of the Convention. A pension fund will qualify for benefits if more than fifty percent of the beneficiaries, members or participants of the organization are individuals resident in either Contracting State. For purposes of this provision, the term "beneficiaries" should be understood to refer to the persons receiving benefits from the organization. On the other hand, a tax-exempt organization other than a pension fund automatically qualifies for benefits, without regard to the residence of its beneficiaries or members. Entities qualifying under this rule generally are those that are exempt from tax in their State of residence and that are organized and operated exclusively to fulfill religious, charitable, scientific, artistic, cultural, or educational purposes.

Ownership/Base Erosion — Subparagraph 2(e)

Subparagraph 2(e) provides an additional method to qualify for treaty benefits that applies to any form of legal entity that is a resident of a Contracting State. The test provided in subparagraph (e), the so-called ownership and base erosion test, is a two-part test. Both prongs of the test must be satisfied for the resident to be entitled to treaty benefits under subparagraph 2(e).

The ownership prong of the test, under clause (i), requires that 50 percent or more of each class of shares or other beneficial interests in the person is owned, directly or indirectly, on at least half the days of the person's taxable year by persons who are residents of the Contracting State of which that person is a resident and that are themselves entitled to treaty benefits under subparagraphs (a), (b), (d) or clause (i) of subparagraph (c) of paragraph 2. In the case of indirect owners, however, each of the intermediate owners must be a resident of that Contracting State.

Trusts may be entitled to benefits under this provision if they are treated as residents under Article 4 (Residence) and they otherwise satisfy the requirements of this subparagraph. For purposes of this subparagraph, the beneficial interests in a trust will be considered to be owned by its beneficiaries in proportion to each beneficiary's actuarial interest in the trust. The interest of a remainder beneficiary will be equal to 100 percent less the aggregate percentages held by income beneficiaries. A beneficiary's interest in a trust will not be considered to be owned by a person entitled to benefits under the other provisions of paragraph 2 if it is not possible to determine the beneficiary's actuarial interest. Consequently, if it is not possible to determine the actuarial interest of the beneficiaries in a trust, the ownership test under clause i) cannot be satisfied, unless all possible beneficiaries are persons entitled to benefits under the other subparagraphs of paragraph 2.

The base erosion prong of clause (ii) of subparagraph (e) is satisfied with respect to a person if less than 50 percent of the person's gross income for the taxable year, as determined under the tax law in the person's State of residence, is paid or accrued to persons who are not residents of either Contracting State entitled to benefits under subparagraphs (a), (b), (d) or clause (i) of subparagraph (c) of paragraph 2, in the form of payments deductible for tax purposes in the payer's State of residence. These amounts do not include arm's-length payments in the ordinary course of business for services or tangible property. To the extent they are deductible from the taxable base, trust distributions are deductible payments. However, depreciation and amortization deductions, which do not represent payments or accruals to other persons, are disregarded for this purpose.

Paragraph 3

Paragraph 3 sets forth an alternative test under which a resident of a Contracting State may receive treaty benefits with respect to certain items of income that are connected to an active trade or business conducted in its State of residence. A resident of a Contracting State may qualify for benefits under paragraph 3 whether or not it also qualifies under paragraph 2.

Subparagraph (a) sets forth the general rule that a resident of a Contracting State engaged in the active conduct of a trade or business in that State may obtain the benefits of the Convention with respect to an item of income derived in the other Contracting State. The item of income, however, must be derived in connection with or incidental to that trade or business.

The term "trade or business" is not defined in the Convention. Pursuant to paragraph 2 of Article 3 (General Definitions), when determining whether a resident of the other Contracting State is entitled to the benefits of the Convention under paragraph 3 of this Article with respect to an item of income derived from sources within the United States, the United States will ascribe to this term the meaning that it has under the law of the United States. Accordingly, the U.S. competent authority will refer to the regulations issued under section 367(a) for the definition of the term "trade or business." In general, therefore, a trade or business will be considered to be a specific unified group of activities that constitute or could constitute an independent economic enterprise carried on for profit. Furthermore, a corporation generally will be considered to carry on a trade or business only if the officers and employees of the corporation conduct substantial managerial and operational activities.

The business of making or managing investments for the resident's own account will be considered to be a trade or business only when part of banking, insurance or securities activities conducted by a bank, an insurance company, or a registered securities dealer. Such activities conducted by a person other than a bank, insurance company or registered securities dealer will not be considered to be the conduct of an active trade or business, nor would they be considered to be the conduct of an active trade or business if conducted by a bank, insurance company or registered securities dealer but not as part of the company's banking, insurance or dealer business. Because a headquarters operation is in the business of managing investments, a company that functions solely as a headquarters company will not be considered to be engaged in an active trade or business for purposes of paragraph 3.

An item of income is derived in connection with a trade or business if the income-producing activity in the State of source is a line of business that "forms a part of" or is "complementary" to the trade or business conducted in the State of residence by the income recipient.

A business activity generally will be considered to form part of a business activity conducted in the State of source if the two activities involve the design, manufacture or sale of the same products or type of products, or the provision of similar services. The line of business in the State of residence may be upstream, downstream, or parallel to the activity conducted in the State of source. Thus, the line of business may provide inputs for a manufacturing process that occurs in the State of source, may sell the output of that manufacturing process, or simply may sell the same sorts of products that are being sold by the trade or business carried on in the State of source.

Example 1. USCo is a corporation resident in the United States. USCo is engaged in an active manufacturing business in the United States. USCo owns 100 percent of the shares of FCo, a corporation resident in the other Contracting State. FCo distributes USCo products in the other Contracting State. Since the business activities conducted by the two corporations involve the same products, FCo's distribution business is considered to form a part of USCo's manufacturing business.

Example 2. The facts are the same as in Example 1, except that USCo does not manufacture. Rather, USCo operates a large research and development facility in the United States that licenses intellectual property to affiliates worldwide, including FCo. FCo and other USCo affiliates then manufacture and market the USCo-designed products in their respective markets. Since the activities conducted by FCo and USCo involve the same product lines, these activities are considered to form a part of the same trade or business.

For two activities to be considered to be "complementary," the activities need not relate to the same types of products or services, but they should be part of the same overall industry and be related in the sense that the success or failure of one activity will tend to result in success or failure for the other. Where more than one trade or business is conducted in the State of source and only one of the trades or businesses forms a part of or is complementary to a trade or business conducted in the State of residence, it is necessary to identify the trade or business to which an item of income is attributable. Royalties generally will be considered to be derived in connection with the trade or business to which the underlying intangible property is attributable. Dividends will be deemed to be derived first out of earnings and profits of the treaty-benefited trade or business, and then out of other earnings and profits. Interest income may be allocated under any reasonable method consistently applied. A method that conforms to U.S. principles for expense allocation will be considered a reasonable method.

Example 3. Americair is a corporation resident in the United States that operates an international airline. FSub is a wholly-owned subsidiary of Americair resident in the other Contracting State. FSub operates a chain of hotels in the other Contracting State that are located near airports served by Americair flights. Americair frequently sells tour packages that include air travel to the other Contracting State and lodging at FSub hotels. Although both companies are engaged in the active conduct of a trade or business, the businesses of operating a chain of hotels and operating an airline are distinct trades or businesses. Therefore FSub's business does not form a part of Americair's business. However, FSub's business is considered to be complementary to Americair's business because they are part of the same overall industry (travel) and the links between their operations tend to make them interdependent.

Example 4. The facts are the same as in Example 3, except that FSub owns an office building in the other Contracting State instead of a hotel chain. No part of Americair's business is conducted through the office building. FSub's business is not considered to form a part of or to be complementary to Americair's business. They are engaged in distinct trades or businesses in separate industries, and there is no economic dependence between the two operations.

Example 5. USFlower is a corporation resident in the United States. USFlower produces and sells flowers in the United States and other countries. USFlower owns all the shares of ForHolding, a corporation resident in the other Contracting State. ForHolding is a holding company that is not engaged in a trade or business. ForHolding owns all the shares of three corporations that are resident in the other Contracting State: ForFlower, ForLawn, and ForFish. ForFlower distributes USFlower flowers under the USFlower trademark in the other State. ForLawn markets a line of lawn care products in the other State under the USFlower trademark. In addition to being sold under the same trademark, ForLawn and ForFlower products are sold in the same stores and sales of each company's products tend to generate increased sales of the other's products. ForFish imports fish from the United States and distributes it to fish wholesalers in the other State. For purposes of paragraph 3, the business of ForFlower forms a part of the business of USFlower, the business of ForLawn is complementary to the business of USFlower, and the business of ForFish is neither part of nor complementary to that of USFlower.

An item of income derived from the State of source is "incidental to" the trade or business carried on in the State of residence if production of the item facilitates the conduct of the trade or business in the State of residence. An example of incidental income is the temporary investment of working capital of a person in the State of residence in securities issued by persons in the State of source.

Subparagraph (b) of paragraph 3 states a further condition to the general rule in subparagraph (a) in cases where the trade or business generating the item of income in question is carried on either by the person deriving the income or by any associated enterprises. Subparagraph (b) states that the trade or business carried on in the State of residence, under these circumstances, must be substantial in relation to the activity in the State of source. The substantiality requirement is intended to prevent a narrow case of treaty-shopping abuses in which a company attempts to qualify for benefits by engaging in de minimis connected business activities in the treaty country in which it is resident (*i.e.*, activities that have little economic cost or effect with respect to the company business as a whole).

The determination of substantiality is made based upon all the facts and circumstances and takes into account the comparative sizes of the trades or businesses in each Contracting State the nature of the activities performed in each Contracting State, and the relative contributions made to that trade or business in each Contracting State. In any case, in making each determination or comparison, due regard will be given to the relative sizes of the economies in the two Contracting States.

The determination in subparagraph (b) also is made separately for each item of income derived from the State of source. It therefore is possible that a person would be entitled to the benefits of the Convention with respect to one item of income but not with respect to another. If a resident of a Contracting State is entitled to treaty benefits with respect to a particular item of income under paragraph 3, the resident is entitled to all benefits of the Convention insofar as they affect the taxation of that item of income in the State of source.

The application of the substantiality requirement only to income from related parties focuses only on potential abuse cases, and does not hamper certain other kinds of non-abusive activities, even though the income recipient resident in a Contracting State may be very small in relation to the entity generating income in the other Contracting State. For example, if a small U.S. research firm develops a process that it licenses to a very large, unrelated, pharmaceutical manufacturer in the other Contracting State, the size of the U.S. research firm would not have to be tested against the size of the manufacturer. Similarly, a small U.S. bank that makes a loan to a very large unrelated company operating a business in the other Contracting State would not have to pass a substantiality test to receive treaty benefits under Paragraph 3.

Subparagraph (c) of paragraph 3 provides special attribution rules for purposes of applying the substantive rules of subparagraphs (a) and (b). Thus, these rules apply for purposes of determining whether a person meets the requirement in subparagraph (a) that it be engaged in the active conduct of a trade or business and that the item of income is derived in connection with that active trade or business, and for making the comparison required by the "substantiality" requirement in subparagraph (b). Subparagraph (c) attributes to a person activities conducted by persons "connected" to such person. A person ("X") is connected to another person ("Y") if X possesses 50 percent or more of the beneficial interest in Y (or if Y possesses 50 percent or more of the beneficial interest in X). For this purpose, X is connected to a company if X owns shares representing fifty percent or more of the aggregate voting power and value of the company or fifty percent or more of the beneficial equity interest in the company. X also is connected to Y if a third person possesses fifty percent or more of the beneficial interest in both X and Y. For this purpose, if X or Y is a company, the threshold relationship with respect to such company or companies is fifty percent or more of the aggregate voting power and value or fifty percent or more of the beneficial equity interest. Finally, X is connected to Y if, based upon all the facts and circumstances, X controls Y, Y controls X, or X and Y are controlled by the same person or persons.

Paragraph 4

Paragraph 4 provides that a resident of one of the States that is not entitled to the benefits of the Convention as a result of paragraphs 1 through 3 still may be granted benefits under the Convention at the discretion of the competent authority of the State from which benefits are claimed. In making determinations under paragraph 4, that competent authority will take into account as its guideline whether the establishment, acquisition, or maintenance of the person seeking benefits under the Convention, or the conduct of such person's operations, has or had as one of its principal purposes the obtaining of benefits under the Convention. Benefits will not be granted, however, solely because a company was established prior to the effective date of a treaty or protocol. In that case a company would still be required to establish to the satisfaction of the Competent Authority clear non-tax business reasons for its formation in a Contracting State, or that the allowance of benefits would not otherwise be contrary to the purposes of the treaty. Thus, persons that establish operations in one of the States with a principal purpose of obtaining the benefits of the Convention ordinarily will not be granted relief under paragraph 4.

The competent authority's discretion is quite broad. It may grant all of the benefits of the Convention to the taxpayer making the request, or it may grant only certain benefits. For instance, it may grant benefits only with respect to a particular item of income in a manner similar to paragraph 3. Further, the competent authority may establish conditions, such as setting time limits on the duration of any relief granted.

For purposes of implementing paragraph 4, a taxpayer will be permitted to present his case to the relevant competent authority for an advance determination based on the facts. In these circumstances, it is also expected that, if the competent authority determines that benefits are to be allowed, they will be allowed retroactively to the time of entry into force of the relevant treaty provision or the establishment of the structure in question, whichever is later.

Finally, there may be cases in which a resident of a Contracting State may apply for discretionary relief to the competent authority of his State of residence. This would arise, for example, if the benefit it is claiming is provided by the residence country, and not by the source country. So, for example, if a company that is a resident of the United States would like to claim the benefit of the re-sourcing rule of paragraph 3 of Article 23, but it does not meet any of the objective tests of paragraphs 2 and 3, it may apply to the U.S. competent authority for discretionary relief.

Paragraph 5

Paragraph 5 defines several key terms for purposes of Article 22. Each of the defined terms is discussed above in the context in which it is used.

ARTICLE 23   (RELIEF FROM DOUBLE TAXATION)

This Article describes the manner in which each Contracting State undertakes to relieve double taxation. The United States uses the foreign tax credit method under its internal law, and by treaty.

Paragraph 1

Paragraph 1 provides that the other Contracting State will provide relief from double taxation through [the credit method/the exemption method/a mixture of the credit and exemption methods.]

Paragraph 2

The United States agrees, in paragraph 2, to allow to its citizens and residents a credit against U.S. tax for income taxes paid or accrued to the other Contracting State. Paragraph 2 also provides that the other Contracting State's covered taxes are income taxes for U.S. purposes. This provision is based on the Department of the Treasury's review of the other Contracting State's laws.

Subparagraph (b) provides for a deemed-paid credit, consistent with section 902 of the Code, to a U.S. corporation in respect of dividends received from a corporation resident in the other Contracting State of which the U.S. corporation owns at least 10 percent of the voting stock. This credit is for the tax paid by the corporation to the other Contracting State on the profits out of which the dividends are considered paid.

The credits allowed under paragraph 2 are allowed in accordance with the provisions and subject to the limitations of U.S. law, as that law may be amended over time, so long as the general principle of the Article, that is, the allowance of a credit, is retained. Thus, although the Convention provides for a foreign tax credit, the terms of the credit are determined by the provisions, at the time a credit is given, of the U.S. statutory credit.

Therefore, the U.S. credit under the Convention is subject to the various limitations of U.S. law (see, *e.g.*, Code sections 901-908). For example, the credit against U.S. tax generally is limited to the amount of U.S. tax due with respect to net foreign source income within the relevant foreign tax credit limitation category (see Code section 904(a) and (d)), and the dollar amount of the credit is determined in accordance with U.S. currency translation rules (see, *e.g.*, Code section 986). Similarly, U.S. law applies to determine carryover periods for excess credits and other inter-year adjustments.

Paragraph 3

Paragraph 3 provides a re-sourcing rule for gross income covered by paragraph 2. Paragraph 3 is intended to ensure that a U.S. resident can obtain an appropriate amount of U.S. foreign tax credit for income taxes paid to the other Contracting State when the Convention assigns to the other Contracting State primary taxing rights over an item of gross income.

Accordingly, if the Convention allows the other Contracting State to tax an item of gross income (as defined under U.S. law) derived by a resident of the United States, the United States will treat that item of gross income as gross income from sources within the other Contracting State for U.S. foreign tax credit purposes. In the case of a U.S.-owned foreign corporation, however, section 904(g)(10) may apply for purposes of determining the U.S. foreign tax credit with respect to income subject to this re-sourcing rule. Section 904(g)(10) generally applies the foreign tax credit limitation separately to re-sourced income. Furthermore, the paragraph 2 resourcing rule applies to gross income, not net income. Accordingly, U.S. expense allocation and apportionment rules, see, *e.g.*, Treas. Reg. section 1.861-9, continue to apply to income resourced under paragraph 2.

Paragraph 4

Paragraph 4 provides special rules for the tax treatment in both States of certain types of income derived from U.S. sources by U.S. citizens who are residents of the other Contracting State. Since U.S. citizens, regardless of residence, are subject to United States tax at ordinary progressive rates on their worldwide income, the U.S. tax on the U.S. source income of a U.S. citizen resident in the other Contracting State may exceed the U.S. tax that may be imposed under the Convention on an item of U.S. source income derived by a resident of the other Contracting State who is not a U.S. citizen. The provisions of paragraph 4 ensure that the other Contracting State does not bear the cost of U.S. taxation of its citizens who are residents of the other Contracting State.

Subparagraph (a) provides, with respect to items of income from sources within the United States, special credit rules for the other Contracting State. These rules apply to items of U.S.-source income that would be either exempt from U.S. tax or subject to reduced rates of U.S. tax under the provisions of the Convention if they had been received by a resident of the other Contracting State who is not a U.S. citizen. The tax credit allowed under paragraph 4 with respect to such items need not exceed the U.S. tax that may be imposed under the Convention, other than tax imposed solely by reason of the U.S. citizenship of the taxpayer under the provisions of the saving clause of paragraph 4 of Article 1 (General Scope).

For example, if a U.S. citizen resident in the other Contracting State receives portfolio dividends from sources within the United States, the foreign tax credit granted by the other Contracting State would be limited to 15 percent of the dividend — the U.S. tax that may be imposed under subparagraph (b) of paragraph 2 of Article 10 (Dividends) — even if the shareholder is subject to U.S. net income tax because of his U.S. citizenship. With respect to royalty or interest income, the other Contracting State would allow no foreign tax credit, because its residents are exempt from U.S. tax on these classes of income under the provisions of Articles 11 (Interest) and 12 (Royalties).

Paragraph 4(b) eliminates the potential for double taxation that can arise because subparagraph 4(a) provides that the other Contracting State need not provide full relief for the U.S. tax imposed on its citizens resident in the other Contracting State. The subparagraph provides that the United States will credit the income tax paid or accrued to the other Contracting State, after the application of subparagraph 4(a). It further provides that in allowing the credit, the United States will not reduce its tax below the amount that is taken into account in the other Contracting State in applying subparagraph 4(a).

Since the income described in paragraph 4(a) generally will be U.S. source income, special rules are required to re-source some of the income to the other Contracting State in order for the United States to be able to credit the tax paid to the other Contracting State. This resourcing is provided for in subparagraph 4(c), which deems the items of income referred to in subparagraph 4(a) to be from foreign sources to the extent necessary to avoid double taxation under paragraph 4(b). Subparagraph 3(c)(iii) of Article 25 (Mutual Agreement Procedure) provides a mechanism by which the competent authorities can resolve any disputes regarding whether income is from sources within the United States.

The following two examples illustrate the application of paragraph 4 in the case of a U.S.-source portfolio dividend received by a U.S. citizen resident in the other Contracting State. In both examples, the U.S. rate of tax on residents of the other Contracting State, under subparagraph (b) of paragraph 2 of Article 10 (Dividends) of the Convention, is 15 percent. In both examples, the U.S. income tax rate on the U.S. citizen is 35 percent. In example 1, the rate of income tax imposed in the other Contracting State on its resident (the U.S. citizen) is 25 percent (below the U.S. rate), and in example 2, the rate imposed on its resident is 40 percent (above the U.S. rate).

	Example 1	Example 2
Subparagraph (a)		
U.S. dividend declared	$100.00	$100.00
Notional U.S. withholding tax (Article 10(2)(b))	15.00	15.00
Taxable income in other Contracting State	100.00	100.00
Other Contracting State tax before credit	25.00	40.00
Less: tax credit for notional U.S. withholding tax	15.00	15.00
Net post-credit tax paid to other Contracting State	10.00	25.00
Subparagraphs (b) and (c)		
U.S. pre-tax income	$100.00	$100.00
U.S. pre-credit citizenship tax	35.00	35.00
Notional U.S. withholding tax	15.00	15.00
U.S. tax eligible to be offset by credit	20.00	20.00
Tax paid to other Contracting State	10.00	25.00
Income re-sourced from U.S. to foreign source (see below)	28.57	57.14
U.S. pre-credit tax on re-sourced income	10.00	20.00
U.S. credit for tax paid to the other Contracting State	10.00	20.00
Net post-credit U.S. tax	10.00	0.00
Total U.S. tax	25.00	15.00

In both examples, in the application of subparagraph (a), the other Contracting State credits a 15 percent U.S. tax against its residence tax on the U.S. citizen. In the first example, the net tax paid to the other Contracting State after the foreign tax credit is $10.00; in the second example, it is $25.00. In the application of subparagraphs (b) and (c), from the U.S. tax due before credit of $35.00, the United States subtracts the amount of the U.S. source tax of $15.00, against which no U.S. foreign tax credit is allowed. This subtraction ensures that the United States collects the tax that it is due under the Convention as the State of source.

In both examples, given the 35 percent U.S. tax rate, the maximum amount of U.S. tax against which credit for the tax paid to the other Contracting State may be claimed is $20 ($35 U.S. tax minus $15 U.S. withholding tax). Initially, all of the income in both examples was from sources within the United States. For a U.S. foreign tax credit to be allowed for the full amount of the tax paid to the other Contracting State, an appropriate amount of the income must be resourced to the other Contracting State under subparagraph (c).

The amount that must be re-sourced depends on the amount of tax for which the U.S. citizen is claiming a U.S. foreign tax credit. In example 1, the tax paid to the other Contracting State was $10. For this amount to be creditable against U.S. tax, $28.57 ($10 tax divided by 35 percent U.S. tax rate) must be resourced to the other Contracting State. When the tax is credited against the $10 of U.S. tax on this resourced income, there is a net U.S. tax of $10 due after credit ($20 U.S. tax eligible to be offset by credit, minus $10 tax paid to the other Contracting State). Thus, in example 1, there is a total of $25 in U.S. tax ($15 U.S. withholding tax plus $10 residual U.S. tax).

In example 2, the tax paid to the other Contracting State was $25, but, because the United States subtracts the U.S. withholding tax of $15 from the total U.S. tax of $35, only $20 of U.S. taxes may be offset by taxes paid to the other Contracting State. Accordingly, the amount that must be resourced to the other Contracting State is limited to the amount necessary to ensure a U.S. foreign tax credit for $20 of tax paid to the other Contracting State, or $57.14 ($20 tax paid to the other Contracting State divided by 35 percent U.S. tax rate). When the tax paid to the other Contracting State is credited against the U.S. tax on this re-sourced income, there is no residual U.S. tax ($20 U.S. tax minus $25 tax paid to the other Contracting State, subject to the U.S. limit of $20). Thus, in example 2, there is a total of $15 in U.S. tax ($15 U.S. withholding tax plus $0 residual U.S. tax). Because the tax paid to the other Contracting State was $25 and the U.S. tax eligible to be offset by credit was $20, there is $5 of excess foreign tax credit available for carryover.

Relationship to other Articles

By virtue of subparagraph (a) of paragraph 5 of Article 1 (General Scope), Article 23 is not subject to the saving clause of paragraph 4 of Article 1. Thus, the United States will allow a credit to its citizens and residents in accordance with the Article, even if such credit were to provide a benefit not available under the Code (such as the re-sourcing provided by paragraph 3 and subparagraph 4(c)).

ARTICLE 24   (NON-DISCRIMINATION)

This Article ensures that nationals of a Contracting State, in the case of paragraph 1, and residents of a Contracting State, in the case of paragraphs 2 through 5, will not be subject, directly or indirectly, to discriminatory taxation in the other Contracting State. Not all differences in tax treatment, either as between nationals of the two States, or between residents of the two States, are violations of the prohibition against discrimination. Rather, the nondiscrimination obligations of this Article apply only if the nationals or residents of the two States are comparably situated.

Each of the relevant paragraphs of the Article provides that two persons that are comparably situated must be treated similarly. Although the actual words differ from paragraph to paragraph (*e.g.*, paragraph 1 refers to two nationals "in the same circumstances," paragraph 2 refers to two enterprises "carrying on the same activities" and paragraph 4 refers to two enterprises that are "similar"), the common underlying premise is that if the difference in treatment is directly related to a tax-relevant difference in the situations of the domestic and foreign persons being compared, that difference is not to be treated as discriminatory (i.e., if one person is taxable in a Contracting State on worldwide income and the other is not, or tax may be collectible from one person at a later stage, but not from the other, distinctions in treatment would be justified under paragraph 1). Other examples of such factors that can lead to nondiscriminatory differences in treatment are noted in the discussions of each paragraph.

The operative paragraphs of the Article also use different language to identify the kinds of differences in taxation treatment that will be considered discriminatory. For example, paragraphs 1 and 4 speak of "any taxation or any requirement connected therewith that is more burdensome," while paragraph 2 specifies that a tax "shall not be less favorably levied." Regardless of these differences in language, only differences in tax treatment that materially disadvantage the foreign person relative to the domestic person are properly the subject of the Article.

Paragraph 1

Paragraph 1 provides that a national of one Contracting State may not be subject to taxation or connected requirements in the other Contracting State that are more burdensome than the taxes and connected requirements imposed upon a national of that other State in the same circumstances. The OECD Model prohibits taxation that is "other than or more burdensome" than that imposed on U.S. persons. This Convention omits the reference to taxation that is "other than" that imposed on U.S. persons because the only relevant question under this provision should be whether the requirement imposed on a national of the other Contracting State is more burdensome. A requirement may be different from the requirements imposed on U.S. nationals without being more burdensome.

The term "national" in relation to a Contracting State is defined in subparagraph 1(j) of Article 3 (General Definitions). The term includes both individuals and juridical persons. A national of a Contracting State is afforded protection under this paragraph even if the national is not a resident of either Contracting State. Thus, a U.S. citizen who is resident in a third country is entitled, under this paragraph, to the same treatment in the other Contracting State as a national of the other Contracting State who is in similar circumstances (i.e., presumably one who is resident in a third State).

As noted above, whether or not the two persons are both taxable on worldwide income is a significant circumstance for this purpose. For this reason, paragraph 1 specifically states that the United States is not obligated to apply the same taxing regime to a national of the other Contracting State who is not resident in the United States as it applies to a U.S. national who is not resident in the United States. United States citizens who are not residents of the United States but who are, nevertheless, subject to United States tax on their worldwide income are not in the same circumstances with respect to United States taxation as citizens of the other Contracting State who are not United States residents. Thus, for example, Article 24 would not entitle a national of the other Contracting State resident in a third country to taxation at graduated rates on U.S. source dividends or other investment income that applies to a U.S. citizen resident in the same third country.

Paragraph 2

Paragraph 2 of the Article, provides that a Contracting State may not tax a permanent establishment of an enterprise of the other Contracting State less favorably than an enterprise of that first-mentioned State that is carrying on the same activities.

The fact that a U.S. permanent establishment of an enterprise of the other Contracting State is subject to U.S. tax only on income that is attributable to the permanent establishment, while a U.S. corporation engaged in the same activities is taxable on its worldwide income is not, in itself, a sufficient difference to provide different treatment for the permanent establishment. There are cases, however, where the two enterprises would not be similarly situated and differences in treatment may be warranted. For instance, it would not be a violation of the non-discrimination protection of paragraph 2 to require the foreign enterprise to provide information in a reasonable manner that may be different from the information requirements imposed on a resident enterprise, because information may not be as readily available to the Internal Revenue Service from a foreign as from a domestic enterprise. Similarly, it would not be a violation of paragraph 2 to impose penalties on persons who fail to comply with such a requirement (see, *e.g.*, sections 874(a) and 882(c)(2)). Further, a determination that income and expenses have been attributed or allocated to a permanent establishment in conformity with the principles of Article 7 (Business Profits) implies that the attribution or allocation was not discriminatory.

Section 1446 of the Code imposes on any partnership with income that is effectively connected with a U.S. trade or business the obligation to withhold tax on amounts allocable to a foreign partner. In the context of the Convention, this obligation applies with respect to a share of the partnership income of a partner resident in the other Contracting State, and attributable to a U.S. permanent establishment. There is no similar obligation with respect to the distributive shares of U.S. resident partners. It is understood, however, that this distinction is not a form of discrimination within the meaning of paragraph 2 of the Article. No distinction is made between U.S. and non-U.S. partnerships, since the law requires that partnerships of both U.S. and non-U.S. domicile withhold tax in respect of the partnership shares of non-U.S. partners. Furthermore, in distinguishing between U.S. and non-U.S. partners, the requirement to withhold on the non-U.S. but not the U.S. partner's share is not discriminatory taxation, but, like other withholding on nonresident aliens, is merely a reasonable method for the collection of tax from persons who are not continually present in the United States, and as to whom it otherwise may be difficult for the United States to enforce its tax jurisdiction. If tax has been over-withheld, the partner can, as in other cases of over-withholding, file for a refund.

Paragraph 3

Paragraph 3 makes clear that the provisions of paragraphs 1 and 2 do not obligate a Contracting State to grant to a resident of the other Contracting State any tax allowances, reliefs, etc., that it grants to its own residents on account of their civil status or family responsibilities. Thus, if a sole proprietor who is a resident of the other Contracting State has a permanent establishment in the United States, in assessing income tax on the profits attributable to the permanent establishment, the United States is not obligated to allow to the resident of the other Contracting State the personal allowances for himself and his family that he would be permitted to take if the permanent establishment were a sole proprietorship owned and operated by a U.S. resident, despite the fact that the individual income tax rates would apply.

Paragraph 4

Paragraph 3 prohibits discrimination in the allowance of deductions. When a resident or an enterprise of a Contracting State pays interest, royalties or other disbursements to a resident of the other Contracting State, the first-mentioned Contracting State must allow a deduction for those payments in computing the taxable profits of the resident or enterprise as if the payment had been made under the same conditions to a resident of the first-mentioned Contracting State. Paragraph 3, however, does not require a Contracting State to give non-residents more favorable treatment than it gives to its own residents. Consequently, a Contracting State does not have to allow non-residents a deduction for items that are not deductible under its domestic law (for example, expenses of a capital nature).

The term "other disbursements" is understood to include a reasonable allocation of executive and general administrative expenses, research and development expenses and other expenses incurred for the benefit of a group of related persons that includes the person incurring the expense.

An exception to the rule of paragraph 4 is provided for cases where the provisions of paragraph 1 of Article 9 (Associated Enterprises), paragraph 5 of Article 11 (Interest) or paragraph 4 of Article 12 (Royalties) apply. All of these provisions permit the denial of deductions in certain circumstances in respect of transactions between related persons. Neither State is forced to apply the non-discrimination principle in such cases. The exception with respect to paragraph 4 of Article 11 would include the denial or deferral of certain interest deductions under Code section 163(j).

Paragraph 4 also provides that any debts of an enterprise of a Contracting State to a resident of the other Contracting State are deductible in the first-mentioned Contracting State for purposes of computing the capital tax of the enterprise under the same conditions as if the debt had been contracted to a resident of the first-mentioned Contracting State. Even though, for general purposes, the Convention covers only income taxes, under paragraph 7 of this Article, the nondiscrimination provisions apply to all taxes levied in both Contracting States, at all levels of government. Thus, this provision may be relevant for both States. The other Contracting State may have capital taxes and in the United States such taxes frequently are imposed by local governments.

Paragraph 5

Paragraph 5 requires that a Contracting State not impose more burdensome taxation or connected requirements on an enterprise of that State that is wholly or partly owned or controlled, directly or indirectly, by one or more residents of the other Contracting State than the taxation or connected requirements that it imposes on other similar enterprises of that first-mentioned Contracting State. For this purpose it is understood that "similar" refers to similar activities or ownership of the enterprise.

This rule, like all non-discrimination provisions, does not prohibit differing treatment of entities that are in differing circumstances. Rather, a protected enterprise is only required to be treated in the same manner as other enterprises that, from the point of view of the application of the tax law, are in substantially similar circumstances both in law and in fact. The taxation of a distributing corporation under section 367(e) on an applicable distribution to foreign shareholders does not violate paragraph 5 of the Article because a foreign-owned corporation is not similar to a domestically-owned corporation that is accorded non-recognition treatment under sections 337 and 355.

For the reasons given above in connection with the discussion of paragraph 2 of the Article, it is also understood that the provision in section 1446 of the Code for withholding of tax on non-U.S. partners does not violate paragraph 5 of the Article.

It is further understood that the ineligibility of a U.S. corporation with nonresident alien shareholders to make an election to be an "S" corporation does not violate paragraph 5 of the Article. If a corporation elects to be an S corporation, it is generally not subject to income tax and the shareholders take into account their pro rata shares of the corporation's items of income, loss, deduction or credit. (The purpose of the provision is to allow an individual or small group of individuals the protections of conducting business in corporate form while paying taxes at individual rates as if the business were conducted directly.) A nonresident alien does not pay U.S. tax on a net basis, and, thus, does not generally take into account items of loss, deduction or credit. Thus, the S corporation provisions do not exclude corporations with nonresident alien shareholders because such shareholders are foreign, but only because they are not net-basis taxpayers. Similarly, the provisions exclude corporations with other types of shareholders where the purpose of the provisions cannot be fulfilled or their mechanics implemented. For example, corporations with corporate shareholders are excluded because the purpose of the provision to permit individuals to conduct a business in corporate form at individual tax rates would not be furthered by their inclusion.

Finally, it is understood that paragraph 5 does not require a Contracting State to allow foreign corporations to join in filing a consolidated return with a domestic corporation or to allow similar benefits between domestic and foreign enterprises.

Paragraph 6

Paragraph 6 of the Article confirms that no provision of the Article will prevent either Contracting State from imposing the branch profits tax described in paragraph 8 of Article 10 (Dividends).

Paragraph 7

As noted above, notwithstanding the specification of taxes covered by the Convention in Article 2 (Taxes Covered) for general purposes, for purposes of providing nondiscrimination protection this Article applies to taxes of every kind and description imposed by a Contracting State or a political subdivision or local authority thereof. Customs duties are not considered to be taxes for this purpose.

Relationship to Other Articles

The saving clause of paragraph 4 of Article 1 (General Scope) does not apply to this Article by virtue of the exceptions in paragraph 5(a) of Article 1. Thus, for example, a U.S. citizen who is a resident of the other Contracting State may claim benefits in the United States under this Article.

Nationals of a Contracting State may claim the benefits of paragraph 1 regardless of whether they are entitled to benefits under Article 22 (Limitation on Benefits), because that paragraph applies to nationals and not residents. They may not claim the benefits of the other paragraphs of this Article with respect to an item of income unless they are generally entitled to treaty benefits with respect to that income under a provision of Article 22.

ARTICLE 25   (MUTUAL AGREEMENT PROCEDURE)

This Article provides the mechanism for taxpayers to bring to the attention of competent authorities issues and problems that may arise under the Convention. It also provides the authority for cooperation between the competent authorities of the Contracting States to resolve disputes and clarify issues that may arise under the Convention and to resolve cases of double taxation not provided for in the Convention. The competent authorities of the two Contracting States are identified in paragraph 1(g) of Article 3 (General Definitions).

Paragraph 1

This paragraph provides that where a resident of a Contracting State considers that the actions of one or both Contracting States will result in taxation that is not in accordance with the Convention he may present his case to the competent authority of either Contracting State. This rule is more generous than in most treaties, which generally allow taxpayers to bring competent authority cases only to the competent authority of their country of residence, or citizen-ship/nationality. Under this more generous rule, a U.S. permanent establishment of a corporation resident in the treaty partner that faces inconsistent treatment in the two countries would be able to bring its complaint to the U.S. competent authority. If the U.S. competent authority can resolve the issue on its own, then the taxpayer need never involve the other competent authority. Thus, the rule provides flexibility that might result in greater efficiency.

Although the typical cases brought under this paragraph will involve economic double taxation arising from transfer pricing adjustments, the scope of this paragraph is not limited to such cases. For example, a taxpayer could request assistance from the competent authority if one Contracting State determines that the taxpayer has received deferred compensation taxable at source under Article 14 (Income from Employment), while the taxpayer believes that such income should be treated as a pension that is taxable only in his country of residence pursuant to Article 17 (Pensions, Social Security, Annuities, Alimony, and Child Support).

It is not necessary for a person bringing a complaint first to have exhausted the remedies provided under the national laws of the Contracting States before presenting a case to the competent authorities, nor does the fact that the statute of limitations may have passed for seeking a refund preclude bringing a case to the competent authority. Unlike the OECD Model, no time limit is provided within which a case must be brought.

Paragraph 2

Paragraph 2 sets out the framework within which the competent authorities will deal with cases brought by taxpayers under paragraph 1. It provides that, if the competent authority of the Contracting State to which the case is presented judges the case to have merit, and cannot reach a unilateral solution, it shall seek an agreement with the competent authority of the other Contracting State pursuant to which taxation not in accordance with the Convention will be avoided.

Any agreement is to be implemented even if such implementation otherwise would be barred by the statute of limitations or by some other procedural limitation, such as a closing agreement. Paragraph 2, however, does not prevent the application of domestic-law procedural limitations that give effect to the agreement (*e.g.*, a domestic-law requirement that the taxpayer file a return reflecting the agreement within one year of the date of the agreement).

Where the taxpayer has entered a closing agreement (or other written settlement) with the United States before bringing a case to the competent authorities, the U.S. competent authority will endeavor only to obtain a correlative adjustment from the other Contracting State. *See* Rev. Proc. 2002-52, 2002-31 I.R.B. 242, § 7.04. Because, as specified in paragraph 2 of Article 1 (General Scope), the Convention cannot operate to increase a taxpayer's liability, temporal or other procedural limitations can be overridden only for the purpose of making refunds and not to impose additional tax.

Paragraph 3

Paragraph 3 authorizes the competent authorities to resolve difficulties or doubts that may arise as to the application or interpretation of the Convention. The paragraph includes a non- exhaustive list of examples of the kinds of matters about which the competent authorities may reach agreement. This list is purely illustrative; it does not grant any authority that is not implicitly present as a result of the introductory sentence of paragraph 3.

The competent authorities may, for example, agree to the same allocation of income, deductions, credits or allowances between an enterprise in one Contracting

State and its permanent establishment in the other or between related persons. These allocations are to be made in accordance with the arm's length principle underlying Article 7 (Business Profits) and Article 9 (Associated Enterprises). Agreements reached under these subparagraphs may include agreement on a methodology for determining an appropriate transfer price, common treatment of a taxpayer's cost sharing arrangement, or upon an acceptable range of results under that methodology.

As indicated in subparagraph (c), the competent authorities also may agree to settle a variety of conflicting applications of the Convention. They may agree to settle conflicts regarding the characterization of particular items of income, the characterization of persons, the application of source rules to particular items of income, the meaning of a term, or the timing of an item of income.

They also may agree as to advance pricing arrangements. They also may agree as to the application of the provisions of domestic law regarding penalties, fines, and interest in a manner consistent with the purposes of the Convention.

Since the list under paragraph 3 is not exhaustive, the competent authorities may reach agreement on issues not enumerated in paragraph 3 if necessary to avoid double taxation. For example, the competent authorities may seek agreement on a uniform set of standards for the use of exchange rates. Agreements reached by the competent authorities under paragraph 3 need not conform to the internal law provisions of either Contracting State.

Finally, paragraph 3 authorizes the competent authorities to consult for the purpose of eliminating double taxation in cases not provided for in the Convention and to resolve any difficulties or doubts arising as to the interpretation or application of the Convention. This provision is intended to permit the competent authorities to implement the treaty in particular cases in a manner that is consistent with its expressed general purposes. It permits the competent authorities to deal with cases that are within the spirit of the provisions but that are not specifically covered. An example of such a case might be double taxation arising from a transfer pricing adjustment between two permanent establishments of a third-country resident, one in the United States and one in the other Contracting State. Since no resident of a Contracting State is involved in the case, the Convention does not apply, but the competent authorities nevertheless may use the authority of this Article to prevent the double taxation of income.

Paragraph 4

Paragraph 4 authorizes the competent authorities to increase any dollar amounts referred to in the Convention to reflect economic and monetary developments. Under the Model, this refers only to Article 17 (Entertainers and Sportsmen); Article 19 (Students, Trainees, Teachers and Researchers) separately instructs the competent authorities to adjust the exemption amount for students and trainees in accordance with specified guidelines. The rule under paragraph 4 is intended to operate as follows: if, for example, after the Convention has been in force for some time, inflation rates have been such as to make the $20,000 exemption threshold for entertainers unrealistically low in terms of the original objectives intended in setting the threshold, the competent authorities may agree to a higher threshold without the need for formal amendment to the treaty and ratification by the Contracting States. This authority can be exercised, however, only to the extent necessary to restore those original objectives. This provision can be applied only to the benefit of taxpayers (i.e., only to increase thresholds, not to reduce them).

Paragraph 5

Paragraph 5 provides that the competent authorities may communicate with each other for the purpose of reaching an agreement. This makes clear that the competent authorities of the two Contracting States may communicate without going through diplomatic channels. Such communication may be in various forms, including, where appropriate, through face-to-face meetings of representatives of the competent authorities.

Treaty termination in relation to competent authority dispute resolution

A case may be raised by a taxpayer under a treaty with respect to a year for which a treaty was in force after the treaty has been terminated. In such a case the ability of the competent authorities to act is limited. They may not exchange confidential information, nor may they reach a solution that varies from that specified in its law.

Triangular competent authority solutions

International tax cases may involve more than two taxing jurisdictions (e.g., transactions among a parent corporation resident in country A and its subsidiaries resident in countries B and C). As long as there is a complete network of treaties among the three countries, it should be possible, under the full combination of bilateral authorities, for the competent authorities of the three States to work together on a three-sided solution. Although country A may not be able to give information received under Article 26 (Exchange of Information) from country B to the authorities of country C, if the competent authorities of the three countries are working together, it should not be a problem for them to arrange for the authorities of country B to give the necessary information directly to the tax authorities of country C, as well as to those of country A. Each bilateral part of the trilateral solution must, of course, not exceed the scope of the authority of the competent authorities under the relevant bilateral treaty.

Relationship to Other Articles

This Article is not subject to the saving clause of paragraph 4 of Article 1 (General Scope) by virtue of the exceptions in paragraph 5(a) of that Article. Thus, rules, definitions, procedures, etc. that are agreed upon by the competent authorities under this Article may be applied by the United States with respect to its citizens and residents even if they differ from the comparable Code provisions. Similarly, as indicated above, U.S. law may be overridden to provide refunds of tax to a U.S. citizen or resident under this Article. A person may seek relief under Article 25 regardless of whether he is generally entitled to benefits under Article

22 (Limitation on Benefits). As in all other cases, the competent authority is vested with the discretion to decide whether the claim for relief is justified.

ARTICLE 26 (EXCHANGE OF INFORMATION AND ADMINISTRATIVE ASSISTANCE)

This Article provides for the exchange of information and administrative assistance between the competent authorities of the Contracting States.

Paragraph 1

The obligation to obtain and provide information to the other Contracting State is set out in Paragraph 1. The information to be exchanged is that which may be relevant for carrying out the provisions of the Convention or the domestic laws of the United States or of the other Contracting State concerning taxes of every kind applied at the national level. This language incorporates the standard in 26 U.S.C. Section 7602 which authorizes the IRS to examine "any books, papers, records, or other data which may be relevant or material." (Emphasis added.) In United States v. Arthur Young & Co., 465 U.S. 805, 814 (1984), the Supreme Court stated that the language "may be" reflects Congress's express intention to allow the IRS to obtain "items of even potential relevance to an ongoing investigation, without reference to its admissibility." (Emphasis in original.) However, the language "may be" would not support a request in which a Contracting State simply asked for information regarding all bank accounts maintained by residents of that Contracting State in the other Contracting State, or even all accounts maintained by its residents with respect to a particular bank.

Exchange of information with respect to each State's domestic law is authorized to the extent that taxation under domestic law is not contrary to the Convention. Thus, for example, information may be exchanged with respect to a covered tax, even if the transaction to which the information relates is a purely domestic transaction in the requesting State and, therefore, the exchange is not made to carry out the Convention. An example of such a case is provided in the OECD Commentary: a company resident in the United States and a company resident in the other Contracting State transact business between themselves through a third-country resident company. Neither Contracting State has a treaty with the third State. To enforce their internal laws with respect to transactions of their residents with the third-country company (since there is no relevant treaty in force), the Contracting States may exchange information regarding the prices that their residents paid in their transactions with the third-country resident.

Paragraph 1 clarifies that information may be exchanged that relates to the assessment or collection of, the enforcement or prosecution in respect of, or the determination of appeals in relation to, the taxes covered by the Convention. Thus, the competent authorities may request and provide information for cases under examination or criminal investigation, in collection, on appeals, or under prosecution.

The taxes covered by the Convention for purposes of this Article constitute a broader category of taxes than those referred to in Article 2 (Taxes Covered).

Exchange of information is authorized with respect to taxes of every kind imposed by a Contracting State at the national level. Accordingly, information may be exchanged with respect to U.S. estate and gift taxes, excise taxes or, with respect to the other Contracting State, value added taxes.

Information exchange is not restricted by paragraph 1 of Article 1 (General Scope). Accordingly, information may be requested and provided under this article with respect to persons who are not residents of either Contracting State. For example, if a third-country resident has a permanent establishment in the other Contracting State, and that permanent establishment engages in transactions with a U.S. enterprise, the United States could request information with respect to that permanent establishment, even though the third-country resident is not a resident of either Contracting State. Similarly, if a third-country resident maintains a bank account in the other Contracting State, and the Internal Revenue Service has reason to believe that funds in that account should have been reported for U.S. tax purposes but have not been so reported, information can be requested from the other Contracting State with respect to that person's account, even though that person is not the taxpayer under examination.

Although the term "United States" does not encompass U.S. possessions for most purposes of the Convention, Section 7651 of the Code authorizes the Internal Revenue Service to utilize the provisions of the Internal Revenue Code to obtain information from the U.S. possessions pursuant to a proper request made under Article 26. If necessary to obtain requested information, the Internal Revenue Service could issue and enforce an administrative summons to the taxpayer, a tax authority (or a government agency in a U.S. possession), or a third party located in a U.S. possession.

Paragraph 2

Paragraph 2 also provides assurances that any information exchanged will be treated as secret, subject to the same disclosure constraints as information obtained under the laws of the requesting State. Information received may be disclosed only to persons, including courts and administrative bodies, involved in the assessment, collection, or administration of, the enforcement or prosecution in respect of, or the determination of the of appeals in relation to, the taxes covered by the Convention. The information must be used by these persons in connection with the specified functions. Information may also be disclosed to legislative bodies, such as the tax-writing committees of Congress and the Government Accountability Office, engaged in the oversight of the preceding activities. Information received by these bodies must be for use in the performance of their role in overseeing the administration of U.S. tax laws. Information received may be disclosed in public court proceedings or in judicial decisions.

Paragraph 3

Paragraph 3 provides that the obligations undertaken in paragraphs 1 and 2 to exchange information do not require a Contracting State to carry out administrative measures that are at variance with the laws or administrative practice of either State. Nor is a Contracting State required to supply information not obtainable under the laws or administrative practice of either State, or to disclose trade secrets or other information, the disclosure of which would be contrary to public policy.

Thus, a requesting State may be denied information from the other State if the information would be obtained pursuant to procedures or measures that are broader than those available in the requesting State. However, the statute of limitations of the Contracting State making the request for information should govern a request for information. Thus, the Contracting State of which the request is made should attempt to obtain the information even if its own statute of limitations has passed. In many cases, relevant information will still exist in the business records of the taxpayer or a third party, even though it is no longer required to be kept for domestic tax purposes.

While paragraph 3 states conditions under which a Contracting State is not obligated to comply with a request from the other Contracting State for information, the requested State is not precluded from providing such information, and may, at its discretion, do so subject to the limitations of its internal law.

Paragraph 4

Paragraph 4 provides that when information is requested by a Contracting State in accordance with this Article, the other Contracting State is obligated to obtain the requested information as if the tax in question were the tax of the requested State, even if that State has no direct tax interest in the case to which the request relates. In the absence of such a paragraph, some taxpayers have argued that paragraph 3(a) prevents a Contracting State from requesting information from a bank or fiduciary that the Contracting State does not need for its own tax purposes. This paragraph clarifies that paragraph 3 does not impose such a restriction and that a Contracting State is not limited to providing only the information that it already has in its own files.

Paragraph 5

Paragraph 5 provides that a Contracting State may not decline to provide information because that information is held by financial institutions, nominees or persons acting in an agency or fiduciary capacity. Thus, paragraph 5 would effectively prevent a Contracting State from relying on paragraph 3 to argue that its domestic bank secrecy laws (or similar legislation relating to disclosure of financial information by financial institutions or intermediaries) override its obligation to provide information under paragraph 1. This paragraph also requires the disclosure of information regarding the beneficial owner of an interest in a person, such as the identity of a beneficial owner of bearer shares.

Paragraph 6

Paragraph 6 provides that the requesting State may specify the form in which information is to be provided (e.g., depositions of witnesses and authenticated copies of original documents). The intention is to ensure that the information may be introduced as evidence in the judicial proceedings of the requesting State. The requested State should, if possible, provide the information in the form requested to the same extent that it can obtain information in that form under its own laws and administrative practices with respect to its own taxes.

Paragraph 7

Paragraph 7 provides for assistance in collection of taxes to the extent necessary to ensure that treaty benefits are enjoyed only by persons entitled to those benefits under the terms of the Convention. Under paragraph 7, a Contracting State will endeavor to collect on behalf of the other State only those amounts necessary to ensure that any exemption or reduced rate of tax at source granted under the Convention by that other State is not enjoyed by persons not entitled to those benefits. For example, if the payer of a U.S.-source portfolio dividend receives a Form W-8BEN or other appropriate documentation from the payee, the withholding agent is permitted to withhold at the portfolio dividend rate of 15 percent. If, however, the addressee is merely acting as a nominee on behalf of a third-country resident, paragraph 7 would obligate the other Contracting State to withhold and remit to the United States the additional tax that should have been collected by the U.S. withholding agent.

This paragraph also makes clear that the Contracting State asked to collect the tax is not obligated, in the process of providing collection assistance, to carry out administrative measures that are different from those used in the collection of its own taxes, or that would be contrary to its sovereignty, security or public policy.

Paragraph 8

Paragraph 8 provides that the requested State shall allow representatives of the applicant State to enter the requested State to interview individuals and examine books and records with the consent of the persons subject to examination.

Paragraph 9

Paragraph 9 states that the competent authorities of the Contracting States may develop an agreement upon the mode of application of the Article. The article authorizes the competent authorities to exchange information on a routine basis, on request in relation to a specific case, or spontaneously. It is contemplated that the Contracting States will utilize this authority to engage in all of these forms of information exchange, as appropriate.

The competent authorities may also agree on specific procedures and timetables for the exchange of information. In particular, the competent authorities may agree on minimum thresholds regarding tax at stake or take other measures aimed at ensuring some measure of reciprocity with respect to the overall exchange of information between the Contracting States.

Treaty effective dates and termination in relation to exchange of information

Once the Convention is in force, the competent authority may seek information under the Convention with respect to a year prior to the entry into force of the

Convention. Even if an earlier Convention with more restrictive provisions, or even no Convention, was in effect during the years in which the transaction at issue occurred, the exchange of information provisions of the Convention apply. In that case, the competent authorities have available to them the full range of information exchange provisions afforded under this Article. Paragraph 3 of Article 28 (Entry into Force) confirms this understanding with respect to the effective date of the Article.

A tax administration may also seek information with respect to a year for which a treaty was in force after the treaty has been terminated. In such a case the ability of the other tax administration to act is limited. The treaty no longer provides authority for the tax administrations to exchange confidential information. They may only exchange information pursuant to domestic law or other international agreement or arrangement.

ARTICLE 27   (MEMBERS OF DIPLOMATIC MISSIONS AND CONSULAR POSTS)

This Article confirms that any fiscal privileges to which diplomatic or consular officials are entitled under general provisions of international law or under special agreements will apply notwithstanding any provisions to the contrary in the Convention. The agreements referred to include any bilateral agreements, such as consular conventions, that affect the taxation of diplomats and consular officials and any multilateral agreements dealing with these issues, such as the Vienna Convention on Diplomatic Relations and the Vienna Convention on Consular Relations. The U.S. generally adheres to the latter because its terms are consistent with customary international law.

The Article does not independently provide any benefits to diplomatic agents and consular officers. Article 19 (Government Service) does so, as do Code section 893 and a number of bilateral and multilateral agreements. In the event that there is a conflict between the Convention and international law or such other treaties, under which the diplomatic agent or consular official is entitled to greater benefits under the latter, the latter laws or agreements shall have precedence. Conversely, if the Convention confers a greater benefit than another agreement, the affected person could claim the benefit of the tax treaty.

Pursuant to subparagraph 5(b) of Article 1, the saving clause of paragraph 4 of Article 1 (General Scope) does not apply to override any benefits of this Article available to an individual who is neither a citizen of the United States nor has immigrant status in the United States.

ARTICLE 28   (ENTRY INTO FORCE)

This Article contains the rules for bringing the Convention into force and giving effect to its provisions.

Paragraph 1

Paragraph 1 provides for the ratification of the Convention by both Contracting States according to their constitutional and statutory requirements. Instruments of ratification shall be exchanged as soon as possible.

In the United States, the process leading to ratification and entry into force is as follows: Once a treaty has been signed by authorized representatives of the two Contracting States, the Department of State sends the treaty to the President who formally transmits it to the Senate for its advice and consent to ratification, which requires approval by two-thirds of the Senators present and voting. Prior to this vote, however, it generally has been the practice for the Senate Committee on Foreign Relations to hold hearings on the treaty and make a recommendation regarding its approval to the full Senate. Both Government and private sector witnesses may testify at these hearings. After the Senate gives its advice and consent to ratification of the protocol or treaty, an instrument of ratification is drafted for the President's signature. The President's signature completes the process in the United States.

Paragraph 2

Paragraph 2 provides that the Convention will enter into force upon the exchange of instruments of ratification. The date on which a treaty enters into force is not necessarily the date on which its provisions take effect. Paragraph 2, therefore, also contains rules that determine when the provisions of the treaty will have effect.

Under paragraph 2(a), the Convention will have effect with respect to taxes withheld at source (principally dividends, interest and royalties) for amounts paid or credited on or after the first day of the second month following the date on which the Convention enters into force. For example, if instruments of ratification are exchanged on April 25 of a given year, the withholding rates specified in paragraph 2 of Article 10 (Dividends) would be applicable to any dividends paid or credited on or after June 1 of that year. This rule allows the benefits of the withholding reductions to be put into effect as soon as possible, without waiting until the following year. The delay of one to two months is required to allow sufficient time for withholding agents to be informed about the change in withholding rates. If for some reason a withholding agent withholds at a higher rate than that provided by the Convention (perhaps because it was not able to re-program its computers before the payment is made), a beneficial owner of the income that is a resident of the other Contracting State may make a claim for refund pursuant to section 1464 of the Code.

For all other taxes, paragraph 2(b) specifies that the Convention will have effect for any taxable period beginning on or after January 1 of the year following entry into force.

As discussed under Articles 25 (Mutual Agreement Procedure) and 26 (Exchange of Information), the powers afforded the competent authority under these articles apply retroactively to taxable periods preceding entry into force.

ARTICLE 29   (TERMINATION)

The Convention is to remain in effect indefinitely, unless terminated by one of the Contracting States in accordance with the provisions of Article 29. The Convention may be terminated at any time after the year in which the Convention enters into force. If notice of termination is given, the provisions of the Convention with respect to withholding at source will cease to have effect after the expiration of a period of 6 months beginning with the delivery of notice of termination. For other taxes, the Convention will cease to have effect as of taxable periods beginning after the expiration of this 6 month period.

Article 29 relates only to unilateral termination of the Convention by a Contracting State. Nothing in that Article should be construed as preventing the Contracting States from concluding a new bilateral agreement, subject to ratification, that supersedes, amends or terminates provisions of the Convention without the six-month notification period.

Customary international law observed by the United States and other countries, as reflected in the Vienna Convention on Treaties, allows termination by one Contracting State at any time in the event of a "material breach" of the agreement by the other Contracting State.

INCOME TAX CONVENTION BETWEEN
CANADA AND THE UNITED STATES

Signed September 26, 1980; In Force as of August 16, 1984
As Amended by Subsequent Protocols through 2007

This convention, signed September 26, 1980, has been amended by protocols signed June 14, 1983, March 28, 1984, March 17, 1995, July 29, 1997 and September 21, 2007

The United States of America and Canada,

Desiring to conclude a Convention for the avoidance of double taxation and the prevention of fiscal evasion with respect to taxes on income and on capital,

Have agreed as follows:

Article I   Personal Scope

This Convention is generally applicable to persons who are residents of one or both of the Contracting States.

Article II   Taxes Covered

1. This Convention shall apply to taxes on income and on capital imposed on behalf of each Contracting State, irrespective of the manner in which they are levied.

2. Notwithstanding paragraph 1, the taxes existing on March 17, 1995 to which the Convention shall apply are:

(a) In the case of Canada, the taxes imposed by the Government of Canada under the Income Tax Act; and

(b) In the case of the United States, the Federal income taxes imposed by the Internal Revenue Code of 1986. However, the Convention shall apply to:

(i) The United States accumulated earnings tax and personal holding company tax, to the extent, and only to the extent, necessary to implement the provisions of paragraphs 5 and 8 of Article X (Dividends);

(ii) The United States excise taxes imposed with respect to private foundations, to the extent, and only to the extent, necessary to implement the provisions of paragraph 4 of Article XXI (Exempt Organizations);

(iii) The United States social security taxes, to the extent, and only to the extent, necessary to implement the provisions of paragraph 2 of Article XXIV (Elimination of Double Taxation) and paragraph 4 of Article XXIX (Miscellaneous Rules); and

(iv) The United States estate taxes imposed by the Internal Revenue Code of 1986, to the extent, and only to the extent, necessary to implement the provisions of paragraph 3(g) of Article XXVI (Mutual Agreement Procedure) and Article XXIX B (Taxes Imposed by Reason of Death).

3. The Convention shall apply also to:

(a) Any taxes identical or substantially similar to those taxes to which the Convention applies under paragraph 2; and

(b) Taxes on capital;

which are imposed after March 17, 1995 in addition to, or in place of, the taxes to which the Convention applies under paragraph 2.

Article III   General Definitions

1. For the purposes of this Convention, unless the context otherwise requires:

(a) When used in a geographical sense, the term "Canada" means the territory of Canada, including any area beyond the territorial seas of Canada which, in accordance with international law and the laws of Canada, is an area within which Canada may exercise rights with respect to the seabed and subsoil and their natural resources;

(b) The term "United States" means:

(i) The United States of America, but does not include Puerto Rico, the Virgin Islands, Guam or any other United States possession or territory; and

(ii) When used in a geographical sense, such term also includes any area beyond the territorial seas of the United States which, in accordance with international law and the laws of the United States, is an area within which the United States, may exercise rights with respect to the seabed and subsoil and their natural resources;

(c) The term "Canadian tax" means the taxes referred to in Article II (Taxes Covered) that are imposed on income by Canada;

(d) The term "United States tax" means the taxes referred to in Article II (Taxes Covered), other than in subparagraph (b)(i) to (iv) of paragraph 2 thereof, that are imposed on income by the United States;

(e) The term "person" includes an individual, an estate, a trust, a company and any other body of persons;

(f) The term "company" means any body corporate or any entity which is treated as a body corporate for tax purposes;

(g) The term "competent authority" means:

(i) In the case of Canada, the Minister of National Revenue or his authorized representative; and

(ii) In the case of the United States, the Secretary of the Treasury or his delegate;

(h) The term "international traffic" with references to a resident of a Contracting State means any voyage of a ship or aircraft to transport passengers or property (whether or not operated or used by that resident) except where the principal purpose of the voyage is to transport passengers or property between places within the other Contracting State;

(i) The term "State" means any national State, whether or not a Contracting State;

(j) The term "the 1942 Convention" means the Convention and Protocol between the United States and Canada for the Avoidance of Double Taxation and the Prevention of Fiscal Evasion in the case of Income Taxes signed at Washington on March 4, 1942, as amended by the Convention signed at Ottawa on June 12, 1950, by the Convention signed at Ottawa on August 8, 1956 and by the Supplementary Convention signed at Washington on October 25, 1966; and

(k) The term "national" of a Contracting State means:

(i) Any individual possessing the citizenship or nationality of that State; and

(ii) Any legal person, partnership or association deriving its status as such from the laws in force in that State.

2. As regards the application of the Convention by a Contracting State any term not defined therein shall, unless the context otherwise requires and subject to the provisions of Article XXVI (Mutual Agreement Procedure), have the meaning which it has under the law of that State concerning the taxes to which the Convention applies.

Article IV   Residence

1. For the purposes of this Convention, the term "resident" of a Contracting State means any person that, under the laws of that State, is liable to tax therein by reason of that persons domicile, residence, citizenship, place of management, place of incorporation or any other criterion of a similar nature, but in the case of an estate or trust, only to the extent that income derived by the estate or trust is liable to tax in that State, either in its hands or in the hands of its beneficiaries. For the purposes of this paragraph, an individual who is not a resident of Canada under this paragraph and who is a United States citizen or an alien admitted to the United States for permanent residence (a "green card" holder) is a resident of the United States only if the individual has a substantial presence, permanent home or habitual abode in the United States, and that individuals personal and economic relations are closer to the United States than to any third State. The term "resident" of a Contracting State is understood to include:

(a) The Government of that State or a political subdivision or local authority thereof or any agency or instrumentality of any such government, subdivision or authority, and

(b) (i) A trust, organization or other arrangement that is operated exclusively to administer or provide pension, retirement or employee benefits; and

(ii) A not-for-profit organization that was constituted in that State and that is, by reason of its nature as such, generally exempt from income taxation in that State.

2. Where by reason of the provisions of paragraph 1 an individual is a resident of both Contracting States, then his status shall be determined as follows:

(a) He shall be deemed to be a resident of the Contracting State in which he has a permanent home available to him; if he has a permanent home available to him in both States or in neither State, he shall be deemed to be a resident of the Contracting State with which his personal and economic relations are closer (centre of vital interests);

(b) If the Contracting State in which he has the centre of vital interests cannot be determined, he shall be deemed to be a resident of the Contracting State in which he has an habitual abode;

(c) If he has an habitual abode in both States or in neither State, he shall be deemed to be a resident of the Contracting State of which he is a citizen; and

(d) If he is a citizen of both States or of neither of them, the competent authorities of the Contracting States shall settle the question by mutual agreement.

3. Where by reason of the provisions of paragraph 1, a company is a resident of both Contracting States, then

(a) If it is created under the laws in force in a Contracting State, but not under the laws in force in the other Contracting State, it shall be deemed to be a resident only of the first-mentioned State; and

(b) In any other case, the competent authorities of the Contracting States shall endeavor to settle the question of residency by mutual agreement and determine the mode of application of this Convention to the company. In the absence of such agreement, the company shall not be considered a resident of either Contracting State for purposes of claiming any benefits under this Convention.

4. Where by reason of the provisions of paragraph 1 an estate, trust or other person (other than an individual or a company) is a resident of both Contracting States, the competent authorities of the States shall by mutual agreement endeavor to settle the question and to determine the mode of application of the Convention to such person.

5. Notwithstanding the provisions of the preceding paragraphs, an individual shall be deemed to be a resident of a Contracting State if:

(a) The individual is an employee of that State or of a political subdivision, local authority or instrumentality thereof rendering services in the discharge of functions of a governmental nature in the other Contracting State or in a third State; and

(b) The individual is subjected in the first-mentioned State to similar obligations in respect of taxes on income as are residents of the first-mentioned State.

The spouse and dependent children residing with such an individual and meeting the requirements of subparagraph (b) above shall also be deemed to be residents of the first-mentioned State.

6. An amount of income, profit or gain shall be considered to be derived by a person who is a resident of a Contracting State where:

(a) The person is considered under the taxation law of that State to have derived the amount through an entity (other than an entity that is a resident of the other Contracting State); and

(b) By reason of the entity being treated as fiscally transparent under the laws of the first-mentioned State, the treatment of the amount under the taxation law of that State is the same as its treatment would be if that amount had been derived directly by that person.

7. An amount of income, profit or gain shall be considered not to be paid to or derived by a person who is a resident of a Contracting State where:

(a) The person is considered under the taxation law of the other Contracting State to have derived the amount through an entity that is not a resident of the first-mentioned State, but by reason of the entity not being treated as fiscally transparent under the laws of that State, the treatment of the amount under the taxation law of that State is not the same as its treatment would be if that amount had been derived directly by that person; or

(b) The person is considered under the taxation law of the other Contracting State to have received the amount from an entity that is a resident of that other State, but by reason of the entity being treated as fiscally transparent under the laws of the first-mentioned State, the treatment of the amount under the taxation law of that State is not the same as its treatment would be if that entity were not treated as fiscally transparent under the laws of that State.

Article V   Permanent Establishment

1. For the purposes of this Convention, the term "permanent establishment" means a fixed place of business through which the business of a resident of a Contracting State is wholly or partly carried on.

2. The term "permanent establishment" shall include especially:

(a) A place of management;

(b) A branch;

(c) An office;

(d) A factory;

(e) A workshop; and

(f) A mine, an oil or gas well, a quarry or any other place of extraction of natural resources.

3. A building site or construction or installation project constitutes a permanent establishment if, but only if, it lasts more than 12 months.

4. The use of an installation or drilling rig or ship in a Contracting State to explore for or exploit natural resources constitutes a permanent establishment if, but only if, such use is for more than three months in any twelve-month period.

5. A person acting in a Contracting State on behalf of a resident of the other Contracting State — other than an agent of an independent status to whom paragraph 7 applies — shall be deemed to be a permanent establishment in the first-mentioned State if such person has, and habitually exercises in that State, an authority to conclude contracts in the name of the resident.

6. Notwithstanding the provisions of paragraphs 1, 2, 5 and 9, the term "permanent establishment" shall be deemed not to include a fixed place of business used solely for, or a person referred to in paragraph 5 engaged solely in, one or more of the following activities:

(a) The use of facilities for the purpose of storage, display or delivery of goods or merchandise belonging to the resident;

(b) The maintenance of a stock of goods or merchandise belonging to the resident for the purpose of storage, display or delivery;

(c) The maintenance of a stock of goods or merchandise belonging to the resident for the purpose of processing by another person;

(d) The purchase of goods or merchandise, or the collection of information, for the resident; and

(e) Advertising, the supply of information, scientific research or similar activities which have a preparatory or auxiliary character, for the resident.

7. A resident of a Contracting State shall not be deemed to have a permanent establishment in the other Contracting State merely because such resident carries on business in that other State through a broker, general commission agent or any other agent of an independent status, provided that such persons are acting in the ordinary course of their business.

8. The fact that a company which is a resident of a Contracting State controls or is controlled by a company which is a resident of the other Contracting State, or which carries on business in that other State (whether through a permanent establishment or otherwise), shall not constitute either company a permanent establishment of the other.

9. Subject to paragraph 3, where an enterprise of a Contracting State provides services in the other Contracting State, if that enterprise is found not to have a permanent establishment in that other State by virtue of the preceding paragraphs

of this Article, that enterprise shall be deemed to provide those services through a permanent establishment in that other State if and only if:

(a) Those services are performed in that other State by an individual who is present in that other State for a period or periods aggregating 183 days or more in any twelve-month period, and, during that period or periods, more than 50 percent of the gross active business revenues of the enterprise consists of income derived from the services performed in that other State by that individual; or

(b) The services are provided in that other State for an aggregate of 183 days or more in any twelve-month period with respect to the same or connected project for customers who are either residents of that other State or who maintain a permanent establishment in that other State and the services are provided in respect of that permanent establishment. 10. For the purposes of this Convention, the provisions of this Article shall be applied in determining whether any person has a permanent establishment in any State.

Article VI　Income From Real Property

1. Income derived by a resident of a Contracting State from real property (including income from agriculture, forestry or other natural resources) situated in the other Contracting State may be taxed in that other State.

2. For the purposes of this Convention, the term "real property" shall have the meaning which it has under the taxation laws of the Contracting State in which the property in question is situated and shall include any option or similar right in respect thereof. The term shall in any case include usufruct of real property, rights to explore for or to exploit mineral deposits, sources and other natural resources and rights to amounts computed by reference to the amount or value of production from such resources; ships and aircraft shall not be regarded as real property.

3. The provisions of paragraph 1 shall apply to income derived from the direct use, letting or use in any other form of real property and to income from the alienation of such property.

Article VII　Business Profits

1. The business profits of a resident of a Contracting State shall be taxable only in that State unless the resident carries on business in the other Contracting State through a permanent establishment situated therein. If the resident carries on, or has carried on, business as aforesaid, the business profits of the resident may be taxed in the other State but only so much of them as is attributable to that permanent establishment.

2. Subject to the provisions of paragraph 3, where a resident of a Contracting State carries on, or has carried on, business in the other Contracting State through a permanent establishment situated therein, there shall in each Contracting State be attributed to that permanent establishment the business profits which it might be expected to make if it were a distinct and separate person engaged in the same or similar activities under the same or similar conditions and dealing wholly

independently with the resident and with any other person related to the resident (within the meaning of paragraph 2 of Article IX (Related Persons)).

3. In determining the business profits of a permanent establishment, there shall be allowed as deductions expenses which are incurred for the purposes of the permanent establishment, including executive and general administrative expenses so incurred, whether in the State in which the permanent establishment is situated or elsewhere. Nothing in this paragraph shall require a Contracting State to allow the deduction of any expenditure which, by reason of its nature, is not generally allowed as a deduction under the taxation laws of that State.

4. No business profits shall be attributed to a permanent establishment of a resident of a Contracting State by reason of the use thereof for either the mere purchase of goods or merchandise or the mere provision of executive, managerial or administrative facilities or services for such resident.

5. For the purposes of the preceding paragraphs, the business profits to be attributed to a permanent establishment shall be determined by the same method year by year unless there is good and sufficient reason to the contrary.

6. Where business profits include items of income which are dealt with separately in other Articles of this Convention, then the provisions of those Articles shall not be affected by the provisions of this Article.

7. For the purposes of the Convention, the business profits attributable to a permanent establishment shall include only those profits derived from the assets or activities of the permanent establishment.

Article VIII   Transportation

1. Notwithstanding the provisions of Articles VII (Business Profits), XII (Royalties) and XIII (Gains), profits derived by a resident of a Contracting State from the operation of ships or aircraft in international traffic, and gains derived by a resident of a Contracting State from the alienation of ships, aircraft or containers (including trailers and related equipment for the transport of containers) used principally in international traffic, shall be exempt from tax in the other Contracting State.

2. For the purposes of this Convention, profits derived by a resident of a Contracting State from the operation of ships or aircraft in international traffic include profits from:

(a) The rental of ships or aircraft operated in international traffic;

(b) The use, maintenance or rental of containers (including trailers and related equipment for the transport of containers) used in international traffic; and

(c) The rental of ships, aircraft or containers (including trailers and related equipment for the transport of containers) provided that such profits are incidental to profits referred to in paragraph 1, 2(a) or 2(b).

3. Notwithstanding the provisions of Article VII (Business Profits), profits derived by a resident of a Contracting State from a voyage of a ship where the

principal purpose of the voyage is to transport passengers or property between places in the other Contracting State may be taxed in that other State.

4. Notwithstanding the provisions of Articles VII (Business Profits) and XII (Royalties), profits of a resident of a Contracting State engaged in the operation of motor vehicles or a railway as a common carrier or a contract carrier derived from:

(a) The transportation of passengers or property between a point outside the other Contracting State and any other point; or

(b) The rental of motor vehicles (including trailers) or railway rolling stock, or the use, maintenance or rental of containers (including trailers and related equipment for the transport of containers) used to transport passengers or property between a point outside the other Contracting State and any other point.

shall be exempt from tax in that other Contracting State.

5. The provisions of paragraphs 1, 3 and 4 shall also apply to profits or gains referred to in those paragraphs derived by a resident of a Contracting State from the participation in a pool, a joint business or an international operating agency.

6. Notwithstanding the provisions of Article XII (Royalties), profits derived by a resident of a Contracting State from the use, maintenance or rental of railway rolling stock, motor vehicles, trailers or containers (including trailers and related equipment for the transport of containers) used in the other Contracting State for a period or periods not expected to exceed in the aggregate 183 days in any twelve-month period shall be exempt from tax in the other Contracting State except to the extent that such profits are attributable to a permanent establishment in the other State and liable to tax in the other State by reason of Article VII (Business Profits).

Article IX   Related Persons

1. Where a person in a Contracting State and a person in the other Contracting State are related and where the arrangements between them differ from those which would be made between unrelated persons, each State may adjust the amount of the income, loss or tax payable to reflect the income, deductions, credits or allowances which would, but for those arrangements, have been taken into account in computing such income, loss or tax.

2. For the purposes of this Article, a person shall be deemed to be related to another person if either person participates directly or indirectly in the management or control of the other, or if any third person or persons participate directly or indirectly in the management or control of both.

3. Where an adjustment is made or to be made by a Contracting State in accordance with paragraph 1, the other Contracting State shall (notwithstanding any time or procedural limitations in the domestic law of that other State) make a corresponding adjustment to the income, loss or tax of the related person in that other State if:

(a) It agrees with the first mentioned adjustment; and

(b) Within six years from the end of the taxable year to which the first-mentioned adjustment relates, the competent authority of the other State has been notified of the first-mentioned adjustment. The competent authorities, however, may agree to consider cases where the corresponding adjustment would not otherwise be barred by any time or procedural limitations in the other State, even if the notification is not made within the six-year period.

4. In the event that the notification referred to in paragraph 3 is not given within the time period referred to therein, and the competent authorities have not agreed to otherwise consider the case in accordance with paragraph 3(b), the competent authority of the Contracting State which has made or is to make the first-mentioned adjustment may provide relief from double taxation where appropriate.

5. The provisions of paragraphs 3 and 4 shall not apply in the case of fraud, willful default or neglect or gross negligence.

Article X   Dividends

1. Dividends paid by a company which is a resident of a Contracting State to a resident of the other Contracting State may be taxed in that other State.

2. However, such dividends may also be taxed in the Contracting State of which the company paying the dividends is a resident and according to the laws of that State; but if a resident of the other Contracting State is the beneficial owner of such dividends, the tax so charged shall not exceed:

(a) 5 percent of the gross amount of the dividends if the beneficial owner is a company which owns at least 10 percent of the voting stock of the company paying the dividends (for this purpose, a company that is a resident of a Contracting State shall be considered to own the voting stock owned by an entity that is considered fiscally transparent under the laws of that State and that is not a resident of the Contracting State of which the company paying the dividends is a resident, in proportion to the company's ownership interest in that entity);

(b) 15 per cent of the gross amount of the dividends in all other cases.

This paragraph shall not affect the taxation of the company in respect of the profits out of which the dividends are paid.

3. For the purposes of this Article, the term "dividends" means income from shares or other rights, not being debt-claims, participating in profits, as well as income that is subjected to the same taxation treatment as income from shares under the laws of the State of which the payer is a resident.

4. The provisions of paragraph 2 shall not apply if the beneficial owner of the dividends, being a resident of a Contracting State, carries on, or has carried on, business in the other Contracting State of which the company paying the dividends is a resident, through a permanent establishment situated therein, and the holding in respect of which the dividends are paid is effectively connected to such permanent establishment. In such case, the provisions of Article VII (Business Profits) shall apply.

5. Where a company is a resident of a Contracting State, the other Contracting State may not impose any tax on the dividends paid by the company, except insofar as such dividends are paid to a resident of that other State or insofar as the holding in respect of which the dividends are paid is effectively connected with a permanent establishment situated in that other State, nor subject the companys undistributed profits to a tax, even if the dividends paid or the undistributed profits consist wholly or partly of profits or income arising in such other State.

6. Nothing in this Convention shall be construed as preventing a Contracting State from imposing a tax on the earnings of a company attributable to permanent establishments in that State, in addition to the tax which would be chargeable on the earnings of a company which is a resident of that State, provided that any additional tax so imposed shall not exceed 5 per cent of the amount of such earnings which have not been subjected to such additional tax in previous taxation years. For the purposes of this paragraph, the term "earnings" means the amount by which the business profits attributable to permanent establishments in a Contracting State (including gains from the alienation of property forming part of the business property of such permanent establishments) in a year and previous years exceeds the sum of:

(a) Business losses attributable to such permanent establishments (including losses from the alienation of property forming part of the business property of such permanent establishments) in such year and previous years;

(b) All taxes, other than the additional tax referred to in this paragraph, imposed on such profits in that State;

(c) The profits reinvested in that State, provided that where that State is Canada, such amount shall be determined in accordance with the existing provisions of the law of Canada regarding the computation of the allowance in respect of investment in property in Canada, and any subsequent modification of those provisions, which shall not affect the general principle hereof; and

(d) Five hundred thousand Canadian dollars ($500,000) or its equivalent in United States currency, less any amounts deducted by the company, or by an associated company with respect to the same or a similar business, under this subparagraph (d); for the purposes of this subparagraph (d) a company is associated with another company if one company directly or indirectly controls the other, or both companies are directly or indirectly controlled by the same person or persons, or if the two companies deal with each other not at arms length.

7. Notwithstanding the provisions of paragraph 2,

(a) Dividends paid by a company that is a resident of Canada and a non-resident-owned investment corporation to a company that is a resident of the United States, that owns at least 10 per cent of the voting stock of the company paying the dividends and that is the beneficial owner of such dividends, may be taxed in Canada at a rate not exceeding 10 per cent of the gross amount of the dividends;

(b) Paragraph 2(b) and not paragraph 2(a) shall apply in the case of dividends paid by a resident of the United States that is a Regulated Investment Company; and

(c) Subparagraph 2(a) shall not apply to dividends paid by a resident of the United States that is a Real Estate Investment Trust (REIT), and subparagraph 2(b) shall apply

only if:

(i) The beneficial owner of the dividends is an individual holding an interest of not more than 10 percent in the REIT;

(ii) The dividends are paid with respect to a class of stock that is publicly traded and the beneficial owner of the dividends is a person holding an interest of not more than 5 percent in any class of the REITs stock; or

(iii) The beneficial owner of the dividends is a person holding an interest of not more than 10 percent in the REIT and the REIT is diversified.

Otherwise, the rate of tax applicable under the domestic law of the United States shall apply. Where an estate or testamentary trust acquired its interest in a REIT as a consequence of an individuals death, for purposes of this subparagraph the estate or trust shall for the five-year period following the death be deemed with respect to that interest to be an individual.

8. Notwithstanding the provisions of paragraph 5, a company which is a resident of Canada and which has income subject to tax in the United States (without regard to the provisions of the Convention) may be liable to the United States accumulated earnings tax and personal holding company tax but only if 50 per cent or more in value of the outstanding voting shares of the company is owned, directly or indirectly, throughout the last half of its taxable year by citizens and residents of the United States (other than citizens of Canada who do not have immigrant status in the United States or who have not been residents in the United States for more than three taxable years) or by residents of a third State.

Article XI   Interest

1. Interest arising in a Contracting State and beneficially owned by a resident of the other Contracting State may be taxed only in that other State.

2. The term "interest" as used in this Article means income from debt-claims of every kind, whether or not secured by mortgage, and whether or not carrying a right to participate in the debtors profits, and in particular, income from government securities and income from bonds or debentures, including premiums or prizes attaching to such securities, bonds or debentures, as well as income assimilated to income from money lent by the taxation laws of the Contracting State in which the income arises. However, the term "interest" does not include income dealt with in Article X (Dividends).

3. The provisions of paragraph 1 shall not apply if the beneficial owner of the interest, being a resident of a Contracting State, carries on, or has carried on, business in the other Contracting State in which the interest arises, through a permanent establishment situated therein, and the debt-claim in respect of which the interest is paid is effectively connected with such permanent establishment. In such case the provisions of Article VII (Business Profits) shall apply.

4. For the purposes of this Article, interest shall be deemed to arise in a Contracting State when the payer is that State itself, or a political subdivision, local authority or a resident of that State. Where, however, the person paying the interest, whether he is a resident of a Contracting State or not, has in a State other than that of which he is a resident a permanent establishment in connection with which the indebtedness on which the interest is paid was incurred, and such interest is borne by such permanent establishment, then such interest shall be deemed to arise in the State in which the permanent establishment is situated and not in the State of which the payer is a resident.

5. Where, by reason of a special relationship between the payer and the beneficial owner or between both of them and some other person, the amount of the interest, having regard to the debt-claim for which it is paid, exceeds the amount which would have been agreed upon by the payer and the beneficial owner in the absence of such relationship, the provisions of this Article shall apply only to the last-mentioned amount. In such case the excess part of the payments shall remain taxable according to the laws of each Contracting State, due regard being had to the other provisions of this Convention.

6. Notwithstanding the provisions of paragraph 1:

(a) Interest arising in the United States that is contingent interest of a type that does not qualify as portfolio interest under United States law may be taxed by the United States but, if the beneficial owner of the interest is a resident of Canada, the gross amount of the interest may be taxed at a rate not exceeding the rate prescribed in subparagraph (b) of paragraph 2 of Article X (Dividends);

(b) Interest arising in Canada that is determined with reference to receipts, sales, income, profits or other cash flow of the debtor or a related person, to any change in the value of any property of the debtor or a related person or to any dividend, partnership distribution or similar payment made by the debtor to a related person may be taxed by Canada, and according to the laws of Canada, but if the beneficial owner is a resident of the United States, the gross amount of the interest may be taxed at a rate not exceeding the rate prescribed in subparagraph (b) of paragraph 2 of Article X (Dividends); and

(c) Interest that is an excess inclusion with respect to a residual interest in a real estate mortgage investment conduit may be taxed by each State in accordance with its domestic law.

7. Where a resident of a Contracting State pays interest to a person other than a resident of the other Contracting State, that other State may not impose any tax on such interest except insofar as it arises in that other State or insofar as the

debt-claim in respect of which the interest is paid is effectively connected with a permanent establishment situated in that other State.

Article XII   Royalties

1. Royalties arising in a Contracting State and paid to a resident of the other Contracting State may be taxed in that other State.

2. However, such royalties may also be taxed in the Contracting State in which they arise, and according to the laws of that State; but if a resident of the other Contracting State is the beneficial owner of such royalties, the tax so charged shall not exceed 10 per cent of the gross amount of the royalties.

3. Notwithstanding the provisions of paragraph 2,

   (a) Copyright royalties and other like payments in respect of the production or reproduction of any literary, dramatic, musical or artistic work (other than payments in respect of motion pictures and works on film, videotape or other means of reproduction for use in connection with television);

   (b) Payments for the use of, or the right to use, computer software;

   (c) Payments for the use of, or the right to use, any patent or any information concerning industrial, commercial or scientific experience (but not including any such information provided in connection with a rental or franchise agreement); and

   (d) Payments with respect to broadcasting as may be agreed for the purposes of this paragraph in an exchange of notes between the Contracting States;

arising in a Contracting State and beneficially owned by a resident of the other Contracting State shall be taxable only in that other State.

4. The term "royalties" as used in this Article means payments of any kind received as a consideration for the use of, or the right to use, any copyright of literary, artistic or scientific work (including motion pictures and works on film, videotape or other means of reproduction for use in connection with television), any patent, trademark, design or model, plan, secret formula or process, or for the use of, or the right to use, tangible personal property or for information concerning industrial, commercial or scientific experience, and, notwithstanding the provisions of Article XIII (Gains), includes gains from the alienation of any intangible property or rights described in this paragraph to the extent that such gains are contingent on the productivity, use or subsequent disposition of such property or rights.

5. The provisions of paragraphs 2 and 3 shall not apply if the beneficial owner of the royalties, being a resident of a Contracting State, carries on, or has carried on, business in the other Contracting State in which the royalties arise, through a permanent establishment situated therein, and the right or property in respect of which the royalties are paid is effectively connected to such permanent establishment. In such case the provisions of Article VII (Business Profits) shall apply.

6. For the purposes of this Article,

(a) Royalties shall be deemed to arise in a Contracting State when the payer is a resident of that State. Where, however, the person paying the royalties, whether he is a resident of a Contracting State or not, has in a State a permanent establishment in connection with which the obligation to pay the royalties was incurred, and such royalties are borne by such permanent establishment, then such royalties shall be deemed to arise in the State in which the permanent establishment is situated and not in any other State of which the payer is a resident; and

(b) Where subparagraph (a) does not operate to treat royalties as arising in either Contracting State and the royalties are for the use of, or the right to use, intangible property or tangible personal property in a Contracting State, then such royalties shall be deemed to arise in that State.

7. Where, by reason of a special relationship between the payer and the beneficial owner or between both of them and some other person, the amount of the royalties, having regard to the use, right or information for which they are paid, exceeds the amount which would have been agreed upon by the payer and the beneficial owner in the absence of such relationship, the provisions of this Article shall apply only to the last-mentioned amount. In such case, the excess part of the payments shall remain taxable according to the laws of each Contracting State, due regard being had to the other provisions of this Convention.

8. Where a resident of a Contracting State pays royalties to a person other than a resident of the other Contracting State, that other State may not impose any tax on such royalties except insofar as they arise in that other State or insofar as the right or property in respect of which the royalties are paid is effectively connected with a permanent establishment situated in that other State.

Article XIII Gains

1. Gains derived by a resident of a Contracting State from the alienation of real property situated in the other Contracting State may be taxed in that other State.

2. Gains from the alienation of personal property forming part of the business property of a permanent establishment which a resident of a Contracting State has or had (within the twelve-month period preceding the date of alienation) in the other Contracting State, including such gains from the alienation of such a permanent establishment, may be taxed in that other State.

3. For the purposes of this Article the term "real property situated in the other Contracting State"

(a) In the case of real property situated in the United States, means a United States real property interest and real property referred to in Article VI (Income from Real Property) situated in the United States, but does not include a share of the capital stock of a company that is not a resident of the United States; and

(b) In the case of real property situated in Canada means:

(i) Real property referred to in Article VI (Income from Real Property) situated in Canada;

(ii) A share of the capital stock of a company that is a resident of Canada, the value of whose shares is derived principally from real property situated in Canada; and

(iii) An interest in a partnership, trust or estate, the value of which is derived principally from real property situated in Canada.

4. Gains from the alienation of any property other than that referred to in paragraphs 1, 2 and 3 shall be taxable only in the Contracting State of which the alienator is a resident.

5. The provisions of paragraph 4 shall not affect the right of a Contracting State to levy, according to its domestic law, a tax on gains from the alienation of any property derived by an individual who is a resident of the other Contracting State if:

(a) The individual was a resident of the first-mentioned State:

(i) For at least 120 months during any period of 20 consecutive years preceding the alienation of the property; and

(ii) At any time during the 10 years immediately preceding the alienation of the property; and

(b) The property (or property for which such property was substituted in an alienation the gain on which was not recognized for the purposes of taxation in the first-mentioned State):

(i) Was owned by the individual at the time the individual ceased to be a resident of the first-mentioned State; and

(ii) Was not a property that the individual was treated as having alienated by reason of ceasing to be a resident of the first-mentioned State and becoming a resident of the other Contracting State.

6. Where an individual (other than a citizen of the United States) who was a resident of Canada became a resident of the United States, in determining his liability to United States taxation in respect of any gain from the alienation of a principal residence in Canada owned by him at the time he ceased to be a resident of Canada, the adjusted basis of such property shall be no less than its fair market value at that time.

7. Where at any time an individual is treated for the purposes of taxation by a Contracting State as having alienated a property and is taxed in that State by reason thereof, the individual may elect to be treated for the purposes of taxation in the other Contracting State, in the year that includes that time and all subsequent years, as if the individual had, immediately before that time, sold and repurchased the property for an amount equal to its fair market value at that time.

8. Where a resident of a Contracting State alienates property in the course of a corporate or other organization, reorganization, amalgamation, division or similar transaction and profit, gain or income with respect to such alienation is not recognized for the purpose of taxation in that State, if requested to do so by the person who acquires the property, the competent authority of the other Contracting

State may agree, in order to avoid double taxation and subject to terms and conditions satisfactory to such competent authority, to defer the recognition of the profit, gain or income with respect to such property for the purpose of taxation in that other State until such time and in such manner as may be stipulated in the agreement.

9. Where a person who is a resident of a Contracting State alienates a capital asset which may in accordance with this Article be taxed in the other Contracting State and

(a) That person owned the asset on September 26, 1980 and was resident in the first-mentioned State on that date; or

(b) The asset was acquired by that person in an alienation of property which qualified as a non-recognition transaction for the purposes of taxation in that other State;

the amount of the gain which is liable to tax in that other State in accordance with this Article shall be reduced by the proportion of the gain attributable on a monthly basis to the period ending on December 31 of the year in which the Convention enters into force, or such greater portion of the gain as is shown to the satisfaction of the competent authority of the other State to be reasonably attributable to that period. For the purposes of this paragraph the term "non-recognition transaction" includes a transaction to which paragraph 8 applies and, in the case of taxation in the United States, a transaction that would have been a non-recognition transaction but for Sections 897(d) and 897(e) of the Internal Revenue Code. The provisions of this paragraph shall not apply to

(c) An asset that on September 26, 1980 formed part of the business property of a permanent establishment of a resident of a Contracting State situated in the other Contracting State;

(d) An alienation by a resident of a Contracting State of an asset that was owned at any time after September 26, 1980 and before such alienation by a person who was not at all times after that date while the asset was owned by such person a resident of that States; or

(e) An alienation of an asset that was acquired by a person at any time after September 26, 1980 and before such alienation in a transaction other than a non-recognition transaction.

Article XIV   Independent Personal Services

[Deleted]

Article XV   Income From Employment

1. Subject to the provisions of Articles XVIII (Pensions and Annuities) and XIX (Government Service), salaries, wages and other remuneration derived by a resident of a Contracting State in respect of an employment shall be taxable only in that State unless the employment is exercised in the other Contracting State. If the employment is so exercised, such remuneration as is derived therefrom may be taxed in that other State.

2. Notwithstanding the provisions of paragraph 1, remuneration derived by a resident of a Contracting State in respect of an employment exercised in the other Contracting State shall be taxable only in the first-mentioned State if:

(a) Such remuneration does not exceed ten thousand dollars ($10,000) in the currency of that other State; or

(b) The recipient is present in that other State for a period or periods not exceeding in the aggregate 183 days in any twelve-month period commencing or ending in the fiscal year concerned, and the remuneration is not paid by, or on behalf of, a person who is a resident of that other State and is not borne by a permanent establishment in that other State.

3. Notwithstanding the provisions of paragraphs 1 and 2, remuneration derived by a resident of a Contracting State in respect of an employment regularly exercised in more than one State on a ship, aircraft, motor vehicle or train operated by a resident of that Contracting State shall be taxable only in that State.

Article XVI   Artistes and Athletes

1. Notwithstanding the provisions of Articles VII (Business Profits) and XV (Income From Employment), income derived by a resident of a Contracting State as an entertainer, such as a theatre, motion picture, radio or television artiste, or a musician, or as an athlete, from his personal activities as such exercised in the other Contracting State, may be taxed in that other State, except where the amount of the gross receipts derived by such entertainer or athlete, including expenses reimbursed to him or borne on his behalf, from such activities do not exceed fifteen thousand dollars ($15,000) in the currency of that other State for the calendar year concerned.

2. Where income in respect of personal activities exercised by an entertainer or an athlete in his capacity as such accrues not to the entertainer or athlete but to another person, that income may, notwithstanding the provisions of Articles VII (Business Profits), and XV (Income From Employment), be taxed in the Contracting State in which the activities of the entertainer or athlete are exercised. For the purposes of the preceding sentence, income of an entertainer or athlete shall be deemed not to accrue to another person if it is established that neither the entertainer or athlete, nor person related thereto, participate directly or indirectly in the profits of such other person in any manner, including the receipt of deferred remuneration, bonuses, fees, dividends, partnership distributions or other distributions.

3. The provisions of paragraphs 1 and 2 shall not apply to the income of:

(a) An athlete in respect of his activities as an employee of a team which participates in a league with regularly scheduled games in both Contracting State; or

(b) A team described in subparagraph (a).

4. Notwithstanding the provisions of Articles VII (Business Profits) and XV (Income From Employment) an amount paid by a resident of a Contracting State to a resident of the other Contracting State as an inducement to sign an agreement

relating to the performance of the services of an athlete (other than an amount referred to in paragraph 1 of Article XV (Income From Employment)) may be taxed in the first-mentioned State, but the tax so charged shall not exceed 15 per cent of the gross amount of such payment.

Article XVII   Witholding of Taxes in Respect of Personal Services

[Deleted]

Article XVIII   Pensions and Annuities

1. Pensions and annuities arising in a Contracting State and paid to a resident of the other Contracting State may be taxed in that other State, but the amount of any such pension that would be excluded from taxable income in the first-mentioned State if the recipient were a resident thereof shall be exempt from taxation in that other State.

2. However:

(a) Pensions may also be taxed in the Contracting State in which they arise and according to the laws of that State; but if a resident of the other Contracting State is the beneficial owner of a periodic pension payment, the tax so charged shall not exceed 15 per cent of the gross amount of such payment; and

(b) Annuities may also be taxed in the Contracting State in which they arise and according to the laws of that State; but if a resident of the other Contracting State is the beneficial owner of an annuity payment, the tax so charged shall not exceed 15 per cent of the portion of such payment that would not be excluded from taxable income in the first-mentioned State if the beneficial owner were a resident thereof.

3. For the purposes of this Convention:

(a) The term "pensions" includes any payment under a superannuation, pension or other retirement arrangement, Armed Forces retirement pay, war veterans pensions and allowances and amounts paid under a sickness, accident or disability plan, but does not include payments under an income-averaging annuity contract or, except for the purposes of Article XIX (Government Service), any benefit referred to in paragraph 5; and

(b) The term "pensions" also includes a Roth IRA, within the meaning of section 408A of the Internal Revenue Code, or a plan or arrangement created pursuant to legislation enacted by a Contracting State after September 21, 2007 that the competent authorities have agreed is similar thereto. Notwithstanding the provisions of the preceding sentence, from such time that contributions have been made to the Roth IRA or similar plan or arrangement, by or for the benefit of a resident of the other Contracting State (other than rollover contributions from a Roth IRA or similar plan or arrangement described in the previous sentence that is a pension within the meaning of this subparagraph), to the extent of accretions from such time, such Roth IRA or similar plan or arrangement shall cease to be considered a pension for purposes of the provisions of this Article.

4. For the purposes of this Convention:

(a) The term "annuity" means a stated sum paid periodically at stated times during life or during a specified number of years, under an obligation to make the payments in return for adequate and full consideration (other than services rendered), but does not include a payment that is not a periodic payment or any annuity the cost of which was deductible for the purposes of taxation in the Contracting State in which it was acquired; and

(b) An annuity or other amount paid in respect of a life insurance or annuity contract (including a withdrawal in respect of the cash value thereof) shall be deemed to arise in a Contracting State if the person paying the annuity or other amount (in this subparagraph referred to as the "payer") is a resident of that State. However, if the payer, whether a resident of a Contracting State or not, has in a State other than that of which the payer is a resident a permanent establishment in connection with which the obligation giving rise to the annuity or other amount was incurred, and the annuity or other amount is borne by the permanent establishment, then the annuity or other amount shall be deemed to arise in the State in which the permanent establishment is situated and not in the State of which the payer is a resident.

5. Benefits under the social security legislation in a Contracting State (including tier 1 railroad retirement benefits but not including unemployment benefits) paid to a resident of the other Contracting State shall be taxable only in that other State, subject to the following conditions:

(a) a benefit under the social security legislation in the United States paid to a resident of Canada shall be taxable in Canada as though it were a benefit under the Canada Pension Plan, except that 15 per cent of the amount of the benefit shall be exempt from Canadian tax; and

(b) a benefit under the social security legislation in Canada paid to a resident of the United States shall be taxable in the United States as though it were a benefit under the Social Security Act, except that a type of benefit that is not subject to Canadian tax when paid to residents of Canada shall be exempt from United States tax.

6. Alimony and other similar amounts (including child support payments) arising in a Contracting State and paid to a resident of the other Contracting State shall be taxable as follows:

(a) Such amounts shall be taxable only in that other State;

(b) Notwithstanding the provisions of subparagraph (a), the amount that would be excluded from taxable income in the first-mentioned State if the recipient were a resident thereof shall be exempt from taxation in that other State.

7. A natural person who is a citizen or resident of a Contracting State and a beneficiary of a trust, company, organization or other arrangement that is a resident of the other Contracting State, generally exempt from income taxation in that other State and operated exclusively to provide pension or employee benefits may elect to defer taxation in the first-mentioned State, subject to rules established by the competent authority of that State, with respect to any income accrued in the plan but not distributed by the plan, until such time as and to the extent that a distribution is made from the plan or any plan substituted therefor.

8. Contributions made to, or benefits accrued under, a qualifying retirement plan in a Contracting State by or on behalf of an individual shall be deductible or excludible in computing the individuals taxable income in the other Contracting State, and contributions made to the plan by the individuals employer shall be allowed as a deduction in computing the employers profits in that other State, where:

(a) The individual performs services as an employee in that other State the remuneration from which is taxable in that other State;

(b) The individual was participating in the plan (or another similar plan for which this plan was substituted) immediately before the individual began performing the services in that other State;

(c) The individual was not a resident of that other State immediately before the individual began performing the services in that other State;

(d) The individual has performed services in that other State for the same employer (or a related employer) for no more than 60 of the 120 months preceding the individuals current taxation year;

(e) The contributions and benefits are attributable to the services performed by the individual in that other State, and are made or accrued during the period in which the individual performs those services; and

(f) With respect to contributions and benefits that are attributable to services performed during a period in the individuals current taxation year, no contributions in respect of the period are made by or on behalf of the individual to, and no services performed in that other State during the period are otherwise taken into account for purposes of determining the individuals entitlement to benefits under, any plan that would be a qualifying retirement plan in that other State if paragraph 15 of this Article were read without reference to subparagraphs (b) and (c) of that paragraph.

This paragraph shall apply only to the extent that the contributions or benefits would qualify for tax relief in the first-mentioned State if the individual was a resident of and performed the services in that State.

9. For the purposes of United States taxation, the benefits granted under paragraph 8 to a citizen of the United States shall not exceed the benefits that would be allowed by the United States to its residents for contributions to, or benefits otherwise accrued under, a generally corresponding pension or retirement plan established in and recognized for tax purposes by the United States.

10. Contributions made to, or benefits accrued under, a qualifying retirement plan in a Contracting State by or on behalf of an individual who is a resident of the other Contracting State shall be deductible or excludible in computing the individuals taxable income in that other State, where:

(a) The individual performs services as an employee in the firstmentioned state the remuneration from which is taxable in that State and is borne by an employer who is a resident of that State or by a permanent establishment which the employer has in that State; and

(b) The contributions and benefits are attributable to those services and are made or accrued during the period in which the individual performs those services.

This paragraph shall apply only to the extent that the contributions or benefits qualify for tax relief in the first-mentioned State.

11. For the purposes of Canadian taxation, the amount of contributions otherwise allowed as a deduction under paragraph 10 to an individual for a taxation year shall not exceed the individuals deduction limit under the law of Canada for the year for contributions to registered retirement savings plans remaining after taking into account the amount of contributions to registered retirement savings plans deducted by the individual under the law of Canada for the year. The amount deducted by an individual under paragraph 10 for a taxation year shall be taken into account in computing the individuals deduction limit under the law of Canada for subsequent taxation years for contributions to registered retirement savings plans.

12. For the purposes of United States taxation, the benefits granted under paragraph 10 shall not exceed the benefits that would be allowed by the United States to its residents for contributions to, or benefits otherwise accrued under, a generally corresponding pension or retirement plan established in and recognized for tax purposes by the United States. For purposes of determining an individuals eligibility to participate in and receive tax benefits with respect to a pension or retirement plan or other retirement arrangement established in and recognized for tax purposes by the United States, contributions made to, or benefits accrued under, a qualifying retirement plan in Canada by or on behalf of the individual shall be treated as contributions or benefits under a generally corresponding pension or retirement plan established in and recognized for tax purposes by the United States.

13. Contributions made to, or benefits accrued under, a qualifying retirement plan in Canada by or on behalf of a citizen of the United States who is a resident of Canada shall be deductible or excludible in computing the citizens taxable income in the United States, where:

(a) The citizen performs services as an employee in Canada the remuneration from which is taxable in Canada and is borne by an employer who is a resident of Canada or by a permanent establishment which the employer has in Canada; and

(b) The contributions and benefits are attributable to those services and are made or accrued during the period in which the citizen performs those services.

This paragraph shall apply only to the extent that the contributions or benefits qualify for tax relief in Canada.

14. The benefits granted under paragraph 13 shall not exceed the benefits that would be allowed by the United States to its residents for contributions to, or benefits otherwise accrued under, a generally corresponding pension or retirement plan established in and recognized for tax purposes by the United States. For purposes of determining an individuals eligibility to participate in and receive tax benefits with respect to a pension or retirement plan or other retirement arrangement established in and recognized for tax purposes by the United States, contributions made to, or benefits accrued under, a qualifying retirement plan in Canada by or on behalf of the individual shall be treated as contributions or benefits under a generally corresponding pension or retirement plan established in and recognized for tax purposes by the United States.

15. For purposes of paragraphs 8 to 14, a qualifying retirement plan in a Contracting State means a trust, company, organization or other arrangement:

(a) That is a resident of that State, generally exempt from income taxation in that State and operated primarily to provide pension or retirement benefits;

(b) That is not an individual arrangement in respect of which the individuals employer has no involvement; and

(c) Which the competent authority of the other Contracting State agrees generally corresponds to a pension or retirement plan established in and recognized for tax purposes by that other State.

16. For purposes of this Article, a distribution from a pension or retirement plan that is reasonably attributable to a contribution or benefit for which a benefit was allowed pursuant to paragraph 8, 10 or 13 shall be deemed to arise in the Contracting State in which the plan is established.

17. Paragraphs 8 to 16 apply, with such modifications as the circumstances require, as though the relationship between a partnership that carries on a business, and an individual who is a member of the partnership, were that of employer and employee.

Article XIX   Government Service

Remuneration, other than a pension, paid by a Contracting State or a political subdivision or local authority thereof to a citizen of that State in respect of services rendered in the discharge of functions of a governmental nature shall be taxable only in the State. However, the provisions of Article VII (Business Profits), XV (Income From Employment) or XVI (Artistes and Athletes), as the case may be, shall apply, and the preceding sentence shall not apply, to remuneration paid in respect of services rendered in connection with a trade or business carried on by a Contracting State or a political subdivision or local authority thereof.

Article XX   Students

Payments received by an individual who is a student, apprentice, or business trainee, and is, or was immediately before visiting a Contracting State, a resident of the other Contracting State, and who is present in the first-mentioned State for the purpose of the individuals full-time education or full-time training, shall not be taxed in that State, provided that such payments arise outside that State, and are for the purpose of the maintenance, education or training of the individual. The provisions of this Article shall apply to an apprentice or business trainee only for a period of time not exceeding one year from the date the individual first arrives in the first-mentioned State for the purpose of the individuals training.

Article XXI   Exempt Organizations

1. Subject to the provisions of paragraph 4, income derived by a religious, scientific, literary, educational or charitable organization shall be exempt from tax in a Contracting State if it is resident in the other Contracting State, but only to the extent that such income is exempt from tax in that other State.

2. Subject to the provisions of paragraph 4, income referred to in Articles X (Dividends) and XI (Interest) derived by a trust, company, organization or other arrangement that is a resident of a Contracting State, generally exempt from income taxation in a taxable year in that State and operated exclusively to administer or provide pension, retirement or employee benefits shall be exempt from income taxation in that taxable year in the other Contracting State.

3. Subject to the provisions of paragraph 4, income referred to in Articles X (Dividends) and XI (Interest) derived by a trust, company, organization or other arrangement that is a resident of a Contracting State, generally exempt from income taxation in a taxable year in that State and operated exclusively to earn income for the benefit of one or more of the following:

    (a) An organization referred to in paragraph 1; or

    (b) A trust, company, organization or other arrangement referred to in paragraph 2;

shall be exempt from income taxation in that taxable year in the other Contracting State.

4. The provisions of paragraphs 1, 2 and 3 shall not apply with respect to the income of a trust, company, organization or other arrangement from carrying on a trade or business or from a related person other than a person referred to in paragraphs 1, 2 or 3.

5. A religious, scientific, literary, educational or charitable organization which is resident in Canada and which has received substantially all of its support from persons other than citizens or residents of the United States shall be exempt in the United States from the United States excise taxes imposed with respect to private foundations.

6. For the purposes of United States taxation, contributions by a citizen or resident of the United States to an organization which is resident in Canada, which

is generally exempt from Canadian tax and which could qualify in the United States to receive deductible contributions if it were resident in the United States shall be treated as charitable contributions; however, such contributions (other than such contributions to a college or university at which the citizen or resident or a member of his family is or was enrolled) shall not be deductible in any taxable year to the extent that they exceed an amount determined by applying the percentage limitations of the laws of the United States in respect of the deductibility of charitable contributions to the income of such citizen or resident arising in Canada. The preceding sentence shall not be interpreted to allow in any taxable year deductions for charitable contributions in excess of the amount allowed under the percentage limitations of the laws of the United States in respect of the deductibility of charitable contributions. For the purposes of this paragraph, a company that is a resident of Canada and that is taxable in the United States as if it were a resident of the United States shall be deemed to be a resident of the United States.

7. For the purposes of Canadian taxation, gifts by a resident of Canada to an organization that is a resident of the United States, that is generally exempt from United States tax and that could qualify in Canada as a registered charity if it were a resident of Canada and created or established in Canada, shall be treated as gifts to a registered charity; however, no relief from taxation shall be available in any taxation year with respect to such gifts (other than such gifts to a college or university at which the resident or a member of the residents family is or was enrolled) to the extent that such relief would exceed the amount of relief that would be available under the Income Tax Act if the only income of the resident for that year were the residents income arising in the United States. The preceding sentence shall not be interpreted to allow in any taxation year relief from taxation for gifts to registered charities in excess of the amount of relief allowed under the percentage limitations of the laws of Canada in respect of relief for gifts to registered charities.

Article XXII   Other Income

1. Items of income of a resident of a Contracting State, wherever arising, not dealt with in the foregoing Articles of this Convention shall be taxable only in that State, except that if such income arises in the other Contracting State it may also be taxed in that other State.

2. To the extent that income distributed by an estate or trust is subject to the provisions of paragraph 1, then, notwithstanding such provisions, income distributed by an estate or trust which is a resident of a Contracting State to a resident of the other Contracting State who is a beneficiary of the estate or trust may be taxed in the first-mentioned State and according to the laws of that State, but the tax so charged shall not exceed 15 per cent of the gross amount of the income; provided, however, that such income shall be exempt from tax in the first-mentioned State to the extent of any amount distributed out of income arising outside that State.

3. Losses incurred by a resident of a Contracting State with respect to wagering transactions the gains on which may be taxed in the other Contracting State shall, for the purpose of taxation in that other State, be deductible to the same extent that

such losses would be deductible if they were incurred by a resident of that other State.

4. Notwithstanding the provisions of paragraph 1, compensation derived by a resident of a Contracting State in respect of the provision of a guarantee of indebtedness shall be taxable only in that State, unless such compensation is business profits attributable to a permanent establishment situated in the other Contracting State, in which case the provisions of Article VII (Business Profits) shall apply.

Article XXIII   Capital

1. Capital represented by real property, owned by a resident of a Contracting State and situated in the other Contracting State, may be taxed in that other State.

2. Capital represented by personal property forming part of the business property of a permanent establishment which a resident of a Contracting State has in the other Contracting State may be taxed in that other State.

3. Capital represented by ships and aircraft operated by a resident of a Contracting State in international traffic, and by personal property pertaining to the operation of such ships and aircraft, shall be taxable only in that State.

4. All other elements of capital of a resident of a Contracting State shall be taxable only in that State.

Article XXIV   Elimination of Double Taxation

1. In the case of the United States, subject to the provisions of paragraphs 4, 5 and 6, double taxation shall be avoided as follows: In accordance with the provisions and subject to the limitations of the law of the United States (as it may be amended from time to time without changing the general principle hereof), the United States shall allow to a citizen or resident of the United States, or to a company electing to be treated as a domestic corporation, as a credit against the United States tax on income the appropriate amount of income tax paid or accrued to Canada; and, in the case of a company which is a resident of the United States owning at least 10 per cent of the voting stock of a company which is a resident of Canada from which it receives dividends in any taxable year, the United States shall allow as a credit against the United States tax on income the appropriate amount of income tax paid or accrued to Canada by that company with respect to the profits out of which such dividends are paid.

2. In the case of Canada, subject to the provisions of paragraphs 4, 5 and 6, double taxation shall be avoided as follows:

(a) Subject to the provisions of the law of Canada regarding the deduction from tax payable in Canada of tax paid in a territory outside Canada and to any subsequent modification of those provisions (which shall not affect the general principle hereof)

(i) Income tax paid or accrued to the United States on profits, income or gains arising in the United States, and

(ii) In the case of an individual, any social security taxes paid to the United States (other than taxes relating to unemployment insurance benefits) by the individual on such profits, income or gains shall be deducted from any Canadian tax payable in respect of such profits, income or gains;

(b) In the case of a company which is a resident of Canada owning at least 10 percent of the voting stock of a company which is a resident of the United States from which it receives dividends in any taxable year, Canada shall allow as a credit against the Canadian tax on income the appropriate amount of income tax paid or accrued to the United States by the second company with respect to the profits out of which the dividends are paid.

(c) Notwithstanding the provisions of subparagraph (a), where Canada imposes a tax on gains from the alienation of property that, but for the provisions of paragraph 5 of Article XIII (Gains), would not be taxable in Canada, income tax paid or accrued to the United States on such gains shall be deducted from any Canadian tax payable in respect of such gains.

3. For the purposes of this Article:

(a) Profits, income or gains (other than gains to which paragraph 5 of Article XIII (Gains) applies) of a resident of a Contracting State which may be taxed in the other Contracting State in accordance with the Convention (without regard to paragraph 2 of Article XXIX (Miscellaneous Rules)) shall be deemed to arise in that other State; and

(b) Profits, income or gains of a resident of a Contracting State which may not be taxed in the other Contracting State in accordance with the Convention (without regard to paragraph 2 of Article XXIX (Miscellaneous Rules)) or to which paragraph 5 of Article XIII (Gains) applies shall be deemed to arise in the first-mentioned State.

4. Where a United States citizen is a resident of Canada, the following rules shall apply:

(a) Canada shall allow a deduction from the Canadian tax in respect of income tax paid or accrued to the United States in respect of profits, income or gains which arise (within the meaning of paragraph 3) in the United States, except that such deduction need not exceed the amount of the tax that would be paid to the United States if the resident were not a United States citizen; and

(b) For the purposes of computing the United States tax, the United States shall allow as a credit against United States tax the income tax paid or accrued to Canada after the deduction referred to in subparagraph (a). The credit so allowed shall not reduce that portion of the United States tax that is deductible from Canadian tax in accordance with subparagraph (a).

5. Notwithstanding the provisions of paragraph 4, where a United States citizen is a resident of Canada, the following rules shall apply in respect of the items of income referred to in Article X (Dividends), XI (Interest) or XII (Royalties) that arise (within the meaning of paragraph 3) in the United States and that would be

subject to United States tax if the resident of Canada were not a citizen of the United States, as long as the law in force in Canada allows a deduction in computing income for the portion of any foreign tax paid in respect of such items which exceeds 15 per cent of the amount thereof:

(a) The deduction so allowed in Canada shall not be reduced by any credit or deduction for income tax paid or accrued to Canada allowed in computing the United States tax on such items;

(b) Canada shall allow a deduction from Canadian tax on such items in respect of income tax paid or accrued to the United States on such items, except that such deduction need not exceed the amount of the tax that would be paid on such items to the United States if the resident of Canada were not a United States citizen; and

(c) For the purposes of computing the United States tax on such items, the United States shall allow as a credit against United States tax the income tax paid or accrued to Canada after the deduction referred to in subparagraph (b). The credit so allowed shall reduce only that portion of the United States tax on such items which exceeds the amount of tax that would be paid to the United States on such items if the resident of Canada were not a United States citizen.

6. Where a United States citizen is a resident of Canada, items of income referred to in paragraph 4 or 5 shall, notwithstanding the provisions of paragraph 3, be deemed to arise in Canada to the extent necessary to avoid the double taxation of such income under paragraph 4(b) or paragraph 5(c).

7. For the purposes of this Article, any reference to "income tax paid or accrued" to a Contracting State shall include Canadian tax and United States tax, as the case may be, and taxes of general application which are paid or accrued to a political subdivision or local authority of that State, which are not imposed by that political subdivision or local authority in a manner inconsistent with the provisions of the Convention and which are substantially similar to the Canadian tax or United States tax, as the case may be.

8. Where a resident of a Contracting State owns capital which, in accordance with the provisions of the Convention, may be taxed in the other Contracting State, the first-mentioned State shall allow as a deduction from the tax on the capital of that resident an amount equal to the capital tax paid in that other State. The deduction shall not, however, exceed that part of the capital tax, as computed before the deduction is given, which is attributable to the capital which may be taxed in that other State.

9. The provisions of this Article relating to the source of profits, income or gains shall not apply for the purpose of determining a credit against United States tax for any foreign taxes other than income taxes paid or accrued to Canada.

10. Where in accordance with any provision of the Convention income derived or capital owned by a resident of a Contracting State is exempt from tax in that State, such State may nevertheless, in calculating the amount of tax on other income or capital, take into account the exempted income or capital.

Article XXV   Non-Discrimination

1. Nationals of a Contracting State shall not be subjected in the other Contracting State to any taxation or any requirement connected therewith that is more burdensome than the taxation and connected requirements to which nationals of that other State in the same circumstances, particularly with respect to taxation on worldwide income, are or may be subjected. This provision shall also apply to individuals who are not residents of one or both of the Contracting States.

2. In determining the taxable income or tax payable of an individual who is a resident of a Contracting State, there shall be allowed as a deduction in respect of any other person who is a resident of the other Contracting State and who is dependent on the individual for support the amount that would be so allowed if that other person were a resident of the first-mentioned State.

3. Where a married individual who is a resident of Canada and not a citizen of the United States has income that is taxable in the United States pursuant to Article XV (Income from Employment), the United States tax with respect to such income shall not exceed such proportion of the total United States tax that would be payable for the taxable year if both the individual and his spouse were United States citizens as the individuals taxable income determined without regard to this paragraph bears to the amount that would be the total taxable income of the individual and his spouse. For the purposes of this paragraph,

(a) The "total United States tax" shall be determined as if all the income of the individual and his spouse arose in the United States; and

(b) A deficit of the spouse shall not be taken into account in determining taxable income.

4. Any company which is a resident of a Contracting State, the capital of which is wholly or partly owned or controlled, directly or indirectly, by one or more residents of the other Contracting State, shall not be subjected in the first-mentioned State to any taxation or any requirement connected therewith which is other or more burdensome than the taxation and connected requirements to which other similar companies of the first-mentioned State, the capital of which is wholly or partly owned or controlled, directly or indirectly, by one or more residents of a third State, are or may be subjected.

5. Notwithstanding the provisions of Article XXIV (Elimination of Double Taxation), the taxation on a permanent establishment which a resident of a Contracting State has in the other Contracting State shall not be less favorable levied in the other State than the taxation levied on residents of the other State carrying on the same activities. This paragraph shall not be construed as obliging a Contracting State:

(a) To grant to a resident of the other Contracting State any personal allowances, reliefs and reductions for taxation purposes on account of civil status or family responsibilities which it grants to its own residents; or

(b) To grant to a company which is a resident of the other Contracting State the same tax relief that it provides to a company which is a resident of the first-mentioned State with respect to dividends received by it from a company.

6. Except where the provisions of paragraph 1 of Article IX (Related Persons), paragraph 7 of Article XI (Interest) or paragraph 7 of Article XII (Royalties) apply, interest, royalties and other disbursements paid by a resident of a Contracting State to a resident of the other Contracting State shall, for the purposes of determining the taxable profits of the first-mentioned resident, be deductible under the same conditions as if they had been paid to a resident of the first-mentioned State. Similarly, any debts of a resident of a Contracting State to a resident of the other Contracting State shall, for the purposes of determining the taxable capital of the first-mentioned resident, be deductible under the same conditions as if they had been contracted to a resident of the first-mentioned State.

7. The provisions of paragraph 7 shall not affect the operation of any provision of the taxation laws of a Contracting State:

(a) Relating to the deductibility of interest and which is in force on the date of signature of this Convention (including any subsequent modification of such provisions that does not change the general nature thereof); or

(b) Adopted after such date by a Contracting State and which is designed to ensure that a person who is not a resident of that state does not enjoy, under the laws of that State, a tax treatment that is more favorable than that enjoyed by residents of that State.

8. Expenses incurred by a citizen or resident of a Contracting State with respect to any convention (including any seminar, meeting, congress or other function of a similar nature) held in the other Contracting State shall, for the purposes of taxation in the first-mentioned State, be deductible to the same extent that such expenses would be deductible if the convention were held in the first-mentioned State.

9. Notwithstanding the provisions of Article II (Taxes Covered), this Article shall apply to all taxes imposed by a Contracting State.

Article XXVI   Mutual Agreement Procedure

1. Where a person considers that the actions of one or both of the Contracting States result or will result for him in taxation not in accordance with the provisions of this Convention, he may, irrespective of the remedies provided by the domestic law of those States, present his case in writing to the competent authority of the Contracting State of which he is a resident or, if he is a resident of neither Contracting State, of which he is a national.

2. The competent authority of the Contracting State to which the case has been presented shall endeavor, if the objection appears to it to be justified and if it is not itself able to arrive at a satisfactory solution, to resolve the case by mutual agreement with the competent authority of the other Contracting State, with a view to the avoidance of taxation which is not in accordance with the Convention. Except where the provisions of Article IX (Related Persons) apply, any agreement reached shall be implemented notwithstanding any time or other procedural limitations in

the domestic law of the Contracting States, provided that the competent authority of the other Contracting State has received notification that such a case exists within six years from the end of the taxable year to which the case relates.

3. The competent authorities of the Contracting States shall endeavor to resolve by mutual agreement any difficulties or doubts arising as to the interpretation or application of the Convention. In particular, the competent authorities of the Contracting States may agree:

(a) To the same attribution of profits to a resident of a Contracting State and its permanent establishment situated in the other Contracting State;

(b) To the same allocation of income, deductions, credits or allowances between persons;

(c) To the same determination of the source, and the same characterization, of particular items of income;

(d) To a common meaning of any term used in the Convention;

(e) To the elimination of double taxation with respect to income distributed by an estate or trust;

(f) To the elimination of double taxation with respect to a partnership;

(g) To provide relief from double taxation resulting from the application of the estate tax imposed by the United States or the Canadian tax as a result of a distribution or disposition of property by a trust that is a qualified domestic trust within the meaning of section 2056A of the Internal Revenue Code, or is described in subsection 70(6) of the Income Tax Act or is treated as such under paragraph 5 of Article XXIX B (Taxes Imposed by Reason of Death), in cases where no relief is otherwise available; or

(h) To increases in any dollar amounts referred to in the Convention to reflect monetary or economic developments.

They may also consult together for the elimination of double taxation in cases not provided for in the Convention.

4. Each of the Contracting States will endeavor to collect on behalf of the other Contracting State such amounts as may be necessary to ensure that relief granted by the Convention from taxation imposed by that other State does not inure to the benefit of persons not entitled thereto. However, nothing in this paragraph shall be construed as imposing on either of the Contracting States the obligation to carry out administrative measures of a different nature from those used in the collection of its own tax or which would be contrary to its public policy (ordre public).

5. The competent authorities of the Contracting States may communicate with each other directly for the purpose of reaching an agreement in the sense of the preceding paragraphs.

6. Where, pursuant to a mutual agreement procedure under this Article, the competent authorities have endeavored but are unable to reach a complete agreement in a case, the case shall be resolved through arbitration conducted in the manner prescribed by, and subject to, the requirements of paragraph 7 and any

rules or procedures agreed upon by the Contracting States by notes to be exchanged through diplomatic channels, if:

(a) Tax returns have been filed with at least one of the Contracting States with respect to the taxable years at issue in the case;

(b) The case:

(i) Is a case that:

(A) Involves the application of one or more Articles that the competent authorities have agreed in an exchange of notes shall be the subject of arbitration; and

(B) Is not a particular case that the competent authorities agree, before the date on which arbitration proceedings would otherwise have begun, is not suitable for determination by arbitration; or

(ii) Is a particular case that the competent authorities agree is suitable for determination by arbitration; and

(c) All concerned persons agree according to the provisions of subparagraph 7(d).

7. For the purposes of paragraph 6 and this paragraph, the following rules and definitions shall apply:

(a) The term "concerned person" means the presenter of a case to a competent authority for consideration under this Article and all other persons, if any, whose tax liability to either Contracting State may be directly affected by a mutual agreement arising from that consideration;

(b) The "commencement date" for a case is the earliest date on which the information necessary to undertake substantive consideration for a mutual agreement has been received by both competent authorities;

(c) Arbitration proceedings in a case shall begin on the later of:

(i) Two years after the commencement date of that case, unless both competent authorities have previously agreed to a different date, and

(ii) The earliest date upon which the agreement required by subparagraph (d) has been received by both competent authorities;

(d) The concerned person(s), and their authorized representatives or agents, must agree prior to the beginning of arbitration proceedings not to disclose to any other person any information received during the course of the arbitration proceeding from either Contracting State or the arbitration board, other than the determination of such board;

(e) Unless a concerned person does not accept the determination of an arbitration board, the determination shall constitute a resolution by mutual agreement under this Article and shall be binding on both Contracting States with respect to that case; and

(f) For purposes of an arbitration proceeding under paragraph 6 and this paragraph, the members of the arbitration board and their staffs shall be considered "persons or authorities" to whom information may be disclosed under Article XXVII (Exchange of Information) of this Convention.

Article XXVI A   Assistance in Collection

1. The Contracting States undertake to lend assistance to each other in the collection of taxes referred to in paragraph 9, together with interest, costs, additions to such taxes and civil penalties, referred to in this Article as a "revenue claim".

2. An application for assistance in the collection of a revenue claim shall include a certification by the competent authority of the applicant State that, under the laws of that State, the revenue claim has been finally determined. For the purposes of this Article, a revenue claim is finally determined when the applicant State has the right under its internal law to collect the revenue claim and all administrative and judicial rights of the taxpayer to restrain collection in the applicant State have lapsed or been exhausted.

3. A revenue claim of the applicant State that has been finally determined may be accepted for collection by the competent authority of the requested State and, subject to the provisions of paragraph 7, if accepted shall be collected by the requested State as though such revenue claim were the requested States own revenue claim finally determined in accordance with the laws applicable to the collection of the requested States own taxes.

4. Where an application for collection of a revenue claim in respect of a taxpayer is accepted

(a) By the United States, the revenue claim shall be treated by the United States as an assessment under United States laws against the taxpayer as of the time the application is received; and

(b) By Canada, the revenue claim shall be treated by Canada as an amount payable under the Income Tax Act, the collection of which is not subject to any restriction.

5. Nothing in this Article shall be construed as creating or providing any rights of administrative or judicial review of the applicant States finally determined revenue claim by the requested State, based on any such rights that may be available under the laws of either Contracting State. If, at any time pending execution of a request for assistance under this Article, the applicant State loses the right under its internal law to collect the revenue claim, the competent authority of the applicant State shall promptly withdraw the request for assistance in collection.

6. Subject to this paragraph, amounts collected by the requested State pursuant to this Article shall be forwarded to the competent authority of the applicant State. Unless the competent authorities of the Contracting States otherwise agree, the ordinary costs incurred in providing collection assistance shall be borne by the requested State and any extraordinary costs so incurred shall be borne by the applicant State.

7. A revenue claim of an applicant State accepted for collection shall not have in the requested State any priority accorded to the revenue claims of the requested State.

8. No assistance shall be provided under this Article for a revenue claim in respect of a taxpayer to the extent that the taxpayer can demonstrate that

(a) Where the taxpayer is an individual, the revenue claim relates either to a taxable period in which the taxpayer was a citizen of the requested State or, if the taxpayer became a citizen of the requested State at any time before November 9, 1995 and is such a citizen at the time the applicant State applies for collection of the claim, to a taxable period that ended before November 9, 1995; and

(b) Where the taxpayer is an entity that is a company, estate or trust, the revenue claim relates to a taxable period in which the taxpayer derived its status as such an entity from the laws in force in the requested State.

9. Notwithstanding the provisions of Article II (Taxes Covered), the provisions of this Article shall apply to all categories of taxes collected, and to contributions to social security and employment insurance premiums levied, by or on behalf of the Government of a Contracting State.

10. Nothing in this Article shall be construed as:

(a) Limiting the assistance provided for in paragraph 4 of Article XXVI (Mutual Agreement Procedure); or

(b) Imposing on either Contracting State the obligation to carry out administrative measures of a different nature from those used in the collection of its own taxes or that would be contrary to its public policy (ordre public).

11. The competent authorities of the Contracting States shall agree upon the mode of application of this Article, including agreement to ensure comparable levels of assistance to each of the Contracting States.

Article XXVII   Exchange of Information

1. The competent authorities of the Contracting States shall exchange such information as may be relevant for carrying out the provisions of this Convention or of the domestic laws of the Contracting States concerning taxes to which this Convention applies insofar as the taxation thereunder is not contrary to this Convention. The exchange of information is not restricted by Article I (Personal Scope). Any information received by a Contracting State shall be treated as secret in the same manner as information obtained under the taxation laws of that State and shall be disclosed only to persons or authorities (including courts and administrative bodies) involved in the assessment or collection of, the administration and enforcement in respect of, or the determination of appeals in relation to the taxes to which this Convention applies or, notwithstanding paragraph 4, in relation to taxes imposed by a political subdivision or local authority of a Contracting State that are substantially similar to the taxes covered by this Convention under Article II (Taxes Covered). Such persons or authorities shall use the information only for

such purposes. They may disclose the information in public court proceedings or in judicial decisions. The competent authorities may release to an arbitration board established pursuant to paragraph 6 of Article XXVI (Mutual Agreement Procedure) such information as is necessary for carrying out the arbitration procedure; the members of the arbitration board shall be subject to the limitations on disclosure described in this Article.

2. If information is requested by a Contracting State in accordance with this Article, the other Contracting State shall use its information gathering measures to obtain the requested information, even though that other State may not need such information for its own tax purposes. The obligation contained in the preceding sentence is subject to the limitations of paragraph 3 but in no case shall such limitations be construed to permit a Contracting State to decline to supply information because it has no domestic interest in such information.

3. In no case shall the provisions of paragraph 1 and 2 be construed so as to impose on a Contracting State the obligation:

(a) To carry out administrative measures at variance with the laws and administrative practice of that State or of the other Contracting State;

(b) To supply information which is not obtainable under the laws or in the normal course of the administration of that State or of the other Contracting State; or

(c) To supply information which would disclose any trade, business, industrial, commercial or professional secret or trade process, or information the disclosure of which would be contrary to public policy (ordre public).

4. For the purposes of this Article, this Convention shall apply, notwithstanding the provisions of Article II (Taxes Covered):

(a) To all taxes imposed by a Contracting State; and

(b) To other taxes to which any other provision of this Convention applies, but only to the extent that the information may be relevant for the purposes of the application of that provision.

5. In no case shall the provisions of paragraph 3 be construed to permit a Contracting State to decline to supply information because the information is held by a bank, other financial institution, nominee or person acting in an agency or a fiduciary capacity or because it relates to ownership interests in a person.

6. If specifically requested by the competent authority of a Contracting State, the competent authority of the other Contracting State shall provide information under this Article in the form of depositions of witnesses and authenticated copies of unedited original documents (including books, papers, statements, records, accounts, and writings).

7. The requested State shall allow representatives of the requesting State to enter the requested State to interview individuals and examine books and records with the consent of the persons subject to examination.

Article XXVIII   Diplomatic Agents and Consular Officers

Nothing in this Convention shall affect the fiscal privileges of diplomatic agents or consular officers under the general rules of international law or under the provisions of special agreements.

Article XXIX   Miscellaneous Rules

1. The provisions of this Convention shall not restrict in any manner any exclusion, exemption, deduction, credit or other allowances now or hereafter accorded by the laws of a Contracting State in the determination of the tax imposed by that State.

2. (a) Except to the extent provided in paragraph 3, this Convention shall not affect the taxation by a Contracting State of its residents (as determined under Article IV (Residence)) and, in the case of the United States, its citizens and companies electing to be treated as domestic corporations.

(b) Notwithstanding the other provisions of this Convention, a former citizen or former long-term resident of the United States, may, for the period of ten years following the loss of such status, be taxed in accordance with the laws of the United States with respect to income from sources within the United States (including income deemed under the domestic law of the United States to arise from such sources).

3. The provisions of paragraph 2 shall not affect the obligations undertaken by a Contracting State:

(a) Under paragraphs 3 and 4 of Article IX (Related Persons), paragraphs 6 and 7 of Article XIII (Gains), paragraphs 1, 3, 4, 5, 6(b), 7, 8, 10 and 13 of Article XVIII (Pensions and Annuities), paragraph 5 of Article XXIX (Miscellaneous Rules), paragraphs 1, 5, and 6 of Article XXIX B (Taxes Imposed by Reason of Death), paragraphs 2, 3, 4, and 7 of Article XXIX B (Taxes Imposed by Reason of Death) as applied to estates of persons other than former citizens referred to in paragraph 2 of this Article, paragraphs 3 and 5 of Article XXX (Entry into Force), and Articles XIX (Government Service), XXI (Exempt Organizations), XXIV (Elimination of Double Taxation), XXV (Non-Discrimination) and XXVI (Mutual Agreement Procedure);

(b) Under Article XX (Students), toward individuals who are neither citizens of, nor have immigrant status in, that State.

4. With respect to taxable years not barred by the statute of limitations ending on or before December 31 of the year before the year in which the Social Security Agreement between Canada and the United States (signed in Ottawa on March 11, 1981) enters into force, income from personal services not subject to tax by the United States under the Convention or the 1942 Convention shall not be considered wages or net earnings from self-employment for purposes of social security taxes imposed under the Internal Revenue Code.

5. Where a person who is a resident of Canada and a shareholder of a United States S corporation requests the competent authority of Canada to do so, the

competent authority may agree, subject to terms and conditions satisfactory to such competent authority, to apply the following rules for the purposes of taxation in Canada with respect to the period during which the agreement is effective:

(a) The corporation shall be deemed to be a controlled foreign affiliate of the person;

(b) All the income of the corporation shall be deemed to be foreign accrual property income;

(c) For the purposes of subsection 20(11) of the Income Tax Act, the amount of the corporations income that is included in the persons income shall be deemed not to be income from a property; and

(d) Each dividend paid to the person on a share of the capital stock of the corporation shall be excluded from the persons income and shall be deducted in computing the adjusted cost base to the person of the share.

6. For purposes of paragraph 3 of Article XXII (Consultation) of the General Agreement on Trade in Services, the Contracting States agree that:

(a) A measure falls within the scope of the Convention only if:

(i) The measure relates to a tax to which Article XXV (Non-Discrimination) of the Convention applies; or

(ii) The measure relates to a tax to which Article XXV (Non-Discrimination) of the Convention does not apply and to which any other provision of the Convention applies, but only to the extent that the measure relates to a matter dealt with in that other provision of the Convention; and

(b) Notwithstanding paragraph 3 of Article XXII (Consultation) of the General Agreement on Trade in Services, any doubt as to the interpretation of subparagraph (a) will be resolved under paragraph 3 of Article XXVI (Mutual Agreement Procedure) of the Convention or any other procedure agreed to by both Contracting States.

7. The appropriate authority of a Contracting State may request consultations with the appropriate authority of the other Contracting State to determine whether change to the Convention is appropriate to respond to changes in the law or policy of that other State. Where domestic legislation enacted by a Contracting State unilaterally removes or significantly limits any material benefit otherwise provided by the Convention, the appropriate authorities shall promptly consult for the purpose of considering an appropriate change to the Convention.

Article XXIX A   Limitation on Benefits

1. For the purposes of the application of this Convention by a Contracting State,

(a) a qualifying person shall be entitled to all of the benefits of this Convention; and

(b) except as provided in paragraphs 3, 4 and 6, a person that is not a qualifying person shall not be entitled to any benefits of this Convention.

2. For the purposes of this Article, a qualifying person is a resident of a Contracting State that is:

(a) a natural person;

(b) a Contracting State or a political subdivision or local authority thereof, or any agency or instrumentality of any such State, subdivision or authority;

(c) a company or trust whose principal class of shares or units (and any disproportionate class of shares or units) is primarily and regularly traded on one or more recognized stock exchanges;

(d) a company, if five or fewer persons each of which is a company or trust referred to in subparagraph (c) own directly or indirectly more than 50 percent of the aggregate vote and value of the shares and more than 50 percent of the vote and value of each disproportionate class of shares (in neither case including debt substitute shares), provided that each company or trust in the chain of ownership is a qualifying person;

(e) (i) a company, 50 percent or more of the aggregate vote and value of the shares of which and 50 percent or more of the vote and value of each disproportionate class of shares (in neither case including debt substitute shares) of which is not owned, directly or indirectly, by persons other than qualifying persons; or

(ii) a trust, 50 percent or more of the beneficial interest in which and 50 percent or more of each disproportionate interest in which, is not owned, directly or indirectly, by persons other than qualifying persons;

where the amount of the expenses deductible from gross income (as determined in the State of residence of the company or trust) that are paid or payable by the company or trust, as the case may be, for its preceding fiscal period (or, in the case of its first fiscal period, that period) directly or indirectly, to persons that are not qualifying persons is less than 50 percent of its gross income for that period;

(f) an estate;

(g) a not-for-profit organization, provided that more than half of the beneficiaries, members or participants of the organization are qualifying persons;

(h) a trust, company, organization or other arrangement described in paragraph 2 of Article XXI (Exempt Organizations) and established for the purpose of providing benefits primarily to individuals who are qualifying persons, or persons who were qualifying persons within the five preceding years; or

(i) a trust, company, organization or other arrangement described in paragraph 3 of Article XXI (Exempt Organizations) provided that the beneficiaries of the trust, company, organization or other arrangement are described in subparagraph (g) or (h).

3. Where a person is a resident of a Contracting State and is not a qualifying person, and that person, or a person related thereto, is engaged in the active conduct of a trade or business in that State (other than the business of making or managing investments, unless those activities are carried on with customers in the ordinary course of business by a bank, an insurance company, a registered securities dealer or a deposit-taking financial institution), the benefits of this Convention shall apply to that resident person with respect to income derived from the other Contracting State in connection with or incidental to that trade or business (including any such income derived directly or indirectly by that resident person through one or more other persons that are residents of that other State), but only if that trade or business is substantial in relation to the activity carried on in that other State giving rise to the income in respect of which benefits provided under this Convention by that other State are claimed.

4. A company that is a resident of a Contracting State shall also be entitled to the benefits of Articles X (Dividends), XI (Interest) and XII (Royalties) if:

(a) Its shares that represent more than 90 percent of the aggregate vote and value of all of its shares and at least 50 percent of the vote and value of any disproportionate class of shares (in neither case including debt substitute shares) are owned, directly or indirectly, by persons each of whom is a qualifying person or a person who:

(i) Is a resident of a country with which the other Contracting State has a comprehensive income tax convention and is entitled to all of the benefits provided by that other State under that convention;

(ii) Would qualify for benefits under paragraphs 2 or 3 if that person were a resident of the first-mentioned State (and, for the purposes of paragraph 3, if the business it carried on in the country of which it is a resident were carried on by it in the first mentioned State); and

(iii) Would be entitled to a rate of tax in the other Contracting State under the convention between that persons country of residence and that other State, in respect of the particular class of income for which benefits are being claimed under this Convention, that is at least as low as the rate applicable under this Convention; and

(b) The amount of the expenses deductible from gross income (as determined in the company's State of residence) that are paid or payable by the company for its preceding fiscal period (or, in the case of its first fiscal period, that period) directly or indirectly to persons that are not qualifying persons is less than 50 percent of the company's gross income for that period.

5. For the purposes of this Article,

(a) The term "debt substitute share" means:

(i) A share described in paragraph (e) of the definition "term preferred share" in the Income Tax Act, as it may be amended from time to time without changing the general principle thereof; and

(ii) Such other type of share as may be agreed upon by the competent authorities of the Contracting States.

(b) The term "disproportionate class of shares" means any class of shares of a company resident in one of the Contracting States that entitles the shareholder to disproportionately higher participation, through dividends, redemption payments or otherwise, in the earnings generated in the other State by particular assets or activities of the company;

(c) The term "disproportionate interest in a trust" means any interest in a trust resident in one of the Contracting States that entitles the interest holder to disproportionately higher participation in, or claim to, the earnings generated in the other State by particular assets or activities of the trust;

(d) The term "not-for-profit organization" of a Contracting State means an entity created or established in that State and that is, by reason of its not-for-profit status, generally exempt from income taxation in that State, and includes a private foundation, charity, trade union, trade association or similar organization;

(e) The term "principal class of shares" of a company means the ordinary or common shares of the company, provided that such class of shares represents the majority of the voting power and value of the company. If no single class of ordinary or common shares represents the majority of the aggregate voting power and value of the company, the "principal class of shares" are those classes that in the aggregate represent a majority of the aggregate voting power and value of the company; and

(f) The term "recognized stock exchange" means:

(i) The NASDAQ System owned by the National Association of Securities Dealers, Inc. and any stock exchange registered with the Securities and Exchange Commission as a national securities exchange for purposes of the Securities Exchange Act of 1934;

(ii) Canadian stock exchanges that are "prescribed stock exchanges" or "designated stock exchanges" under the Income Tax Act; and

(iii) Any other stock exchange agreed upon by the Contracting States in an exchange of notes or by the competent authorities of the Contracting States.

6. Where a person that is a resident of a Contracting State is not entitled under the preceding provisions of this Article to the benefits provided under this Convention by the other Contracting State, the competent authority of that other State shall, upon that persons request, determine on the basis of all factors including the history, structure, ownership and operations of that person whether:

(a) Its creation and existence did not have as a principal purpose the obtaining of benefits under this Convention that would not otherwise be available; or

(b) It would not be appropriate, having regard to the purpose of this Article, to deny the benefits of this Convention to that person.

The person shall be granted the benefits of this Convention by that other State where the competent authority determines that subparagraph (a) or (b) applies.

7. It is understood that this Article shall not be construed as restricting in any manner the right of a Contracting State to deny benefits under this Convention where it can reasonably be concluded that to do otherwise would result in an abuse of the provisions of this Convention.

Article XXIX B   Taxes Imposed by Reason of Death

1. Where the property of an individual who is a resident of a Contracting State passes by reason of the individuals death to an organization that is referred to in paragraph 1 of Article XXI (Exempt Organizations) and that is a resident of the other Contracting State,

(a) If the individual is a resident of the United States and the organization is a resident of Canada, the tax consequences in the United States arising out of the passing of the property shall apply as if the organization were a resident of the United States; and

(b) If the individual is a resident of Canada and the organization is a resident of the United States, the tax consequences in Canada arising out of the passing of the property shall apply as if the individual had disposed of the property for proceeds equal to an amount elected on behalf of the individual for this purpose (in a manner specified by the competent authority of Canada), which amount shall be no less than the individuals cost of the property as determined for purposes of Canadian tax and no greater than the fair market value of the property.

2. In determining the estate tax imposed by the United States, the estate of an individual (other than a citizen of the United States) who was a resident of Canada at the time of the individuals death shall be allowed a unified credit equal to the greater of

(a) The amount that bears the same ratio to the credit allowed under the law of the United States to the estate of a citizen of the United States as the value of the part of the individuals gross estate that at the time of the individuals death is situated in the United States bears to the value of the individuals entire gross estate wherever situated; and

(b) The unified credit allowed to the estate of a nonresident not a citizen of the United States under the law of the United States.

The amount of any unified credit otherwise allowable under this paragraph shall be reduced by the amount of any credit previously allowed with respect to any gift made by the individual. A credit otherwise allowable under subparagraph (a) shall be allowed only if all information necessary for the verification and computation of the credit is provided.

3. In determining the estate tax imposed by the United States on an individuals estate with respect to property that passes to the surviving spouse of the individual (within the meaning of the law of the United States) and that would qualify for the estate tax marital deduction under the law of the United States if the surviving spouse were a citizen of the United States and all applicable elections were properly made (in this paragraph and paragraph 4 referred to as "qualifying property"), a non-refundable credit computed in accordance with the provisions of paragraph 4 shall be allowed in addition to the unified credit allowed to the estate under paragraph 2 or under the law of the United States, provided that

(a) The individual was at the time of death a citizen of the United States or a resident of either Contracting State;

(b) The surviving spouse was at the time of the individuals death a resident of either Contracting State;

(c) If both the individual and the surviving spouse were residents of the United States at the time of the individuals death, one or both was a citizen of Canada; and

(d) The executor of the decedents estate elects the benefits of this paragraph and waives irrevocably the benefits of any estate tax marital deduction that would be allowed under the law of the United States on a United States Federal estate tax return filed for the individuals estate by the date on which a qualified domestic trust election could be made under the law of the United States.

4. The amount of the credit allowed under paragraph 3 shall equal the lesser of

(a) The unified credit allowed under paragraph 2 or under the law of the United States (determined without regard to any credit allowed previously with respect to any gift made by the individual), and

(b) The amount of estate tax that would otherwise be imposed by the United States on the transfer of qualifying property.

The amount of estate tax that would otherwise be imposed by the United States on the transfer of qualifying property shall equal the amount by which the estate tax (before allowable credits) that would be imposed by the United States if the qualifying property were included in computing the taxable estate exceeds the estate tax (before allowable credits) that would be so imposed if the qualifying property were not so included. Solely for purposes of determining other credits allowed under the law of the United States, the credit provided under paragraph 3 shall be allowed after such other credits.

5. Where an individual was a resident of the United States immediately before the individuals death, for the purposes of subsections 70(5.2) and (6) of the Income Tax Act, both the individual and the individuals spouse shall be deemed to have been resident in Canada immediately before the individuals death. Where a trust that would be a trust described in subsection 70(6) of that Act, if its trustees that were residents or citizens of the United States or domestic corporations under the law of the United States were residents of Canada, requests the competent authority of Canada to do so, the competent authority may agree, subject to terms and

conditions satisfactory to such competent authority, to treat the trust for the purposes of that Act as being resident in Canada for such time and with respect to such property as may be stipulated in the agreement.

6. In determining the amount of Canadian tax payable by an individual who immediately before death was a resident of Canada, or by a trust described in subsection 70(6) of the Income Tax Act (or a trust which is treated as being resident in Canada under the provisions of paragraph 5), the amount of any Federal or state estate or inheritance taxes payable in the United States (not exceeding, where the individual was a citizen of the United States or a former citizen referred to in paragraph 2 of Article XXIX (Miscellaneous Rules), the amount of estate and inheritance taxes that would have been payable if the individual were not a citizen or former citizen of the United States) in respect of property situated within the United States shall,

(a) To the extent that such estate or inheritance taxes are imposed upon the individuals death, be allowed as a deduction from the amount of any Canadian tax otherwise payable by the individual for the taxation year in which the individual died on the total of

(i) Any income, profits or gains of the individual arising (within the meaning of paragraph 3 of Article XXIV (Elimination of Double Taxation)) in the United States in that year, and

(ii) Where the value at the time of the individuals death of the individuals entire gross estate wherever situated (determined under the law of the United States) exceeded 1.2 million U.S. dollars or its equivalent in Canadian dollars, any income, profits or gains of the individual for that year from property situated in the United States at that time, and

(b) To the extent that such estate or inheritance taxes are imposed upon the death of the individuals surviving spouse, be allowed as a deduction from the amount of any Canadian tax otherwise payable by the trust for its taxation year in which that spouse dies on any income, profits or gains of the trust for that year arising (within the meaning of paragraph 3 of Article XXIV (Elimination of Double Taxation)) in the United States or from property situated in the United States at the time of death of the spouse.

For purposes of this paragraph, property shall be treated as situated within the United States if it is so treated for estate tax purposes under the law of the United States as in effect on March 17, 1995, subject to any subsequent changes thereof that the competent authorities of the Contracting States have agreed to apply for the purposes of this paragraph. The deduction allowed under this paragraph shall take into account the deduction for any income tax paid or accrued to the United States that is provided under paragraph 2(a), 4(a) or 5(b) of Article XXIV (Elimination of Double Taxation).

7. In determining the amount of estate tax imposed by the United States on the estate of an individual who was a resident or citizen of the United States at the time of death, or upon the death of a surviving spouse with respect to a qualified domestic trust created by such an individual or the individuals executor or surviving spouse,

a credit shall be allowed against such tax imposed in respect of property situated outside the United States, for the federal and provincial income taxes payable in Canada in respect of such property by reason of the death of the individual or, in the case of a qualified domestic trust, the individuals surviving spouse. Such credit shall be computed in accordance with the following rules:

(a) A credit otherwise allowable under this paragraph shall be allowed regardless of whether the identity of the taxpayer under the law of Canada corresponds to that under the law of the United States.

(b) The amount of a credit allowed under this paragraph shall be computed in accordance with the provisions and subject to the limitations of the law of the United States regarding credit for foreign death taxes (as it may be amended from time to time without changing the general principle hereof), as though the income tax imposed by Canada were a creditable tax under that law.

(c) A credit may be claimed under this paragraph for an amount of federal or provincial income tax payable in Canada only to the extent that no credit or deduction is claimed for such amount in determining any other tax imposed by the United States, other than the estate tax imposed on property in a qualified domestic trust upon the death of the surviving spouse.

8. Provided that the value, at the time of death, of the entire gross estate wherever situated of an individual who was a resident of Canada (other than a citizen of the United states) at the time of death does not exceed 1.2 million U.S. dollars or its equivalent in Canadian dollars, the United States may impose its estate tax upon property forming part of the estate of the individual only if any gain derived by the individual from the alienation of such property would have been subject to income taxation by the United States in accordance with Article XIII (Gains).

Article XXX   Entry Into Force

1. This Convention shall be subject to ratification in accordance with the applicable procedures of each Contracting State and instruments of ratification shall be exchanged at Ottawa as soon as possible.

2. The Convention shall enter into force upon the exchange of instruments of ratification and, subject to the provisions of paragraph 3, its provisions shall have effect:

(a) For tax withheld at the source on income referred to in Articles X (Dividends), XI (Interest), XII (Royalties) and XVIII (Pensions and Annuities), with respect to amounts paid or credited on or after the first day of the second month next following the date on which the Convention enters into force;

(b) For other taxes, with respect to taxable years beginning on or after the first day of January next following the date on which the Convention enters into force; and

(c) Notwithstanding the provisions of subparagraph (b), for the taxes covered by paragraph 4 of Article XXIX (Miscellaneous Rules) with respect to all taxable years referred to in that paragraph.

3. For the purposes of applying the United States foreign tax credit in relation to taxes paid or accrued to Canada:

(a) Notwithstanding the provisions of paragraph 2(a) of Article II (Taxes Covered), the tax on 1971 undistributed income on hand imposed by Part IX of the Income Tax Act of Canada shall be considered to be an income tax for distributions made on or after the first day of January 1972 and before the first day of January 1979 and shall be considered to be imposed upon the recipient of a distribution, in the proportion that the distribution out of undistributed income with respect to which the tax has been paid bears to 85 per cent of such undistributed income;

(b) The principles of paragraph 6 of Article XXIV (Elimination of Double Taxation) shall have effect for taxable years beginning on or after the first day of January 1976; and

(c) The provisions of paragraph 1 of Article XXIV shall have effect for taxable years beginning on or after the first day of January 1981.

Any claim for refund based on the provisions of this paragraph may be filed on or before June 30 of the calendar year following that in which the Convention enters into force, notwithstanding any rule of domestic law to the contrary.

4. Subject to the provisions of paragraph 5, the 1942 Convention shall cease to have effect for taxes for which this Convention has effect in accordance with the provisions of paragraph 2.

5. Where any greater relief from tax would have been afforded by any provision of the 1942 Convention than under this Convention, any such provision shall continue to have effect for the first taxable year with respect to which the provisions of this Convention have effect under paragraph 2(b).

6. The 1942 Convention shall terminate on the last date on which it has effect in accordance with the preceding provisions of this Article.

7. The Exchange of Notes between the United States and Canada dated August 2 and September 17, 1928, providing for relief from double income taxation on shipping profits, is terminated. Its provisions shall cease to have effect with respect to taxable years beginning on or after the first day of January next following the date on which this Convention enters into force.

8. The provisions of the Convention between the Government of Canada and the Government of the United States of America for the Avoidance of Double Taxation and the Prevention of Fiscal Evasion with Respect to Taxes on the Estates of Deceased Persons signed at Washington on February 17, 1961 shall continue to have effect with respect to estates of persons deceased prior to the first day of January next following the date on which this Convention enters into force but shall cease to have effect with respect to estates of persons deceased on or after that date. Such Convention shall terminate on the last date on which it has effect in accordance

with the preceding sentence.

Article XXXI   Termination

1. This Convention shall remain in force until terminated by a Contracting State.

2. Either Contracting State may terminate the Convention at any time after 5 years from the date on which the Convention enters into force provided that at least 6 months prior notice of termination has been given through diplomatic channels.

3. Where a Contracting State considers that a significant change introduced in the taxation laws of the other Contracting State should be accommodated by a modification of the Convention, the Contracting States shall consult together with a view to resolving the matter; if the matter cannot be satisfactorily resolved, the first-mentioned State may terminate the Convention in accordance with the procedures set forth in paragraph 2, but without regard to the 5 year limitation provided therein.

4. In the event the Convention is terminated, the Convention shall cease to have effect:

(a) For tax withheld at the source on income referred to in Articles X (Dividends), XI (Interest), XII (Royalties), XVIII (Pensions and Annuities) and paragraph 2 of Article XXII (Other Income), with respect to amounts paid or credited on or after the first day of January next following the expiration of the 6 months period referred to in paragraph 2; and

(b) For other taxes, with respect to taxable years beginning on or after the first day of January next following the expiration of the 6 months period referred to in paragraph 2.

In witness whereof, the undersigned, being duly authorized thereto by their respective Governments, have signed this Convention.

Done in two copies at Washington this twenty-sixth day of September, 1980, in the English and French languages, each text being equally authentic.

TREASURY DEPARTMENT TECHNICAL EXPLANATION OF THE [1980] CONVENTION BETWEEN THE UNITED STATES OF AMERICA AND CANADA WITH RESPECT TO TAXES ON INCOME AND CAPITAL

(April 26, 1984)

INTRODUCTION

This is a technical explanation of the Convention between the United States and Canada signed on September 26, 1980, as amended by the Protocols signed on June 14, 1983 and March 28, 1984. ("the Convention"). References are made to the Convention and Protocol between Canada and the United States with respect to Income Taxes signed on March 4, 1942, as amended by the Convention signed on June 12, 1950, the Convention signed on August 8, 1956 and the Supplementary Convention signed on October 25, 1966 (the "1942 Convention"). These references are intended to put various provisions of the Convention into context. The technical explanation does not, however, provide a complete comparison between the Convention and the 1942 Convention. Moreover, neither the Convention nor the technical explanation is intended to have implications for the interpretation of the 1942 Convention.

The technical explanation is an official guide to the Convention. It reflects policies behind particular Convention provisions, as well as understandings reached with respect to the interpretation and application of the Convention.

Table of Articles

ARTICLE I   Personal Scope

Article I provides that the Convention is generally applicable to persons who are residents of either Canada or the United States or both Canada and the United States. The word "generally" is used because certain provisions of the Convention apply to persons who are residents of neither Canada nor the United States.

ARTICLE II   Taxes Covered

Paragraph I states that the Convention applies to taxes "on income and on capital" imposed on behalf of Canada and the United States, irrespective of the manner in which such taxes are levied. Neither Canada nor the United States presently impose taxes on capital. Paragraph 1 is not intended either to broaden or to limit paragraph 2, which provides that the Convention shall apply, in the case of Canada, to the taxes imposed by the Government of Canada under Parts I, XIII, and XIV of the Income Tax Act and, in the case of the United States, to the Federal income taxes imposed by the Internal Revenue Code ("the Code").

National taxes not generally covered by the Convention include, in the case of the United States, the estate, gift, and generation-skipping transfer taxes, the Windfall Profits Tax, Federal unemployment taxes, social security taxes imposed under sections 1401, 3101, and 3111 of the Code, and the excise tax on insurance premiums imposed under Code section 4371. The Convention also does not generally cover the Canadian excise tax on net insurance premiums paid by residents of Canada for coverage of a risk situated in Canada, the Petroleum and Gas Revenue Tax (PGRT) and the Incremental Oil Revenue Tax (IORT). However, the Convention has the effect of covering the Canadian social security tax in certain respects because under Canadian domestic tax law no such tax is due if there is no income subject to tax under the Income Tax Act of Canada. Taxes imposed by the states of the United States, and by the provinces of Canada, are not generally covered by the Convention. However, if such taxes are imposed in accordance with the provisions of the Convention, a foreign tax credit is ensured by paragraph 7 of Article XXIV (Elimination of Double Taxation).

Paragraph 2 contrasts with paragraph 1 of the Protocol to the 1942 Convention, which refers to "Dominion income taxes." In addition, unlike the 1942 Convention, the Convention does not contain a reference to "surtaxes and excess-profits taxes."

Paragraph 3 provides that the Convention also applies to any taxes identical or substantially similar to the taxes on income in existence on September 26, 1980 which are imposed in addition to or in place of the taxes existing on that date. Similarly, taxes on capital imposed after that date are to be covered.

It was agreed that Part I of the Income Tax Act of Canada is a covered tax even though Canada has made certain modifications in the Income Tax Act after the signature of the Convention and before the signature of the 1983 Protocol. In particular, Canada has enacted a low flat rate tax on petroleum production (the PGRT) which, at the time of the signature of the 1983 Protocol, is imposed generally at the statutory rate of 14.67 percent for the period June 1, 1982 to May 31, 1983, and at 16 percent thereafter, generally reduced to an effective rate of 11 percent or 12 percent after deducting a 25 percent resource allowance. The PGRT is not deductible in computing income for Canadian income tax purposes. This agreement is not intended to have implications for any other convention or for the interpretation of Code sections 901 and 903. Further, the PGRT and IORT are not taxes described in paragraphs 2 or 3.

Paragraph 4 provides that, notwithstanding paragraphs 2 and 3 the Convention applies to certain United States taxes for certain specified purposes: the accumulated earnings tax and personal holding company tax are covered only to the extent necessary to implement the provisions of paragraphs 5 and 8 of Article X (Dividends); the excise taxes imposed with respect to private foundations are covered only to the extent necessary to implement the provisions of paragraph 4 of Article XXI (Exempt Organizations); and the social security taxes imposed under sections 1401, 3101, and 3111 of the Code are covered only to the extent necessary to implement the provisions of paragraph 4 of Article XXIX (Miscellaneous Rules). The pertinent provisions of Articles X, XXI, and XXIX are described below. Canada has no national taxes similar to the United States accumulated earnings tax, personal holding company tax, or excise taxes imposed with respect to private foundations.

Article II does not specifically refer to interest, fines and penalties. Thus, each Contracting State may, in general, impose interest, fines, and penalties or pay interest pursuant to its domestic laws. Any question whether such items are being imposed or paid in connection with covered taxes in a manner consistent with provisions of the Convention, such as Article XXV (Non-Discrimination), may, however, be resolved by the competent authorities pursuant to Article XXVI (Mutual Agreement Procedure). See, however, the discussion below of the treatment of certain interest under Articles XXIX (Miscellaneous Rules) and XXX (Entry Into Force).

ARTICLE III   General Definitions

Article III provides definitions and general rules of interpretation for the Convention. . . .

Paragraph 1(a) states that the term "Canada," when used in a geographical sense, means the territory of Canada, including any area beyond the territorial seas of Canada which, under international law and the laws of Canada, is an area within which Canada may exercise rights with respect to the seabed and subsoil and their natural resources. This definition differs only in form from the definition of Canada in the 1942 Convention; paragraph 1(a) omits the reference in the 1942 Convention to "the Provinces, the Territories and Sable Island" as unnecessary.

Paragraph 1(b)(i) defines the term "United States" to mean the United States of America. The term does not include Puerto Rico, the Virgin Islands, Guam, or any other United States possession or territory.

Paragraph 1(b)(ii) states that when the term "United States" is used in a geographical sense the term also includes any area beyond the territorial seas of the United States which, under international law and the laws of the United States, is an area within which the United States may exercise rights with respect to the seabed and subsoil and their natural resources.

Paragraph 1(c) defines the term "Canadian tax" to mean the taxes imposed by the Government of Canada under Parts I, XIII, and XIV of the Income Tax Act as in existence on September 26, 1980 and any identical or substantially similar taxes on income imposed by the Government of Canada after that date and which are in addition to or in place of the then existing taxes. The term does not extend to capital taxes, if and when such taxes are ever imposed by Canada.

Paragraph 1(d) defines the term "United States tax" to mean the Federal income taxes imposed by the Internal Revenue Code as in existence on September 26, 1980 and any identical or substantially similar taxes on income imposed by the United States after that date in addition to or in place of the then existing taxes. The term does not extend to capital taxes, nor to the United States taxes identified in paragraph 4 of Article II (Taxes Covered).

Paragraph 1(e) provides that the term "person" includes an individual, an estate, a trust, a company, and any other body of persons. Although both the United States and Canada do not regard partnerships as taxable entities, the definition in the paragraph is broad enough to include partnerships where necessary.

Paragraph 1(f) defines the term "company" to mean any body corporate or any entity which is treated as a body corporate for tax purposes.

The term "competent authority" is defined in paragraph 1(g) to mean, in the case of Canada, the Minister of National Revenue or his authorized representative and, in the case of the United States, the Secretary of the Treasury or his delegate. The Secretary of the Treasury has delegated the general authority to act as competent authority to the Commissioner of the Internal Revenue Service, who has redelegated such authority to the Associate Commissioner (Operations). The Assistant Commissioner (Examination) has been delegated the authority to administer programs for simultaneous, spontaneous and industry wide exchanges of information. The Director, Foreign Operations District, has been delegated the authority to administer programs for routine and specific exchanges of information and mutual assistance in collection. The Assistant Commissioner (Criminal Investigations) has been delegated the authority to administer the simultaneous criminal investigation program with Canada.

Paragraph 1(h) defines the term "international traffic" to mean, with reference to a resident of a Contracting State, any voyage of a ship or aircraft to transport passengers or property (whether or not operated or used by that resident), except where the principal purpose of the voyage is transport between points within the other Contracting State. For example, in determining for Canadian tax purposes whether a United States resident has derived profits from the operation of ships or aircraft in international traffic, a voyage of a ship or aircraft (whether or not operated or used by that resident) that includes stops in both Contracting States will not be international traffic if the principal purpose of the voyage is to transport passengers or property from one point in Canada to another point in Canada.

Paragraph 1(i) defines the term "State" to mean any national State, whether or not a Contracting State.

Paragraph 1(j) establishes "the 1942 Convention" as the term to be used throughout the Convention for referring to the pre-existing income tax treaty relationship between the United States and Canada.

Paragraph 2 provides that, in the case of a term not defined in the Convention, the domestic tax law of the Contracting State applying to the Convention shall control, unless the context in which the term is used requires a definition independent of domestic tax law or the competent authorities reach agreement on a meaning pursuant to Article XXVI (Mutual Agreement Procedure). The term "context" refers to the purpose and background of the provision in which the term appears.

Pursuant to the provisions of Article XXVI, the competent authorities of the Contracting States may resolve any difficulties or doubts as to the interpretation or application of the Convention. An agreement by the competent authorities with respect to the meaning of a term used in the Convention would supersede conflicting meanings in the domestic laws of the Contracting States.

ARTICLE IV   Residence

Article IV provides a detailed definition of the term "resident of a Contracting State." The definition begins with a person's liability to tax as a resident under the respective taxation laws of the Contracting States. A person who, under those laws, is a resident of one Contracting State and not the other need look no further. However, the Convention definition is also designed to assign residence to one State or the other for purposes of the Convention in circumstances where each of the Contracting States believes a person to be its resident. The Convention definition is, of course, exclusively for purposes of the Convention.

Paragraph 1 provides that the term "resident of a Contracting State" means any person who, under the laws of that State, is liable to tax therein by reason of his domicile, residence, place of management, place of incorporation, or any other criterion of a similar nature. The phrase "any other criterion of a similar nature" includes, for U.S. purposes, an election under the Code to be treated as a U.S. resident. An estate or trust is, however, considered to be a resident of a Contracting State only to the extent that income derived by such estate or trust is liable to tax in that State either in its hands or in the hands of its beneficiaries. To the extent that an estate or trust is considered a resident of a Contracting State under this provision, it can be a "beneficial owner" of items of income specified in other articles of the Convention - e.g., paragraph 2 of Article X (Dividends).

Paragraphs 2, 3, and 4 provide rules to determine a single residence for purposes of the Convention for persons resident in both Contracting States under the rules set forth in paragraph 1. Paragraph 2 deals with individuals. A "dual resident" individual is initially deemed to be a resident of the Contracting State in which he has a permanent home available to him in both States or in neither, he is deemed to be a resident of the Contracting State with which his personal and economic relations are closer. If the personal and economic relations of an individual are not closer to one Contracting State than to the other, the individual is deemed to be a resident of the Contracting State in which he has an habitual abode. If he has such an abode in both States or in neither State, he is deemed to be a resident of the Contracting State of which he is a citizen. If the individual is a citizen of both States or of neither, the competent authorities are to settle the status of the individual by mutual agreement.

Paragraph 3 provides that if, under the provisions of paragraph 1, a company is a resident of both Canada and the United States, then it shall be deemed to be a resident of the State under whose laws (including laws of political subdivisions) it was created. Paragraph 3 does not refer to the State in which a company is organized, thus making clear that the tie-breaker rule for a company is controlled by the State of the company's original creation. Various jurisdictions may allow local incorporation of an entity that is already organized and incorporated under the laws of another country. Paragraph 3 provides certainty in both the United States and Canada with respect to the treatment of such an entity for purposes of the Convention.

Paragraph 4 provides that where, by reason of the provisions of paragraph 1, an estate, trust, or other person, other than an individual or a company, is a resident of both Contracting States, the competent authorities of the States shall by mutual agreement endeavor to settle the question and determine the mode of application of the Convention to such person. This delegation of authority to the competent authorities complements the provisions of Article XXVI (Mutual Agreement Procedure), which implicitly grant such authority.

Paragraph 5 provides a special rule for certain government employees, their spouses, and dependent children. An individual is deemed to be a resident of a Contracting State if he is an employee of that State or of a political subdivision, local authority, or instrumentality of that State, is rendering services in the discharge of functions of a governmental nature in any State, and is subjected in the first-mentioned State to "similar obligations" in respect of taxes on income as are residents of the first-mentioned State. Paragraph 5 provides further that a spouse and dependent children residing with a government employee and also subject to "similar obligations" in respect of income taxes as residents if the first-mentioned State are also deemed to be residents of that State. Paragraph 5 overrides the normal tie-breaker rule of paragraph 2. A U.S. citizen or resident who is an employee of the U.S. government in a foreign country or who is a spouse or dependent of such employee is considered to be subject in the United States to "similar obligations" in respect of taxes on income as those imposed on residents of the United States, notwithstanding that such person may be entitled to the benefits allowed by sections 911 or 912 of the Code.

ARTICLE V   Permanent Establishment

Paragraph 1 provides that for the purposes of the Convention the term "permanent establishment" means a fixed place of business through which the business of a resident of a Contracting State is wholly or partly carried on. Article V does not use. the term "enterprise of a Contracting State," which appears in the 1942 Convention. Thus, paragraph 1 avoids introducing an additional term into the Convention. The omission of the term is not intended to have any implications for the interpretation of the 1942 Convention.

Paragraph 2 provides that the term "permanent establishment" includes especially a place of management, a branch, an office, a factory, a workshop, and a mine, oil or gas well, quarry, or any other place of extraction of natural resources. Paragraph 3 adds that a building site or construction or installation project constitutes a permanent establishment if and only if it lasts for more than 12 months. Paragraph 4 provides that a permanent establishment exists in a Contracting State if the use of an installation or drilling rig or drilling ship in that State to explore for or exploit natural resources lasts for more than 3 months in any 12 month period, but not if such activity exists for a lesser period of time. The competent authorities have entered into an agreement under the 1942 Convention setting forth guidelines as to certain aspects of Canadian taxation of drilling rigs owned by U.S. persons that constitute Canadian permanent establishments. The agreement will be renewed when this Convention enters into force.

Paragraph 5 provides that a person acting in a Contracting State on behalf of a resident of the other Contracting State is deemed to be a permanent establishment of the resident if such person has and habitually exercises in the first-mentioned State the authority to conclude contracts in the name of the resident. This rule does not apply to an agent of independent status, covered by paragraph 7. Under the provisions of paragraph 5, a permanent establishment may exist even in the absence of a fixed place of business. If, however, the activities of a person described in paragraph 5 are limited to the ancillary activities described in paragraph 6, then a permanent establishment does not exist solely on account of the person's activities. There are a number of minor differences between the provisions of paragraphs 1 through 5 and the analogous provisions of the 1942 Convention. One important deviation is elimination of the rule of the 1942 Convention which deems a permanent establishment to exist in any circumstance where a resident of one State uses substantial equipment in the other State for any period of time. The Convention thus generally raises the thresh-hold for source basis taxation of activities that involve substantial equipment (and that do not otherwise constitute a permanent establishment). Another deviation of some significance is elimination of the rule of the 1942 Convention that considers a permanent establishment to exist where a resident of one State carries on business in the other State through an agent or employee who has a stock of merchandise from which he regularly fills orders that he receives. The Convention provides that a person other than an agent of independent status who is engaged solely in the maintenance of a stock of goods or merchandise belonging to a resident of the other State for the purpose of storage, display or delivery does not constitute a permanent establishment.

Paragraph 6 provides that a fixed place of business used solely for, or an employee described in paragraph 5 engaged solely in, certain specified activities is not a permanent establishment, notwithstanding the provisions of paragraphs 1, 2, and 5. The specified activities are:

(a)   the use of facilities for the purpose of storage, display, or delivery of goods or merchandise belonging to the resident whose business is being carried on;

(b)   the maintenance of a stock of goods or merchandise belonging to the resident for the purpose of storage, display, or delivery;

(c)   the maintenance of a stock of goods or merchandise belonging to the resident for the purpose of processing by another person;

(d)   the purchase of goods or merchandise, or the collection of information, for the resident; and

(e)   advertising, the supply of information, scientific research, or similar activities which have a preparatory or auxiliary character, for the resident.

Combinations of the specified activities have the same status as any one of the activities. Thus, unlike the OECD Model Convention, a combination of the activities described in subparagraphs 6(a) through 6(e) need not be of a preparatory or auxiliary character (except as required by subparagraph 6(e)) in order to avoid the creation of a permanent establishment. The reference in paragraph 6(e) to specific activities does not imply that any other particular activities - for example, the servicing of a patent or a know-how contract or the inspection of the implementation of engineering plans - do not fall within the scope of paragraph 6(e) provided that, based on the facts and circumstances, such activities have a preparatory or auxiliary character.

Paragraph 7 provides that a resident of a Contracting State is not deemed .to have a permanent establishment in the other Contracting State merely because such resident carries on business in the other State through a broker, general commission agent, or any other agent of independent status, provided that such persons are acting in the ordinary course of their business.

Paragraph 8 states that the fact that a company which is a resident of one Contracting State controls or is controlled by a company which is either a resident of the other Contracting State or which is carrying on a business in the other State, whether through a permanent establishment or otherwise, does not automatically render either company a permanent establishment of the other.

Paragraph 9 provides that, for purposes of the Convention, the provisions of Article V apply in determining whether any person has a permanent establishment in any State. Thus, these provisions would determine whether a person other than a resident of Canada or the United States has a permanent establishment in Canada or the United States, and whether a person resident in Canada or the United States, has a permanent establishment in a third State.

ARTICLE VI   Income From Real Property

Paragraph 1 provides that income derived by a resident of a Contracting State from real property situated in the other Contracting State may be taxed by that other State. Income from real property includes, for purposes of Article VI, income from agriculture, forestry or other natural resources. Also, while "income derived . . . from real property" includes income from rights such as an overriding royalty or a net profits interest in a natural resource, it does not include income in the form of rights to explore for or exploit natural resources which a party receives as compensation for services (e.g., exploration services); the latter income is subject to the provisions of Article VII (Business Profits), XIV (Independent Personal Services), or XV (Dependent Personal Services), as the case may be. As provided by paragraph 3, paragraph 1 applies to income derived from the direct use, letting or use in any other form of real property and to income from the alienation of such property.

Generally speaking, the term "real property" has the meaning which it has under the taxation laws of the Contracting State in which the property in question is situated, in accordance with paragraph 2. In any case, the term includes any option or similar right in respect of real property, the usufruct of real property, and rights to explore for or to exploit mineral deposits, sources, and other natural resources. The reference to "rights to explore for or to exploit mineral deposits, sources and other natural resources" includes rights generating either variable (e.g., computed by reference to the amount of value or production) or fixed payments. The term "real property" does not include ships and aircraft.

Unlike Article XIII A of the 1942 Convention, Article VI does not contain an election to allow a resident of a Contracting State to compute tax on income from real property situated in the other State on a net basis. Both the Internal Revenue Code and the Income Tax Act of Canada generally allow for net basis taxation with respect to real estate rental income, although Canada does not permit such an election for natural resource royalties. Also, unlike the 1942 Convention which in Article XI imposes a 15 percent limitation on the source basis taxation of rental or royalty income from real property, Article VI of the Convention allows a Contracting State to impose tax on such income under its internal law. In Canada the rate of tax on resource royalties is 25 percent of the gross amount of the royalty, if the income is not attributable to a business carried on in Canada. In an exchange of notes to the Protocol, the United States and Canada agreed to resume negotiations, upon request by either country, to provide an appropriate limit on taxation in the State of source if either country subsequently increases its statutory tax rate now applicable to such royalties (25 percent in the case of Canada and 30 percent in the case of the United States).

ARTICLE VII   Business Profits

Paragraph 1 provides that business profits of a resident of a Contracting State are taxable only in that State unless the resident carries on business in the other Contracting State through a permanent establishment situated in that other State. If the resident carries on, or has carried on, business through such a permanent establishment, the other State may tax such business profits but only so much of them as are attributable to the permanent establishment. The reference to a prior permanent establishment ("or has carried on") makes clear that a Contracting State in which a permanent establishment existed has the right to tax the business profits attributable to that permanent establishment, even if there is a delay in the receipt or accrual of such profits until after the permanent establishment has been terminated.

Any business profits received or accrued in taxable years in which the Convention has effect, in accordance with Article XXX (Entry Into Force), which are attributable to a permanent establishment that was previously terminated are subject to tax in the Contracting State in which such permanent establishment existed under the provisions of Article VII.

Paragraph 2 provides that where a resident of either Canada or the United States carries on business in the other Contracting State through a permanent establishment in that other State, both Canada and the United States shall attribute to that permanent establishment business profits which the permanent establishment might be expected to make if it were a distinct and separate person engaged in the same or similar activities under the same or similar conditions and dealing wholly independently with the resident and with any other person related to the resident. The term "related to the resident" is to be interpreted in accordance with paragraph 2 of Article IX (Related Persons). The reference to other related persons is intended to make clear that the test of paragraph 2 is not restricted to independence between a permanent establishment and a home office.

Paragraph 3 provides that, in determining business profits of a permanent establishment, there are to be allowed as deductions those expenses which are incurred for the purposes of the permanent establishment, including executive and administrative expenses, whether incurred in the State in which the permanent establishment is situated or in any other State. However, nothing in the paragraph requires Canada or the United States to allow a deduction for any expenditure which would not generally be allowed as a deduction under its taxation laws. The language of this provision differs from that of paragraph 1 of Article III of the 1942 Convention, which states that in the determination of net industrial and commercial profits of a permanent establishment there shall be allowed as deductions "all expenses, wherever incurred" as long as such expenses are reasonably allocable to the permanent establishment. Paragraph 3 of Article VII of the Convention is not intended to have any implications for interpretation of the 1942 Convention, but is intended to assure that under the Convention deductions are allowed by a Contracting State which are generally allowable by that State.

Paragraph 4 provides that no business profits are to be attributed to a permanent establishment of a resident of a Contracting State by reason of the use of the permanent establishment for merely purchasing goods or merchandise or merely providing executive, managerial, or administrative facilities or services for the resident. Thus, if a company resident in a Contracting State has a permanent establishment in the other State, and uses the permanent establishment for the mere performance of stewardship or other managerial services carried on for the benefit of the resident, this activity will not result in profits being attributed to the permanent establishment.

Paragraph 5 provides that business profits are to be attributed to a permanent establishment by the same method in every taxable period unless there is good and sufficient reason to change such method. In the United States, such a change may be a change in accounting method requiring the approval of the Internal Revenue Service.

Paragraph 6 explains the relationship between the provisions of Article VII and other provisions of the Convention. Where business profits include items of income which are dealt with separately in other Articles of the Convention, those other Articles are controlling.

Paragraph 7 provides a definition for the term "attributable to". Profits "attributable to" a permanent establishment are those derived from the assets or activities of the permanent establishment. Paragraph 7 does not preclude Canada or the United States from using appropriate domestic tax law rules of attribution. The "attributable to" definition does not, for example, preclude a taxpayer from using the rules of section 1, 864-4(c)(5) of the Treasury Regulations to assure for U.S. tax purposes that interest arising in the United States is attributable to a permanent establishment in the United States. (Interest arising outside the United States is attributable to a permanent establishment in the United States based on the principles of Regulations sections 1.864-5 and 1.864-6 and Revenue Ruling 75-253, 1975-2 C.B. 203.) Income that would be taxable under the Code and that is "attributable to" a permanent establishment under paragraph 7 is taxable pursuant to Article VII, however, even if such income might under the Code be treated as fixed or determinable annual or periodical gains or income not effectively connected with the conduct of a trade or business within the United States. The "attributable to" definition means that the limited "force-of-attraction" rule of Code section 864(c)(3) does not apply for U.S. tax purposes under the Convention.

ARTICLE VIII   Transportation

Paragraph 1 provides that profits derived by a resident of a Contracting State from the operation of ships or aircraft in international traffic are exempt from tax in the other Contracting State, even if, under Article VII (Business Profits), such profits are attributable to a permanent establishment. Paragraph 1 also provides that gains derived by a resident of a Contracting State from the alienation of ships, aircraft or containers (including trailers and related equipment for the transport of containers) used principally in international traffic are exempt from tax in the other Contracting State even if, under Article XIII (Gains), those gains would be taxable in that other State. These rules differ from Article V of the 1942 Convention, which conditions the exemption in the State of source on registration of the ship or aircraft in the other State. Paragraph 1 also applies notwithstanding the provisions of Article XII (Royalties). Thus, to the extent that profits described in paragraph 2 would also fall within Article XII (Royalties) (e.g., rent from the lease of a container), the provisions of Article VIII are controlling.

Paragraph 2(a) provides that profits covered by paragraph 1 include profits from the rental of ships or aircraft operated in international traffic. Such rental profits are included whether the rental is on a time, voyage, or bareboat basis, and irrespective of the State of residence of the operator.

Paragraph 2(b) provides that profits covered by paragraph 1 include profits derived from the use, maintenance or rental of containers, including trailers and related equipment for the transport of containers, if such containers are used in international traffic.

Paragraph 2(c) provides that profits covered by paragraph 1 include profits derived by a resident of a Contracting State from the rental of ships, aircraft, or containers (including trailers and related equipment for the transport of containers), even if not operated in international traffic, as long as such profits are incidental to profits of such person referred to in paragraphs 1, 2(a), or 2(b).

Paragraph 3 states that profits derived by a resident of a Contracting State from a voyage of a ship where the principal purpose of the voyage is to transport passengers or property between points in the other Contracting State is taxable in that other State, whether or not the resident maintains a permanent establishment there. Paragraph 3 overrides the provisions of Article VII. Profits from such a voyage do not qualify for exemption under Article VIII by virtue of the definition of "international traffic" in paragraph 1(h) of Article III (General Definitions). However, profits from a similar voyage by aircraft are taxable in the Contracting State of source only if the profits are attributable to a permanent establishment maintained in that State.

Paragraph 4 provides that profits derived by a resident of a Contracting State engaged in the operation of motor vehicles or a railway as a common carrier or contract carrier, and attributable to the transportation of passengers or property between a point outside the other Contracting State and any other point are exempt from tax in that other State. In addition, profits of such a person from the rental of motor vehicles (including trailers) or railway rolling stock, or from the use, maintenance, or rental of containers (including trailers and related equipment for the transport of containers) used to transport passengers or property between a point outside the other Contracting State and any other point are exempt from tax in that other State.

Paragraph 5 provides that a resident of a Contracting State that participates in a pool, a joint business, or an international operating agency is subject to the provisions of paragraphs 1, 3, and 4 with respect to the profits or gains referred to in paragraphs 1, 3, and 4.

Paragraph 6 states that profits derived by a resident of a Contracting State from the use, maintenance, or rental of railway rolling stock, motor vehicles, trailers, or containers (including trailers and related equipment for the transport of containers) used in the other Contracting State for a period not expected to exceed 183 days in the aggregate in any 12-month period are exempt from tax in that other State except to the extent that the profits are attributable to a permanent establishment, in which case the State of source has the right to tax under Article VII. The provisions of paragraph 6, unlike the provisions of paragraph 4, apply whether or not the resident is engaged in the operation of motor vehicles or a railway as a common carrier or contract carrier. Paragraph 6 overrides the provisions of Article XII (Royalties), which would otherwise permit taxation in the State of source in the circumstances described.

Gains from the alienation of motor vehicles and railway rolling stock derived by a resident of a Contracting State are not affected by paragraph 4 or 6. Such gains would be taxable in the other Contracting State, however, only if the motor vehicles or rolling stock formed part of a permanent establishment maintained there. See paragraphs 2 and 4 of Article XIII.

ARTICLE IX   Related Persons

Paragraph 1 authorizes Canada and the United States, as the case may be, to adjust the amount of income, loss, or tax payable by a person with respect to arrangements between that person and a related person in the other Contracting State. Such adjustment may be made when arrangements between related persons differ from those that would obtain between unrelated persons. The term "person" encompasses a company resident in a third State with, for example, a permanent establishment in a Contracting State.

Paragraph 2 provides that, for the purposes of Article IX, a person is deemed to be related to another person if either participates directly or indirectly in the management or control of the other or if any third person or persons participate directly or indirectly in the management or control of both. Thus, if a resident of any State controls directly or indirectly a company resident in Canada and a company resident in the United States, such companies are considered to be related persons for purposes of Article IX. Article IX and the definition of "related person" in paragraph 2 may encompass situations that would not be covered by provisions in the domestic laws of the Contracting States. Nor is the paragraph 2 definition controlling for the definition of "related person" or similar terms appearing in other Articles of the Convention. Those terms are defined as provided in paragraph 2 of Article III (General Definitions).

Paragraph 3 provides that where, pursuant to paragraph 1, an adjustment is made or to be made by a Contracting State, the other Contracting State shall make a corresponding adjustment to the income, loss, or tax of the related person in that other State, provided that the other State agrees with the adjustment and, within six years from the end of the taxable year of the person in the first State to which the adjustment relates, the competent authority of the other State has been notified in writing of the adjustment. The reference to an adjustment which "is made or to be made" does not require a Contracting State to formally propose an adjustment before paragraph 3 becomes pertinent. The notification required by paragraph 3 may be made by any of the related persons involved or by the competent authority of the State which makes or is to make the initial adjustment. The notification must give details regarding the adjustment sufficient to apprize the competent authority receiving the notification of the nature of the adjustment.

If the requirements of paragraph 3 are complied with, the corresponding adjustment will be made by the other Contracting State notwithstanding any time or procedural limitations in the domestic law of that State.

Paragraph 4 provides that in a case where the other Contracting State has not been notified as provided in paragraph 3 and if the person whose income, loss, or tax is being adjusted has not received notification of the adjustment within five and one-half years from the end of its taxable year to which the adjustment relates, such adjustment shall not be made to the extent that the adjustment would give rise to double taxation between the United States and Canada. Again, the notification referred to in this paragraph need not be a formal adjustment, but it must be in writing and must contain sufficient details to permit the taxpayer to give the notification referred to in paragraph 3.

If, for example, the Internal Revenue Service proposes to make an adjustment to the income of a U.S. company pursuant to Code section 482, and the adjustment involves an allocation of income from a related Canadian company, the competent authority of Canada must receive written notification of the proposed IRS adjustment within six years from the end of the taxable year of the U.S. company to which the adjustment relates. If such notification is not received in a timely fashion and if the U.S. company does not receive written notification of the adjustment from the IRS within 5-1/2 years from the end of its relevant taxable year, the IRS will unilaterally recede on the proposed section 482 adjustment to the extent that this adjustment would otherwise give rise to double taxation between the United States and Canada. The Internal Revenue Service will determine whether and to what extent the adjustment would give rise to double taxation with respect to income arising in Canada by examining the relevant facts and circumstances such as the amount of foreign tax credits attributable to Canadian taxes paid by the U.S. company, including any carry-overs and credits for deemed paid taxes.

Paragraph 5 provides that neither a corresponding adjustment described in paragraph 3 nor the canceling of an adjustment described in paragraph 4 will be made in any case of fraud, willful default, neglect, or gross negligence on the part of the taxpayer or any related person.

Paragraphs 3 and 4 of Article IX are exceptions to the "saving clause" contained in paragraph 2 of Article XXIX (Miscellaneous Rules), as provided in paragraph 3(a) of Article XXIX. Paragraphs 3 and 4 of Article IX apply to adjustments made or to be made with respect to taxable years for which the Convention has effect as provided in paragraphs 2 and 5 of Article XXX (Entry Into Force).

ARTICLE X   Dividends

Paragraph 1 allows a Contracting State to impose tax on its residents with respect to dividends paid by a company which is a resident of the other Contracting State.

Paragraph 2 limits the amount of tax that may be imposed on such dividends by the Contracting State in which the company paying the dividends is resident if the beneficial owner of the dividends is a resident of the other Contracting State. The limitation is 10 percent of the gross amount of the dividends if the beneficial owner is a company that owns 10 percent or more of the voting stock of the company paying the dividends; and 15 percent of the gross amount of the dividends in all other cases. Paragraph 2 does not impose any restrictions with respect to taxation of the profits out of which the dividends are paid.

Paragraph 3 defines the term "dividends," as the term is used in this Article. Each Contracting State is permitted to apply its domestic law rules for differentiating dividends from interest and other disbursements.

Paragraph 4 provides that the limitations of paragraph 2 do not apply if the beneficial owner of the dividends carries on business in the State in which the company paying the dividends is a resident through a permanent establishment or fixed base situated there, and the stockholding in respect of which the dividends are paid is effectively connected with such permanent establishment or fixed base. In such a case, the dividends are taxable pursuant to the provisions of Article VII (Business Profits) or Article XIV (Independent Personal Services), as the case may be. Thus, dividends paid in respect of holdings forming part of the assets of a permanent establishment or fixed base or which are otherwise effectively connected with such permanent establishment or fixed base (i.e., dividends attributable to the permanent establishment or fixed base) will be taxed on a net basis using the rates and rules of taxation generally applicable to residents of the State in which the permanent establishment or fixed base is situated.

Paragraph 5 imposes limitations on the right of Canada or the United States, as the case may be, to impose tax on dividends paid by a company which is a resident of the other Contracting State. The State in which the company is not resident may not tax such dividends except insofar as they are paid to a resident of that State or the holding in respect of which the dividends are paid is effectively connected with a permanent establishment or fixed base in that State. In the case of the United States such dividends may also be in the hands of a U.S. citizen and certain former citizens, pursuant the "saving clause" of paragraph 2 of Article XXIX (Miscellaneous Rules). In addition, the Contracting State in which the company is not resident may not subject such company's undistributed profits to any tax. See, however, paragraphs 6, 7, and 8 which, in certain circumstances, qualify the rules of paragraph 5. Neither paragraph 5 nor any other provision of the Convention restricts the ability of the United States to apply the provisions of the Code concerning foreign personal holding companies and controlled foreign corporations.

Paragraph 6 provides that, notwithstanding paragraph 5, a Contracting State in which is maintained permanent establishment or permanent establishments of a company resident in the other Contracting State may impose tax on such company's earnings, in addition to the tax that would be charged on the earnings of a company resident in that State. The additional tax may not, however, exceed 10 percent of amount of the earnings which have not been subjected to such additional tax in previous taxation years. Thus, Canada, which has a branch profits tax in force, may impose that tax up to the 10 percent limitation in the case of a United States company with one or more permanent establishments in Canada. This branch profits tax may be imposed notwithstanding other rules of the Convention, including paragraph 6 of Article XXV (Non-Discrimination).

For purposes of paragraph 6, the term "earnings" means the excess of business profits attributable to all permanent establishments for a year and previous years over the sum of:

(a) business losses attributable to such permanent establishments for such years;

(b) all taxes on profits, whether or not covered by the Convention (e.g., provincial taxes on profits and provincial resource royalties (which Canada considers "taxes") in excess of the mineral resource allowance provided for under the law of Canada), other than the additional tax referred to in paragraph 6;

(c) profits reinvested in such State; and

(d) $500,000 (Canadian, or its equivalent in U.S. dollars) less any amounts deducted under paragraph 6(d) with respect to the same or a similar business by the company or an associated company.

The deduction under paragraph 6(d) is available as of the first year for which the Convention has effect, regardless of the prior earnings and tax expenses, if any, of the permanent establishment. The $500,000 deduction is taken into account after other deductions, and is permanent. For the purpose of paragraph 6, references to business profits and business losses include gains and losses from the alienation of property forming part of the business property of a permanent establishment. The term "associated company" includes a company which directly or indirectly controls another company or two companies directly or indirectly controlled by the same person or persons, as well as any two companies that deal with each other not at arm's length. This definition differs from the definition of "related persons" in paragraph 2 of Article IX (Related Persons).

Paragraph 7 provides that, notwithstanding paragraph 5, a Contracting State that does not impose a branch profits tax as described in paragraph 6 (i.e., under current law, the United States) may tax a dividend paid by a company which is a resident of the other Contracting State if at least 50 percent of the company's gross income from all sources was included in the computation of business profits attributable to one or more permanent establishments which such company had in the first-mentioned State. The dividend subject to such a tax must, however, be attributable to profits earned by the company in taxable years beginning after September 26, 1980 and the 50 percent test must be met for the three-year period preceding the taxable year of the company in which the dividend is declared (including years ending on or before September 26, 1980) or such shorter period as the company had been in existence prior to that taxable year. Dividends will be deemed to be distributed, for purposes of paragraph 7, first out of profits of the taxation year of the company in which the distribution is made and then out of the profits of the preceding year or years of the company. Paragraph 7 provides further that if a resident of the other Contracting State is the beneficial owner of such dividends, any tax imposed under paragraph 7 is subject to the 10 or 15 percent limitation of paragraph 2 or the rules of paragraph 4 (providing for dividends to be taxed as business profits or income from independent personal services), as the case may be.

Paragraph 8 provides that, notwithstanding paragraph 5, a company which is a resident of Canada and which, absent the provisions of the Convention, has income subject to tax by the United States may be liable for the United States accumulated earnings tax and personal holding company tax. These taxes can be applied, however, only if 50 percent or more in value of the outstanding voting shares of the company is owned, directly or indirectly, throughout the last half of its taxable year by residents of a third State or by citizens or residents of the United States, other than citizens of Canada who are resident in the United States but who either do not have immigrant status in the United States or who have not been resident in the United States for more than three taxable years. The accumulated earnings tax is applied to accumulated taxable income calculated without the benefits of the Convention. Similarly, the personal holding company tax is applied to undistributed personal holding company income computed as if the Convention had not come into force.

Article X does not apply to dividends paid by a company which is not a resident of either Contracting State. Such dividends, if they are income of a resident of one of the Contracting States, are subject to tax as provided in Article XXII (Other Income).

ARTICLE XI   Interest

Paragraph 1 allows interest arising in Canada or the United States and paid to a resident of the other State to be taxed in the latter State. Paragraph 2 provides that such interest may also be taxed in the Contracting State where it arises, but if a resident of the other Contracting State is the beneficial owner, the tax imposed by the State of source is limited to 15 percent of the gross amount of the interest.

Paragraph 3 provides a number of exceptions to the right of the source State to impose a 15 percent tax under paragraph 2. The following types of interest beneficially owned by a resident of a Contracting State are exempt from tax in the State of source:

(a)   interest beneficially owned by a Contracting State, a political subdivision, or a local authority thereof, or an instrumentality of such State, subdivision, or authority, which interest is not subject to tax by such State;

(b)   interest beneficially owned by a resident of a Contracting State and paid with respect to debt obligations issued at arm's length which are guaranteed or insured by such State or a political subdivision thereof, or by an instrumentality of such State or subdivision (not by a local authority or an instrumentality thereof), but only if the guarantor or insurer is not subject to tax by that State;

(c)   interest paid by a Contracting State, a political subdivision, or a local authority thereof, or by an instrumentality of such State, subdivision, or authority, but only if the payor is not subject to tax by such State; and

(d)   interest beneficially owned by a seller of equipment, merchandise, or services, but only if the interest is paid in connection with a sale on credit

of equipment, merchandise, or services and the sale was made at arm's
length.

Whether such a transaction is made at arm's length will be determined in the
United States under the facts and circumstances. The relationship between the
parties is a factor, but not the only factor, taken into account in making this
determination. Furthermore, interest paid by a company resident in the other
Contracting State with respect to an obligation entered into before September 26,
1980 is exempt from tax in the State of source (irrespective of the State of
residence of the beneficial owner), provided that such interest would have been
exempt from tax in the Contracting State of source under Article XII of the 1942
Convention. Thus, interest paid by a United States corporation whose business is
not managed and controlled in Canada to a recipient not resident in Canada or to
a corporation not managed and controlled in Canada would be exempt from
Canadian tax as long as the debt obligation was entered into before September 26,
1980. The phrase "not subject to tax by that State" in paragraph 3(a), (b), and (c)
refers to taxation at the Federal levels of Canada and the United States.

The phrase "obligation entered into before the date of signature of this
Convention" means:

(1)   any obligation under which funds were dispersed prior to September 26,
      1980;

(2)   any obligation under which funds are dispersed on or after September 26,
      1980, pursuant to a written contract binding prior to and on such date, and
      at all times thereafter until the obligation is satisfied; or

(3)   any obligation with respect to which, prior to September 26, 1980, a lender
      had taken every action to signify approval under procedures ordinarily
      employed by such lender in similar transactions and had sent or deposited
      for delivery to the person to whom the loan is to be made written evidence
      of such approval in the form of a document setting forth, or referring to a
      document sent by the person to whom the loan is to be made that sets
      forth, the principal terms of such loan.

Paragraph 4 defines the term "interest," as used in Article XI, to include, among
other things, debt claims of every kind as well as income assimilated to income
from money lent by the taxation laws of the Contracting State in which the income
arises. In no event, however, is income dealt with in Article X (Dividends) to be
considered interest.

Paragraph 5 provides that neither the 15 percent limitation on tax in the
Contracting State of source provided in paragraph 2 nor the various exemptions
from tax in such State provided in paragraph 3 apply if the beneficial owner of the
interest is a resident of the other Contracting State carrying on business in the
State of source through a permanent establishment or fixed base, and the debt
claim in respect of which the interest is paid is effectively connected with such
permanent establishment or fixed base (i.e., the interest is attributable to the
permanent establishment or fixed base). In this case, interest income is to be taxed
in the Contracting State of source as business profits - that is, on a net basis.

Paragraph 6 establishes the source of interest for purposes of Article XI. Interest is considered to arise in a Contracting State if the payer is that State, or a political subdivision, local authority, or resident of that State. However, in cases where the person paying the interest, whether a resident of a Contracting State or of a third State, has in a State other than that of which he is a resident a permanent establishment or fixed base in connection with which the indebtedness on which the interest was paid was incurred, and such interest is borne by the permanent establishment or fixed base, then such interest is deemed to arise in the State in which the permanent establishment or fixed base is situated and not in the State of the payer's residence. Thus, pursuant to paragraphs 6 and 2, and Article XXII (Other Income), Canadian tax will not be imposed on interest paid to a U.S. resident by a company resident in Canada if the indebtedness is incurred in connection with, and the interest is borne by, a permanent establishment of the company situated in a third State. "Borne by" means allowable as a deduction in computing taxable income.

Paragraph 7 provides that in cases involving special relationships between persons Article XI does not apply to amounts in excess of the amount which would have been agreed upon between persons having no special relationship; any such excess amount remains taxable according to the laws of Canada and the United States, consistent with any relevant provisions of the Convention.

Paragraph 8 restricts the right of a Contracting State to impose tax on interest paid by a resident of the other Contracting State. The first State may not impose any tax on such interest except insofar as the interest is paid to a resident of that State or arises in that State or the debt claim in respect of which the interest is paid is effectively connected with a permanent establishment or fixed base situated in that State. Thus, pursuant to paragraph 8 the United States has agreed not to impose tax on certain interest paid by Canadian companies to persons not resident in the United States, to the extent that such companies would pay U.S.- source interest under Code section 861(a)(1)(C) but not under the source rule of paragraph 6. It is to be noted that paragraph 8 is subject to the "saving clause" of paragraph 2 of Article XXIX (Miscellaneous Rules), so the United States may in all events impose its tax on interest received by U.S. citizens.

ARTICLE XII   Royalties

Generally speaking, under the 1942 Convention royalties, including royalties with respect to motion picture films, which are derived by a resident of one Contracting State from sources within the other Contracting State are taxed at a maximum rate of 15 percent in the latter State; copyright royalties are exempt from tax in the State of source, if the resident does not have a permanent establishment in that State. See Articles II, III, XIII C, and paragraph 1 of Article XI of the 1942 Convention, and paragraph 6(a) of the Protocol to the 1942 Convention.

Paragraph 1 of Article XII of the Convention provides that a Contracting State may tax its residents with respect to royalties arising in the other Contracting State. Paragraph 2 provides that such royalties may also be taxed in the Contracting State in which they arise, but that if a resident of the other

Contracting State is the beneficial owner of the royalties the tax in the Contracting State of source is limited to 10 percent of the gross amount of the royalties.

Paragraph 3 provides that, notwithstanding paragraph 2, copyright royalties and other like payments in respect of the production or reproduction of any literary, dramatic, musical, or artistic work, including royalties from such works on videotape or other means of reproduction for private (home) use, if beneficially owned by a resident of the other Contracting State, may not be taxed by the Contracting State of source. This exemption at source does not apply to royalties in respect of motion pictures, and of works on film, videotape or other means of reproduction for use in connection with television broadcasting. Such royalties are subject to tax at a maximum rate of 10 percent in the Contracting State in which they arise, as provided in paragraph 2 (unless the provisions of paragraph 5, described below, apply).

Paragraph 4 defines the term "royalties" for purposes of Article XII. "Royalties" means payments of any kind received as consideration for the use of or the right to use any copyright of literary, artistic, or scientific work, including motion pictures, and works on film, videotape or other means of reproduction for use in connection with television broadcasting, any patent, trademark, design or model, plan, secret formula or process, or any payment for the use of or the right to use tangible personal property or for information concerning industrial, commercial, or scientific experience. The term "royalties" also includes gains from the alienation of any intangible property or rights described in paragraph 4 to the extent that such gains are contingent on the productivity, use, or subsequent disposition of such intangible property or rights. Thus, a guaranteed minimum payment derived from the alienation of (but not the use of) any right or property described in paragraph 4 is not a "royalty." Any amounts deemed contingent on use by reason of Code section 871(e) are, however, royalties under paragraph 2 of Article III (General Definitions), subject to Article XXVI (Mutual Agreement Procedure). The term "royalties" does not encompass management fees, which are covered by the provisions of Article VII (Business Profits) or XIV (Independent Personal Services), or payments under a bona fide cost - sharing arrangement. Technical service fees may be royalties in cases where the fees are periodic and dependent upon productivity or a similar measure.

Paragraph 5 provides that the 10 percent limitation on tax in the Contracting State of source provided by paragraph 2, and the exemption in the Contracting State of source for certain copyright royalties provided by paragraph 3, do not apply if the beneficial owner of the royalties carries on business in the State of source through a permanent establishment or fixed base and the right or property in respect of which the royalties are paid is effectively connected with such permanent establishment or fixed base (i.e., the royalties are attributable to the permanent establishment or fixed base). In that event, the royalty income would be taxable under the provisions of Article VII (Business Profits) or XIV (Independent Personal Services), as the case may be.

Paragraph 6 establishes rules to determine the source of royalties for purposes of Article XII. The first rule is that royalties arise in a Contracting State when the payer is that State, or a political subdivision, local authority, or resident of that

State. Notwithstanding that rule, royalties arise not in the State of the payer's residence but in any State, whether or not a Contracting State, in which is situated a permanent establishment or fixed base in connection with which the obligation to pay royalties was incurred, if such royalties are borne by such permanent establishment or fixed base. Thus, royalties paid to a resident of the United States by a company resident in Canada for the use of property in a third State will not be subject to tax in Canada if the obligation to pay the royalties is incurred in connection with, and the royalties are borne by, a permanent establishment of the company in a third State. "Borne by" means allowable as a deduction in computing taxable income.

A third rule, which overrides both the residence rule and the permanent establishment rule just described, provides that royalties for the use of, or the right to use, intangible property or tangible personal property in a Contracting State arise in that State. Thus, consistent with the provisions of Code section 861(a)(4), if a resident of a third State pays royalties to a resident of Canada for the use of or the right to use intangible property or tangible personal property in the United States, such royalties are considered to arise in the United States and are subject to taxation by the United States consistent with the Convention. Similarly, if a resident of Canada pays royalties to a resident of a third State, such royalties are considered to arise in the United States and are subject to U.S. taxation if they are for the use of or the right to use intangible property or tangible personal property in the United States. The term "intangible property" encompasses all the items described in paragraph 4, other than tangible personal property.

Paragraph 7 provides that in cases involving special relationships between persons the benefits of Article XII do not apply to amounts in excess of the amount which would have been agreed upon between persons with no special relationship; any such excess amount remains taxable according to the laws of Canada and the United States, consistent with any relevant provisions of the Convention.

Paragraph 8 restricts the right of a Contracting State to impose tax on royalties paid by a resident of the other Contracting State. The first State may not impose any tax on such royalties except insofar as they arise in that State or they are paid to a resident of that State or the right or property in respect of which the royalties are paid is effectively connected with a permanent establishment or fixed base situated in that State. This rule parallels the rule in paragraph 8 of Article XI (Interest) and paragraph 5 of Article X (Dividends). Again, U.S. citizens remain subject to U.S. taxation on royalties received despite this rule, by virtue of paragraph 2 of Article XXIX (Miscellaneous Rules).

ARTICLE XIII   Gains

Paragraph 1 provides that Canada and the United States may each tax gains from the alienation of real property situated within that State which are derived by a resident of the other Contracting State. The term "real property situated in the other Contracting State" is defined for this purpose in paragraph 3 of this Article. The term "alienation" used in paragraph 1 and other paragraphs of Article XIII means sales, exchanges and other dispositions or deemed dispositions (e.g., change of use, gifts, distributions, death) that are taxable events under the taxation laws of the Contracting State applying the provisions of the Article.

Paragraph 2 of Article XIII provides that the Contracting State in which a resident of the other Contracting State "has or had" a permanent establishment or fixed base may tax gains from the alienation of personal property constituting business property if such gains are attributable to such permanent establishment or fixed base. Unlike paragraph 1 of Article VII (Business Profits), paragraph 2 limits the right of the source State to tax such gains to a twelve-month period following the termination of the permanent establishment or fixed base.

Paragraph 3 provides a definition of the term "real property situated in the other Contracting State." Where the United States is the other Contracting State, the term includes real property (as defined in Article VI (Income from Real Property)) situated in the United States and a United States real property interest. Thus, the United States retains the ability to exercise its full taxing right under the Foreign Investment in Real Property Tax Act (Code section 897). (For a transition rule from the 1942 Convention, see paragraph 9 of this Article.) Where Canada is the other Contracting State, the term means real property (as defined in Article VI) situated in Canada; shares of stock of a company, the value of whose shares consists principally of Canadian real property; and an interest in a partnership, trust or estate, the value of which consists principally of Canadian real property. The term "principally" means more than 50 percent. Taxation in Canada is preserved through several tiers of entities if the value of the company's shares or the partnership, trust or estate is ultimately dependent principally upon real property situated in Canada.

Paragraph 4 reserves to the Contracting State of residence the sole right to tax gains from the alienation of any property other than property referred to in paragraphs 1, 2, and 3.

Paragraph 5 states that, despite paragraph 4, a Contracting State may impose tax on gains derived by an individual who is a resident of the other Contracting State if such individual was a resident of the first-mentioned State for 120 months (whether or not consecutive) during any period of 20 consecutive years preceding the alienation of the property, and was a resident of that State at any time during the 10-year period immediately preceding the alienation of the property. The property (or property received in substitution in a tax-free transaction in the first-mentioned State) must have been owned by the individual at the time he ceased to be a resident of the first-mentioned State.

Paragraph 6 provides a rule to coordinate Canadian and United States taxation of gains from the alienation of a principal residence situated in Canada. An individual (not a citizen of the United States) who was a resident of Canada and becomes a resident of the United States may determine his liability for U.S. income tax purposes in respect of gain from the alienation of a principal residence in Canada owned by him at the time he ceased to be a resident of Canada by claiming an adjusted basis for such residence in an amount no less than the fair market value of the residence at that time. Under paragraph 2(b) of Article XXX, the rule of paragraph 6 applies to gains realized for U.S. income tax purposes in taxable years beginning on or after the first day of January next following the date when instruments of ratification are exchanged, even if a particular individual described in paragraph 6 ceased to be a resident of Canada prior to such date. Paragraph 6 supplements any benefits available to a taxpayer pursuant to the provisions of the Code, e.g., section 1034.

Paragraph 7 provides a rule to coordinate U.S. and Canadian taxation of gains in circumstances where an individual is subject to tax in both Contracting States and one Contracting State deems a taxable alienation of property by such person to have occurred, while the other Contracting State at that time does not find a realization or recognition of income and thus defers, but does not forgive taxation. In such a case the individual may elect in his annual return of income for the year of such alienation to be liable to tax in the latter Contracting State as if he had sold and repurchased the property for an amount equal to its fair market value at a time immediately prior to the deemed alienation. The provision would, for example, apply in the case of a gift by a U.S. citizen or a U.S. resident individual which Canada deems to be an income producing event for its tax purposes but with respect to which the United States defers taxation while assigning the donor's basis to the donee. The provision would also apply in the case of a U.S. citizen who, for Canadian tax purposes, is deemed to recognize income upon his departure from Canada, but not to a Canadian resident (not a U.S. citizen) who is deemed to recognize such income. The rule does not apply in the case death, although Canada also deems that to be a taxable event, because the United States in effect forgives income taxation of economic gains at death. If in one Contracting State there are losses and gains from deemed alienations of different properties, then paragraph 7 must be applied consistently in the other Contracting State within the taxable period with respect to all such properties. Paragraph 7 only applies, however, if the deemed alienations of the properties result in a net gain.

Paragraph 8 concerns the coordination of Canadian and U.S. rules with respect to the recognition of gain on corporate organizations, reorganizations, amalgamations, divisions, and similar transactions. Where a resident of a Contracting State alienates property in such a transaction, and profit, gain, or income with respect to such alienation is not recognized for income tax purposes in the Contracting State of residence, the competent authority of the other Contracting State may agree, pursuant to paragraph 8, if requested by the person who acquires the property, to defer recognition of the profit, gain, or income with respect to such property for income tax purposes. This deferral shall be for such time and under such other conditions as are stipulated between the person who acquires the property and the competent authority. The agreement of the competent authority of the State of source is entirely discretionary and will be granted only to the extent necessary to avoid double taxation of income. This provision means, for example, that the United States competent authority may agree to defer recognition of gain with respect to a transaction if the alienator would otherwise recognize gain for U.S. tax purposes and would not recognize gain under Canada's law. The provision only applies, however, if alienations described in paragraph 8 result in a net gain. In the absence of extraordinary circumstances the provisions of the paragraph must be applied consistently within a taxable period with respect to alienations described in the paragraph that take place within that period.

Paragraph 9 provides a transitional rule reflecting the fact that under Article VIII of the 1942 Convention gains from the sale or exchange of capital assets are exempt from taxation in the State of source provided the taxpayer had no permanent establishment in that State. Paragraph 9 applies to deemed, as well as actual, alienations or dispositions. In addition, paragraph 9 applies to a gain described in paragraph 1, even though such gain is also income within the meaning of paragraph 3 of Article VI. Paragraph 9 will apply to transactions notwithstanding section 1125(c) of the Foreign Investment in Real Property Tax Act, Public Law 96-499 ("FIRPTA").

Paragraph 9 applies to capital assets alienated by a resident of a Contracting State if

(a)   that person owned the asset on September 26, 1980 and was a resident of that Contracting State on September 26, 1980 (and at all times after that date until the alienation), or

(b)   the asset was acquired by that person in an alienation of property which qualified as a non-recognition transaction for tax purposes in the other Contracting State.

For purposes of subparagraph 9(b), a non-recognition transaction is a transaction in which gain resulting therefrom is, in effect, deferred for tax purposes, but is not permanently forgiven. Thus, in the United States, certain tax-free organizations, reorganizations, liquidations and like kind exchanges will qualify as non-recognition transactions. However, a transfer of property at death will not constitute a non-recognition transaction, since any gain due to appreciation in the property is permanently forgiven in the United States due to the fair market value basis taken by the recipient of the property. If a transaction is a non-recognition transaction for tax purposes, the transfer of non-qualified property, or "boot," which may cause some portion of the gain on the transaction to be recognized, will not cause the transaction to lose its character as a nonrecognition transaction for purposes of subparagraph 9(b). In addition, a transaction that would have been a non-recognition transaction in the United States but for the application of sections 897(d) and 897(e) of the Code will also constitute a non-recognition transaction for purposes of subparagraph 9(b). Further, a transaction which is not a non-recognition transaction under U.S. law, but to which non-recognition treatment is granted pursuant to the agreement of the competent authority under paragraph 8 of this Article, is a non-recognition transaction for purposes of subparagraph 9(b). However, a transaction which is not a non-recognition transaction under U.S. law does not become a non-recognition transaction for purposes of subparagraph 9(b) merely because the basis of the property in the hands of the transferee is reduced under section 1125(d) of FIRPTA.

The benefits of paragraph 9 are not available to the alienation or disposition by a resident of a Contracting State of an asset that

(a)   on September 26, 1980 formed part of the business property of a permanent establishment or pertained to a fixed base which a resident of that Contracting State had in the other Contracting State,

(b) was alienated after September 26, 1980 and before the alienation in question in any transaction that was not a non-recognition transaction, as described above, or

(c) was owned at any time prior to the alienation in question and after September 26, 1980 by a person who was not a resident of that same Contracting State after September 26, 1980 while such person held the asset.

Thus, for example, in order for paragraph 9 to be availed of by a Canadian resident who did not own the alienated asset on September 26, 1980, the asset must have been owned by other Canadian residents continuously after September 26, 1980 and must have been transferred only in transactions which were non-recognition transactions for U.S. tax purposes.

The availability of the benefits of paragraph 9 is illustrated by the following examples. It should be noted that the examples do not purport to fully describe the U.S. and Canadian tax consequences resulting from the transactions described therein. Any condition for the application of paragraph 9 which is not discussed in an example should be assumed to be satisfied.

Example 1.   A, an individual resident of Canada, owned an appreciated U.S. real property interest on September 26, 1980. On January 1, 1982, A transferred the U.S. real property interest to X, a Canadian corporation, in exchange for 100 percent of X's voting stock. A's gain on the transfer to X is exempt from U.S. tax under Article VIII of the 1942 Convention. Since the transaction qualifies as a non-recognition transaction for U.S. tax purposes, as described above, X is entitled to the benefits of paragraph 9, pursuant to subparagraph 9(b), upon a subsequent disposition of the U.S. real property interest occurring after the entry into force of this Convention. If A's transfer to X had instead occurred after the entry into force of this Convention, A would be entitled to the benefits of paragraph 9, pursuant to subparagraph 9(a), with respect to U.S. taxation of that portion of the gain resulting from the transfer to X that is attributable on a monthly basis to the period ending on December 31 of the year in which the Convention enters into force (or a greater portion of the gain as is shown to the satisfaction of the U.S. competent authority). X would be entitled to the benefits of paragraph 9 pursuant to subparagraph 9(b), upon a subsequent disposition of the U.S. real property interest.

Example 2.   The facts are the same as in Example 1, except that A is a corporation which is resident in Canada. Assuming that the transfer of the U.S. real property interest to X is a section 351 transaction or a tax-free reorganization for U.S. tax purposes, the results are the same as in Example 1.

Example 3.   The facts are the same as in Example 1, except that X is a U.S. corporation. If the transfer to X by A took place on January 1, 1982, A's gain on the transfer to X would be exempt from tax under Article VIII of the 1942 Convention and A would be entitled to the benefits of paragraph 9, pursuant to subparagraph 9(b), upon a subsequent disposition of the stock of X occurring after the entry into force of this Convention. If the transfer to X by A took place after the entry into force of this Convention, A would be entitled to the benefits of paragraph 9, pursuant to subparagraph 9(a), with respect to U.S. taxation (if any) of the gain resulting from the transfer to X, and would also be entitled to the benefits of paragraph 9, pursuant to subparagraph 9(b), upon a subsequent disposition of the stock of X. For several reasons, including the fact that X is a U.S. corporation, paragraph 9 has no impact on the U.S. tax consequences of a subsequent disposition by X of the U.S. real property interest in either case.

Example 4. B, a corporation resident in Canada, owns all of the stock of C, which is also a corporation resident in Canada. C owns a U.S. real property interest. After the Convention enters into force, B liquidates C in a section 332 liquidation. The transaction is treated as a non-recognition transaction for U.S. tax purposes under the definition of a non-recognition transaction described above. C is entitled to the benefits of paragraph 9, pursuant to subparagraph 9(a), with respect to gain taxed (if any) under section 897(d), and B is entitled to the benefits of paragraph 9, pursuant to subparagraph 9(b), upon a subsequent disposition of the U.S. real property interest. Generally, the United States would not subject B to tax upon the liquidation of C.

Example 5. The facts are the same as in Example 4, except that C is a U.S. corporation. B is entitled to the benefits of paragraph 9, pursuant to subparagraph 9(a), with respect to U.S. taxation (if any) of the gain resulting from the liquidation of C. B is not entitled to the benefits of paragraph 9 upon a subsequent disposition of the U.S. real property interest since that asset was held after September 26, 1980 by a person who was not a resident of Canada. The U.S. tax consequences to C are governed by the internal law of the United States.

Example 6. D, an individual resident of the United States, owns Canadian real estate. On January 1, 1982, D transfers the Canadian real estate to E, a corporation resident in Canada, in exchange for all of E's stock. This transfer is treated as a taxable transaction under the Income Tax Act of Canada. However, D's gain on the transfer is exempt from Canadian tax under Article VIII of the 1942 Convention. D is not entitled to the benefits of subparagraph 9(b) upon a subsequent disposition of the stock of E since the stock was not transferred in a transaction which was a nonrecognition transaction for Canadian tax purposes. E is not entitled to Canadian benefits under this paragraph since, inter alia, it is a Canadian resident. (However, under Canadian law, both D and E would have a basis for tax purposes equal to the fair market value of the property at the time of D's transfer). If the transfer to E had taken place after entry into force of this Convention, D would be entitled to the benefits of paragraph 9, pursuant to subparagraph 9(a), with respect to Canadian tax resulting from the transfer to E, but would not be entitled to the benefits of subparagraph 9(b) upon a subsequent disposition of the E stock. (Note that E could seek to have the transaction treated as a non-recognition transaction under paragraph 8 of this Article, with the result that, if the competent authority agrees, D will take a carryover basis in the stock of E and be entitled to the benefits of subparagraph 9(b) upon a subsequent disposition thereof).

Example 7. The facts are the same as in Example 6, except that E is a U.S. corporation. This transaction is also a recognition event under Canadian law at the shareholder level. The results are generally the same as in Example 6. However, if the transfer to E had been granted non-recognition treatment in Canada pursuant to paragraph 8, both D and E would be entitled to the benefits of paragraph 9 for Canadian tax purposes, pursuant to subparagraph 9(b), upon subsequent dispositions of the stock of E or the Canadian real estate, respectively.

Example 8. F, an individual resident of the United States, owns all of the stock of G, a Canadian corporation, which in turn owns Canadian real estate. F causes G to be amalgamated in a merger with another Canadian corporation. This is a nonrecognition transaction under Canadian law and F is entitled, for Canadian tax purposes, to the benefits of paragraph 9, pursuant to subparagraph 9(b) upon a subsequent disposition of the stock of the other Canadian corporation.

Example 9. H, a U.S. corporation, owns all of the stock of J, another U.S. corporation. J owns Canadian real estate. H liquidates J. For Canadian tax purposes, no tax is imposed on H as a result of the liquidation and H received a fair market value basis in the Canadian real estate. Accordingly, since gain has been forgiven due to the fair market value basis (rather than postponed in a non-recognition transaction), H would not be entitled to the benefits of subparagraph 9(b) upon the subsequent disposition of the Canadian real estate. Canada would impose a tax on J, but J would be entitled to the benefits of paragraph 9, pursuant to subparagraph 9(a), with respect to Canadian tax imposed on the liquidation.

Example 10. The facts are the same as in Example 9, except that J is a Canadian corporation. Paragraph 9 does not affect the Canadian taxation of J. While H is subject to Canadian tax on the liquidation of J, H is entitled to the benefits of paragraph 9, pursuant to subparagraph 9(a), with respect to such Canadian taxation. H will take a fair market value basis (rather than have gain postponed in a non-recognition transaction) in the Canadian real estate for Canadian tax purposes and is thus not entitled to the benefits of paragraph 9 upon a subsequent disposition of the Canadian real estate (since, inter alia, the gain has been forgiven due to the fair market value basis).

Example 11. K, a U.S. corporation, owns the stock of L, another U.S. corporation, which in turn owns Canadian real estate. K causes L to be merged into another U.S. corporation. For Canadian tax purposes, such a transaction treated as a recognition event, but Canada will not impose a tax on K under its internal law. Canada would impose tax on L, but L is entitled to the benefits of paragraph 9, pursuant to subparagraph 9(a), with respect to Canadian taxation of gain resulting from the merger. The acquiring U.S. corporation would take a fair market value basis in the Canadian real estate, and would thus not be entitled to the benefits of subparagraph 9(b) upon subsequent disposition of the real estate. (Note that the acquiring U.S. corporation could seek to obtain non-recognition treatment under paragraph 8 of this Article, with the results that, if approved by the competent authority it would obtain a carryover basis in the property and be entitled to the benefits of subparagraph 9(b) upon a subsequent disposition of the Canadian real estate.)

Paragraph 9 provides that where a resident of Canada or the United States is subject to tax pursuant to Article XIII in the other Contracting State on gains from the alienation of a capital asset, and if the other conditions of paragraph 9 are satisfied, the amount of the gain shall be reduced for tax purposes in that other State by the amount of the gain attributable to the period during which the property was held up to and including December 31 of the year in which the documents of ratification are exchanged. The gain attributable to such person is normally determined by dividing the total gain by the number of full calendar months the property was held by such person, including, in the case of an alienation described in paragraph 9(b), the number of months in which a predecessor in interest held the property, and multiplying such monthly amount by the number of full calendar months ending on or before December 31 of the year in which the instruments of ratification are exchanged.

Upon a clear showing, however, a taxpayer may prove that a greater portion of the gain was attributable to the specified period. Thus, in the United States the fair market value of the alienated property at the treaty valuation date may be established under paragraph 9 in the manner and with the evidence that is generally required by U.S. Federal Income, estate, and gift tax regulations. For this purpose a taxpayer may use valid appraisal techniques for valuing real estate such as the comparable sales approach (see Rev. Proc. 79-24, 1979-1 C.B. 565) and the reproduction cost approach. If more than one property is alienated in a single transaction each property will be considered individually.

A taxpayer who desires to make this alternate showing for U.S. tax purposes must so indicate on his U.S. income tax return for the year of the sale or exchange and must attach to the return a statement describing the relevant evidence. The U.S. competent authority or his authorized delegate will determine whether the taxpayer has satisfied the requirements of paragraph 9.

The amount of gain which is reduced by reason of the application of paragraph 9 is not to be treated for U.S. tax purposes as an amount of "non-taxed gain" under section 1125(d)(2)(B) of FIRPTA, where that section would otherwise apply. (Note that gain not taxed by virtue of the 1942 Convention is "non-taxed gain".)

U.S. residents, citizens and former citizens remain subject to U.S. taxation on gains as provided by the Code notwithstanding the provisions of Article XIII, other than paragraphs 6 and 7. See paragraphs 2 and 3(a) of Article XXIX (Miscellaneous Rules).

ARTICLE XIV   Independent Personal Services

Article XIV concerns the taxation of income derived by an individual in respect of the performance of independent personal services. Such income may be taxed in the Contracting State of which such individual is a resident. It may also be taxed in the other Contracting State if the individual has or had a fixed base regularly available to him in the other State for the purpose of performing his activities, but only to the extent that the income is attributable to that fixed base. The use of the term "has or had" ensures that a Contracting State in which a fixed base existed has the right to tax income attributable to that fixed base even if there is a delay between the termination of the fixed base and the receipt or accrual of such income.

Unlike Article VII of the 1942 Convention, which provides a limited exemption from tax at source on income from independent personal services, Article XIV does not restrict the exemption to persons present in the State of source for fewer than 184 days. Furthermore, Article XIV does not allow the $5,000 exemption at source of the 1942 Convention, which was available even if services were performed through a fixed base. However, Article XIV provides complete exemption at source if a fixed base does not exist.

ARTICLE XV   Dependent Personal Services

Paragraph 1 provides that, in general, salaries, wages, and other similar remuneration derived by a resident of a Contracting State in respect of an employment are taxable only in that State unless the employment is exercised in the other Contracting State. If the employment is exercised in the other Contracting State, the entire remuneration derived therefrom may be taxed in that other State but only if, as provided by paragraph 2, the recipient is present in the other State for a period or periods exceeding 183 days in the calendar year, or the remuneration is borne by an employer who is a resident of that other State or by a permanent establishment or fixed base which the employer has in that other State. However, in all cases where the employee earns $10,000 or less in the currency of the State of source, such earnings are exempt from tax in that State. "Borne by" means allowable as a deduction in computing taxable income. Thus, if a Canadian resident individual employed at the Canadian permanent establishment of a U.S. company performs services in the United States, the income earned by the employee from such services is not exempt from U.S. tax under paragraph 1 if such income exceeds $10,000 (U.S.) because the U.S. company is entitled to a deduction for such wages in computing its taxable income.

Paragraph 3 provides that a resident of a Contracting State is exempt from tax in the other Contracting State with respect to remuneration derived in respect of an employment regularly exercised in more than one State on a ship, aircraft, motor vehicle, or train operated by a resident of the taxpayer's State of residence.

The word "regularly" is intended to distinguish crew members from persons occasionally employed on a ship, aircraft, motor vehicle, or train. Only the Contracting State of which the employee and operator are resident has the right to tax such remuneration. However, this provision is subject to the "saving clause" of paragraph 2 of Article XXIX (Miscellaneous Rules), which permits the United States to tax its citizens despite paragraph 3.

Article XV states that its provisions are overridden by the more specific rules of Article XVIII (Pensions and Annuities) and Article XIX (Government Services).

ARTICLE XVI   Artistes and Athletes

Article XVI concerns income derived by a resident of a Contracting State as an entertainer, such as a theatre, motion picture, radio, or television artiste, or a musician, or as an athlete, from his personal activities as such exercised in the other Contracting State. Article XVI overrides Articles XIV (Independent Personal Services) and XV (Dependent Personal Services) to allow source basis taxation of an entertainer or athlete in cases where the latter Articles would not permit such taxation. Thus, paragraph 1 provides that certain income of an entertainer or athlete may be taxed in the State of source in all cases where the amount of gross receipts derived by the entertainer or athlete, including expenses reimbursed to him or borne on his behalf, exceeds $15,000 in the currency of that other State for the calendar year concerned. For example, where a resident of Canada who is an entertainer derives income from his personal activities as an entertainer in the United States, he is taxable in the United States on all such income in any case where his gross receipts are greater than $15,000 for the calendar year. Article XVI does not restrict the right of the State of source to apply the provisions of Articles XIV and XV. Thus, an entertainer or athlete resident in a Contracting State and earning $14,000 in wages borne by a permanent establishment in the other State may be taxed in the other State as provided in Article XV.

Paragraph 2 provides that where income in respect of personal activities exercised by an entertainer or an athlete accrues not to the entertainer or athlete himself but to another person, that income may, notwithstanding the provisions of Article VII (Business Profits), Article XIV, and Article XV, be taxed in the Contracting State in which the activities are exercised. The anti-avoidance rule of paragraph 2 does not apply if it is established by the entertainer or athlete that neither he nor persons related to him participate directly or indirectly in the profits of the other person in any manner, including the receipt of deferred remuneration, bonuses, fees, dividends, partnership distributions, or other distributions.

Thus, if an entertainer who is a resident of Canada is under contract with a company and the arrangement between the entertainer and the company provides for payments to the entertainer based on the profits of the company, all of the income of the company attributable to the performer's U.S. activities may be taxed in the United States irrespective of whether the company maintains a permanent establishment in the United States. Paragraph 2 does not affect the rule of paragraph 1 that applies to the entertainer or athlete himself.

Paragraph 3 provides that paragraphs 1 and 2 of Article XVI do not apply to the income of an athlete in respect of an employment with a team which participates in a league with regularly scheduled games in both Canada and the United States, nor do those paragraphs apply to the income of such a team. Such an athlete is subject to the rules of Article XV. Thus, the athlete's remuneration would be exempt from tax in the Contracting State of source if he is a resident of the other Contracting State and earns $10,000 or less in the currency of the State of source, or if he is present in that State for a period or periods not exceeding in the aggregate 183 days in the calendar year, and his remuneration is not borne by a resident of that State or a permanent establishment or fixed base in that State. In addition, a team described in paragraph 3 may not be taxed in a Contracting State under paragraph 2 of this Article solely by reason of the fact that a member of the team may participate in the profits of the team through the receipt of a bonus based, for example, on ticket sales. The employer may be taxable pursuant to other articles of the Convention, such as Article VII.

Paragraph 4 provides that, notwithstanding Articles XIV and XV, an amount paid by a resident of a Contracting State to a resident of the other State as an inducement to sign an agreement relating to the performance of the services of an athlete may be taxed in the first-mentioned State. However, the tax imposed may not exceed 15 percent of the gross amount of the payment. The provision clarifies the taxation of signing bonuses in a manner consistent with their treatment under U.S. interpretations of the 1942 Convention. Amounts paid as salary or other remuneration for the performance of the athletic services themselves are not taxable under this provision but are subject to the provisions of paragraphs 1 and 3 of this Article, or Articles XIV or XV, as the case may be. The paragraph covers all amounts paid (to the athlete or another person) as an inducement to sign an agreement for the services of an athlete, such as a bonus to sign a contract not to perform for other teams. An amount described in this paragraph is not to be included in determining the amount of gross receipts derived by an athlete in a calendar year for purposes of paragraph 1. Thus, if an athlete receives a $50,000 signing bonus and a $12,000 salary for a taxable year, the State of source would not be entitled to tax the salary portion of the receipt of the athlete for that year under paragraph 1 of this Article.

ARTICLE XVII   Withholding of Taxes in Respect of Personal Services

Article XVII confirms that a Contracting State may require withholding of tax on account of tax liability with respect to remuneration paid to an individual who is a resident of the other Contracting State, including an entertainer or athlete, in respect of the performance of independent personal services in the first-mentioned State. However, withholding with respect to the first $5,000 (in the currency of the State of source) of such remuneration paid in that taxable year by each payor shall not exceed 10 percent of such payment. In the United States, the withholding described in paragraph 1 relates to withholding with respect to income tax liability and does not relate to withholding with respect to other taxes, such as social security taxes. Nor is the paragraph intended to suggest that withholding in circumstances not specifically mentioned, such as withholding with respect to dependent personal services, is precluded by the Convention.

Paragraph 2 provides that in any case where the competent authority of Canada or the United States believes that withholding with respect to remuneration for the performance of personal services is excessive in relation to the estimated tax liability of an individual to that State for a taxable year, it may determine that a lesser amount will be deducted or withheld. In the case of independent personal services, paragraph 2 may thus result in a lesser withholding than the maximum authorized by paragraph 1.

Paragraph 3 states that the provisions of Article XVII do not affect the liability of a resident of a Contracting State for taxes imposed by the other Contracting State. The Article deals only with the method of collecting taxes and not with substantive tax liability.

Article XVIII A of the 1942 Convention authorizes the issuance of regulations to specify circumstances under which residents of the United States temporarily performing personal services in Canada may be exempted from deduction and withholding of United States tax. This provision is omitted from the Convention as unnecessary. The Code and regulations provide sufficient authority to avoid excessive withholding of U.S. income tax. Further, paragraph 2 provides for adjustments in the amount of withholding where appropriate.

ARTICLE XVIII   Pensions and Annuities

Paragraph 1 provides that a resident of a Contracting State is taxable in that State with respect to pensions and annuities arising in the other Contracting State. However, the State of residence shall exempt from taxation the amount of any such pension that would be excluded from taxable income in the State of source if the recipient were a resident thereof. Thus, if a $10,000 pension payment arising in a Contracting State is paid to a resident of the Contracting State and $5,000 of such payment would be excluded from taxable income as a return of capital in the first-mentioned State if the recipient were a resident of the first-mentioned State, the State of residence shall exempt from tax $5,000 of the payment. Only $5,000 would be so exempt even if the first-mentioned State would also grant a personal allowance as a deduction from gross income if the recipient were a resident thereof. Paragraph 1 imposes no such restriction with respect to the amount that may be taxed in the State of residence in the case of annuities.

Paragraph 2 provides rules with respect to the taxation of pensions and annuities in the Contracting State in which they arise. If the beneficial owner of a periodic pension payment is a resident of the other Contracting State, the tax imposed in the State of source is limited to 15 percent of the gross amount of such payment. Thus, the State of source is not required to allow a deduction or exclusion for a return of capital to the pensioner, but its tax is limited in amount in the case of a periodic payment. Other pension payments may be taxed in the State of source without limit.

In the case of annuities beneficially owned by a resident of a Contracting State, the Contracting State of source is limited to a 15 percent tax on the portion of the payment that would not be excluded from taxable income (i.e., as a return of capital) in that State if the beneficial owner were a resident thereof.

Paragraph 3 defines the term "pensions" for purposes of the Convention to include any payment under a superannuation, pension, or retirement plan, Armed-Forces retirement pay, war veterans pensions and allowances, and amounts paid under a sickness, accident, or disability plan. Thus, the term "pension" includes pensions paid by private employers as well as any pension paid by a Contracting State in respect of services rendered to that State. A pension for government service is covered. The term "pensions" does not include payments under an income averaging annuity contact or benefits paid under social security legislation. The latter benefits are taxed, pursuant to paragraph 5, only in the Contracting State paying the benefit. Income derived from an income averaging annuity contract is taxable pursuant to the provisions of Article XXII (Other Income).

Paragraph 4 provides that, for purposes of the Convention, the term "annuities" means a stated sum paid periodically at stated times during life or during a specified number of years, under an obligation to make payments in return for adequate and full consideration other than services rendered. The term does not include a payment that is not periodic or any annuity the cost of which was deductible for tax purposes in the Contracting State where the annuity was acquired. Items excluded from the definition of "annuities" are subject to the rules of Article XXII.

Paragraph 5, as amended by the 1984 Protocol, provides that benefits under social security legislation in Canada or the United States paid to a resident of the other Contracting State are taxable only in the State in which the recipient is resident. However, the State of residence must exempt from taxation one-half of the total amount of such benefits paid in a taxable year. Thus, if U.S. social security benefits are paid to a resident of Canada, the United States will exempt such benefits from tax and Canada will exempt one-half of the benefits from taxation. The exemption of one-half of the benefits in the State of residence is an exception to the saving clause under subparagraph 3(a) of Article XXIX (Miscellaneous Rules). The United States will not exempt U.S. social security benefits from tax if the Canadian resident receiving such benefits is a U.S. citizen. If a U.S. citizen and resident receives Canadian social security benefits, Canada will not tax such benefits and the United States will exempt from tax one-half of the total amount of such benefits. The United States will also exempt one-half of Canadian social security benefits from tax if the recipient is a U.S. citizen who is a resident of Canada, under paragraph 7 of Article XXIX. Paragraph 5 encompasses benefits paid under social security legislation of a political subdivision, such as a province of Canada.

Paragraph 6(a) provides that only the State of which a person is resident has the right to tax alimony and other similar amounts (including child support payments) arising in the other Contracting State and paid to such person. However, under paragraph 6(b), the State of residence shall exempt from taxation the amount that would be excluded from taxable income in the State of source if the recipient were a resident thereof. Thus, if child support payments are made by a U.S. resident to a resident of Canada, Canada shall exempt from tax the amount of such payments which would be excluded from taxable income under section 71(b) of the Internal

Revenue Code. Paragraph 6 does not define the term "alimony"; the term is defined pursuant to the provisions of paragraph 2 of Article III (General Definitions).

Article XVIII does not provide rules to determine the State in which pensions, annuities, alimony, and other similar amounts arise. The provisions of paragraph 2 of Article III are used to determine where such amounts arise for purposes of determining whether a Contracting State has the right to tax such amounts.

Paragraphs 1, 3, 4, 5(b) and 6(b) of Article XVIII are, by reason of paragraph 3(a) of Article XXIX (Miscellaneous Rules), exceptions to the "saving clause." Thus, the rules in those paragraphs change U.S. taxation of U.S. citizens and residents.

ARTICLE XIX   Government Service

Article XIX provides that remuneration, other than a pension, paid by a Contracting State or political subdivision or local authority thereof to a citizen of that State in respect of services rendered in the discharge of governmental functions shall be taxable only in that State. (Pursuant to paragraph 5 of Article IV (Residence), other income of such a citizen may also be exempt from tax, or subject to reduced rates of tax, in the State in which he is performing services, in accordance with other provisions of the Convention.) However, if the services are rendered in connection with a trade or business, then the provisions of Article XIV (Independent Personal Services), Article XV (Dependent Personal Services), or Article XVI (Artistes and Athletes), as the case may be, are controlling. Whether functions are of a governmental nature may be determined by a comparison with the concept of a governmental function in the State in which the income arises.

Pursuant to paragraph 3(a) of Article XIX (Miscellaneous Rules), Article XIX is an exception to the "saving clause." As a result, a U.S. citizen resident in Canada and performing services in Canada in the discharge of functions of a governmental nature for the United States is taxable only in the United States on remuneration for such services.

This provision differs from the rules of Article VI of the 1942 Convention. For example, Article XIX allows the United States to impose tax on a person other than a citizen of Canada who earns remuneration paid by Canada in respect of services rendered in the discharge of governmental functions in the United States. (Such a person may, however, be entitled to an exemption from U.S. tax as provided in Code section 893.) Also, under the provisions of Article XIX Canada will not impose tax on amounts paid by the United States in respect of services rendered in the discharge of governmental functions to a U.S. citizen who is ordinarily resident in Canada for purposes other than rendering governmental services. Under paragraph 1 of Article VI of the 1942 Convention, such amounts would be taxable by Canada.

ARTICLE XX   Students

Article XX provides that a student, apprentice, or business trainee temporarily present in a Contracting State for the purpose of his full-time education or training is exempt from tax in that State with respect to amounts received from outside that

State for the purpose of his maintenance, education, or training, if the individual is or was a resident of the other Contracting State immediately before visiting the first-mentioned State. There is no limitation on the number of years or the amount of income to which the exemption applies.

The Convention does not contain provisions relating specifically to professors and teachers. Teachers are treated under the Convention pursuant to the rules established in Articles XIV (Independent Personal Services) and XV (Dependent Personal Services), in the same manner as other persons performing services. In Article VIII A of the 1942 Convention there is a 2-year exemption in the Contracting State of source in the case of a professor or teacher who is a resident of the other Contracting State.

ARTICLE XXI   Exempt Organizations

Paragraph 1 provides that a religious, scientific, literary, educational, or charitable organization resident in a Contracting State shall be exempt from tax on income arising in the other Contracting State but only to the extent that such income is exempt from taxation in the Contracting State in which the organization is resident. Since this paragraph, and the remainder of Article XXI, deal with entities that are not normally taxable, the test of "resident in" is intended to be similar - but cannot be identical - to the one outlined in paragraph 1 of Article IV (Residence). Paragraph 3 provides that paragraph 1 does not exempt from tax, income of a trust, company, or other organization from carrying on a trade or business, or income from a "related person" other than a person referred to in paragraph 1 or 2.

Paragraph 2 provides that a trust, company, or other organization that is resident in a Contracting State constituted and operated exclusively to administer or provide employee benefits or benefits for the self-employed under one or more funds or plans established to provide pension or retirement benefits or other employee benefits is exempt from taxation on dividend and interest income arising in the other Contracting State in a taxable year, if the income of such, organization is generally exempt from taxation for that year in the Contracting State in which it is resident. In addition, a trust, company, or other organization resident in a Contracting State and not taxed in a taxable year in that State shall be exempt from taxation in the other State in that year on dividend and interest income arising in that other State if it is constituted and operated exclusively to earn, income for the benefit of an organization described in the preceding sentence. Pursuant to paragraph 3 the exemption at source provided by paragraph 2 does not apply to dividends or interest from carrying on trade or business or from a "related person," other than a person referred to in paragraph 1 or 2. The term "related person" is not necessarily defined by paragraph 2 of Article IX (Related Persons).

Paragraph 4 provides an exemption from U.S. excise taxes on private foundations in the case of a religious, scientific, literary, educational, or charitable organization which is resident in Canada but only if such organization has received substantially all of its support from persons other than citizens or residents of the United States.

Paragraph 5 provides that contributions by a citizen or resident of the United States to an organization which is resident in Canada and is generally exempt from Canadian tax are treated as charitable contributions, but only if the organization could qualify in the United States to receive deductible contributions if it were resident in (i.e., organized in) the United States. Paragraph 5 generally limits the amount of contributions made deductible by the Convention to the income of the U.S. citizen or resident arising in Canada, as determined under the Convention. In the case of contributions to a college or university at which the U.S. citizen or resident or a member of his family is or was enrolled, the special limitation to income arising in Canada is not required. The percentage limitations of Code section 170 in respect of the deductibility of charitable contributions apply after the limitations established by the Convention. Any amounts treated as charitable contributions by paragraph 5 which are in excess of amounts deductible in a taxable year pursuant to paragraph 5 may be carried over and deducted in subsequent taxable years, subject to the limitations of paragraph 5.

Paragraph 6 provides rules for purposes of Canadian taxation with respect to the deductibility of gifts to a U.S. resident organization by a resident of Canada. The rules of paragraph 6 parallel the rules of paragraph 5. The current limitations in Canadian law provide that deductions for gifts to charitable organizations may not exceed 20 percent of income. Excess deductions may be carried forward for one year. The term "family" used in paragraphs 5 and 6 is defined in paragraph 2 of the Exchange of Notes accompanying the Convention to mean an individual's brothers and sisters (whether by whole or half-blood, or by adoption), spouse, ancestors, lineal descendants, and adopted descendants. Paragraph 2 of the Exchange of Notes also provides that the competent authorities of Canada and the United States will review procedures and requirements for organizations to establish their exempt status under paragraph 1 of Article XXI or as an eligible recipient of charitable contributions or gifts under paragraphs 5 and 6 of Article XXI. It is contemplated that such review will lead to the avoidance of duplicative administrative efforts in determining such status and eligibility.

The provisions of paragraph 5 and 6 generally parallel the rules of Article XIII D of the 1942 Convention. However, paragraphs 5 and 6 permit greater deductions for certain contributions to colleges and universities than do the provisions of the 1942 Convention.

ARTICLE XXII   Other Income

Paragraph 1 provides that a Contracting State of which a person is a resident has the sole right to tax items of income, wherever arising, if such income is not dealt with in the prior Articles of the Convention. If such income arises in the other Contracting State, however, it may also be taxed in that State. The determination of where income arises for this purpose is made under the domestic laws of the respective Contracting States unless the Convention specifies where the income arises (e.g., paragraph 6 of Article XI (Interest)) for purposes of determining the right to tax, in which case the provisions of the Convention control.

Paragraph 2 provides that to the extent that income distributed by an estate or trust resident in one Contracting State is deemed under the domestic law of that

State to be a separate type of income "arising" within that State, such income distributed to a beneficiary resident in the other Contracting State may be taxed in the State of source at a maximum rate of 15 percent of the gross amount of such distribution. Such a distribution will, however, be exempt from tax in the State of source to the extent that the income distributed by the estate or trust was derived by the estate or trust from sources outside that State. Thus, in a case where the law of Canada treats a distribution made by a trust resident in Canada as a separate type of income arising in Canada, Canadian tax is limited by paragraph 2 to 15 percent of the gross amount distributed to a U.S. resident beneficiary. Although the Code imposes tax on certain domestic trusts (e.g., accumulation trusts) and such trusts are residents of the United States for purposes of Article IV (Residence) and paragraph 2 of Article XXII, paragraph 2 does not apply to distributions by such trusts because, pursuant to Code sections 667(e) and 662(b), these distributions have the same character in the hands of a nonresident beneficiary as they do in the hands of the trust. Thus, a distribution by a domestic accumulation trust is not a separate type of income for U.S. purposes. The taxation of such a distribution in the United States is governed by the distribution's character, the provisions of the Code and the provisions of the Convention other than the provision in paragraph 2 limiting the tax at source to 15 percent.

ARTICLE XXIII   Capital

Although neither Canada nor the United States currently has national taxes on capital, Article XXIII provides rules for the eventuality that such taxes might be enacted in the future. Paragraph 1 provides that capital represented by real property (as defined in paragraph 2 of Article VI (Income From Real Property)) owned by a resident of a Contracting State and situated in the other Contracting State may be taxed in that other State.

Paragraph 2 provides that capital represented by either personal property forming part of the business property of a permanent establishment or personal property pertaining to a fixed base in a Contracting State may be taxed in that State.

Paragraph 3 provides that capital represented by ships and aircraft operated by a resident of a Contracting State in international traffic and by personal property pertaining to the operation of such ships and aircraft are taxable only in the Contracting State of residence.

Paragraph 4 provides that all elements of capital other than those covered by paragraphs 1,2, and 3 are taxable only in the Contracting State of residence. Thus, capital represented by motor vehicles or railway cars, not pertaining to a permanent establishment or fixed base in a Contracting State, would be taxable only in the Contracting State of which the taxpayer is a resident.

ARTICLE XXIV   Elimination of Double Taxation

Paragraph 1 provides the general rules that will apply under the Convention with respect to foreign tax credits for Canadian taxes paid or accrued. The United States undertakes to allow to a citizen or resident of the United States, or to a company electing under Code section 1504(d) to be treated as a domestic corporation, a credit against the Federal income taxes imposed by the Code for the appropriate amount of income tax paid or accrued to Canada. In the case of a company which is a resident of the United States owning 10 percent or more of the voting stock of a company which is a resident of Canada (which for this purpose does not include a company electing under Code section 1504(d) to be treated as a domestic corporation), and from which it receives dividends in a taxable year, the United States shall allow as a credit against income taxes imposed by the Code the appropriate amount of income tax paid or accrued to Canada by the Canadian company with respect to the profits out of which such company paid the dividends.

The direct and deemed-paid credits allowed by paragraph 1 are subject to the limitations of the Code as they may be amended from time to time without changing the general principle of paragraph 1. Thus, as is generally the case under U.S. income tax conventions, provisions such as Code sections 901(c), 904, 905, 907, 908, and 911 apply for purposes of computing the allowable credit under paragraph 1. In addition, the United States is not required to maintain the overall limitation currently provided by U.S. law.

The term "income tax paid or accrued" is defined in paragraph 7 of Article XXIV to include certain specified taxes which are paid or accrued. The Convention only provides a credit for amounts paid or accrued. The determination of whether an amount is paid or accrued is made under the Code. Paragraph 1 provides a credit for these specified taxes whether or not they qualify as creditable under Code section 901 or 903. A taxpayer who claims credit under the Convention for Canadian taxes made creditable solely by paragraph 1 is not, as a result of the Protocol, subject to a per-country limitation with respect to Canadian taxes. Thus, credit for such Canadian taxes would be computed under the overall limitation currently provided by U.S. law. (However, see the discussion below of the source rules of paragraphs 3 and 9 for a restriction on the use of third country taxes to offset the U.S. tax imposed on resourced income.)

A taxpayer claiming credits for Canadian taxes under the Convention must apply the source rules of the Convention, and must apply those source rules in their entirety. Similarly, a taxpayer claiming credit for Canadian taxes which are creditable under the Code and who wishes to use the source rules of the Convention in computing that credit must apply the source rules of the Convention in their entirety.

Paragraph 3 provides source rules for purposes of applying Article XXIV. Profits, income or gains of a resident of a Contracting State which may be taxed in the other Contracting State in accordance with the Convention, for reasons other than the saving clause of paragraph 2 of Article XXIX (Miscellaneous Rules) (e.g., pensions and annuities taxable where arising pursuant to Article XVIII (Pensions and Annuities)), are deemed to arise in the latter State. This rule does not, however, apply to gains taxable under paragraph 5 of Article XIII (Gains) (i.e., gains taxed by a Contracting State derived from the alienation of property by a former resident of that State). Gains from such an alienation arise, pursuant to paragraph 3(b), in the State of which the alienator is a resident. Thus, if in accordance with paragraph 5 of Article XIII, Canada imposes tax on certain gains of a U.S. resident such gains are deemed, pursuant to paragraphs 2 and 3(b) of

Article XXIV, to arise in the United States for purposes of computing the deduction against Canadian tax for the U.S. tax on such gain. Under the Convention such gains arise in the United States for purposes of the United States foreign tax credit. Paragraph 3(b) also provides that profits, income, or gains arise in the Contracting State of which a person is a resident if they may not be taxed in the other Contracting State under the provisions of the Convention (e.g., alimony), other than the "saving clause" of paragraph 2 of Article XXIX.

Paragraph 9 provides clarification that the source rules of this Article shall not be used to determine the credit available against U.S. tax for foreign taxes other than income taxes paid or accrued to Canada (i.e., taxes of third countries). Thus, creditable third country taxes may not offset the U.S. tax on income treated as arising in Canada under the source rules of the Convention. A person claiming credit for income taxes of a third country may not rely upon the rules of paragraphs 3 and 6 for purposes of treating income that would otherwise have a U.S. source as having a foreign source. Thus, if the taxpayer elects to compute the foreign tax credit for any year using the special source rules set forth in paragraphs 3 and 6, paragraph 9 requires that a separate limitation be computed for taxes not covered by paragraph 1 without regard to the source rules of paragraphs 3 and 6, and the credit for such taxes may not exceed such limitation. The credit allowed under this separate limitation may not exceed the proportion of the Federal income taxes imposed by the Code that the taxpayer's taxable income from foreign sources (under the Code) not included in taxable income arising in Canada (and not in excess of total foreign source taxable income under the Code) bears to the taxpayer's worldwide taxable income. In any case the credit for taxes covered by paragraph 1 and the credit for other foreign taxes is limited to the amount allowed under overall limitation computed by aggregating taxable income arising in Canada and other foreign source taxable income.

If creditable Canadian taxes exceed the proportion of U.S. tax that taxable income arising in Canada bears to the entire taxable income, such taxes may qualify to be absorbed by any excess in the separate limitation computed with respect to other taxes.

In a case where a taxpayer has different types of income subject to separate limitations under the Code (e.g., section 904(d)(l)(B) DISC dividends) the Convention rules just described apply in the context of each of the separate Code limitations.

A taxpayer may, for any year, claim a credit pursuant to the rules of the Code. In such case, the taxpayer would be subject to the limitations established in the Code, and would forego the rules of the Convention that determine where taxable income arises. In addition, any Canadian taxes covered by paragraph 1 which are not creditable under the Code would not be credited. Thus, where a taxpayer elects to use the special source rules of this Article to compute the foreign tax credit for any year, the following computations must be made:

Step 1(a): Compute a hypothetical foreign tax credit limitation for Canadian income and taxes using the source rules of the Convention.

Step 1(b): Compute a hypothetical foreign tax credit limitation for third country income and taxes using the source rules of the Code.

Step 1(c): Compute an overall foreign tax credit limitation using the source rules of the Convention to the extent they resource Canadian source income as U.S. source income or U.S. source income as Canadian source income, and using the source rules of the Code with respect to any other income.

Step 2: Allocate the amount of creditable Canadian taxes to the amount of the limitation computed under step 1(a), and allocate the amount of creditable third country taxes to the amount of the limitation computed under step 1(b). The amount of credit to be so allocated may not exceed the amount of the respective limitation.

Step 3:

(1) If the total credits allocated under step 2 exceed the amount of the limitation computed under step 1(c), the amount of allowable credits must be reduced to that limitation (see Rev. Rule. 82-215, 1982-2 C.B. 153 for the method of such reduction).

(2) If the total credits allocated under step 2 are less than the amount of the limitation computed under step 1(c), then

(a) any amount of creditable Canadian taxes in excess of the amount of the step 1(a) limitation may be credited to the extent of the excess of the step 1(c) limitation over the total step 2 allocation, and

(b) any amount of third country taxes in excess of the amount of the step 1(b) limitation may not be credited.

The following examples (in which the taxpayer's U.S. tax rate is presumed to be 46%) illustrate the application of the source rules of Article XXIV:

Example 1.

(a) A U.S. corporate taxpayer has for the taxable year $100 of taxable income having a U.S. source under both the Convention and the Code; $100 of taxable income having a Canadian source under both the Convention and the Code; $50 of taxable income having a Canadian source under the Convention but a U.S. source under the Code (see, for example, paragraph 1 of Article VII (Business Profits) and paragraph 3(a) of Article XXIV); and $80 of taxable income having a foreign (non-Canadian) source under the Code. The taxpayer pays $75 of Canadian income taxes and $45 of third country income taxes. All the foreign source income of the taxpayer constitutes "other" income described in Code section 904(d)(l)(C).

The source rules of the Convention are applied as follows to compute the taxpayer's foreign tax credit:

Step 1(a):

$$\frac{\$150 \text{ (Canadian source taxable income under convention)}}{\$330 \text{ (total taxable income)}}$$
x $151.80 = $69 limit for Canadian taxes.

Step 1(b):

$$\frac{\$ 80 \text{ (third country source taxable income under Code)}}{\$330 \text{ (total taxable income)}}$$
x $151.80 = $36.80 limit for third country taxes.

Step 1(c):

$$\frac{\$230 \text{ (overall foreign taxable income under source rules described above)}}{\$330 \text{ (total taxable income)}}$$
x $151.80 = $105.80 total limit.

Step 2: The taxpayer may tentatively credit $69 of the $75 Canadian income taxes under the step 1(a) limitation, and $36.80 of the third country income taxes under the step 1(b) limitation.

Step 3: Since the total amount of taxes credited under step 2 equals the taxpayer's total limitation of $105.80 under step 1(c), no additional taxes may be credited. The taxpayer has a $6 Canadian income tax carryover and a $8.20 third country income tax carryover for U.S. foreign tax credit purposes.

(b) If the taxpayer had paid only $30 of third country taxes, he would credit that $30 in step 2. Since the total amount of credits allowed under step 2 ($99) is less than the taxpayer's total limit of $105.80, and since the taxpayer has $6 of excess Canadian taxes not credited under step 2, he may also claim a credit for that $6 of Canadian income taxes, for a total credit of $105.

(c) If the taxpayer had paid $45 of third country income taxes and $65 of Canadian income taxes, the computation would be as follows:

Step 2: The taxpayer would credit the $65 of Canadian income taxes, and would also credit $36.80 of the $45 of third country income taxes.

Step 3: Although the total amount of credits computed under step 2 ($101.80) is less than the taxpayer's total limitation of $105.80, no additional credits can be claimed since the taxpayer has only excess third country income taxes. The excess third country income taxes are thus not permitted to offset U.S. tax on income that is Canadian source income under the Convention. The taxpayer would have $8.20 of third country income taxes as a carryover for U.S. foreign tax credit purposes.

Example 2.

A United States corporate taxpayer has for the taxable year $100 of taxable income having a Canadian source under the Convention but a U.S. source under the Code; $100 of taxable income having a U.S. source under both the Convention and the Code; $80 of taxable income having a foreign (non-Canadian) source under the Code; and ($50) of loss allocated or apportioned to Canadian source income. The taxpayer pays $50 of foreign (non-Canadian) income taxes, and $20 of Canadian income taxes.

The source rules of the Convention are applied as follows to compute the taxpayer's foreign tax credit:

Step 1(a): $\dfrac{\$\ 50\ \text{(Canadian source taxable income under Contention)}}{\$230\ \text{(total taxable income)}}$

x $105.80 = $23 limit for Canadian taxes.

Step 1(b): $\dfrac{\$\ 80\ \text{(third country source taxable income under Code)}}{\$230\ \text{(total taxable income)}}$

x $105.80 = $36.80 limit for third country taxes.

Step 1(c): $\dfrac{\$130\ \text{(overall foreign taxable income under source rules described above)}}{\$230\ \text{(total taxable income)}}$

x $105.80 = $59.80 total limit.

Step 2: Since the taxpayer paid $20 of Canadian income taxes, he may credit that amount in full since the step 1(a) limit is $23. Since the step 1(b) limit is $36.80, the taxpayer may credit $36.80 of the $50 foreign income taxes paid.

Step 3: Although the total taxes credited under step 2 ($56.80) is less than the taxpayer's total limit of $59.80, no additional credits may be claimed since the only excess taxes are third country income taxes, and those may not be used to offset any excess limitation in step 3. The $13.20 of foreign taxes not allowed as a credit is available as a foreign tax credit carryover.

Example 3:

The facts are the same as in Example 2, except that foreign (non-Canadian) operations result in a loss of ($30) rather than taxable income of $80, and no foreign (non-Canadian) income taxes are paid. The taxpayer's credit is computed as follows:

Step 1(a): $\dfrac{\$\ 50}{\$120}$ x $55.20 = $23 limit for Canadian taxes.

Step 1(b):   Since there is no third country source taxable income under the Code, the limit for third country income taxes is zero.

Step 1(c): $\dfrac{\$\ 20}{\$120}$ x $55.20 = $9.20 total limit.

Step 2: Since the taxpayer paid $20 of Canadian income tax, he may tentatively credit that amount in full since the step 1(a) limit is $23.

Step 3: Since the total taxes credited under step 2 ($20) exceeds the taxpayer's total limit of $9.20, the taxpayer must reduce the total amount claimed as a credit of $9.20. The remaining $10.80 of Canadian income taxes are available as a foreign tax credit carryover.

Example 4.

The facts are the same as in Example 2, except that the first $100 of taxable income mentioned in Example 2 has a Canadian source under both the Convention and the Code.

Step 1(a): $\dfrac{\$\ 50}{\$120}$ x $105.80 = $23 limit for Canadian taxes.

Step 1(b): $\dfrac{\$\ 80}{\$120}$ x $105.80 = $36.80 limit for third country income taxes.

Step 1(c): $\dfrac{\$130}{\$230}$ x $105.80 = $59.80 total limit.

Step 2: The taxpayer credits the $20 of Canadian income tax and $36.80 of third country income tax.

Step 3: As explained in Example 2, the taxpayer's total credit is limited to $56.80. In this case, however, if the Canadian taxes covered by the Convention are creditable under the Code, the taxpayer could elect the Code limitation of

$$\$59.80\ (\dfrac{\$130}{\$230} \text{ x } \$105.80),$$

which is more advantageous than the Convention limitation because that limitation does not permit third country income taxes to be credited against the U.S. tax on income arising in Canada under the Convention.

Example 5.

The facts are the same as in Example 2, except that the corporation pays $25 of Canadian income taxes and $12 of foreign (non-Canadian) income taxes. Under step 2, the taxpayer would credit $23 of the $25 of Canadian income taxes and the full $12 of third country income taxes. Since the total amount of income taxes credited under step 2 is $35, which is less than the taxpayer's total limit of $59.80, the taxpayer may credit an amount of Canadian income taxes up to the $24.80

excess. Here, the taxpayer may claim a credit for the additional $2 of Canadian income taxes not credited under step 2, and has a total credit of $37.

Example 6.

(a) A U.S. corporate taxpayer has for the taxable year $100 of taxable income having a Canadian source under the Convention and the Code; $50 of taxable income having a Canadian source under the Convention but a U.S. source under the Code; $80 of taxable income having a foreign (non-Canadian) source under the Code; and ($50) of loss allocated or apportioned to U.S. source income. The taxpayer pays $65 of Canadian income taxes, and $45 of third country income taxes.

Step 1(a): $\dfrac{\$150}{\$180}$ x $82.80 = $69 limit for Canadian income taxes.

Step 1(b): $\dfrac{\$\ 80}{\$180}$ x $82.80 = $36.80 limit for third country income taxes.

Step 1(c): $\dfrac{\$180}{\$180}$ x $82.80 = $82.80 total limit.

Step 2: The taxpayer tentatively credits the $65 of Canadian income taxes against the $69 limit of step 1(a), and $36.80 of the $45 of third country income taxes against the $36.80 limit of step 1(b).

Step 3: Since the total amount of credits tentatively allowed under step 2 ($101.80) exceeds the taxpayer's total limit of $82.80 under step 1(c), the taxpayer's allowable credit is reduced to $82.80 under the method provided by Rev. Rul. 82-215.

(b) If the taxpayer had paid only $40 of Canadian income taxes, the total credits tentatively allowed under step 2 is $76.80. Although that amount is less than the $82.80 total limit under step 1(c), no additional taxes may be credited since the taxpayer only has excess third country income taxes. The $8.20 of excess third country income taxes would be allowed as a foreign tax credit carryover.

The general rule for avoiding double taxation in Canada is provided in paragraph 2. Pursuant to paragraph 2(a) Canada undertakes to allow to a resident of Canada a credit against income taxes imposed under the Income Tax Act for the appropriate amount of income taxes paid or accrued to the United States. Paragraph 2(b) provides for the deduction by a Canadian company, in computing taxable income, of any dividend received out of the exempt surplus of a U.S. company which is an affiliate. The provisions of paragraphs 2(a) and (b) are subject to the provisions of the Income Tax Act as they may be amended from time to time without changing the general principle of paragraph 2. Paragraph 2(c) provides that where Canada imposes a tax on the alienation of property pursuant to the provisions of paragraph 5 of Article XIII (Gains), Canada will allow a credit for the income tax paid or accrued to the United States on such gain.

The rules of paragraph 1 are modified in certain respects by rules in paragraphs 4 and 5 for income derived by United States citizens who are residents of Canada. Paragraph 4 provides two steps for the elimination of double taxation in such a case. First, paragraph 4(a) provides that Canada shall allow a deduction from (credit against) Canadian tax in respect of income tax paid or accrued to the United States in respect of profits, income, or gains which arise in the United States (within the meaning of paragraph 3(a)); the deduction against Canadian tax need not, however, exceed the amount of income tax that would be paid or accrued to the United States if the individual were not a U.S. citizen, after taking into account any relief available under the Convention.

The second step, as provided in paragraph 4(b), is that the United States allows as a credit against United States tax, subject to the rules of paragraph 1, the income tax paid or accrued to Canada after the Canadian credit for U.S. tax provided by paragraph 4(a). The credit so allowed by the United States is not to reduce the portion of the United States tax that is creditable against Canadian tax in accordance with paragraph 4(a).

The following example illustrates the application of paragraph 4.

Example A

— A U.S. citizen who is a resident of Canada earns $175 of income from the performance of independent personal services, of which $100 is derived from services performed in Canada and $75 from services performed in the United States. That is his total world-wide income.

If he were not a U.S. citizen, the United States could tax $75 of that amount under Article XIV (Independent Personal Services). By reason of paragraph 3(a), the $75 that may be taxed by the United States under Article XIV is deemed to arise in the United States. Assume that the U.S. tax on the $75 would be $25 if the taxpayer were not a U.S. citizen.

— However, since the individual is a U. S. citizen, he is subject to U.S. tax on his worldwide income of $175. After excluding $75 under section 911, his taxable income is $100 and his U.S. tax is $40.

— Because he is a resident of Canada, he is also subject to Canadian tax on his world-wide income. Assume that Canada taxes the $175 at $75.

— Canada will credit against its tax of $75 the U.S. tax at source of $25, leaving a net Canadian tax of $50.

— The United States will credit against its tax of $40 the Canadian tax net of credit, but without reducing its source basis tax of $25; thus, the allowable credit is $40 - $25 = $15.

— To use a credit of $15 requires Canadian source taxable income of $37.50 ($37.50/$100 x $40 = $15). Without any special treaty rule, Canadian source taxable income would be only $25 ($100 less the section 911 exclusion of $75). Paragraph 6 provides for resourcing an additional $12.50 of income to Canada, so that the credit of $15 can be fully used.

Paragraph 5 provides special rules for the elimination of double taxation in the case of dividends, interest, and royalties earned by a U.S. citizen resident in Canada. These rules apply notwithstanding the provisions of paragraph 4, but only as long as the law in Canada allows a deduction in computing income for the portion of any foreign tax paid in respect of dividends, interest, or royalties which exceeds 15 percent of the amount of such items of income, and only with respect to those items of income. The rules of paragraph 4 apply with respect to other items of income; moreover, if the law in force in Canada regarding the deduction for foreign taxes changes, the provisions of paragraph 5 shall not apply and the U.S. foreign tax credit for Canadian taxes and the Canadian credit for U.S. taxes will be determined solely pursuant to the provisions of paragraph 4.

The calculations under paragraph 5 are as follows. First, the deduction allowed in Canada in computing income shall be made with respect to U.S. tax on the dividends, interest and royalties before any foreign tax credit by the United States with respect to income taxes paid or accrued to Canada. Second, Canada shall allow a deduction from (credit against) Canadian tax for U.S. tax paid or accrued with respect to the dividends, interest, royalties, but such credit need not exceed 15 percent of the gross amount of such items income that have been included in computed income for Canadian tax purposes. (The credit may, however, exceed the amount of tax that the United States would be entitled to levy under the Convention upon a Canadian resident who is not a U.S. citizen.) Third, for purposes of computing the U.S. tax on such dividends, interest, and royalties, the United States shall allow as a credit against the U.S. tax the income tax paid or accrued to Canada after the 15 percent credit against Canadian tax for income tax paid or accrued to the United States. The United States is in no event obliged to give a credit for Canadian income tax which will reduce the U.S. tax below 15 percent of the amount of the dividends, interest, and royalties.

The rules of paragraph 5 are illustrated by the following examples.

Example B

— A U.S. citizen who is a resident of Canada has $100 of royalty income arising in the United States. The tentative U.S. tax before foreign tax credit is $40.

— Canada, under its law, allows a deduction for the U.S. tax in excess of 15 percent or, in this case, a deduction of $25 ($40 - $15). The Canadian taxable income is $75 and the Canadian tax on that amount is $35.

— Canada gives a credit of $15 (the maximum credit allowed is 15 percent of the gross royalty taken into Canadian income) and collects a net tax of $20.

— The United States allows a credit for the net Canadian tax against its tax in excess of 15 percent. Thus, the maximum credit is $25 ($40 - $15). But since the net Canadian tax paid was $20, the usable credit is $20.

— To be able to use a credit of $20 requires Canadian source taxable income of $50 (50% of the U.S. tentative tax of $40). Under paragraph 6, $50 of the U.S. royalty is resourced to be of Canadian source. The credit of $20 may then be offset against the U.S. tax of $40, leaving a net U.S. tax of $20.

— The combined tax paid to both countries is $40, $20 to Canada and $20 to the United States.

Example C

A U.S. citizen who is a resident of Canada receives $200 of income with respect to personal services performed within Canada and $100 of royalty income arising within the United States. Taxable income for U.S. purposes, taking into account the rules of Code section 911, is $220. U.S. tax (before foreign tax credits) is $92. The $100 of royalty income is deemed to bear U.S. tax (before foreign tax credits) of $41.82

$$\frac{(\$100 \times \$92).}{\$220}$$

Under Canadian law, a deduction of $26.82 (the excess of $41.82 over 15 percent of the $100 royalty income) is allowed in computing income. The Canadian tax on $273.18 of income ($300 less the $26.82 deduction) is $130. Canada then gives a credit against the $130 for $15 (the U.S. tax paid or accrued with respect to the royalty, $41.82, but limited to 15 percent of the gross amount of such income, or $15), leaving a final Canadian tax of $115. Of the $115, $30.80 is attributable to the royalty

$$\frac{(\$\ 73.18\ (\$100\ royalty\ less\ \$26.82\ deduction\ x\ \$115.}{(\$273.18\ (\$300\ income\ less\ \$26.82\ deduction)}$$

Of this amount, $26.82 is creditable against U.S. tax pursuant to paragraph 5. (Although the U.S. allows a credit for the Canadian tax imposed on the royalty, $30.80, the credit may not reduce the U.S. tax below 15 percent of the amount of the royalty. Thus, the maximum allowable credit is the excess of $41.82, the U.S. tax imposed on the royalty income, over $15, which is 15 percent of the $100 royalty). The remaining $3.98 (the Canadian tax of $30.80 less the credit allowed of $26.82) is a foreign tax credit carryover for U.S. purposes, subject to the limitations of paragraph 5. (An additional $50.18 of Canadian tax with respect to Canadian source services income is creditable against U.S. tax pursuant to paragraphs 3 and 4(b). The $50.18 is computed as follows: tentative U.S. tax (before foreign tax credits) is $92; the U.S. tax on Canadian source services income is $50.18 ($92 less the U.S. tax on the royalty income of $41.82); the limitation on the services income is:

$$\frac{\$120\ (taxable\ income\ from\ services)\ x\ \$92.}{\$220\ (total\ taxable\ income)}$$

or $50.18. The credit for Canadian tax paid on the services income is therefore $50.18; the remainder of the Canadian tax on the services income, or $34.02, is a foreign tax credit carryover for U.S. purposes, subject to the limitations of paragraph 5).

Paragraph 6 is necessary to implement the objectives of paragraphs 4(b) and 5(c). Paragraph 6 provides that where a U.S. citizen is a resident of Canada, items of income referred to in paragraph 4 or 5 are deemed for the purposes of Article XXIV to arise in Canada to the extent necessary to avoid double taxation of income by Canada and the United States consistent with the objectives of paragraphs 4(b) and 5(c). Paragraph 6 can override the source rules of paragraph 3 to permit a limited resourcing of income. The principles of paragraph 6 have effect, pursuant to paragraph 3(b) of Article XXX (Entry Into Force), for taxable years beginning on or after January 1, 1976. See the discussion of Article XXX below.

The application of paragraph 6 is illustrated by the following example.

Example D

The facts are the same as in Example C. The United States has undertaken, pursuant to paragraph 5(c) and paragraph 6, to credit $26.82 of Canadian taxes on royalty income that has a U.S. source under both paragraph 3 and the Internal Revenue Code. (As illustrated in Example C, the credit, however, only reduces the U.S. tax on the royalty income which exceeds 15 percent of the amount of such income included in computing U.S. taxable income.) Pursuant to paragraph 6, for purposes of determining the U.S. foreign tax credit limitation under the Convention with respect to Canadian taxes,

$$\$ 64.13 \left(\frac{A}{\$220} \times \$92 = \$26.82; A = \$64.13 \right)$$

of taxable income with respect to the royalties is deemed to arise in Canada.

Paragraph 7 provides that any reference to "income tax paid or accrued" to Canada or the United States includes Canadian tax or United States tax, as the case may be. The terms "Canadian tax" and "United States tax" are defined in paragraphs 1(c) and 1(d) of Article III (General Definitions). References to income taxes paid or accrued also include taxes of general application paid or accrued to a political subdivision or local authority of Canada or the United States which are not imposed by such political subdivision or local authority in a manner inconsistent with the provisions of the Convention and which are substantially similar to taxes of Canada or the United States referred to in paragraphs 2 and 3(a) of Article II (Taxes Covered).

In order for a tax imposed by a political subdivision or local authority to fall within the scope of paragraph 7, such tax must apply to individuals, companies, or other persons generally, and not only to a particular class of individuals or companies or a particular type of business. The tax must also be substantially similar to the national taxes referred to in paragraphs 2 and 3(a) of Article II. Finally, the political subdivision or local authority must apply its tax in a manner not inconsistent with the provisions of the Convention. For example, the political subdivision or local authority must not impose its tax on a resident of the other Contracting State earning business profits within the political subdivision or local authority but not having a permanent establishment there. It is understood that a Canadian provincial income tax that satisfied the conditions of paragraph 7 on

September 26, 1980 also satisfied the conditions of that paragraph on June 14, 1983 — i.e., no significant changes have occurred in the taxes imposed by Canadian provinces.

Paragraph 8 relates to the provisions of Article XXIII (Capital). It provides that where a resident of a Contracting State owns capital which, in accordance with the provisions of Article XXIII, may be taxed in the other Contracting State, the State of residence shall allow as a deduction from (credit against) its tax on capital an amount equal to the capital tax paid in the other Contracting State. The deduction is not, however, to exceed that part of the capital tax, computed before the deduction, which is attributable to capital which may be taxed in the other State.

ARTICLE XXV   Non-Discrimination

Paragraphs 1 and 2 of Article XXV protect individual citizens of a Contracting State from discrimination by the other Contracting State in taxation matters. Paragraph 1 provides that a citizen of a Contracting State who is a resident of the other Contacting State may not be subjected in that other State to any taxation or requirement connected with taxation which is other or more burdensome than the taxation and connected requirements imposed on similarly situated citizens of the other State.

Paragraph 2 assures protection in a case where a citizen of a Contracting State is not a resident of the other Contracting State. Such a citizen may not be subjected in the other State to any taxation or requirement connected to taxation which is other or more burdensome than the taxation and connected requirements to which similarly situated citizens of any third State are subjected. The reference to citizens of a third State "in the same circumstances" includes consideration of the State of residence. Thus, pursuant to paragraph 2, the Canadian taxation with respect to a citizen of the United States resident in, for example, the United Kingdom may not be more burdensome than the taxation of a U.K. citizen resident in the United Kingdom. Any benefits available to the U.K. citizen by virtue of an income tax convention between the United Kingdom and Canada would be available to the U.S. citizen resident in the United Kingdom if he is otherwise in the same circumstances as the U.K. citizen.

Paragraph 3 assures that, in computing taxable income, an individual resident of a Contracting State will be entitled to the same deduction for dependents resident in the other Contracting State that would be allowed if the dependents were residents of the individual's State of residence. The term "dependent" is defined in accordance with the rules set forth in paragraph 2 of Article III (General Definitions). For U.S. tax purposes, paragraph 3 does not expand the benefits currently available to a resident of the United States with a dependent resident in Canada. See Code section 152(b)(3).

Paragraph 4 allows a resident of Canada (not a citizen of the United States) to file a joint return in cases where such person earns salary, wages, or other similar remuneration as an employee and such income is taxable in the United States under the Convention. Paragraph 4 does not apply where the resident of Canada earns wages which are exempt in the United States under Article XV (Dependent Personal Services) or earns only income taxable by the United States under provisions of the Convention other than Article XV.

The benefit provided by paragraph 4 is available regardless of the residence of the taxpayer's spouse. It is limited, however, by a formula designed to ensure that the benefit is available solely with respect to persons whose U.S. source income is entirely, or almost entirely, wage income. The formula limits the United States tax with respect to wage income to that portion of the total U.S. tax that would be payable for the taxable year if both the individual and his spouse were United States citizens as the individual's taxable income (determined without any of the benefits made available by paragraph 4, such as the standard deduction) bears to the total taxable income of the individual and his spouse. The term "total United States tax" used in the formula is total United States tax without regard to any foreign tax credits, as provided in subparagraph 4(a). (Foreign income taxes may, however, be claimed as deductions in computing taxable income, to the extent allowed by the Code.) In determining total taxable income of the individual and his spouse, the benefits made available by paragraph 4 are taken into account, but a deficit of the spouse is not.

The following example illustrates the application of paragraph 4.

A, a Canadian citizen and resident, is married to B who is also a Canadian citizen and resident. A earns $12,000 of wages taxable in the U.S. under Article XV (Dependent Personal Services) and $2,000 of wages taxable only in Canada. B earns $1,000 of U.S. source dividend income, taxed by the United States at 15 percent pursuant to Article X (Dividends). B also earns $2,000 of wages taxable only in Canada. A's taxable income for U.S. Pu poses, determined without regard to paragraph 4, is $11,700 ($12,000 - $2,000 (Code sections 151(b) and 873(b)(3)) + $1,700 (Code sections 63)). The U.S. tax (Code section 1(d)) with respect to such income is $2,084.50. The total U.S. tax payable by A and B if both were U.S. citizens and all their income arose in the United States would be $2,013 under Code section 1(a) on taxable income of $14,800 ($17,000 - $200 (Code section 116) - $2,000 (Code section 151)). Pursuant to paragraph 4, the U.S. tax imposed on A's wages from U.S. sources is limited to B's U.S. tax liability with respect to the U.S. source dividends remains $150.

$$\$1,591.36 \ (\underline{\$11,700} \times \$2,013).$$
$$\$14,800$$

The provisions of paragraph 4 may be elected on a year-by-year basis They are purely computational and do not make either or both spouses residents of the United States for the purpose of other U.S. income tax conventions. The rules relating to the election provided by U.S. law under Code section 6013(g)(see section 1.6013-6 of the Treasury Regulations) do not apply to the election described in this paragraph.

Paragraph 5 protects against discrimination in a case where the capital of a company which is a resident of one Contracting State is wholly or partly owned or controlled, directly or indirectly, by one or more residents of the other Contracting State. Such a company shall not be subjected in the State of which it is a resident to any taxation or requirement connected therewith which is other or more burdensome than the taxation and connected requirements to which are subjected to other similar companies which are residents of that State but whose capital is wholly or partly owned or controlled, directly or indirectly, by one or more residents of a third State.

Paragraph 6 protects against discrimination in the case of a permanent establishment which a resident of one Contracting State has in the other Contracting State. The taxation of such a permanent establishment by the other Contracting State shall not be less favorable than the taxation of residents of that other State carrying on the same activities. The paragraph specifically overrides the provisions of Article XXIV (Elimination of Double Taxation), thus ensuring that permanent establishments will be entitled to relief from double taxation on a basis comparable to the relief, afforded to similarly situated residents. Paragraph 6 does not oblige a Contracting State to grant to a residents of the other Contracting State any personal allowances, reliefs, and reductions for taxation purposes on account of civil status or family responsibilities which it grants to its own residents. In addition, paragraph 6 does not require a Contracting State to grant to a company which is a resident of the other Contracting State the same tax relief that it grants to companies which are resident in the first-mentioned State with respect to intercorporate dividends. This provision is merely clarifying in nature, since neither the United States nor Canada would interpret paragraph 6 to provide for granting the same relief in the absence of a specific denial thereof. The principles of paragraph 6 would apply with respect to a fixed base as well as a permanent establishment. Paragraph 6 does not, however, override the provisions of Code section 906.

Paragraph 7 concerns the right of a resident of a Contracting State to claim deductions for purposes of computing taxable profits in the case of disbursements made to a resident of the other Contracting State. Such disbursements shall be deductible under the same conditions as if they had been made to a resident of the first-mentioned State. Thus, this paragraph does not require Canada to permit a deduction to a Canadian trust for disbursements made to a nonresident beneficiary out of income derived from a business in Canada or Canadian real property; granting such a deduction would result in complete exemption by Canada of such income and would put Canadian trusts with nonresident beneficiaries in a better position than if they had resident beneficiaries. These provisions do not apply to amounts to which paragraph 1 of Article IX (Related Persons), paragraph 7 of Article XI (Interest), or paragraph 7 of Article XII (Royalties) apply. Paragraph 7 of Article XXV also provides that, for purposes of determining the taxable capital of a resident of a Contracting State, any debts of such person to a resident of the other Contracting State shall be deductible under the same conditions as if they had been contracted to a resident of the first-mentioned State. This portion of paragraph 7 relates to Article XXIII (Capital).

Paragraph 8 provides that, notwithstanding the provisions of paragraph 7, a Contracting State may enforce the provisions of its taxation laws relating to the deductibility of interest, in force on September 26, 1980, or as modified subsequent to that date in a manner that does not change the general nature of the provisions in force on September 26, 1980; or which are adopted after September 26, 1980, and are designed to ensure that nonresidents do not enjoy a more favorable tax treatment under the taxation laws of that State than that enjoyed by residents. Thus Canada may continue to limit the deductions for interest paid to certain nonresidents as provided in section 18(4) of Part 1 of the Income Tax Act.

Paragraph 9 provides that expenses incurred by citizens or residents of a Contracting State with respect to any Convention, including any seminar, meeting, congress, or other function of similar nature, held in the other Contracting State, are deductible for purposes of taxation in the first-mentioned State to the same extent that such expenses would be deductible if the convention were held in that first-mentioned State. Thus, for U.S. income tax purposes an individual who is a citizen or resident of the United States and who attends a convention held in Canada may claim deductions for expenses incurred in connection with such convention without regard to the provisions of Code section 274(h). Section 274(h) imposes special restrictions on the deductibility of expenses incurred in connection with foreign conventions. A claim for a deduction for such an expense remains subject, in all events, to the provisions of U.S. law with respect to the deductibility of convention expenses generally (e.g., Code sections 162 and 212). Similarly, in the case of a citizen or resident of Canada attending a convention in the United States, paragraph 9 requires Canada to allow a deduction for expenses relating to such convention as if the convention had taken place in Canada.

Paragraph 10 provides that, notwithstanding the provisions of Article II (Taxes Covered), the provisions of Article XXV apply in the case of Canada to all taxes imposed under the Income Tax Act; and, in the case of the United States, to all taxes imposed under the Code. Article XXV does not apply to taxes imposed by political subdivisions or local authorities of Canada or the United States.

Article XXV substantially broadens the protection against discrimination provided by the 1942 Convention, which contains only one provision dealing specifically with this subject. That provision, paragraph 11 of the Protocol to the 1942 Convention, states that citizens of one of the Contracting States residing within the other Contracting State are not to be subjected to the payment of more burdensome taxes than the citizens of the other State.

The benefits of Article XXV may affect the tax liability of a U.S. citizen or resident with respect to the United States. See paragraphs 2 and 3 of Article XXIX (Miscellaneous Rules).

ARTICLE XXVI   Mutual Agreement Procedure

Paragraph 1 provides that where a person considers that the actions of one or both of the Contracting States will result in taxation not in accordance with the Convention, he may present his case in writing to the competent authority of the Contracting State of which he is a resident or, if he is a resident of neither Contracting State, of which he is a national. Thus, a resident of Canada must present to the Minister of National Revenue (or his authorized representative) any claim that such resident is being subjected to taxation contrary to the Convention. A person who requests assistance from the competent authority may also avail himself of any remedies available under domestic laws.

Paragraph 2 provides that the competent authority of the Contracting State to which the case is presented shall endeavor to resolve the case by mutual agreement with the competent authority of the other Contracting State, unless he believes that the objection is not justified or he is able to arrive at a satisfactory unilateral solution. Any agreement reached between the competent authorities of Canada and the United States shall be implemented notwithstanding any time or other procedural limitations in the domestic laws of the Contracting States, except where the special mutual agreement provisions of Article IX (Related Persons) apply, provided that the competent authority of the Contracting State asked to waive its domestic time or procedural limitations has received written notification that such a case exists within six years from the end of the taxable year in the first-mentioned State to which the case relates. The notification may be given by the competent authority of the first-mentioned State, the taxpayer who has requested the competent authority to take action, or a person related to the taxpayer. Unlike Article IX, Article XXVI does not require the competent authority of a Contracting State to grant unilateral relief to avoid double taxation in a case where timely notification is not given to the competent authority of the other Contracting State. Such unilateral relief may, however, be granted by the competent authority in its discretion pursuant to the provisions of Article XXVI and in order to achieve the purposes of the Convention. In a case where the provisions of Article IX apply, the provisions of paragraphs 3, 4, and 5 of that Article are controlling with respect to adjustments and corresponding adjustments of income, loss, or tax and the effect of the Convention upon time or procedural limitations of domestic law. Thus, if the provisions of paragraph 2 of Article XXVI do not independently authorize such relief.

Paragraph 3 provides that the competent authorities of the Contacting States shall endeavor to resolve by mutual agreement any difficulties or doubts arising as to the interpretation or application of the Convention. In particular, the competent authorities may agree to the same attribution of profits to a resident of a Contracting State and its permanent establishment in the other Contracting State; the same allocation of income, deductions, credits, or allowances between persons; the same determination of the source of income; the same characterization of particular items of income; a common meaning of any term used in the Convention; rules, guidelines, or procedures for the elimination of double taxation with respect to income distributed by an estate or trust, or with respect to a partnership; or to increase any dollar amounts referred to in the Convention to reflect monetary or economic developments. The competent authorities may also consult and reach agreements on rules, guidelines, or procedures for the elimination of double taxation in cases not provided for in the Convention.

The list of subjects of potential mutual agreement in paragraph 3 is not exhaustive; it merely illustrates the principles set forth in the paragraph. As in the case of other U.S. tax conventions, agreement can be arrived at in the context of determining the tax liability of a specific person or in establishing rules, guidelines, and procedures that will apply generally under the Convention to resolve issues for classes of taxpayers. It is contemplated that paragraph 3 could be utilized by the competent authorities, for example, to resolve conflicts between the domestic laws of Canada and the United States with respect to the allocation and apportionment of deductions. Paragraph 4 provides that each Contracting State will endeavor to collect on behalf of the other State such amounts as may be necessary to ensure that relief granted by the Convention from taxation imposed by the other State does not enure to the benefit of persons not entitled to such relief.

Paragraph 4 does not oblige either Contracting State to carry out administrative measures of a different nature from those that would be used by Canada or the United States in the collection of its own tax or which would be contrary to its public policy.

Paragraph 5 confirms that the competent authorities of Canada and the United States may communicate with each other directly for the purpose of reaching agreement in the sense of paragraphs 1 through 4.

ARTICLE XXVII Exchange of Information

Paragraph 1 authorizes the competent authorities to exchange the information necessary for carrying out the provisions of the Convention or the domestic laws of Canada and the United States concerning taxes covered by the Convention, insofar as the taxation under those domestic laws is not contrary to the Convention. The authority to exchange information granted by paragraph 1 is not restricted by Article I (Personal Scope), and thus need not relate solely to persons otherwise covered by the Convention. It is contemplated that Article XXVII will be utilized by the competent authorities to exchange information upon request, routinely, and spontaneously.

Any information received by a Contracting State pursuant to the Convention is to be treated as secret in the same manner as information is obtained under the taxation laws of that State. Such information shall be disclosed only to persons or authorities, including courts and administrative bodies, involved in the assessment or collection of, the administration and enforcement in respect of, or the determination of appeals in relation to, the taxes covered by the Convention and the information may be used by such persons only for such purposes. (In accordance with paragraph 4, for the purposes of this Article the Convention applies to a broader range of taxes than those covered specifically by Article II (Taxes Covered).

In specific cases a competent authority providing information may, pursuant to paragraph 3, impose such other conditions on the use of information as are necessary. Although the information received by persons described in paragraph 1 is to be treated as secret, it may be disclosed by such persons in public court proceedings or in judicial decisions.

The provisions of paragraph 1 authorize the U.S. competent authority to continue to allow the General Accounting Office to examine tax return information received from Canada when GAO is engaged in a study of the administration of U.S. tax laws pursuant to a directive of Congress. However, the secrecy requirements of paragraph 1 must be met. If a Contracting State requests information in accordance with Article XXVII, the other Contracting State, shall endeavor, pursuant to paragraph 2, to obtain the information to which the request relates in the same manner as if its own taxation were involved, notwithstanding the fact that such States does not need the information. In addition, the competent authority requested to obtain information shall endeavor to provide the information in the particular form requested, such as depositions of witnesses and copies of unedited original documents, to the same extent such depositions and documents can be obtained under the laws or administrative practices of that State with respect to its own taxes.

Paragraph 3 provides that the provisions of paragraphs 1 and 2 do not impose on Canada or the United States the obligation to carry out administrative measures at variance with the laws and administrative practice of either State; to supply information which is not obtainable under the laws or in the normal course of the administration of either State; or to supply information which would disclose any trade, business, industrial, commercial, or professional secret or trade process, or information the disclosure of which would be contrary to public policy. Thus, Article XXVII allows, but does not obligate, the United States and Canada to obtain and provide information that would not be available to the requesting State under its laws or administrative practice or that in different circumstances would not be available to the State requested to provide the information. Further, Article XXVII allows a Contracting State to obtain information for the other Contracting State even if there is no tax liability in the State requested to obtain the information. Thus, the United States will continue to be able to give Canada tax information even if there is no U.S. tax liability at issue.

Paragraph 4 provides that, for the purposes of Article XXVII, the Convention applies, in the case of Canada, to all taxes imposed by the Government of Canada on estates and gifts and under the Income Tax Act and, in the case of the United States, to all taxes imposed under the Internal Revenue Code. Article XXVII does not apply to taxes imposed by political subdivisions or local authorities of the Contracting States. Paragraph 4 is designed to ensure that information exchange will extend to most national level taxes on both sides, and specifically to information gathered for purposes of Canada's taxes on estates and gifts (not effective for deaths or gifts after 1971). This provision is intended to mesh with paragraph 8 of Article XXX (Entry Into Force), which terminates the existing estate tax convention between the United States and Canada.

ARTICLE XXVIII   Diplomatic Agents and Consular Officers

Article XXVIII states that nothing in the Convention affects the fiscal privileges of diplomatic agents or consular officers under the general rules of international law or under the provisions of special agreements. However, various provisions of the Convention could apply to such persons, such as those concerning exchange of information, mutual agreement, and nondiscrimination.

ARTICLE XXIX   Miscellaneous Rules

Paragraph 1 states that the provisions of the Convention do not restrict in any manner any exclusion, exemption, deduction, credit, or other allowance accorded by the laws of a Contracting State in the determination of the tax imposed by that State. Thus, if a deduction would be allowed for an item in computing the taxable income of a Canadian resident under the Code, such deduction is available to such person in computing taxable income under the Convention. Paragraph 1 does not, however, authorize a taxpayer to make inconsistent choices between rules of the Code and rules of the Convention. For example, if a resident of Canada desires to claim the benefits of the "attributable to" rule of paragraphs 1 and 7 of Article VII (Business Profits) with respect to the taxation of business profits of a permanent establishment, such person must use the "attributable to" concept consistently for all items of income and deductions and may not rely upon the "effectively connected" rules of the Code to avoid U.S. tax on other items of attributable income. In no event are the rules of the Convention to increase overall U.S. tax liability from what liability would be if there were no convention.

Paragraph 2 provides a "saving clause" pursuant to which Canada and the United States may each tax its residents, as determined under Article IV (Residence), and the United States may tax its citizens (including any former citizen whose loss of citizenship had as one of its principal purposes the avoidance of tax, but only for a period of 10 years following such loss) and companies electing under Code section 1504(d) to be treated as domestic corporations, as if there were no convention between the United States and Canada with respect to taxes on income and capital.

Paragraph 3 provides that, notwithstanding paragraph 2, the United States and Canada must respect certain specified provisions of the Convention in regard to residents, citizens, and section 1504(d) companies. Paragraph 3(a) lists certain paragraphs and Articles of the Convention that represent exceptions to the "saving clause" in all situations; paragraph 3(b) provides a limited further exception for students who have not acquired immigrant status in the State where they are temporarily present.

Paragraph 4 provides relief with respect to social security taxes imposed on employers, employees, and self-employed persons under Code sections 1401, 3101, and 3111. Income from personal services not subject to tax by the United States under the provisions of this Convention or the 1942 Convention is not to be considered wages or net earnings from self-employment for purposes of the U.S. social security taxes with respect to taxable years of the taxpayer not barred by the statute of limitations relating to refunds (under the Code) ending on or before December 31 of the year before the year in which the Social Security Agreement between Canada and the United States (signed in Ottawa on March 11, 1981) enters into force. Thus, if that agreement enters into force in 1986, a resident of Canada earning income from personal services and such person's employer may apply for refunds of the employee's and employer's shares of U.S. social security tax paid attributable to the employee's income from personal services that is exempt from U.S. tax by virtue of this Convention or the 1942 Convention. In this example, the refunds would be available for social security taxes paid with respect to taxable years not barred by the statute of limitations of the Code ending on or before December 31, 1985. For purposes of Code section 6611, the date of overpayment with respect to refunds of U.S. tax pursuant to paragraph 4 is the later of the date on which the Social Security Agreement between Canada and the United States enters into force and the date on which instruments of ratification of the Convention are exchanged.

Under certain limited circumstances, an employee may, pursuant to paragraph 5 of Article XXX (Entry Into Force), claim an exemption from U.S. tax on wages under the 1942 Convention for one year after the Convention comes into force. The provisions of paragraph 4 would not, however, provide an exemption from U.S. social security taxes for such year.

Paragraph 4 does not modify existing U.S. statutes concerning social security benefits or funding. The Social Security Act requires the general funds of the Treasury to reimburse the social security trust funds on the basis of the records of wages and self-employment income maintained by the Social Security Administration. The Convention does not alter those records. Thus, any refunds of tax made pursuant to paragraph 4 would not affect claims for U.S. quarters of coverage with respect to social security benefits. And such refunds would be charged to general revenue funds, not social security trust funds. Paragraph 5 provides a method to resolve conflicts between the Canadian and U.S. treatment of individual retirement accounts. Certain Canadian retirement plans which are qualified plans for Canadian tax purposes do not meet Code requirements for qualification. As a result, the earnings of such a plan are currently included in income, for U.S. tax purposes, rather than being deferred until actual distributions are made by the plan. Canada defers current taxes on the earnings of such a plan but imposes tax on actual distributions from the plan.

Paragraph 5 is designed to avoid a mismatch of U.S. taxable income and foreign tax credits attributable to the Canadian tax on such distributions. Under the paragraph a beneficiary of a Canadian registered retirement savings plan may elect to defer U.S. taxation with respect to any income accrued in the plan but not distributed by the plan, until such time as a distribution is made from the plan or any substitute plan. The election is to be made under rules established by the competent authority of the United States. The election is not available with respect to income accrued in the plan which is reasonably attributable to contributions made to the plan by the beneficiary while he was not a Canadian resident.

Paragraph 6 provides rules denying the benefits of the Convention in certain situations where both countries believed that granting benefits would be inappropriate. Paragraph 6(a) provides that Articles VI (Income from Real Property) through XXIV (Elimination of Double Taxation) shall not apply to profits, income or gains derived by a trust which is treated as the income of a resident of a Contracting State (see paragraph 1 of Article IV (Residence)), if a principal purpose of the establishment, acquisition or maintenance of the trust was to obtain a benefit under the Convention or the 1942 Convention for persons who are not residents of that State. For example, the provision could be applied to a case where a nonresident of the United States created a United States trust to derive dividend income from Canada and a principal purpose of the establishment or maintenance of the trust was to obtain the reduced rate of Canadian tax under Article X (Dividends) for the nonresident. Paragraph 6(b) provides that Articles VI through XXIV shall not apply to Canadian nonresident owned investment companies, as defined in section 133 of the Income Tax Act, or under a similar provision that is subsequently enacted. This provision operates to deny the benefits of the Convention to a Canadian nonresident owned investment company, and does not effect the grant of benefits to other persons. Thus, for example, a dividend paid by such a company to a shareholder who is a U.S. resident is subject to the reduced rates of tax provided by Article X. The denial of the benefits of Articles VI through XXIV in such cases applies notwithstanding any other provision of the Convention. A Canadian nonresident owned investment company may, however, be entitled to claim the benefits of the 1942 Convention for an additional one-year period, pursuant to paragraph 5 of Article XXX (Entry Into Force). Where the provisions of this paragraph apply, the Contracting State in which the income arises may tax such income under its domestic law.

Paragraph 7 provides rules for the U.S. taxation of Canadian social security benefits paid to a resident of Canada who is a U.S. citizen. These rules are described in the discussion of paragraph 5 of Article XVIII (Pensions and Annuities).

ARTICLE XXX   Entry into Force

Paragraph 1 provides that the Convention is subject to ratification in accordance with the procedures of Canada and the United States. The exchange of instruments of ratification is to take place at Ottawa as soon as possible.

Paragraph 2 provides, subject to paragraph 3, that the Convention shall enter into force upon the exchange of instruments of ratification. It has effect, with respect to source State taxation of dividends, interest, royalties, pensions, annuities, alimony, and child support, for amounts paid or credited on or after the first day of the second calendar month after the date on which the instruments of ratification are exchanged. For other taxes, the Convention takes effect for taxable years beginning on or after January 1 next following the date when instrument of ratification are exchanged. In the case of relief' from United States social security taxes provided by paragraph 4 of Article XXIX (Miscellaneous Rules), the Convention also has effect for taxable year before the date on which instrument of ratification are exchanged.

Paragraph 3 provides special effective date rules for foreign tax credit computations with respect to tax paid or accrued to Canada. Paragraph 3(a) provides that the tax on 1971 undistributed income on hand imposed by Part IX of the Income Tax Act of Canada is considered to be an "income tax" for distribution made on or after January 1, 1972 and before January 1, 1979. Any such tax which is paid or accrued under U.S. standards is considered be imposed at the time of distribution and on the recipient of the distribution, in the proportion that the distribution out of undistributed income with respect to which the tax has been paid bears to 85 percent of undistributed income. A person claiming a credit for tax pursuant to paragraph 3(a) is obligated to compute the amount of the credit in accordance with that paragraph.

Paragraph 3(b) provides that the principles of paragraph 6 of Article XXIV (Elimination of Double Taxation), which provides for resourcing of certain dividend, interest, and royalty income to eliminate double taxation of U.S. citizens residing in Canada, have effect for taxable years beginning on or after January 1, 1976. The paragraph is intended to grant the competent authorities sufficient flexibility to address certain practical problems that have arisen under the 1942 Convention. It is anticipated that the competent authorities will be guided by paragraphs 4 and 5 of Article XXIV in applying paragraph 3(b) of Article XXX. Paragraph 3(c) provides that the provisions of paragraph 1 of Article XXIV (and the source rules of that Article) shall have effect for taxable years beginning on or after January 1,1981.

Any claim for refund based on the provisions of paragraph 3 may be filed on or before June 30 of the calendar year following the year in which instruments of ratification are exchanged, notwithstanding statutes of limitations or other rules of domestic law to the contrary. For purposes of Code section 6611, the date of overpayment is the date on which instruments of ratification are exchanged, with respect to any refunds of U.S. tax pursuant to paragraph 3.

Paragraph 4 provides that, subject to paragraph 5, the 1942 Convention ceases to have effect for taxes for which the Convention has effect under the provisions of paragraph 2. For example, if under paragraph 2 the Convention were to have effect with respect to taxes withheld at source on dividends paid as of October 1, 1984, the 1942 Convention will not have effect with respect to such taxes.

Paragraph 5 modifies the rule of paragraph 4 to allow all of the provisions of the 1942 Convention to continue to have effect for the period through the first taxable year with respect to which the provisions of the Convention would otherwise have effect under paragraph 2(b), if greater relief from tax is available under the 1942 Convention than under the Convention. Paragraph 5 applies to all provisions of the 1942 Convention, not just those provisions of the convention for which the Convention takes effect under paragraph 2(b) of this Article. Thus, for example, assume that the Convention has effect, pursuant to paragraph 2(b), for taxable years of a taxpayer beginning on or after January 1, 1985. Further assume that a U.S. resident with a taxable year beginning on April 1 and ending on March 31 receives natural resource royalties from Canada which are subject to a 25% tax under Article VI (Income from Real Property) of the Convention, as amended by the Protocol, and Canada's internal law, but which would be subject to a 15% tax under Article XI of the 1942 Convention. Pursuant to paragraph 5, the greater benefits of the 1942 Convention would continue to apply to royalties paid or credited to the U.S. resident through March 31, 1986.

Paragraph 6 provides that the 1942 Convention terminates on the last of the dates on which it has effect in accordance with the provisions of paragraphs 4 and 5.

Paragraph 7 terminates the Exchange of Notes between the United States and Canada of August 2 and September 17, 1928 providing for relief from double taxation of shipping profits. The provisions of the Exchange of Notes no longer have effect for taxable years beginning on or after January 1 following the exchange of instruments of ratification of the Convention. The 1942 Convention, in Article V, had suspended the effectiveness of the Exchange of Notes.

Paragraph 8 terminates the Convention between Canada and the United States for the Avoidance of Double Taxation with Respect to Taxes on the Estates of Deceased Persons signed on February 17, 1961. The provisions of that Convention cease to have effect with respect to estates of persons deceased on or after January

1 of the year following the exchange of instruments of ratification of the Convention.

ARTICLE XXXI   Termination

Paragraph 1 provides that the Convention shall remain in force until terminated by Canada or the United States.

Paragraph 2 provides that either Canada or the United States may terminate the Convention at any time after 5 years from the date on which instruments of ratification are exchanged, provided that notice of termination is given through diplomatic channels at least 6 months prior to the date on which the Convention is to terminate.

Paragraph 3 provides a special termination rule in situations where Canada or the United States changes its taxation laws and the other Contracting State believes that such change is significant enough to warrant modification of the Convention. In such a circumstance, the Canadian Ministry of Finance and the United States Department of the Treasury would consult with a view to resolving the matter. If the matter cannot be satisfactorily resolved, the Contracting State requesting an accommodation because of the change in the other Contracting State's taxation laws may terminate the Convention by giving the 6 months' prior notice required by paragraph 2, without regard to whether the Convention has been in force for 5 years.

Paragraph 4 provides that, in the event of termination, the Convention ceases to have effect for tax withheld at source under Articles X (Dividends), XI (Interest), XII (Royalties), and XVIII (Pensions and Annuities), and under paragraph 2 of Article XXII (Other Income), with respect to amounts paid or credited on or after the first day of January following the expiration of the 6 month period referred to in paragraph 2. In the case of other taxes, the Convention shall cease to have effect in the event of termination with respect to taxable years beginning on or after January 1 following the expiration of the 6 month period referred to in paragraph 2.

TREASURY DEPARTMENT TECHNICAL EXPLANATION OF THE [1995] PROTOCOL AMENDING THE CONVENTION BETWEEN THE UNITED STATES OF AMERICA AND CANADA WITH RESPECT TO TAXES ON INCOME AND CAPITAL

(June 13, 1995)

The Protocol, signed at Washington on March 17, 1995 (the "Protocol"), amends the Convention Between the United States of America and Canada with Respect to Taxes on Income and on Capital, signed at Washington on September 26, 1980, as amended by the Protocols signed on June 14, 1983 and March 28, 1984 (collectively referred to as the "Convention"). This technical explanation is an official guide to the Protocol. It explains policies behind particular provisions, as well as understandings reached during the negotiations with respect to the interpretation and application of the Protocol. The technical explanation is not intended to provide a complete comparison between the Protocol and the Articles of the Convention that it amends. To the extent that the Convention has not been amended by the Protocol, the Technical Explanation of the Convention remains the official explanation. References to "he" or "his" should be read to mean "he" or "she" or "his" or "her."

ARTICLE 1

Article 1 of the Protocol amends Article II (Taxes Covered) of the Convention. Article II identifies the taxes to which the Convention applies. Paragraph 1 of Article 1 replaces paragraphs 2 through 4 of Article II of the Convention with new paragraphs 2 and 3. For each Contracting State, new paragraph 2 of Article II specifies the taxes existing on the date of signature of the Protocol to which the Convention applies. New paragraph 3 provides that the Convention will also apply to taxes identical or substantially similar to those specified in paragraph 2, and to any new capital taxes, that are imposed after the date of signature of the Protocol.

New paragraph 2(a) of Article II describes the Canadian taxes covered by the Convention. As amended by the Protocol, the Convention will apply to all taxes imposed by the Government of Canada under the Income Tax Act.

New paragraph 2(b) of Article II amends the provisions identifying the U.S. taxes covered by the Convention in several respects. The Protocol incorporates into paragraph 2(b) the special rules found in paragraph 4 of Article II of the present Convention. New paragraph 2(b)(iii) conforms the rule previously found in paragraph 4(c) of Article II to the amended provisions of Article XXIV (Elimination of Double Taxation), under which Canada has agreed to grant a foreign tax credit for U.S. social security taxes. In addition, the Protocol adds a fourth special rule to reflect the addition to the Convention of new Article XXIX B (Taxes Imposed by Reason of Death) and related provisions in new paragraph 3(g) of Article XXVI (Mutual Agreement Procedure).

Article 1 of the Protocol also makes minor clarifying, nonsubstantive amendments to paragraphs 2 and 3 of the Article.

ARTICLE 2

This Article of the Protocol amends paragraphs 1(c) and 1(d) of Article III (General Definitions) of the Convention. These paragraphs define the terms "Canadian tax" and "United States tax," respectively. The present Convention defines "Canadian tax" to mean the Canadian taxes specified in paragraph 2(a) or 3(a) of Article II (Taxes Covered), i.e., Canadian income taxes. It similarly defines the term "United States tax" to mean the U.S. taxes specified in paragraph 2(b) or 3(a) of Article II, i.e., U.S. income taxes.

As amended by the Protocol, paragraph 2(a) of Article II of the Convention covers all taxes imposed by Canada under its Income Tax Act, including certain taxes that are not *income* taxes. As explained below, paragraph 2(b) is similarly amended by the Protocol to include certain U.S. taxes that are not *income* taxes. It was, therefore, necessary to amend the terms "Canadian tax" and "United States tax" so that they would continue to refer exclusively to the *income* taxes imposed by each Contracting State. The amendment to the definition of the term "Canadian tax" ensures, for example, that the Protocol will not obligate the United States to give a foreign tax credit under Article XXIV (Elimination of Double Taxation) for covered taxes other than income taxes.

The definition of "United States tax," as amended, excludes certain United States taxes that are covered in Article II only for certain limited purposes under the Convention. These include the accumulated earnings tax, the personal holding company tax, foundation excise taxes, social security taxes, and estate taxes. To the extent that these are to be creditable taxes in Canada, that fact is specified elsewhere in the Convention. A Canadian income tax credit for U.S. social security taxes is provided in new paragraph 2(a)(ii) of Article XXIV (Elimination of Double Taxation). A Canadian income tax credit for the U.S. estate taxes is provided in paragraph 6 of new Article XXIX B (Taxes Imposed by Reason of Death).

ARTICLE 3

Article 3 of the Protocol amends Article IV (Residence) of the Convention. It clarifies the meaning of the term "resident" in certain cases and adds a special rule, found in a number of recent U.S. treaties, for determining the residence of U.S. citizens and "green card" holders.

The first sentence of paragraph 1 of Article IV sets forth the general criteria for determining residence under the Convention. It is amended by the Protocol to state explicitly that a person will be considered a resident of a Contracting State for purposes of the Convention if he is liable to tax in that Contracting State by reason of citizenship. Although the sentence applies to both Contracting States, only the United States taxes its nonresident citizens in the same manner as its residents. Aliens admitted to the United States for permanent residence ("green card" holders) continue to qualify as U.S. residents under the first sentence of paragraph 1, because they are taxed by the United States as residents, regardless of where they physically reside.

U.S. citizens and green card holders who reside outside the United States, however, may have relatively little personal or economic nexus with the United States. The Protocol adds a second sentence to paragraph 1 that acknowledges this fact by limiting the circumstances under which such persons are to be treated, for purposes of the Convention, as U.S. residents.

Under that sentence, a U.S. citizen or green card holder will be treated as a resident of the United States for purposes of the Convention, and, thereby, be entitled to treaty benefits, only if

(1) the individual has a substantial presence, permanent home, or habitual abode in the United States, and

(2) the individual's personal and economic relations with the United States are closer than those with any third country.

If, however, such an individual is a resident of both the United States and Canada under the first sentence of the paragraph, his residence for purposes of the Convention is determined instead under the "tie-breaker" rules of paragraph 2 of the Article.

The fact that a U.S. citizen who does not have close ties to the United States may not be treated as a U.S. resident under Article IV of the Convention does not alter the application of the saving clause of paragraph 2 of Article XXIX (Miscellaneous Rules) to that citizen. However, like any other individual that is a resident alien under U.S. law, a green card holder is treated as a resident of the United States for purposes of the saving clause only if he qualifies as such under Article IV.

New paragraph 1(a) confirms that the term "resident" of a Contracting State includes the Government of that State or a political subdivision or local authority of that State, as well as any agency or instrumentality of one of these governmental entities. This is implicit in the current Convention and in other U.S. and Canadian treaties, even where not specified.

New paragraph 1 also clarifies, in subparagraph (b), that trusts, organizations, or other arrangements operated exclusively to provide retirement or employee benefits, and other not-for-profit organizations, such as organizations described in section 501(c) of the Internal Revenue Code, are residents of a Contracting State if they are constituted in that State and are generally exempt from income taxation in that State by reason of their nature as described above. This change clarifies that the specified entities are to be treated as residents of one of the Contracting States. This corresponds to the interpretation that had previously been adopted by the Contracting States. Such entities, therefore, will be entitled to the benefits of the Convention with respect to the other Contracting State, provided that they satisfy the requirements of new Article XXIX A (Limitation on Benefits) (discussed below).

Article 3 of the Protocol adds a sentence to paragraph 3 of Article IV of the current Convention to address the residence of certain dual resident corporations. Certain jurisdictions allow local incorporation of an entity that is already organized and incorporated under the laws of another country. Under Canadian law, such an entity is referred to as having been "continued" into the other country. Although the Protocol uses the Canadian term, the provision operates reciprocally. The new sentence states that such a corporation will be considered a resident of the State into which it is continued. Paragraph 5 of Article 21 of the Protocol governs the effective date of this provision.

ARTICLE 4

Article 4 of the Protocol amends paragraphs 3 and 4 of Article IX (Related Persons) of the Convention. Paragraph 1 of Article IX authorizes a Contracting State to adjust the amount of income, loss, or tax payable by a person with respect to arrangements between that person and a related person in the other Contracting State, when such arrangements differ from those that would obtain between unrelated persons. Under the present Convention, if an adjustment is made or to be made by a Contracting State under paragraph 1, paragraph 3 obligates the other Contracting State to make a corresponding adjustment if two conditions are satisfied:

(1) the other Contracting State agrees with the adjustment made or to be made by the first Contracting State, and

(2) the competent authority of the other Contracting State has received notice of the first adjustment within six years of the end of the taxable year to which that adjustment relates.

If notice is not given within the six-year period, and if the person to whom the first adjustment relates is not notified of the adjustment at least six months prior to the end of the six-year period, paragraph 4 of Article IX of the present Convention requires that the first Contracting State withdraw its adjustment, to the extent necessary to avoid double taxation.

Article 4 of the Protocol amends paragraphs 3 and 4 of Article IX to prevent taxpayers from using the notification requirements of the present Convention to avoid adjustments. Paragraph 4, as amended, eliminates the requirement that a Contracting State withdraw an adjustment if the notification requirement of paragraph 3 has not been met. Paragraph 4 is also amended to delete the requirement that the taxpayer be notified at least six months before expiration of the six-year period specified in paragraph 3.

As amended by the Protocol, Article IX also explicitly authorizes the competent authorities to relieve double taxation in appropriate cases, even if the notification requirement is not satisfied. Paragraph 3 confirms that the competent authorities may agree to a corresponding adjustment if such an adjustment is not otherwise barred by time or procedural limitations such as the statute of limitations. Paragraph 4 provides that the competent authority of the State making the initial adjustment may grant unilateral relief from double taxation in other cases, although such relief is not obligatory.

ARTICLE 5

Article 5 of the Protocol amends Article X (Dividends) of the Convention. Paragraph 1 of Article 5 amends paragraph 2(a) of Article X to reduce from 10 percent to 5 percent the maximum rate of tax that may be imposed by a Contracting State on the gross amount of dividends beneficially owned by a company resident in the other Contracting State that owns at least 10 percent of the voting stock of the company paying the dividends. The rate at which the branch profits tax may be imposed under paragraph 6 is also reduced by paragraph 1 of Article 5 from 10 percent to 5 percent. Under the entry-into-force provisions of Article 21 of the Protocol, these reductions will be phased in over a three-year period.

Paragraph 2 of Article 5 of the Protocol replaces paragraph 7 of Article X of the Convention with a new paragraph 7. Paragraph 7 of the existing Convention is no longer relevant because it applies only in the case where a Contracting State does not impose a branch profits tax. Both Contracting States now do impose such a tax.

New paragraph 7 makes the 5 percent withholding rate of new paragraph 2(a) inapplicable in certain situations. Under new paragraph 7(b), dividends paid by U.S. regulated investment companies (RICs) are denied the 5 percent withholding rate even if the Canadian shareholder is a corporation that would otherwise qualify as a direct investor by satisfying the 10-percent ownership requirement. Consequently, all RIC dividends to Canadian beneficial owners are subjected to the 15 percent rate that applies to dividends paid to portfolio investors.

Dividends paid by U.S. real estate investment trusts (REITs) to Canadian beneficial owners are also denied the 5 percent rate under the rules of paragraph 7(c). REIT dividends paid to individuals who own less than a 10 percent interest in the REIT are subject to withholding at a maximum rate of 15 percent. Paragraph 7(c) also provides that dividend distributions by a REIT to an estate or a testamentary trust acquiring the interest in the REIT as a consequence of the death of an individual will be treated as distributions to an individual, for the five-year period following the death. Thus, dividends paid to an estate or testamentary trust in respect of a holding of less than a 10 percent interest in the REIT also will be entitled to the 15 percent rate of withholding, but only for up to five years after the death. REIT dividends paid to other Canadian beneficial owners are subject to the rate of withholding tax that applies under the domestic law of the United States (i.e., 30 percent).

The denial of the 5 percent withholding rate at source to all RIC and REIT shareholders, and the denial of the 15 percent rate to most shareholders of REITs, is intended to prevent the use of these nontaxable conduit entities to gain unjustifiable benefits for certain shareholders. For example, a Canadian corporation that wishes to hold a portfolio of U.S. corporate shares may hold the portfolio directly and pay a U.S. withholding tax of 15 percent on all of the dividends that it receives. Alternatively, it may place the portfolio of U.S. stocks in a RIC, in which the Canadian corporation owns more than 10 percent of the shares, but in which there are enough small shareholders to satisfy the RIC diversified ownership requirements. Since the RIC is a pure conduit, there are no U.S. tax costs to the Canadian corporation of interposing the RIC as an intermediary in the chain of ownership. It is unlikely that a 10 percent shareholding in a RIC will constitute a 10 percent share holding in any company from which the dividends originate. In the absence of the special rules in paragraph 7(b), however, interposition of a RIC would transform what should be portfolio dividends into direct investment dividends taxable at source by the United States only at 5 percent. The special rules of paragraph 7 prevent this.

Similarly, a resident of Canada may hold U.S. real property directly and pay U.S. tax either at a 30 percent rate on the gross income or at the income tax rates specified in the Internal Revenue Code on the net income. By placing the real estate holding in a REIT, the Canadian investor could transform real estate income into dividend income and thus transform high-taxed income into much lower-taxed income. In the absence of the special rule, if the REIT shareholder were a Canadian corporation that owned at least a 10 percent interest in the REIT, the withholding rate would be 5 percent; in all other cases, it would be 15 percent. In either event, with one exception, a tax rate of 30 percent or more would be significantly reduced. The exception is the relatively small individual Canadian investor who might be subject to U.S. tax at a rate of only 15 percent on the net income even if he earned the real estate income directly. Under the rule in paragraph 7(c), such individuals, defined as those holding less than a 10 percent interest in the REIT, remain taxable at source at a 15 percent rate.

Subparagraph (a) of paragraph 7 provides a special rule for certain dividends paid by Canadian non-resident-owned investment corporations ("NROs"). The subparagraph provides for a maximum rate of 10 percent (instead of the standard rate of 5 percent) for dividends paid by NROs that are Canadian residents to a U.S. company that owns 10 percent or more of the voting stock of the NRO and that is the beneficial owner of the dividend. This rule maintains the rate available under the current Convention for dividends from NROs. Canada wanted the withholding rate for direct investment NRO dividends to be no lower than the maximum withholding rates under the Convention on interest and royalties, to make sure that a foreign investor cannot transform interest or royalty income subject to a 10 percent withholding tax into direct dividends qualifying for a 5 percent withholding tax by passing it through to an NRO.

ARTICLE 6

Article 6 of the Protocol amends Article XI (Interest) of the Convention. Paragraph 1 of the Article reduces the general maximum withholding rate on interest under paragraph 2 of Article XI from 15 percent to 10 percent.

Paragraph 3 of Article XI of the Convention provides that, notwithstanding the general withholding rate applicable to interest payments under paragraph 2, certain specified categories of interest are exempt from withholding at source. Paragraph 2 of Article 6 of the Protocol amends paragraph 3(d) of the Convention, which deals with interest paid on indebtedness arising in connection with a sale on credit of equipment, merchandise, or services. The exemption provided by that paragraph in the Convention is broadened under the Protocol to apply to interest that is beneficially owned either by the seller in the underlying transaction, as under the present Convention, or by any beneficial owner of interest paid with respect to an indebtedness arising as a result of the sale on credit of equipment, merchandise, or services. This exemption, however, does not apply in cases where the purchaser is related to the seller or the debtor is related to the beneficial owner of the interest. The negotiators agreed that this exemption is subject, as are the other provisions of the Convention, to any anti-avoidance rules applicable under the respective domestic law of the Contracting States.

The reference to "related persons" in paragraph 3(d) of Article XI of the Convention, as amended, is a change from the present Convention, which refers to "persons dealing at arm's length." The term "related person" as used in this Article is not defined for purposes of the Convention. Accordingly, the meaning of the term, and, therefore, the application of this Article, will be governed by the domestic law of each Contracting State (as is true with the use of the term "arm's length" under the current Convention) under the interpretative rule of paragraph 2 of Article III (General Definitions). The United States will define the term "related person" as under section 482 of the Internal Revenue Code, to include organizations, trades, or businesses (whether or not incorporated, whether or not organized in the United States, and whether or not affiliated) owned or controlled directly or indirectly by the same interests. The Canadian definition of "related persons" is found in section 251 of the Income Tax Act.

Paragraph 3 of Article 6 of the Protocol adds a new paragraph 9 to Article XI of the Convention. Although the definition of "interest" in paragraph 4 includes an excess inclusion with respect to a residual interest in a real estate mortgage investment conduit (REMIC) described in section 86OG of the Internal Revenue Code, new paragraph 9 provides that the reduced rates of tax at source for interest provided for in paragraphs 2 and 3 do not apply to such income. This class of interest, therefore, remains subject to the statutory 30 percent U.S. rate of tax at source. The legislation that created REMICs in 1986 provided that such excess inclusions were to be taxed at the full 30 percent statutory rate, regardless of any then-existing treaty provisions to the contrary. The 30 percent rate of tax on excess inclusions received by residents of Canada is consistent with this expression of Congressional intent.

ARTICLE 7

Article 7 of the Protocol modifies Article XII (Royalties) of the Convention by expanding the classes of royalties exempt from withholding of tax at source. Paragraph 3, as amended by the Protocol, identifies four classes of royalty payments arising in one Contracting State and beneficially owned by a resident of the other that are exempt at source:

(1) subparagraph (a) preserves the exemption in paragraph 3 of the present Convention for copyright royalties in respect of literary and other works, other than certain such payments in respect of motion pictures, videotapes, and similar payments;

(2) subparagraph (b) specifies that computer software royalties are also exempt;

(3) subparagraph (c) adds royalties paid for the use of, or the right to use, patents and information concerning industrial, commercial, and scientific experience, other than payments in connection with rental or franchise agreements; and

(4) subparagraph (d) allows the Contracting States to reach an agreement, through an exchange of diplomatic notes, with respect to the application of paragraph 3 of Article XII to payments in respect of certain live broadcasting transmissions.

The specific reference to software in subparagraph (b) is not intended to suggest that the United States views the term "copyright" as excluding software in other U.S. treaties (including the current treaty with Canada).

The negotiators agreed that royalties paid for the use of, or the right to use, designs or models, plans, secret formulas, or processes are included under subparagraph 3(c) to the extent that they represent payments for the use of, or the right to use, information concerning industrial, commercial, or scientific experience. In addition, they agreed that royalties paid for the use of, or the right to use, "know how," as defined in paragraph 11 of the Commentary on Article 12 of the OECD Model Income Tax Treaty, constitute payments for the use of, or the right to use, information concerning industrial, commercial, or scientific experience. The negotiators further agreed that a royalty paid under a "mixed contract," "package fee," or similar arrangement will be treated as exempt at source by virtue of paragraph 3 to the extent of any portion that is paid for the use of, or the right to use, property or information with respect to which paragraph 3 grants an exemption.

The exemption granted under subparagraph 3(c) does not, however, extend to payments made for information concerning industrial, commercial, or scientific experience that is provided in connection with a rental or franchise agreement. For this purpose, the negotiators agreed that a franchise is to be distinguished from other arrangements resulting in the transfer of intangible property. They agreed that a license to use intangibles (whether or not including a trademark) in a territory, in and of itself, would not constitute a franchise agreement for purposes of subparagraph 3(c) in the absence of other rights and obligations in the license agreement or in any other agreement that would indicate that the arrangement in its totality constituted a franchise agreement. For example, a resident of one Contracting State may acquire a right to use a secret formula to manufacture a particular product (e.g., a perfume), together with the right to use a trademark for that product and to market it at a non-retail level, in the other Contracting State. such an arrangement would not constitute a franchise in the absence of any other rights or obligations under that arrangement or any other agreement that would indicate that the arrangement in its totality constituted a franchise agreement. Therefore, the royalty payment under that arrangement would be exempt from withholding tax in the other Contracting State to the extent made for the use of, or the right to use, the secret formula or other information concerning industrial, commercial, or scientific experience; however, it would be subject to withholding tax at a rate of 10 percent, to the extent made for the use of, or the right to use, the trademark.

The provisions of paragraph 3 do not fully reflect the U.S. treaty policy of exempting all types of royalty payments from taxation at source, but Canada was not prepared to grant a complete exemption for all types of royalties in the Protocol. Although the Protocol makes several important changes to the royalty provisions of the present Convention in the direction of bringing Article XII into conformity with U.S. policy, the United States remains concerned about the imposition of withholding tax on some classes of royalties and about the associated administrative burdens. In this connection, the Contracting States have affirmed their intention to collaborate to resolve in good faith any administrative issues that may arise in applying the provisions of subparagraph 3(c). The United States intends to continue to pursue a zero rate of withholding for all royalties in future negotiations with Canada, including discussions under Article 20 of the Protocol, as well as in negotiations with other countries.

As noted above, new subparagraph 3(d) enables the Contracting States to provide an exemption for royalties paid with respect to broadcasting through an exchange of notes. This provision was included because Canada was not prepared at the time of the negotiations to commit to an exemption for broadcasting royalties. Subparagraph 3(d) was included to enable the Senate to give its advice and consent in advance to such an exemption, in the hope that such an exemption could be obtained without awaiting the negotiation of another full protocol. Any agreement reached under the exchange of notes authorized by subparagraph 3(d) would lower the withholding rate from 10 percent to zero and, thus, bring the Convention into greater conformity with established U.S. treaty policy.

Paragraph 2 of Article 7 of the Protocol amends the rules in paragraph 6 of Article XII of the Convention for determining the source of royalty payments. Under the present Convention, royalties generally are deemed to arise in a Contracting State if paid by a resident of that State. However, if the obligation to pay the royalties was incurred in connection with a permanent establishment or a fixed base in one of the Contracting States that bears the expense, the royalties are deemed to arise in that State.

The Protocol continues to apply these basic rules but changes the scope of an exception provided under the present Convention. Under the present Convention, a royalty paid for the use of, or the right to use, property in a Contracting State is deemed to arise in that State. Under the Protocol, this "place of use1, exception applies only if the Convention does not otherwise deem the royalties to arise in one of the Contracting States. Thus, the "place of use" exception will apply only if royalties are neither paid by a resident of one of the Contracting States nor borne by a permanent establishment or fixed base in either State. For example, if a Canadian resident were to grant franchise rights to a resident of Chile for use in the United States, the royalty paid by the Chilean resident to the Canadian resident for those rights would be U.S. source income under this Article, subject to U.S. withholding at the 10 percent rate provided in paragraph 2.

The rules of this Article differ from those provided under U.S. domestic law. Under U.S. domestic law, a royalty is considered to be from U.S. sources if it is paid for the use of, or the privilege of using, an intangible within the United States; the residence of the payor is irrelevant. If paid to a nonresident alien individual or other foreign person, a U.S. source royalty is generally subject to withholding tax at a rate of 30 percent under U.S. domestic law. By reason of paragraph 1 of Article XXIX (Miscellaneous Rules), a Canadian resident would be permitted to apply the rules of U.S. domestic law to its royalty income if those rules produced a more favorable result in its case than those of this Article. However, under a basic principle of tax treaty interpretation recognized by both Contracting States, the prohibition against so-called "cherry-picking," the Canadian resident would be precluded from claiming selected benefits under the Convention (e.g., the tax rates only) and other benefits under U.S. domestic law (e.g., the source rules only) with respect to its royalties. See, e.g., Rev. Rul. 84-17, 1984-1 C.B. 308. For example, if a Canadian company granted franchise rights to a resident of the United States for use 50 percent in the United States and 50 percent in Chile, the Convention would permit the Canadian company to treat all of its royalty income from that single transaction as U.S. source income entitled to the withholding tax reduction under paragraph 2. U.S. domestic law would permit the Canadian company to treat 50 percent of its royalty income as U.S. source income subject to a 30 percent withholding tax and the other 50 percent as foreign source income exempt from U.S. tax. The Canadian company could choose to apply either the provisions of U.S. domestic law or the provisions of the Convention to the transaction, but would not be permitted to claim both the U.S. domestic law exemption for 50 percent of the income and the Convention's reduced withholding rate for the remainder of the income.

Royalties generally are considered borne by a permanent establishment or fixed base if they are deductible in computing the taxable income of that permanent establishment or fixed base.

Since the definition of "resident" of a Contracting State in Article IV (Residence), as amended by Article 3 of the Protocol, specifies that this term includes the Contracting States and their political subdivisions and local authorities, the source rule does not include a specific reference to these governmental entities.

ARTICLE 8

Article 8 of the Protocol broadens the scope of paragraph 8 of Article XIII (Gains) of the Convention to cover organizations, reorganizations, amalgamations, and similar transactions involving either corporations or other entities. The present Convention covers only transactions involving corporations. The amendment is intended to make the paragraph applicable to transactions involving other types of entities, such as trusts and partnerships.

As in the case of transactions covered by the present Convention, the deferral allowed under this provision shall be for such time and under such other conditions as are stipulated between the person acquiring the property and the competent authority. The agreement of the competent authority of the State of source is entirely discretionary and, when granted, will be granted only to the extent necessary to avoid double taxation.

ARTICLE 9

Article 9 of the Protocol amends Article XVIII (Pensions and Annuities) of the Convention. Paragraph 3 of Article XVIII defines the term "pensions" for purposes of the Convention, including the rules for the taxation of cross-border pensions in paragraphs 1 and 2 of the Article, the rules in paragraphs 2 and 3 of Article XXI (Exempt Organizations) for certain income derived by pension funds, and the rules in paragraph 1(b)(i) of Article IV (Residence) regarding the residence of pension funds and certain other entities. The Protocol amends the present definition by substituting the phrase "other retirement arrangement" for the phrase "retirement plan." The purpose of this change is to clarify that the definition of "pensions" includes, for example, payments from Individual Retirement Accounts (IRAs) in the United States and to provide that "pensions" includes, for example, Registered

Retirement Savings Plans (RRSPS) and Registered Retirement Income Funds (RRIFs) in Canada. The term "pensions" also would include amounts paid by other retirement plans or arrangements, whether or not they are qualified plans under U.S. domestic law; this would include, for example, plans and arrangements described in section 457 or 414(d) of the Internal Revenue Code.

Paragraph 2 of Article 9 of the Protocol amends paragraph 5 of Article XVIII to modify the treatment of social security benefits under the Convention. Under the amended paragraph, benefits paid under the U.S. or Canadian social security legislation to a resident of the other Contracting State, or, in the case of Canadian benefits, to a U.S. citizen, are taxable exclusively in the paying State. This amendment brings the Convention into line with current U.S. treaty policy. Social security benefits are defined, for this purpose, to include tier 1 railroad retirement benefits but not unemployment benefits (which therefore fall under Article XXII (Other Income) of the Convention). Pensions in respect of government service are covered not by this rule but by the rules of paragraphs 1 and 2 of Article XVIII.

The special rule regarding U.S. citizens is intended to clarify that only Canada, and not the United States, may tax a social security payment by Canada to a U.S. citizen not resident in the United States. This is consistent with the intention of the general rule, which is to give each Contracting State exclusive taxing jurisdiction over its social security payments. Since paragraph 5 is an exception to the saving clause, Canada will retain exclusive taxing jurisdiction over Canadian social security benefits paid to U.S. residents and citizens, and vice versa. It was not necessary to provide a special rule to clarify the taxation of U.S. social security payments to Canadian citizens, because Canada does not tax on the basis of citizenship and, therefore, does not include citizens within the scope of its saving clause.

A new paragraph 7 is added to Article XVIII by Article 9 of the Protocol. This paragraph replaces paragraph 5 of Article XXIX (Miscellaneous Rules) of the present Convention. The new paragraph makes reciprocal the rule that it replaced and expands its scope, so that it no longer applies only to residents and citizens of the United States who are beneficiaries of Canadian RRSPs. As amended, paragraph 7 applies to an individual who is a citizen or resident of a Contracting State and a beneficiary of a trust, company, organization, or other arrangement that is a resident of the other Contracting State and that is both generally exempt from income taxation in its State of residence and operated exclusively to provide pension, retirement, or employee benefits. Under this rule, the beneficiary may elect to defer taxation in his State of residence on income accrued in the plan until it is distributed or rolled over into another plan. The new rule also broadens the types of arrangements covered by this paragraph in a manner consistent with other pension-related provisions of the Protocol.

ARTICLE 10

Article 10 of the Protocol amends Article XXI (Exempt Organizations) of the Convention. Paragraph 1 of Article 10 amends paragraphs 2 and 3 of Article XXI. The most significant changes are those that conform the language of the two paragraphs to the revised definition of the term "pension" in paragraph 3 of Article XVIII (Pensions and Annuities). The revision adds the term "arrangement" to "trust, company or organization" in describing the residents of a Contracting State that may receive dividend and interest income exempt from current income taxation by the other Contracting State. This clarifies that IRAs, for example, are eligible for the benefits of paragraph 2, subject to the exception in paragraph 3, and makes Canadian RRSPs and RRIFs, for example, similarly eligible (provided that they are operated exclusively to administer or provide pension, retirement, or employee benefits).

The other changes, all in paragraph 2, are intended to improve and clarify the language. For example, the reference to "tax" in the present Convention is changed to a reference to "income taxation." This is intended to clarify that if an otherwise exempt organization is subject to an excise tax, for example, it will not lose the benefits of this paragraph. In subparagraph 2 (b), the phrase "not taxed in a taxable year" was changed to "generally exempt from income taxation in a taxable year" to ensure uniformity throughout the Convention; this change was not intended to disqualify a trust or other arrangement that qualifies for the exemption under the wording of the present Convention.

Paragraph 2 of Article 10 adds a sentence to paragraph 5 of Article XXI of the Convention. The paragraph in the present Convention provides that a U.S. citizen or resident may deduct, for U.S. income tax purposes, contributions made to Canadian charities under certain circumstances. The added sentence makes clear that the benefits of the paragraph are available to a company that is a resident of Canada but is treated by the United States as a domestic corporation under the consolidated return rules of section 1504(d) of the Internal Revenue Code. Thus, such a company will be able to deduct, for U.S. income tax purposes, contributions to Canadian charities that are deductible to a U.S. resident under the provisions of the paragraph.

Paragraph 3 of Article 10 amends paragraph 6 of Article XXI of the Convention to replace references to "deductions" for Canadian tax purposes with references to "relief" from tax. These changes clarify that the provisions of paragraph 6 apply to the credit for charitable contributions allowed under current Canadian law. The Protocol also makes other non-substantive drafting changes to paragraph 6.

ARTICLE 11

Article 11 of the Protocol adds a new paragraph 3 to Article XXII (Other Income) of the Convention. This Article entitles residents of one Contracting State who are taxable by the other State on gains from wagering transactions to deduct losses from wagering transactions for the purposes of taxation in that other State. However, losses are to be deductible only to the extent that they are incurred with respect to wagering transactions, the gains on which could be taxable in the other State, and only to the extent that such losses would be deductible if incurred by a resident of that other State.

This Article does not affect the collection of tax by a Contracting State. Thus, in the case of a resident of Canada, this Article does not affect, for example, the imposition of U.S. withholding taxes under section 1441 or section 1442 of the Internal Revenue Code on the gross amount of gains from wagering transactions. However, in computing its U.S. income tax liability on net income for the taxable year concerned, the Canadian resident may reduce its gains from wagering transactions subject to taxation in the United States by any wagering losses incurred on such transactions, to the extent that those losses are deductible under the provisions of new paragraph 3. Under U.S. domestic law, the deduction of wagering losses is governed by section 165 of the Internal Revenue Code. It is intended that the resident of Canada file a nonresident income tax return in order to substantiate the deduction for losses and to claim a refund of any overpayment of U.S. taxes collected by withholding.

ARTICLE 12

Article 12 of the Protocol amends Article XXIV (Elimination of Double Taxation) of the Convention. Paragraph 1 of Article 12 amends the rules for Canadian double taxation relief in subparagraphs (a) and (b) of paragraph 2 of Article XXIV. The amendment to subparagraph (a) obligates Canada to give a foreign tax credit for U.S. social security taxes paid by individuals. The amendment to subparagraph (b) of paragraph 2 does not alter the substantive effect of the rule, but conforms the language to current Canadian law. Under the provision as amended, Canada generally continues to allow an exemption to a Canadian corporation for direct dividends paid from the exempt surplus of a U.S. affiliate.

Paragraphs 4 and 5 of Article XXIV of the Convention provide double taxation relief rules, for both the United States and Canada, with respect to U.S. source income derived by a U.S. citizen who is resident in Canada. These rules address the fact that a U.S. citizen resident in Canada remains subject to U.S. tax on his worldwide income at ordinary progressive rates, and may, therefore, be subject to U.S. tax at a higher rate than a resident of Canada who is not a U.S. citizen. In essence, these paragraphs limit the foreign tax credit that Canada is obliged to allow such a U.S. citizen to the amount of tax on his U.S. source income that the United States would be allowed to collect from a Canadian resident who is not a U.S. citizen. They also oblige the United States to allow the U.S. citizen a credit for any income tax paid to Canada on the remainder of his income. Paragraph 4 deals with items of income other than dividends, interest, and royalties and is not changed by the Protocol. Paragraph 5, which deals with dividends, interest, and royalties, is amended by paragraph 2 of Article 12 of the Protocol.

The amendments to paragraph 5 of the Article make that paragraph applicable only to dividend, interest, and royalty income that would be subject to a positive rate of U.S. tax if paid to a Canadian resident who is not a U.S. citizen. This means that the rules of paragraph 4, not paragraph 5, will apply to items of interest and royalties, such as portfolio interest, that would be exempt from U.S. tax if paid to a non-U.S. citizen resident in Canada. Under paragraph 4, Canada will not allow a credit for the U.S. tax on such income, and the United States will credit the Canadian tax to the extent necessary to avoid double taxation.

Paragraph 2 of Article 12 of the Protocol makes further technical amendments to paragraph 5 of Article XXIV of the Convention. The existing Technical Explanation of paragraphs 5 and 6 of Article XXIV of the Convention should be read as follows to reflect the amendments made by the Protocol.

Paragraph 5 provides special rules for the elimination of double taxation in the case of dividends, interest, and royalties earned by a U.S. citizen resident in Canada. These rules apply notwithstanding the provisions of paragraph 4, but only as long as the law in Canada allows a deduction in computing income for the portion of any foreign tax paid in respect of dividends, interest, or royalties which exceeds 15 percent of the amount of such items of income, and only with respect to those items of income. The rules of paragraph 4 apply with respect to other items of income; moreover, if the law in force in Canada regarding the deduction for foreign taxes is changed so as to no longer allow such a deduction, the provisions of paragraph 5 shall not apply and the U.S. foreign tax credit for Canadian taxes and the Canadian credit for U.S. taxes will be determined solely pursuant to the provisions of paragraph 4.

The calculations under paragraph 5 are as follows. First, the deduction allowed in Canada in computing income shall be made with respect to U.S. tax on the dividends, interest, and royalties before any foreign tax credit by the United States with respect to income tax paid or accrued to Canada. Second, Canada shall allow a deduction from (credit against) Canadian tax for U.S. tax paid or accrued with respect to the dividends, interest, and royalties, but such credit need not exceed the amount of income tax that would be paid or accrued to the United States on such items of income if the individual were not a U.S. citizen after taking into account any relief available under the Convention. Third, for purposes of computing the U.S. tax on such dividends, interest, and royalties, the United States shall allow as a credit against the U.S. tax the income tax paid or accrued to Canada after the credit against Canadian tax for income tax paid or accrued to the United States. The United States is in no event obliged to give a credit for Canadian income tax which will reduce the U.S. tax below the amount of income tax that would be paid or accrued to the United States on the amount of the dividends, interest, and royalties if the individual were not a U.S. citizen after taking into account any relief available under the Convention.

The rules of paragraph 5 are illustrated by the following examples.

Example B

— A U.S. citizen who is a resident of Canada has $100 of dividend income arising in the United States. The tentative U.S. tax before foreign tax credit is $40.

— Canada, under its law, allows a deduction for the U.S. tax in excess of 15 percent or, in this case, a deduction of $25 ($40 - $15). The Canadian taxable income is $75 and the Canadian tax on that amount is $35.

— Canada gives a credit of $15 (the maximum credit allowed is 15 percent of the gross dividend taken into Canadian income) and collects a net tax of $20.

— The United States allows a credit for the net Canadian tax against its tax in excess of 15 percent. Thus, the maximum credit is $25 ($40 - $15). But since the net Canadian tax paid was $20, the usable credit is $20.

— To be able to use a credit of $20 requires Canadian source taxable income of $50 (50% of the U.S. tentative tax of $40). Under paragraph 6, $50 of the U.S. dividend is resourced to be of Canadian source. The credit of $20 may then be offset against the U.S. tax of $40, leaving a net U.S. tax of $20.

— The combined tax paid to both countries is $40, $20 to Canada and $20 to the United States.

Example C

— A U.S. citizen who is a resident of Canada receives $200 of income with respect to personal services performed within Canada and $100 of dividend income arising within the United States. Taxable income for U.S. purposes, taking into account the rules of Code section 911, is $220. U.S. tax (before foreign tax credits) is $92. The $100 of dividend income is deemed to bear U.S. tax (before foreign tax credits) of $41.82 ($100/$200 x $92). Under Canadian law, a deduction of $26.82 (the excess of $41.82 over 15 percent of the $100 dividend income) is allowed in computing income. The Canadian tax on $273.18 of income ($300 less the $26.82 deduction) is $130. Canada then gives a credit against the $130 for $15 (the U.S. tax paid or accrued with respect to the dividend, $41.82 but limited to 15 percent of the gross amount of such income, or $15), leaving a final Canadian tax of $115. Of the $115, $30.80 is attributable to the dividend:

$$\frac{\$73.18\ (\$100\ \text{dividend less}\ \$26.82\ \text{deduction}) \times \$115}{\$273.18\ (\$300\ \text{income less}\ \$26.82\ \text{deduction})}$$

Of this amount, $26.82 is creditable against U.S. tax pursuant to paragraph 5. (Although the U.S. allows a credit for the Canadian tax imposed on the dividend, $30.80, the credit may not reduce the U.S. tax below 15 percent of the amount of the dividend. Thus, the maximum allowable credit is the excess of $41.82, the U.S. tax imposed on the dividend income, over $15, which is 15 percent of the $100 dividend.) The remaining $3.98 (the Canadian tax of $30.80 less the credit allowed of $26.82) is a foreign tax credit carryover for U.S. purposes, subject to the limitations of paragraph 5. (An additional $50.18 of Canadian tax with respect to Canadian source services income is creditable against U.S. tax pursuant to paragraphs 3 and 4(b). The $50.18 is computed as follows: tentative U.S. tax (before foreign tax credits) is $92; the U.S. tax on Canadian source services income is $50.18 ($92 less the U.S. tax on the dividend income of $41.82); the limitation on the services income is:

$$\frac{\$120\ (\text{taxable income from services}) \times \$92}{\$220\ (\text{total taxable income}),}$$

or $50.18. The credit for Canadian tax paid on the services income is therefore $50.18; the remainder of the Canadian tax on the services income, or $34.02, is a foreign tax credit carryover for U.S. purposes, subject to the limitations of paragraph 5.)

Paragraph 6 is necessary to implement the objectives of paragraphs 4(b) and 5(c). Paragraph 6 provides that where a U.S. citizen is a resident of Canada, items of income referred to in paragraph 4 or 5 are deemed for the purposes of Article XXIV to arise in Canada to the extent necessary to avoid double taxation of income by Canada and the United States consistent with the objectives of paragraphs 4(b) and 5(c). Paragraph 6 can override the source rules of paragraph 3 to permit a limited resourcing of income. The principles of paragraph 3 have effect, pursuant to paragraph 3(b) of Article XXX (Entry Into Force) of the Convention, for taxable years beginning on or after January 1, 1976. See the discussion of Article XXX below.

The application of paragraph 6 is illustrated by the following example.

Example D

The facts are the same as in Example C. The United States has undertaken, pursuant to paragraph 5(c) and paragraph 6, to credit $26.82 of Canadian taxes on dividend income that has a U.S. source under both paragraph 3 and the Internal Revenue Code. (As illustrated in Example C, the credit, however, only reduces the U.S. tax on the dividend income which exceeds the amount of income tax that would be paid or accrued to the United States on such income if the individual were not a U.S. citizen after taking into account any relief available under the Convention. Pursuant to paragraph 6, for purposes of determining the U.S. foreign tax credit limitation under the Convention with respect to Canadian taxes,

$$\$64.13 \left(\frac{A}{\$220} \text{ x } \$92 \ \$26.82; A = \$64.13 \right.$$

of taxable income with respect to the dividends is deemed to arise in Canada.

Paragraph 3 of Article 12 of the Protocol makes a technical amendment to paragraph 7 of Article XXIV. It conforms the reference to U.S. and Canadian taxes to the amended definitions of "United States tax" and "Canadian tax" in subparagraphs (c) and (d) of paragraph 1 of Article III (General Definitions). No substantive change in the effect of the paragraph is intended.

Paragraph 4 of Article 12 of the Protocol adds a new paragraph 10 to Article XXIV of the Convention. This paragraph provides for the application of the rule of "exemption with progression" by a Contracting State in cases where an item of income of a resident of that State is exempt from tax in that State by virtue of a provision of the Convention. For example, where under Canadian law a tax benefit, such as the goods and services tax credit, to a Canadian resident individual is reduced as the income of that individual, or the individual's spouse or other dependent, increases, and any of these persons receives U.S. social security benefits that are exempt from tax in Canada under the Convention, Canada may, nevertheless, take the U.S. social security benefits into account in determining whether, and to what extent, the benefit should be reduced.

New Article XXIX B (Taxes Imposed by Reason of Death), added by Article 19 of the Protocol, also provides relief from double taxation in certain circumstances in connection with Canadian income tax imposed by reason of death and U.S. estate taxes. However, subparagraph 7(c) of Article XXIX B generally denies relief from U.S. estate tax under that Article to the extent that a credit or deduction has been claimed for the same amount in determining any other tax imposed by the United States. This restriction would operate to deny relief, for example, to the extent that relief from U.S. income tax is claimed under Article XXIV in respect of the same amount of Canadian tax. There is, however, no requirement that relief from U.S. tax be claimed first (or exclusively) under Article XXIV. Paragraph 6 of Article XXIX B also prevents the claiming of double relief from Canadian income taxation under both that Article and Article XXIV, by providing that the credit provided by Article XXIX B applies only after the application of the credit provided by Article XXIV.

ARTICLE 13

Article 13 of the Protocol amends Article XXV (Non-Discrimination) of the Convention. Paragraph 1 of Article 13 amends paragraph 3 of Article XXV to conform the treaty language to a change in Canadian law. The paragraph is intended to allow the treatment of dependents under the income tax law of a Contracting State to apply with respect to dependents who are residents of the other Contracting State. As drafted in the present Convention, the rule deals specifically only with deductions; the amendments made by the Protocol clarify that it also applies to the credits now provided by Canadian law.

Paragraph 2 of Article 13 of the Protocol amends paragraph 10 of Article XXV of the Convention to broaden the scope of the non-discrimination protection provided by the Convention. As amended, Article XXV will apply to all taxes imposed by a Contracting State. Under the present Convention, non-discrimination protection is limited in the case of Canadian taxes to taxes imposed under the Income Tax Act. As amended by the Protocol, nondiscrimination protection will extend, for example, to the Canadian goods and services tax and other Canadian excise taxes.

ARTICLE 14

Article 14 of the Protocol makes two changes to Article XXVI (Mutual Agreement Procedure) of the Convention. First, it adds a new subparagraph 3(g) specifically authorizing the competent authorities to provide relief from double taxation in certain cases involving the distribution or disposition of property by a U.S. qualified domestic trust or a Canadian spousal trust, where relief is not otherwise available.

Article 14 also adds a new paragraph 6 to Article XXVI (Mutual Agreement Procedure). Paragraph 6 provides for a voluntary arbitration procedure, to be implemented only upon the exchange of diplomatic notes between the United States and Canada. Similar provisions are found in the recent U.S. treaties with the Federal Republic of Germany, the Netherlands, and Mexico. Paragraph 6 provides that where the competent authorities have been unable, pursuant to the other provisions of Article XXVI, to resolve a disagreement regarding the interpretation or application of the Convention, the disagreement may, with the consent of the taxpayer and both competent authorities, be submitted for arbitration, provided the taxpayer agrees in writing to be bound by the decision of the arbitration board. Nothing in the provision requires that any case be submitted for arbitration. However, if a case is submitted to an arbitration board, the board's decision in that case will be binding on both Contracting States and on the taxpayer with respect to that case.

The United States was reluctant to implement an arbitration procedure until there has been an opportunity to evaluate the process in practice under other agreements that allow for arbitration, particularly the U.S.-Germany Convention. It was agreed, therefore, as specified in paragraph 6, that the provisions of the Convention calling for an arbitration procedure will not take effect until the two Contracting States have agreed through an exchange of diplomatic notes to do so. This is similar to the approach taken with the Netherlands and Mexico. Paragraph 6 also provides that the procedures to be followed in applying arbitration will be agreed through an exchange of notes by the Contracting States. It is expected that such procedures will ensure that arbitration will not generally be available where matters of either State's tax policy or domestic law are involved.

Paragraph 2 of Article 20 of the Protocol provides that the appropriate authorities of the Contracting State will consult after three years following entry into force of the Protocol to determine whether the diplomatic notes implementing the arbitration procedure should be exchanged.

ARTICLE 15

Article 15 of the Protocol adds to the Convention a new Article XXVI A (Assistance in Collection). Collection assistance provisions are included in several other U.S. income tax treaties, including the recent treaty with the Netherlands, and in many U.S. estate tax treaties. U.S. negotiators initially raised with Canada the possibility of including collection assistance provisions in the Protocol, because the Internal Revenue Service has claims pending against persons in Canada that would be subject to collection under these provisions. However, the ultimate decision of the U.S. and Canadian negotiators to add the collection assistance article was attributable to the confluence of several unusual factors.

Of critical importance was the similarity between the laws of the United States and Canada. The Internal Revenue Service, the Justice Department, and other U.S. negotiators were reassured by the close similarity of the legal and procedural protections afforded by the Contracting States to their citizens and residents and by the fact that these protections apply to the tax collection procedures used by each State. In addition, the U.S. negotiators were confident, given their extensive experience in working with their Canadian counterparts, that the agreed procedures could be administered appropriately, effectively, and efficiently. Finally, given the close cooperation already developed between the United States and Canada in the exchange of tax information, the U.S. and Canadian negotiators concluded that the potential benefits to both countries of obtaining such assistance would be immediate and substantial and would far outweigh any cost involved.

Under paragraph 1 of Article XXVI A, each Contracting State agrees, subject to the exercise of its discretion and to the conditions explicitly provided later in the Article, to lend assistance and support to the other in the collection of revenue claims. The term "revenue claim" is defined in paragraph 1 to include all taxes referred to in paragraph 9 of the Article, as well as interest, costs, additions to such taxes, and civil penalties. Paragraph 9 provides that, notwithstanding the provisions of Article II (Taxes Covered) of the Convention, Article XXVI A shall apply to all categories of taxes collected by or on behalf of the Government of a

Contracting State.

Paragraph 2 of the Article requires the Contracting State applying for collection assistance (the "applicant State") to certify that the revenue claim for which collection assistance is sought has been "finally determined." A revenue claim has been finally determined when the applicant State has the right under its internal law to collect the revenue claim and all administrative and judicial rights of the taxpayer to restrain collection in the applicant State have lapsed or been exhausted.

Paragraph 3 of the Article clarifies that the Contracting State from which assistance was requested (the "requested State") has discretion as to whether to accept a particular application for collection assistance. However, if the application for assistance is accepted, paragraph 3 requires that the requested State grant assistance under its existing procedures as though the claim were the requested State's own revenue claim finally determined under the laws of that State. This obligation under paragraph 3 is limited by paragraph 7 of the Article, which provides that, although generally treated as a revenue claim of the requested State, a claim for which collection assistance is granted shall not have any priority accorded to the revenue claims of the requested State.

Paragraph 4 of Article XXVI A provides that, when the United States accepts a request for assistance in collection, the claim will be treated by the United States as an assessment as of the time the application was received. Similarly, when Canada accepts a request, a revenue claim shall be treated as an amount payable under the Income Tax Act, the collection of which is not subject to any restriction.

Paragraph 5 of the Article provides that nothing in Article XXVI A shall be construed as creating in the requested State any rights of administrative or judicial review of the applicant State's finally determined revenue claim. Thus, when an application for collection assistance has been accepted, the substantive validity of the applicant State's revenue claim cannot be challenged in an action in the requested State. Paragraph 5 further provides, however, that if the applicant State's revenue claim ceases to be finally determined, the applicant State is obligated to withdraw promptly any request that had been based on that claim.

Paragraph 6 provides that, as a general rule, the requested State is to forward the entire amount collected to the competent authority of the applicant State. The ordinary costs incurred in providing collection assistance will normally be borne by the requested State and only extraordinary costs will be borne by the applicant State. The application of this paragraph, including rules specifying which collection costs are to be borne by each State and the time and manner of payment of the amounts collected, will be agreed upon by the competent authorities, as provided for in paragraph 11.

Paragraph 8 provides that no assistance is to be given under this Article for a claim in respect of an individual taxpayer, to the extent that the taxpayer can demonstrate that he was a citizen of the requested State during the taxable period to which the revenue claim relates. Similarly, in the case of a company, estate, or trust, no assistance is to be given to the extent that the entity can demonstrate that it derived its status as such under the laws in force in the requested State during the taxable period to which the claim relates.

Subparagraph (a) of paragraph 10 clarifies that Article XXVI A supplements the provisions of paragraph 4 of Article XXVI (Mutual Agreement Procedure). The Mutual Agreement Procedure paragraph, which is more common in U.S. tax treaties, provides for collection assistance in cases in which a Contracting State seeks assistance in reclaiming treaty benefits that have been granted to a person that is not entitled to those benefits. Subparagraph (b) of paragraph 10 makes clear that nothing in Article XXVI A can require a Contracting State to carry out administrative measures of a different nature from those used in the collection of its own taxes, or that would be contrary to its public policy (ordre public).

Paragraph 11 requires the competent authorities to agree upon the mode of application of Article XXVI A, including agreement to ensure comparable levels of assistance to each of the Contracting States.

Paragraph 3 of Article 21 of the Protocol allows collection assistance under Article XXVI A to be sought for revenue claims that have been finally determined at any time within the 10 years preceding the date on which the Protocol enters into force.

ARTICLE 16

Article 16 of the Protocol amends Article XXVII (Exchange of Information) of the Convention. Paragraph 1 of Article 16 amends paragraph 1 of Article XXVII. The first change is a wording change to make it clear that information must be exchanged if it is "relevant" for carrying out the provisions of the Convention or of the domestic laws of the Contracting States, even if it is not "necessary." Neither the United States nor Canada views this as a substantive change. The second amendment merely conforms the language of the paragraph to the language of Article II (Taxes Covered), as amended, by referring to the taxes "to which the Convention applies" rather than to the taxes "covered by the Convention."

The Protocol further amends paragraph 1 to allow a Contracting State to provide information received from the other Contracting State to its states, provinces, or local authorities, if it relates to a tax imposed by that state, province, or local authority that is substantially similar to a national-level tax covered under Article II (Taxes Covered). However, this provision does not authorize a Contracting State to request information on behalf of a state, province, or local authority. The Protocol also amends paragraph 1 to authorize the competent authorities to release information to any arbitration panel that may be established under the provisions of new paragraph 6 of Article XXVI (Mutual Agreement Procedure). Any information provided to a state, province, or local authority or to an arbitration panel is subject to the same use and disclosure provisions as is information received by the national Governments and used for their purposes.

Paragraph 2 of Article 16 amends paragraph 4 of Article XXVII, which describes the applicable taxes for the purposes of this Article. Under the present Convention, the Article applies in Canada to taxes imposed by the Government of Canada under the Income Tax Act and on estates and gifts and in the United States to all taxes imposed under the Internal Revenue Code. The Protocol broadens the scope of the Article to apply to "all taxes imposed by a Contracting State." This change allows information to be exchanged, for example, with respect to Canadian excise taxes, as is the case with respect to U.S. excise taxes under the present Convention. Paragraph 4 is also amended to authorize the exchange of information with respect to other taxes, to the extent relevant to any other provision of the Convention.

ARTICLE 17

Article 17 of the Protocol amends Article XXIX (Miscellaneous Rules) of the Convention. Paragraph 1 of Article 17 modifies paragraph 3(a), the exceptions to the saving clause, to conform the cross-references in the paragraph to changes in other parts of the Convention. The paragraph also adds to the exceptions to the saving clause certain provisions of Article XXIX B (Taxes Imposed by Reason of Death). Thus, certain benefits under that Article will be granted by a Contracting State to its residents and, in the case of the United States, to its citizens, notwithstanding the saving clause of paragraph 2 of Article XXIX.

Paragraph 2 of Article 17 replaces paragraphs 5 through 7 of Article XXIX of the present Convention with three new paragraphs. (Paragraph 5 in the present Convention was moved to paragraph 7 of Article XVIII (Pensions and Annuities), and paragraphs 6 and 7 were deleted as unnecessary.) New paragraph 5 provides a rule for the taxation by Canada of a Canadian resident that is a shareholder in a U.S. S corporation. The application of this rule is relatively limited, because U.S. domestic law requires that S corporation shareholders be either U.S. citizens or U.S. residents. Therefore, the rule provided by paragraph 5 would apply only to an S corporation shareholder who is a resident of both the United States and Canada (i.e., a "dual resident" who meets certain requirements), determined before application of the "tie-breaker" rules of Article IV (Residence), or a U.S. citizen resident in Canada. Since the shareholder would be subject to U.S. tax on its share of the income of the S corporation as it is earned by the S corporation and, under Canadian statutory law, would be subject to tax only when the income is distributed, there could be a timing mismatch resulting in unrelieved double taxation. Under paragraph 5, the shareholder can make a request to the Canadian competent authority for relief under the special rules of the paragraph. Under these rules, the Canadian shareholder will be subject to Canadian tax on essentially the same basis as he is subject to U.S. tax, thus eliminating the timing mismatch.

The Protocol adds to Article XXIX a new paragraph 6, which provides a coordination rule for the Convention and the General Agreement on Trade in Services ("GATS"). Paragraph 6(a) provides that, for purposes of paragraph 3 of Article XXII (Consultation) of the GATS, a measure falls within the scope of the Convention only if the measure relates to a tax

    (1)   to which Article XXV (Non-Discrimination) of the Convention applies, or

    (2)   to which Article XXV does not apply and to which any other provision of the Convention applies, but only to the extent that the measure relates to a matter dealt with in that other provision.

Under paragraph 6(b), notwithstanding paragraph 3 of Article XXII of the GATS, any doubt as to the interpretation of subparagraph (a) will be resolved under paragraph 3 of Article XXVI (Mutual Agreement Procedure) of the Convention or any other procedure agreed to by both Contracting States.

GATS generally obliges its Members to provide national treatment and most-favored-nation treatment to services and service suppliers of other Members. A very broad exception from the national treatment obligation applies to direct taxes. An exception from the most-favored-nation obligation applies to a difference in treatment resulting from an international agreement on the avoidance of double taxation (a "tax agreement") or from provisions on the avoidance of double taxation in any other international agreement or arrangement by which the Member is bound.

Article XXII(3) of GATS specifically provides that there will be no access to GATS procedures to settle a national treatment dispute concerning a measure that falls within the scope of a tax agreement. This provision preserves the exclusive application of nondiscrimination obligations in the tax agreement and clarifies that the competent authority mechanism provided by the tax agreement will apply, instead of GATS procedures, to resolve nondiscrimination disputes involving the taxation of services and service suppliers.

In the event of a disagreement between Members as to whether a measure falls within the scope of a tax agreement that existed at the time of the entry into force of the Agreement establishing the World Trade Organization, Article XXII(2), footnote 11, of GATS reserves the resolution of the dispute to the Contracting States under the tax agreement. In such a case, the issue of the scope of- a tax agreement may be resolved under GATS procedures (rather than tax treaty procedures) only if both parties to the existing tax agreement consent. With respect to subsequent tax agreements, GATS provides that either Member may bring the jurisdictional matter before the Council for Trade In Services, which will refer the matter to arbitration for a decision that will be final and binding on the Members.

Both Canada and the United States agree that a protocol to a convention that is grandfathered under Article XXII(2), footnote 11, of GATS is also grandfathered. Nevertheless, since the Protocol extends the application of the Convention, and particularly the nondiscrimination article, to additional taxes (e.g., some non-income taxes imposed by Canada), the negotiators sought to remove any ambiguity and agreed to a provision that clarified the scope of the Convention and the relationship between the Convention and GATS.

The purpose of new paragraph 6(a) of the Convention is to provide the agreement of the Contracting States as to the measures considered to fall within the scope of the Convention in applying Article XXII(3) of GATS between the Contracting States. The purpose of new paragraph 6(b) is to reserve the resolution of the issue of the scope of the Convention for purposes of Article XXII(3) of GATS to the competent authorities under the Convention rather than to settlement under GATS procedures.

The Protocol also adds to Article XXIX a new paragraph 7, relating to certain changes in the law or treaty policy of either of the Contracting States. Paragraph 7 provides, first, that in response to a change in the law or policy of either State, the appropriate authority of either State may request consultations with its counterpart in the other State to determine whether a change in the Convention is appropriate. If a change in domestic legislation has unilaterally removed or significantly limited a material benefit provided by the Convention, the appropriate authorities are instructed by the paragraph to consult promptly to consider an appropriate amendment to the Convention. The "appropriate authorities" may be the Contracting States themselves or the competent authorities under the Convention. The consultations may be initiated by the authority of the Contracting State making the change in law or policy or by the authority of the other State. Any change in the Convention recommended as a result of this process can be implemented only through the negotiation, signature, ratification, and entry into force of a new protocol to the Convention.

ARTICLE 18

In general.

Article 18 of the Protocol adds a new Article XXIX A (Limitation on Benefits) to the Convention. Article XXIX A addresses the problem of "treaty shopping" by requiring, in most cases, that the person seeking U.S. treaty benefits not only be a Canadian resident but also satisfy other tests. In a typical case of treaty shopping, a resident of a third State might establish an entity resident in Canada for the purpose of deriving income from the United States and claiming U.S. treaty benefits with respect to that income. Article XXIX A limits the benefits granted by the United States under the Convention to those persons whose residence in Canada is not considered to have been motivated by the existence of the Convention. Absent Article XXIX A, the entity would be entitled to U.S. benefits under the Convention as a resident of Canada, unless it were denied benefits as a result of limitations (e.g., business purpose, substance-over-form, step transaction, or conduit principles or other anti-avoidance rules) applicable to a particular transaction or arrangement. General anti-abuse provisions of this sort apply in conjunction with the Convention in both the United States and Canada. In the case of the United States, such anti-abuse provisions complement the explicit anti-treaty-shopping rules of Article XXIX A. While the anti-treaty- shopping rules determine whether a person has a sufficient nexus to Canada to be entitled to treaty benefits, general anti-abuse provisions determine whether a particular transaction should be recast in accordance with the substance of the transaction.

The present Convention deals with treaty-shopping in a very limited manner, in paragraph 6 of Article XXIX, by denying benefits to Canadian residents that benefit from specified provisions of Canadian law. The Protocol removes that paragraph 6 from Article XXIX, because it is superseded by the more general provisions of Article XXIX A.

The Article is not reciprocal, except for paragraph 7. Canada prefers to rely on general anti-avoidance rules to counter arrangements involving treaty-shopping through the United States.

The structure of the Article is as follows: Paragraph 1 states that, in determining whether a resident of Canada is entitled to U.S. benefits under the Convention, a "qualifying person" is entitled to all of the benefits of the Convention, and other persons are not entitled to benefits, except where paragraphs 3, 4, or 6 provide otherwise. Paragraph 2 lists a number of characteristics any one of which will make a Canadian resident a qualifying person. These are essentially mechanical tests. Paragraph 3 provides an alternative rule, under which a Canadian resident that is not a qualifying person under paragraph 2 may claim U.S. benefits with respect to those items of U.S. source income that are connected with the active conduct of a trade or business in Canada. . . . Paragraph 6 requires the U.S. competent authority to grant benefits to a resident of Canada that does not qualify for benefits under any other provision of the Article, where the competent authority determines, on the basis of all factors, that benefits should be granted. Paragraph 7 clarifies the application of general anti-abuse provisions.

Individuals and governmental entities.

Under paragraph 2, the first two categories of qualifying persons are

(1) individual residents of Canada, and

(2) the Government of Canada, a political subdivision or local authority thereof, or an agency or instrumentality of that Government, political subdivision, or local authority.

It is considered unlikely that persons falling into these two categories can be used, as the beneficial owner of income, to derive treaty benefits on behalf of a third-country person. If a person is receiving income as a nominee on behalf of a third-country resident, benefits will be denied with respect to those items of income under the articles of the Convention that grant the benefit, because of the requirements in those articles that the beneficial owner of the income be a resident of a Contracting State.

Publicly traded entities.

Under subparagraph (c) of paragraph 2, a Canadian resident company or trust is a qualifying person if there is substantial and regular trading in the company's principal class of shares, or in the trust's units, on a recognized stock exchange. The term "recognized stock exchange" is defined in paragraph 5(a) of the Article to mean, in the United States, the NASDAQ System and any stock exchange registered as a national securities exchange with the Securities and Exchange Commission, and, in Canada, any Canadian stock exchanges that are "prescribed stock exchanges" under the Income Tax Act. These are, at the time of signature of the Protocol, the Alberta, Montreal, Toronto, Vancouver, and Winnipeg Stock Exchanges. Additional exchanges may be added to the list of recognized exchanges by exchange of notes between the Contracting States or by agreement between the competent authorities.

Certain companies owned by publicly traded corporations also may be qualifying persons. Under subparagraph (d) of paragraph 2, a Canadian resident company will be a qualifying person, even if not publicly traded, if more than 50 percent of the vote and value of its shares is owned (directly or indirectly) by five or fewer persons that would be qualifying persons under subparagraph (c). In addition, each company in the chain of ownership must be a qualifying person or a U.S. citizen or resident. Thus, for example, a Canadian company that is not publicly traded but that is owned, one4hird each, by three companies, two of which are Canadian resident corporations whose principal classes of shares are substantially and regularly traded on a recognized stock exchange, will qualify under subparagraph (d).

The 50-percent test under subparagraph (d) applies only to shares other than "debt substitute shares." The term "debt substitute shares" is defined in paragraph 5 to mean shares defined in paragraph (e) of the definition in the Canadian Income Tax Act of "term preferred shares" (see section 248(1) of the Income Tax Act), which relates to certain shares received in debt-restructuring arrangements undertaken by reason of financial difficulty or insolvency. Paragraph 5 also provides that the competent authorities may agree to treat other types of shares as debt substitute shares.

Ownership/base erosion test.

Subparagraph (e) of paragraph 2 provides a two-part test under which certain other entities may be qualifying persons, based on ownership and "base erosion." Under the first of these tests, benefits will be granted to a Canadian resident company if 50 percent or more of the vote and value of its shares (other than debt substitute shares), or to a Canadian resident trust if 50 percent or more of its beneficial interest, is not owned, directly or indirectly, by persons other than qualifying persons or U.S. residents or citizens. The wording of these tests is intended to make clear that, for example, if a Canadian company is more than 50 percent owned by a U.S. resident corporation that is, itself, wholly owned by a third-country resident other than a U.S. citizen, the Canadian company would not pass the ownership test. This is because more than 50 percent of its shares is owned indirectly by a person (the third-country resident) that is not a qualifying person or a citizen or resident of the United States.

For purposes of this subparagraph (e) and other provisions of this Article, the term "shares" includes, in the case of a mutual insurance company, any certificate or contract entitling the holder to voting power in the corporation. This is consistent with the interpretation of similar limitation on benefits provisions in other U.S. treaties.

The second test of subparagraph (e) is the so-called "base erosion" test. A Canadian company or trust that passes the ownership test must also pass this test to be a qualifying person. This test requires that the amount of expenses that are paid or payable by the Canadian entity in question to persons that are not qualifying persons or U.S. citizens or residents, and that are deductible from gross income, be less than 50 percent of the gross income of the company or trust. This test is applied for the fiscal period immediately preceding the period for which the qualifying person test is being applied. If it is the first fiscal period of the person, the test is applied for the current period.

The ownership/base erosion test recognizes that the benefits of the Convention can be enjoyed indirectly not only by equity holders of an entity, but also by that entity's obligees, such as lenders, licensers, service providers, insurers and reinsurers, and others. For example, a third-country resident could license technology to Canadian-owned Canadian corporation to be sub licensed to a U.S. resident. The U.S. source royalty income of the Canadian corporation would be exempt from U.S. withholding tax under Article XII (Royalties) of the Convention (as amended by the Protocol). While the Canadian corporation would be subject to Canadian corporation income tax, its taxable income could be reduced to near zero as a result of the deductible royalties paid to the third-country resident. If, under a Convention between Canada and the third country, those royalties were either exempt from Canadian tax or subject to tax at a low rate, the U.S. treaty benefit with respect to the U.S. source royalty income would have flowed to the third-country resident at little or no tax cost, with no reciprocal benefit to the United States from the third country. The ownership/base erosion test therefore requires both that qualifying persons or U.S. residents or citizens substantially own the entity and that the entity's deductible payments be made in substantial part to such persons.

Other qualifying persons.

Under subparagraph (f) of paragraph 2, a Canadian resident estate is a qualifying person, entitled to the benefits of the Convention with respect to its U.S. source income.

Subparagraphs (g) and (h) specify the circumstances under which certain types of not-for-profit organizations will be qualifying persons. Subparagraph (g) of paragraph 2 provides that a not-for-profit organization that is a resident of Canada is a qualifying person, and thus entitled to U.S. benefits, if more than half of the beneficiaries, members, or participants in the organization are qualifying persons or citizens or residents of the United States. The term "not-for-profit organization" of a Contracting State is defined in subparagraph (b) of paragraph 5 of the Article to mean an entity created or established in that State that is generally exempt from income taxation in that State by reason of its not-for-profit status. The term includes charities, private foundations, trade unions, trade associations, and similar organizations.

Subparagraph (h) of paragraph 2 specifies that certain organizations described in paragraph 2 of Article XXI (Exempt Organizations), as amended by Article 10 of the Protocol, are qualifying persons. To be a qualifying person, such an organization must be established primarily for the purpose of providing pension, retirement, or employee benefits to individual residents of Canada who are (or were, within any of the five preceding years) qualifying persons, or to citizens or residents of the United States. An organization will be considered to be established "primarily" for this purpose if more than 50 percent of its beneficiaries, members, or participants are such persons. Thus, for example, a Canadian Registered Retirement Savings Plan ("RRSP") of a former resident of Canada who is working temporarily outside of Canada would continue to be a qualifying person during the period of the individual's absence from Canada or for five years, whichever is shorter. A Canadian pension fund established to provide benefits to persons employed by a company would be a qualifying person only if most of the beneficiaries of the fund are (or were within the five preceding years) individual residents of Canada or residents or citizens of the United States.

The provisions of paragraph 2 are self-executing, unlike the provisions of paragraph 6, discussed below. The tax authorities may, of course, on review, determine that the taxpayer has improperly interpreted the paragraph and is not entitled to the benefits claimed.

Active trade or business test.

Paragraph 3 provides an eligibility test for benefits for residents of Canada that are not qualifying persons under paragraph 2. This is the so-called "active trade or business" test. Unlike the tests of paragraph 2, the active trade or business test looks not solely at the characteristics of the person deriving the income, but also at the nature of the activity engaged in by that person and the connection between the income and that activity. Under the active trade or business test, a resident of Canada deriving an item of income from the United States is entitled to benefits with respect to that income if that person (or a person related to that person under the principles of Internal Revenue Code section 482) is engaged in an active trade or business in Canada and the income in question is derived in connection with, or is incidental to, that trade or business.

Income that is derived in connection with, or is incidental to, the business of making or managing investments will not qualify for benefits under this provision, unless those investment activities are carried on with customers in the ordinary course of the business of a bank, insurance company, registered securities dealer, or deposit-taking financial institution.

Income is considered derived "in connection" with an active trade or business in the United States if, for example, the income-generating activity in the United States is "upstream," "downstream," or parallel to that conducted in Canada. Thus, if the U.S. activity consisted of selling the output of a Canadian manufacturer or providing inputs to the manufacturing process, or of manufacturing or selling in the United States the same sorts of products that were being sold by the Canadian trade or business in Canada, the income generated by that activity would be treated as earned in connection with the Canadian trade or business. Income is considered "incidental" to the Canadian trade or business if, for example, it arises from the short-term investment of working capital of the Canadian resident in U.S. securities.

An item of income will be considered to be earned in connection with or to be incidental to an active trade or business in Canada if the income is derived by the resident of Canada claiming the benefits directly or indirectly through one or more other persons that are residents of the United States. Thus, for example, a Canadian resident could claim benefits with respect to an item of income earned by a U.S. operating subsidiary but derived by the Canadian resident indirectly through a wholly-owned U.S. holding company interposed between it and the operating subsidiary. This language would also permit a Canadian resident to derive income from the United States through one or more U.S. residents that it does not wholly own. For example, a Canadian partnership in which three unrelated Canadian companies each hold a one-third interest could form a wholly-owned U.S. holding company with a U.S. operating subsidiary. The "directly or indirectly" language would allow otherwise available treaty benefits to be claimed with respect to income derived by the three Canadian partners through the U.S. holding company, even if the partners were not considered to be related to the U.S. holding company under the principles of Internal Revenue Code section 482.

Income that is derived in connection with, or is incidental to, an active trade or business in Canada, must pass an additional test to qualify for U.S. treaty benefits. The trade or business in Canada must be substantial in relation to the activity in the United States that gave rise to the income in respect of which treaty benefits are being claimed. To be considered substantial, it is not necessary that the Canadian trade or business be as large as the U.S. income-generating activity. The Canadian trade or business cannot, however, in terms of income, assets, or other similar measures, represent only a very small percentage of the size of the U.S. activity.

The substantiality requirement is intended to prevent treaty-shopping. For example, a third-country resident may want to acquire a U.S. company that manufactures television sets for worldwide markets; however, since its country of residence has no tax treaty with the United States, any dividends generated by the investment would be subject to a U.S. withholding tax of 30 percent. Absent a substantiality test, the investor could establish a Canadian corporation that would operate a small outlet in Canada to sell a few of the television sets manufactured by the U.S. company and earn a very small amount of income. That Canadian corporation could then acquire the U.S. manufacturer with capital provided by the third-country resident and produce a very large number of sets for sale in several countries, generating a much larger amount of income. It might attempt to argue that the U.S. source income is generated from business activities in the United States related to the television sales activity of the Canadian parent and that the dividend income should be subject to U.S. tax at the 5 percent rate provided by Article X of the Convention, as amended by the Protocol. However, the substantiality test would not be met in this example, so the dividends would remain subject to withholding in the United States at a rate of 30 percent.

In general, it is expected that if a person qualifies for benefits under one of the tests of paragraph 2, no inquiry will be made into qualification for benefits under paragraph 3. Upon satisfaction of any of the tests of paragraph 2, any income derived by the beneficial owner from the other Contracting State is entitled to treaty benefits. Under paragraph 3, however, the test is applied separately to each item of income.

Derivative benefits test.

Paragraph 4 of Article XXIX A contains a so-called "derivative benefits" rule not generally found in U.S. treaties. This rule was included in the Protocol because of the special economic relationship between the United States and Canada and the close coordination between the tax administrations of the two countries.

Under the derivative benefits rule, a Canadian resident company may receive the benefits of Articles X (Dividends), XI (Interest), and XII (Royalties), even if the company is not a qualifying person and does not satisfy the active trade or business test of paragraph 3. To qualify under this paragraph, the Canadian company must satisfy both

   (i)   the base erosion test under subparagraph (e) of paragraph 2, and

   (ii) an ownership test.

The derivative benefits ownership test requires that shares (other than debt substitute shares) representing more than 90 percent of the vote and value of the Canadian company be owned directly or indirectly by either

   (i)   qualifying persons or U.S. citizens or residents, or

   (ii) other persons that satisfy each of three tests. The three tests that must be satisfied by these other persons are as follows:

First, the person must be a resident of a third State with which the United States has a comprehensive income tax convention and be entitled to all of the benefits under that convention. Thus, if the person fails to satisfy the limitation on benefits tests, if any, of that convention, no benefits would be granted under this paragraph. Qualification for benefits under an active trade or business test does not suffice for these purposes, because that test grants benefits only for certain items of income, not for all purposes of the convention.

Second, the person must be a person that would qualify for benefits with respect to the item of income for which benefits are sought under one or more of the tests of paragraph 2 or 3 of this Convention, if the person were a resident of Canada and, for purposes of paragraph 3, the business were carried on in Canada. For example, a person resident in a third country would be deemed to be a person that would qualify under the publicly-traded test of paragraph 2 of this Convention if the principal class of its shares were substantially and regularly traded on a stock exchange recognized either under the treaty between the United States and Canada or under the treaty between the United States and the third country. Similarly, a company resident in a third country would be deemed to satisfy the ownership/base erosion test of paragraph 2 under this hypothetical analysis if, for example, it were wholly owned by an individual resident in that third country and most of its deductible payments were made to individual residents of that country (i.e., it satisfied base erosion).

The third requirement is that the rate of U.S. withholding tax on the item of income in respect of which benefits are sought must be at least as low under the convention between the person's country of residence and the United States as under this Convention.

Competent authority discretion.

Paragraph 6 provides that when a resident of Canada derives income from the United States and is not entitled to the benefits of the Convention under other provisions of the Article, benefits may, nevertheless be granted at the discretion of the U.S. competent authority. In making a determination under this paragraph, the competent authority will take into account all relevant facts and circumstances relating to the person requesting the benefits. In particular, the competent authority will consider the history, structure, ownership (including ultimate beneficial ownership), and operations of the person. In addition, the competent authority is to consider

(1) whether the creation and existence of the person did not have as a principal purpose obtaining treaty benefits that would not otherwise be available to the person, and

(2) whether it would not be appropriate, in view of the purpose of the Article, to deny benefits.

The paragraph specifies that if the U.S. competent authority determines that either of these two standards is satisfied, benefits shall be granted.

For purposes of implementing paragraph 6, a taxpayer will be expected to present his case to the competent authority for an advance determination based on the facts. The taxpayer will not be required to wait until it has been determined that benefits are denied under one of the other provisions of the Article. It also is expected that, if and when the competent authority determines that benefits are to be allowed, they will be allowed retroactively to the time of entry into force of the relevant treaty provision or the establishment of the structure in question, whichever is later (assuming that the taxpayer also qualifies under the relevant facts for the earlier period).

General anti-abuse provisions.

Paragraph 7 was added at Canada's request to confirm that the specific provisions of Article XXIX A and the fact that these provisions apply only for the purposes of the application of the Convention by the United States should not be construed so as to limit the right of each Contracting State to invoke applicable anti- abuse rules. Thus, for example, Canada remains free to apply such rules to counter abusive arrangements involving "treaty-shopping" through the United States, and the United States remains free to apply its substance-over-form and anti-conduit rules, for example, in relation to Canadian residents. This principle is recognized by the Organization for Economic Cooperation and Development in the Commentaries to its Model Tax Convention on Income and on Capital, and the United States and Canada agree that it is inherent in the Convention. The agreement to state this principle explicitly in the Protocol is not intended to suggest that the principle is not also inherent in other tax conventions, including the current Convention with Canada.

ARTICLE 19

In general.

Article 19 of the Protocol adds to the Convention a new Article XXIX B (Taxes Imposed by Reason of Death). The purpose of Article XXIX B is to better coordinate the operation of the death tax regimes of the two Contracting States. Such coordination is necessary because the United States imposes an estate tax, while Canada now applies an income tax on gains deemed realized at death rather than an estate tax. Article XXIX B also contains other provisions designed to alleviate death taxes in certain situations.

For purposes of new Article XXIX B, the term "resident" has the meaning provided by Article IV (Residence) of the Convention, as amended by Article 3 of the Protocol. The meaning of the term "resident" for purposes of Article XXIX B, therefore, differs in some respects from its meaning under the estate, gift, and generation-skipping transfer tax provisions of the Internal Revenue Code.

Charitable bequests.

Paragraph 1 of new Article XXIX B facilitates certain charitable bequests. It provides that a Contracting State shall accord the same death tax treatment to a bequest by an individual resident in one of the Contracting States to a qualifying exempt organization resident in the other Contracting State as it would have accorded if the organization had been a resident of the first Contracting State. The organizations covered by this provision are those referred to in paragraph 1 of Article XXI (Exempt Organizations) of the Convention. A bequest by a U.S. citizen or U.S. resident (as defined for estate tax purposes under the Internal Revenue Code) to such an exempt organization generally is deductible for U.S. estate tax purposes under section 2055 of the Internal Revenue Code, without regard to whether the organization is a U.S. corporation. However, if the decedent is not a U.S. citizen or U.S. resident (as defined for estate tax purposes under the Internal Revenue Code), such a bequest is deductible for U.S. estate tax purposes, under section 2106(a)(2) of the Internal Revenue Code, only if the recipient organization is a U.S. corporation. Under paragraph 1 of Article XXIX B, a U.S. estate tax deduction also will be allowed for a bequest by a Canadian resident (as defined under Article IV (Residence)) to a qualifying exempt organization that is a Canadian corporation. However, paragraph 1 does not allow a deduction for U.S. estate tax purposes with respect to any transfer of property that is not subject to U.S. estate tax.

Unified credit.

Paragraph 2 of Article XXIX B grants a "pro rata" unified credit to the estate of a Canadian resident decedent, for purposes of computing U.S. estate tax. Although the Congress anticipated the negotiation of such pro rata unified credits in Internal Revenue Code section 2102(c)(3)(A), this is the first convention in which the United States has agreed to give such a credit. However, certain exemption provisions of existing estate and gift tax conventions have been interpreted as providing a pro rata unified credit.

Under the Internal Revenue Code, the estate of a nonresident not a citizen of the United States is subject to U.S. estate tax only on its U.S. situs assets and is entitled to a unified credit of $13,000, while the estate of a U.S. citizen or U.S. resident is subject to U.S. estate tax on its entire worldwide assets and is entitled to a unified credit of $192,800. (For purposes of these Internal Revenue Code provisions, the term "resident" has the meaning provided for estate tax purposes under the Internal Revenue Code.) A lower unified credit is provided for the former category of estates because it is assumed that the estate of a nonresident not a citizen generally will hold fewer U.S. situs assets, as a percentage of the estate's total assets, and thus will have a lower U.S. estate tax liability. The pro rata unified credit provisions of paragraph 2 increase the credit allowed to the estate of a Canadian resident decedent to an amount between $13,000 and $192,800 in appropriate cases, to take into account the extent to which the assets of the estate are situated in the United States. Paragraph 2 provides that the amount of the unified credit allowed to the estate of a Canadian resident decedent will in no event be less than the $13,000 allowed under the Internal Revenue Code to the estate of a nonresident not a citizen of the United States (subject to the adjustment for prior gift tax unified credits, discussed below). Paragraph 2 does not apply to the estates of U.S. citizen decedents, whether resident in Canada or elsewhere, because such estates receive a unified credit of $192,800 under the Internal Revenue Code.

Subject to the adjustment for gift tax unified credits, the pro rata credit allowed under paragraph 2 is determined by multiplying $192,800 by a fraction, the numerator of which is the value of the part of the gross estate situated in the United States and he denominator of which is the value of the entire gross estate wherever situated. Thus, if half of the entire gross estate (by value) of a decedent who was a resident and citizen of Canada were situated in the United States, the estate would be entitled to a pro rata unified credit of $96,400 (provided that the U.S. estate tax due is not less than that amount). For purposes of the denominator, the entire gross estate wherever situated (i.e., the worldwide estate, determined under U.S. domestic law) is to be taken into account for purposes of the computation. For purposes of the numerator, an estate's assets will be treated as situated in the United States if they are so treated under U.S. domestic law. However, if enacted, a technical correction now pending before the Congress will amend U.S. domestic law to clarify that assets will not be treated as U.S. situs assets for purposes of the pro rata unified credit computation if the United States is precluded from taxing them by reason of a treaty obligation. This technical correction will affect the interpretation of both this paragraph 2 and the analogous provisions in existing conventions. As currently proposed, it will take effect on the date of enactment.

Paragraph 2 restricts the availability of the pro rata unified credit in two respects. First, the amount of the unified credit otherwise allowable under paragraph 2 is reduced by the amount of any unified credit previously allowed against U.S. gift tax imposed on any gift by the decedent. This rule reflects the fact that, under U.S. domestic law, a U.S. citizen or U.S. resident individual is allowed a unified credit against the U.S. gift tax on lifetime transfers. However, as a result of the estate tax computation, the individual is entitled only to a total unified credit of $192,800, and the amount of the unified credit available for use against U.S. estate tax on the individual's estate is effectively reduced by the amount of any unified credit that has been allowed in respect of gifts by the individual. This rule is reflected by reducing the amount of the pro rata unified credit otherwise allowed to the estate of a decedent individual under paragraph 2 by the amount of any unified credit previously allowed with respect to lifetime gifts by that individual. This reduction will be relevant only in rare cases, where the decedent made gifts subject to the U.S. gift tax while a U.S. citizen or U.S. resident (as defined under the Internal Revenue Code for U.S. gift tax purposes).

Paragraph 2 also conditions allowance of the pro rata unified credit upon the provision of all information necessary to verify and compute the credit. Thus, for example, the estate's representatives will be required to demonstrate satisfactorily both the value of the worldwide estate and the value of the U.S. portion of the estate. Substantiation requirements also apply, of course, with respect to other provisions of the Protocol and the Convention. However, the negotiators believed it advisable to emphasize the substantiation requirements in connection with this provision, because the computation of the pro rata unified credit involves certain information not otherwise relevant for U.S. estate tax purposes.

In addition, the amount of the pro rata unified credit is limited to the amount of U.S. estate tax imposed on the estate. See section 2102(c)(4) of the Internal Revenue Code.

Marital credit.

Paragraph 3 of Article XXIX B allows a special "marital credit" against U.S. estate tax in respect of certain transfers to a surviving spouse. The purpose of this marital credit is to alleviate, in appropriate cases, the impact of the estate tax marital deduction restrictions enacted by the Congress in the Technical and Miscellaneous Revenue Act of 1988 ("TAMRA"). It is the firm position of the U.S. Treasury Department that the TAMRA provisions do not violate the nondiscrimination provisions of this Convention or any other convention to which the United States is a party. This is because the estate--not the surviving spouse--is the taxpayer, and the TAMRA provisions treat the estates of nonresidents not citizens of the United States in the same manner as the estates of U.S. citizen and U.S. resident decedents. However, the U.S. negotiators believed that it was not inappropriate, in the context of the Protocol, to ease the impact of those TAMRA provisions upon certain estates of limited value.

Paragraph 3 allows a non-refundable marital credit in addition to the pro rata unified credit allowed under paragraph 2 (or, in the case of a U.S. citizen or U.S. resident decedent, the unified credit allowed under U.S. domestic law). However, the marital credit is allowed only in connection with transfers satisfying each of the five conditions set forth in paragraph 3. First, the property must be "qualifying property," i.e., it must pass to the surviving spouse (within the meaning of U.S. domestic law) and be property that would have qualified for the estate tax marital deduction under U.S. domestic law if the surviving spouse had been a U.S. citizen and all applicable elections specified by U.S. domestic law had been properly made. Second, the decedent must have been, at the time of death, either a resident of Canada or the United States or a citizen of the United States. Third, the surviving spouse must have been, at the time of the decedent's death, a resident of either Canada or the United States. Fourth, if both the decedent and the surviving spouse were residents of the United States at the time of the decedent's death, at least one of them must have been a citizen of Canada. Finally, to limit the benefits of paragraph 3 to relatively small estates, the executor of the decedent's estate is required to elect the benefits of paragraph 3, and to waive irrevocably the benefits of any estate tax marital deduction that would be allowed under U.S. domestic law, on a U.S. Federal estate tax return filed by the deadline for making a qualified domestic trust election under Internal Revenue Code section 2056A(d). In the case of the estate of a decedent for which the U.S. Federal estate tax return is filed on or before the date on which this Protocol enters into force, this election and waiver must be made on any return filed to claim a refund pursuant to the special effective date applicable to such estates (discussed below).

Paragraph 4 governs the computation of the marital credit allowed under paragraph 3. It provides that the amount of the marital credit shall equal the lesser of

(i)   the amount of the unified credit allowed to the estate under paragraph 2 or, where applicable, under U.S. domestic law (before reduction for any gift tax unified credit), or

(ii)   the amount of U.S. estate tax that would otherwise be imposed on the transfer of qualifying property to the surviving spouse.

For this purpose, the amount of U.S. estate tax that would otherwise be imposed on the transfer of qualifying property equals the amount by which

(i)   the estate tax (before allowable credits) that would be imposed if that property were included in computing the taxable estate exceeds

(ii)   the estate tax (before allowable credits) that would be imposed if the property were not so included.

Property that, by reason of the provisions of paragraph 8 of this Article, is not subject to U.S. estate tax is not taken into account for purposes of this hypothetical computation.

Finally, paragraph 4 provides taxpayers with an ordering rule. The rule states that, solely for purposes of determining any other credits (e.g., the credits for foreign and state death taxes) that may be allowed under U.S. domestic law to the estate, the marital credit shall be allowed after such other credits.

In certain cases, the provisions of paragraphs 3 and 4 may affect the U.S. estate taxation of a trust that would meet the requirements for a qualified terminable interest property ("QTIP") election, for example, a trust with a life income interest for the surviving spouse and a remainder interest for other family members. If, in lieu of making the QTIP election and the qualified domestic trust election, the decedent's executor makes the election described in paragraph 3(d) of this Article, the provisions of Internal Revenue Code sections 2044 (regarding inclusion in the estate of the second spouse of certain property for which the marital deduction was previously allowed), 2056A (regarding qualified domestic trusts), and 2519 (regarding dispositions of certain life estates) will not apply. To obtain this treatment, however, tile executor is required, under paragraph 3, to irrevocably waive the benefit of any marital deduction allowable under the Internal Revenue Code with respect to the trust.

The following examples illustrate the operation of the marital credit and its interaction with other credits. Unless otherwise stated, assume for purposes of illustration that H, the decedent, and W, his surviving spouse, are Canadian citizens resident in Canada at the time of the decedent's death. Assume further that all conditions set forth in paragraphs 2 and 3 of this Article XXIX B are satisfied (including the condition that the executor waive the estate tax marital deduction), that no deductions are available under the Internal Revenue Code in computing the U.S. estate tax liability, and that there are no adjusted taxable gifts within the meaning of Internal Revenue Code section 2001(b) or 2101(c). Also assume that the applicable U.S. domestic estate and gift tax laws are those that were in effect on the date the Protocol was signed.

Example 1.   H has a worldwide gross estate of $1,200,000. He bequeaths U.S. real property worth $600,000 to W. The remainder of H's estate consists of Canadian situs property. H's estate would be entitled to a pro rata unified credit of $96,400 (= $192,800 x ($600,000/$1,200,000)) and to a marital credit in the same amount (the lesser of the unified credit allowed ($96,400) and the U.S. estate tax that would otherwise be imposed on the property transferred to W ($192,800 [tax on U.S. taxable estate of $600,000])). The pro rata unified credit and the marital credit combined would eliminate all U.S. estate tax with respect to the property transferred to W.

Example 2.   H has a worldwide gross estate of $1,200,000, all of which is situated in the United States. He bequeaths U.S. real property worth $600,000 to W and U.S. real property worth $600,000 to a child, C. H's estate would be entitled to a pro rata unified credit of $192,800 (= $192,800 x $1,200,000/$1,200,000) and to a marital credit of $192,800 (the lesser of the unified credit ($192,800) and the U.S. estate tax that would otherwise be imposed on the property transferred to W ($235,000, i.e., $427,800 [tax on U.S. taxable estate of $1,200,000] less $192,800 [tax on U.S. taxable estate of $600,000])). This would reduce the estate's total U.S. estate tax liability of $427,800 by $385,600.

Example 3.   H has a worldwide gross estate of $700,000, of which $500,000 is real property situated in the United States. H bequeaths U.S. real property valued at $100,000 to W. The remainder of H's gross estate, consisting of U.S. and Canadian situs real property, is bequeathed to H's child, C. H's estate would be entitled to a pro rata unified credit of $137,714 ($192,800 x $500,000/$700,000). In addition, H's estate would be entitled to a marital credit of $34,000, which equals the lesser of the unified credit ($137,714) and $34,000 (the U.S. estate tax that would otherwise be imposed on the property transferred to W before allowance of any credits, i.e., $155,800 [tax on U.S. taxable estate of $500,000] less $121,800 [tax on U.S. taxable estate of $400,000]).

Example 4.   H has a worldwide gross estate of $5,000,000, $2,000,000 of which consists of U.S. real property situated in State X. State X imposes a state death tax equal to the federal credit allowed under Internal Revenue Code section 2011. H bequeaths U.S. situs real property worth $1,000,000 to W and U.S. situs real property worth $1,000,000 to his child, C. The remainder of H's estate ($3,000,000) consists of Canadian situs property passing to C. H's estate would be entitled to a pro rata unified credit of $77,120 ($192,800 x $2,000,000/$5,000,000). H's estate would be entitled to a state death tax credit under Internal Revenue Code section 2102 of $99,600 (determined under Internal

Revenue Code section 2011(b) with respect to an adjusted taxable estate of $1,940,000). H's estate also would be entitled to a marital credit of $77,120, which equals the lesser of the unified credit ($77,120) and $435,000 (the U.S. estate tax that would otherwise be imposed on the property transferred to W before allowance of any credits, i.e., $780,000 [tax on U.S. taxable estate of $2,000,000] less $345,800 [tax on U.S. taxable estate of $1,000,000]).

Example 5. The facts are the same as in Example 4, except that H and W are Canadian citizens who are resident in the United States at the time of H's death. Canadian Federal and provincial income taxes totaling $500,000 are imposed by reason of H's death. H's estate would be entitled to a unified credit of $192,800 and to a state death tax credit of $300,880 under Internal Revenue Code sections 2010 and 2011(b), respectively. Under paragraph 6 of Article XXIX B, H's estate would be entitled to a credit for the Canadian income tax imposed by reason of death, equal to the lesser of $500,000 (the Canadian taxes paid) or $1,138,272 ($2,390,800 (tax on $5,000,000 taxable estate) less total of unified and state death tax credits ($493,680) x $3,000,000/$5,000,000). H's estate also would be entitled to a marital credit of $192,800, which equals the lesser of the unified credit ($192,800) and $550,000 (the U.S. estate tax that would otherwise be imposed on the property transferred to W before allowance of any credits, i.e., $2,390,800 (tax on U.S. taxable estate of $5,000,000] less $1,840,800 [tax on U.S. taxable estate of $4,000,000]).

Canadian treatment of certain transfers.

The provisions of paragraph 5 relate to the operation of Canadian law. They are intended to provide deferral ("rollover") of the Canadian tax at death for certain transfers to a surviving spouse and to permit the Canadian competent authority to allow such deferral for certain transfers to a trust. For example, they would enable the competent authority to treat a trust that is a qualified domestic trust for U.S. estate tax purposes as a Canadian spousal trust as well for purposes of certain provisions of Canadian tax law and of the Convention. These provisions do not affect U.S. domestic law regarding qualified domestic trusts. Nor do they affect the status of U.S. resident individuals for any other purpose.

Credit for U.S. taxes.

Under paragraph 6, Canada agrees to give Canadian residents and Canadian resident spousal trusts (or trusts treated as such by virtue of paragraph 5) a deduction from tax (i.e., a credit) for U.S. Federal or state estate or inheritance taxes imposed on U.S. situs property of the decedent or the trust. This credit is allowed against the income tax imposed by Canada, in an amount computed in accordance with subparagraph 6(a) or 6(b).

Subparagraph 6(a) covers the first set of cases---where the U.S. tax is imposed upon a decedent's death. Subparagraph 6(a)(i) allows a credit for U.S. tax against the total amount of Canadian income tax payable by the decedent in the taxable year of death on any income, profits, or gains arising in the United States (within the meaning of paragraph 3 of Article XXIV(Elimination of Double Taxation)). For purposes of subparagraph 6(a)(i), income, profits, or gains arising in the United States within the meaning of paragraph 3 of Article XXIV include gains deemed realized at death on U.S. situs real property and on personal property forming part of the business property of a U.S. permanent establishment or fixed base. (As explained below, these are the only types of property on which the United States may impose its estate tax if the estate is worth $1.2 million or less.) Income, profits, or gains arising in the United States also include income and profits earned by the decedent during the taxable year of death, to the extent that the United States may tax such amounts under the Convention (e.g., dividends received from a U.S. corporation and wages from the performance of personal services in the United States).

Where the value of the decedent's entire gross estate exceeds $1.2 million, subparagraph 6(a)(ii) allows a credit against the Canadian income tax on any income, profits, or gains from any U.S. situs property, in addition to any credit allowed by subparagraph 6(a)(i). This provision is broader in scope than is the general rule under subparagraph 6(a)(i), because the United States has retained the right to impose its estate tax on all types of property in the case of larger estates. Subparagraph 6(b) provides rules for a second category of cases----where the U.S. tax is imposed upon the death of the surviving spouse. In these cases, Canada agrees to allow a credit against the Canadian tax payable by a trust for its taxable year during which the surviving spouse dies on any income, profits, or gains

(i)   arising in the United States on U.S. situs real property or business property, or

(ii) from property situated in the United States.

These rules are intended to provide a credit for taxes imposed as a result of the death of the surviving spouse in situations involving trusts. To the extent that taxes are imposed on the estate of the surviving spouse, subparagraph 6(a) would apply as well. In addition, the competent authorities are authorized to provide relief from double taxation in certain additional circumstances involving trusts, as described above in connection with Article 14 of the Protocol.

The credit allowed under paragraph 6 is subject to certain conditions. First, where the decedent was a U.S. citizen or former citizen (described in paragraph 2 of Article XXIX (Miscellaneous Rules)), paragraph 6 does not obligate Canada to provide a credit for U.S. taxes in excess of the amount of U.S. taxes that would have been payable if the decedent had not been a U.S. citizen or former citizen. Second, the credit allowed under paragraph 6 will be computed after taking into account any deduction for U.S. income tax provided under paragraph 2(a), 4(a), or 5(b) of Article XXIV (Elimination of Double Taxation). This clarifies that no double credit will be allowed for any amount and provides an ordering rule. Finally, because Canadian domestic law does not contain a definition of U.S. situs property for death tax purposes, such a definition is provided for purposes of paragraph 6. To maximize coordination of the credit provisions, the Contracting States agreed to follow the U.S. estate tax law definition as in effect on the date of signature of the

Protocol and, subject to competent authority agreement, as it may be amended in the future.

Credit for Canadian taxes.

Under paragraph 7, the United States agrees to allow a credit against U.S. Federal estate tax imposed on the estate of a U.S. resident or U.S. citizen decedent, or upon the death of a surviving spouse with respect to a qualified; domestic trust created by such a decedent (or the decedent's executor or surviving spouse). The credit is allowed for <u>Canadian Federal and provincial income taxes</u> imposed at death with respect to property of the estate or trust that is situated outside of the United States. As in the case under paragraph 6, the competent authorities also are authorized to provide relief from double taxation in certain cases involving trusts (see discussion of Article 14, above).

The amount of the credit generally will be determined as though the income tax imposed by Canada were a creditable tax under the U.S. estate tax provisions regarding credit for foreign death taxes, in accordance with the provisions and subject to the limitations of Internal Revenue Code section 2014. However, subparagraph 7(a) clarifies that a credit otherwise allowable under paragraph 7 will not be denied merely because of inconsistencies between U.S. and Canadian law regarding the identity of the taxpayer in the case of a particular taxable event. For example, the fact that the taxpayer is the decedent's estate for purposes of U.S. estate taxation and the decedent for purposes of Canadian income taxation will not prevent the allowance of a credit under paragraph 7 for Canadian income taxes imposed by reason of the death of the decedent.

In addition, subparagraph 7(c) clarifies that the credit against the U.S. estate tax generally may be claimed only to the extent that no credit or deduction is claimed for the same amount of Canadian tax in determining any other U.S. tax. This makes clear, for example, that a credit may not be claimed for the same amount under both this provision and Article XXIV (Elimination of Double Taxation). To prevent double taxation, an exception to this restriction is provided for certain taxes imposed with respect to qualified domestic trusts. Subject to the limitations of subparagraph 7(c), the taxpayer may choose between relief under Article XXIV, relief under this paragraph 7, or some combination of the two.

Relief for small estates.

Under paragraph 8, the United States agrees to limit the application of its estate tax in the case of certain small estates of Canadian resident decedents. This provision is intended to eliminate the "trap for the unwary" that exists for such decedents, in the absence of an estate tax convention between the United States and Canada. In the absence of sophisticated estate tax planning, such decedents may inadvertently subject their estates to U.S. estate tax liability by holding shares of U.S. corporate stock or other U.S. situs property. U.S. resident decedents are already protected in this regard by the provisions of Article XIII (Gains) of the present Convention, which prohibit Canada from imposing its income tax on gains deemed realized at death by U.S. residents on such property.

Paragraph 8 provides relief only in the case of Canadian resident decedents whose entire gross estates wherever situated (i.e., worldwide gross estates determined under U.S. law) have a value, at the time of death, not exceeding $1.2 million. Paragraph 8 provides that the United States may impose its estate tax upon property forming part of such estates only if any gain on alienation of the property would have been subject to U.S. income taxation under Article XIII (Gains). For estates with a total value not exceeding $1.2 million, this provision has the effect of permitting the United States to impose its estate tax only on real property situated in the United States within the meaning of Article XIII, and personal property forming part of the business property of a U.S. permanent establishment or fixed base.

Saving clause exceptions.

Certain provisions of Article XXIX B are included in the list of exceptions to the general "saving clause" of Article XXIX (Miscellaneous Rules), as amended by Article 17 of the Protocol. To the extent that an exception from the saving clause is provided for a provision, each Contracting State is required to allow the benefits of that provision to its residents (and, in the case of the United States, its citizens), notwithstanding the saving clause. General saving clause exceptions are provided for paragraphs 1, 5, and 6 of Article XXIX B. Saving clause exceptions are provided for paragraphs 2, 3, 4, and 7, except for the estates of former U.S. citizens referred to in paragraph 2 of Article XXIX.

Effective dates.

Article 21 of the Protocol contains special retrospective effective date provisions for paragraphs 2 through 8 of Article XXIX B and certain related provisions of the Protocol. Paragraphs 2 through 8 of Article XXIX B and the specified related provisions generally will take effect with respect to deaths occurring after the date on which the Protocol enters into force (i.e., the date on which the instruments of ratification are exchanged). However, the benefits of those provisions will also be available with respect to deaths occurring after November 10, 1988, provided that a claim for refund due as a result of these provisions is filed by the later of one year from the date on which the Protocol enters into force or the date on which the applicable period for filing such a claim expires under the domestic law of the Contracting State concerned. The general effective dates set forth in Article 21 of the Protocol otherwise apply.

It is unusual for the United States to agree to retrospective effective dates. In this case, however, the negotiators believed that retrospective application was not inappropriate, given the fact that the TAMRA provisions were the impetus for negotiation of the Protocol and that the negotiations commenced soon after the enactment of TAMRA. The United States has agreed to retrospective effective dates in certain other instances (e.g., in the case of the U.S.-Germany estate tax treaty). The retrospective effective dates apply reciprocally, so that they will benefit the estates of U.S. decedents as well as Canadian decedents.

ARTICLE 20

Article 20 of the Protocol does not amend the text of the Convention. It states two understandings between the Contracting States regarding future action relating to matters dealt with in the Protocol. Paragraph 1 requires the appropriate authorities of the Contracting States to consult on two matters within three years from the date on which the Protocol enters into force. First, they will consult with a view to agreeing to further reductions in withholding rates on dividends, interest and royalties under Articles X, XI, and XII, respectively. This provision reflects the fact that, although the Protocol does significantly reduce withholding rates, the United States remains interested in even greater reductions, to further open the capital markets and fulfill the objectives of the North American Free Trade Agreement. Second, the appropriate authorities of the Contracting States will consult about the rules in Article XXIX A (Limitation on Benefits). By that time, both Contracting States will have had an opportunity to observe the operation of the Article, and the United States will have had greater experience with the corresponding provisions in other recent U.S. tax conventions.

Paragraph 2 of Article 20 also requires consultations between the appropriate authorities, after the three-year period from the date on which the Protocol enters into force, to determine whether to implement the arbitration procedure provided for in paragraph 6 of Article XXVI (Mutual Agreement Procedure), added by Article 14 of the Protocol. The three-year period is intended to give the authorities an opportunity to consider how arbitration has functioned in other tax conventions, such as the U.S.-Germany Convention, before implementing it under this Convention.

ARTICLE 21

Article 21 of the Protocol provides the rules for the entry into force of the Protocol provisions. The Protocol will be subject to ratification according to the normal procedures in both Contracting States and instruments of ratification will be exchanged as soon as possible. Upon the exchange of instruments, the Protocol will enter into force.

Paragraph 2(a) of Article 21 generally governs the entry into force of the provisions of the Protocol for taxes withheld at source, while paragraph 2(b) generally governs for other taxes. Paragraphs 3, 4, and 5 provide special rules for certain provisions.

Paragraph 2(a) provides that the Protocol generally will have effect for taxes withheld at source on dividends, interest, royalties, and pensions and annuities (other than social security benefits), under Articles X, XI, XII, and XVIII, respectively, with respect to amounts paid or credited on or after the first day of the second month following the date on which the Protocol enters into force (i.e., the date on which instruments of ratification are exchanged). However, with respect to direct investment dividends, the 5 percent rate specified in paragraph 2(a) of Article X will be phased in as follows:

    (1)   for dividends paid or credited after the first day of the second month referred to above, and during 1995, the rate of withholding will be 7

percent;

(2) for dividends paid or credited after the first day of the second month, and during 1996, the rate will be 6 percent; and

(3) for dividends paid or credited after the first day of the second month and after 1996, the rate will be 5 percent.

For taxes other than those withheld at source and for the provisions of the Protocol relating to taxes withheld on social security benefits, the Protocol will have effect with respect to taxable years beginning on or after the first day of January following the date on which the Protocol enters into force. However, the rate of tax applicable to the branch tax under paragraph 6 of Article X (Dividends) will be phased in a manner similar to the direct investment dividend withholding tax rate; that is, a rate of 6 percent will apply for taxable years beginning in 1996 and a rate of 5 percent will apply for taxable years beginning in 1997 and subsequent years.

Paragraph 3 of Article 21 provides a special effective date for the provisions of the new Article XXVI A (Assistance in Collection) of the Convention, introduced by Article 15 of the Protocol. Collection assistance may be granted by a Contracting State with respect to a request by the other Contracting State for a claim finally determined by the requesting State after the date that is ten years before the date of the entry into force of the Protocol. Thus, for example, if instruments of ratification are exchanged on July 1,1995, assistance may be given by Canada under Article XXVI A for a claim that was finally determined in the United States at any time after July 1, 1985.

Paragraph 4 of Article 21 provides special effective date provisions for paragraphs 2 through 7 of the new Article XXIX B (Taxes Imposed by Reason of Death) of the Convention, introduced by Article 18 of the Protocol, and certain related provisions elsewhere in the Convention. These special effective date provisions are discussed above in connection with Article 18.

Finally, paragraph 5 of Article 21 provides a special effective date for paragraph 2 of Article 3 of the Protocol, which provides a new residence rule for certain "continued" corporations. Under paragraph 5, the new residence rule for such corporations will have effect for taxable years beginning on or after the first day of January following the date on which the Protocol enters into force.

TREASURY DEPARTMENT TECHNICAL EXPLANATION
OF THE [2007] PROTOCOL AMENDING THE CONVENTION BETWEEN THE UNITED STATES OF AMERICA AND CANADA WITH RESPECT TO TAXES ON INCOME AND CAPITAL

Done at Washington on September 26, 1980,

As Amended by the Protocols Done on June 14, 1983,

March 28, 1994, March 17, 1995, and July 29, 1997

INTRODUCTION

This is a Technical Explanation of the Protocol signed at Chelsea on September 21, 2007 (the "Protocol"), amending the Convention between the United States of America and Canada with Respect to Taxes on Income and on Capital done at Washington on September 26, 1980, as amended by the Protocols done on June 14, 1983, March 28, 1994, March 17, 1995, and July 29, 1997 (the "existing Convention"). The existing Convention as modified by the Protocol shall be referred to as the "Convention."

Negotiation of the Protocol took into account the U.S. Treasury Department's current tax treaty policy and the Treasury Department's Model Income Tax Convention, published on November 15, 2006 (the "U.S. Model"). Negotiations also took into account the Model Tax Convention on Income and on Capital, published by the Organisation for Economic Cooperation and Development (the "OECD Model"), and recent tax treaties concluded by both countries.

The Technical Explanation is an official United States guide to the Protocol. The Government of Canada has reviewed this document and subscribes to its contents. In the view of both governments, this document accurately reflects the policies behind particular Protocol provisions, as well as understandings reached with respect to the application and interpretation of the Protocol and the Convention.

References made to the "existing Convention" are intended to put various provisions of the Protocol into context. The Technical Explanation does not, however, provide a complete comparison between the provisions of the existing Convention and the amendments made by the Protocol. The Technical Explanation is not intended to provide a complete guide to the existing Convention as amended by the Protocol. To the extent that the existing Convention has not been amended by the Protocol, the prior technical explanations of the Convention remain the official explanations. References in this Technical Explanation to "he" or "his" should be read to mean "he or she" or "his or her." References to the "Code" are to the Internal Revenue Code.

On the date of signing of the Protocol, the United States and Canada exchanged two sets of diplomatic notes. Each of these notes sets forth provisions and understandings related to the Protocol and the Convention, and comprises an integral part of the overall agreement between the United States and Canada. The first note, the "Arbitration Note," relates to the implementation of new paragraphs 6 and 7 of Article XXVI (Mutual Agreement Procedure), which provide for binding arbitration of certain disputes between the competent authorities. The second note, the "General Note," relates more generally to issues of interpretation or application of various provisions of the Protocol.

Article 1

Article 1 of the Protocol adds subparagraph 1(k) to Article III (General Definitions) to address the definition of "national" of a Contracting State as used in the Convention. The Contracting States recognize that Canadian tax law does not draw distinctions based on nationality as such. Nevertheless, at the request of the United States, the definition was added and contains references to both citizenship and nationality. The definition includes any individual possessing the citizenship or nationality of a Contracting State and any legal person, partnership or association whose status is determined by reference to the laws in force in a Contracting State. The existing Convention contains one reference to the term "national" in paragraph 1 of Article XXVI (Mutual Agreement Procedure). The Protocol adds another reference in paragraph 1 of Article XXV (Non-Discrimination) to ensure that nationals of the United States are covered by the non-discrimination provisions of the Convention. The definition added by the Protocol is consistent with the definition provided in other U.S. tax treaties.

The General Note provides that for purposes of paragraph 2 of Article III, as regards the application at any time of the Convention, any term not defined in the Convention shall, unless the context otherwise requires or the competent authorities otherwise agree to a common meaning pursuant to Article XXVI (Mutual Agreement Procedure), have the meaning which it has at that time under the law of that State for the purposes of the taxes to which the Convention apply, any meaning under the applicable tax laws of that State prevailing over a meaning given to the term under other laws of that State.

Article 2

Article 2 of the Protocol replaces paragraph 3 of Article IV (Residence) of the existing Convention to address the treatment of so-called dual resident companies. Article 2 of the Protocol also adds new paragraphs 6 and 7 to Article IV to determine whether income is considered to be derived by a resident of a Contracting State when such income is derived through a fiscally transparent entity.

Paragraph 3 of Article IV — Dual resident companies

Paragraph 3, which addresses companies that are otherwise considered resident in each of the Contracting States, is replaced. The provisions of paragraph 3, and the date upon which these provisions are effective, are consistent with an understanding reached between the United States and Canada on September 18, 2000, to clarify the residence of a company under the Convention when the company has engaged in a so-called corporate "continuance" transaction. The paragraph applies only where, by reason of the rules set forth in paragraph 1 of Article IV (Residence), a company is a resident of both Contracting States.

Subparagraph 3(a) provides a rule to address the situation when a company is a resident of both Contracting States but is created under the laws in force in only one of the Contracting States. In such a case, the rule provides that the company is a resident only of the Contracting State under which it is created. For example, if a company is incorporated in the United States but the company is also otherwise considered a resident of Canada because the company is managed in Canada, subparagraph 3(a) provides that the company shall be considered a resident only of the United States for purposes of the Convention. Subparagraph 3(a) is intended to operate in a manner similar to the first sentence of former paragraph 3. However, subparagraph 3(a) clarifies that such a company must be considered created in only one of the Contracting States to fall within the scope of subparagraph 3(a). In some cases, a company may engage in a corporate continuance transaction and retain its charter in the Contracting State from which it continued, while also being considered as created in the State to which the company continued. In such cases, the provisions of subparagraph 3(a) shall not apply because the company would be considered created in both of the Contracting States.

Subparagraph 3(b) addresses all cases involving a dual resident company that are not addressed in subparagraph 3(a). Thus, subparagraph 3(b) applies to continuance transactions occurring between the Contracting States if, as a result, a company otherwise would be considered created under the laws of each Contracting State, *e.g.*, because the corporation retained its charter in the first State. Subparagraph 3(b) would also address so-called serial continuance transactions where, for example, a company continues from one of the Contracting States to a third country and then continues into the other Contracting State without having ceased to be treated as resident in the first Contracting State.

Subparagraph 3(b) provides that if a company is considered to be a resident of both Contracting States, and the residence of such company is not resolved by subparagraph 3(a), then the competent authorities of the Contracting States shall endeavor to settle the question of residency by a mutual agreement procedure and determine the mode of application of the Convention to such company. Subparagraph3(b) also provides that in the absence of such agreement, the company shall not be considered a resident of either Contracting State for purposes of claiming any benefits under the Convention.

Paragraphs 6 and 7 of Article IV — income, profit, or gain derived through fiscally transparent entities

New paragraphs 6 and 7 are added to Article IV to provide specific rules for the treatment of amounts of income, profit or gain derived through or paid by fiscally transparent entities such as partnerships and certain trusts. Fiscally transparent entities, as explained more fully below, are in general entities the income of which is taxed at the beneficiary, member, or participant level. Entities that are subject to tax, but with respect to which tax may be relieved under an integrated system, are not considered fiscally transparent entities. Entities that are fiscally transparent for

U.S. tax purposes include partnerships, common investment trusts under section 584, grantor trusts, and business entities such as a limited liability company ("LLC") that is treated as a partnership or is disregarded as an entity separate from its owner for U.S. tax purposes. Entities falling within this description in Canada are (except to the extent the law provides otherwise) partnerships and what are known as "bare" trusts.

United States tax law also considers a corporation that has made a valid election to be taxed under Subchapter S of Chapter 1 of the Internal Revenue Code (an "S corporation") to be fiscally transparent within the meaning explained below. Thus, if a U.S. resident derives income from Canada through an S corporation, the U.S. resident will under new paragraph 6 be considered for purposes of the Convention as the person who derived the income. Exceptionally, because Canada will ordinarily accept that an S corporation is itself resident in the United States for purposes of the Convention, Canada will allow benefits under the Convention to the S corporation in its own right. In a reverse case, however — that is, where the S corporation is owned by a resident of Canada and has U.S.-source income, profits or gains — the Canadian resident will not be considered as deriving the income by virtue of subparagraph 7 (a) as Canada does not see the S corporation as fiscally transparent.

Under both paragraph 6 and paragraph 7, it is relevant whether the treatment of an amount of income, profit or gain derived by a person through an entity under the tax law of the residence State is "the same as its treatment would be if that amount had been derived directly." For purposes of paragraphs 6 and 7, whether the treatment of an amount derived by a person through an entity under the tax law of the residence State is the same as its treatment would be if that amount had been derived directly by that person shall be determined in accordance with the principles set forth in Code section 894 and the regulations under that section concerning whether an entity will be treated as fiscally transparent with respect to an item of income received by the entity. Treas. Reg. section1.894-1(d)(3)(iii) provides that an entity will be fiscally transparent under the laws of an interest holder's jurisdiction with respect to an item of income to the extent that the laws of that jurisdiction require the interest holder resident in that jurisdiction to separately take into account on a current basis the interest holder's respective share of the item of income paid to the entity, whether or not distributed to the interest holder, and the character and source of the item in the hands of the interest holder are determined as if such item were realized directly from the source from which realized by the entity. Although Canada does not have analogous provisions in its domestic law, it is anticipated that principles comparable to those described above will apply.

Paragraph 6

Under paragraph 6, an amount of income, profit or gain is considered to be derived by a resident of a Contracting State (residence State) if 1) the amount is derived by that person through an entity (other than an entity that is a resident of the other Contracting State (source State), and 2) by reason of that entity being considered fiscally transparent under the laws of the residence State, the treatment of the amount under the tax law of the residence State is the same as its treatment would be if that amount had been derived directly by that person. These two requirements are set forth in subparagraphs 6(a) and 6(b), respectively.

For example, if a U.S. resident owns a French entity that earns Canadian-source dividends and the entity is considered fiscally transparent under U.S. tax law, the U.S. resident is considered to derive the Canadian-source dividends for purposes of Article IV (and thus, the dividends are considered as being "paid to" the resident) because the U.S. resident is considered under the tax law of the United States to have derived the dividend through the French entity and, because the entity is treated as fiscally transparent under U.S. tax law, the treatment of the income under U.S. tax law is the same as its treatment would be if that amount had been derived directly by the U.S. resident. This result obtains even if the French entity is viewed differently under the tax laws of Canada or of France (*i.e.*, the French entity is treated under Canadian law or under French tax law as not fiscally transparent).

Similarly, if a Canadian resident derives U.S.-source income, profit or gain through an entity created under Canadian law that is considered a partnership for Canadian tax purposes but a corporation for U.S. tax purposes, U.S.-source income, profit or gain derived through such entity by the Canadian resident will be considered to be derived by the Canadian resident in considering the application of the Convention.

Application of paragraph 6 and related treaty provisions by Canada

In determining the entitlement of a resident of the United States to the benefits of the Convention, Canada shall apply the Convention within its own legal framework.

For example, assume that from the perspective of Canadian law an amount of income is seen as being paid from a source in Canada to USLLC, an entity that is entirely owned by U.S. persons and is fiscally transparent for U.S. tax purposes, but that Canada considers a corporation and, thus, under Canadian law, a taxpayer in its own right. Since USLLC is not itself taxable in the United States, it is not considered to be a U.S. resident under the Convention; but for new paragraph 6 Canada would not apply the Convention in taxing the income.

If new paragraph 6 applies in respect of an amount of income, profit or gain, such amount is considered as having been derived by one or more U.S. resident shareholders of USLLC, and Canada shall grant benefits of the Convention to the payment to USLLC and eliminate or reduce Canadian tax as provided in the Convention. The effect of the rule is to suppress Canadian taxation of USLLC to give effect to the benefits available under the Convention to the U.S. residents in respect of the particular amount of income, profit or gain.

However, for Canadian tax purposes, USLLC remains the only "visible" taxpayer in relation to this amount. In other words, the Canadian tax treatment of this taxpayer (USLLC) is modified because of the entitlement of its U.S. resident shareholders to benefits under the Convention, but this does not alter USLLC's status under Canadian law. Canada does not, for example, treat USLLC as though it did not exist, substituting the shareholders for it in the role of taxpayer under Canada's system.

Some of the implications of this are as follows. First, Canada will not require the shareholders of USLLC to file Canadian tax returns in respect of income that benefits from new paragraph 6. Instead, USLLC itself will file a Canadian tax return in which it will claim the benefit of the paragraph and supply any documentation required to support the claim. (The Canada Revenue Agency will supply additional practical guidance in this regard, including instructions for seeking to establish entitlement to Convention benefits in advance of payment.) Second, as is explained in greater detail below, if the income in question is business profits, it will be necessary to determine whether the income was earned through a permanent establishment in Canada. This determination will be based on the presence and activities in Canada of USLLC itself, not of its shareholders acting in their own right.

Determination of the existence of a permanent establishment from the business activities of a fiscally transparent entity

New paragraph 6 applies not only in respect of amounts of dividends, interest and royalties, but also profit (business income), gains and other income. It may thus be relevant in cases where a resident of one Contracting State carries on business in the other State through an entity that has a different characterization in each of the two Contracting States.

Application of new paragraph 6 and the provisions of Article V (Permanent Establishment) by Canada

Assume, for instance, that a resident of the United States is part owner of a U.S. limited liability company (USLLC) that is treated in the United States as a fiscally transparent entity, but in Canada as a corporation. Assume one of the other two shareholders of USLLC is resident in a country that does not have a tax treaty with Canada and that the remaining shareholder is resident in a country with which Canada does have a tax treaty, but that the treaty does not include a provision analogous to paragraph 6.

Assume further that USLLC carries on business in Canada, but does not do so through a permanent establishment there. (Note that from the Canadian perspective, the presence or absence of a permanent establishment is evaluated with respect to USLLC only, which Canada sees as a potentially taxable entity in its own right.) Regarding Canada's application of the provisions of the Convention, the portion of USLLC's profits that belongs to the U.S. resident shareholder will not be taxable in Canada, provided that the U.S. resident meets the Convention's limitation on benefits provisions. Under paragraph 6, that portion is seen as having been derived by the U.S. resident shareholder, who is entitled to rely on Article VII (Business Profits). The balance of USLLC's profits will, however, remain taxable in Canada. Since USLLC is not itself resident in the United States for purposes of the Convention, in respect of that portion of its profits that is not considered to have been derived by a U.S. resident (or a resident of another country whose treaty with Canada includes a rule comparable to paragraph 6) it is not relevant whether or not it has a permanent establishment in Canada.

Another example would be the situation where a USLLC that is wholly owned by a resident of the U.S. carries on business in Canada through a permanent establishment. If the USLLC is fiscally transparent for U.S. tax purposes (and therefore, the conditions for the application of paragraph 6 are satisfied) then the USLLC's profits will be treated as having been derived by its U.S. resident owner inclusive of all attributes of that income (*e.g.*, such as having been earned through a permanent establishment). However, since the USLLC remains the only "visible" taxpayer for Canadian tax purposes, it is the USLLC, and not the U.S. shareholder, that is subject to tax on the profits that are attributable to the permanent establishment.

Application of new paragraph 6 and the provisions of Article V (Permanent Establishment) by the United States

It should be noted that in the situation where a person is considered to derive income through an entity, the United States looks in addition to such person's activities in order to determine whether he has a permanent establishment. Assume that a Canadian resident and a resident in a country that does not have a tax treaty with the United States are owners of CanLP. Assume further that Can LP is an entity that is considered fiscally transparent for Canadian tax purposes but is not considered fiscally transparent for U.S. tax purposes, and that CanLP carries on business in the United States. If CanLP carries on the business through a permanent establishment, that permanent establishment may be attributed to the partners. Moreover, in determining whether there is a permanent establishment, the activities of both the entity and its partners will be considered. If CanLP does not carry on the business through a permanent establishment, the Canadian resident, who derives income through the partnership, may claim the benefits of Article VII (Business Profits) of the Convention with respect to such income, assuming that the income is not otherwise attributable to a permanent establishment of the partner. In any case, the third country partner cannot claim the benefits of Article VII of the Convention between the United States and Canada.

Paragraph 7

Paragraph 7 addresses situations where an item of income, profit or gain is considered not to be paid to or derived by a person who is a resident of a Contracting State. The paragraph is divided into two subparagraphs.

Under subparagraph 7(a), an amount of income, profit or gain is considered not to be paid to or derived by a person who is a resident of a Contracting State (the residence State) if (1) the other Contracting State (the source State) views the person as deriving the amount through an entity that is not a resident of the residence State, and (2) by reason of the entity not being treated as fiscally transparent under the laws of the residence State, the treatment of the amount under the tax law of the residence State is not the same as its treatment would be if that amount had been derived directly by the person.

For example, assume USCo, a company resident in the United States, is a part owner of CanLP, an entity that is considered fiscally transparent for Canadian tax purposes, but is not considered fiscally transparent for U.S. tax purposes. CanLP receives a dividend from a Canadian company in which it owns stock. Under Canadian tax law USCo is viewed as deriving a Canadian-source dividend through CanLP. For U.S. tax purposes, CanLP, and not USCo, is viewed as deriving the dividend. Because the treatment of the dividend under U.S. tax law in this case is not the same as the treatment under U.S. law if USCo derived the dividend directly, subparagraph 7(a) provides that USCo will not be considered as having derived the dividend. The result would be the same if CanLP were a third-country entity that was viewed by the United States as not fiscally transparent, but was viewed by Canada as fiscally transparent. Similarly, income from U.S. sources received by an entity organized under the laws of the United States that is treated for Canadian tax purposes as a corporation and is owned by shareholders who are residents of Canada is not considered derived by the shareholders of that U.S. entity even if, under U.S. tax law, the entity is treated as fiscally transparent.

Subparagraph 7(b) provides that an amount of income, profit or gain is not considered to be paid to or derived by a person who is a resident of a Contracting State (the residence State) where the person is considered under the tax law of the other Contracting State (the source State) to have received the amount from an entity that is a resident of that other State (the source State), but by reason of the entity being treated as fiscally transparent under the laws of the Contracting State of which the person is resident (the residence State), the treatment of such amount under the tax law of that State (the residence State) is not the same as the treatment would be if that entity were not treated as fiscally transparent under the laws of that State (the residence State).

That is, under subparagraph 7(b), an amount of income, profit or gain is not considered to be paid to or derived by a resident of a Contracting State (the residence State) if: (1) the other Contracting State (the source State) views such person as receiving the amount from an entity resident in the source State; (2) the entity is viewed as fiscally transparent under the laws of the residence State; and (3) by reason of the entity being treated as fiscally transparent under the laws of the residence State, the treatment of the amount received by that person under the tax law of the residence State is not the same as its treatment would be if the entity were not treated as fiscally transparent under the laws of the residence State.

For example, assume that USCo, a company resident in the United States is the sole owner of CanCo, an entity that is considered under Canadian tax law to be a corporation that is resident in Canada but is considered under U.S. tax law to be disregarded as an entity separate from its owner. Assume further that USCo is considered under Canadian tax law to have received a dividend from CanCo.

In such a case, Canada, the source State, views USCo as receiving income (*i.e.*, a dividend) from a corporation that is a resident of Canada (CanCo), CanCo is viewed as fiscally transparent under the laws of the United States, the residence State, and by reason of CanCo being disregarded under U.S. tax law, the treatment under U.S. tax law of the payment is not the same as its treatment would be if the entity were regarded as a corporation under U.S. tax law. That is, the payment is disregarded for U.S. tax purposes, whereas if U.S. tax law regarded CanCo as a corporation, the payment would be treated as a dividend. Therefore, subparagraph 7(b) would apply to provide that the income is not considered to be paid to or derived by USCo.

The same result obtains if, in the above example, USCo is considered under Canadian tax law to have received an interest or royalty payment (instead of a dividend) from CanCo. Under U.S. law, because CanCo is disregarded as an entity separate from its owner, the payment is disregarded, whereas if CanCo were treated as not fiscally transparent, the payment would be treated as interest or a royalty, as the case may be. Therefore, subparagraph 7(b) would apply to provide that such amount is not considered to be paid to or derived by USCo.

The application of subparagraph 7(b) differs if, in the above example, USCo (as well as other persons) are owners of CanCo, a Canadian entity that is considered under Canadian tax law to be a corporation that is resident in Canada but is considered under U.S. tax law to be a partnership (as opposed to being disregarded). Assume that USCo is considered under Canadian tax law to have received a dividend from CanCo. Such payment is viewed under Canadian tax law as a dividend, but under U.S. tax law is viewed as a partnership distribution. In such a case, Canada views USCo as receiving income (*i.e.*, a dividend) from an entity that is a resident of Canada (CanCo), CanCo is viewed as fiscally transparent under the laws of the United States, the residence State, and by reason of CanCo being treated as a partnership under U.S. tax law, the treatment under U.S. tax law of the payment (as a partnership distribution) is not the same as the treatment would be if CanCo were not fiscally transparent under U.S. tax law (as a dividend). As a result, subparagraph 7(b) would apply to provide that such amount is not considered paid to or derived by the U.S. resident.

As another example, assume that CanCo, a company resident in Canada, is the owner of USLP, an entity that is considered under U.S. tax law (by virtue of an election) to be a corporation resident in the United States, but that is considered under Canadian tax law to be a branch of CanCo. Assume further that CanCo is considered under U.S. tax law to have received a dividend from USLP. In this case, the United States views CanCo as receiving income (*i.e.*, a dividend) from an entity that is resident in the United States (USLP), but by reason of USLP being a branch under Canadian tax law, the treatment under Canadian tax law of the payment is not the same as its treatment would be if USLP were a company under Canadian tax law. That is, the payment is treated as a branch remittance for Canadian tax purposes, whereas if Canadian tax law regarded USLP as a corporation, the payment would be treated as a dividend. Therefore, subparagraph 7(b) would apply to provide that the income is not considered to be paid to or derived by CanCo. The same result would obtain in the case of interest or royalties paid by USLP to CanCo.

Paragraphs 6 and 7 apply to determine whether an amount is considered to be derived by (or paid to) a person who is a resident of Canada or the United States. If, as a result of paragraph 7, a person is not considered to have derived or received an amount of income, profit or gain, that person shall not be entitled to the benefits of the Convention with respect to such amount. Additionally, for purposes of application of the Convention by the United States, the treatment of such payments under Code section 894(c) and the regulations there under would not be relevant.

New paragraphs 6 and 7 are not an exception to the saving clause of paragraph 2 of Article XXIX (Miscellaneous Rules). Accordingly, subparagraph 7(b) does not prevent a Contracting State from taxing an entity that is treated as a resident of that State under its tax law. For example, if a U.S. partnership with members who are residents of Canada elects to be taxed as a corporation for U.S. tax purposes, the United States will tax that partnership on its worldwide income on a net basis, even if Canada views the partnership as fiscally transparent.

Interaction of paragraphs 6 and 7 with the determination of "beneficial ownership"

With respect to payments of income, profits or gain arising in a Contracting State and derived directly by a resident of the other Contracting State (and not through a fiscally transparent entity), the term "beneficial owner" is defined under the internal law of the country imposing tax (*i.e.*, the source State). Thus, if the payment arising in a Contracting State is derived by a resident of the other State who under the laws of the first-mentioned State is determined to be a nominee or agent acting on behalf of a person that is not a resident of that other State, the payment will not be entitled to the benefits of the Convention. However, payments arising in a Contracting State and derived by a nominee on behalf of a resident of that other State would be entitled to benefits. These limitations are confirmed by paragraph 12 of the Commentary to Article 10 of the OECD Model.

Special rules apply in the case of income, profits or gains derived through a fiscally transparent entity, as described in new paragraph 6 of Article IV. Residence State principles determine who derives the income, profits or gains, to assure that the income, profits or gains for which the source State grants benefits of the Convention will be taken into account for tax purposes by a resident of the residence State. Source country principles of beneficial ownership apply to determine whether the person who derives the income, profits or gains, or another resident of the other Contracting State, is the beneficial owner of the income, profits or gains. The source State may conclude that the person who derives the income, profits or gains in the residence State is a mere nominee, agent, conduit, etc., for a third country resident and deny benefits of the Convention. If the person who derives the income, profits or gains under paragraph 6 of Article IV would not be treated under the source State's principles for determining beneficial ownership as a nominee, agent, custodian, conduit, etc., that person will be treated as the beneficial owner of the income, profits or gains for purposes of the Convention.

Assume, for instance, that interest arising in the United States is paid to CanLP, an entity established in Canada which is treated as fiscally transparent for Canadian tax purposes but is treated as a company for U.S. tax purposes. CanCo, a company incorporated in Canada, is the sole interest holder in CanLP. Paragraph 6 of Article IV provides that CanCo derives the interest. However, if under the laws of the United States regarding payments to nominees, agents, custodians and conduits, CanCo is found be a nominee, agent, custodian or conduit for a person who is not a resident of Canada, CanCo will not be considered the beneficial owner of the interest and will not be entitled to the benefits of Article XI with respect to such interest. The payment may be entitled to benefits, however, if CanCo is found to be a nominee, agent, custodian or conduit for a person who is a resident of Canada.

With respect to Canadian-source income, profit or gains, beneficial ownership is to be determined under Canadian law. For example, assume that LLC, an entity that is treated as fiscally transparent for U.S. tax purposes, but as a corporation for Canadian tax purposes, is owned by USCo, a U.S. resident company. LLC receives Canadian-source income. The question of the beneficial ownership of the income received by LLC is determined under Canadian law. If LLC is considered the beneficial owner of the income under Canadian law, paragraph 6 shall apply to extend benefits of the Convention to the income received by LLC to the extent that the Canadian-source income is derived by U.S. resident members of LLC.

Article 3

Article 3 of the Protocol amends Article V (Permanent Establishment) of the Convention. Paragraph 1 of Article 3 of the Protocol adds a reference in Paragraph 6 of Article IV to new paragraph 9 of Article V. Paragraph 2 of Article 3 of the Protocol sets forth new paragraphs 9 and 10 of Article V.

Paragraph 9 of Article V

New paragraph 9 provides a special rule (subject to the provisions of paragraph 3) for an enterprise of a Contracting State that provides services in the other Contracting State, but that does not have a permanent establishment by virtue of the preceding paragraphs of the Article. If (and only if) such an enterprise meets either of two tests as provided in subparagraphs 9(a) and 9(b), the enterprise will be deemed to provide those services through a permanent establishment in the other State.

The first test as provided in subparagraph 9(a) has two parts. First, the services must be performed in the other State by an individual who is present in that other State for a period or periods aggregating 183 days or more in any twelve-month period. Second, during that period or periods, more than 50 percent of the gross active business revenues of the enterprise (including revenue from active business activities unrelated to the provision of services) must consist of income derived from the services performed in that State by that individual. If the enterprise meets both of these tests, the enterprise will be deemed to provide the services through a permanent establishment. This test is employed to determine whether an enterprise is deemed to have a permanent establishment by virtue of the presence of a single individual (*i.e.*, a natural person).

For the purposes of subparagraph 9(a), the term "gross active business revenues" shall mean the gross revenues attributable to active business activities that the enterprise has charged or should charge for its active business activities, regardless of when the actual billing will occur or of domestic law rules concerning when such revenues should be taken into account for tax purposes. Such active business activities are not restricted to the activities related to the provision of services. However, the term does not include income from passive investment activities.

As an example of the application of subparagraph 9(a), assume that Mr. X, an individual resident in the United States, is one of the two shareholders and employees of USCo, a company resident in the United States that provides engineering services. During the 12-month period beginning December 20 of Year 1 and ending December 19 of Year 2, Mr. X is present in Canada for periods totaling 190 days, and during those periods, 70 percent of all of the gross active business revenues of USCo attributable to business activities are derived from the services that Mr. X performs in Canada. Because both of the criteria of subparagraph 9(a) are satisfied, USCo will be deemed to have a permanent establishment in Canada by virtue of that subparagraph.

The second test as provided in subparagraph 9(b) provides that an enterprise will have a permanent establishment if the services are provided in the other State for an aggregate of 183 days or more in any twelve-month period with respect to the same or connected projects for customers who either are residents of the other State or maintain a permanent establishment in the other State with respect to which the services are provided. The various conditions that have to be satisfied in order for subparagraph 9(b) to have application are described in detail below.

In addition to meeting the 183-day threshold, the services must be provided for customers who either are residents of the other State or maintain a permanent establishment in that State. The intent of this requirement is to reinforce the concept that unless there is a customer in the other State, such enterprise will not be deemed as participating sufficiently in the economic life of that other State to warrant being deemed to have a permanent establishment.

Assume for example, that CanCo, a Canadian company, wishes to acquire USCo, a company in the United States. In preparation for the acquisition, CanCo hires Canlaw, a Canadian law firm, to conduct a due diligence evaluation of USCo's legal and financial standing in the United States. Canlaw sends a staff attorney to the United States to perform the due diligence analysis of USCo. That attorney is present and working in the United States for greater than 183 days. If the remuneration paid to Canlaw for the attorney's services does not constitute more than 50 percent of Canlaw's gross active business revenues for the period during which the attorney is present in the United States, Canlaw will not be deemed to provide the services through a permanent establishment in the United States by virtue of subparagraph 9(a). Additionally, because the services are being provided for a customer (CanCo) who neither is a resident of the United States nor maintains a permanent establishment in the United States to which the services are provided, Canlaw will also not have a permanent establishment in the United States by virtue of subparagraph 9(b).

Paragraph 9 applies only to the provision of services, and only to services provided by an enterprise to third parties. Thus, the provision does not have the effect of deeming an enterprise to have a permanent establishment merely because services are provided to that enterprise. Paragraph 9 only applies to services that are performed or provided by an enterprise of a Contracting State within the other Contracting State. It is therefore not sufficient that the relevant services be merely furnished to a resident of the other Contracting State. Where, for example, an enterprise provides customer support or other services by telephone or computer to customers located in the other State, those would not be covered by paragraph 9 because they are not performed or provided by that enterprise within the other State. Another example would be that of an architect who is hired to design blueprints for the construction of a building in the other State. As part of completing the project, the architect must make site visits to that other State, and his days of presence there would be counted for purposes of determining whether the 183-day threshold is satisfied. However, the days that the architect spends working on the blueprint in his home office shall not count for purposes of the 183-day threshold, because the architect is not performing or providing those services within the other State.

For purposes of determining whether the time threshold has been met, subparagraph 9(b) permits the aggregation of services that are provided with respect to connected projects. Paragraph 2 of the General Note provides that for purposes of subparagraph 9(b), projects shall be considered to be connected if they constitute a coherent whole, commercially and geographically. The determination of whether projects are connected should be determined from the point of view of the enterprise (not that of the customer), and will depend on the facts and circumstances of each case. In determining the existence of commercial coherence, factors that would be relevant include: 1) whether the projects would, in the absence of tax planning considerations, have been concluded pursuant to a single contract; 2) whether the nature of the work involved under different projects is the same; and 3) whether the same individuals are providing the services under the different projects. Whether the work provided is covered by one or multiple contracts may be relevant, but not determinative, in finding that projects are commercially coherent.

The aggregation rule addresses, for example, potentially abusive situations in which work has been artificially divided into separate components in order to avoid meeting the 183-day threshold. Assume for example, that a technology consultant has been hired to install a new computer system for a company in the other country. The work will take ten months to complete. However, the consultant purports to divide the work into two five-month projects with the intention of circumventing the rule in subparagraph 9(b). In such case, even if the two projects were considered separate, they will be considered to be commercially coherent. Accordingly, subject to the additional requirement of geographic coherence, the two projects could be considered to be connected, and could therefore be aggregated for purposes of subparagraph 9(b). In contrast, assume that the technology consultant is contracted to install a particular computer system for a company, and is also hired by that same company, pursuant to a separate contract, to train its employees on the use of another computer software that is unrelated to the first system. In this second case, even though the contracts are both concluded between the same two parties, there is no commercial coherence to the two projects, and the time spent fulfilling the two contracts may not be aggregated for purposes of subparagraph 9(b). Another example of projects that do not have commercial coherence would be the case of a law firm which, as one project provides tax advice to a customer from one portion of its staff, and as another project provides trade advice from another portion of its staff, both to the same customer.

Additionally, projects, in order to be considered connected, must also constitute a geographic whole. An example of projects that lack geographic coherence would be a case in which a consultant is hired to execute separate auditing projects at different branches of a bank located in different cities pursuant to a single contract. In such an example, while the consultant's projects are commercially coherent, they are not geographically coherent and accordingly the services provided in the various branches shall not be aggregated for purposes of applying subparagraph 9(b). The services provided in each branch should be considered separately for purposes of subparagraph 9(b).

The method of counting days for purposes of subparagraph 9(a) differs slightly from the method for subparagraph 9(b). Subparagraph 9(a) refers to days in which an individual is present in the other country. Accordingly, physical presence during a day is sufficient. In contrast, subparagraph 9(b) refers to days during which services are provided by the enterprise in the other country. Accordingly, non-working days such as weekends or holidays would not count for purposes of subparagraph 9(b), as long as no services are actually being provided while in the other country on those days. For the purposes of both subparagraphs, even if the enterprise sends many individuals simultaneously to the other country to provide services, their collective presence during one calendar day will count for only one day of the enterprise's presence in the other country. For instance, if an enterprise sends 20 employees to the other country to provide services to a client in the other country for 10 days, the enterprise will be considered present in the other country only for 10 days, not 200 days (20 employees x 10 days).

By deeming the enterprise to provide services through a permanent establishment in the other Contracting State, paragraph 9 allows the application of Article VII (Business Profits), and accordingly, the taxation of the services shall be on a net-basis. Such taxation is also limited to the profits attributable to the activities carried on in performing the relevant services. It will be important to ensure that only the profits properly attributable to the functions performed and risks assumed by provision of the services will be attributed to the deemed permanent establishment.

In addition to new paragraph 9, Article 3 of the Protocol amends paragraph 6 of Article V of the Convention to include a reference to paragraph 9. Therefore, in no case will paragraph 9 apply to deem services to be provided through a permanent establishment if the services are limited to those mentioned in paragraph 6 which, if performed through a fixed place of business, would not make the fixed place of business a permanent establishment under the provisions of that paragraph.

The competent authorities are encouraged to consider adopting rules to reduce the potential for excess withholding or estimated tax payments with respect to employee wages that may result from the application of this paragraph. Further, because paragraph 6 of Article V applies notwithstanding paragraph 9, days spent on preparatory or auxiliary activities shall not be taken into account for purposes of applying subparagraph 9(b).

Paragraph 10 of Article V

Paragraph 2 of Article 3 of the Protocol also sets forth new paragraph 10 of Article V. The provisions of new paragraph 10 are identical to paragraph 9 of Article V as it existed prior to the Protocol. New paragraph 10 provides that the provisions of Article V shall be applied in determining whether any person has a permanent establishment in any State.

Article 4

Article 4 of the Protocol replaces paragraph 2 of Article VII (Business Profits).

New paragraph 2 provides that where a resident of either Canada or the United States carries on (or has carried on) business in the other Contracting State through a permanent establishment in that other State, both Canada and the United States shall attribute to permanent establishments in their respective states those business profits which the permanent establishment might be expected to make if it were a distinct and separate person engaged in the same or similar activities under the same or similar conditions and dealing wholly independently with the resident and with any other person related to the resident. The term "related to the resident" is to be interpreted in accordance with paragraph 2 of Article IX (Related Persons). The reference to other related persons is intended to make clear that the test of paragraph 2 is not restricted to independence between a permanent establishment and a home office.

New paragraph 2 is substantially similar to paragraph 2 as it existed before the Protocol. However, in addition to the reference to a resident of a Contracting State who "carries on" business in the other Contracting State, the Protocol incorporates into the Convention the rule of Code section 864(c)(6) by adding "or has carried on" to address circumstances where, as a result of timing, income may be attributable to a permanent establishment that no longer exists in one of the Contracting States. In such cases, the income is properly within the scope of Article VII. Conforming changes are also made in the Protocol to Articles X (Dividends), XI (Interest), and XII (Royalties) of the Convention where Article VII would apply. As is explained in paragraph 5 of the General Note, these revisions to the Convention are only intended to clarify the application of the existing provisions of the Convention.

The following example illustrates the application of paragraph 2. Assume a company that is a resident of Canada and that maintains a permanent establishment in the United States winds up the permanent establishment's business and sells the permanent establishment's inventory and assets to a U.S. buyer at the end of year 1 in exchange for an installment obligation payable in full at the end of year 3. Despite the fact that the company has no permanent establishment in the United States in year 3, the United States may tax the deferred income payment recognized by the company in year 3.

The "attributable to" concept of paragraph 2 provides an alternative to the analogous but somewhat different "effectively connected" concept in Code section 864(c). Depending on the circumstances, the amount of income "attributable to" a permanent establishment under Article VII may be greater or less than the amount of income that would be treated as "effectively connected" to a U.S. trade or business under Code section 864. In particular, in the case of financial institutions, the use of internal dealings to allocate income within an enterprise may produce results under Article VII that are significantly different than the results under the effectively connected income rules. For example, income from interbranch notional principal contracts may be taken into account under Article VII, notwithstanding that such transactions may be ignored for purposes of U.S. domestic law. A taxpayer may use the treaty to reduce its taxable income, but may not use both treaty and Code rules where doing so would thwart the intent of either set of rules. *See* Rev. Rul. 84-17, 1984-1 C.B. 308.

The profits attributable to a permanent establishment may be from sources within or without a Contracting State. However, as stated in the General Note, the business profits attributable to a permanent establishment include only those profits derived from the assets used, risks assumed, and activities performed by the permanent establishment.

The language of paragraph 2, when combined with paragraph 3 dealing with the allowance of deductions for expenses incurred for the purposes of earning the profits, incorporates the arm's length standard for purposes of determining the profits attributable to a permanent establishment. The United States and Canada generally interpret the arm's length standard in a manner consistent with the OECD Transfer Pricing Guidelines.

Paragraph 9 of the General Note confirms that the arm's length method of paragraphs 2 and 3 consists of applying the OECD Transfer Pricing Guidelines, but taking into account the different economic and legal circumstances of a single legal entity (as opposed to separate but associated enterprises). Thus, any of the methods used in the Transfer Pricing Guidelines, including profits methods, may be used as appropriate and in accordance with the Transfer Pricing Guidelines. However, the use of the Transfer Pricing Guidelines applies only for purposes of attributing profits within the legal entity. It does not create legal obligations or other tax consequences that would result from transactions having independent legal significance. Thus, the Contracting States agree that the notional payments used to compute the profits that are attributable to a permanent establishment will not be taxed as if they were actual payments for purposes of other taxing provisions of the Convention, for example, for purposes of taxing a notional royalty under Article XII (Royalties).

One example of the different circumstances of a single legal entity is that an entity that operates through branches rather than separate subsidiaries generally will have lower capital requirements because all of the assets of the entity are available to support all of the entity's liabilities (with some exceptions attributable to local regulatory restrictions). This is the reason that most commercial banks and some insurance companies operate through branches rather than subsidiaries. The benefit that comes from such lower capital costs must be allocated among the branches in an appropriate manner. This issue does not arise in the case of an enterprise that operates through separate entities, since each entity will have to be separately capitalized or will have to compensate another entity for providing capital (usually through a guarantee).

Under U.S. domestic regulations, internal "transactions" generally are not recognized because they do not have legal significance. In contrast, the rule provided by the General Note is that such internal dealings may be used to attribute income to a permanent establishment in cases where the dealings accurately reflect the allocation of risk within the enterprise. One example is that of global trading in securities. In many cases, banks use internal swap transactions to transfer risk from one branch to a central location where traders have the expertise to manage that particular type of risk. Under paragraph 2 as set forth in the Protocol, such a bank may also use such swap transactions as a means of attributing income between the branches, if use of that method is the "best method" within the meaning of regulation section 1.482-1(c). The books of a branch will not be respected, however, when the results are inconsistent with a functional analysis. So, for example, income from a transaction that is booked in a particular branch (or home office) will not be treated as attributable to that location if the sales and risk management functions that generate the income are performed in another location.

The understanding in the General Note also affects the interpretation of paragraph 3 of Article VII. Paragraph 3 provides that in determining the business profits of a permanent establishment, deductions shall be allowed for the expenses incurred for the purposes of the permanent establishment, ensuring that business profits will be taxed on a net basis. This rule is not limited to expenses incurred exclusively for the purposes of the permanent establishment, but includes expenses incurred for the purposes of the enterprise as a whole, or that part of the enterprise that includes the permanent establishment. Deductions are to be allowed regardless of which accounting unit of the enterprise books the expenses, so long as they are incurred for the purposes of the permanent establishment. For example, a portion of the interest expense recorded on the books of the home office in one State may be deducted by a permanent establishment in the other. The amount of the expense that must be allowed as a deduction is determined by applying the arm's length principle.

As noted above, paragraph 9 of the General Note provides that the OECD Transfer Pricing Guidelines apply, by analogy, in determining the profits attributable to a permanent establishment. Accordingly, a permanent establishment may deduct payments made to its head office or another branch in compensation for services performed for the benefit of the branch. The method to be used in calculating that amount will depend on the terms of the arrangements between the branches and head office. For example, the enterprise could have a policy, expressed in writing, under which each business unit could use the services of lawyers employed by the head office. At the end of each year, the costs of employing the lawyers would be charged to each business unit according to the amount of services used by that business unit during the year. Since this has the characteristics of a cost-sharing arrangement and the allocation of costs is based on the benefits received by each business unit, such a cost allocation would be an acceptable means of determining a permanent establishment's deduction for legal expenses. Alternatively, the head office could agree to employ lawyers at its own risk, and to charge an arm's length price for legal services performed for a particular business unit. If the lawyers were under-utilized, and the "fees" received from the business units were less than the cost of employing the lawyers, then the head office would bear the excess cost. If the "fees" exceeded the cost of employing the lawyers, then the head office would keep the excess to compensate it for assuming the risk of employing the lawyers. If the enterprise acted in accordance with this agreement, this method would be an acceptable alternative method for calculating a permanent establishment's deduction for legal expenses.

The General Note also makes clear that a permanent establishment cannot be funded entirely with debt, but must have sufficient capital to carry on its activities as if it were a distinct and separate enterprise. To the extent that the permanent establishment has not been attributed capital for profit attribution purposes, a Contracting State may attribute such capital to the permanent establishment, in accordance with the arm's length principle, and deny an interest deduction to the extent necessary to reflect that capital attribution. The method prescribed by U.S. domestic law for making this attribution is found in Treas. Reg. section 1.882-5. Both section 1.882-5 and the method prescribed in the General Note start from the premise that all of the capital of the enterprise supports all of the assets and risks of the enterprise, and therefore the entire capital of the enterprise must be allocated to its various businesses and offices.

However, section 1.882-5 does not take into account the fact that some assets create more risk for the enterprise than do other assets. An independent enterprise would need less capital to support a perfectly-hedged U.S. Treasury security than it would need to support an equity security or other asset with significant market and/or credit risk. Accordingly, in some cases section 1.882-5 would require a taxpayer to allocate more capital to the United States, and therefore would reduce the taxpayer's interest deduction more, than is appropriate. To address these cases, the General Note allows a taxpayer to apply a more flexible approach that takes into account the relative risk of its assets in the various jurisdictions in which it does business. In particular, in the case of financial institutions other than insurance companies, the amount of capital attributable to a permanent establishment is determined by allocating the institution's total equity between its various offices on the basis of the proportion of the financial institution's risk-weighted assets attributable to each of them. This recognizes the fact that financial institutions are in many cases required to risk-weight their assets for regulatory purposes and, in other cases, will do so for business reasons even if not required to do so by regulators. However, risk-weighting is more complicated than the method prescribed by section 1.882-5. Accordingly, to ease this administrative burden, taxpayers may choose to apply the principles of Treas. Reg. section 1.882-5(c) to determine the amount of capital allocable to its U.S. permanent establishment, in lieu of determining its allocable capital under the risk-weighted capital allocation method provided by the General Note, even if it has otherwise chosen the principles of Article VII rather than the effectively connected income rules of U.S. domestic law. It is understood that this election is not binding for purposes of Canadian taxation unless the result is in accordance with the arm's length principle.

As noted in the Convention, nothing in paragraph 3 requires a Contracting State to allow the deduction of any expenditure which, by reason of its nature, is not generally allowed as a deduction under the tax laws in that State.

Article 5

Article 5 makes a number of amendments to Article X (Dividends) of the existing Convention. As with other benefits of the Convention, the benefits of Article X are available to a resident of a Contracting State only if that resident is entitled to those benefits under the provisions of Article XXIX A (Limitation on Benefits).

See the Technical Explanation for new paragraphs 6 and 7 of Article IV(Residence) for discussion regarding the interaction between domestic law concepts of beneficial ownership and the treaty rules to determine when a person is considered to derive an item of income for purposes of obtaining benefits of the Convention such as withholding rate reductions.

Paragraph 1

Paragraph 1 of Article 5 of the Protocol replaces subparagraph 2(a) of Article X of the Convention. In general, paragraph 2 limits the amount of tax that may be imposed on dividends by the Contracting State in which the company paying the dividends is resident if the beneficial owner of the dividends is a resident of the other Contracting State. Subparagraph 2(a) limits the rate to 5 percent of the gross amount of the dividends if the beneficial owner is a company that owns 10 percent or more of the voting stock of the company paying the dividends.

The Protocol adds a parenthetical to address the determination of the requisite ownership set forth in subparagraph 2(a) when the beneficial owner of dividends receives the dividends through an entity that is considered fiscally transparent in the beneficial owner's Contracting State. The added parenthetical stipulates that voting stock in a company paying the dividends that is indirectly held through an entity that is considered fiscally transparent in the beneficial owner's Contracting State is taken into account, provided the entity is not a resident of the other Contracting State. The United States views the new parenthetical as merely a clarification.

For example, assume USCo, a U.S. corporation, directly owns 2 percent of the voting stock of CanCo, a Canadian company that is considered a corporation in the United States and Canada. Further, assume that USCo owns 18 percent of the interests in LLC, an entity that in turn owns 50 percent of the voting stock of CanCo. CanCo pays a dividend to each of its shareholders. Provided that LLC is fiscally transparent in the United States and not considered a resident of Canada, USCo's 9 percent ownership in CanCo through LLC (50 percent x 18 percent) is taken into account in determining whether USCo meets the 10 percent ownership threshold set forth in subparagraph 2(a). In this example, USCo may aggregate its voting stock interests in CanCo that it owns directly and through LLC to determine if it satisfies the ownership requirement of subparagraph 2(a). Accordingly, USCo will be entitled to the 5 percent rate of withholding on dividends paid with respect to both its voting stock held through LLC and its voting stock held directly. Alternatively, if, for example, all of the shareholders of LLC were natural persons, the 5 percent rate would not apply.

Paragraph 2

Paragraph 2 of Article 5 of the Protocol replaces the definition of the term "dividends" provided in paragraph 3 of Article X of the Convention. The new definition conforms to the U.S. Model formulation. Paragraph 3 defines the term dividends broadly and flexibly. The definition is intended to cover all arrangements that yield a return on an equity investment in a corporation as determined under the tax law of the source State, as well as arrangements that might be developed in the future.

The term dividends includes income from shares, or other corporate rights that are not treated as debt under the law of the source State, that participate in the profits of the company. The term also includes income that is subjected to the same tax treatment as income from shares by the law of the source State. Thus, for example, a constructive dividend that results from a non-arm's length transaction between a corporation and a related party is a dividend. In the case of the United States the term "dividend" includes amounts treated as a dividend under U.S. law upon the sale or redemption of shares or upon a transfer of shares in a reorganization. *See, e.g.*, Rev. Rul. 92-85, 1992-2 C.B. 69 (sale of foreign subsidiary's stock to U.S. sister company is a deemed dividend to extent of the subsidiary's and sister company's earnings and profits). Further, a distribution from a U.S. publicly traded limited partnership that is taxed as a corporation under U.S. law is a dividend for purposes of Article X. However, a distribution by a limited liability company is not considered by the United States to be a dividend for purposes of Article X, provided the limited liability company is not characterized as an association taxable as a corporation under U.S. law.

Paragraph 3 of the General Note states that distributions from Canadian income trusts and royalty trusts that are treated as dividends as a result of changes to Canada's taxation of income and royalty trusts enacted in 2007 (S.C. 2007, c. 29) shall be treated as dividends for the purposes of Article X.

Additionally, a payment denominated as interest that is made by a thinly capitalized corporation may be treated as a dividend to the extent that the debt is recharacterized as equity under the laws of the source State. At the time the Protocol was signed, interest payments subject to Canada's thin-capitalization rules were not recharacterized as dividends.

Paragraph 3

Paragraph 3 of Article 5 of the Protocol replaces paragraph 4 of Article X. New paragraph 4 is substantially similar to paragraph 4 as it existed prior to the Protocol. New paragraph 4, however, adds clarifying language consistent with the changes made in Articles 4, 6, and 7 of the Protocol with respect to income attributable to a permanent establishment that has ceased to exist. Paragraph 4 provides that the limitations of paragraph 2 do not apply if the beneficial owner of the dividends carries on or has carried on business in the State in which the company paying the dividends is a resident through a permanent establishment situated there, and the stockholding in respect of which the dividends are paid is effectively connected to such permanent establishment. In such a case, the dividends are taxable pursuant to the provisions of Article VII (Business Profits). Thus, dividends paid in respect of holdings forming part of the assets of a permanent establishment or which are otherwise effectively connected to such permanent establishment will be taxed on a net basis using the rates and rules of taxation generally applicable to residents of the State in which the permanent establishment is situated.

To conform with Article 9 of the Protocol, which deletes Article XIV (Independent Personal Services) of the Convention, paragraph 4 of Article 5 of the Protocol also amends paragraph 5 of Article X by omitting the reference to a "fixed base."

Paragraph 4

To conform with Article 9 of the Protocol, which deletes Article XIV (Independent Personal Services) of the Convention, paragraph 4 of Article 5 of the Protocol amends paragraph 5 of Article X by omitting the reference to a "fixed base."

Paragraph 5

Paragraph 5 of Article 5 of the Protocol replaces subparagraph 7(c) of Article X of the existing Convention. Consistent with current U.S. tax treaty policy, new subparagraph 7(c) provides rules that expand the application of subparagraph 2(b) for the treatment of dividends paid by a Real Estate Investment Trust (REIT). New subparagraph 7(c) maintains the rule of the existing Convention that dividends paid by a REIT are not eligible for the 5 percent maximum rate of withholding tax of subparagraph 2(a), and provides that the 15 percent maximum rate of withholding tax of subparagraph 2(b) applies to dividends paid by REITs only if one of three conditions is met.

First, the dividend will qualify for the 15 percent maximum rate if the beneficial owner of the dividend is an individual holding an interest of not more than 10 percent in the REIT. For this purpose, subparagraph 7(c) also provides that where an estate or testamentary trust acquired its interest in a REIT as a consequence of the death of an individual, the estate or trust will be treated as an individual for the five-year period following the death. Thus, dividends paid to an estate or testamentary trust in respect of a holding of less than a 10 percent interest in the REIT also will be entitled to the 15 percent rate of withholding, but only for up to five years after the death.

Second, the dividend will qualify for the 15 percent maximum rate if it is paid with respect to a class of stock that is publicly traded and the beneficial owner of the dividend is a person holding an interest of not more than 5 percent of any class of the REIT's stock.

Third, the dividend will qualify for the 15 percent maximum rate if the beneficial owner of the dividend holds an interest in the REIT of 10 percent or less and the REIT is "diversified." A REIT is diversified if the gross value of no single interest in real property held by the REIT exceeds 10 percent of the gross value of the REIT's total interest in real property. For purposes of this diversification test, foreclosure property is not considered an interest in real property, and a REIT holding a partnership interest is treated as owning its proportionate share of any interest in real property held by the partnership.

A resident of Canada directly holding U.S. real property would pay U.S. tax either at a 30 percent rate of withholding tax on the gross income or at graduated rates on the net income. By placing the real property in a REIT, the investor absent a special rule could transform real estate income into dividend income, taxable at the rates provided in Article X, significantly reducing the U.S. tax that otherwise would be imposed. Subparagraph 7(c) prevents this result and thereby avoids a disparity between the taxation of direct real estate investments and real estate investments made through REIT conduits. In the cases in which subparagraph 7(c) allows a dividend from a REIT to be eligible for the 15 percent maximum rate of withholding tax, the holding in the REIT is not considered the equivalent of a direct holding in the underlying real property.

Article 6

Article 6 of the Protocol replaces Article XI (Interest) of the existing Convention. Article XI specifies the taxing jurisdictions over interest income of the States of source and residence and defines the terms necessary to apply Article XI. As with other benefits of the Convention, the benefits of Article XI are available to a resident of a Contracting State only if that resident is entitled to those benefits under the provisions of Article XXIX A (Limitation on Benefits).

Paragraph 1 of Article XI

New paragraph 1 generally grants to the residence State the exclusive right to tax interest beneficially owned by its residents and arising in the other Contracting State. See the Technical Explanation for new paragraphs 6 and 7 of Article IV (Residence) for discussion regarding the interaction between domestic law concepts of beneficial ownership and the treaty rules to determine when a person is considered to derive an item of income for purposes of obtaining benefits under the Convention such as withholding rate reductions.

Subparagraph 3(d) of Article 27 of the Protocol provides an additional rule regarding the application of paragraph 1 during the first two years that end after the Protocol's entry into force. This rule is described in detail in the Technical Explanation to Article 27.

Paragraph 2 of Article XI

Paragraph 2 of new Article XI is substantially identical to paragraph 4 of Article XI of the existing Convention.

Paragraph 2 defines the term "interest" as used in Article XI to include, *inter alia*, income from debt claims of every kind, whether or not secured by a mortgage. Interest that is paid or accrued subject to a contingency is within the ambit of Article XI. This includes income from a debt obligation carrying the right to participate in profits. The term does not, however, include amounts that are treated as dividends under Article X (Dividends).

The term "interest" also includes amounts subject to the same tax treatment as income from money lent under the law of the State in which the income arises. Thus, for purposes of the Convention, amounts that the United States will treat as interest include (i) the difference between the issue price and the stated redemption price at maturity of a debt instrument (*i.e.*, original issue discount (OID)), which may be wholly or partially realized on the disposition of a debt instrument (section 1273), (ii) amounts that are imputed interest on a deferred sales contract (section 483), (iii) amounts treated as interest or OID under the stripped bond rules (section 1286),

(iv) amounts treated as original issue discount under the below-market interest rate rules (section 7872), (v) a partner's distributive share of a partnership's interest income (section 702), (vi) the interest portion of periodic payments made under a "finance lease" or similar contractual arrangement that in substance is a borrowing by the nominal lessee to finance the acquisition of property, (vii) amounts included in the income of a holder of a residual interest in a real estate mortgage investment conduit (REMIC) (section 860E), because these amounts generally are subject to the same taxation treatment as interest under U.S. tax law, and (viii) interest with respect to notional principal contracts that are re-characterized as loans because of a "substantial non-periodic payment."

Paragraph 3 of Article XI

Paragraph 3 is in all material respects the same as paragraph 5 of Article XI of the existing Convention. New paragraph 3 adds clarifying language consistent with the changes made in Articles 4, 5, and 7 of the Protocol with respect to income attributable to a permanent establishment that has ceased to exist. Also, consistent with the changes described in Article 9 of the Protocol, discussed below, paragraph 3 does not contain references to the performance of independent personal services through a fixed base.

Paragraph 3 provides an exception to the exclusive residence taxation rule of paragraph 1 in cases where the beneficial owner of the interest carries on business through a permanent establishment in the State of source and the interest is effectively connected to that permanent establishment. In such cases the provisions of Article VII(Business Profits) will apply and the source State will retain the right to impose tax on such interest income.

Paragraph 4 of Article XI

Paragraph 4 is in all material respects the same as paragraph 6 of Article XI of the existing Convention. The only difference is that, consistent with the changes described below with respect to Article 9 of the Protocol, paragraph 4 does not contain references to a fixed base.

Paragraph 4 establishes the source of interest for purposes of Article XI. Interest is considered to arise in a Contracting State if the payer is that State, or a political subdivision, local authority, or resident of that State. However, in cases where the person paying the interest, whether a resident of a Contracting State or of a third State, has in a State other than that of which he is a resident a permanent establishment in connection with which the indebtedness on which the interest was paid was incurred, and such interest is borne by the permanent establishment, then such interest is deemed to arise in the State in which the permanent establishment is situated and not in the State of the payer's residence. Furthermore, pursuant to paragraphs 1 and 4, and Article XXII (Other Income), Canadian tax will not be imposed on interest paid to a U.S. resident by a company resident in Canada if the indebtedness is incurred in connection with, and the interest is borne by, a permanent establishment of the company situated in a third State. For the purposes of this Article, "borne by" means allowable as a deduction in computing taxable income.

Paragraph 5 of Article XI

Paragraph 5 is identical to paragraph 7 of Article XI of the existing Convention.

Paragraph 5 provides that in cases involving special relationships between the payer and the beneficial owner of interest income or between both of them and some other person, Article XI applies only to that portion of the total interest payments that would have been made absent such special relationships (*i.e.*, an arm's-length interest payment). Any excess amount of interest paid remains taxable according to the laws of the United States and Canada, respectively, with due regard to the other provisions of the Convention.

Paragraph 6 of Article XI

New paragraph 6 provides anti-abuse exceptions to exclusive residence State taxation in paragraph 1 for two classes of interest payments.

The first class of interest, dealt with in subparagraphs 6(a) and 6(b), is so-called "contingent interest." With respect to interest arising in the United States, subparagraph 6(a) refers to contingent interest of a type that does not qualify as portfolio interest under U.S. domestic law. The cross-reference to the U.S. definition of contingent interest, which is found in Code section 871(h)(4), is intended to ensure that the exceptions of Code section 871(h)(4)(C) will apply. With respect to Canada, such interest is defined in subparagraph 6(b) as any interest arising in Canada that is determined by reference to the receipts, sales, income, profits or other cash flow of the debtor or a related person, to any change in the value of any property of the debtor or a related person or to any dividend, partnership distribution or similar payment made by the debtor or a related person. Any such interest may be taxed in Canada according to the laws of Canada.

Under subparagraph 6(a) or 6(b), if the beneficial owner is a resident of the other Contracting State, the gross amount of the "contingent interest" may be taxed at a rate not exceeding 15 percent.

The second class of interest is dealt with in subparagraph 6(c). This exception is consistent with the policy of Code sections 860E(e) and 860G(b) that excess inclusions with respect to a real estate mortgage investment conduit (REMIC) should bear full U.S. tax in all cases. Without a full tax at source, foreign purchasers of residual interests would have a competitive advantage over U.S. purchasers at the time these interests are initially offered. Also, absent this rule, the U.S. fisc would suffer a revenue loss with respect to mortgages held in a REMIC because of opportunities for tax avoidance created by differences in the timing of taxable and economic income produced by these interests.

Therefore, subparagraph 6(c) provides a bilateral provision that interest that is an excess inclusion with respect to a residual interest in a REMIC may be taxed by each State in accordance with its domestic law. While the provision is written reciprocally, at the time the Protocol was signed, the provision had no application in respect of Canadian-source interest, as Canada did not have REMICs.

Paragraph 7 of Article XI

Paragraph 7 is in all material respects the same as paragraph 8 of Article XI of the existing Convention. The only difference is that, consistent with the changes made in Article 9 of the Protocol, paragraph 7 removes the references to a fixed base.

Paragraph 7 restricts the right of a Contracting State to impose tax on interest paid by a resident of the other Contracting State. The first State may not impose any tax on such interest except insofar as the interest is paid to a resident of that State or arises in that State or the debt claim in respect of which the interest is paid is effectively connected with a permanent establishment situated in that State.

New subparagraph 6(b) of Article XI erroneously refers to a "similar payment made by the debtor to a related person." The correct formulation, which the Contracting States agree to apply, is "similar payment made by the debtor or a related person."

Relationship to other Articles

Notwithstanding the foregoing limitations on source State taxation of interest, the saving clause of paragraph 2 of Article XXIX (Miscellaneous Rules) permits the United States to tax its residents and citizens, subject to the special foreign tax credit rules of paragraph 5 of Article XXIV (Elimination of Double Taxation), as if the Convention had not come into force.

Article 7

Article 7 of the Protocol amends Article XII (Royalties) of the existing Convention. As with other benefits of the Convention, the benefits of Article XII are available to a resident of a Contracting State only if that resident is entitled to those benefits under the provisions of Article XXIX A (Limitation on Benefits).

See the Technical Explanation for new paragraphs 6 and 7 of Article IV(Residence) for discussion regarding the interaction between domestic law concepts of beneficial ownership and the treaty rules to determine when a person is considered to derive an item of income for purposes of obtaining benefits of the Convention such as withholding rate reductions.

Paragraph 1

Paragraph 1 of Article 7 of the Protocol replaces paragraph 5 of Article XII of the Convention. In all material respects, new paragraph 5 is the same as paragraph 5 of Article XII of the existing Convention. However, new paragraph 5 adds clarifying language consistent with the changes made in Articles 4, 5, and 6 of the Protocol with respect to income attributable to a permanent establishment that has ceased to exist. To conform with Article 9 of the Protocol, which deletes Article XIV (Independent Personal Services) of the Convention, paragraph 1 of Article 7 of the Protocol also amends paragraph 5 of Article XII by omitting the reference to a "fixed base."

New paragraph 5 provides that the 10 percent limitation on tax in the source State provided by paragraph 2, and the exemption in the source State for certain royalties provided by paragraph 3, do not apply if the beneficial owner of the royalties carries on or has carried on business in the source State through a permanent establishment and the right or property in respect of which the royalties are paid is attributable to such permanent establishment. In such case, the royalty income would be taxable by the source State under the provisions of Article VII (Business Profits).

Paragraph 2

Paragraph 2 of Article 7 of the Protocol sets forth a new subparagraph 6(a) of Article XII that is in all material respects the same as subparagraph 6(a) of Article XII of the existing Convention. The only difference is that, consistent with the changes made in Article 9 of the Protocol, new subparagraph 6(a) omits references to a "fixed base."

Paragraph 3

Paragraph 3 of Article 7 of Protocol amends paragraph 8 of Article XII of the Convention to remove references to a "fixed base." In addition, paragraph 8 of the General Note confirms the intent of the Contracting States that the reference in subparagraph 3(c) of Article XII of the Convention to information provided in connection with a franchise agreement generally refers only to information that governs or otherwise deals with the operation (whether by the payer or by another person) of the franchise, and not to other information concerning industrial, commercial or scientific experience that is held for resale or license.

Article 8

Paragraph 1

Paragraph 1 of Article 8 of the Protocol replaces paragraph 2 of Article XIII (Gains) of the existing Convention. Consistent with Article 9 of the Protocol, new paragraph 2 does not contain any reference to property pertaining to a fixed base or to the performance of independent personal services.

New paragraph 2 of Article XIII provides that the Contracting State in which a resident of the other Contracting State has or had a permanent establishment may tax gains from the alienation of personal property constituting business property if such gains are attributable to such permanent establishment. Unlike paragraph 1 of Article VII(Business Profits), paragraph 2 limits the right of the source State to tax such gains to a twelve-month period following the termination of the permanent establishment.

Paragraph 2

Paragraph 2 of Article 8 of the Protocol replaces paragraph 5 of Article XIII of the existing Convention. In general, new paragraph 5 provides an exception to the general rule stated in paragraph 4 that gains from the alienation of any property, other than property referred to in paragraphs 1, 2, and 3, shall be taxable only in the Contracting State of which the alienator is a resident. Paragraph 5 provides that a Contracting State may, according to its domestic law, impose tax on gains derived by an individual who is a resident of the other Contracting State if such individual was a resident of the first-mentioned State for 120 months (whether or not consecutive) during any period of 20 consecutive years preceding the alienation of the property, and was a resident of that State at any time during the 10-year period immediately preceding the alienation of the property. Further, the property (or property received in substitution in a tax-free transaction in the first-mentioned State) must have been owned by the individual at the time he ceased to be a resident of the first-mentioned State and must not have been property that the individual was treated as having alienated by reason of ceasing to be a resident of the first-mentioned State and becoming a resident of the other Contracting State.

The provisions of new paragraph 5 are substantially similar to paragraph 5 of Article XIII of the existing Convention. However, the Protocol adds a new requirement to paragraph 5 that the property not be "a property that the individual was treated as having alienated by reason of ceasing to be a resident of the first-mentioned State and becoming a resident of the other Contracting State." This new requirement reflects the fact that the main purpose of paragraph 5 — ensuring that gains that accrue while an individual is resident in a Contracting State remain taxable for the stated time after the individual has moved to the other State — is met if that pre-departure gain is taxed in the first State immediately before the individual's emigration. This rule applies whether or not the individual makes the election provided by paragraph 7 of Article XIII, as amended, which is described below.

Paragraph 3

Paragraph 3 of Article 8 of the Protocol replaces paragraph 7 of Article XIII.

The purpose of paragraph 7, in both its former and revised form, is to provide a rule to coordinate U.S. and Canadian taxation of gains in the case of a timing mismatch. Such a mismatch may occur, for example, where a Canadian resident is deemed, for Canadian tax purposes, to recognize capital gain upon emigrating from Canada to the United States, or in the case of a gift that Canada deems to be an income producing event for its tax purposes but with respect to which the United States defers taxation while assigning the donor's basis to the donee. The former paragraph 7 resolved the timing mismatch of taxable events by allowing the individual to elect to be liable to tax in the deferring Contracting State as if he had sold and repurchased the property for an amount equal to its fair market value at a time immediately prior to the deemed alienation.

The election under former paragraph 7 was not available to certain non-U.S. citizens subject to tax in Canada by virtue of a deemed alienation because such individuals could not elect to be liable to tax in the United States. To address this problem, the Protocol replaces the election provided in former paragraph 7, with an election by the taxpayer to be treated by a Contracting State as having sold and repurchased the property for its fair market value immediately before the taxable event in the other Contracting State. The election in new paragraph 7 therefore will be available to any individual who emigrates from Canada to the United States, without regard to whether the person is a U.S. citizen immediately before ceasing to be a resident of Canada. If the individual is not subject to U.S. tax at that time, the effect of the election will be to give the individual an adjusted basis for U.S. tax purposes equal to the fair market value of the property as of the date of the deemed alienation in Canada, with the result that only post-emigration gain will be subject to U.S. tax when there is an actual alienation. If the Canadian resident is also a U.S. citizen at the time of his emigration from Canada, then the provisions of new paragraph 7 would allow the U.S. citizen to accelerate the tax under U.S. tax law and allow tax credits to be used to avoid double taxation. This would also be the case if the person, while not a U.S. citizen, would otherwise be subject to taxation in the United States on a disposition of the property.

In the case of Canadian taxation of appreciated property given as a gift, absent paragraph 7, the donor could be subject to tax in Canada upon making the gift, and the donee may be subject to tax in the United States upon a later disposition of the property on all or a portion of the same gain in the property without the availability of any foreign tax credit for the tax paid to Canada. Under new paragraph 7, the election will be available to any individual who pays taxes in Canada on a gain arising from the individual's gifting of a property, without regard to whether the person is a U.S. taxpayer at the time of the gift. The effect of the election in such case will be to give the donee an adjusted basis for U.S. tax purposes equal to the fair market value as of the date of the gift. If the donor is a U.S. taxpayer, the effect of the election will be the realization of gain or loss for U.S. purposes immediately before the gift. The acceleration of the U.S. tax liability by reason of the election in such case enables the donor to utilize foreign tax credits and avoid double taxation with respect to the disposition of the property.

Generally, the rule does not apply in the case of death. Note, however, that Article XXIX B (Taxes Imposed by Reason of Death) of the Convention provides rules that coordinate the income tax that Canada imposes by reason of death with the U.S. estate tax.

If in one Contracting State there are losses and gains from deemed alienations of different properties, then paragraph 7 must be applied consistently in the other Contracting State within the taxable period with respect to all such properties. Paragraph 7 only applies, however, if the deemed alienations of the properties result in a net gain.

Taxpayers may make the election provided by new paragraph 7 only with respect to property that is subject to a Contracting State's deemed disposition rules and with respect to which gain on a deemed alienation is recognized for that Contracting State's tax purposes in the taxable year of the deemed alienation. At the time the Protocol was signed, the following were the main types of property that were excluded from the deemed disposition rules in the case of individuals (including trusts) who cease to be residents of Canada: real property situated in Canada; interests and rights in respect of pensions; life insurance policies (other than segregated fund (investment) policies); rights in respect of annuities; interests in testamentary trusts, unless acquired for consideration; employee stock options; property used in a business carried on through a permanent establishment in

Canada (including intangibles and inventory); interests in most Canadian personal trusts; Canadian resource property; and timber resource property.

Paragraph 4

Consistent with the provisions of Article 9 of the Protocol, paragraph 4 of Article 8 of the Protocol amends subparagraph 9(c) of Article XIII of the existing Convention to remove the words "or pertained to a fixed base."

Relationship to Other Articles

The changes to Article XIII set forth in paragraph 3 were announced in a press release issued by the Treasury Department on September 18, 2000. Consistent with that press release, subparagraph 3(e) of Article 27 of the Protocol provides that the changes, jointly effectuated by paragraphs 2 and 3, will be generally effective for alienations of property that occur after September 17, 2000.

Article 9

To conform with the current U.S. and OECD Model Conventions, Article 9 of the Protocol deletes Article XIV (Independent Personal Services) of the Convention. The subsequent articles of the Convention are not renumbered. Paragraph 4 of the General Note elaborates that current tax treaty practice omits separate articles for independent personal services because a determination of the existence of a fixed base is qualitatively the same as the determination of the existence of a permanent establishment. Accordingly, the taxation of income from independent personal services is adequately governed by the provisions of Articles V (Permanent Establishment) and VII (Business Profits).

Article 10

Article 10 of the Protocol renames Article XV of the Convention as "Income from Employment" to conform with the current U.S. and OECD Model Conventions, and replaces paragraphs 1 and 2 of that renamed article consistent with the OECD Model Convention.

Paragraph 1

New paragraph 1 of Article XV provides that, in general, salaries, wages, and other remuneration derived by a resident of a Contracting State in respect of an employment are taxable only in that State unless the employment is exercised in the other Contracting State. If the employment is exercised in the other Contracting State, the entire remuneration derived therefrom may be taxed in that other State, subject to the provisions of paragraph 2.

New paragraph 1 of Article XV does not contain a reference to "similar" remuneration. This change was intended to clarify that Article XV applies to any form of compensation for employment, including payments in kind. This interpretation is consistent with paragraph 2.1 of the Commentary to Article 15 (Income from Employment) of the OECD Model and the Technical Explanation of the 2006 U.S. Model.

Paragraph 2

New paragraph 2 of Article XV provides two limitations on the right of a source State to tax remuneration for services rendered in that State. New paragraph 2 is divided into two subparagraphs that each sets forth a rule which, notwithstanding any contrary result due to the application of paragraph 1 of Article XV, prevents the source State from taxing income from employment in that State.

First, subparagraph 2(a) provides a safe harbor rule that the remuneration may not be taxed in the source State if such remuneration is $10,000 or less in the currency of the source State. This rule is identical to the rule in subparagraph 2(a) of Article XV of the existing Convention. It is understood that, consistent with the prior rule, the safe harbor will apply on a calendar-year basis.

Second, if the remuneration is not exempt from tax in the source State by virtue of subparagraph 2(a), subparagraph 2(b) provides an additional rule that the source State may not tax remuneration for services rendered in that State if the recipient is present in the source State for a period (or periods) that does not exceed in the aggregate 183 days in any twelve-month period commencing or ending in the fiscal year concerned, and the remuneration is not paid by or on behalf of a person who is a resident of that other State or borne by a permanent establishment in that other State. For purposes of this article, "borne by" means allowable as a deduction in computing taxable income.

Assume, for example, that Mr. X, an individual resident in Canada, is an employee of the Canadian permanent establishment of USCo, a U.S. company. Mr. X is sent to the United States to perform services and is present in the United States for less than 183 days. Mr. X receives more than $10,000 (U.S.) in the calendar year(s) in question. The remuneration paid to Mr. X for such services is not exempt from U.S. tax under paragraph 1, because his employer, USCo, is a resident of the United States and pays his remuneration. If instead Mr. X received less than $10,000 (U.S.), such earnings would be exempt from tax in the United States, because in all cases where an employee earns less than $10,000 in the currency of the source State, such earnings are exempt from tax in the source State.

As another example, assume Ms. Y, an individual resident in the United States is employed by USCo, a U.S. company. Ms. Y is sent to Canada to provide services in the Canadian permanent establishment of USCo. Ms. Y is present in Canada for less than183 days. Ms. Y receives more than $10,000 (Canadian) in the calendar year(s) in question. USCo charges the Canadian permanent establishment for Ms. Y's remuneration, which the permanent establishment takes as a deduction in computing its taxable income. The remuneration paid to Ms. Y for such services is not exempt from Canadian tax under paragraph 1, because her remuneration is borne by the Canadian permanent establishment.

New subparagraph 2(b) refers to remuneration that is paid by or on behalf of a "person" who is a resident of the other Contracting State, as opposed to an "employer." This change is intended only to clarify that both the United States and Canada understand that in certain abusive cases, substance over form principles may be applied to recharacterize an employment relationship, as prescribed in paragraph 8 of the Commentary to Article 15 (Income from Employment) of the OECD Model. Subparagraph 2(b) is intended to have the same meaning as the analogous provisions in the U.S. and OECD Models.

Paragraph 6 of the General Note

Paragraph 6 of the General Note contains special rules regarding employee stock options. There are no similar rules in the U.S. Model or the OECD Model, although the issue is discussed in detail in paragraph 12 of the Commentary to Article 15 (Income from Employment) of the OECD Model.

The General Note sets forth principles that apply for purposes of applying Article XV and Article XXIV (Elimination of Double Taxation) to income of an individual in connection with the exercise or other disposal (including a deemed exercise or disposal) of an option that was granted to the individual as an employee of a corporation or mutual fund trust to acquire shares or units ("securities") of the employer in respect of services rendered or to be rendered by such individual, or in connection with the disposal (including a deemed disposal) of a security acquired under such an option. For this purpose, the term "employer" is considered to include any entity related to the service recipient. The reference to a disposal (or deemed disposal) reflects the fact that under Canadian law and under certain provisions of U.S. law, income or gain attributable to the granting or exercising of the option may, in some cases, not be recognized until disposition of the securities.

Subparagraph 6(a) of the General Note provides a specific rule to address situations where, under the domestic law of the Contracting States, an employee would be taxable by both Contracting States in respect of the income in connection with the exercise or disposal of the option. The rule provides an allocation of taxing rights where (1) an employee has been granted a stock option in the course of employment in one of the Contracting States, and (2) his principal place of employment has been situated in one or both of the Contracting States during the period between grant and exercise (or disposal) of the option. In this situation, each Contracting State may tax as Contracting State of source only that proportion of the income that relates to the period or periods between the grant and the exercise (or disposal) of the option during which the individual's principal place of employment was situated in that Contracting State. The proportion attributable to a Contracting State is determined by multiplying the income by a fraction, the numerator of which is the number of days between the grant and exercise (or disposal) of the option during which the employee's principal place of employment was situated in that Contracting State and the denominator of which is the total number of days between grant and exercise (or disposal) of the option that the employee was employed by the employer.

If the individual is a resident of one of the Contracting States at the time he exercises the option, that Contracting State will have the right, as the State of residence, to tax all of the income under the first sentence of paragraph 1 of Article XV. However, to the extent that the employee renders his employment in the other Contracting State for some period of time between the date of the grant of the option and the date of the exercise (or disposal) of the option, the proportion of the income that is allocated to the other Contracting State under subparagraph 6(a) of the General Note will, subject to paragraph 2, be taxable by that other State under the second sentence of paragraph 1 of Article XV of the Convention. For this purpose, the tests of paragraph 2 of Article XV are applied to the year or years in which the relevant services were performed in the other Contracting State (and not to the year in which the option is exercised or disposed). To the extent the same income is subject to taxation in both Contracting States after application of Article XV, double taxation will be alleviated under the rules of Article XXIV (Elimination of Double Taxation).

Subparagraph 6(b) of the General Note provides that notwithstanding subparagraph 6(a), if the competent authorities of both Contracting States agree that the terms of the option were such that the grant of the option is appropriately treated as transfer of ownership of the securities (*e.g.*, because the options were in-the-money or not subject to a substantial vesting period), then they may agree to attribute income accordingly.

Article 11

Consistent with Article 9 and paragraph 1 of Article 10 of the Protocol, paragraphs 1, 2, and 3 of Article 11 of the Protocol revise paragraphs 1, 2, and 4 of Article XVI (Artistes and Athletes) of the existing Convention by deleting references to former Article XIV (Independent Personal Services) of the Convention and deleting and replacing other language in acknowledgement of the renaming of Article XV (Income from Employment).

Article 12

Article 12 of the Protocol deletes Article XVII (Withholding of Taxes in Respect of Personal Services) from the Convention. However, the subsequent Articles are not renumbered.

Article 13

Article 13 of the Protocol replaces paragraphs 3, 4, and 7 and adds paragraphs 8 through 17 to Article XVIII (Pensions and Annuities) of the Convention.

Paragraph 1

Roth IRAs

Paragraph 1 of Article 13 of the Protocol separates the provisions of paragraph 3 of Article XVIII into two subparagraphs. Subparagraph 3(a) contains the existing definition of the term "pensions," while subparagraph 3(b) adds a new rule to address the treatment of Roth IRAs or similar plan (as described below).

Subparagraph 3(a) of Article XVIII provides that the term "pensions" for purposes of the Convention includes any payment under a superannuation, pension, or other retirement arrangement, Armed-Forces retirement pay, war veterans pensions and allowances, and amounts paid under a sickness, accident, or disability plan, but does not include payments under an income-averaging annuity contract (which are subject to Article XXII (Other Income)) or social security benefits, including social security benefits in respect of government services (which are subject to paragraph 5 of Article XVIII). Thus, the term "pensions" includes pensions paid by private employers (including pre-tax and Roth 401(k) arrangements) as well as any pension paid in respect of government services. Further, the definition of "pensions" includes, for example, payments from individual retirement accounts (IRAs) in the United States and from registered retirement savings plans (RRSPs) and registered retirement income funds (RRIFs) in Canada.

Subparagraph 3(b) of Article XVIII provides that the term "pensions" generally includes a Roth IRA, within the meaning of Code section 408A (or a similar plan described below). Consequently, under paragraph 1 of Article XVIII, distributions from a Roth IRA to a resident of Canada generally continue to be exempt from Canadian tax to the extent they would have been exempt from U.S. tax if paid to a resident of the United States. In addition, residents of Canada generally may make an election under paragraph 7 of Article XVIII to defer any taxation in Canada with respect to income accrued in a Roth IRA but not distributed by the Roth IRA, until such time as and to the extent that a distribution is made from the Roth IRA or any plan substituted therefore. Because distributions will be exempt from Canadian tax to the extent they would have been exempt from U.S. tax if paid to a resident of the United States, the effect of these rules is that, in most cases, no portion of the Roth IRA will be subject to taxation in Canada.

However, subparagraph 3(b) also provides that if an individual who is a resident of Canada makes contributions to his or her Roth IRA while a resident of Canada, other than rollover contributions from another Roth IRA (or a similar plan described below), the Roth IRA will cease to be considered a pension at that time with respect to contributions and accretions from such time and accretions from such time will be subject to tax in Canada in the year of accrual. Thus, the Roth IRA will in effect be bifurcated into a "frozen" pension that continues to be subject to the rules of Article XVIII and a savings account that is not subject to the rules of Article XVIII. It is understood by the Contracting States that, following a rollover contribution from a Roth 401(k) arrangement to a Roth IRA, the Roth IRA will continue to be treated as a pension subject to the rules of Article XVIII.

Assume, for example, that Mr. X moves to Canada on July 1, 2008. Mr. X has a Roth IRA with a balance of 1,100 on July 1, 2008. Mr. X elects under paragraph 7 of Article XVIII to defer any taxation in Canada with respect to income accrued in his Roth IRA while he is a resident of Canada. Mr. X makes no additional contributions to his Roth IRA until July 1, 2010, when he makes an after-tax contribution of 100. There are accretions of 20 during the period July 1, 2008 through June 30, 2010, which are not taxed in Canada by reason of the election under paragraph 7 of Article XVIII. There are additional accretions of 50 during the period July 1, 2010 through June 30, 2015, which are subject to tax in Canada in the year of accrual. On July 1, 2015, while Mr. X is still resident of Canada, Mr. X receives a lump-sum distribution of 1,270 from his Roth IRA. The 1,120 that was in the Roth IRA on June 30, 2010 is treated as a distribution from a pension plan that, pursuant to paragraph 1 of Article XVIII, is exempt from tax in Canada provided it would be exempt from tax in the United States under the Internal Revenue Code if paid to a resident of the United States. The remaining 150 comprises the after-tax contribution of 100 in 2010 and accretions of 50 that were subject to Canadian tax in the year of accrual.

The rules of new subparagraph 3(b) of Article XVIII also will apply to any plan or arrangement created pursuant to legislation enacted by either Contracting State after September 21, 2007 (the date of signature of the Protocol) that the competent authorities agree is similar to a Roth IRA.

Source of payments under life insurance and annuity contracts

Paragraph 1 of Article 13 also replaces paragraph 4 of Article XVIII. Subparagraph 4(a) contains the existing definition of annuity, while subparagraph 4(b) adds a source rule to address the treatment of certain payments by branches of insurance companies.

Subparagraph 4(a) provides that, for purposes of the Convention, the term "annuity" means a stated sum paid periodically at stated times during life or during a specified number of years, under an obligation to make the payments in return for adequate and full consideration other than services rendered. The term does not include a payment that is not periodic or any annuity the cost of which was deductible for tax purposes in the Contracting State where the annuity was acquired. Items excluded from the definition of "annuity" and not dealt with under another Article of the Convention are subject to the rules of Article XXII (Other Income).

Under the existing Convention, payments under life insurance and annuity contracts to a resident of Canada by a Canadian branch of a U.S. insurance company are subject to either a 15-percent withholding tax under subparagraph 2(b) of Article XVIII or, unless dealt with under another Article of the Convention, an unreduced 30-percent withholding tax under paragraph 1 of Article XXII, depending on whether the payments constitute annuities within the meaning of paragraph 4 of Article XVIII.

On July 12, 2004, the Internal Revenue Service issued Revenue Ruling 2004-75,2004-2 C.B. 109, which provides in relevant part that annuity payments under, and withdrawals of cash value from, life insurance or annuity contracts issued by a foreign branch of a U.S. life insurance company are U.S.-source income that, when paid to a nonresident alien individual, is generally subject to a 30-percent withholding tax under Code sections 871(a) and 1441. Revenue Ruling 2004-97, 2004-2 C.B. 516, provided that Revenue Ruling 2004-75 would not be applied to payments that were made before January 1, 2005, provided that such payments were made pursuant to binding life insurance or annuity contracts issued on or before July 12, 2004.

Under new subparagraph 4(b) of Article XVIII, an annuity or other amount paid in respect of a life insurance or annuity contract (including a withdrawal in respect of the cash value thereof), will generally be deemed to arise in the Contracting State where the person paying the annuity or other amount (the "payer") is resident. However, if the payer, whether a resident of a Contracting State or not, has a permanent establishment in a Contracting State other than a Contracting State in which the payer is a resident, the payment will be deemed to arise in the

Contracting State in which the permanent establishment is situated if both of the following requirements are satisfied: (i) the obligation giving rise to the annuity or other amount must have been incurred in connection with the permanent establishment, and (ii) the annuity or other amount must be borne by the permanent establishment. When these requirements are satisfied, payments by a Canadian branch of a U.S. insurance company will be deemed to arise in Canada.

Paragraph 2

Paragraph 2 of Article 13 of the Protocol replaces paragraph 7 of Article XVIII of the existing Convention. Paragraph 7 continues to provide a rule with respect to the taxation of a natural person on income accrued in a pension or employee benefit plan in the other Contracting State. Thus, paragraph 7 applies where an individual is a citizen or resident of a Contracting State and is a beneficiary of a trust, company, organization, or other arrangement that is a resident of the other Contracting State, where such trust, company, organization, or other arrangement is generally exempt from income taxation in that other State, and is operated exclusively to provide pension, or employee benefits. In such cases, the beneficiary may elect to defer taxation in his State of residence on income accrued in the plan until it is distributed from the plan (or from another plan in that other Contracting State to which the income is transferred pursuant to the domestic law of that other Contracting State).

Paragraph 2 of Article 13 of the Protocol makes two changes to paragraph 7 of Article XVIII of the existing Convention. The first change is that the phrase "pension, retirement or employee benefits" is changed to "pension or employee benefits" solely to reflect the fact that in certain cases, discussed above, Roth IRAs will not be treated as pensions for purposes of Article XVIII. The second change is that "under" is changed to "subject to" to make it clear that an election to defer taxation with respect to undistributed income accrued in a plan may be made whether or not the competent authority of the first-mentioned State has prescribed rules for making an election. For the U.S. rules, see Revenue Procedure 2002-23, 2002-1 C.B. 744. As of the date the Protocol was signed, the competent authority of Canada had not prescribed rules.

Paragraph 3

Paragraph 3 of Article 13 of the Protocol adds paragraphs 8 through 17 to Article XVIII to deal with cross-border pension contributions. These paragraphs are intended to remove barriers to the flow of personal services between the Contracting States that could otherwise result from discontinuities in the laws of the Contracting States regarding the deductibility of pension contributions. Such discontinuities may arise where a country allows deductions or exclusions to its residents for contributions, made by them or on their behalf, to resident pension plans, but does not allow deductions or exclusions for payments made to plans resident in another country, even if the structure and legal requirements of such plans in the two countries are similar.

There is no comparable set of rules in the OECD Model, although the issue is discussed in detail in the Commentary to Article 18 (Pensions). The 2006 U.S. Model deals with this issue in paragraphs 2 through 4 of Article 18 (Pension Funds).

Workers on short-term assignments in the other Contracting State

Paragraphs 8 and 9 of Article XVIII address the case of a short-term assignment where an individual who is participating in a "qualifying retirement plan" (as defined in paragraph 15 of Article XVIII) in one Contracting State (the "home State") performs services as an employee for a limited period of time in the other Contracting State (the "host State"). If certain requirements are satisfied, contributions made to, or benefits accrued under, the plan by or on behalf of the individual will be deductible or excludible in computing the individual's income in the host State. In addition, contributions made to the plan by the individual's employer will be allowed as a deduction in computing the employer's profits in the host State.

In order for paragraph 8 to apply, the remuneration that the individual receives with respect to the services performed in the host State must be taxable in the host State. This means, for example, that where the United States is the host State, paragraph 8 would not apply if the remuneration that the individual receives with respect to the services performed in the United States is exempt from taxation in the United States under Code section 893.

The individual also must have been participating in the plan, or in another similar plan for which the plan was substituted, immediately before he began performing services in the host State. The rule regarding a successor plan would apply if, for example, the employer has been acquired by another corporation that replaces the existing plan with its own plan, transferring membership in the old plan over into the new plan.

In addition, the individual must not have been a resident (as determined under Article IV (Residence)) of the host State immediately before he began performing services in the host State. It is irrelevant for purposes of paragraph 8 whether the individual becomes a resident of the host State while he performs services there. A citizen of the United States who has been a resident of Canada may be entitled to benefits under paragraph 8 if (a) he performs services in the United States for a limited period of time and (b) he was a resident of Canada immediately before he began performing such services.

Benefits are available under paragraph 8 only for so long as the individual has not performed services in the host State for the same employer (or a related employer) for more than 60 of the 120 months preceding the individual's current taxable year. The purpose of this rule is to limit the period of time for which the host State will be required to provide benefits for contributions to a plan from which it is unlikely to be able to tax the distributions. If the individual continues to perform services in the host State beyond this time limit, he is expected to become a participant in a plan in the host State. Canada's domestic law provides preferential tax treatment for employer contributions to foreign pension plans in respect of services rendered in Canada by short-term residents, but such treatment ceases once the individual has been resident in Canada for at least 60 of the preceding 72 months.

The contributions and benefits must be attributable to services performed by the individual in the host State, and must be made or accrued during the period in which the individual performs those services. This rule prevents individuals who render services in the host State for a very short period of time from making dispropor- tionately large contributions to home State plans in order to offset the tax liability associated with the income earned in the host State. In the case where the United States is the host State, contributions will be deemed to have been made on the last day of the preceding taxable year if the payment is on account of such taxable year and is treated under U.S. law as a contribution made on the last day of the preceding taxable year.

If an individual receives benefits in the host State with respect to contributions to a plan in the home State, the services to which the contributions relate may not be taken into account for purposes of determining the individual's entitlement to benefits under any trust, company, organization, or other arrangement that is a resident of the host State, generally exempt from income taxation in that State and operated to provide pension or retirement benefits. The purpose of this rule is to prevent double benefits for contributions to both a home State plan and a host State plan with respect to the same services. Thus, for example, an individual who is working temporarily in the United States and making contributions to a qualifying retirement plan in Canada with respect to services performed in the United States may not make contributions to an individual retirement account (within the meaning of Code section 408(a)) in the United States with respect to the same services.

Paragraph 8 states that it applies only to the extent that the contributions or benefits would qualify for tax relief in the home State if the individual were a resident of and performed services in that State. Thus, benefits would be limited in the same fashion as if the individual continued to be a resident of the home State. However, paragraph 9 provides that if the host State is the United States and the individual is a citizen of the United States, the benefits granted to the individual under paragraph 8 may not exceed the benefits that would be allowed by the United States to its residents for contributions to, or benefits otherwise accrued under, a generally corresponding pension or retirement plan established in and recognized for tax purposes by the United States. Thus, the lower of the two limits applies. This rule ensures that U.S. citizens working temporarily in the United States and participating in a Canadian plan will not get more favorable U.S. tax treatment than U.S. citizens participating in a U.S. plan.

Where the United States is the home State, the amount of contributions that may be excluded from the employee's income under paragraph 8 for Canadian purposes is limited to the U.S. dollar amount specified in Code section 415 or the U.S. dollar amount specified in Code section 402(g)(1) to the extent contributions are made from the employee's compensation. For this purpose, the dollar limit specified in Code section 402(g)(1) means the amount applicable under Code section 402(g)(1) (including the age 50 catch-up amount in Code section 402(g)(1)(C)) or, if applicable, the parallel dollar limit applicable under Code section 457(e)(15) plus the age 50 catch-up amount under Code section 414(v)(2)(B)(i) for a Code section 457(g) trust.

Where Canada is the home State, the amount of contributions that may be excluded from the employee's income under paragraph 8 for U.S. purposes is subject to the limitations specified in subsections 146(5), 147(8), 147.1(8) and (9) and 147.2(1) and (4) of the Income Tax Act and paragraph 8503(4)(a) of the Income Tax

Regulations, as applicable. If the employee is a citizen of the United States, then the amount of contributions that may be excluded is the lesser of the amounts determined under the limitations specified in the previous sentence and the amounts specified in the previous paragraph.

The provisions described above provide benefits to employees. Paragraph 8 also provides that contributions made to the home State plan by an individual's employer will be allowed as a deduction in computing the employer's profits in the host State, even though such a deduction might not be allowable under the domestic law of the host State. This rule applies whether the employer is a resident of the host State or a permanent establishment that the employer has in the host State. The rule also applies to contributions by a person related to the individual's employer, such as contributions by a parent corporation for its subsidiary, that are treated under the law of the host State as contributions by the individual's employer. For example, if an individual who is participating in a qualifying retirement plan in Canada performs services for a limited period of time in the United States for a U.S. subsidiary of a Canadian company, a contribution to the Canadian plan by the parent company in Canada that is treated under U.S. law as a contribution by the U.S. subsidiary would be covered by the rule.

The amount of the allowable deduction is to be determined under the laws of the home State. Thus, where the United States is the home State, the amount of the deduction that is allowable in Canada will be subject to the limitations of Code section 404 (including the Code section 401(a)(17) and 415 limitations). Where Canada is the home State, the amount of the deduction that is allowable in the United States is subject to the limitations specified in subsections 147(8), 147.1(8) and (9) and 147.2(1) of the Income Tax Act, as applicable.

Cross-border commuters

Paragraphs 10, 11, and 12 of Article XVIII address the case of a commuter who is a resident of one Contracting State (the "residence State") and performs services as an employee in the other Contracting State (the "services State") and is a member of a "qualifying retirement plan" (as defined in paragraph 15 of Article XVIII) in the services State. If certain requirements are satisfied, contributions made to, or benefits accrued under, the qualifying retirement plan by or on behalf of the individual will be deductible or excludible in computing the individual's income in the residence State.

In order for paragraph 10 to apply, the individual must perform services as an employee in the services State the remuneration from which is taxable in the services State and is borne by either an employer who is a resident of the services State or by a permanent establishment that the employer has in the services State. The contributions and benefits must be attributable to those services and must be made or accrued during the period in which the individual performs those services. In the case where the United States is the residence State, contributions will be deemed to have been made on the last day of the preceding taxable year if the payment is on account of such taxable year and is treated under U.S. law as a contribution made on the last day of the preceding taxable year.

Paragraph 10 states that it applies only to the extent that the contributions or benefits qualify for tax relief in the services State. Thus, the benefits granted in the residence State are available only to the extent that the contributions or benefits accrued qualify for relief in the services State. Where the United States is the services State, the amount of contributions that may be excluded under paragraph 10 is the U.S. dollar amount specified in Code section 415 or the U.S. dollar amount specified in Code section 402(g)(1) (as defined above) to the extent contributions are made from the employee's compensation. Where Canada is the services State, the amount of contributions that may be excluded from the employee's income under paragraph 10 is subject to the limitations specified in subsections 146(5), 147(8), 147.1(8) and (9) and 147.2(1) and (4) of the Income Tax Act and paragraph 8503(4)(a) of the Income Tax Regulations, as applicable.

However, paragraphs 11 and 12 further provide that the benefits granted under paragraph 10 by the residence State may not exceed certain benefits that would be allowable under the domestic law of the residence State.

Paragraph 11 provides that where Canada is the residence State, the amount of contributions otherwise allowable as a deduction under paragraph 10 may not exceed the individual's deduction limit for contributions to registered retirement savings plans (RRSPs) remaining after taking into account the amount of contributions to RRSPs deducted by the individual under the law of Canada for the year. The amount deducted by the individual under paragraph 10 will be taken into account in computing the individual's deduction limit for subsequent taxation years for contributions to RRSPs. This rule prevents double benefits for contributions to both an RRSP and a qualifying retirement plan in the United States with respect to the same services.

Paragraph 12 provides that if the United States is the residence State, the benefits granted to an individual under paragraph 10 may not exceed the benefits that would be allowed by the United States to its residents for contributions to, or benefits otherwise accrued under, a generally corresponding pension or retirement plan established in and recognized for tax purposes by the United States. For purposes of determining an individual's eligibility to participate in and receive tax benefits with respect to a pension or retirement plan or other retirement arrangement in the United States, contributions made to, or benefits accrued under, a qualifying retirement plan in Canada by or on behalf of the individual are treated as contributions or benefits under a generally corresponding pension or retirement plan established in and recognized for tax purposes by the United States. Thus, for example, the qualifying retirement plan in Canada would be taken into account for purposes of determining whether the individual is an "active participant" within the meaning of Code section 219(g)(5), with the result that the individual's ability to make deductible contributions to an individual retirement account in the United States would be limited.

Paragraph 10 does not address employer deductions because the employer is located in the services State and is already eligible for deductions under the domestic law of the services State.

U.S. citizens resident in Canada

Paragraphs 13 and 14 of Article XVIII address the special case of a U.S. citizen who is a resident of Canada (as determined under Article IV (Residence)) and who performs services as an employee in Canada and participates in a qualifying retirement plan (as defined in paragraph 15 of Article XVIII) in Canada. If certain requirements are satisfied, contributions made to, or benefits accrued under, a qualifying retirement plan in Canada by or on behalf of the U.S. citizen will be deductible or excludible in computing his or her taxable income in the United States. These provisions are generally consistent with paragraph 4 of Article 18 of the U.S. Model treaty.

In order for paragraph 13 to apply, the U.S. citizen must perform services as an employee in Canada the remuneration from which is taxable in Canada and is borne by an employer who is a resident of Canada or by a permanent establishment that the employer has in Canada. The contributions and benefits must be attributable to those services and must be made or accrued during the period in which the U.S. citizen performs those services. Contributions will be deemed to have been made on the last day of the preceding taxable year if the payment is on account of such taxable year and is treated under U.S. law as a contribution made on the last day of the preceding taxable year.

Paragraph 13 states that it applies only to the extent the contributions or benefits qualify for tax relief in Canada. However, paragraph 14 provides that the benefits granted under paragraph 13 may not exceed the benefits that would be allowed by the United States to its residents for contributions to, or benefits otherwise accrued under, a generally corresponding pension or retirement plan established in and recognized for tax purposes by the United States. Thus, the lower of the two limits applies. This rule ensures that a U.S. citizen living and working in Canada does not receive better U.S. treatment than a U.S. citizen living and working in the United States. The amount of contributions that may be excluded from the employee's income under paragraph 13 is the U.S. dollar amount specified in Code section 415 or the U.S. dollar amount specified in Code section 402(g)(1) (as defined above) to the extent contributions are made from the employee's compensation. In addition, pursuant to Code section 911(d)(6), an individual may not claim benefits under paragraph 13 with respect to services the remuneration for which is excluded from the individual's gross income under Code section 911(a).

For purposes of determining the individual's eligibility to participate in and receive tax benefits with respect to a pension or retirement plan or other retirement arrangement established in and recognized for tax purposes by the United States, contributions made to, or benefits accrued under, a qualifying retirement plan in Canada by or on behalf of the individual are treated as contributions or benefits under a generally corresponding pension or retirement plan established in and recognized for tax purposes by the United States. Thus, for example, the qualifying retirement plan in Canada would be taken into account for purposes of determining whether the individual is an "active participant" within the meaning of Code section 219(g)(5), with the result that the individual's ability to make deductible contributions to an individual retirement account in the United States would be limited.

Paragraph 13 does not address employer deductions because the employer is located in Canada and is already eligible for deductions under the domestic law of Canada.

Definition of "qualifying retirement plan"

Paragraph 15 of Article XVIII provides that for purposes of paragraphs 8 through 14, a "qualifying retirement plan" in a Contracting State is a trust, company, organization, or other arrangement that (a) is a resident of that State, generally exempt from income taxation in that State and operated primarily to provide pension or retirement benefits; (b) is not an individual arrangement in respect of which the individual's employer has no involvement; and (c) the competent authority of the other Contracting State agrees generally corresponds to a pension or retirement plan established in and recognized for tax purposes in that State. Thus, U.S. individual retirement accounts (IRAs) and Canadian registered retirement savings plans (RRSPs) are not treated as qualifying retirement plans unless addressed in paragraph 10 of the General Note (as discussed below). In addition, a Canadian retirement compensation arrangement (RCA) is not a qualifying retirement plan because it is not considered to be generally exempt from income taxation in Canada.

Paragraph 10 of the General Note provides that the types of Canadian plans that constitute qualifying retirement plans for purposes of paragraph 15 include the following and any identical or substantially similar plan that is established pursuant to legislation introduced after the date of signature of the Protocol (September 21, 2007): registered pension plans under section 147.1 of the Income Tax Act, registered retirement savings plans under section 146 that are part of a group arrangement described in subsection 204.2(1.32), deferred profit sharing plans under section 147, and any registered retirement savings plan under section 146, or registered retirement income fund under section 146.3, that is funded exclusively by rollover contributions from one or more of the preceding plans.

Paragraph 10 of the General Note also provides that the types of U.S. plans that constitute qualifying retirement plans for purposes of paragraph 15 include the following and any identical or substantially similar plan that is established pursuant to legislation introduced after the date of signature of the Protocol (September 21, 2007): qualified plans under Code section 401(a) (including Code section 401(k) arrangements), individual retirement plans that are part of a simplified employee pension plan that satisfies Code section 408(k), Code section 408(p) simple retirement accounts, Code section 403(a) qualified annuity plans, Code section 403(b) plans, Code section 457(g) trusts providing benefits under Code section 457(b) plans, the Thrift Savings Fund (Code section 7701(j)), and any individual retirement account under Code section 408(a) that is funded exclusively by rollover contributions from one or more of the preceding plans.

If a particular plan in one Contracting State is of a type specified in paragraph 10 of the General Note with respect to paragraph 15 of Article XVIII, it will not be necessary for taxpayers to obtain a determination from the competent authority of the other Contracting State that the plan generally corresponds to a pension or retirement plan established in and recognized for tax purposes in that State. A taxpayer who believes a particular plan in one Contracting State that is not described in paragraph 10 of the General Note nevertheless satisfies the requirements of paragraph 15 may request a determination from the competent authority of the other Contracting State that the plan generally corresponds to a pension or retirement plan established in and recognized for tax purposes in that State. In the case of the United States, such a determination must be requested under Revenue Procedure 2006-54, 2006-49 I.R.B. 655 (or any applicable analogous provision). In the case of Canada, the current version of Information Circular 71-17 provides guidance on obtaining assistance from the Canadian competent authority.

Source rule

Paragraph 16 of Article XVIII provides that a distribution from a pension or retirement plan that is reasonably attributable to a contribution or benefit for which a benefit was allowed pursuant to paragraph 8, 10, or 13 of Article XVIII will be deemed to arise in the Contracting State in which the plan is established. This ensures that the Contracting State in which the plan is established will have the right to tax the gross amount of the distribution under subparagraph 2(a) of Article XVIII, even if a portion of the services to which the distribution relates were not performed in such Contracting State.

Partnerships

Paragraph 17 of Article XVIII provides that paragraphs 8 through 16 of Article XVIII apply, with such modifications as the circumstances require, as though the relationship between a partnership that carries on a business, and an individual who is a member of the partnership, were that of employer and employee. This rule is needed because paragraphs 8, 10, and 13, by their terms, apply only with respect to contributions made to, or benefits accrued under, qualifying retirement plans by or on behalf of individuals who perform services as an employee. Thus, benefits are not available with respect to retirement plans for self-employed individuals, who may be deemed under U.S. law to be employees for certain pension purposes. Paragraph 17 ensures that partners participating in a plan established by their partnership may be eligible for the benefits provided by paragraphs 8, 10, and 13.

Relationship to Other Articles

Paragraphs 8, 10, and 13 of Article XVIII are not subject to the saving clause of paragraph 2 of Article XXIX (Miscellaneous Rules) by reason of the exception in subparagraph 3(a) of Article XXIX.

Article 14

Consistent with Articles 9 and 10 of the Protocol, Article 14 of the Protocol amends Article XIX (Government Service) of the Convention by deleting the reference to "Article XIV (Independent Personal Services)" and replacing such reference with the reference to "Article VII (Business Profits)" and by reflecting the new name of Article XV (Income from Employment).

Article 15

Article 15 of the Protocol replaces Article XX (Students) of the Convention. Article XX provides rules for host-country taxation of visiting students and business trainees. Persons who meet the tests of Article XX will be exempt from tax in the State that they are visiting with respect to designated classes of income. Several conditions must be satisfied in order for an individual to be entitled to the benefits of this Article.

First, the visitor must have been, either at the time of his arrival in the host State or immediately before, a resident of the other Contracting State.

Second, the purpose of the visit must be the full-time education or training of the visitor. Thus, if the visitor comes principally to work in the host State but also is a part-time student, he would not be entitled to the benefits of this Article, even with respect to any payments he may receive from abroad for his maintenance or education, and regardless of whether or not he is in a degree program. Whether a student is to be considered full-time will be determined by the rules of the educational institution at which he is studying.

The host State exemption in Article XX applies to payments received by the student or business trainee for the purpose of his maintenance, education or training that arise outside the host State. A payment will be considered to arise outside the host State if the payer is located outside the host State. Thus, if an employer from one of the Contracting States sends an employee to the other Contracting State for full-time training, the payments the trainee receives from abroad from his employer for his maintenance or training while he is present in the host State will be exempt from tax in the host State. Where appropriate, substance prevails over form in determining the identity of the payer. Thus, for example, payments made directly or indirectly by a U.S. person with whom the visitor is training, but which have been routed through a source outside the United States (*e.g.*, a foreign subsidiary), are not treated as arising outside the United States for this purpose.

In the case of an apprentice or business trainee, the benefits of Article XX will extend only for a period of one year from the time that the individual first arrives in the host country for the purpose of the individual's training. If, however, an apprentice or trainee remains in the host country for a second year, thus losing the benefits of the Article, he would not retroactively lose the benefits of the Article for the first year.

Relationship to other Articles

The saving clause of paragraph 2 of Article XXIX (Miscellaneous Rules) does not apply to Article XX with respect to an individual who neither is a citizen of the host State nor has been admitted for permanent residence there. The saving clause, however, does apply with respect to citizens and permanent residents of the host State. Thus, a U.S. citizen who is a resident of Canada and who visits the United States as a full-time student at an accredited university will not be exempt from U.S. tax on remittances from abroad that otherwise constitute U.S. taxable income. However, an individual who is not a U.S. citizen, and who visits the United States as a student and remains long enough to become a resident under U.S. law, but does not become a permanent resident (*i.e.*, does not acquire a green card), will be entitled to the full benefits of the Article.

Article 16

Article 16 of the Protocol revises Article XXI (Exempt Organizations) of the existing Convention.

Paragraph 1

Paragraph 1 amends Article XXI by renumbering paragraphs 4, 5, and 6 as 5, 6, and 7, respectively.

Paragraph 2

Paragraph 2 replaces paragraphs 1 through 3 of Article XXI with four new paragraphs. In general, the provisions of former paragraphs 1 through 3 have been retained.

New paragraph 1 provides that a religious, scientific, literary, educational, or charitable organization resident in a Contracting State shall be exempt from tax on income arising in the other Contracting State but only to the extent that such income is exempt from taxation in the Contracting State in which the organization is resident.

New paragraph 2 retains the provisions of former subparagraph 2(a), and provides that a trust, company, organization, or other arrangement that is resident in a Contracting State and operated exclusively to administer or provide pension, retirement or employee benefits or benefits for the self-employed under one or more funds or plans established to provide pension or retirement benefits or other employee benefits is exempt from taxation on dividend and interest income arising in the other Contracting State in a taxable year, if the income of such organization or other arrangement is generally exempt from taxation for that year in the Contracting State in which it is resident.

New paragraph 3 replaces and expands the scope of former subparagraph 2(b) Former subparagraph 2(b) provided that, subject to the provisions of paragraph 3 (new paragraph 4), a trust, company, organization or other arrangement that was a resident of a Contracting State, generally exempt from income taxation in that State and operated exclusively to earn income for the benefit of one or more organizations described in subparagraph 2(a) (new paragraph 2) was exempt from taxation on dividend and interest income arising in the other Contracting State in a taxable year. The Internal Revenue Service concluded in private letter rulings (PLR 200111027 and PLR 200111037) that a pooled investment fund that included as investors one or more organizations described in paragraph 1 could not qualify for benefits under former subparagraph 2(b). New paragraph 3 now allows organizations described in paragraph 1 to invest in pooled funds with trusts, companies, organizations, or other arrangements described in new paragraph 2.

Former subparagraph 2(b) did not exempt income earned by a trust, company or other arrangement for the benefit of religious, scientific, literary, educational or charitable organizations exempt from tax under paragraph 1. Therefore, the Protocol expands the scope of paragraph 3 to include such income.

As noted above with respect to Article X (Dividends), paragraph 3 of the General Note explains that distributions from Canadian income trusts and royalty trusts that are treated as dividends as a result of changes to Canada's law regarding taxation of income and royalty trusts shall be treated as dividends for the purposes of Article X. Accordingly, such distributions will also be entitled to the benefits of Article XXI.

New paragraph 4 replaces paragraph 3 and provides that the exemptions provided by paragraphs 1, 2, 3 do not apply with respect to the income of a trust, company, organization or other arrangement from carrying on a trade or business or from a related person, other than a person referred to in paragraph 1, 2 or 3. The term "related person" is not necessarily defined by paragraph 2 of Article IX (Related Person).

Article 17

Article 17 of the Protocol amends Article XXII (Other Income) of the Convention by adding a new paragraph 4. Article XXII generally assigns taxing jurisdiction over income not dealt with in the other articles (Articles VI through XXI) of the Convention.

New paragraph 4 provides a specific rule for residence State taxation of compensation derived in respect of a guarantee of indebtedness. New paragraph 4 provides that compensation derived by a resident of a Contracting State in respect of the provision of a guarantee of indebtedness shall be taxable only in that State, unless the compensation is business profits attributable to a permanent establishment situated in the other Contracting State, in which case the provisions of Article VII (Business Profits) shall apply. The clarification that Article VII shall apply when the compensation is considered business profits was included at the request of the United States. Compensation paid to a financial services entity to provide a guarantee in the ordinary course of its business of providing such guarantees to customers constitutes business profits dealt with under the provisions of Article VII. However, provision of guarantees with respect to debt of related parties is ordinarily not an independent economic undertaking that would generate business profits, and thus compensation in respect of such related-party guarantees is, in most cases, covered by Article XXII.

Article 18

Article 18 of the Protocol amends paragraph 2 of Article XXIII (Capital) of the Convention by deleting language contained in that paragraph consistent with the changes made by Article 9 of the Protocol.

Article 19

Article 19 of the Protocol deletes subparagraph 2(b) of Article XXIV (Elimination of Double Taxation) of the Convention and replaces it with a new subparagraph.

New subparagraph 2(b) allows a Canadian company receiving a dividend from a U.S. resident company of which it owns at least 10 percent of the voting stock, a credit against Canadian income tax of the appropriate amount of income tax paid or accrued to the United States by the dividend paying company with respect to the profits out of which the dividends are paid. The third Protocol to the Convention, signed March 17, 1995, had amended subparagraph (b) to allow a Canadian company to deduct in computing its Canadian taxable income any dividend received by it out of the exempt surplus of a foreign affiliate which is a resident of the United States. This change is consistent with current Canadian tax treaty practice: it does not indicate any present intention to change Canada's "exempt surplus" rules, and those rules remain in effect.

Article 20

Article 20 of the Protocol revises Article XXV (Non-Discrimination) of the existing Convention to bring that Article into closer conformity to U.S. tax treaty policy.

Paragraphs 1 and 2

Paragraph 1 replaces paragraph 1 of Article XXV of the existing Convention. New paragraph 1 provides that a national of one Contracting State may not be subject to taxation or connected requirements in the other Contracting State that are more burdensome than the taxes and connected requirements imposed upon a national of that other State in the same circumstances. The OECD Model would prohibit taxation that is "other than or more burdensome" than that imposed on U.S. persons. Paragraph 1 omits the words "other than or" because the only relevant question under this provision should be whether the requirement imposed on a national of the other Contracting State is more burdensome. A requirement may be different from the requirements imposed on U.S. nationals without being more burdensome.

The term "national" in relation to a Contracting State is defined in subparagraph 1(k) of Article III (General Definitions). The term includes both individuals and juridical persons. A national of a Contracting State is afforded protection under this paragraph even if the national is not a resident of either Contracting State. Thus, a U.S. citizen who is resident in a third country is entitled, under this paragraph, to the same treatment in Canada as a national of Canada in the same or similar circumstances (*i.e.*, one who is resident in a third State).

Whether or not the two persons are both taxable on worldwide income is a significant circumstance for this purpose. For this reason, paragraph 1 specifically refers to taxation or any requirement connected therewith, particularly with respect to taxation on worldwide income, as relevant circumstances. This language means that the United States is not obliged to apply the same taxing regime to a national of Canada who is not resident in the United States as it applies to a U.S. national who is not resident in the United States. U.S. citizens who are not resident in the United States but who are, nevertheless, subject to U.S. tax on their worldwide income are not in the same circumstances with respect to U.S. taxation as citizens of Canada who are not U.S. residents. Thus, for example, Article XXV would not entitle a national of Canada residing in a third country to taxation at graduated rates on U.S.-source dividends or other investment income that applies to a U.S. citizen residing in the same third country.

Because of the increased coverage of paragraph 1 with respect to the treatment of nationals wherever they are resident, paragraph 2 of this Article no longer has application, and therefore has been omitted.

Paragraph 3

Paragraph 3 makes changes to renumbered paragraph 3 of Article XXV in order to conform with Article 10 of the Protocol by deleting the reference to "Article XV (Dependent Personal Services)" and replacing it with a reference to "Article XV (Income from Employment)."

Article 21

Paragraph 1 of Article 21 of the Protocol replaces paragraph 6 of Article XXVI (Mutual Agreement Procedure) of the Convention with new paragraphs 6 and 7. New paragraphs 6 and 7 provide a mandatory binding arbitration proceeding (Arbitration Proceeding). The Arbitration Note details additional rules and procedures that apply to a case considered under the arbitration provisions.

New paragraph 6 provides that a case shall be resolved through arbitration when the competent authorities have endeavored but are unable through negotiation to reach a complete agreement regarding a case and the following three conditions are satisfied. First, tax returns have been filed with at least one of the Contracting States with respect to the taxable years at issue in the case. Second, the case (i) involves the application of one or more Articles that the competent authorities have agreed in an exchange of notes shall be the subject of arbitration and is not a case that the competent authorities agree before the date on which an Arbitration Proceeding would otherwise have begun, is not suitable for determination by arbitration; or (ii) is a case that the competent authorities agree is suitable for determination by arbitration. Third, all concerned persons and their authorized representatives agree, according to the provisions of subparagraph 7(d), not to disclose to any other person any information received during the course of the Arbitration Proceeding from either Contracting State or the arbitration board, other than the determination of the board (confidentiality agreement). The confidentiality agreement may also be executed by any concerned person that has the legal authority to bind any other concerned person on the matter. For example, a parent corporation with the legal authority to bind its subsidiary with respect to confidentiality may execute a comprehensive confidentiality agreement on its own behalf and that of its subsidiary.

The United States and Canada have agreed in the Arbitration Note to submit cases regarding the application of one or more of the following Articles to mandatory binding arbitration under the provisions of paragraphs 6 and 7 of Article XXVI: IV (Residence), but only insofar as it relates to the residence of a natural person, V (Permanent Establishment), VII (Business Profits), IX (Related Persons), and XII (Royalties) (but only (i) insofar as Article XII might apply in transactions involving related persons to whom Article IX might apply, or (ii) to an allocation of amounts between royalties that are taxable under paragraph 2 thereof and royalties that are exempt under paragraph 3 thereof). The competent authorities may, however, agree, before the date on which an Arbitration Proceeding would otherwise have begun, that a particular case is not suitable for arbitration.

New paragraph 7 provides six subparagraphs that detail the general rules and definitions to be used in applying the arbitration provisions.

Subparagraph 7(a) provides that the term "concerned person" means the person that brought the case to competent authority for consideration under Article XXVI (Mutual Agreement Procedure) and includes all other persons, if any, whose tax liability to either Contracting State may be directly affected by a mutual agreement arising from that consideration. For example, a concerned person does not only include a U.S. corporation that brings a transfer pricing case with respect to a transaction entered into with its Canadian subsidiary for resolution to the U.S. competent authority, but also the Canadian subsidiary, which may have a correlative adjustment as a result of the resolution of the case.

Subparagraph 7(c) provides that an Arbitration Proceeding begins on the later of two dates: two years from the "commencement date" of the case (unless the competent authorities have previously agreed to a different date), or the earliest date upon which all concerned persons have entered into a confidentiality agreement and the agreements have been received by both competent authorities. The "commencement date" of the case is defined by subparagraph 7(b) as the earliest date the information necessary to undertake substantive consideration for a mutual agreement has been received by both competent authorities.

Paragraph 16 of the Arbitration Note provides that each competent authority will confirm in writing to the other competent authority and to the concerned persons the date of its receipt of the information necessary to undertake substantive consideration for a mutual agreement. In the case of the United States, this information is (i) the information that must be submitted to the U.S. competent authority under Section 4.05 of Rev. Proc. 2006-54, 2006-49 I.R.B. 1035 (or any applicable successor publication), and (ii) for cases initially submitted as a request for an Advance Pricing Agreement, the information that must be submitted to the Internal Revenue Service under Rev. Proc. 2006-9, 2006-2

I.R.B. 278 (or any applicable successor publication). In the case of Canada, this information is the information required to be submitted to the Canadian competent authority under Information Circular 71-17 (or any applicable successor publication). The information shall not be considered received until both competent authorities have received copies of all materials submitted to either Contracting State by the concerned person(s) in connection with the mutual agreement procedure. It is understood that confirmation of the "information necessary to undertake substantive consideration for a mutual agreement" is envisioned to ordinarily occur within 30 days after the necessary information is provided to the competent authority.

The Arbitration Note also provides for several procedural rules once an Arbitration Proceeding under paragraph 6 of Article XXVI ("Proceeding") has commenced, but the competent authorities may modify or supplement these rules as necessary. In addition, the arbitration board may adopt any procedures necessary for the conduct of its business, provided the procedures are not inconsistent with any provision of Article XXVI of the Convention.

Paragraph 5 of the Arbitration Note provides that each Contracting State has 60 days from the date on which the Arbitration Proceeding begins to send a written communication to the other Contracting State appointing one member of the arbitration board. Within 60 days of the date the second of such communications is sent, these two board members will appoint a third member to serve as the chair of the board. It is agreed that this third member ordinarily should not be a citizen of either of the Contracting States.

In the event that any members of the board are not appointed (including as a result of the failure of the two members appointed by the Contracting States to agree on a third member) by the requisite date, the remaining members are appointed by the highest ranking member of the Secretariat at the Centre for Tax Policy and Administration of the Organisation for Economic Co-operation and Development (OECD) who is not a citizen of either Contracting State, by written notice to both Contracting States within 60 days of the date of such failure.

Paragraph 7 of the Arbitration Note establishes deadlines for submission of materials by the Contracting States to the arbitration board. Each competent authority has 60 days from the date of appointment of the chair to submit a Proposed Resolution describing the proposed disposition of the specific monetary amounts of income, expense or taxation at issue in the case, and a supporting Position Paper. Copies of each State's submissions are to be provided by the board to the other Contracting State on the date the later of the submissions is submitted to the board. Each of the Contracting States may submit a Reply Submission to the board within 120 days of the appointment of the chair to address points raised in the other State's Proposed Resolution or Position Paper. If one Contracting State fails to submit a Proposed Resolution within the requisite time, the Proposed Resolution of the other Contracting State is deemed to be the determination of the arbitration board. Additional information may be supplied to the arbitration board by a Contracting State only at the request of the arbitration board. The board will provide copies of any such requested information, along with the board's request, to the other Contracting State on the date the request is made or the response is received.

All communication with the board is to be in writing between the chair of the board and the designated competent authorities with the exception of communication regarding logistical matters.

In making its determination, the arbitration board will apply the following authorities as necessary: (i) the provisions of the Convention, (ii) any agreed commentaries or explanation of the Contracting States concerning the Convention as amended, (iii) the laws of the Contracting States to the extent they are not inconsistent with each other, and (iv) any OECD Commentary, Guidelines or Reports regarding relevant analogous portions of the OECD Model Tax Convention.

The arbitration board must deliver a determination in writing to the Contracting States within six months of the appointment of the chair. The determination must be one of the two Proposed Resolutions submitted by the Contracting States. The determination shall provide a determination regarding only the amount of income, expense or tax reportable to the Contracting States. The determination has no precedential value and consequently the rationale behind a board's determination would not be beneficial and shall not be provided by the board.

Paragraph 11 of the Arbitration Note provides that, unless any concerned person does not accept the decision of the arbitration board, the determination of the board constitutes a resolution by mutual agreement under Article XXVI and, consequently, is binding on both Contracting States. Each concerned person must, within 30 days of receiving the determination from the competent authority to which the case was first presented, advise that competent authority whether the person accepts the determination. The failure to advise the competent authority within the requisite time is considered a rejection of the determination. If a determination is rejected, the case cannot be the subject of a subsequent MAP procedure on the same issue(s) determined by the panel, including a subsequent Arbitration Proceeding. After the commencement of an Arbitration Proceeding but before a decision of the board has been accepted by all concerned persons, the competent authorities may reach a mutual agreement to resolve the case and terminate the Proceeding.

For purposes of the Arbitration Proceeding, the members of the arbitration board and their staffs shall be considered "persons or authorities" to whom information may be disclosed under Article XXVII (Exchange of Information). The Arbitration Note provides that all materials prepared in the course of, or relating to, the Arbitration Proceeding are considered information exchanged between the Contracting States. No information relating to the Arbitration Proceeding or the board's determination may be disclosed by members of the arbitration board or their staffs or by either competent authority, except as permitted by the Convention and the domestic laws of the Contracting States. Members of the arbitration board and their staffs must agree in statements sent to each of the Contracting States in confirmation of their appointment to the arbitration board to abide by and be subject to the confidentiality and nondisclosure provisions of Article XXVII of the Convention and the applicable domestic laws of the Contracting States, with the most restrictive of the provisions applying.

The applicable domestic law of the Contracting States determines the treatment of any interest or penalties associated with a competent authority agreement achieved through arbitration.

In general, fees and expenses are borne equally by the Contracting States, including the cost of translation services. However, meeting facilities, related resources, financial management, other logistical support, and general and administrative coordination of the Arbitration Proceeding will be provided, at its own cost, by the Contracting State that initiated the Mutual Agreement Procedure. The fees and expenses of members of the board will be set in accordance with the International Centre for Settlement of Investment Disputes (ICSID) Schedule of Fees for arbitrators (in effect on the date on which the arbitration board proceedings begin). All other costs are to be borne by the Contracting State that incurs them. Since arbitration of MAP cases is intended to assist taxpayers in resolving a governmental difference of opinion regarding the taxation of their income, and is merely an extension of the competent authority process, no fees will be chargeable to a taxpayer in connection with arbitration.

Article 22

Article 22 of the Protocol amends Article XXVI A (Assistance in Collection) of the existing Convention. Article XXVI A sets forth provisions under which the United States and Canada have agreed to assist each other in the collection of taxes.

Paragraph 1

Paragraph 1 replaces subparagraph 8(a) of Article XXVI A. In general, new subparagraph 8(a) provides the circumstances under which no assistance is to be given under the Article for a claim in respect of an individual taxpayer. New subparagraph 8(a) contains language that is in substance the same as subparagraph 8(a) of Article XXVI A of the existing Convention. However, the revised subparagraph also provides that no assistance in collection is to be given for a revenue claim from a taxable period that ended before November 9, 1995 in respect of an individual taxpayer, if the taxpayer became a citizen of the requested State at any time before November 9, 1995 and is such a citizen at the time the applicant State applies for collection of the claim.

The additional language is intended to avoid the potentially discriminating application of former subparagraph 8(a) as applied to persons who were not citizens of the requested State in the taxable period to which a particular collection request related, but who became citizens of the requested State at a time prior to the entry into force of Article XXVI A as set forth in the third protocol signed March 17, 1995. New subparagraph 8(a) addresses this situation by treating the citizenship of a person in the requested State at anytime prior to November 9, 1995 as comparable to citizenship in the requested State during the period for which the claim for assistance relates if 1) the person is a citizen of the requested state at the time of the request for assistance in collection, and 2) the request relates to a taxable period ending prior to November 9, 1995. As is provided in subparagraph 3(g) of Article 27, this change will have effect for revenue claims finally determined after November 9, 1985, the effective date of the adoption of collection assistance in the third protocol signed March 17, 1995.

Paragraph 2

Paragraph 2 replaces paragraph 9 of Article XXVI A of the Convention. Under paragraph 1 of Article XXVI A, each Contracting State generally agrees to lend assistance and support to the other in the collection of revenue claims. The term "revenue claim" is defined in paragraph 1 to include all taxes referred to in paragraph 9 of the Article, as well as interest, costs, additions to such taxes, and civil penalties. New paragraph 9 provides that, notwithstanding the provisions of Article II (Taxes Covered) of the Convention, Article XXVI A shall apply to all categories of taxes collected, and to contributions to social security and employment insurance premiums levied, by or on behalf of the Government of a Contracting State. Prior to the Protocol, paragraph 9 did not contain a specific reference to contributions to social security and employment insurance premiums. Although the prior language covered U.S. federal social security and unemployment taxes, the language did not cover Canada's social security (*e.g.*, Canada Pension Plan) and employment insurance programs, contributions to which are not considered taxes under Canadian law and therefore would not otherwise have come within the scope of the paragraph.

Article 23

Article 23 of the Protocol replaces Article XXVII (Exchange of Information) of the Convention.

Paragraph 1 of Article XXVII

New paragraph 1 of Article XXVII is substantially the same as paragraph 1 of Article XXVII of the existing Convention. Paragraph 1 authorizes the competent authorities to exchange information as may be relevant for carrying out the provisions of the Convention or the domestic laws of Canada and the United States concerning taxes covered by the Convention, insofar as the taxation under those domestic laws is not contrary to the Convention. New paragraph 1 changes the phrase "is relevant" to "maybe relevant" to clarify that the language incorporates the standard in Code section 7602 which authorizes the Internal Revenue Service to examine "any books, papers, records, or other data which *may be relevant* or material." (Emphasis added.) In *United States v. Arthur Young & Co.*, 465 U.S. 805, 814 (1984), the Supreme Court stated that "the language 'may be' reflects Congress's express intention to allow the Internal Revenue Service to obtain 'items of even *potential* relevance to an ongoing investigation, without reference to its admissibility.'" (Emphasis in original.) However, the language "may be" would not support a request in which a Contracting State simply asked for information regarding all bank accounts maintained by residents of that Contracting State in the other Contracting State, or even all accounts maintained by its residents with respect to a particular bank.

The authority to exchange information granted by paragraph 1 is not restricted by Article I (Personal Scope), and thus need not relate solely to persons otherwise covered by the Convention. Under paragraph 1, information may be exchanged for use in all phases of the taxation process including assessment, collection, enforcement or the determination of appeals. Thus, the competent authorities may request and provide information for cases under examination or criminal investigation, in collection, on appeals, or under prosecution.

Any information received by a Contracting State pursuant to the Convention is to be treated as secret in the same manner as information obtained under the tax laws of that State. Such information shall be disclosed only to persons or authorities, including courts and administrative bodies, involved in the assessment or collection of, the administration and enforcement in respect of, or the determination of appeals in relation to, the taxes covered by the Convention and the information may be used by such persons only for such purposes. (In accordance with paragraph 4, for the purposes of this Article the Convention applies to a broader range of taxes than those covered specifically by Article II (Taxes Covered)). Although the information received by persons described in paragraph 1 is to be treated as secret, it may be disclosed by such persons in public court proceedings or in judicial decisions.

Paragraph 1 also permits, however, a Contracting State to provide information received from the other Contracting State to its states, provinces, or local authorities, if it relates to a tax imposed by that state, province, or local authority that is substantially similar to a national-level tax covered under Article II (Taxes Covered). This provision does not authorize a Contracting State to request information on behalf of a state, province, or local authority. Paragraph 1 also authorizes the competent authorities to release information to any arbitration panel that may be established under the provisions of new paragraph 6 of Article XXVI (Mutual Agreement Procedure). Any information provided to a state, province, or local authority or to an arbitration panel is subject to the same use and disclosure provisions as is information received by the national Governments and used for their purposes.

The provisions of paragraph 1 authorize the U.S. competent authority to continue to allow legislative bodies, such as the tax-writing committees of Congress and the Government Accountability Office to examine tax return information received from Canada when such bodies or offices are engaged in overseeing the administration of U.S. tax laws or a study of the administration of U.S. tax laws pursuant to a directive of Congress. However, the secrecy requirements of paragraph 1 must be met.

It is contemplated that Article XXVII will be utilized by the competent authorities to exchange information upon request, routinely, and spontaneously.

Paragraph 2 of Article XXVII

New paragraph 2 conforms with the corresponding U.S. and OECD Model provisions. The substance of the second sentence of former paragraph 2 is found in new paragraph 6 of the Article, discussed below.

Paragraph 2 provides that if a Contracting State requests information in accordance with Article XXVII, the other Contracting State shall use its information gathering measures to obtain the requested information. The instruction to the requested State to "use its information gathering measures" to obtain the requested information communicates the same instruction to the requested State as the language of former paragraph 2 that stated that the requested State shall obtain the information "in the same way as if its own taxation was involved." Paragraph 2 makes clear that the obligation to provide information is limited by the provisions of paragraph 3, but that such limitations shall not be construed to permit a Contracting State to decline to obtain and supply information because it has no domestic tax interest in such information.

In the absence of such a paragraph, some taxpayers have argued that subparagraph 3(a) prevents a Contracting State from requesting information from a bank or fiduciary that the Contracting State does not need for its own tax purposes. This paragraph clarifies that paragraph 3 does not impose such a restriction and that a Contracting State is not limited to providing only the information that it already has in its own files.

Paragraph 3 of Article XXVII

New paragraph 3 is substantively the same as paragraph 3 of Article XXVII of the existing Convention. Paragraph 3 provides that the provisions of paragraphs 1 and 2 do not impose on Canada or the United States the obligation to carry out administrative measures at variance with the laws and administrative practice of either State; to supply information which is not obtainable under the laws or in the normal course of the administration of either State; or to supply information which would disclose any trade, business, industrial, commercial, or professional secret or trade process, or information the disclosure of which would be contrary to public policy.

Thus, a requesting State may be denied information from the other State if the information would be obtained pursuant to procedures or measures that are broader than those available in the requesting State. However, the statute of limitations of the Contracting State making the request for information should govern a request for information. Thus, the Contracting State of which the request is made should attempt to obtain the information even if its own statute of limitations has passed. In many cases, relevant information will still exist in the business records of the taxpayer or a third party, even though it is no longer required to be kept for domestic tax purposes.

While paragraph 3 states conditions under which a Contracting State is not obligated to comply with a request from the other Contracting State for information, the requested State is not precluded from providing such information, and may, at its discretion, do so subject to the limitations of its internal law.

As discussed with respect to paragraph 2, in no case shall the limitations in paragraph 3 be construed to permit a Contracting State to decline to obtain information and supply information because it has no domestic tax interest in such information.

Paragraph 4 of Article XXVII

The language of new paragraph 4 is substantially similar to former paragraph 4. New paragraph 4, however, consistent with new paragraph 1, discussed above, replaces the words "is relevant" with "may be relevant" in subparagraph 4(b).

Paragraph 4 provides that, for the purposes of Article XXVII, the Convention applies to all taxes imposed by a Contracting State, and to other taxes to which any other provision of the Convention applies, but only to the extent that the information may be relevant for the purposes of the application of that provision.

Article XXVII does not apply to taxes imposed by political subdivisions or local authorities of the Contracting States. Paragraph 4 is designed to ensure that information exchange will extend to taxes of every kind (including, for example, estate, gift, excise, and value added taxes) at the national level in the United States and Canada.

Paragraph 5 of Article XXVII

New paragraph 5 conforms with the corresponding U.S. and OECD Model provisions. Paragraph 5 provides that a Contracting State may not decline to provide information because that information is held by a financial institution, nominee or person acting in an agency or fiduciary capacity. Thus, paragraph 5 would effectively prevent a Contracting State from relying on paragraph 3 to argue that its domestic bank secrecy laws (or similar legislation relating to disclosure of financial information by financial institutions or intermediaries) override its obligation to provide information under paragraph 1. This paragraph also requires the disclosure of information regarding the beneficial owner of an interest in a person.

Paragraph 6 of Article XXVII

The substance of new paragraph 6 is similar to the second sentence of paragraph 2 of Article XXVII of the existing Convention. New paragraph 6 adopts the language of paragraph 6 of Article 26 (Exchange of Information and Administrative Assistance) of the U.S. Model. New paragraph 6 provides that the requesting State may specify the form in which information is to be provided (*e.g.*, depositions of witnesses and authenticated copies of original documents). The intention is to ensure that the information may be introduced as evidence in the judicial proceedings of the requesting State.

The requested State should, if possible, provide the information in the form requested to the same extent that it can obtain information in that form under its own laws and administrative practices with respect to its own taxes.

Paragraph 7 of Article XXVII

New paragraph 7 is consistent with paragraph 8 of Article 26 (Exchange of Information and Administrative Assistance) of the U.S. Model. Paragraph 7 provides that the requested State shall allow representatives of the requesting State to enter the requested State to interview individuals and examine books and records with the consent of the persons subject to examination. Paragraph 7 was intended to reinforce that the administrations can conduct consensual tax examinations abroad, and was not intended to limit travel or supersede any arrangements or procedures the competent authorities may have previously had in place regarding travel for tax administration purposes.

Paragraph 13 of General Note

As is explained in paragraph 13 of the General Note, the United States and Canada understand and agree that the standards and practices described in Article XXVII of the Convention are to be in no respect less effective than those described in the Model Agreement on Exchange of Information on Tax Matters developed by the OECD Global Forum Working Group on Effective Exchange of Information.

Article 24

Article 24 amends Article XXIX (Miscellaneous Rules) of the Convention.

Paragraph 1

Paragraph 1 replaces paragraph 2 of Article XXIX of the existing Convention. New paragraph 2 is divided into two subparagraphs. In general, subparagraph 2(a) provides a "saving clause" pursuant to which the United States and Canada may each tax its residents, as determined under Article IV (Residence), and the United States may tax its citizens and companies, including those electing to be treated as domestic corporations (*e.g.* under Code section 1504(d)), as if there were no convention between the United States and Canada with respect to taxes on income and capital. Subparagraph 2(a) contains language that generally corresponds to former paragraph 2, but omits certain language pertaining to former citizens, which are addressed in new subparagraph 2(b).

New subparagraph 2(b) generally corresponds to the provisions of former paragraph 2 addressing former citizens of the United States. However, new subparagraph 2(b) also includes a reference to former long-term residents of the United States. This addition, as well as other changes in subparagraph 2(b), brings the Convention in conformity with the U.S. taxation of former citizens and long-term residents under Code section 877.

Similar to subparagraph 2(a), new subparagraph 2(b) operates as a "saving clause" and provides that notwithstanding the other provisions of the Convention, a former citizen or former long-term resident of the United States, may, for a period of ten years following the loss of such status, be taxed in accordance with the laws of the United States with respect to income from sources within the United States (including income deemed under the domestic law of the United States to arise from such sources).

Paragraphs 11 and 12 of the General Note provide definitions based on Code section 877 that are relevant to the application of paragraph 2 of Article XXIX. Paragraph 11 of the General Note provides that the term "long-term resident" means any individual who is a lawful permanent resident of the United States in eight or more taxable years during the preceding 15 taxable years. In determining whether the eight-year threshold is met, one does not count any year in which the individual is treated as a resident of Canada under this Convention (or as a resident of any country other than the United States under the provisions of any other U.S. tax treaty), and the individual does not waive the benefits of such treaty applicable to residents of the other country. This understanding is consistent with how this provision is generally interpreted in U.S. tax treaties.

Paragraph 12 of the General Note provides that the phrase "income deemed under the domestic law of the United States to arise from such sources" as used in new subparagraph 2(b) includes gains from the sale or exchange of stock of a U.S. company or debt obligations of a U.S. person, the United States, a State, or a political subdivision thereof, or the District of Columbia, gains from property (other than stock or debt obligations) located in the United States, and, in certain cases, income or gain derived from the sale of stock of a non-U.S. company or a disposition of property contributed to such non-U.S. company where such company would be a controlled foreign corporation with respect to the individual if such person had continued to be a U.S. person. In addition, an individual who exchanges property that gives rise or would give rise to U.S. source income for property that gives rise to foreign-source income will be treated as if he had sold the property that would give rise to U.S.-source income for its fair market value, and any consequent gain shall be deemed to be income from sources within the United States.

Paragraph 2

Paragraph 2 replaces subparagraph 3(a) of Article XXIX of the existing Convention. Paragraph 3 provides that, notwithstanding paragraph 2 of Article XXIX, the United States and Canada must respect specified provisions of the Convention in regard to certain persons, including residents and citizens. Therefore, subparagraph 3(a) lists certain paragraphs and Articles of the Convention that represent exceptions to the "saving clause" in all situations. New subparagraph 3(a) is substantially similar to former subparagraph 3(a), but now contains a reference to paragraphs 8, 10, and 13 of Article XVIII (Pensions and Annuities) to reflect the changes made to that article in paragraph 3 of Article 13 of the Protocol.

Article 25

Article 25 of the Protocol replaces Article XXIX A (Limitation on Benefits) of the existing Convention, which was added to the Convention by the Protocol done on March 17, 1995. Article XXIX A addresses the problem of "treaty shopping" by residents of third States by requiring, in most cases, that the person seeking benefits not only be a U.S. resident or Canadian resident but also satisfy other tests. For example, a resident of a third State might establish an entity resident in Canada for the purpose of deriving income from the United States and claiming U.S. treaty benefits with respect to that income. Article XXIX A limits the benefits granted by the United States or Canada under the Convention to those persons whose residence in the other Contracting State is not considered to have been motivated by the existence of the Convention. As replaced by the Protocol, new Article XXIX A is reciprocal, and many of the changes to the former paragraphs of Article XXIX A are made to effectuate this reciprocal application.

Absent Article XXIX A, an entity resident in one of the Contracting States would be entitled to benefits under the Convention, unless it were denied such benefits as a result of limitations under domestic law (*e.g.*, business purpose, substance-over-form, step transaction, or conduit principles or other anti-avoidance rules) applicable to a particular transaction or arrangement. As noted below in the explanation of paragraph 7, general anti-abuse provisions of this sort apply in conjunction with the Convention in both the United States and Canada. In the case of the United States, such anti-abuse provisions complement the explicit anti-treaty-shopping rules of Article XXIX A. While the anti-treaty-shopping rules determine whether a person has a sufficient nexus to Canada to be entitled to benefits under the Convention, the anti-abuse provisions under U.S. domestic law determine whether a particular transaction should be recast in accordance with the substance of the transaction.

Paragraph 1 of Article XXIX A

New paragraph 1 of Article XXIX A provides that, for the purposes of the application of the Convention, a "qualifying person" shall be entitled to all of the benefits of the Convention and, except as provided in paragraphs 3, 4, and 6, a person that is not a qualifying person shall not be entitled to any benefits of the Convention.

Paragraph 2 of Article XXIX A

New paragraph 2 lists a number of characteristics any one of which will make a United States or Canadian resident a qualifying person. The "look-through" principles introduced by the Protocol (e.g. paragraph 6 of Article IV (Residence)) are to be applied in conjunction with Article XXIX A. Accordingly, the provisions of Article IV shall determine the person who derives an item of income, and the objective tests of Article XXIX A shall be applied to that person to determine whether benefits shall be granted. The rules are essentially mechanical tests and are discussed below.

Individuals and governmental entities

Under new paragraph 2, the first two categories of qualifying persons are (1) natural persons resident in the United States or Canada (as listed in subparagraph 2(a)), and (2) the Contracting States, political subdivisions or local authorities thereof, and any agency or instrumentality of such Government, political subdivision or local authority (as listed in subparagraph 2(b)). Persons falling into these two categories are unlikely to be used, as the beneficial owner of income, to derive benefits under the Convention on behalf of a third-country person. If such a person receives income as a nominee on behalf of a third-country resident, benefits will be denied with respect to those items of income under the articles of the Convention that would otherwise grant the benefit, because of the requirements in those articles that the beneficial owner of the income be a resident of a Contracting State.

Publicly traded entities

Under new subparagraph 2(c), a company or trust resident in a Contracting State is a qualifying person if the company's principal class of shares, and any disproportionate class of shares, or the trust's units, or disproportionate interest in a trust, are primarily and regularly traded on one or more recognized stock exchanges. The term "recognized stock exchange" is defined in subparagraph 5(f) of the Article to mean, in the United States, the NASDAQ System and any stock exchange registered as a national securities exchange with the Securities and Exchange Commission, and, in Canada, any Canadian stock exchanges that are "prescribed stock exchanges" or "designated stock exchanges" under the Income Tax Act. These are, at the time of signature of the Protocol, the Montreal Stock Exchange, the Toronto Stock Exchange, and Tiers 1 and 2 of the TSX Venture Exchange. Additional exchanges may be added to the list of recognized exchanges by exchange of notes between the Contracting States or by agreement between the competent authorities.

If a company has only one class of shares, it is only necessary to consider whether the shares of that class meet the relevant trading requirements. If the company has more than one class of shares, it is necessary as an initial matter to determine which class or classes constitute the "principal class of shares." The term "principal class of shares" is defined in subparagraph 5(e) of the Article to mean the ordinary or common shares of the company representing the majority of the aggregate voting power and value of the company. If the company does not have a class of ordinary or common shares representing the majority of the aggregate voting power and value of the company, then the "principal class of shares" is that class or any combination of classes of shares that represents, in the aggregate, a majority of the voting power and value of the company. Although in a particular case involving a company with several classes of shares it is conceivable that more than one group of classes could be identified that account for more than 50% of the voting power and value of the shares of the company, it is only necessary for one such group to satisfy the requirements of this subparagraph in order for the company to be entitled to benefits. Benefits would not be denied to the company even if a second, non-qualifying, group of shares with more than half of the company's voting power and value could be identified.

A company whose principal class of shares is regularly traded on a recognized stock exchange will nevertheless not qualify for benefits under subparagraph 2(c) if it has a disproportionate class of shares that is not regularly traded on a recognized stock exchange. The term "disproportionate class of shares" is defined in subparagraph 5(b) of the Article. A company has a disproportionate class of shares if it has outstanding a class of shares which is subject to terms or other arrangements that entitle the holder to a larger portion of the company's income, profit, or gain in the other Contracting State than that to which the holder would be entitled in the absence of such terms or arrangements. Thus, for example, a company has a disproportionate class of shares if it has outstanding a class of "tracking stock" that pays dividends based upon a formula that approximates the company's return on its assets employed in the United States. Similar principles apply to determine whether or not there are disproportionate interests in a trust.

The following example illustrates the application of subparagraph 5(b).

Example. OCo is a corporation resident in Canada. OCo has two classes of shares: Common and Preferred. The Common shares are listed and regularly traded on a designated stock exchange in Canada. The Preferred shares have no voting rights and are entitled to receive dividends equal in amount to interest payments that OCo receives from unrelated borrowers in the United States. The Preferred shares are owned entirely by a single investor that is a resident of a country with which the United States does not have a tax treaty. The Common shares account for more than 50 percent of the value of OCo and for 100 percent of the voting power. Because the owner of the Preferred shares is entitled to receive payments corresponding to the U.S.-source interest income earned by OCo, the Preferred shares are a disproportionate class of shares. Because the Preferred shares are not primarily and regularly traded on a recognized stock exchange, OCo will not qualify for benefits under subparagraph 2(c).

The term "regularly traded" is not defined in the Convention. In accordance with paragraph 2 of Article III (General Definitions) and paragraph 1 of the General Note, this term will be defined by reference to the domestic tax laws of the State from which benefits of the Convention are sought, generally the source State. In the case of the United States, this term is understood to have the meaning it has under Treas. Reg. section 1.884-5(d)(4)(i)(B), relating to the branch tax provisions of the Code, as may be amended from time to time. Under these regulations, a class of shares is considered to be "regularly traded" if two requirements are met: trades in the class of shares are made in more than de minimis quantities on at least 60 days during the taxable year, and the aggregate number of shares in the class traded during the year is at least 10 percent of the average number of shares outstanding during the year. Sections 1.884-5(d)(4)(i)(A), (ii) and (iii) will not be taken into account for purposes of defining the term "regularly traded" under the Convention.

The regularly-traded requirement can be met by trading on one or more recognized stock exchanges. Therefore, trading may be aggregated for purposes of this requirement. Thus, a U.S. company could satisfy the regularly traded requirement through trading, in whole or in part, on a recognized stock exchange located in Canada. Authorized but unissued shares are not considered for purposes of this test.

The term "primarily traded" is not defined in the Convention. In accordance with paragraph 2 of Article III (General Definitions) and paragraph 1 of the General Note, this term will have the meaning it has under the laws of the State concerning the taxes to which the Convention applies, generally the source State. In the case of the United States, this term is understood to have the meaning it has under Treas. Reg. section 1.884-5(d)(3), as may be amended from time to time, relating to the branch tax provisions of the Code. Accordingly, stock of a corporation is "primarily traded" if the number of shares in the company's principal class of shares that are traded during the taxable year on all recognized stock exchanges exceeds the number of shares in the company's principal class of shares that are traded during that year on all other established securities markets.

Subject to the adoption by Canada of other definitions, the U.S. interpretation of "regularly traded" and "primarily traded" will be considered to apply, with such modifications as circumstances require, under the Convention for purposes of Canadian taxation.

Subsidiaries of publicly traded entities

Certain companies owned by publicly traded corporations also may be qualifying persons. Under subparagraph 2(d), a company resident in the United States or Canada will be a qualifying person, even if not publicly traded, if more than 50 percent of the vote and value of its shares, and more than 50 percent of the vote and value of each disproportionate class of shares, is owned (directly or indirectly) by five or fewer persons that are qualifying persons under subparagraph 2(c). In addition, each company in the chain of ownership must be a qualifying person. Thus, for example, a company that is a resident of Canada, all the shares of which are owned by another company that is a resident of Canada, would qualify for benefits of the Convention if the principal class of shares (and any disproportionate classes of shares) of the parent company are regularly and primarily traded on a recognized stock exchange. However, such a subsidiary would not qualify for benefits under subparagraph 2(d) if the publicly traded parent company were a resident of a third state, for example, and not a resident of the United States or Canada. Furthermore, if a parent company qualifying for benefits under subparagraph 2(c) indirectly owned the bottom-tier company through a chain of subsidiaries, each subsidiary in the chain, as an intermediate owner, must be a qualifying person in order for the bottom-tier subsidiary to meet the test in subparagraph 2(d).

Subparagraph 2(d) provides that a subsidiary can take into account ownership by as many as five companies, each of which qualifies for benefits under subparagraph 2(c) to determine if the subsidiary qualifies for benefits under subparagraph 2(d). For example, a Canadian company that is not publicly traded but that is owned, one-third each, by three companies, two of which are Canadian resident corporations whose principal classes of shares are primarily and regularly traded on a recognized stock exchange, will qualify under subparagraph 2(d).

By applying the principles introduced by the Protocol (e.g. paragraph 6 of Article IV) in the context of this rule, one "looks through" entities in the chain of ownership that are viewed as fiscally transparent under the domestic laws of the State of residence (other than entities that are resident in the State of source).

The 50-percent test under subparagraph 2(d) applies only to shares other than "debt substitute shares." The term "debt substitute shares" is defined in subparagraph 5(a) to mean shares defined in paragraph (e) of the definition in the Canadian Income Tax Act of "term preferred shares" (see subsection 248(1) of the Income Tax Act), which relates to certain shares received in debt-restructuring arrangements undertaken by reason of financial difficulty or insolvency. Subparagraph 5(a) also provides that the competent authorities may agree to treat other types of shares as debt substitute shares.

Ownership/base erosion test

Subparagraph 2(e) provides a two-part test under which certain other entities may be qualifying persons, based on ownership and lack of "base erosion." A company resident in the United States or Canada will satisfy the first of these tests if 50 percent or more of the vote and value of its shares and 50 percent or more of the vote and value of each disproportionate class of shares, in both cases not including debt substitute shares, is not owned, directly or indirectly, by persons other than qualifying persons. Similarly, a trust resident in the United States or Canada will satisfy this first test if 50 percent or more of its beneficial interests, and 50 percent or more of each disproportionate interest, is not owned, directly or indirectly, by persons other than qualifying persons. The wording of these tests is intended to make clear that, for example, if a Canadian company is more than 50 percent owned, either directly or indirectly (including cumulative indirect ownership through a chain of entities), by a U.S. resident corporation that is, itself, wholly owned by a third-country resident other than a qualifying person, the Canadian company would not pass the ownership test. This is because more than 50 percent of its shares is owned indirectly by a person (the third-country resident) that is not a qualifying person.

It is understood by the Contracting States that in determining whether a company satisfies the ownership test described in subparagraph 2(e)(i), a company, 50 percent of more of the aggregate vote and value of the shares of which and 50 percent or more of the vote and value of each disproportionate class of shares (in neither case including debt substitute shares) of which is owned, directly or indirectly, by a company described in subparagraph 2(c) will satisfy the ownership test of subparagraph 2(e)(i). In such case, no further analysis of the ownership of the company described in subparagraph 2(c) is required. Similarly, in determining whether a trust satisfies the ownership test described in subparagraph 2(e)(ii), a trust, 50 percent or more of the beneficial interest in which and 50 percent or more of each disproportionate interest in which, is owned, directly or indirectly, by a trust described in subparagraph (2)(c) will satisfy the ownership test of subparagraph (2)(e)(ii), and no further analysis of the ownership of the trust described in subparagraph 2(c) is required.

The second test of subparagraph 2(e) is the so-called "base erosion" test. A company or trust that passes the ownership test must also pass this test to be a qualifying person under this subparagraph. This test requires that the amount of expenses that are paid or payable by the entity in question, directly or indirectly, to persons that are not qualifying persons, and that are deductible from gross income (with both deductibility and gross income as determined under the tax laws of the State of residence of the company or trust), be less than 50 percent of the gross income of the company or trust. This test is applied for the fiscal period immediately preceding the period for which the qualifying person test is being applied. If it is the first fiscal period of the person, the test is applied for the current period.

The ownership/base erosion test recognizes that the benefits of the Convention can be enjoyed indirectly not only by equity holders of an entity, but also by that entity's obligees, such as lenders, licensors, service providers, insurers and reinsurers, and others. For example, a third-country resident could license technology to a Canadian-owned Canadian corporation to be sub-licensed to a U.S. resident. The U.S.-source royalty income of the Canadian corporation would be exempt from U.S. withholding tax under Article XII (Royalties) of the Convention. While the Canadian corporation would be subject to Canadian corporation income tax, its taxable income could be reduced to near zero as a result of the deductible royalties paid to the third-country resident. If, under a convention between Canada and the third country, those royalties were either exempt from Canadian tax or subject to tax at a low rate, the U.S. treaty benefit with respect to the U.S.-source royalty income would have flowed to the third-country resident at little or no tax cost, with no reciprocal benefit to the United States from the third country. The ownership/ base erosion test therefore requires both that qualifying persons substantially own the entity and that the entity's tax base is not substantially eroded by payments (directly or indirectly) to nonqualifying persons.

For purposes of this subparagraph 2(e) and other provisions of this Article, the term "shares" includes, in the case of a mutual insurance company, any certificate or contract entitling the holder to voting power in the corporation. This is consistent with the interpretation of similar limitation on benefits provisions in other U.S. treaties. In Canada, the principles that are reflected in subsection 256(8.1) of the Income Tax Act will be applied, in effect treating memberships, policies or other interests in a corporation incorporated without share capital as representing an appropriate number of shares.

The look-through principles introduced by the Protocol (*e.g.*, new paragraph 6 of Article IV) are to be taken into account when applying the ownership and base erosion provisions of Article XXIX A. Therefore, one "looks through" an entity that is viewed as fiscally transparent under the domestic laws of the residence State (other than entities that are resident in the source State) when applying the ownership/base erosion test. Assume, for example, that USCo, a company incorporated in the United States, wishes to obtain treaty benefits by virtue of the ownership and base erosion rule. USCo is owned by USLLC, an entity that is treated as fiscally transparent in the United States. USLLC in turn is wholly owned in equal shares by 10 individuals who are residents of the United States. Because the United States views USLLC as fiscally transparent, the 10 U.S. individuals shall be regarded as the owners of USCo for purposes of the ownership test. Accordingly, USCo would satisfy the ownership requirement of the ownership/base erosion test. However, if USLLC were instead owned in equal shares by four U.S. individuals and six individuals who are not residents of either the United States or Canada, USCo would not satisfy the ownership requirement. Similarly, for purposes of the base erosion test, deductible payments made to USLLC will be treated as made to USLLC's owners.

Other qualifying persons

Under new subparagraph 2(f), an estate resident in the United States or Canada is a qualifying person entitled to the benefits of the Convention.

New subparagraphs 2(g) and 2(h) specify the circumstances under which certain types of not-for-profit organizations will be qualifying persons. Subparagraph 2(g) provides that a not-for-profit organization that is resident in the United States or Canada is a qualifying person, and thus entitled to benefits, if more than half of the beneficiaries, members, or participants in the organization are qualifying persons. The term "not-for profit organization" of a Contracting State is defined in subparagraph 5(d) of the Article to mean an entity created or established in that State that is generally exempt from income taxation in that State by reason of its not-for-profit status. The term includes charities, private foundations, trade unions, trade associations, and similar organizations.

New subparagraph 2(h) specifies that certain trusts, companies, organizations, or other arrangements described in paragraph 2 of Article XXI (Exempt Organizations) are qualifying persons. To be a qualifying person, the trust, company, organization or other arrangement must be established for the purpose of providing pension, retirement, or employee benefits primarily to individuals who are (or were, within any of the five preceding years) qualifying persons. A trust, company, organization, or other arrangement will be considered to be established for the purpose of providing benefits primarily to such persons if more than 50 percent of its beneficiaries, members, or participants are such persons. Thus, for example, a Canadian Registered Retirement Savings Plan ("RRSP") of a former resident of Canada who is working temporarily outside of Canada would continue to be a qualifying person during the period of the individual's absence from Canada or for five years, whichever is shorter. A Canadian pension fund established to provide benefits to persons employed by a company would be a qualifying person only if most of the beneficiaries of the fund are (or were within the five preceding years) individual residents of Canada or residents or citizens of the United States.

New subparagraph 2(i) specifies that certain trusts, companies, organizations, or other arrangements described in paragraph 3 of Article XXI (Exempt Organizations) are qualifying persons. To be a qualifying person, the beneficiaries of a trust, company, organization or other arrangement must be described in subparagraph 2(g) or 2(h).

The provisions of paragraph 2 are self-executing, unlike the provisions of paragraph 6, discussed below. The tax authorities may, of course, on review, determine that the taxpayer has improperly interpreted the paragraph and is not entitled to the benefits claimed.

Paragraph 3 of Article XXIX A

Paragraph 3 provides an alternative rule, under which a United States or Canadian resident that is not a qualifying person under paragraph 2 may claim benefits with respect to those items of income that are connected with the active conduct of a trade or business in its State of residence.

This is the so-called "active trade or business" test. Unlike the tests of paragraph 2, the active trade or business test looks not solely at the characteristics of the person deriving the income, but also at the nature of the person's activity and the connection between the income and that activity. Under the active trade or business test, a resident of a Contracting State deriving an item of income from the other Contracting State is entitled to benefits with respect to that income if that person (or a person related to that person under the principles of Code section 482, or in the case of Canada, section 251 of the Income Tax Act) is engaged in an active trade or business in the State where it is resident, the income in question is derived in connection with, or is incidental to, that trade or business, and the size of the active trade or business in the residence State is substantial relative to the activity in the other State that gives rise to the income for which benefits are sought. Further details on the application of the substantiality requirement are provided below.

Income that is derived in connection with, or is incidental to, the business of making or managing investments will not qualify for benefits under this provision, unless those investment activities are carried on with customers in the ordinary course of the business of a bank, insurance company, registered securities dealer, or deposit-taking financial institution.

Income is considered derived "in connection" with an active trade or business if, for example, the income-generating activity in the State is "upstream," "down-stream," or parallel to that conducted in the other Contracting State. Thus, for example, if the U.S. activity of a Canadian resident company consisted of selling the output of a Canadian manufacturer or providing inputs to the manufacturing process, or of manufacturing or selling in the United States the same sorts of products that were being sold by the Canadian trade or business in Canada, the income generated by that activity would be treated as earned in connection with the Canadian trade or business. Income is considered "incidental" to a trade or business if, for example, it arises from the short-term investment of working capital of the resident in securities issued by persons in the State of source.

An item of income may be considered to be earned in connection with or to be incidental to an active trade or business in the United States or Canada even though the resident claiming the benefits derives the income directly or indirectly through one or more other persons that are residents of the other Contracting State. Thus, for example, a Canadian resident could claim benefits with respect to an item of income earned by a U.S. operating subsidiary but derived by the Canadian resident indirectly through a wholly-owned U.S. holding company interposed between it and the operating subsidiary. This language would also permit a resident to derive income from the other Contracting State through one or more residents of that other State that it does not wholly own. For example, a Canadian partnership in which three unrelated Canadian companies each hold a one-third interest could form a wholly-owned U.S. holding company with a U.S. operating subsidiary. The "directly or indirectly" language would allow otherwise unavailable treaty benefits to be claimed with respect to income derived by the three Canadian partners through the U.S. holding company, even if the partners were not considered to be related to the U.S. holding company under the principles of Code section 482.

As described above, income that is derived in connection with, or is incidental to, an active trade or business in a Contracting State, must pass the substantiality requirement to qualify for benefits under the Convention. The trade or business must be substantial in relation to the activity in the other Contracting State that gave rise to the income in respect of which benefits under the Convention are being claimed. To be considered substantial, it is not necessary that the trade or business be as large as the income-generating activity. The trade or business cannot, however, in terms of income, assets, or other similar measures, represent only a very small percentage of the size of the activity in the other State.

The substantiality requirement is intended to prevent treaty shopping. For example, a third-country resident may want to acquire a U.S. company that manufactures television sets for worldwide markets; however, since its country of residence has no tax treaty with the United States, any dividends generated by the investment would be subject to a U.S. withholding tax of 30 percent. Absent a substantiality test, the investor could establish a Canadian corporation that would operate a small outlet in Canada to sell a few of the television sets manufactured by the U.S. company and earn a very small amount of income. That Canadian corporation could then acquire the U.S. manufacturer with capital provided by the third-country resident and produce a very large number of sets for sale in several countries, generating a much larger amount of income. It might attempt to argue that the U.S.-source income is generated from business activities in the United States related to the television sales activity of the Canadian parent and that the dividend income should be subject to U.S. tax at the 5 percent rate provided by Article X (Dividends) of the Convention. However, the substantiality test would not be met in this example, so the dividends would remain subject to withholding in the United States at a rate of 30 percent.

It is expected that if a person qualifies for benefits under one of the tests of paragraph 2, no inquiry will be made into qualification for benefits under paragraph 3. Upon satisfaction of any of the tests of paragraph 2, any income derived by the beneficial owner from the other Contracting State is entitled to treaty benefits. Under paragraph 3, however, the test is applied separately to each item of income.

Paragraph 4 of Article XXIX A

Paragraph 4 provides a limited "derivative benefits" test that entitles a company that is a resident of the United States or Canada to the benefits of Articles X (Dividends), XI (Interest), and XII (Royalties), even if the company is not a qualifying person and does not satisfy the active trade or business test of paragraph 3. In general, a derivative benefits test entitles the resident of a Contracting State to treaty benefits if the owner of the resident would have been entitled to the same benefit had the income in question been earned directly by that owner. To qualify under this paragraph, the company must satisfy both the ownership test in subparagraph 4(a) and the base erosion test of subparagraph 4(b).

Under subparagraph 4(a), the derivative benefits ownership test requires that the company's shares representing more than 90 percent of the aggregate vote and value of all of the shares of the company, and at least 50 percent of the vote and value of any disproportionate class of shares, in neither case including debt substitute shares, be owned directly or indirectly by persons each of whom is either (i) a qualifying person or (ii) another person that satisfies each of three tests. The three tests of subparagraph 4(a) that must be satisfied by these other persons are as follows:

First, the other person must be a resident of a third State with which the Contracting State that is granting benefits has a comprehensive income tax convention. The other person must be entitled to all of the benefits under that convention. Thus, if the person fails to satisfy the limitation on benefits tests, if any, of that convention, no benefits would be granted under this paragraph. Qualification for benefits under an active trade or business test does not suffice for these purposes, because that test grants benefits only for certain items of income, not for all purposes of the convention.

Second, the other person must be a person that would qualify for benefits with respect to the item of income for which benefits are sought under one or more of the tests of paragraph 2 or 3 of Article XXIX A, if the person were a resident of the Contracting State that is not providing benefits for the item of income and, for purposes of paragraph 3, the business were carried on in that State. For example, a person resident in a third country would be deemed to be a person that would qualify under the publicly-traded test of paragraph 2 of Article XXIX A if the principal class of its shares were primarily and regularly traded on a stock exchange recognized either under the Convention between the United States and Canada or under the treaty between the Contracting State granting benefits and the third country. Similarly, a company resident in a third country would be deemed to satisfy the ownership/base erosion test of paragraph 2 under this hypothetical analysis if, for example, it were wholly owned by an individual resident in that third country and the company's tax base were not substantially eroded by payments (directly or indirectly) to nonqualifying persons.

The third requirement is that the rate of tax on the item of income in respect of which benefits are sought must be at least as low under the convention between the person's country of residence and the Contracting State granting benefits as it is under the Convention.

Subparagraph 4(b) sets forth the base erosion test. This test requires that the amount of expenses that are paid or payable by the company in question, directly or indirectly, to persons that are not qualifying persons under the Convention, and that are deductible from gross income (with both deductibility and gross income as determined under the tax laws of the State of residence of the company), be less than 50 percent of the gross income of the company. This test is applied for the fiscal period immediately preceding the period for which the test is being applied. If it is the first fiscal period of the person, the test is applied for the current period. This test is qualitatively the same as the base erosion test of subparagraph 2(e).

Paragraph 5 of Article XXIX A

Paragraph 5 defines certain terms used in the Article. These terms were identified and discussed in connection with new paragraph 2, above.

Paragraph 6 of Article XXIX A

Paragraph 6 provides that when a resident of a Contracting State derives income from the other Contracting State and is not entitled to the benefits of the Convention under other provisions of the Article, benefits may, nevertheless be granted at the discretion of the competent authority of the other Contracting State. This determination can be made with respect to all benefits under the Convention or on an item by item basis. In making a determination under this paragraph, the competent authority will take into account all relevant facts and circumstances relating to the person requesting the benefits. In particular, the competent authority will consider the history, structure, ownership (including ultimate beneficial ownership), and operations of the person. In addition, the competent authority is to consider (1) whether the creation and existence of the person did not have as a principal purpose obtaining treaty benefits that would not otherwise be available to the person, and (2) whether it would not be appropriate, in view of the purpose of the Article, to deny benefits. If the competent authority of the other Contracting State determines that either of these two standards is satisfied, benefits shall be granted.

For purposes of implementing new paragraph 6, a taxpayer will be permitted to present his case to the competent authority for an advance determination based on a full disclosure of all pertinent information. The taxpayer will not be required to wait until it has been determined that benefits are denied under one of the other provisions of the Article. It also is expected that, if and when the competent authority determines that benefits are to be allowed, they will be allowed retroactively to the time of entry into force of the relevant provision of the Convention or the establishment of the structure in question, whichever is later (assuming that the taxpayer also qualifies under the relevant facts for the earlier period).

Paragraph 7 of Article XXIX A

New paragraph 7 is in substance similar to paragraph 7 of Article XXIX A of the existing Convention and clarifies the application of general anti-abuse provisions. New paragraph 7 provides that paragraphs 1 through 6 of Article XXIX A shall not be construed as limiting in any manner the right of a Contracting State to deny benefits under the Convention where it can reasonably be concluded that to do otherwise would result in an abuse of the provisions of the Convention. This provision permits a Contracting State to rely on general anti-avoidance rules to counter arrangements involving treaty shopping through the other Contracting State.

Thus, Canada may apply its domestic law rules to counter abusive arrangements involving "treaty shopping" through the United States, and the United States may apply its substance-over-form and anti-conduit rules, for example, in relation to Canadian residents. This principle is recognized by the OECD in the Commentaries to its Model Tax Convention on Income and on Capital, and the United States and Canada agree that it is inherent in the Convention. The statement of this principle explicitly in the Protocol is not intended to suggest that the principle is not also inherent in other tax conventions concluded by the United States or Canada.

Article 26

Article 26 of the Protocol replaces paragraphs 1 and 5 of Article XXIX B (Taxes Imposed by Reason of Death) of the Convention. In addition, paragraph 7 of the General Note provides certain clarifications for purposes of paragraphs 6 and 7 of Article XXIX B.

Paragraph 1

Paragraph 1 of Article XXIX B of the existing Convention generally addresses the situation where a resident of a Contracting State passes property by reason of the individual's death to an organization referred to in paragraph 1 of Article XXI (Exempt Organizations) of the Convention. The paragraph provided that the tax consequences in a Contracting State arising out of the passing of the property shall apply as if the organization were a resident of that State.

The Protocol replaces paragraph 1, and the changes set forth in new paragraph 1 are intended to specifically address questions that have arisen about the application of former paragraph 1 where property of an individual who is a resident of Canada passes by reason of the individual's death to a charitable organization in the United States that is not a "registered charity" under Canadian law. Under one view, paragraph 1 of Article XXIX B requires Canada to treat the passing of the property as a contribution to a "registered charity" and thus to allow all of the same deductions for Canadian tax purposes as if the U.S. charity had been a "registered charity" under Canadian law. Under another view, paragraph 6 of Article XXI (Exempt Organizations) of the Convention continues to limit the amount of the income tax charitable deduction in Canada to the individual's income arising in the United States. The changes set forth in new paragraph 1 are intended to provide relief from the Canadian tax on gain deemed recognized by reason of death that would otherwise give rise to Canadian tax when the individual passes the property to a charitable organization in the United States, but, for purposes of the separate Canadian income tax, do not eliminate the limitation under paragraph 6 of Article XXI on the amount of the deduction in Canada for the charitable donation to the individual's income arising in the United States.

As revised, paragraph 1 is divided into two subparagraphs. New subparagraph 1(a) applies where property of an individual who is a resident of the United States passes by reason of the individual's death to a qualifying exempt organization that is a resident of Canada. In such case, the tax consequences in the United States arising from the passing of such property apply as if the organization were a resident of the United States. A bequest by a U.S. citizen or U.S. resident (as defined for estate tax purposes under the Code) to an exempt organization generally is deductible for U.S. federal estate tax purposes under Code section 2055, without regard to whether the organization is a U.S. corporation. Thus, generally, the individual's estate will be entitled to a charitable deduction for Federal estate tax purposes equal to the value of the property transferred to the organization. Generally, the effect is that no Federal estate tax will be imposed on the value of the property.

New subparagraph 1(b) applies where property of an individual who is a resident of Canada passes by reason of the individual's death to a qualifying exempt organization that is a resident of the United States. In such case, for purposes of the Canadian capital gains tax imposed at death, the tax consequences arising out of the passing of the property shall apply as if the individual disposed of the property for proceeds equal to an amount elected on behalf of the individual. For this purpose, the amount elected shall be no less than the individual's cost of the property as determined for purposes of Canadian tax, and no greater than the fair market value of the property. The manner in which the individual's representative shall make this election shall be specified by the competent authority of Canada. Generally, in the event of a full exercise of the election under new subparagraph 1(b), no capital gains tax will be imposed in Canada by reason of the death with regard to that property.

New paragraph 1 does not address the situation in which a resident of one Contracting State bequeaths property with a situs in the other Contracting State to a qualifying exempt organization in the Contracting State of the decedent's residence. In such a situation, the other Contracting State may impose tax by reason of death, for example, if the property is real property situated in that State.

Paragraph 2

Paragraph 2 of Article 26 of the Protocol replaces paragraph 5 of Article XXIX B of the existing Convention. The provisions of new paragraph 5 relate to the operation of Canadian law. Because Canadian law requires both spouses to have been Canadian residents in order to be eligible for the rollover, these provisions are intended to provide deferral ("rollover") of the Canadian tax at death for certain transfers to a surviving spouse and to permit the Canadian competent authority to allow such deferral for certain transfers to a trust. For example, they would enable the competent authority to treat a trust that is a qualified domestic trust for U.S. estate tax purposes as a Canadian spousal trust as well for purposes of certain provisions of Canadian tax law and of the Convention. These provisions do not affect U.S. domestic law regarding qualified domestic trusts. Nor do they affect the status of U.S. resident individuals for any other purpose.

New paragraph 5 adds a reference to subsection 70(5.2) of the Canadian Income Tax Act. This change is needed because the rollover in respect of certain kinds of property is provided in that subsection. Further, new paragraph 5 adds a clause "and with respect to such property" near the end of the second sentence to make it clear that the trust is treated as a resident of Canada only with respect to its Canadian property.

For example, assume that a U.S. decedent with a Canadian spouse sets up a qualified domestic trust holding U.S. and Canadian real property, and that the decedent's executor elects, for Federal estate tax purposes, to treat the entire trust as qualifying for the Federal estate tax marital deduction. Under Canadian law, because the decedent is not a Canadian resident, Canada would impose capital gains tax on the deemed disposition of the Canadian real property immediately before death. In order to defer the Canadian tax that might otherwise be imposed by reason of the decedent's death, under new paragraph 5 of Article XXIX B, the competent authority of Canada shall, at the request of the trustee, treat the trust as a Canadian spousal trust with respect to the Canadian real property. The effect of such treatment is to defer the tax on the deemed distribution of the Canadian real property until an appropriate triggering event such as the death of the surviving spouse.

Paragraph 7 of the General Note

In addition to the foregoing, paragraph 7 of the General Note provides certain clarifications for purposes of paragraphs 6 and 7 of Article XXIX B. These clarifications ensure that tax credits will be available in cases where there are inconsistencies in the way the two Contracting States view the income and the property.

Subparagraph 7(a) of the General Note applies where an individual who immediately before death was a resident of Canada held at the time of death a share or option in respect of a share that constitutes property situated in the United States for the purposes of Article XXIX B and that Canada views as giving rise to employment income (for example, a share or option granted by an employer). The United States imposes estate tax on the share or option in respect of a share, while Canada imposes income tax on income from employment. Subparagraph 7(a) provides that for purposes of clause 6(a)(ii) of Article XXIX B, any employment income in respect of the share or option constitutes income from property situated in the United States. This provision ensures that the estate tax paid on the share or option in the United States will be allowable as a deduction from the Canadian income tax.

Subparagraph 7(b) of the General Note applies where an individual who immediately before death was a resident of Canada held at the time of death a registered retirement savings plan (RRSP) or other entity that is a resident of Canada and that is described in subparagraph 1(b) of Article IV (Residence) and such RRSP or other entity held property situated in the United States for the purposes of Article XXIX B. The United States would impose estate tax on the value of the property held by the RRSP or other entity (to the extent such property is subject to Federal estate tax), while Canada would impose income tax on a deemed distribution of the property in the RRSP or other entity. Subparagraph 7(b) provides that any income out of or under the entity in respect of the property is, for the purpose of subparagraph 6(a)(ii) of Article XXIX B, income from property situated in the United States. This provision ensures that the estate tax paid on the underlying property in the United States (if any) will be allowable as a deduction from the Canadian income tax.

Subparagraph 7(c) of the General Note applies where an individual who immediately before death was a resident or citizen of the United States held at the time of death an RRSP or other entity that is a resident of Canada and that is described in subparagraph 1(b) of Article IV (Residence). The United States would impose estate tax on the value of the property held by the RRSP or other entity, while Canada would impose income tax on a deemed distribution of the property in the RRSP or other entity. Subparagraph 7(c) provides that for the purpose of paragraph 7 of Article XXIX B, the tax imposed in Canada is imposed in respect of property situated in Canada. This provision ensures that the Canadian income tax will be allowable as a credit against the U.S. estate tax.

Article 27

Article 27 of the Protocol provides the entry into force and effective date of the provisions of the Protocol.

Paragraph 1

Paragraph 1 provides generally that the Protocol is subject to ratification in accordance with the applicable procedures in the United States and Canada. Further, the Contracting States shall notify each other by written notification, through diplomatic channels, when their respective applicable procedures have been satisfied.

Paragraph 2

The first sentence of paragraph 2 generally provides that the Protocol shall enter into force on the date of the later of the notifications referred to in paragraph 1, or January 1, 2008, whichever is later. The relevant date is the date on the second of these notification documents, and not the date on which the second notification is provided to the other Contracting State. The January 1, 2008 date is intended to ensure that the provisions of the Protocol will generally not be effective before that date.

Subparagraph 2(a) provides that the provisions of the Protocol shall have effect in respect of taxes withheld at source, for amounts paid or credited on or after the first day of the second month that begins after the date on which the Protocol enters into force. Further, subparagraph 2(b) provides that the Protocol shall have effect in respect of other taxes, for taxable years that begin after (or, if the later of the notifications referred to in paragraph 1 is dated in 2007, taxable years that begin in and after) the calendar year in which the Protocol enters into force. These provisions are generally consistent with the formulation in the U.S. Model treaty, with the exception that a parenthetical was added in subparagraph 2(b) to address the contingency that the written notifications provided pursuant to paragraph 1 may occur in the 2007 calendar year. Further, subparagraph 3(d) of Article 27 of the Protocol contains special provisions with respect to the taxation of cross-border interest payments that have effect for the first two calendar years that end after the date the Protocol enters into force. Therefore, during this period, cross-border interest payments are not subject to the effective date provisions of subparagraph 2(a).

Paragraph 3

Paragraph 3 sets forth exceptions to the general effective date rules set forth in paragraph 2 of Article 27 of the Protocol.

Dual corporate residence tie-breaker

Subparagraph 3(a) of Article 27 of the Protocol provides that paragraph 1 of Article 2 of the Protocol relating to Article IV (Residence) shall have effect with respect to corporate continuations effected after September 17, 2000. This date corresponds to a press release issued on September 18, 2000 in which the United States and Canada identified certain issues with respect to these transactions and stated their intention to negotiate a protocol that, if approved, would address the issues effective as of the date of the press release.

Certain payments through fiscally transparent entities

Subparagraph 3(b) of Article 27 of the Protocol provides that new paragraph 7 of Article IV (Residence) set forth in paragraph 2 of Article 2 of the Protocol shall have effect as of the first day of the third calendar year that ends after the Protocol enters into force.

Permanent establishment from the provision of services

Subparagraph 3(c) of Article 27 of the Protocol sets forth the effective date for the provisions of Article 3 of the Protocol, pertaining to Article V (Permanent Establishment) of the Convention. The provisions pertaining to Article V shall have effect as of the third taxable year that ends after the Protocol enters into force, but in no event shall it apply to include, in the determination of whether an enterprise is deemed to provide services through a permanent establishment under paragraph 9 of Article V of the Convention, any days of presence, services rendered, or gross active business revenues that occur or arise prior to January 1, 2010. Therefore, the provision will apply beginning no earlier than January 1, 2010 and shall not apply with regard to any presence, services or related revenues that occur or arise prior to that date.

Withholding rates on cross-border interest payments

Subparagraph 3(d) of Article 27 of the Protocol sets forth special effective date rules pertaining to Article 6 of the Protocol relating to Article XI (Interest) of the Convention. Article 6 of the Protocol sets forth a new Article XI of the Convention that provides for exclusive residence State taxation regardless of the relationship between the payer and the beneficial owner of the interest. Subparagraph 3(d), however, phases in the application of paragraph 1 of Article XI during the first two calendar years that end after the date the Protocol enters into force. During that period, paragraph 1 of Article XI of the Convention permits source State taxation of interest if the payer and the beneficial owner are related or deemed to be related by reason of paragraph 2 of Article IX (Related Persons) of the Convention ("related party interest"), and the interest would not otherwise be exempt under the provisions of paragraph 3 of Article XI as it read prior to the Protocol. However, subparagraph 3(d) also provides that the source State taxation on such related party interest is limited to 7 percent in the first calendar year that ends after entry into force of the Protocol and 4 percent in the second calendar year that ends after entry into force of the Protocol.

Subparagraph 3(d) makes clear that the provisions of the Protocol with respect to exclusive residence based taxation of interest when the payer and the beneficial owner are not related or deemed related ("unrelated party interest") applies for interest paid or credited during the first two calendar years that end after entry into force of the Protocol.

The withholding rate reductions for related party interest and exemptions for unrelated party interest will likely apply retroactively. For example, if the Protocol enters into force on June 30, 2008, paragraph 1 of Article XI, as it reads under subparagraph 3(d) of Article 27, will have the following effect during the first two calendar years. First, unrelated party interest that is paid or credited on or after January 1, 2008 will be exempt from taxation in the source State. Second, related party interest paid or credited on or after January 1, 2008 and before January 1, 2009, will be subject to source State taxation but at a rate not to exceed 7 percent of the gross amount of the interest. Third, related party interest paid or credited on or after January 1, 2009 and before January 1, 2010, will be subject to source State taxation but at a rate not to exceed 4 percent of the gross amount of the interest. Finally, all interest paid or credited after January 1, 2010, will be subject to the regular rules of Article XI without regard to subparagraph 3(d) of Article 27.

Further, the provisions of subparagraph 3(d) ensure that even with respect to circumstances where the payer and the beneficial owner are related or deemed related under the provisions of paragraph 2 of Article IX, the source State taxation of such cross-border interest shall be no greater than the taxation of such interest prior to the Protocol.

Gains

Subparagraph 3(e) of Article 27 of the Protocol provides the effective date for paragraphs 2 and 3 of Article 8 of this Protocol, which relate to the changes made to paragraphs 5 and 7 of Article XIII (Gains) of the Convention. The changes set forth in those paragraphs shall have effect with respect to alienations of property that occur (including, for greater certainty, those that are deemed under the law of a Contracting State to occur) after September 17, 2000. This date corresponds to the press release issued on September 18, 2000 which announced the intention of the United States and Canada to negotiate a protocol that, if approved, would incorporate the changes set forth in these paragraphs to coordinate the tax treatment of an emigrant's gains in the United States and Canada.

Arbitration

Subparagraph 3(f) of Article 27 of the Protocol pertains to Article 21 of the Protocol which implements the new arbitration provisions. An arbitration proceeding will generally begin two years after the date on which the competent authorities of the Contracting States began consideration of a case. Subparagraph 3(f), however, makes clear that the arbitration provisions shall apply to cases that are already under consideration by the competent authorities when the Protocol enters into force, and in such cases, for purposes of applying the arbitration provisions, the commencement date shall be the date the Protocol enters into force. Further, the provisions of Article 21 of the Protocol shall be effective for cases that come into consideration by the competent authorities after the date that the Protocol enters into force. In order to avoid the potential for a large number of MAP cases becoming subject to arbitration immediately upon the expiration of two years from entry into force, the competent authorities are encouraged to develop and implement procedures for arbitration by January 1, 2009, and begin scheduling arbitration of otherwise unresolvable MAP cases in inventory (and meeting the agreed criteria) prior to two years from entry into force.

Assistance in collection

Subparagraph 3(g) of Article 27 of the Protocol pertains to the date when the changes set forth in Article 22 of the Protocol, relating to assistance in collection of taxes, shall have effect. Consistent with the third protocol that entered into force on November 9, 1995, and which had effect for requests for assistance on claims finally determined after November 9, 1985, the provisions of Article 22 of the Protocol shall have effect for revenue claims finally determined by an applicant State after November 9, 1985.

TABLE OF CASES

[References are to pages.]

TABLE OF STATUTES

[References are to pages.]

[References are to pages.]

[References are to pages.]

[References are to pages.]

[References are to pages.]

INTERNAL REVENUE CODE OF 1939

INTERNAL REVENUE CODE OF 1954

INTERNAL REVENUE CODE OF 1962

JOBS ACT OF 2004

PASSIVE FOREIGN INVESTMENT COMPANIES RULES

TAX INCREASE PREVENTION AND RECONCILIATION ACT OF 2005 (TIRPA)

TAX REFORM ACT OF 1986

[References are to pages.]

[References are to pages.]

[References are to pages.]

TABLE OF SECONDARY AUTHORITIES

[References are to pages.]

[References are to pages.]

INDEX

[References are to sections.]

[References are to sections.]

[References are to sections.]

[References are to sections.]

[References are to sections.]